'This book will be a vital encyclopaedia for all those tasked with the production, amendment, finalisation and administration of FIDIC contracts in the Asia Pacific. It provides a valuable guide to those aspects of mandatory and non-mandatory law that should be taken into account when drafting Particular Conditions of contract.'

— **Nick Longley**, *HFW*

'Such is the comprehensive nature of the guidance and explanations within the opening chapters that it will undoubtedly be regarded as one of the definitive guides to what FIDIC is, and how to use it.'

— **Bill Barton**, *Barton Legal*

'*FIDIC Contracts in Asia Pacific* will be an invaluable resource when it comes to understanding the FIDIC suite and assisting the industry in maximising the benefit from the suite, whether or not any particular project adopts one of the FIDIC contracts.'

— **Phillip Greenham**, *JBM Advisory*

'I can highly commend this book on multiple levels—from its intention to provide a practical tool by which to draft the Particular Conditions to a FIDIC Contract to its secondary benefits providing invaluable insight into the operation of construction law across multiple jurisdictions.'

— **Kiri Parr**, *Member of FIDIC Contracts Committee*

FIDIC CONTRACTS IN ASIA PACIFIC

FIDIC contracts are the most widely used contracts for international construction around the world and are used in many different jurisdictions, both common law and civil law. For any construction project, the General Conditions of Contract published by FIDIC need to be supplemented by Particular Conditions that specify the specific requirements of that project subject to the relevant laws.

FIDIC Contracts in Asia Pacific provides readers with detailed guidance and resources for the preparation of the Particular Conditions that will comply with the requirements of the applicable laws for a number of the jurisdictions in which FIDIC contracts are used. The laws that apply to the governing law of the contract, construction works and dispute resolution in each jurisdiction are identified. This book offers chapters on the FIDIC Conditions of Contract for Underground Works, and the perspective of a bilateral aid agency on the use of FIDIC contracts. Each jurisdiction features an outline of its construction industry and information on the impact of Covid-19 on both the execution of construction projects and the operation of construction contracts.

This book is essential reading for construction professionals, lawyers and students of construction law using FIDIC contracts.

Donald Charrett practises in construction law as an arbitrator, mediator, dispute board member and expert. Prior to becoming a lawyer, he worked as a consulting engineer for over 30 years. He has published widely on legal and engineering subjects, including as the author/joint author/editor of five books on construction law.

PRACTICAL LEGAL GUIDES FOR CONSTRUCTION AND TECHNOLOGY PROJECTS

Series editor: Donald Charrett

The books in this series provide lawyers and construction professionals with the relevant knowledge, resources and practical guidance to understand the contemporary construction industry and the law necessary to achieve successful outcomes for construction projects. The topics covered include front-end issues such as project procurement, the production, negotiation and administration of contracts, and the avoidance of disputes, as well as backend issues such as taking part in, managing or resolving disputes. The series aims to keep abreast of the technologies that have increasing impact in changing traditional ways of working, contracting and resolving disputes.

FIDIC Contracts in Asia Pacific
A Practical Guide to Application
Edited by Donald Charrett

Contracts for Construction and Engineering Projects
Second Edition
Donald Charrett

For more information, please visit: www.routledge.com/Practical-Legal-Guides-for-Construction-and-Technology-Projects/book-series/PLGCTP

FIDIC CONTRACTS IN ASIA PACIFIC

A Practical Guide to Application

EDITED BY
DONALD CHARRETT

informa law
from Routledge

Cover image: © Donald Charrett

First published 2022
by Informa Law from Routledge
2 Park Square, Milton Park, Abingdon, Oxon OX14 4RN

and by Informa Law from Routledge
605 Third Avenue, New York, NY 10158

Informa Law from Routledge is an imprint of the Taylor & Francis Group, an informa business

British Library Cataloguing-in-Publication Data
A catalogue record for this book is available from the British Library

Library of Congress Cataloging-in-Publication Data
Names: Charrett, D. E. (Donald Eric), editor.
Title: FIDIC contracts in Asia Pacific : a practical guide to application /
edited by Donald Charrett.
Other titles: International Federation of Consulting Engineers contracts in Asia Pacific
Description: Abingdon, Oxon [UK] ; New York, NY : Routledge, 2021. |
Includes bibliographical references and index.
Identifiers: LCCN 2021017932 (print) | LCCN 2021017933 (ebook) |
ISBN 9781032061436 (hardback) | ISBN 9781003200901 (ebook)
Subjects: LCSH: Construction contracts—Pacific Area. | Engineering contracts—Pacific Area. |
Standardized terms of contract—Pacific Area.
Classification: LCC KVC839 .F53 2021 (print) |
LCC KVC839 (ebook) | DDC 343.182307/8624—dc23
LC record available at https://lccn.loc.gov/2021017932
LC ebook record available at https://lccn.loc.gov/2021017933

ISBN: 978-1-032-06143-6 (hbk)
ISBN: 978-1-032-05597-8 (pbk)
ISBN: 978-1-003-20090-1 (ebk)

DOI: 10.4324/9781003200901

Typeset in Times New Roman
by codeMantra

This book is dedicated with grateful thanks to my wife, Jeyami, without whose understanding of and tolerance for the time-consuming demands entailed by my writing activities, this book would not have been possible.

CONTENTS

FIGURES AND TABLES

Figures

Tables

ACKNOWLEDGEMENTS

DONALD CHARRETT

FIDIC Contracts in Asia Pacific: A Practical Guide to Application was inspired by the success of the book *The International Application of FIDIC Contracts: A Practical Guide*, published by Routledge in 2020. One of the reviewers of that book opined: ‘In time and if its contents were allowed to spread to other jurisdictions in which FIDIC contracts are commonly used, it will develop into a vital encyclopaedia for all those tasked with the production, amendment and finalisation of a FIDIC construction contract.’[1]

This book is the first outcome of that challenge, comprising chapters on most of the major jurisdictions in the Asia Pacific region. The contents covered in each jurisdiction chapter in *FIDIC Contracts in Asia Pacific* have been expanded to include a section on the construction industry, and sections on the impacts of Covid-19 on the execution of construction projects and the operation of construction contracts. The book also includes a new chapter on the FIDIC Emerald Book, and a chapter on the Japan International Cooperation Agency’s perspectives on the use of FIDIC contracts.

This book has the ambitious aim of addressing the specific legal requirements of the applicable construction law in a number of jurisdictions in Asia Pacific. Each of these jurisdictions has its own particular legal landscape that impacts on the application of FIDIC (and other) construction contracts. Articulating the breadth and complexity of construction law in each of these jurisdictions required the skill and knowledge of expert local construction law practitioners. The chapter authors and their profiles and affiliations are identified in the following author profile sections. Each of those profiles demonstrate a deep well of legal and practical experience in local construction law in general, and the requirements of FIDIC contracts in particular. The authors are all eminent professionals who have had to fit the writing for their chapters into their busy schedules, in circumstances where normal professional life in every country was severely impacted by the ravages of Covid-19 and the new ways of working that entailed. I am very grateful to each of them for their commitment and hard work, and for delivering their chapters within the demanding timeframe that I set (albeit extensions of time were requested and granted due to the inevitable impact of the Covid-19 pandemic). The authors of the jurisdiction chapters closely followed a template that I provided; accordingly, any deficiencies in the scope of topics covered by the jurisdiction chapters are my responsibility, not those of the chapter authors. To state the obvious, this book could not have been written without the skill and expertise of the authors of the jurisdiction chapters.

1 Nick Longley, ‘Book Review: The International Application of FIDIC Contracts: A Practical Guide’ (2020) 1 *International Construction Law Review* 96, 98.

I also sincerely thank Bill Howard, President of FIDIC, for writing the Foreword, and the Honourable Peter Vickery QC for writing the chapter on the FIDIC Emerald Book. I am most grateful to Takashi Ito and Michino Yamaguchi for writing the chapter on JICA's perspectives, which provides an important view of the proper use of FIDIC contracts from an agency that is focused on obtaining the best value from the substantial bilateral aid funds that it dispenses.

In addition to those named above, I acknowledge and thank the many colleagues I have met at international FIDIC conferences and training courses who have contributed to my knowledge and interest in the international application of FIDIC contracts.

I also thank Terry Clague, Guy Loft and Julia Pollacco of Routledge, who have been unfailingly encouraging and helpful in publishing this book. Nicola Prior has done an excellent job on the difficult task of editing the manuscript and ensuring consistency of style and presentation, for which I am most grateful.

FOREWORD

It is indeed an honour to present this Foreword on *FIDIC Contracts in Asia Pacific: A Practical Guide to Application* edited by Dr Donald Charrett. Donald is a world-renowned expert in the application of FIDIC Conditions of Contract. As such, on behalf of the entire FIDIC family, I thank him immensely for editing this comprehensive treatise of the application of FIDIC Conditions of Contract in the Asia Pacific region.

FIDIC has proudly been preparing Conditions of Contract for global use for over 60 years. In all cases, we strive to develop documents which are fair to all parties and which appropriately balance risk. We also constantly seek feedback on the use of our Conditions of Contract in order, via our Contracts Committee, to keep them up to date.

Over the years, Donald has helped us in this endeavour, by leading task forces, conducting training, reviewing documents and in many other ways. By producing this book, he continues to serve FIDIC and the construction industry in a valuable way.

I am especially pleased to note that Donald has included in this book a chapter on the FIDIC Golden Principles. In the complex world global firms practising in the infrastructure space, their clients and the various funding agencies they work with operate in, there is a need to delineate some basic principles regarding the use of FIDIC Conditions of Contract. These Golden Principles address this need, and we encourage everyone to follow them. We firmly believe that following these five principles will dramatically increase the probability of a successful project. The principles are designed to protect everyone's interests. We respectfully suggest that not following them can lead to serious project problems, as well as negatively albeit unfairly impact the perception of FIDIC's Conditions of Contract. Thus, we strongly encourage everyone to follow them and, again, are pleased that Donald has featured them in the text.

This book also includes information from a number of Asia Pacific countries, many of which have very large infrastructure programmes underway or planned. Thus, Donald's timing in producing it is excellent.

I am confident that you will find this book to be a very valuable resource in your practice. Once again, Donald, thank you very much for preparing it and thank you for all you do for FIDIC.

Bill Howard
FIDIC President 2019–2020

ABOUT THE EDITOR

DR DONALD CHARRETT

BE(Hons), LLB(Hons), MConstLaw, PhD, ProfCertArb, Dip International Arbitration, FIEAust, FCIArb

Dr Charrett is a barrister, arbitrator, mediator, expert and dispute board member practising in technology, engineering and construction (TEC) disputes. Prior to joining the Victorian Bar, he worked as a solicitor at a large Australian law firm. His construction law briefs have included litigation, mediation, expert determination, facilitation of experts' conferences, arbitration and membership of dispute boards. He is a member of the FIDIC President's List of Adjudicators and a Fellow of the Chartered Institute of Arbitrators. He was named as Best Construction Law Practitioner, Australia 2016 by *Business Worldwide Magazine*. In 2019 and 2020, Who's Who Legal included him on their list of Thought Leaders – Construction, saying 'Donald Charrett is looked on with enormous favour by sources for his vast experience in construction and engineering disputes'.

Prior to becoming a lawyer, he worked as an engineer for over 30 years, including 12 years as a director of a consulting engineering firm. Dr Charrett's engineering experience included computer applications, structural design, managing engineering projects, acting as an expert witness and management roles in contract negotiation and administration, insurance, international joint ventures and corporate restructuring. From 2012 to 2014 he was non-executive chairman of consulting engineering company AMOG.

Dr Charrett has published widely on legal and engineering subjects, and presented conference papers, workshops and training courses in Australia and internationally. He is a Senior Fellow at the University of Melbourne, teaching a Master of Construction Law subject on international construction law.

His legal publications include articles on expert evidence, FIDIC contracts, dispute boards, dispute avoidance and resolution, contract risk, forensic engineering, contractual lessons from past projects, design and construct contracts, *quantum meruit*, solidary liability, construction insurance, professional indemnity insurance and reinsurance. He is the author of *The Application of Contracts in Engineering and Construction* Contracts, joint author of *The Application of Contracts in Developing Oil and Gas Projects* and the editor of *The International Application of FIDIC Contracts: A Practical* Guide, and *Global Challenges Shared Solutions.*

CONTRIBUTORS

Mr Aditya Ajay (India) Aditya is a practising advocate with SKV Law Offices with experience in the field of dispute resolution, energy laws and infrastructure. He has been a part of teams representing national conglomerates before the Supreme Court of India, various High Courts and tribunals. He has a keen interest in the field of international commercial arbitration and investment laws. He has also represented the Central Government before the Delhi High Court in matters of national importance.

Contact details: aditya.ajay@skvlawoffices.com

Reynaldo Albertiny ST (Indonesia) graduated in 2017 from Harapan Bangsa Institute of Technology, Bandung majoring in industrial engineering. He began his career in construction dispute resolution in 2018 at the Indonesian Construction Arbitration and Alternative Dispute Resolution Centre (BADAPSKI) and also at the Institute of Dispute Board for Construction (PADSK). He has been involved in construction dispute resolution for several power plant and toll road projects in Indonesia by providing assistance to Prof Dr Ir Sarwono Hardjomuljadi. Together with Prof Dr Ir Sarwono Hardjomuljadi, he has been involved in the translation of the FIDIC Pink Book (MDB Harmonised Edition) 2010.

Mr Chamaka Ambagahawita (Sri Lanka) was admitted as an Attorney-at-Law of the Supreme Court of Sri Lanka in 2018. He presently serves the Bar as Junior Counsel to Dr Harsha Cabral, President's Counsel under whose guidance Mr Ambagahawita continues to specialise the fields of commercial arbitration (both domestic and international), company law, intellectual property law, commercial agreements and international trade law.

Mr Ambagahawita passed with a Second Class Honours at the Final Examination for the admission as an Attorney-at-Law conducted by the Sri Lanka Law College in October 2016. He read for his Bachelor's Degree in Laws (LLB) from the Faculty of Law, University of Colombo, Sri Lanka. In addition, he holds a Diploma in Law from the University of London, United Kingdom. Furthermore, presently, Mr Ambagahawita is following the Diploma in Arbitration organised by the Institute for the Development of Commercial Law and Practice (ICLP) in Sri Lanka.

In addition to his practice as a Junior Counsel, Mr Ambagahawita has been engaged in academia through the publication of journal articles. He also had the good fortune of assisting Dr Cabral in his latest publication on commercial arbitration titled *Law and Practice of Commercial Arbitration in Sri Lanka* (2018).

Contact details: cja91@yahoo.com

Mr Joseph Barbaro (Papua New Guinea) is a partner in Corrs Chambers Westgarth specialising in construction and infrastructure in the areas of project delivery, outsourcing and dispute resolution. He advises government and the private sector (including financiers, sponsors, principals and contractors) on all aspects of project and infrastructure delivery across a range of sectors, including education, health, property, energy and resources, transport and water.

He immerses himself in projects during the tender phase, rolling up his sleeves to understand the technical detail and then supports his clients through project delivery with strategic and practical guidance. His experience through all these phases gives him keen insight into the issues and risks facing clients implementing large and complex projects. Deploying this experience for clients early during tender contract design and negotiation proves invaluable.

Joseph's experience spans the full range of contract delivery models, from traditional D&C and EPC using FIDIC and Australian Standard form contracts, through to DBOM, BOOT and relationship-based alliance contracting. He represents clients in superior courts, arbitration, expert determinations and statutory adjudications.

Contact details: Joseph.Barbaro@corrs.com.au

Mr Nicholas Barnes (Fiji) is a Suva-based lawyer, notary public and managing partner in Fiji's largest private firm, Munro Leys. Nicholas graduated with a Bachelor of Laws degree from Newcastle Polytechnic in the UK. He was admitted to the English and Welsh Bar in 1991 and since then in Tuvalu (1997) (former People's Lawyer), Fiji (1998), New Zealand (2002) and Grenada (2002). He has over 27 years of legal experience in both public and private practice.

Nicholas practises in a wide variety of commercial litigation and advisory work, including employment negotiations/disputes, civil and commercial litigation, construction/engineering contracts, high-end criminal defence, ADR, general commercial advice, aviation and environment law. Nicholas led the team that drafted Fiji's Environmental Management Act. He is a trained mediator. Nicholas has advised governments on human rights obligations and has represented several commonwealth country governments in judicial review applications.

Nicholas is a former in-house counsel for Greenpeace, former vice chair of Fiji Environmental Law Association and former board member of Habitat for Humanity. Nicholas is the honorary solicitor for Fiji Association of Sports and Olympics Committee, current honorary legal adviser British High Commission and board member of FRIEND Fiji (NGO). Nicholas has provided contractual and legislative advice in PNG.

Contact details: nicholas.barnes@munroleyslaw.com.fj

Mr Ben Bury (Hong Kong and Malaysia) is a partner in Holman Fenwick Willan's Hong Kong and Singapore offices. For more than 15 years, Ben has assisted clients to resolve disputes arising out of complex and high value construction projects.

Ben has been based in Asia since 2011 and has advised on disputes arising out of some of the largest and most significant projects in the region. This includes the construction of multi-billion dollar onshore and offshore oil and gas facilities, power plants, underground railways and tunnelling projects, ports, roads, refineries, mines and processing plants, and reclamation works.

Highly recommended by the independent directories that review the legal market, Ben is described as 'an accomplished and impressive lawyer, responsive, friendly, personable and a delight to work with' (Legal 500 Asia Pacific 2020); he is also praised as being an 'arbitration specialist' and 'very, very smart, with a strategic mind and huge knowledge of international construction' (Legal 500 Asia Pacific 2019).

Ben has worked for or against corporations or on projects connected to almost every country in Asia-Pacific including China, Hong Kong, South Korea, Japan, India, Bangladesh, Thailand, Vietnam, Malaysia, Indonesia, the Philippines, Singapore and Australia.

He has acted as counsel on arbitrations seated in numerous jurisdictions and subject to the institutional rules of the ICC, SIAC, HKIAC and LCIA, as well as *ad hoc* arbitrations subject to the UNCITRAL rules.

Qualified in Hong Kong and England & Wales, Ben has been granted full registration as a Registered Foreign Lawyer in the Singapore International Commercial Court. He is also the secretary and international liaison officer for the Society of Construction Law in Hong Kong.

Contact details: ben.bury@hfw.com

Dr Harsha Cabral (Sri Lanka) is a President's Counsel in Sri Lanka with 30 years' experience in the fields of company law, intellectual property law, commercial law, international trade law and commercial arbitration. He has been a President's Counsel for 12 years and commands an extensive practice in the Commercial High Courts and the Supreme Courts of Sri Lanka. He holds a doctorate in corporate law from the University of Canberra, Australia and is a sitting member of the International Chamber of Commerce ICC International Court of Arbitration in Paris.

Dr Cabral is a member of the Law Commission of Sri Lanka, a Council Member of the University of Colombo and a member of the UGC Standing Committee on Legal Matters. As a member of the Advisory Commission on Company Law in Sri Lanka, he was one of the architects of the *Companies Act No. 7 of 2007*, the current Act. He is a Council Member of the Institute for the Development of Commercial Law & Practice (ICLP) and is the Course Director for the Diploma in Commercial Arbitration. As a member of the Council of Legal Education in Sri Lanka, as a member the Ministerial Committee appointed to reform Commercial Arbitration in Sri Lanka, and as a Founder Board Member of the Sri Lanka International Arbitration Centre, Dr Cabral has contributed immensely to the legal academia and the corporate community of Sri Lanka.

Dr Cabral is a visiting lecturer at several universities and is a regular speaker at public seminars, author of several books and has presented several papers on corporate law, intellectual property law, international trade law and commercial arbitration here and abroad. In addition to his active practice in courts and lecturing, he has been a counsel in many arbitrations and has served as sole-arbitrator, co-arbitrator and chairman in a large number of arbitrations, domestic and international.

Contact details: harshacabral@yahoo.com

Mr Salvador P. Castro, Jr. (Philippines) ASEAN Chartered Professional Engineer (ACPE), APEC and ASEAN Engineer. He is an accredited arbitrator and mediator of Construction Industry Arbitration Commission (Philippines), Philippine Dispute

Resolution Center and Hong Kong International Arbitration Centre. He is member of the ADR Committee of the Philippine Judicial Academy-Supreme Court. He is Philippines Country Representative to DRBF, Member of CIArb (UK) and SoCL (UK). Listed in the Accepted Adjudicators of CECOPHIL, FIDIC's MA in the Philippines, after passing the ADB-FIDIC-JICA Adjudicator's Assessment Workshop.

As FIDIC Contracts International Accredited Trainer, he lectures on FIDIC Contracts and dispute boards within ASEAN and non-ASEAN countries. He lectures for JICA on the FIDIC MDB Contract and dispute boards focusing on dispute avoidance for JICA ODA Loan Projects under the Philippines' Build Infrastructure Program. He is a FIDIC Affiliate Member.

With over 40 years' experience in project management, one of his achievements was the Presidential Citation for Filipino Individuals & Organizations Overseas in 1998 as Project Director of Guinness Book of World Record's biggest residential palace – Istana Nurul Iman of The Sultan of Brunei Darussalam. He is elected as a Fellow of Association of Project Management (UK).

SP Castro is founding chairman and CEO of SPCastro, Inc (Philippines) and SPCastro & Associates Sdn Bhd (Brunei Darussalam).

Contact details: spcjr@spcastro.com

Mr Melvin Chand (Fiji) is a Savusavu-based in-house lawyer at one of Fiji's top-tier projects, the Nawi Island Project. The Project is developing Fiji's largest boutique and integrated gold standard 'green' tourism marina (130 berths with 19 superyacht capacity) and central facility with an attached 5-star resort and spa, and private real estate. The project will feature a cyclone 5 rated 200 boats dry dock storage and maintenance yard.

Melvin graduated in 2015 from the University of the South Pacific with a Bachelor of Laws and a Bachelor of Commerce (in International Business and Marketing) degrees. In the same year he completed the Professional Diploma in Legal Practice and was admitted to the Fiji Bar.

Since admission, Melvin has practised in Fiji's largest private law firm Munro Leys in their litigation team with Mr Nicholas Barnes until November 2020. At Munro Leys, Melvin practised in a wide variety of commercial litigation and advisory work, including employment negotiations and litigating in the Employment Relations Tribunal, civil and commercial litigation including contract and tort-based negligence such as medical and professional negligence, construction law disputes, ADR and general commercial law advice. He has a keen interest in human rights law.

Melvin is an accredited mediator with the Fiji Mediation Centre trained by the Singapore Mediation Centre.

Contact details: melvin@nawiisland.com

Ms Kanika Chugh (India) is an advocate with SKV Law Offices with experience in varied commercial litigation and telecom disputes. She has represented Indian and multinational clients in corporate and commercial disputes before various courts and tribunals in India. A substantial part of her practice has been advising and representing telecom giants on all their issues, including disputes with shareholders, regulatory disputes and disputes with various vendors in the telecom industry. She

has also managed commercial disputes for telecom companies in various forums, including arbitrations before the Singapore International Arbitration Centre (SIAC).
Contact details: kanika.chugh@skvlawoffices.com

Mr Tanka Prasad Dulal (Nepal) is a Senior Advocate practising in the Supreme Court of Nepal and a member of Supreme Court Bar Association Nepal. He has 29 years' legal practice and experience in the field of corporate law including construction law, policy and rules and regulations of Nepal. Mr Dulal has additional experience especially in the field of the public procurement law and policy. He is legal adviser/consultant to the Federation of Contractors' Association of Nepal (FCAN). As law consultant for the Nepal Government Law Commission and other organisations he has developed legislative drafting manuals, organisation and academic administration rules, employees' services rules and procurement and financial administration rules. Mr Dulal was legal adviser to the policy research, evaluation and analyst consultant for the three-year interim Nepal national plan and policy to the Action Aid International and national women's rights forum. Mr Dulal is chairperson of the Development and Business Law Institute.
Contact details: tp.dulal@gmail.com

Ms Yvonne Foo (Singapore) is a partner in the Construction and Engineering Practice Group of Harry Elias Partnership LLP in Singapore. Yvonne has extensive experience in advising international, regional and local clients on construction-related disputes relating to issues such as variations, claims for extensions of time, liquidated damages, termination, risk management and, recently, Covid-related issues. A specialist in construction law, Yvonne has advised on a wide range of projects including airports, ports, rail, hospitals, stadium and other public infrastructure projects; residential, hospitality and commercial real estate and property projects; water and waste treatment plants, food processing and other industrial treatment plants; oil and gas, hydro and other renewable energy projects, etc. She has been involved in various prominent projects globally.

Yvonne regularly advises on dispute resolution and dispute avoidance matters. She is highly experienced in alternative dispute resolution mechanisms including arbitration, adjudication and mediation. Yvonne is a Fellow of the Chartered Institute of Arbitrators (FCIArb), and also an associate mediator with the Singapore Mediation Centre.

Yvonne was called to the Singapore Bar, and has practised thereafter in both common law and civil law jurisdictions. She often assist clients on construction projects involving international elements in Singapore, Southeast Asia and the Middle East.
Contact details: YvonneFoo@harryelias.com

Mr Mino Han (South Korea) is a partner at Peter & Kim (Seoul). He has acted as counsel in various international construction arbitrations conducted under the auspices of the ICC, SIAC, KCAB and JCAA. These disputes concerned the design and construction of combined cycle power plants, solar power production facilities, refineries, high-rise buildings, convention centres and infrastructure facilities. The projects were based in the Middle East, Asia, Eastern Europe, Africa or Latin America. Mino also regularly advises clients on issuing or defending claims during a project arising out of standard form contracts including the FIDIC Suite of Contracts. He majored in law at Seoul National University (LLB 2006), after which he passed the Korean Bar Exam in 2006. He also received a Master of Laws degree in international arbitration law from Seoul National University in 2012. In 2018, Mino received an MSc degree for construction law and dispute resolution at King's College London. His dissertation for this MSc programme entitled 'The meaning and scope of "consequential loss" exclusion clauses: A comparative law analysis between English law and Korean law' was awarded with a distinction grade. In July 2019, Mino was admitted to the roll of solicitors in England and Wales.

Contact details: MinoHan@peterandkim.com

Prof Dr Sarwono Hardjomuljadi MSc, MH (Indonesia). Sarwono has 40 years' experience in international construction contracts, including project manager for several hydropower plant projects owned by PT PLN (Persero). He has been appointed arbitrator and dispute board member for international contracts and is an accredited trainer for FIDIC Conditions of Contract. He is professor in legal aspects and construction contract management and dispute resolution at Mercu Buana University, Jakarta and several other universities including Tarumanagara Jakarta, Parahyangan Bandung, Atma Jaya Yogyakarta and Muhammadiyah Jakarta.

Recently he was elected a member of the board of directors of Fédération Internationale des Ingénieurs-Conseils (FIDIC) (2019–2023), and the board of directors for Region 2 of the Dispute Resolution Board Foundation (DRBF) (2017–2022).

Sarwono provided consultancy services to the Government of Indonesia in the preparation of *Law No 2/2017 for Construction Services*. He has also worked as special adviser to the Minister of Public Works and Housing of Indonesia; formerly Vice President of PT PLN (Persero), the State Electricity Corporation, Deputy Director for Capability Development of PT PLN (Persero), Director of PT Geodipa Energi (Persero); Board of Supervisors Indonesian National Board for Construction Services Development (LPJK); Founder and Vice Chairman of Indonesian Construction Arbitration and Alternative Dispute Resolution Centre (BADAPSKI); President of the Institute of Dispute Board for Construction (PADSK); Member of Committee for Construction Safety (Komite K2). He was a reviewer of the FIDIC rainbow suite 2017 and together with his team has translated the 1999 FIDIC rainbow suite and the Pink Book (MDB Harmonised Edition) 2006 and 2010 into Bahasa Indonesia.

Contact details: sarwonohm2@yahoo.co.id

Henrico Hariandja ST, MT (Indonesia) has 10 years' experience in the Indonesian construction industry. He earned a Bachelor's degree in Industrial Engineering from Bandung Institute Technology (ITB), Indonesia in 2006, and a Master's Degree in Construction Project Management from Parahyangan University in 2014. He started his career in 2009 in the Ministry of Public Works and Housing in a variety of working fields such as construction business development, construction institutional development, public private partnership and construction procurement. Recently he was appointed as Head of Procurement Division for construction projects of the Ministry of Public Works and Housing for Bangka-Belitung Province. He is also active in the Institute of Dispute Board for Construction (PADSK) as Treasurer. Together with Prof Dr Ir Sarwono Hardjomuljadi he translated the 1999 FIDIC Yellow Book into the Indonesian Language.

Dr Nguyen Thi Hoa (Vietnam) is a lecturer at Ho Chi Minh City University of Law (from 9/2019). She worked as a legal adviser in the Department of Justice of Ho Chi Minh City in Vietnam (2010–9/2019), and her job involves counselling about: Public-Private Partnership contracts; construction law; investment law; international dispute resolution; promotion of commercial arbitration; recognition and enforcement of decisions of foreign authorities, etc. She finished her PhD thesis with honours at University Pantheon-Assas Paris II, on the topic of 'Dispute resolution procedures under FIDIC contracts' in December 2018. She worked as an intern in a construction law firm in Paris from September to December 2018.

Contact details: nguyenthihoa_5787@yahoo.com.vn

Mr Le The Hung (Vietnam) is recognised as an experienced real estate and construction lawyer, and regularly advises project developers, contractors, and various consultants on investment, construction, and real estate in Vietnam. Hung's clients include Hoa Binh Group, How Yu, Lecade, Eurowindow, PVInvest, Nha Trang Bay Investment Group, Kurihara, COFICO, Pado and Sinh Nam.

Hung's extensive experience and solid relationships has provided these clients with exceptional and valuable legal advice and wide range of services, ranging from contracts, construction, and real estate to dispute resolution.

Ranked as one of a few lawyers in Vietnam who understands real estate and the construction industry in depth, Hung regularly conducts comprehensive FIDIC contract management training courses. Hung's sole purpose is to help Vietnamese practitioners to be consistent with that of international standards with respect to construction contracts and real estate.

Contact details: hung.le@cnccounsel.com

Mr Naoki Iguchi (Japan) is a partner at Nagashima Ohno & Tsunematsu. He studied law at the University of Tokyo (LLB, LLM) and Stanford Law School (LLM). He has served as the representative of Japan at the Dispute Resolution Board Foundation (DRBF), Director of the International Academy of Construction Lawyers (IACL) and Co-Chair of the International Construction Project Committee of the Inter-Pacific Bar Association (IPBA). His practice experience covers a wide range of construction projects, including EPC projects in all regions. He has advised on contentious and non-contentious matters in construction/operation and maintenance projects of railway/metro, highways, renewable/coal/gas/nuclear power stations and power grids, chemical/agricultural plants, oil/gas pipelines and development of commercial properties. He has taught construction and project law at Keio University Law School. He also devoted himself to the development of international arbitration practice in Japan, having served as a Director of the Japan Association of Arbitrators (JAA) and as a member of the ICC Japan Committee. He has also taught an international arbitration law course at Keio University Law School. He speaks, reads and writes Japanese, English, Mandarin and Spanish. He is a member of the Society of Construction Law (SCL) and the Swiss Arbitration Association (ASA).

Contact details: naoki_iguchi@noandt.com

Mr Kenneth Imako (Papua New Guinea) is Special Counsel in the Corrs Chambers Westgarth's Papua New Guinea litigation department. He has extensive experience in commercial litigation in the District, National and Supreme Court of Papua New Guinea as well as the Local and Provincial Land Court. Kenneth has advised on and acted as counsel in litigation involving employment issues, personal injury claims, fraud claims, liquidation and insolvency matters, alternative dispute resolution, banking and finance litigation and insurance claims.

Kenneth is also an Honorary member of the Victorian Bar, having read and signed the Roll of Overseas Practitioners in 2005.

Contact details: kenneth.imako@corrs.com.au

Mr Takashi Ito (JICA: Japan) Deputy Director General, Infrastructure Engineering Department, Japan International Cooperation Agency (JICA). Takashi ITO focuses on promotion of sound contract implementation in the projects funded by JICA. His enhanced knowledge of international construction contracts, in particular different FIDIC contract forms, helps JICA's clients and other stakeholders for their projects/contracts moving in a better direction at different stages (ie project formulation, bidding, contract administration, etc). He has represented JICA in many FIDIC gatherings and has been appointed as JICA's representative to FIDIC's IFI committee. He also played a leading role to introduce the system of standard bidding documents using FIDIC MDB Harmonised Edition and the Yellow Book for the first time in the history of JICA's Official Development Assistance (ODA) loans. In the context of promotion of sound contract implementation, dispute resolution has been the area that his energy has particularly been devoted to. Some of his outstanding achievements are, for example, creation of the National List of Adjudicators in Japan, publication of a 'Dispute Board Manual' for practitioners, etc., all in close collaboration with different FIDIC experts.

Contact details: Ito.Takashi.2@jica.go.jp

Ms Julie-Anne Mallis (nee Pemberton) (Hong Kong & Malaysia) is an associate in Holman Fenwick Willan's Hong Kong Office. She specialises in dispute resolution, primarily focusing on high-value disputes arising out of complex construction, engineering, major infrastructure and energy and resources projects. She has experience acting for principals including government, contractors and subcontractors in litigation and arbitration in Asia and Australia. Julie-Anne has experience in domestic and international arbitration seated in Hong Kong and Singapore and subject to the institutional rules of the HKIAC and SIAC.

Julie-Anne also has experience in insolvency and has previously worked on a range of general commercial litigation matters.

Julie-Anne completed her Bachelor of Laws (Honours)/Bachelor of Arts at the University of Notre Dame Australia. She is qualified in Western Australia and Hong Kong.

Contact details: julie-anne.mallis@hfw.com

Mr Andrew McCormack (Papua New Guinea) is a partner of Corrs Chambers Westgarth with over 20 years' experience working in major projects and procurement. He provides tailored advice to clients which is delivered with regard to the prevailing commercial circumstances.

His previous experience as in-house legal counsel gives Andrew valuable insight into the business operations and corporate governance structures his clients operate within. Andrew offers a solution-based approach and is not afraid to explore alternative contracting strategies.

He is renowned for his major transaction and projects work in the construction, mining, energy and resources and infrastructure sectors, including in recent years the world first CSG to LNG QCLNG project, as well as the Cross River Rail and Brisbane Metro projects.

He provides expert advice on a wide range of contracts including EPC, EPCM, PPP, Alliance Agreements, mining services contracts and drilling contracts, using both bespoke and standard forms such as FIDIC and Australian Standards.

He offers advice from strategic planning and the selection of a contracting model, through to procurement and contract delivery (including claims management). Andrew's client base includes blue chip companies such as QGC/Shell, Puma Energy, Thiess, Laing O'Rourke, Spiecapag, MACH Energy, Queensland Rail and Aurizon.

Contact details: Andrew.McCormack@corrs.com.au

Mr Malith Mendis (Sri Lanka) is a civil engineer, arbitrator and adjudicator and is a FIDIC accredited lecturer/trainer in management of construction contracts and a reviewer of the 2017 FIDIC Contracts.

He is a Past President of the Association of Consulting Engineers Sri Lanka, a Fellow and a Council Member of the Institution of Engineers Sri Lanka, a Fellow and Country Representative of the Institution of Civil Engineers UK, Member of the Society of Structural Engineers Sri Lanka, Member and Country Representative of the Dispute Resolution Board Foundation and an Associate member of the Chartered Institute of Arbitrators UK. He has served and currently serves on many standing and *ad hoc* dispute adjudication boards and on arbitral tribunals. He is on the panel of Arbitrators and Adjudicators of the Institution of Engineers, Sri Lanka, and on the panel of Adjudicators, Association of Consulting Engineers, Sri Lanka. He is a faculty member/lecturer at the Institute for the Development of Commercial Law and Practice (ICLP).

Mr Mendis has served as Council Member of the Chamber of Construction Industry Sri Lanka, and on the Advisory Council on Export of Professional Services of the Export Development Board.

He has worked on many large projects worldwide as employer's representative, consultant and contractor in hydropower projects, industrial building projects, hospitals, ports & harbours and other projects specialising in contract management, claims analysis and dispute resolution.

Mr Mendis is a former CEO of the Lanka Hydraulic Institute, Sri Lanka. He is currently Chairman of Mendis Cobain Consultants (Pvt) Ltd.

Contact details: mm@mendiscobain.com

Mr Khawaja Hamid Mushtaq (Pakistan) is an engineer-lawyer, with over 16 years of international experience in project procurement, contract administration and dispute resolution of multiple billion-dollar infrastructure projects. Hamid has completed his Bachelor of Civil Engineering from Mehran University, Jamshoro, Pakistan, Master of Construction Law from Melbourne Law School, University of Melbourne, Australia, Chartered Institute of Arbitrators' Post Graduate Diploma in International

Commercial Arbitration held at Jesus College, Oxford University and certification in PMP from Project Management Institute (PMI) in addition to many other on job training and certifications.

He currently works with the National Highway Authority, Pakistan as a deputy director in the procurement and contract administration section. His key responsibilities in this role include leading teams in the procurement of road infrastructure projects including works and services, managing contractor and employer claims, providing expert opinions on contractual matters to project authorities and contesting adjudications and arbitrations on multiple projects, nationally and internationally.

He regularly conducts training on FIDIC contracts, construction claims and arbitration in various public and private sector organisations including the Highway Research and Training Centre, Burhan, National University of Science & Technology, Islamabad and WAPDA Staff College, Islamabad.

Contact details: hanny_khawaja@hotmail.com

Dr Peni Jati Setyowati SH, MH (Indonesia) is a graduate with a Bachelor's Degree from the Faculty of Law, Airlangga University, Masters in the Faculty of Law, Airlangga University and Doctoral at the Faculty of Law, Airlangga University. Her scientific specialisations are international law, government law, construction law and investment law. She works as a lecturer in the Faculty of Law, Wijaya Kusuma University Surabaya and also as a contract lecturer at the Faculty of Law at the State University of Surabaya and the Faculty of Law at the Vecontterans National Development University Jakarta. She is active as a journal reviewer at *Notaire Journal*, Faculty of Law, Airlangga University Surabaya, *Authentica Journal*, Faculty of Law, Jenderal Soedirman University; and *Novum Journal*, Faculty of Law, Surabaya State University. She is also active as an administrator at the Surabaya State University Development Law Study Center. She is also active in activities of the Institute of Dispute Board for Construction (PADSK).

Mr Aditya Vardhan Sharma (India) Aditya is a practising advocate with SKV Law Offices who specialises in corporate dispute resolution, including litigation and arbitration. He has experience of having advised on high stake litigation with national importance on behalf of prominent players in banking, insurance and the agriculture sectors. Aditya has appeared and conducted cases before various courts, tribunals and quasi-judicial bodies pan India. He has undertaken and led litigation concerning a wide range of subjects including, insolvency and bankruptcy, arbitration, contracts, securitisation, banking, insurance and company laws.

Contact details: aditya.sharma@skvlawoffices.com

Dr Hare Ram Shrestha (Nepal) is a civil engineer with 33 years' experience in road transport for project implementation, policy formulation, training, transport planning and bioengineering. He pioneered, implemented and piloted the Green Roads concept in Nepal, and has worked for various projects as a specialist in Nepal and Bhutan in project planning, project formulation and bioengineering supported by the government and donors such as the World Bank, ADB, USAID, DFID, KfW, WFP (UN) and SDC. Dr Shrestha has worked in transport and environment related projects for 26 years as a consultant, including as project director for more than 20 road projects, and 15 short studies as a transport specialist in Nepal and Bhutan.

He is a member of Visiting Faculty of the Nepal Engineering College, Pokhara University and has given guest lectures, supervised theses and acted as external examiner for the Masters course of Transport Engineering and Management since 2015.

Dr Shrestha has published over 35 papers and presented at national and international conferences and seminars on infrastructure planning, environment, roads and other engineering sectors. He has been involved in organising over 20 conferences and seminars in Nepal.

Contact details: hrs@sidef.com.np

Ir Dona Alisyah Siregar ST, MSc, CRMP (Indonesia) has 16 years' experience in construction contract law, risks and management in the Indonesian construction industry. Her position now is Vice President of Contract Management at PT Hutama Karaya (Persero), an Indonesian state-owned company general contractor. She earned a Bachelor's Degree in civil engineering from Bandung Institute Technology (ITB), Indonesia and a Master's Degree in construction contract management from Malaysia University of Technology (UTM). She started her career in 2005 as contract administrator in PT Wijaya Karya (Persero) Tbk. (WIKA). With WIKA, she was the manager responsible for construction contracts and risk management and has experience in building, infrastructure, mechanical electrical, industrial plant, oil and gas works contracts, claims and disputes. From 2015 to 2018 she was engaged on the High-Speed Railway (HSR) Project, one of the megaprojects in Indonesia, as General Manager Legal and System of the High-Speed Railway Contractor Consortium (HSRCC). Together with Prof Dr Ir Sarwono Hardjomuljadi she translated the FIDIC 1999 Red Book and Yellow Book into the Indonesian language. She is a Certified Risk Management Professional, an Indonesian Government Procurement Expert and National Mediator.

Ms Komal Singh (Fiji) is a Suva-based lawyer working in Munro Leys, in the firm's litigation team. She was admitted to the Fiji Bar in 2014 and has since practised in areas of employment law, commercial dispute resolution, debt recovery and all aspects of general civil litigation including pre-action conduct.

Komal has represented clients in a wide range of litigation in most of Fiji's courts and tribunals. She also provides pro bono services and general assistance on matters involving public interest on an ad hoc basis.

Komal is an active member of the Fiji Law Society.

Contact details: komal.singh@munroleyslaw.com.fj

Ir Enni M. Soetanto MM (Indonesia). Enni has 40 years' experience in the construction industry, since her graduation as Bachelor of Civil Engineering from Parahyangan University Bandung in 1978; and then Master of Management, Gajah Mada University; International Project Management Programme, Bradford University, UK; Applied International Management Program, Sweden.

She was recently Chair of the Fédération Internationale des Ingénieurs-Conseils (FIDIC) Membership Committee and friendly reviewer of the new edition FIDIC Green Book 2019. She has worked at Mott MacDonald Indonesia as Managing Director (2007–2020) and then Executive Director/Senior Adviser (2020–present); PT Virama Karya Consulting Engineers: Head of Bureau Division (2001–2007) and Branch Manager of Eastern Indonesia (1993–2000).

Enni has specialised in general management and planning, design, implementation and project management of major multidisciplinary projects. Her experience also covers water, transportation, building and infrastructure developments. She manages multidisciplinary teams in master planning, design, supervision, training and construction management.

She is has been Project Director for various projects (selected): DED underground Jakarta Mass Rapid Transit (MRT) – 4.5km with four Stations for JO Shimizu, Obayashi, Jaya Konstruksi and Widjaya Karya (FIDIC Yellow Book); Project Management Services (PMS) Jakarta LRT, for Jakarta Propertindo (FIDIC Silver Book); Construction Management Consultancy (CMC) Palembang sewerage system – Client: InDII/KIAT Australia; 50km DED Ngawi Kertosono toll road project for Thiess Australia; Public Private Partnership (PPP) Advisory Services Support Central Unit (P3CU) of National Planning Agency (Bappenas), Jakarta; Basic Design and Construction Management Suramadu Bridge Project – 5.3 km length, connecting East Java and Madura Island for the Ministry of Public Works, Directorate General of Highways.

Mr Ashutosh Kumar Srivastava (India) Ashutosh is an advocate with SKV Law Offices who specialises in the field of regulatory law and policy with a special focus on energy laws. He has been a part of teams representing domestic and international clients before the Supreme Court of India, several High Courts and Tribunals in matters pertaining to tariff and contractual disputes. He has also been involved in various arbitration proceedings pertaining to issues of liquidated damages and disputes arising out of tender documents.

Contact details: ashutosh@skvlawoffices.com

Ms Kaori Sugimoto (Japan) Kaori Sugimoto is a counsel at Nagashima Ohno & Tsunematsu. She studied law at Hitotsubashi Univesity (LLB, LLM) and University of Pennsylvania Law School (LLM with Wharton Business & Law Certificate). Before joining Nagashima Ohno & Tsunematsu, she worked at White & Case LLP (Tokyo office). Her main areas of practice are international construction and infrastructure projects and international dispute resolution (including international arbitration). She has extensive experience in international construction and infrastructure projects, including process/power plant construction projects, solar power projects, railway projects and wind farm projects, in the region of South-East Asia, Middle East Asia and Europe. She is a member of the Engineering Advancement Association of Japan (ENAA) and the Engineering and Consulting Firms Association of Japan (ECFA).

Contact details: kaori_sugimoto@noandt.com

Mr Nick Thorne (Papua New Guinea) is a partner and member of Corrs Chambers Westgarth's Papua New Guinea practice group. He is a major projects and transactions lawyer with a focus on natural resources, energy and infrastructure, both in Australia and Papua New Guinea. Nick has also spent time on secondment in the legal group of one of the world's leading oil and gas companies. He is an Australian legal practitioner and also a Papua New Guinea lawyer admitted in the National Court of Papua New Guinea.

Contact details: Nick.Thorne@corrs.com.au

Mr Nguyen Nam Trung (Vietnam) is interim Chair of Vietnam Contracts and Construction Law Group (VCCLG). He is working as a deputy director of the Business Development Department of EVNPECC3 and as managing partner of NTT Consulting Ltd in Vietnam. Trung has a M.Eng in structural engineering from Asian Institute of Technology and an MBE in international construction: practice and law from the University of Stuttgart. He is a former member of FIDIC YPFSC (2016–2018) and current member of FIDIC CC TG16, FIDIC BPC BIM TG. He is also member of the Dispute Resolution Board Foundation (DRBF).

Contact details: nnamtrung@gmail.com

Mr Shri Venkatesh (India) Shri Venkatesh has over 12 years of experience as an advocate. After working with top tier firms in India, he set up SKV Law Offices in 2013. His practise areas include infrastructure, energy laws, arbitration, consumer protection and environment. Apart from representing national conglomerates, Shri Venkatesh also represents the Central Government as a standing counsel before the Supreme Court of India. He is well versed with the regulatory regimes and policy changes in the infrastructure sector.

Contact details: shri.venkatesh@skvlawoffices.com

The Hon Peter Vickery QC LLB (Melbourne) LLM (Kings College, London) FCIArb FACICA (Australia) is a Queens Counsel (QC) and formerly a judge of the Supreme Court of Victoria (2008–2018). He retired from the Supreme Court on 8 May 2018 after serving as Judge-in-Charge of the Technology, Engineering and Construction List (the TEC List). He now works as an arbitrator, a referee, a DRB panellist, a mediator and an ENE evaluator and conducts expert determinations. He is the patron of the Society of Construction Law, Australia (SOCLA). He lectures at the University of Technology Sydney (UTS) and is a founding member of Underground Works Chambers (UWC) with Professor Arnold Dix (Vice President of the of the International Tunnelling Association) and Lord Robert Mair CBE FREng FICE FRS NAE, Emeritus Professor of Civil Engineering and Director of Research at Cambridge University, Member of the House of Lords. In August 2020, Peter Vickery was appointed as Senior Fellow, Melbourne University, in the Masters in Construction Law Programme.

Contact details: pnv@petervickeryqc.com

Mr Ryan Warokra (Papua New Guinea) is a member of Corrs Chambers Westgarth's PNG and corporate group. He advises on company law, employment, contracts, property, mining and oil and gas law. He has been ranked as an 'associate to watch' by Chambers Asia-Pacific for key supporting roles on major transactions. Ryan routinely advises clients across a range of sectors, including financial services, superannuation, mining and oil & gas and their related service sectors, and power.

Contact details: ryan.warokra@corrs.com.au

Ms Michino Yamaguchi (JICA: Japan) Director, Loan Procurement Policy and Supervision Division, Infrastructure Engineering Department, Japan International Cooperation Agency (JICA). Her major career is Official Development Assistance (ODA) loan operations in Asia, especially procurement supervision of ODA loan projects in Indonesia and Pakistan during assignment as Representative of JICA

Indonesia Office from 2007 to 2010 and Senior Representative of JICA Pakistan Office from 2016 to 2018. From December 2018, she was assigned to the Director of Loan Procurement Policy and Supervision Division. She has played a leading role in updating JICA's standard bidding documents using FIDIC Contract Conditions for further improvement, and disseminating the proper use of FIDIC Contract Conditions and promotion of dispute boards by holding seminars for relevant officials such as the Executing Agency of ODA loan projects, consultants and contractors.

Contact details: Yamaguchi.Michino@jica.go.jp

Ms Sun Yiwen (China) is an in-house legal counsel of China Railway Construction Company Limited, specialising in international infrastructure projects and related legal issues. She is qualified in China. She has provided legal advice in the Mexico City to Santiago de Queretaro train project, the PPP project of high-speed rail linking three airports in Thailand, etc. She has published many articles in renowned journals.

Contact details: sunyiwen@crcc.cn

Ms Jennifer (Eun Kyung) Yoo (South Korea) is an associate at Peter & Kim (Seoul). She was admitted to the Korean bar in 2015. Jennifer has represented and advised clients on a wide range of international commercial arbitration and cross-border litigation cases. In particular, she has ample experience of large-scale overseas construction disputes, involving multiple claims, parties, experts and counsel. She also frequently advises clients on international arbitration procedures, challenges and enforcement of international arbitral awards, and interim measures in respect of arbitration proceedings.

Contact details: JenniferYoo@peterandkim.com

TABLE OF CASES

Australia

China

Fiji

Hong Kong

India

Japan

Korea

Malaysia

Nepal

Pakistan

Papua New Guinea

Vietnam

TABLE OF LEGISLATION

China

Colombia

European Union

Fiji

France

Germany

Hong Kong

India

Indonesia

Japan

Korea

Malaysia

Nepal

New Zealand

Pakistan

Papua New Guinea

Paraguay

Philippines

Russian Federation

Singapore

Sri Lanka

Switzerland

United Kingdom

Vietnam

CHAPTER 1

Introduction

Dr Donald Charrett

DOI: 10.4324/9781003200901-1

1.1 Construction contracts

1.1.1 Overview

Construction contracts can be defined in various ways. The following definition is used for the purposes of this book:

> [a]ny contract where one person [this includes a corporation] agrees for valuable consideration to carry out construction works, which may include building or engineering works, for another.[1]

A contract for design does not involve 'construction' as such, and for the purposes of this book is not considered to be a construction contract. A design and construct contract includes design, but it also involves construction and therefore falls within the definition adopted above. Moreover, a subcontract in which a Subcontractor undertakes construction work for a Contractor is a species of construction contract and may be 'back-to-back' with the Head Contract between the Employer and the Contractor.[2]

In this book, the **Contract** means the construction contract being referred to. In general terms, the parties to a construction contract are the **Employer,** for whom the work is done, and the **Contractor,** who carries out the work. In the case of a subcontract, the Contractor under the **Head Contract** functions as the Employer, and the Subcontractor functions as the Contractor.

Construction contracts have a number of specific features that give them some unique characteristics that distinguish them from other commercial contracts. The following issues arise by operation of law, or because of specific terms that are incorporated in most construction contracts, or because of the nature of construction work. The unique distinguishing features of construction law can be conveniently

1 Stephen Furst and the Hon Sir Vivian Ramsey, *Keating on Construction Contracts* (8th edn, Sweet & Maxwell 2006) 1.

2 Capitalised terms not specifically defined in this book are defined in the relevant FIDIC Conditions of Contract. The Glossary contains definitions of terms specifically defined in this book.

considered under the following headings that address issues generally relevant to all construction projects.

Scope:

- The subject matter of the contract relates to construction of a unique facility that will be affixed to the land at a specific location over a specific period of time.
- The constructed facility becomes part of the real property of the landowner when attached.
- The required design, scope, time, cost and quality requirements of the Works and the finished project are usually defined by extensive and complex technical documentation.
- The Employer (generally) has the right to increase or decrease the originally agreed scope of work by the issue of Variations, and the Contractor is obliged to carry out or omit the varied work.
- The execution of the construction work and/or the performance of the Contract may be supervised by an 'independent' Engineer who is not a party to the Contract.
- The Contract may be an entire contract.
- There are many different types of construction contract: eg construct only, design and construct, engineer procure and construct (**EPC**), engineer procure and construction management (**EPCM**).

Risk:

- There are many risks in a construction project – known knowns, known unknowns, and unknown unknowns.
- Ground conditions are never completely known, including geotechnical conditions, groundwater, contamination, or heritage items.
- Weather conditions can have significant impact on construction activities and delay completion.
- Freedom of contract may be constrained, eg *Security of Payment legislation* that mandates payment obligations and makes some provisions illegal, such as pay when paid clauses.
- Many aspects of a construction project are subject to Government laws and regulations.
- There are usually a series of independent and interrelated contracts between a number of different parties: eg Employer/designer, Employer/Engineer, Employer/Contractor/DAAB or DAB Member, Employer/Contractor, Contractor/Subcontractor, Subcontractor/sub-Subcontractor Employer/Insurer, Contractor/Insurer.
- Construction activities are potentially dangerous, eg heavy machinery, working at heights, confined spaces etc.
- Construction involves significant environmental impacts: noise, dust, smells, vibration, nuisance, water run-off, sediment and erosion.
- Construction may adversely impact adjacent property.

- Insurance of the works is usually mandatory and is a significant risk transfer mechanism.
- Insolvency of parties to interrelated contracts may impact performance.

Time:

- The time for contractual performance may extend over a number of years, including a period after completion of construction (and when the Employer is in possession of the Site) during which the Contractor is liable to rectify defects.
- There are usually significant financial consequences for late contract completion.

Cost:

- The contract sum and cashflow is typically substantial – cash flow is the lifeblood of construction.
- The Contractor is usually required to provide security for its performance.

Quality:

- A construction contract may involve the assumption of obligations that are very long term, eg maintenance or liability for defects arising many years after construction was completed.
- Construction works apparently completed in accordance with contractual requirements may contain latent defects which only manifest themselves many years after construction was completed.

Disputes:

- Disputes are common and frequently involve complex technical issues and large volumes of documents.

Every construction contract is unique: The Site is a unique location in the Country, constructed by a particular Contractor for a particular Employer over a particular period of time for a specific purpose.

1.1.2 Legal systems

There are a number of 'families' or systems of law, the most widespread being the systems considered in this book: common law and civil law. Other legal systems include Shari'a law and Socialist law.

Common law is the body of law developed by judges from around the 11th century in England, and later exported to its various colonies such as Canada, the USA, Australia, Fiji, Hong Kong, India, Malaysia, Pakistan and Singapore. The basic principle is that earlier judicial decisions, usually of the higher courts, made in a similar case, should be followed in subsequent cases. The principle that precedents should be respected is known as **stare decisis** and although it has never been legislated, courts regard it as binding. However superior courts can decide that a previous case was wrongly decided and modify the law accordingly. In addition to the law made by judges in decided cases, common law is also based on statutes, which judges interpret by discerning the intention of Parliament, and apply it accordingly.

Civil law is a system of law in which the laws are codified in a large number of general rules and principals. Pejovic describes civil law in the following terms:

> Civil law has its origin in Roman law, as codified in the Corpus Iuris Civilis of Justinian. Under this influence, in the ensuing period the civil law has been developed in Continental Europe and in many other parts of the world. The main feature of civil law is that it is contained in civil codes, which are described as a 'systematic, authoritative, and guiding statute of broad coverage, breathing the spirit of reform and marking a new start in the legal life of an entire nation.' Most civil codes were adopted in the nineteenth and twentieth centuries: French Code Civil, 1804, Austrian Burgerliches Gesetzbuch, 1811, German Burgerliches Gesetzbuch, 1896, Japanese Minpo, 1896, Swiss Zivilgesetzbuch, 1907, Italian Codice Civile, 1942. Between these codes there are some important differences, and they are often grouped in the Romanic and the Germanic families. Even though the civil codes of different countries are not homogenous, there are certain features of all civil codes which bind them together and 'sets them apart from those who practice under different systems'.
>
> Civil law is largely classified and structured and contains a great number of general rules and principles, often lacking details. One of the basic characteristics of the civil law is that the courts main task is to apply and interpret the law contained in a code, or a statute to case facts. The assumption is that the code regulates all cases that could occur in practice, and when certain cases are not regulated by the code, the courts should apply some of the general principles used to fill the gaps.[3]

Notwithstanding the differences between common law and civil law systems, and the differences between jurisdictions within either of these systems, construction contracts can be executed in the knowledge that, notwithstanding local law differences, there are appropriate methods of dispute resolution, broad agreement on what constitutes a just outcome in most situations and international norms that ensure remedies can be realised.

The differences between the common law and civil law have become much less in recent years:

- The volume of legislation in common law countries has increased substantially over recent decades. Increasingly, more of the law is explicitly stated in legislation, which either codifies or amends the previous common law, or forms new 'social legislation' which achieves legislatively desirable social outcomes not addressed by the common law, eg the *Human Rights Act 1998* (UK), which incorporates the rights and freedoms of the *European Convention on Human Rights* into British law, and the *Housing Grants, Construction and Regeneration Act 1996* (UK), which introduced a statutory right to adjudication of construction disputes.
- Because the answer to a legal issue may not be found in the *Codes* (which may not have been updated recently), the courts in civil law countries are

3 Casalev Pejovic, 'Civil Law and Common Law: Two Different Paths Leading to the Same Goal' [2001] *VUWLawRw* 42; (2001) 32(3) *Victoria University of Wellington Law Review* 817 https://www.wgtn.ac.nz/law/research/publications/about-nzacl/publications/cljpjdcp-journals/volume-7,-2001/Pejovic.pdf (accessed 7 July 2021).

relying to a much greater extent than previously on the precedential value of court judgments on a similar issue, eg in a book on FIDIC contracts, the authors list a significant number of cases from the French and German civil law jurisdictions, as well as cases from various common law jurisdictions.[4]

1.1.3 Contract law

Contract law around the world is based on the two fundamental principles of freedom of contract and *pacta sunt servanda.* These principles are universal in jurisdictions subject to the rule of law, the necessary precondition for the exercise of the parties' autonomy and the enforcement of their rights and obligations. Freedom of contract sets the 'ground rules' which govern the parties' rights to enter into the contract of their choice. *Pacta sunt servanda* governs the performance of a contract after it has been entered into. These two principles of law apply to the entry into, execution and termination of contracts.

1.1.4 Freedom of contract

Freedom of contract is the ability of legal persons to enter into a binding agreement to do anything, providing it is not contrary to the law or public policy (and in some jurisdictions morals). Subject to these qualifications, courts generally uphold freedom of contract, even if one of the parties has accepted risks that it cannot manage or insure for.

This freedom to contract about anything has a long history in the English common law. Well over one hundred years ago Sir George Jessel MR stated that freedom of contract was the paramount public policy in English common law:

> [i]f there is one thing which more than another public policy requires it is that men of full age and competent understanding shall have the utmost liberty of contracting, and that their contracts when entered into freely and voluntarily shall be held sacred and shall be enforced by courts of justice.[5]

India is a common law country, but for over one hundred years it has had a detailed statute that effectively constitutes a default contract code. The *Contracts Act 1972* (India) provides for freedom of contract in the following terms:

> 10 All agreements are contracts if they are made by the free consent of parties competent to contract, for a lawful consideration and with a lawful object, and are not hereby expressly declared to be void. Nothing herein contained shall affect any law in force in India and not hereby expressly repealed by which any contract is required to be made in writing or in the presence of witnesses, or any law relating to the registration of documents.

Malaysia is also a common law country with a *Contracts Act*. The *Contracts Act 1950* (Malaysia) enshrines freedom of contract in statute in the following terms:

> s 1(2) Nothing herein contained shall affect any written law or any usage or custom of trade, or any incident of any contract, not inconsistent with this Act.

4 Axel-Volkmar Jaeger and Götz-Sebastian Hök, *FIDIC – A Guide for Practitioners* (Springer 2010) xix–xxx.

5 *Printing and Numeral Registering Co v Sampson* (1875) LR 19 Eq, 462, 465 (Sir George Jessel MR).

10.(1) All agreements are contracts if they are made by the free consent of parties competent to contract, for a lawful consideration and with a lawful object, and are not hereby expressly declared to be void.

(2) Nothing herein contained shall affect any law by which any contract is required to be made in writing or in the presence of witnesses, or any law relating to the registration of documents.

. . .

24. The consideration or object of an agreement is lawful, unless–

(a) it is forbidden by a law;
(b) it is of such a nature that, if permitted, it would defeat any law;
(c) it is fraudulent;
(d) it involves or implies injury to the person or property of another; or
(e) the court regards it as immoral, or opposed to public policy.

In each of the above cases, the consideration or object of an agreement is said to be unlawful. Every agreement of which the object or consideration is unlawful is void.

However, the very freedom of contract provided in the *Contracts Act 1950* (Malaysia) gives the parties the freedom to derogate from its provisions. In *Ooi Boon Long v Citibank NA*[6] Lord Brightman held that section 1(2) of the *Contracts Act 1950*,

[d]oes not say that the contracting parties are unable by agreement to vary the legal consequences spelt out by the Act. Section 1 (2) has no effect on the freedom of contracting parties to decide upon what terms they desire to contract.

Therefore, if parties desire to oust the application of a certain provision of the *Contracts Act 1950*, their intention should be made clear expressly.

Freedom of contract is also a fundamental principle under civil law systems, for example:

In this jurisdiction [Philippines] contracts are enforced as they are read, and parties who are competent to contract may make such agreements within the limitations of the law and public policy as they desire, and the courts will enforce them according to their terms.[7]

In this case the principle is enshrined in statute – Article 1306 of the *Civil Code of the Philippines* states:

The contracting parties may establish such stipulations, clauses, terms and conditions as they may deem convenient, provided they are not contrary to law, morals, good customs, public order or public policy.

Public policy is largely concerned with the potential for manifest unfairness or injustice in a given situation. Thus, the courts may disregard or refuse to give effect to contractual obligations which, whilst not directly contrary to any express or implied statutory prohibition, nevertheless contravene 'the policy of the law' as discerned from a consideration of the scope and purpose of the particular statute.[8]

Public policy has a very powerful reach in civil law systems. In the European community, most of whose member states have civil law legal systems, parties have a similar freedom of contract to that applying under common law systems and are free to choose (within certain limits) the law which is to apply to their contract. Regulation (EC) number 593/2008 of the European Parliament (**Rome I**) provides in Article 3.1

---

6 [1984] 1 MLJ 222 (Malaysian Privy Council).

7 *Lambert v Fox* 26 Phil 588 [Philippines], cited in Edgardo L Paras, *Civil Code of the Phillipines Annotated Volume Four* (14th edn, 2000) 332.

8 *Nelson v Nelson* [1995] HCA 25, (1995) 184 CLR 538, 552, 611.

that 'A contract shall be governed by the law chosen by the parties'. However, it also provides in Article 21 that:

> The application of a provision of the law of any country specified by this Regulation may be refused only if such application is manifestly incompatible with the public policy (*ordre public*) of the forum.

The universal application of freedom of contract is reinforced by its statement in principles that may be regarded as private codifications or restatements of international contract law (modern statements of the *lex mercatoria*):

UNIDROIT Principles of International Commercial Contracts 2016:[9]

1.1 The parties are free to enter into a contract and to determine its content.

Trans-Lex Principles:[10]

IV.1.1 The parties are free to enter into contracts and to determine their contents (principle of party autonomy).

Thus, one of the consequences of freedom of contract is that, subject to the applicable mandatory law and public policy, parties generally have the freedom to make an explicit choice of the proper or governing law of their contract, irrespective of the laws of the Country.

Governments legislate to restrain freedom of contract in various ways, including:

- Illegality/unenforceability of certain contractual terms
- Implying terms into all contracts of a particular type
- Creating statutory rights that coexist with contractual rights
- Mandating the way in which a court or tribunal is to settle disputes or determine contractual rights.

1.1.5 Pacta sunt servanda

The obverse of the principle of freedom of contract is articulated by the doctrine of ***pacta sunt servanda***, which Latin phrase means that agreements are to be kept. It is a fundamental principle of international law that the provisions of treaties concluded properly are to be observed. The principle means that once parties have exercised their freedom to enter into a contract, they have the legal rights and obligations they have agreed to, and these will be enforced by a court or an arbitrator. Thus, for instance, if the contracting parties have agreed that any disputes will be settled by arbitration, the courts will generally stay any court proceedings commenced in breach of the agreement to arbitrate, on the principle that the parties should be kept to their agreement.

Article 1.3 (Binding character of contract) of the *UNIDROIT Principles of International Commercial Contracts 2016* gives effect to the principal of *pacta sunt servanda* in the following terms:

> A contract validly entered into is binding upon the parties. It can only be modified or terminated in accordance with its terms or by agreement or as otherwise provided in these Principles.

---

9 The UNIDROIT Principles and their application to construction contracts are discussed in: Donald Charrett, *The Application of Contracts in Engineering and Construction Contracts* (1st edn, Informa Law from Routledge 2018) ch 31: 'The use of the Unidroit Principles in international construction contracts.'

10 https://www.trans-lex.org/principles/of-transnational-law- (accessed 30 October 2020).

The universal nature of this principle has been stated as: 'All the world's legal systems focus on the sanctity of contracts, and damages as the remedy for breach of contract.'[11] The consequences are rather reassuring in the context of construction law:

> [t]he principle of *pacta sunt servanda* . . . is universal to all legal systems. This means that the vast majority of construction disputes are fought and won or lost primarily over the wording of the contract (and alleged facts).[12]

Thus, the contract language will generally govern the parties' rights most of the time.

1.1.6 Proper law of the contract

One important aspect of freedom of contract is that parties are generally free to choose the law that governs their contractual relations, known as the **governing law of the contract** or the **proper law of the contract**. In *Garsec v His Majesty the Sultan of Brunei* [2008] NSWCA 211 [128], Campbell JA noted an Australian court's analysis of the factors to be considered if the parties have not made an explicit choice of the proper law:

> An important feature of the proper law of an international contract is that, subject to questions of public policy and bona fides, the parties are free to choose what the proper law will be: *Vita Food Products Inc v Unus Shipping Co Ltd* [1939] AC 277. If, on construing the contract, the court is unable to conclude that the parties intended that contract to be governed by reference to a particular system of law, the court identifies a proper law by ascertaining the system of law with which the transaction has its closest and most real connection: *Bonython v Commonwealth of Australia* [1951] AC 201*; Akai Pty Ltd v People's Insurance Co Limited* [1996] HCA 39; 91996) 188 CLR 418 at 440–1. But whether the proper law is ascertained from the intention of the parties, or under the *Bonython* test, makes no difference to those aspects of the contract – which might, on some accounts of the law, extend to its formation, validity, interpretation, and the rights and obligations of the parties under it – that are decided in accordance with the proper law of the contract. Other systems of law besides that of the forum and the proper law can sometimes come to bear upon the contract – as when its performance is illegal under the law of the place where it is to be performed. However it can be seen that one of the purposes of recognising a proper law of contract is to allow the parties to have freedom of choice about the system of law that will govern their relations, to the extent that other systems of law do not impose themselves upon the formation, performance or enforcement of the contract. That purpose is also advanced by applying the substantive/procedural distinction articulated in *John Pfeiffer v Rogerson* (2000) 203 CLR 503 to litigation concerning international contracts.

In *Attorney-General of Botswana v Aussie Diamond Products Pty Ltd (No 3)* [2010] WASC 14, in dealing with the factors relevant to the ascertainment of the proper law of the contract In Australia, Murphy J noted at paragraphs 207 and 208:

> In my view, the law of Western Australia is the system of law with which the contract is most directly connected, and hence is the proper law of the contract: see *Bonython v the Commonwealth of Australia* (1950) 81 CLR 486, 498: *Akai Pty Ltd v The People's Insurance Co Ltd* (1996) 188 CLR 418, 434. The following features are relevant. The offer, in the quotation dated 13 May 2003, and all subsequent contractual communications, was in English. The consideration provided by the Department was in Australian dollars. It was to be paid by a confirming bank in Australia upon the presentation of documents. The goods were to be supplied from Australia and cif obligations were to be undertaken by

11 Robert Knutson (ed), *FIDIC An Analysis of International Construction Contracts* (Wolters Kluwer 2005) xiv.

12 ibid xvi.

> the defendant in Australia. Although commissioning was to occur in Botswana, that fact alone does not outweigh the other considerations to which I have referred, which point to the law of the contract being the law of Western Australia.
>
> Whilst the question of the proper law is, in each case, dependent on the particular nature and terms of the contract and its surrounding circumstances, the conclusion which I have reached here derives some support, I think, from *Mendelsohn-Zeller Inc v T&C Providores Pty Ltd* [1981] NSWLR 366 and *Power Curber International Ltd v National Bank of Kuwait* [1981] 1 WLR 1233 and the factors considered relevant in those cases.

Where the parties have not made an explicit choice of the governing law of the contract, and there is more than one legal jurisdiction whose laws govern the Contract, there is a conflict of laws. A judge or arbitrator adjudicating a dispute must determine the governing law of the contract by the appropriate conflict of laws rules. The application of conflict of laws rules may involve a complicated interaction between the facts of the case and the procedural law and substantive law of different legal jurisdictions, where there is no unanimity of conflict of laws rules.

In this writer's view, it is highly desirable to make an explicit choice of the governing law of the contract in the Contract Data, to avoid the possibility of subsequent dispute over what it is. As noted in paragraph 1.5.1 below, the default position in the FIDIC rainbow suite of contracts is that the law of the Country will be the governing law of the contract, excluding any conflict of law rules.

1.1.7 International construction contracts

The main focus of the book is on international contracts. An **international construction contract** is a contract for the provision of goods and services in which:

(a) The parties to the Contract have, at the time of the conclusion of their agreement, their places of business in different legal jurisdictions; or
(b) One of the following places is situated outside the legal jurisdiction in which the parties have their places of business:
   i.) the Site; or
   ii.) any place where a substantial part of the obligations for the Works is to be performed.

Although building work is a species of construction, domestic building work is outside the scope of this book, and accordingly there is no reference to any legislation or other provisions that regulate domestic building contracts or work in any jurisdiction.

1.2 *Lex constructionis*[13]

1.2.1 What is it?

The use of FIDIC contracts across jurisdictions is of particular interest in considering the extent to which there is a 'common law of construction contracts' or a '*lex constructionis*', despite the differences in legal systems and jurisdictions.

13 This topic is discussed in more detail in Charrett (n 9) ch 30: 'A common law of construction contracts – or *vive la différence?*' See also, more recently, Donald Charrett, '*Lex constructionis* – or My Country's Rules?' [2021] *International Construction Law Review* 61.

The book by Jaeger and Hök[14] is especially valuable for its commentary on different philosophical approaches to drafting international contracts, and how the FIDIC contracts are applied in civil law jurisdictions. The book edited by Knutson[15] contains chapters on the use of FIDIC contracts in thirteen different countries – four common law, [16] eight civil law[17] and one Shari'a.[18] The commentaries in Knutson's book clearly underscore the differences between legal jurisdictions in the use of FIDIC contracts, leading one to question whether there could be any such concept as *lex constructionis*.

However, notwithstanding the common law genesis of FIDIC contracts, and the significant differences in a number of legal theories, the following observation from the perspective of German law suggests there may be substantive common ground:

> The legal background of the 'Werkvertrag' as contained in the German Civil Code does not lead to a completely different structure of a construction contract compared to the FIDIC-new series model forms, however some features of the FIDIC-new series, which stem from English construction law, are either unknown (eg the Engineer) or differently regulated (eg provisional and final acceptance of the works) in German construction law. Apart from these two major differences both the structure and the system of a construction contract of CONS [red book] and P & DB [yellow book] seem to lead to both in similar legal principles and sometimes even the same results (eg *force majeure*, risk and responsibility, damages and compensation.[19]

Perhaps the clearest pointer to what there is of a *lex constructionis* is the following statement on the fundamental importance of the words of the contract itself, vindicating the twin principles of freedom of contract and *pacta sunt servanda*:

> Finally, deep in the night, with no one else around, most lawyers in their heart of hearts will admit – the Contract usually decides the issues, despite what the law is.[20]

1.2.2 Promotion of best practice for successful projects

It is suggested that *lex constructionis* can promote best practice for successful projects in which the contracting parties' legitimate expectations can be realized. In this writer's view, those legitimate expectations are typically along the following lines:

***Employer*:**

- Completion of the project on time, for the Contract Price and to the agreed standard of quality.
- Timely and adequate communication from the Contractor of any departures from the original scope of Works, the materialisation of risks and any claims.

14 Axel-Volkmar Jaeger and Götz-Sebastian Hök, *FIDIC – A Guide for Practitioners* (Springer 2010).

15 Robert Knutson (ed), *FIDIC An Analysis of International Construction Contracts* (Kluwer Law International, 2005).

16 England, India, Malaysia and the USA.

17 Brazil, Egypt, France, Germany, Japan, the Netherlands, Sweden and Switzerland.

18 Saudi Arabia.

19 Wolfgang Rosener and Gerhard Dorner, 'Germany' in Robert Knutson (ed), *FIDIC An Analysis of International Construction Contracts* (Kluwer Law International 2005) 87, 125.

20 Robert Knutson (ed), *FIDIC An Analysis of International Construction Contracts* (Kluwer Law International 2005) xix.

***Contractor*:**

- Prompt payment of all amounts due under the Contract.
- Freedom to carry out the construction in accordance with the Contract without hindrance by the Employer.
- Timely and adequate communication from the Employer of the materialisation of any risks, communication of instructions and assessment of claims.

It is submitted that the principles proposed below, if followed, would fulfill those expectations. The proposed principles have been formulated taking into account the unique features of construction projects and construction contracts discussed above, the Abrahamson principles of balanced risk allocation, [21] the FIDIC General Conditions in the rainbow suite, the FIDIC Golden Principles[22] and 'social obligations' owed to third parties. They are also influenced by Molyneaux's paper on this topic in which he formulated a 'modest Mosaic ten' principles.[23]

One of the criticisms that could be directed to the proposed (or any) principles of *lex constructionis* is that they cannot cover all situations, nor can they necessarily be applied in their entirety in many situations. The following discussion of principles in the context of *lex mercatoria* is equally applicable to the proposed principles of *lex constructionis*:

> General principles do not necessarily have pre-set conditions for application. Instead they merely constitute 'rules of optimal application' which means that they may be complied with in varying degrees. The required degree of compliance depends not only on the actual but also on the legal options open to the target group. Application of general principles therefore requires a substantial process of weighing up contradictory principles and rules. General principles are therefore always subject to a continual discussion about the effectiveness and scope.[24] (citations omitted)

1.2.3 Proposed principles of lex constructionis

Overarching principles

1. *Pacta sunt servanda.*
2. ***Rebus sic stantibus*** – doctrines or rules relating to changed conditions.
3. The parties must act in accordance with good faith and fair dealing in construction contracts.

Scope

4. The contract defines, in writing, the original scope of Works and the known conditions at the Site.
5. The Employer has the right to instruct Variations consistent with the original scope of the Contract, and the Contractor has the obligation to carry out all such Variations.

---

21 Max W Abrahamson, 'Risk Management' [1983] *International Construction Law Review* 241, 244.

22 See ch 2 below.

23 Charles Molineaux, 'Moving toward a construction lex mercatoria A lex constructionis' (1997) 1 *Journal of International Arbitration* 55.

24 Klaus Peter Berger, *The Creeping Codification of the New Lex Mercatoria* (Wolters Kluwer 2010) 201.

6. Construction Works must be carried out so as to protect the health and safety of workers.
7. Construction Works must not adversely affect the environment or the interests of third parties.
8. Subject to any contractual requirements, the Contractor selects the methods and timing of the Works.

Risk

9. Each risk is allocated to the Party best able to manage and control it and the consequences if it eventuates, or to the Party who will derive any benefit or suffer the least consequences if the risk eventuates.
10. A Party is not allocated risks that it cannot insure for or has insufficient financial resources to bear.
11. The Contractor is responsible for the Works whilst it is in possession of the Site.

Time

12. The parties have a reasonable time to perform their obligations and exercise their rights.
13. The Contractor provides the Employer with prompt and adequate notice of any unexpected conditions that affect its performance, the occurrence of any risk events and any Claims.
14. The Employer provides the Contractor with prompt and adequate notice of the occurrence of any risk events that affect the Contractor, instructions and responses to Claims.
15. The Contractor is liable to pay damages if it does not complete the Works by the contractually agreed date.

Cost

16. The Employer has adequate financial resources to complete the Contract.
17. The Contractor provides security for its performance.
18. The Employer pays the Contractor its contractual entitlements promptly.

Quality

19. The Contractor either rectifies defects in its Works or pays damages to reinstate the Works to the contractually specified quality.

Disputes

20. Unresolved disputes are finally determined by arbitration.

1.2.4 Discussion

Space does not permit a detailed exposition of each of the above principles. Some would probably be accepted as with implied terms that go without saying. Others may be more controversial.

The overarching principles are contained in statements of the *lex mercatoria*, such as the UNIDROIT Principles. In this writer's view they are important for successful execution of construction projects that frequently take place over a long time and involve changed circumstances. In particular, the requirements of honesty, fairness and reasonableness inherent in the good faith principle will necessarily be relied upon to resolve amicably (where possible) many of the expected and unexpected issues that can arise during the execution of a construction contract.

The principles on scope acknowledge the complexity of construction projects, the possibility that the scope may need to change, and that the Works impact on third parties and the environment. Risks are inherent in any construction project, and their appropriate allocation is often critical to achieving a successful project.[25]

The principles on time reiterate the requirement of reasonableness and emphasise the importance of adequate and timely communication from Contractor to Employer and vice versa. Damages for late completion are appropriate to compensate the Employer for its inability to make commercial use of the constructed facility from the agreed date.

Certainty and promptness of payment are usually of great importance to the Contractor and may be critical to its solvency. The requirement for a Contractor to rectify or pay for defect rectification is merely a construction specific implementation of *pacta sunt servanda.*

The near universal implementation of the *New York Convention*, the norms of international arbitration and the finality and enforcement of awards are the basis for arbitration to generally be the most appropriate method for resolving international construction disputes.

1.3 FIDIC contracts

1.3.1 Overview

The Fédération Internationale des Ingénieurs-Conseils **(FIDIC)** (known by its English name of the International Federation of Consulting Engineers) publishes standard form Conditions of Contract that are used in many countries and are probably the most widely used for international construction contracts in the world. Although they have a common law pedigree, they are intended to be used in any legal jurisdiction whether common law, civil law or any other type of law.

FIDIC publishes the standard forms of construction contract between Employer and Contractor shown in Table 1.1.[26]

Table 1.1 FIDIC Conditions of Contract for contracts between Employer and Contractor

1977 Red Book	Conditions of Contract for Works of Civil Engineering Construction – Third Edition 1977
1987 Red Book	Conditions of Contract for Works of Civil Engineering Construction Fourth Edition 1987
1987 Yellow Book	Conditions of Contract for Electrical and Mechanical Works – Third Edition 1987;

25 For a discussion of the consequences of inappropriately allocating risk, see: Japan International Cooperation Agency, 'Checklist for One Sided Contracts' (2011) 1 https://www.jica.go.jp/english/our_work/types_of_assistance/oda_loans/oda_op_info/guide/c8h0vm0000aoeprl-att/guide02.pdf (accessed 9 September 2020).

26 These FIDIC contracts were listed on the FIDIC website (https://www.fidic.org/bookshop) on 4 November 2020.

1995 Orange Book	Conditions of Contract for Design-Build and Turnkey – First Edition 1995
1999 Red Book	Conditions of Contract for Construction – First Edition 1999
1999 Yellow Book	Conditions of Contract for Plant and Design-Build – First Edition 1999
1999 Silver Book	Conditions of Contract for EPC/Turnkey Projects – First Edition 1999
2017 Red Book	Conditions of Contract for Construction – Second Edition 2017
2017 Yellow Book	Conditions of Contract for Plant and Design-Build – Second Edition 2017
2017 Silver Book	Conditions of Contract for EPC/Turnkey Projects – Second Edition 2017
Green Book	Short Form of Contract – First Edition, 1999
Pink Book	Conditions of Contract for Construction – Multilateral Development Bank Harmonised Edition for Building and Engineering Works Designed by the Employer – Version 1: 2005, Version 3: 2010
Gold Book	Conditions of Contract for Design, Build and Operate Projects – First Edition, 2008
Blue-Green Book	Form of Contract for Dredging and Reclamation Works – First Edition 2006, Second Edition 2016
Emerald Book	Conditions of Contract for Underground Works First Edition 2019

The various editions of the FIDIC Conditions of Contract for contracts between Employer and Contractor are tabulated in Table 1.4 in the Annexure to this chapter.

FIDIC publishes the following standard forms of subcontract between Contractor and Subcontractor:[27]

- Conditions of Subcontract for Work of Civil Engineering Construction – First Edition 1994
- Conditions of Subcontract for Construction – First Edition 2011
- Conditions of Subcontract for Plant and Design (Yellow Book 1999) – First Edition 2019.

The **Red Book**, [28] **Yellow Book**, [29] **Silver Book**[30] (and Pink) Books are commonly referred to as the **rainbow suite**. The focus of this book is mainly on the rainbow suite; however, Chapter 4 covers the unique features of the Emerald Book for Underground Works. Except for Chapter 4, sub-clause references in this book refer to the Second Edition 2017 Red, Yellow and Silver Books unless otherwise noted. However, the principles outlined are generally applicable to all the FIDIC standard form contracts.

A number of guides to the use of FIDIC contracts are listed in paragraph 1.10.3 below.

27 These FIDIC contracts were listed on the FIDIC website (https://www.fidic.org/bookshop) on 4 November 2020.

28 References to the Red Book without a year preface refer to the 1999 Red Book and the 2017 Red Book.

29 References to the Yellow Book without a year preface refer to the 1999 Yellow Book and the 2017 Yellow Book.

30 References to the Silver Book without a year preface refer to the 1999 Silver Book and the 2017 Silver Book.

The FIDIC rainbow suite standard forms generally comprise:

- Acknowledgements
- Notes
- General Conditions
- Guidance for the Preparation of Particular Conditions
- Annexes: Forms of Securities
- Forms of letter of tender, letter of acceptance, contract agreement and dispute adjudication/avoidance agreement.

The Acknowledgements list the numerous groups and individuals that contribute to the rigorous process of developing, reviewing, refining and approval of FIDIC standard form contracts. These contributors include the Contracts Committee that draft the documents, the Task Groups that provide input to the Contracts Committee, special advisors and friendly reviewers. The large number of individuals involved from many countries with extensive contract, construction, engineering and legal skills highlights FIDIC's comprehensive process of drafting contracts that acknowledge the importance of the many stakeholders, and their endeavours to produce balanced contracts that represent best international practice.

1.3.2 MDB use of FIDIC contracts

A number of multilateral development banks (**MDBs**) use FIDIC General Conditions in their Standard Bidding Documents (**SBD**s). MDBs that have embraced FIDIC General Conditions include the World Bank, Asian Development Bank, Black Sea Trade and Development Bank, European Bank for Reconstruction and Development, Caribbean Development Bank and the Inter-American Development Bank.

The use of FIDIC General Conditions by MDBs in their SBDs lead to promulgation of the Pink Book in 2005. This was based on the 1999 Red Book, with the addition of a number of provisions required by MDBs to further their development goals of enhancing living standards and protect the MDBs' interests in probity and proper use of loan funds. In particular the Pink Book contains the following additional 12 sub-clauses in the Red Book clause 6 Staff and Labour:

6.12 Foreign personnel
6.13 Supply of foodstuffs
6.14 Supply of water
6.15 Measures against insect and pest nuisance
6.16 Alcoholic liquor and drugs
6.17 Arms and ammunition
6.18 Festivals and religious customs
6.19 Funeral arrangements
6.20 Forced labour
6.21 Child labour
6.22 Employee records of workers
6.23 Workers' organisations.

These 'social provisions' in the Pink Book provide protections for labour, local communities and the environment that may not be adequately covered by legislation is less developed countries. The Pink Book also contains draconian MDB specific provisions on the consequences of corrupt or fraudulent practices by the Contractor or any of its employees.[31]

The extensive international input into the drafting of FIDIC General Conditions and its acceptance as an appropriate contract for international contracts is evidenced by the World Bank's implementation of the 2017 Red Book in its 2019 Standard Procurement Document.[32] The Particular Conditions of Contract in the World Bank Standard Procurement Document does not change the balanced risk/reward allocation in the General Conditions, and mainly comprises 'social provisions' as outlined for the Pink Book above.

Japan International Cooperation Agency **(JICA)** is one of the world's largest bilateral aid agencies supporting socioeconomic development in developing countries in different regions of the world. It is in charge of administering Japan's Official Development Assistance and uses FIDIC General Conditions is some of its SBDs. JICA's rationale for its strong support of FIDIC contracts is explained in Chapter 5 below. As detailed in that chapter, JICA still uses the Pink Book.

1.3.3 FIDIC Contract documents

A 'FIDIC Contract' comprises a number of documents that are to be taken as mutually explanatory of one another, in the order of precedence in the event of inconsistency between them shown in Table 1.2.[33]

Table 1.2 Order of precedence of Contract documents in the FIDIC rainbow suite

	2017 Red Book	***2017 Yellow Book***	***2017 Silver Book***
(a)	the Contract Agreement	the Contract Agreement	the Contract Agreement
(b)	the Letter of Acceptance	the Letter of Acceptance	the Particular Conditions Part A – Contract Data
(c)	the Letter of Tender	the Letter of Tender	the Particular Conditions Part B – Special Provisions
(d)	the Particular Conditions Part A – Contract Data	the Particular Conditions Part A – Contract Data	the General Conditions
(e)	the Particular Conditions Part B – Special Provisions	the Particular Conditions Part B – Special Provisions	the Employer's Requirements
(f)	the General Conditions	the General Conditions	the Schedules
(g)	the Specification	the Employer's Requirements	the Tender
(h)	the drawings	the Schedules	the JV Undertaking (if the Contractor is a JV)
(i)	the Schedules	the Contractor's Proposal	any other documents forming part of the Contract
(j)	the JV Undertaking (if the Contractor is a JV)	the JV Undertaking (if the Contractor is a JV)	
(k)	any other documents forming part of the Contract	any other documents forming part of the Contract	

31 Sub-clause 15.6.

32 http://pubdocs.worldbank.org/en/865231562944956956/SPD-Request-for-Bids-WORKS-after-prequalification.docx (accessed 28 August 2020).

33 Rainbow suite, sub-clause 1.5.

1.3.4 Contract Agreement

The Contract Agreement form is a two-page pro-forma document that requires the essential details of the Contract to be filled in, and formally executed by the Parties. As this document is highest in priority of the Contract documents, it is essential that it be accurate and comprehensive, and executed in accordance with the governing law of the contract. Appropriate legal advice should be sought to ensure that the resulting Contract complies with all of the relevant legal requirements. Particular jurisdictions may require specific formalities for the Contract to be legally binding, such as payment of stamp duty. Specific jurisdiction requirements are discussed in the later chapters.

1.3.5 Particular Conditions

The table of contract documents above highlights that the Particular Conditions (those Conditions of Contract that are specific to the unique Contract) comprise two parts:

- Part A – Contract Data
- Part B – Special Provisions.

1.3.6 Particular Conditions Part A – Contract Data

The Contract Data, as its name implies, contains the data that is required to define all the unique characteristics of the particular contract, eg the Parties, the Site, the Time for Completion, the governing law of the contract, Contract Price, liability, securities, Defects Notification Period etc. It is a pro-forma consisting of five pages of items referring to sub-clauses of the General Conditions which require insertion of data by the Employer (before calling Tenders), or the Contractor (in its Tender). The Annexure to Chapter 3 below shows the Contract Data in the 2017 Yellow Book, annotated with default provisions.

1.3.7 Particular Conditions Part B – Special Provisions

Special Provisions necessary for the particular requirements of the Works may comprise either modifications to the General Conditions, or additional provisions. Such modifications may be necessary or desirable:

- To comply or align with applicable law
- For the specific requirements of the Site or the Works or
- For the Employer's preferences.

Each of these topics is dealt with in more detail in chapter 3.

1.3.8 General Conditions

The General Conditions as printed are FIDIC copyright, and accordingly cannot legally be reproduced or amended without FIDIC permission. In particular this includes scanning to produce a soft copy that is then modified. As noted above, whilst the FIDIC General Conditions have been drafted to be applicable to a wide range of international construction contracts in various jurisdictions, the unique requirements of a particular contract may mean that the FIDIC General Conditions require modification. The use of a single Conditions of Contract document incorporating both Particular Conditions and General Conditions is discussed in paragraph 3.5 below.

1.4 The FIDIC Golden Principles

The Guidance for the Preparation of Particular Conditions in the Emerald Book contains the following recommendation:

> FIDIC strongly recommends that the Employer, the Contractor and all drafters of the Special Provisions take all due regard of the five FIDIC Golden Principles:
>
> GP1: The duties, rights, obligations, roles and responsibilities of all the Contract Participants must be generally as implied in the General Conditions, and appropriate to the requirements of the project.
> GP2: The Particular Conditions must be drafted clearly and unambiguously.
> GP3: The Particular Conditions must not change the balance of risk/reward allocation provided for in the General Conditions.
> GP4: All time periods specified in the Contract for Contract Participants to perform their obligations must be of reasonable duration.
> GP5: Unless there is a conflict with the governing law of the Contract, all formal disputes must be referred to a Dispute Avoidance/Adjudication Board (or a Dispute Adjudication Board, if applicable) for a provisionally binding decision as a condition precedent to arbitration.[34]
>
> These FIDIC Golden Principles are described and explained in the publication FIDIC's Golden Principles (http://http://fidic.org/bookshop), and are necessary to ensure that modifications to the General Conditions:
>
> - Are limited to those necessary for the particular features of the Site and the project, and necessary to comply with the applicable law
> - Do not change the essential fair and balanced character of a FIDIC contract, and
> - The Contract remains recognisable as a FIDIC contract.[35]

A more detailed explanation of the Golden Principles is provided in Chapter 2 below. That chapter includes some general guidance on preparing Particular Conditions to comply with the Golden Principles. The overarching justification for the Golden Principles is to enable a contract to be recognised as a 'FIDIC contract' that complies with widely accepted international norms and promotes best practice in contract execution and administration.

For another view on the FIDIC Golden Principles, see the article in *Construction Law International* by Graeme Christie.[36]

---

34 Since publication of the 2017 editions of the rainbow suite, GP5 has been amended as follows: '*Unless there is a conflict with the governing law of the Contract*, all formal disputes must be referred to a Dispute Avoidance/Adjudication Board (or a Dispute Adjudication Board, if applicable) for a provisionally binding decision as a condition precedent to arbitration' (emphasis added).

35 Emerald Book, Guidance for the Preparation of Particular Conditions, 8. The 2017 Red Book, 2017 Yellow Book and the 2017 Silver Book contain a similar recommendation.

36 Graeme Christie, 'The Golden Principles – FIDIC's Shiny Christmas Present' (2018) 13(2) *Construction Law International* 10.

1.5 Applicable laws

Applicable laws can be mandatory or non-mandatory:

- **Mandatory law** is based on public policy, and as it cannot be excluded by the parties, it will prevail over any Conditions of Contract.
- **Non-mandatory law** will apply to the extent that the parties have not agreed otherwise.

Distinguishing between mandatory and non-mandatory law can generally only be determined by construction of the relevant law itself.

Irrespective of the wording of the Conditions of Contract and notwithstanding freedom of contract, if the General Conditions are incompatible with mandatory law, mandatory law will apply. Applicable mandatory law that may be inconsistent with the General Conditions could be, inter alia, Laws relating to execution of work at the Site or any other location, and/or the governing law of the contract.

As Site personnel and Contract Administrators may not be familiar with all of the applicable law, in this writer's view it is desirable that Special Provisions are included in the Particular Conditions Part B that articulate all the changes to the General Conditions that are necessary to comply with mandatory law. As discussed further in paragraph 3.1 below, it may also be desirable for Particular Conditions to incorporate provisions that are not incompatible with the General Conditions but refer to issues within the scope of the mandatory law that are not referred to in the General Conditions. Such Particular Conditions will ensure that the Conditions of Contract are an accurate and comprehensive contract management manual that can safely be followed.

Each of the jurisdiction Chapters 6–21 below address both Special Provisions necessary for consistency with mandatory law, as well as desirable to articulate issues within the scope of the mandatory law that are not referred to in the General Conditions.

1.5.1 Laws

The 2017 Yellow Book has the following relevant provisions referring to Laws:

> **1.1 Definitions**
> 1.1.49 '**Laws**' means all national (or state or provincial) legislation, statutes, acts, decrees, rules, ordinances, orders, treaties, international law and other laws, and regulations and by-laws of any legally constituted public authority.
> **1.13 Compliance with Laws:**
> The Contractor and the Employer shall, in performing the Contract, comply with all applicable Laws.

The definition of laws includes laws of the Country, as well as the governing law of the contract. Compliance with Laws is referred to in a number of other subclauses in the Yellow Book:

> **3.5 Engineer's Instructions**
> [I]f . . . the Contractor considers that the instruction:
> (b) does not comply with applicable Laws
> the Contractor shall immediately . . . give a Notice to the Engineer with reasons.

4.8 Health and Safety Obligations

The Contractor shall:

(a) comply with all applicable health and safety regulations and Laws;

The Contractor shall . . . maintain records and make reports (in compliance with the applicable health and safety regulations and Laws) concerning the health and safety of persons and any damage to property.

4.10 Use of Site Data

[t]he Contractor shall be deemed . . . to have been satisfied before submitting the Tender as to all matters relevant to the execution of the Works, including:

(d) the Laws, procedures and labour practices of the Country;

4.18 Protection of the Environment

[T]he Contractor shall ensure that emissions, surface discharges, effluent and any other pollutants from the Contractor's activities shall exceed neither the values indicated in the Employer's Requirements nor those prescribed by applicable Laws.

5.1 General Design Obligations

The Contractor shall carry out, and be responsible for, the design of the Works. Design shall be prepared by designers who:

(c) are qualified and entitled under applicable Laws to design the Works.

5.3 Contractor's Undertaking

The Contractor undertakes that the design, the Contractor's Documents, the execution of the Works and the completed Works will be in accordance with:

(a) the Laws of the Country;

5.4 Technical Standards and Regulations

The Contractor's Documents, the execution of the Works and the completed Works (including defects remedied by the Contractor) shall comply with the Country's technical standards, building, construction and environmental Laws, Laws applicable to the product being produced from the Works, and other standards specified in the Employer's Requirements, applicable to the Works, or defined by applicable Laws.

6.2 Rates of Wages and Conditions of Labour

The Contractor shall pay rates of wages, and observe conditions of labour, which comply with all applicable Laws.

6.4 Labour Laws

The Contractor shall comply with all the relevant labour Laws applicable to the Contractor's Personnel, including Laws relating to their employment (including wages and working hours), health, safety, welfare, immigration and emigration, and shall allow them all their legal rights.

The Contractor shall require the Contractor's Personnel to obey all applicable Laws, including those concerning health and safety at work.

7.4 Testing by the Contractor

[T]he Contractor shall provide all apparatus, assistance, documents and other information, temporary supplies of electricity and water, equipment, fuel, consumables, instruments, labour, materials, and suitably qualified, experienced and competent staff, as are necessary to carry out the specified tests efficiently and properly. All apparatus, equipment and instruments shall be calibrated in accordance with the standards specified in the Employer's Requirements or defined by applicable Laws and, if requested by the Engineer, the Contractor shall submit calibration certificates before carrying out testing.

7.7 Ownership of Plant and Materials

Each item of Plant and Materials shall, to the extent consistent with the mandatory requirements of the Laws of the Country, become the property of the Employer at whichever is the earlier of the following times, free from liens and other encumbrances:

11.11 Clearance of Site

[I]f the Contractor fails to comply with sub-paragraphs (a), (b) and/or (c) above within 28 days after the issue of the Performance Certificate, the Employer may sell (to the extent permitted by applicable Laws) or otherwise dispose of any remaining items and/or may reinstate and clean the Site (as may be necessary) at the Contractor's cost.

15.2 Termination for Contractor's Default

15.2.1 Notice

The Employer shall be entitled to give a Notice . . . to the Contractor of the Employer's intention to terminate the Contract or, in the case of sub-paragraph (f), (g) or (h) below a Notice of termination, if the Contractor:

(g) becomes bankrupt or insolvent; goes into liquidation, administration, reorganisation, winding-up or dissolution; becomes subject to the appointment of a liquidator, receiver, administrator, manager or trustee; enters into a composition or arrangement with the Contractor's creditors; or any act is done or any event occurs which is analogous to or has a similar effect to any of these acts or events under applicable Laws;

16.2 Termination by Contractor

16.2.1 Notice

The Contractor shall be entitled to give a Notice . . . to the Employer of the Contractor's intention to terminate the Contract or, in the case of sub-paragraph (g)(ii), (h), (i) or (j) below, a Notice of termination, if:

(i) the Employer becomes bankrupt or insolvent; goes into liquidation, administration, reorganisation, winding-up or dissolution; becomes subject to the appointment of a liquidator, receiver, administrator, manager or trustee; enters into a composition or arrangement with the Employer's creditors; or any act is done or any event occurs which is analogous to or has a similar effect to any of these acts or events under applicable Laws; or . . .

19.2 Insurance to be provided by the Contractor

19.2.6 Other insurances required by Laws and by local practice

The Contractor shall provide all other insurance as required by the Laws of the countries where (any part of) the Works are being carried out, at the Contractor's own cost.

These provisions refer explicitly or implicitly to the Laws of the Country where the Site is located, with the exception of sub-clause 5.1 [General Design Obligations] and 19.2 [Insurance to be Provided by the Contractor] where the relevant Works may be executed in a country other than the Country where the Site is located.

1.5.2 Governing law of the contract

The 2017 Yellow Book refers to the governing law of the contract as follows:

1.4 Law and Language

The Contract shall be governed by the law of the country (or other jurisdiction) stated in the Contract Data (if not stated, the law of the Country), excluding any conflict of law rules.

The governing law is referred to in the following additional sub-clauses of the Yellow Book:

1.16 Contract Termination

Subject to any mandatory requirements under the governing law of the contract, termination of the Contract under any Sub-Clause of these Conditions shall require no action of whatsoever kind by either Party other than as stated in the Sub-Clause.

18.6 Release from Performance under the Law

In addition to any other provision of this Clause, if any event arises outside the control of the Parties (including, but not limited to, an Exceptional Event) which: (a) makes it impossible or unlawful for either Party or both Parties to fulfil their contractual obligations; or (b) under the law governing the Contract, entitles the Parties to be released from further performance of the Contract,

21.2 Failure to Appoint DAAB Member(s)

[T]hereafter, the Parties and the member(s) so appointed shall be deemed to have signed and be bound by a DAAB Agreement under which: . . . (ii) the law governing the DAAB Agreement shall be the governing law of the contract defined in Sub- Clause 1.4 *[Law and Language]*.

The governing law is referred to in the following sub-clauses of the Appendix General Conditions of Dispute Avoidance/Adjudication Agreement:

> 10 Resignation and Termination
>
> 10.9 Subject to any mandatory requirements under the governing law of the DAA's Agreement, termination of the DAA Agreement under this Clause shall require no action of whatsoever kind by the Parties or the DAAB Member (as the case may be) other than as stated in this clause.

1.5.3 Intersection of local laws with the governing law of the contract

The following are a few examples of issues in which the governing law may be inconsistent with applicable and mandatory Laws of the Country:

- Decennial liability and liability generally for the total or partial collapse of structures[37]
- Use of liens[38]
- Local procurement[39]
- Adjudication of disputes[40]
- Termination for reorganisation.[41]

These issues are covered in more detail in chapter 3.

1.5.4 Laws with extra-territorial reach

In addition to obligations that arise under the governing law of the contract, or the Laws applicable to the Site and the Country, there may be laws applying to legal persons in particular jurisdictions that apply irrespective of the jurisdiction of the Site or Country. For example, no matter what jurisdiction they are operating in, anti-trust/corruption laws apply to US companies, and human rights laws apply to European companies. The *Bribery Act 2010* (UK) applies not only to the UK and UK companies, but the UK courts have jurisdiction if an offence is committed by someone with a close connection with the UK, or by a corporation which does business in the UK, regardless of where the alleged offence was carried out.

1.5.5 Laws applicable to the execution of a construction project

Applicable Laws relevant to the execution a construction project may include:

- The law governing the parties' capacity to enter into a contract
- The governing or proper law of the contract

37 See eg David Brown and Michael Conrad, 'France' in Donald Charrett (ed), *The International Application of FIDIC Contracts A Practical Guide* (Informa Law from Routledge 2020) 141, 152.

38 See eg para 7.6.2 below; Johan Beyers, 'South Africa' in Donald Charrett (ed), *The International Application of FIDIC Contracts A Practical Guide* (Informa Law from Routledge 2020) 334, 342; Sam Moss, Tino Schneider and others, 'Switzerland' in Donald Charrett (ed), *The International Application of FIDIC Contracts A Practical Guide* (Informa Law from Routledge 2020) 366, 379.

39 See eg paras 14.6.6, 16.2.2, 17.1.2.2, 18.2.2 and 21.8.1 below.

40 See eg para 6.2.9 below.

41 See eg Thiago Fernandes Moreira and Caio Gabra, 'Brazil' in Donald Charrett (ed), *The International Application of FIDIC Contracts A Practical Guide* (Informa Law from Routledge 2020) 77, 86; Nicola Davide Romano, 'Italy' in Donald Charrett (ed), *The International Application of FIDIC Contracts A Practical Guide* (Informa Law from Routledge 2020) 240, 253.

- Laws relating to the Site where the Works are carried out (referred to in the FIDIC General Conditions as discussed in paragraph 1.5.1 above) (***lex loci rei sitae***)
- The law relating to the disposition of property (***in rem* claims**)
- Procedural law that applies to any court proceedings, including the coercive power of the court in support of arbitration proceedings (**law of the forum** or ***lex fori***)
- Laws applying to a corporation which does business in a country (eg the *Bribery Act 2010* (UK)).

1.5.6 Laws applicable to arbitration of a dispute

The following laws may apply to arbitration of a dispute arising from a construction project:

- The law governing the parties' capacity to enter into an arbitration agreement
- The law governing the substance of the dispute, generally the governing law of the contract
- The law governing the arbitration agreement and the performance of that agreement
- The law governing the existence and operation of the arbitral tribunal (***lex arbitrii***, sometimes referred to as the curial law), generally the law of the 'seat' of arbitration
- The law (or laws) governing the recognition and enforcement of an arbitral award.

The arbitration agreement is usually incorporated in the Contract but is treated for legal purposes as a separate and independent agreement for the purpose of determining its validity or enforceability. This **doctrine of separability** is a generally recognised principle of the law of international arbitration.[42] It is specifically recognised in the *UNCITRAL*[43] *Model Law*, the basis of the arbitration law in 117 jurisdictions and 84 States.[44] In providing the arbitral tribunal competence to rule on its own jurisdiction, Article 16(1) of the *UNCITRAL Model Law* provides:

> The arbitral tribunal may rule on its own jurisdiction, including any objections with respect to the existence or validity of the arbitration agreement. For that purpose, an arbitration clause which forms part of a contract shall be treated as an agreement independent of the other terms of the contract. A decision by the arbitral tribunal that the contract is null and void shall not entail *ipso jure* the invalidity of the arbitration clause.

The doctrine of separability raises the possibility that the governing law of the contract may not be the same as the governing law of the arbitration agreement, ie the law governing the existence and performance of the arbitration agreement. This issue is discussed further in paragraph 3.2.3 below.

42 See eg *Fiona Trust & Holding Corp v Privalov* [2007] UKHL 40, [2007] All ER 951.

43 United Nations Commission on International Trade Law.

44 https://uncitral.un.org/en/texts/arbitration/modellaw/commercial_arbitration/status (accessed 13 November 2020).

1.6 Covid-19

1.6.1 Government responses to Covid-19

The worldwide advent of the Covid-19 pandemic in 2020 had tragic impacts on the lives of many people and resulted in enormous disruption to the economic fabric of countries around the world. Governments responded with legislation that implemented unprecedented policies in containment and border closure, economic assistance and health measures. The Blavatnik School of Government at the University of Oxford collected data from 186 countries and regions on the measures governments have taken to respond to the pandemic, and presented their findings in the Coronavirus Government Response Tracker (Response Tracker).[45] The dataset in the Response Tracker contains 19 indicators and a miscellaneous notes field organised into four groups:

- Containment and closure policies
- Economic policies
- Health system policies
- Miscellaneous policies.

In addition to the 19 individual policy indicators, the Response Tracker calculates several indices to give an overall impression of government activity. The stringency index provides a single index combining all of the eight containment and closure policies, thereby providing one comparative measure of the impact of the pandemic on economic life.[46] The eight containment and closure policies recorded numerical measures for the following:

- C1 – closings of schools and universities
- C2 – closing of workplaces
- C3 – cancelling public events
- C4 – limits on gatherings
- C5 – closing of public transport
- C6 – orders to 'shelter in place' and otherwise confine to the home
- C7 – restrictions on internal movement between cities/regions
- C8 – restrictions on international travel for foreign travellers.[47]

These indices have been plotted for the countries covered in this book for the period 1 January 2020 to 22 February 2021 in the following four figures for clarity – Figure 1.1 (Australia, China, Hong Kong and Singapore), Figure 1.2 (Indonesia, Japan, Korea and the Philippines), Figure 1.3 (India, Sri Lanka, Nepal and Pakistan), and Figure 1.4 (Fiji, Malaysia, Papua New Guinea and Vietnam).

45 Thomas Hale and others, 'Oxford COVID-19 Government Response Tracker' (2020) *Blavatnik School of Government* https://www.bsg.ox.ac.uk/research/research-projects/coronavirus-government-response-tracker#data (accessed 24 February 2021).

46 https://github.com/OxCGRT/covid-policy-tracker/blob/master/documentation/index_methodology.md (accessed 24 February 2021).

47 https://github.com/OxCGRT/covid-policy-tracker/blob/master/documentation/codebook.md (accessed 24 February 2024).

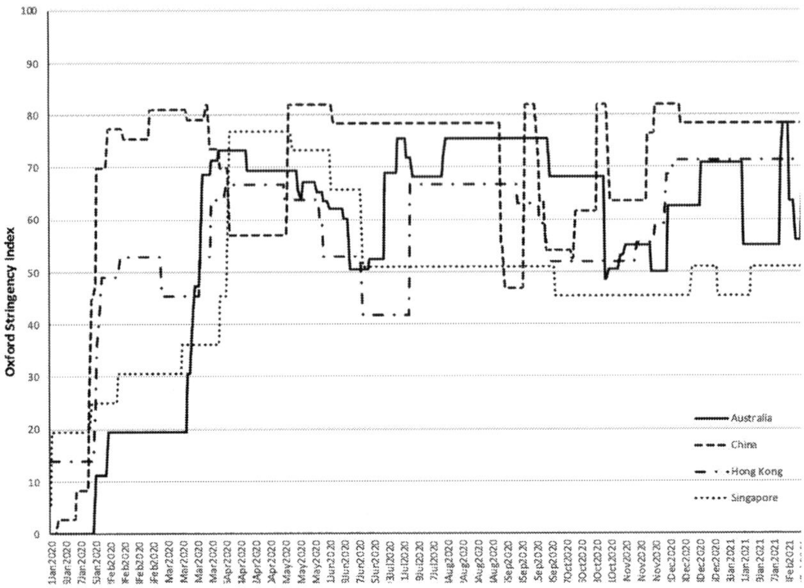

Figure 1.1 Oxford Stringency Index – Australia, China, Hong Kong and Singapore

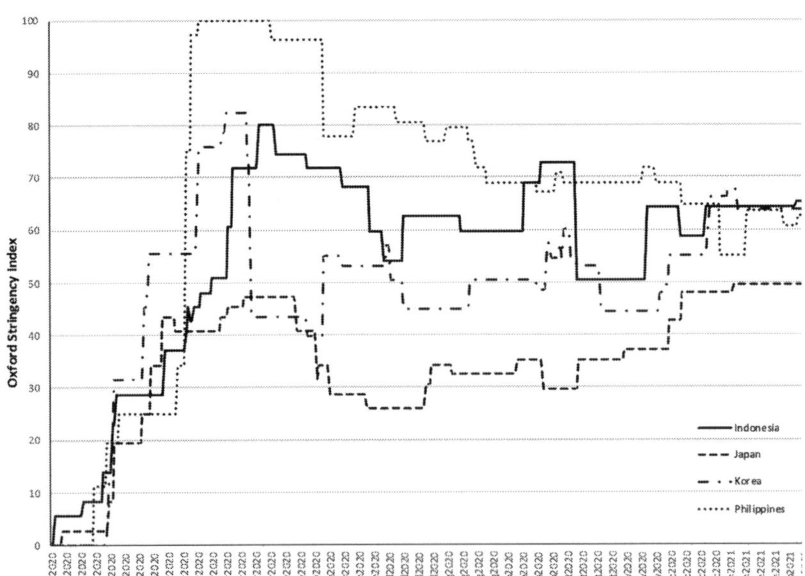

Figure 1.2 Oxford Stringency Index – Indonesia, Japan, Korea and the Philippines

Figure 1.3 Oxford Stringency Index – India, Sri Lanka, Nepal and Pakistan

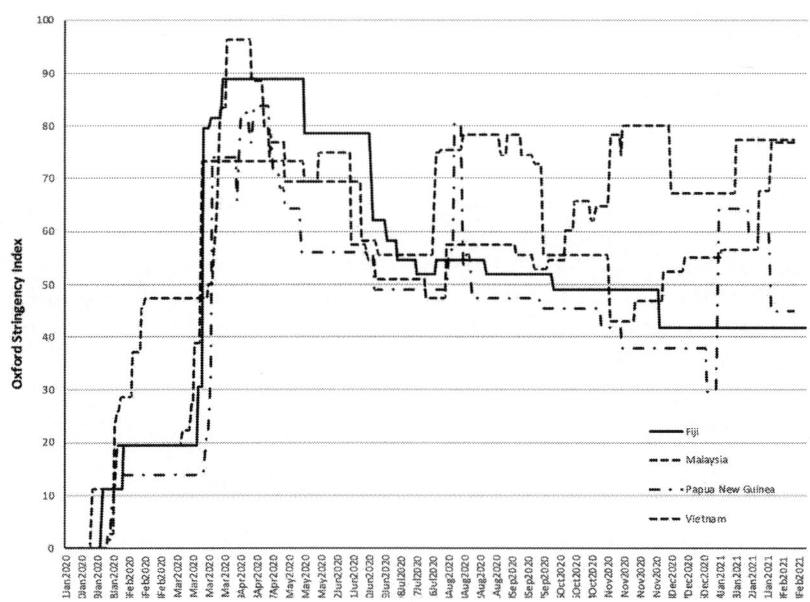

Figure 1.4 Oxford Stringency Index – Fiji, Malaysia, Papua New Guinea and Vietnam

These figures show how rapidly most governments reacted quickly and strongly to the pandemic in February or March 2020. Some countries were able to gradually reduce the level of stringency over the following months, whereas others had subsequent second and third waves that required reintroducing greater stringency. Only two countries had reduced their level of stringency to below 50 (where the maximum recorded for the 16 countries was 100) by 22 February 2021, indicating the persistent impact of significant government containment measures.

1.6.2 The impact of Covid-19 on construction

The closure of borders, shutdown of businesses, restrictions on movement, physical distancing, wearing masks and new health and safety protocols all impacted construction projects, resulting in increased costs and delays. Such impacts have and inevitably will result in claims for time and cost under construction contracts. Some of those claims will no doubt be rejected and result in disputes.

FIDIC responded rapidly to the Covid-19 challenges by running a series of webinars addressing some of the issues that have and will arise under FIDIC contracts. FIDIC also provided resources to assist contracting parties, including the 'FIDIC Covid-19 Guidance Memorandum to Users of FIDIC Standard Forms of Works Contract', prepared by the Contracts Committee.[48] This Guidance Memorandum is discussed in paragraph 1.6.6 below.

The unprecedented array of legislation to deal with the health and economic impacts of Covid-19 significantly constrained freedom of contract in many situations, not least of which were those laws and regulations that impacted construction projects and construction contracts. The legislative interventions that are relevant to construction were measures that constrained:

- The execution of construction projects
- The operation of construction contracts
- Resolution of disputes arising out of Covid-19.

In some jurisdictions the impacts were a result of legislation specifically addressing the construction industry, and others were part of more general government actions to control the spread of Covid-19 or to provide economic support. The following are some examples of the Covid-19 specific measures introduced in various jurisdictions. Each individual jurisdiction chapter below provides details of the measures adopted in that jurisdiction.

1.6.3 Execution of construction projects impacted by Covid-19

Restrictions on travel: countries and regions closed their borders to non-residents, eg Australia closed its borders to non-residents and banned most international travel by residents; most Australian States closed their borders to residents of other States for months.

48 https://fidic.org/sites/default/files/FIDIC%20Guidance%20Memorandum%20to%20Users%20of%20the%201999%20Conditions%20of%20Contract%20dated%201st%20April%202013.pdf (accessed 30 July 2020).

Shut down of construction sites: some countries shut down construction sites after the onset of infection, eg Singapore issued an advisory that all building works as defined in the *Building Control Act* were required to cease with effect from 7 April 2020 to 4 May 2020; Malaysia only permitted 'essential services' to operate in the period from 18 March to 31 March. The Philippines only permitted construction of essential facilities (health care facilities and isolation quarantine facilities) and priority projects under the Build Build Build Infrastructure Program to continue during the period of enhanced community quarantine from 16 March 2020. Small scale construction activities intended for private and personal use were permitted during the subsequent period of modified enhanced community quarantine.

Constraints on working on construction sites: eg following a more severe second wave of infections in Victoria in July 2020, the operation of construction projects was significantly restricted by limiting the number of personnel on construction sites.

Increased hours of working: eg New South Wales permitted construction sites to operate on weekends and public holidays irrespective of what consents might otherwise allow.

Physical distancing was the primary method of protection mandated in many countries, requiring all persons outside their homes (and including construction sites) to be separated by a distance of 1.0, 1.5, 1.8 or 2 metres.

Additional OHS precautions: many jurisdictions required additional health precautions to be implemented, eg wearing of face masks outside the home; Singapore issued an advisory on supporting mental well-being of workers under Covid-19 work arrangements; the Philippines required temperature checks prior to entering workplaces.[49]

Stringent cleaning protocols were required including frequent hand washing and sanitising by regularly and frequently disinfecting contact surfaces in an endeavour to prevent infection, and deep cleaning of premises where infection had occurred.

Enhanced documentation of employees: eg Singapore required mandatory daily declarations and updating by employers of work permits in the construction sector on stay-home notices; Victoria mandated enhanced record keeping to ensure that persons who had been in close contact with an infected person could be identified, advised and tested.

Isolation of infected personnel: personnel diagnosed with Covid-19 were required to isolate from others, typically for a period of 14 days.

Quarantine: many countries required incoming travellers to be quarantined for 14 days. Some countries required particular areas of high risk to be quarantined from outside contact, eg Singapore issued an advisory requiring foreign employees in the construction sector to be quarantined in their accommodation from 20 April to 4 May.

Labour laws: some constraints on the employment of labour were temporarily put in abeyance, eg in Singapore employers were permitted to introduce flexible work schedules to use unused working hours to offset overtime hours; in the Philippines reduction of workhours and/or workdays per week, rotation of workers and forced leave were permitted.

49 Philippines Department of Public Works and Highways (DPWH) Department Order No. 39, series of 2020, dated 19 May 2020.

Labour payments: some countries introduced new requirements to protect the income of infected persons, eg in Indonesia the salary of a documented infected worker was required to be paid in full for up to 14 days, a worker categorised as a suspect Covid-19 infection and quarantined/isolated was required to be paid in full during the quarantine/isolation period and a worker unable to work due to Covid-19 illness was required to be paid wages in accordance with applicable laws.

1.6.4 Operation of construction contracts

1.6.4.1 The Philippines

The Philippines Department of Labor and Employment issued Labor Advisory No 18 of 2020 applying to all employers, including contractors and subcontractors in the private sector that specified:

> The employer shall shoulder the cost of COVID-19 prevention and control measures such as but not limited to the following: testing, disinfection facilities, hand sanitisers, personal protective equipment (PPEs ie face mask), proper orientation and training of workers including IEC materials on COVID-19 prevention and control.[50]

1.6.4.2 Singapore

Singapore acted early to provide significant relief for the impacts of the pandemic in the *Covid-19 (Temporary Measures) Act 2020 (the Act),* passed on 7 April 2020. Part 2 of the *Act* contained a number of measures for temporary relief for inability to perform an obligation in a scheduled contract after 1 February 2020 caused by a Covid-19 event. The *Act* operated for a prescribed period of six months. The *Act* provided that where a party (A) to a scheduled contract (which includes a construction contract) was unable to perform a contractual obligation caused to a material extent by a Covid-19 event and had served a notification for relief with the other party or parties to the contract (B), then despite any law or anything in the contract, B may not take a number of actions for the specified period. Those actions included commencement or continuation of litigation or arbitration, enforcement of security, actions in respect of insolvency, and enforcement of a judgment, arbitral award or an adjudicator's determination. In keeping with the principles of freedom of contract, any applicable *force majeure* clause in the Contract prevailed over the provisions of the *Act*.

The *Act* also provided for specific relief for inability to perform an obligation in a construction or supply contract as a consequence of a Covid-19 event, including extending the term of a performance bond, precluding a call on a performance bond and disregarding delay caused by a Covid-19 event in calculating liquidated damages. The inability to perform an obligation in the Contract to a material extent caused by a Covid19 event is a defence to a claim for a breach of contract.

The *Act* provided for an assessor to exclusively determine whether a party falls within section 5 of the *Act* – i.e. whether their non-performance was in fact due to a Covid-19 event.

50 Guidelines on the Cost of COVID-19 Prevention and Control Measures, 18 May 2020 https://www.dole.gov.ph/news/labor-advisory-no-18-series-of-2020-guidelines-on-the-cost-of-covid-19-prevention-and-control-measures/ (accessed 6 August 2020).

1.6.5 Economic measures

In addition to the measures outlined above that directly impacted the execution of construction projects and the operation of construction contracts, governments provided financial assistance to individuals and businesses that indirectly assisted the construction industry. For example, in Australia the government made a AU$1,500 (US$1,150) per fortnight Jobkeeper payment for a period of six months for each employee in an enterprise that had suffered a 30 per cent (50 per cent for large organisations) reduction in turnover as a result of Covid-19.

The Hong Kong government introduced an Anti-epidemic Fund to implement targeted measures to support the construction industry, paying eligible consultants, contractors and subcontractors HK$50,000 (US$6,500) each and eligible construction workers HK$1,500 (US$200) each in the first round, and further payments to construction workers, contractors and suppliers in the second round. Hong Kong also introduced the Employment Support Scheme of HK$81 billion (US$10 billion) to provide time-limited financial support to employers to retain their employees; the first tranche of the scheme provided wage subsidies for three months from June to August 2020.

The Philippines Government provided an emergency subsidy to low-income households and implemented a small business wage subsidy measure to complement its social amelioration programme.

1.6.6 Claims arising from Covid-19 under FIDIC contracts

Construction projects were significantly delayed, postponed or terminated as a result of Covid-19; those that continued were subject to increased costs as a result of the health measures required to keep workers safe – stringent cleaning and disinfection, physical distancing and increased use of personal protective equipment (**PPE**) among other economic impacts. Contractors will inevitably seek costs and EOTs and a substantial number of claims can therefore be expected. At the time of writing (February 2021) the Covid-19 pandemic is far from over, and there is already anecdotal evidence of claims on many construction projects.

Early in the pandemic (April 2020) FIDIC issued the 'FIDIC Covid-19 Guidance Memorandum to Users of FIDIC Standard Forms of Works Contract'.[51] That Memorandum contains an outline of the provisions in FIDIC's standard forms of contract for works relevant to likely scenarios arising as a consequence of Covid-19:

> FIDIC's core purpose of drafting this Guidance Memorandum is to help Parties to a FIDIC contract to consider mutually satisfactory solutions and avoid disputes arising between them. COVID-19 pandemic is a unique broad scale and extraordinary event which should be recognized as such.

The Guidance Memorandum does not refer to any specific legal system or jurisdiction and cautions that the legal interpretation of the contract will depend upon matters such as the precise wording of the various documents in the Contract and the governing law. The Memorandum takes the approach of outlining a number of possible scenarios and suggests likely relevant responses by reference to relevant provisions of FIDIC contracts.

---

51 https://fidic.org/sites/default/files/FIDIC%20Guidance%20Memorandum%20to%20Users%20of%20the%201999%20Conditions%20of%20Contract%20dated%201st%20April%202013.pdf (accessed 30 July 2020).

FIDIC's list of scenarios identifies the following circumstances that are expected to give rise to claims unique to the impact of Covid-19:[52]

1. The local authorities/government do not promulgate any new piece of legislation or regulation banning construction activity or works on Site. However, the Contractor is facing difficulties in mobilizing personnel, who fear for their safety, and in obtaining Goods due to issues in the supply chain.
2. The Contractor is under the same circumstances as scenario No. 1 above. However, instead of facing difficulties in mobilizing personnel or obtaining Goods, the Contractor is suffering delays caused by the authorities (for example, making repeated health and safety inspections on the Site).
3. The local authorities or government have promulgated changes to the Laws restricting construction activities and works on the Site. The Contractor is still able to proceed with the Works, however it is suffering delay and or incurring additional Cost as a result of those changes.
4. The local authorities/government have issued an order(s)/decree(s) preventing construction activities (including lockdown, curfew, inaccessible quarantined areas, etc), and execution of the Works on Site has now become impossible. Consequently, the Contractor and/or the Employer is prevented from performing obligations under the Contract.
5. Under scenario No. 4 above, can the Contractor subject this scenario to Clause 17 [*Risk and Responsibility/Care of the Works and Indemnities*]? Under Clause 17 the Contractor is entitled to a financial compensation in addition to an EOT, rather than only an EOT, when a natural Force Majeure or Exceptional Event occurs.
6. Under scenarios Nos. 1, 2, or 3, above, can the Employer or the Contractor resort to Clause 19 [*Force Majeure*], Clause 18 [*Exceptional Events*], or Clause 18 [*Exceptional Risks*] (in the relevant FIDIC contract as the case may be), to address such scenarios?
7. There has been no change in Laws of the Country nor real impact on the availability of personnel or on the supply chain so far. However, the personnel of the Employer (including the Engineer or the Employer's Representative, as the case may be) are, as a precaution, working remotely and hence are most of the time away from Site. As a consequence, the Contractor suffers delay and/or incurred additional Cost due to slow decision-making.

1.6.7 Dispute resolution

The spread of Covid-19 prompted government, judicial and other bodies around the globe to adopt measures responding to the need for greater flexibility and remote connectivity on the operation of courts and dispute resolution practice. The IBA documented the impact of Covid-19 on court operations and litigation practice in 37 countries.[53] The Chartered Institute of Arbitrators issued guidance for remote

52 ibid.

53 'The Impact of COVID-19 on Court Operations and Litigation Practice' (June 2020), *International Bar Association* https://www.ibanet.org/Covid-19/Home.aspx (accessed 25 February 2021).

proceedings, [54] as did other arbitral institutions such as HKIAC[55] and AAA-ICDR.[56] The Dispute Resolution Board Foundation recognised the restrictions on in-person meetings during the pandemic and published best practice guidelines and a checklist for virtual Dispute Board proceedings.[57]

1.7 Impact of the applicable laws

In summary, the applicable law can impact the operation of a contract in various ways:

- The provisions of mandatory law will override any contractual provisions.
- A construction contract must be executed in accordance with the applicable Laws irrespective of the contract wording.
- Non-mandatory law may provide default options if they are not covered or explicitly derogated from by the specific terms of the Contract.

It is apparent that in any jurisdiction there is potentially a substantial number of laws that impact on: the entry into, operation of and termination of a contract; the design and execution of the Works; and the resolution of any disputes that arise from or in connection with the Contract. Subject to the desirability of the Conditions of Contract comprising an accurate contract management manual, it is not the place of contract documents to constitute a complete definition of the parties' legal rights and obligations, or a project management manual (nor would it be feasible). Accordingly, the Conditions of Contract, even in a well written and comprehensive FIDIC Contract, can never identify all of the applicable laws that may define the parties' rights and obligations in all circumstances.

Construction of any significant infrastructure or facility in the modern world is a complex undertaking in which the interests of many stakeholders must be considered, and a myriad of legal obligations complied with. Those involved at the 'coalface' of a construction project administering the Contract as Engineer, Employer or Contractor need to be generally aware of their legal obligations under the applicable Laws, so that they can make the appropriate enquiries as to their specific obligations in particular circumstances. Complex or unusual situations will undoubtedly require input from competent construction lawyers experienced in the relevant jurisdiction.

However, except in exceptional circumstances, it is unlikely that such legal advice will be available on a day-to-day basis on the construction Site. The personnel administering the Contract may be engineers or other construction professionals with a general understanding of contract and other law, but they are unlikely to have the

54 'Guidance Note on Remote Dispute Resolution Proceedings' (2020) *Chartered Institute of Arbitrators* https://www.ciarb.org/media/9013/remote-hearings-guidance-note_final_140420.pdf (accessed 25 February 2021).

55 'HKIAC Guidelines for Virtual Hearings' (2020) *HKIAC*.

56 'AAA-ICDR Virtual Hearing Guide for Arbitrators and Parties' (2020) *AAA-ICDR* https://go.adr.org/rs/294-SFS-516/images/AAA268_AAA%20Virtual%20Hearing%20Guide%20for%20Arbitrators%20and%20Parties.pdf (accessed 25 February 2021).

57 'Best Practice Guidelines for Virtual Dispute Board Proceedings' (2020) *Dispute Resolution Board Foundation* http://www.disputeboard.org/wp-content/uploads/2020/07/Best-Practice-Guidelines-for-Virtual-Dispute-Board-Proceedings-5-August-2020.pdf (accessed 25 February 2021); 'Checklist for Dispute Board Members in Preparation for Virtual Dispute Board Proceedings' (2020) *Dispute Resolution Board Foundation* http://www.disputeboard.org/wp-content/uploads/2020/07/DRBF-Checklist-for-Virtual-DB-Proceedings-5-August-2020.pdf (accessed 25 February 2021).

depth of knowledge of an experienced construction lawyer. The challenge for such contract administrators is to have sufficient knowledge of their obligations to know when and where to seek further information and advice on a specific issue. This problem may be particularly acute in a situation where the contract administrator is operating in a jurisdiction in which she/he is unfamiliar.

1.8 Country accessions to international conventions and agreements

Each of the countries considered in this book has acceded to certain international conventions and agreements and incorporated their principles into their domestic law. Table 1.3 identifies, for each country, whether they have a civil law or common law system, and whether they have acceded to various international conventions, agreements or principles of relevance to construction law.

1.8.1 New York Convention

Perhaps the most important international convention for international users of FIDIC contracts is the *1958 New York Arbitration Convention on the Recognition and Enforcement of Foreign Arbitral Awards* (***New York Convention***). This convention ensures that commercial arbitration is an effective means of finally resolving international commercial disputes by means of an award that can be enforced by a court judgment in any state that is a party to the *New York Convention*. It is significant that all the countries covered in this book are party to the *New York Convention.*

The *New York Convention* gives practical effect to the principle of *pacta sunt servanda*, by providing a mechanism to hold parties to the consequences of the bargain they have made. If a dispute arises out of or in connection with a contract, the appointed arbitral tribunal will determine the appropriate remedy in the light of the terms of the contract and the applicable law. Their award is final and binding, and not subject to appeal on findings of fact or law. A court in a Convention State can only set aside or refuse to enforce an award on very narrow jurisdictional grounds.

The *New York Convention* is perhaps the single most important agreement that facilitates international commercial commerce in general, and international construction projects in particular. International arbitration removes a dispute from the jurisdiction of the courts of either party's home jurisdiction that may be perceived as giving one of them an advantage. The arbitration award can be enforced by normal court processes in any jurisdiction that is party to the *New York Convention*, typically in a jurisdiction where the debtor has assets. It is therefore unsurprising that FIDIC General Conditions require international arbitration to finally settle any disputes that have not been avoided or resolved by the decision of a Dispute Avoidance/Adjudication Board or Dispute Adjudication Board.

1.8.2 WTO Agreement on Government Procurement

Purchases of goods and services by government agencies with public resources for public purposes are generally referred to as government/public procurement.

Achieving 'value for money' is a primary aim of most procurement regimes. Open, transparent and non-discriminatory procurement is generally considered to be the best tool to achieve this goal as it optimises competition among suppliers. The liberalisation

Table 1.3 Country Accessions to International Conventions and Agreements

Country	**Civil or common law**	***New York Arbitration Convention on the Recognition and Enforcement of Foreign Arbitral Awards, 1958***[1]	***United Nations Convention on International Settlement Agreements Resulting from Mediation (2018) (the "Singapore Convention on Mediation")***[2]	***Hague Convention of 30 June 2005 on Choice of Court Agreements***[3]	**UNCITRAL Model Law on International Commercial Arbitration (1985 with amendments as adopted in 2006)**[4]	***United Nations Convention of Contracts for the International Sale of Goods* (CISG)**[5]	**Member State of UNIDROIT**[6]	**WTO Agreement on Government Procurement**[7]	**UNCITRAL Model Law on Cross-Border Insolvency (1997)**[8]
Australia	Common law	YES			YES	YES	YES	YES	YES
China	Civil law Based on Germanic civil law with influences from Soviet Socialist law	YES	Signature	Signature		YES	YES	YES	
Fiji	Common law	YES	YES		YES	YES			
Hong Kong	Common law Land tenure – Chinese customary law.	YES			YES			YES	
India	Common law State of Goa & 2 Union Territories– civil law based on Portuguese civil law	YES	Signature		1985		YES	Observer	
Indonesia	Civil law Based on Roman-Dutch civil law and adat (cultural law of Indonesia).	YES					YES	Observer	
Japan	Civil law Based on Germanic civil law. Japanese Civil Code 1895	YES			1985	YES	YES	YES	YES

(*Continued*)

Country	**Civil or common law**	***New York Arbitration Convention on the Recognition and Enforcement of Foreign Arbitral Awards, 1958***[1]	***United Nations Convention on International Settlement Agreements Resulting from Mediation (2018) (the "Singapore Convention on Mediation")***[2]	***Hague Convention of 30 June 2005 on Choice of Court Agreements***[3]	**UNCITRAL Model Law on International Commercial Arbitration (1985 with amendments as adopted in 2006)**[4]	***United Nations Convention of Contracts for the International Sale of Goods (CISG)***[5]	**Member State of UNIDROIT**[6]	**WTO Agreement on Government Procurement**[7]	**UNCITRAL Model Law on Cross-Border Insolvency (1997)**[8]
Korea	Civil law Based on Germanic civil law. Influenced by Japanese civil law.	YES	Signature		YES	YES	YES	YES	YES
Malaysia	Common law	YES	Signature		1985			Observer	
Nepal	Common law	YES							
Pakistan	Common law						YES	Observer	
Papua New Guinea	Common law	YES							
Philippines	Mixed common, civil, Islamic (Sharia) and customary law	YES	Signature		1985		YES	Observer	YES
Singapore	Common law	YES	YES	YES	1985	YES		YES	YES
Sri Lanka	Mixed common law & civil law (Roman–Dutch)	YES	Signature		1985			Observer	
Vietnam	Civil law Communist legal theory and French civil law.	YES				YES		Observer	

of government procurement markets holds the potential to generate benefits both in terms of procurement efficiency and commercial interests. One of the ways the World Trade Organisation (**WTO**) promotes the liberalisation of government is through the Agreement on Government Agreement (**WTO GPA**).

The WTO describes the WTO GPA as follows:

> The GPA is a plurilateral agreement within the framework of the WTO, meaning that not all WTO members are parties to the Agreement. At present, the Agreement has 20 parties comprising 48 WTO members. 36 WTO members/observers participate in the GPA Committee as observers. Out of these, 12 members are in the process of acceding to the Agreement.
>
> The fundamental aim of the GPA is to mutually open government procurement markets among its parties. As a result of several rounds of negotiations, the GPA parties have opened procurement activities worth an estimated US$ 1.7 trillion annually to international competition (i.e. to suppliers from GPA parties offering goods, services or construction services).
>
> The GPA is composed mainly of two parts: the text of the Agreement and parties' market access schedules of commitments.
>
> The text of the Agreement establishes rules requiring that open, fair and transparent conditions of competition be ensured in government procurement. However, these rules do not automatically apply to all procurement activities of each party. Rather, the coverage schedules play a critical role in determining whether a procurement activity is covered by the Agreement or not. Only those procurement activities that are carried out by covered entities purchasing listed goods, services or construction services of a value exceeding specified threshold values are covered by the Agreement.[58]

Under the WTO GPA the coverage schedule of each party contains seven annexes, including Annex 4 goods, Annex 5 services and Annex 6 construction services. The countries listed in Table 1.3 that have acceded to the WTO GPA have defined their coverage of construction services as all construction services in Division 51 of the United Nations Provisional Central Product Classification (CPC Prov.) and the WTO system of classification (MTN.GNS/W/120),[59] procured by the entities in Annexes 1 (central government entities), 2 (sub-central government entities) and 3 (other entities).

The significance of other individual conventions is discussed in the later chapters.

1.9 Aims of the book

One of the aims of this book is to identify, for a range of jurisdictions in the Asia Pacific region in which FIDIC contracts are used, the applicable laws that may impact on the operation of the Contract, the execution of the Works or the determination of disputes arising under or in connection with the Contract.[60] It does not purport to provide guidance on FIDIC contracts per se; there are a number of texts which

58 https://www.wto.org/english/tratop_e/gproc_e/gp_gpa_e.htm (accessed 9 November 2020).

59 MTN.GNS/W/120 (accessed 9 November 2020).

60 *Doing Business in Asia Pacific guidebook* (2020) *International Bar Association* provides details of the business environment in Australia, China, Hong Kong, India, Indonesia, Japan, Malaysia, Singapore, Korea, the Philippines and Vietnam. It focuses on the common pitfalls and cultural differences of doing business throughout Asia Pacific, and includes sections on business and corporate structures, foreign investment, employment industrial relations and WHS, intellectual property and dispute resolution. https://www.ibanet.org/Regional_Fora/Regional_Fora/Asia_Pacific_Forum/Doing-business.aspx (accessed 25 February 2021).

provide an in-depth discussion of FIDIC contracts, including general commentary on what modifications may be required for use in particular jurisdictions. The following section contains a list of references on FIDIC contracts.

This book is intended to be a source book for a contract administrator or lawyer unfamiliar with the requirements of the Particular Conditions of a FIDIC contract or operating with a FIDIC contract in a jurisdiction they are unfamiliar with. It does not provide specific guidance on what Particular Conditions clauses might be necessary or desirable for any jurisdiction; such guidance would always need to be specific to the requirements of the particular project at the particular point in time and require input from a competent construction lawyer. It should also be noted that, although the laws identified are believed to be correct as at December 2020, legislation and case law are constantly changing, another reason why competent advice needs to be sought when necessary.

Chapter 2 provides further details of the FIDIC Golden Principles, which FIDIC recommend should be complied with in preparing Particular Conditions. Chapter 3 provides more specific details of what should be in the Particular Conditions, choosing the governing law of the contract, and guidance on the preparation of Particular Conditions necessary or desirable for particular purposes, without attempting to address the differences between jurisdictions. Chapter 4 discusses the unique features of the FIDIC Emerald Book, a design and construct contract incorporating the specific requirements necessary for appropriate risk allocation in Underground Works. Chapter 5 provides a perspective on the use of FIDIC contracts by the Japan International Cooperation Agency (JICA). As the agency in charge of administering Japan's Official Development Assistance, JICA has an overarching interest in the use of construction contracts that promote the best value for money in construction projects.

Each of the remaining chapters in the book deals with a specific jurisdiction, prepared by one or more construction lawyers and/or engineers, experienced in the application of FIDIC contracts in that jurisdiction. Each of those jurisdiction specific chapters provides a brief overview of the legal landscape and the construction industry, the impact of the Covid-19 pandemic on construction contracts and construction projects, a discussion of any Special Provisions required if the governing law is that jurisdiction, and a listing of the applicable law if the Site is in the jurisdiction. Each chapter also identifies issues that a court or arbitrator may construe differently to that expected from the words of the Contract, because of local law or custom.

1.10 References

1.10.1 Books on construction law

Donald Charrett (ed), *The International Application of FIDIC Contracts A Practical Guide* (Informa Law from Routledge 2020)[61]

Charles O'Neill, *Global Construction Success* (Wiley Blackwell 2019)

Donald Charrett, *The Application of Contracts in Engineering and Construction Projects* (1st edn, Informa Law from Routledge 2018)

61 That book has chapters on the application of FIDIC contracts in the following jurisdictions not included in this book: Brazil, Czech Republic, France, Germany, Ghana, Italy, Peru, Romania, South Africa, Switzerland and the United Arab Emirates.

Stephen Furst and Vivian Ramsey, *Keating on Construction Contracts* (10th edn, Sweet & Maxwell/Thomson Reuters 2018)

Lukas Klee, *International Construction Contract Law* (2nd edn, John Wiley & Sons Inc 2018)

Robert J Gemmell, *Quantification of Delay and Disruption in Construction and Engineering Projects* (Thomson Reuters 2017)

Dimitar Kondev, *Multi-Party and Multi-Contract Arbitration in the Construction Industry* (John Wiley & Sons Inc 2017)

Renato Nazzini, *Transnational Construction Arbitration: Key Themes in the Resolution of Construction Disputes* (Informa Law from Routledge 2017)

John Uff, *Construction law: Law and Practice Relating to the Construction Industry* (12th edn, Sweet & Maxwell/Thomson Reuters 2017)

Arent van Wassenaer, *A Practical Guide to Successful Construction Projects* (Informa Law from Routledge 2017)

Julian Bailey, *Construction Law (Volumes 1–3)* (2nd edn, Informa Law from Routledge 2016)

Andrew Burr (ed), *Delay and Disruption in Construction Contracts* (Informa Law from Routledge 2016)

Cyril Chern, *The Law of Construction Disputes* (2nd edn, Informa Law from Routledge 2016)

Nicholas Dennys and Robert Clay, *Hudson's Building and Engineering Contracts* (13th edn, Sweet & Maxwell 2016)

Darryl Royce, *Adjudication in Construction Law* (Informa Law from Routledge 2016)

Monika Chao-Duivis, *Studies in European Construction Law* (Den Haag: Instituut voor Bouwrecht 2015)

Anthony Edwards and Roger Gibson, *A Practical Guide to Disruption and Productivity Loss on Construction and Engineering Projects* (Wiley 2015)

PJ Keane, Anthony F Caletka, *Delay Analysis in Construction Contracts* (Wiley 2015)

James Pickavance, *A Practical Guide to Construction Adjudication* (Wiley 2015)

Charles O'Neill, *Human Dynamics* (Contract Dynamics Sdn Bhd 2014)

Michael Sergeant and Max Wieliczko, *Construction Contract Variations* (Informa Law from Routledge 2014)

Philip Bryan, *Successful Delivery of Resources Projects* (Clayton Utz 2013)

Donald Charrett (ed), *Global Challenges Shared Solutions* (Society of Construction Law Australia 2013)

Cyril Chern, *Chern on Dispute Boards* (2nd edn, Informa Law from Routledge 2013)

Dr Paula Gerber and Brennan Ong, *Best Practice in Construction Disputes* (Lexis Nexis Butterworths 2013)

Robert Hogarth, Alexandra Anderson and Simon Goldring (eds), *Insurance Law for the Construction Industry* (2nd edn, Oxford University Press 2013)

Sarah Lupton, *Cornes and Lupton's Design Liability in the Construction Industry* (Wiley 2013)

Simon Tolson, *Dictionary of Construction Terms* (Informa Law from Routledge 2012)

Edward W Merrow, *Industrial Megaprojects Concepts, Strategies and Practices for Success* (Wiley 2011)

John Scriven and Nigel Pritchard, *EPC Contracts and Major Projects* (Sweet & Maxwell 2011)

Roger ter Haar QC and Camilla ter Haar, *Remedies in Construction Law* (Informa Law 2010)

David Chappell, Michael Cowlin and Michael Dunn, *Building Law Encyclopedia* (Wiley-Blackwell 2009)

Tom Kendrick, *Identifying and Managing Project Risk* (AMACOM 2009)

David Mosey, *Early Contractor Involvement in Building Procurement* (Wiley-Blackwell 2009)

Michael Furmston, *Powell-Smith and Furmston's Building Contract Case Book* (4th edn, Blackwell 2006)

Alan Redfern and Martin Hunter, *Law and Practice of International Commercial Arbitration* (4th edn, Thomson/Sweet & Maxwell 2004)

1.10.2 Books on FIDIC contracts

Raveed Khalani and Mahdi Saadat Fard, *FIDIC Plant and Design-Build Forms of Contract Illustrated* (Wiley 2015)

Jeremy Glover and Simon Hughes, *Understanding the FIDIC Red Book: A Clause-by-Clause Commentary* (3rd edn, Sweet & Maxwell 2011)

Axel-Volkmar Jaeger and Götz-Sebastian Hök, *FIDIC – A Guide for Practitioners* (Springer 2010)

Ellis Baker, Ben Mellors, Scott Chalmers and Anthony Lavers, *FIDIC Contracts: Law and Practice* (Informa Law 2009)

Brian Totterdill, *FIDIC Users' Guide: A Practical Guide to the 1999 Red and Yellow Books* (Thomas Telford 2006)

Robert Knutson (ed), *FIDIC An Analysis of International Contracts* (Kluwer Law International 2005)

Nael G Bunni, *The FIDIC Forms of Contract* (Blackwell 2005)

1.10.3 Guides on FIDIC contracts[62]

Standard Letters and Notices. For use with the FIDIC Conditions of Contract for Works of Civil Engineering Construction, 4th ed, 1987 Red Book.

Electrical and Mechanical Works Guide (1st edn, 1988). Guide to the Use of the FIDIC Conditions of Contract for Electrical and Mechanical Works 3rd edn, 1987 Yellow Book. Includes Yellow Book 3rd ed 1987 conditions.

Red Book Guide (1st edn, 1989). Guide to the Use of FIDIC Conditions of Contract for Works of Civil Engineering Construction 4th edn, 1987 Red Book. Includes Red Book Conditions.

FIDIC 4th – A Practical Legal Guide (1991). A commentary on the Red Book 4th edn, 1987 by EC Corbett.

Design – Build and Turnkey Guide (1st edn, 1996). Guide to the Use of FIDIC Conditions of Contract for Design-Build and Turnkey. A clause by clause commentary on the provisions contained in Part 1 of the 1995 Orange Book.

FIDIC Contracts Guide to the Construction, Plant and Design-Build and EPC/Turnkey Contracts (1st edn, 2000).

The New EIC Red Book Guide, 2001. European International Contractors (EIC) Contractors Guide to the FIDIC Conditions of Contract for Construction.

The New EIC Yellow Book Guide, 2003. European International Contractors (EIC) Contractors Guide to the FIDIC Conditions of Contract for Plant and Design-Build.

The EIC Silver Book Guide, 2nd edn, 2003. European International Contractors (EIC) Contractors Guide to the FIDIC Conditions of Contract for EPC/Turnkey Projects.

FIDIC Contracts Guide Supplement: MDB Harmonised Construction Contract (2006). Guide to the March 2006 release of the MDB Harmonised Construction Contract.

DBO (2008 Gold Book) Contract Guide 1st edn, 2011.

1.10.4 Journal articles

Lukas Klee and Claudia Adalgiza Teodorescu, 'Romanian Experience with FIDIC Forms in Roads and Bridges Construction' (2013) 30(4) *International Construction Law Review* 432

ICC, 'International Construction Contract Disputes: Third Commentary on ICC Awards Dealing Primarily with FIDIC Contracts' (2012) 23(2) *International Chamber of Commerce Bulletin* 23

62 'Contract advice' https://www.fidic.org/bookshop (accessed 4 November 2020).

Christopher Seppälä, 'The Arbitration Clause in FIDIC Contracts for Major Works' (2005) 22(1) *International Construction Law Review* 4

Michael Black QC, 'Design Risk in FIDIC Contracts' [2005] *Society of Construction Law*

Christopher Seppälä, 'Contractor's Claims under the FIDIC Contracts for Major Works' [2005] 21(4) *Construction Law Journal* 278

Frank Kennedy, 'EIC Contractor's Guide to the FIDIC Conditions of Contract for EPC Turnkey Projects (The Silver Book)' [2000] 17(4) *International Construction Law Review* 504

1.10.5 Internet resources

Construction and Engineering Laws and Regulations 2018 https://iclg.com/practice-areas/construction-and-engineering-law-laws-and-regulations (accessed 17 March 2019)

1.10.6 Case law

A list of cases and publicly available arbitration awards is available at: http://corbett.co.uk/wp-content/uploads/Table-of-FIDIC-Cases.pdf

ANNEXURE

TABLE 1.4 EDITIONS OF FIDIC CONDITIONS OF CONTRACT FOR CONTRACTS BETWEEN EMPLOYER AND CONTRACTOR

Short Form of Contract [Green Book]	Construction [Red Book]	Construction [MDB edition] [Pink Book]	Plant and Design Build [Yellow Book]	EPC/ Turnkey [Silver Book]	Design, Build and Operate [Gold Book]	Under-ground Works [Emerald Book]	Dredging and Reclamation Works [Blue-Green Book]
	1st ed. 1957		1st edn, 1963				
	2nd edn, 1969						
	3rd edn, 1977		2nd edn, 1980				
	4th edn, 1987		3rd edn, 1987				
	1992 Revised edn	2005 edn					
	1996 DAB Supplement	2006 Revised edn		1995 Orange Book			
Short Form of Contract First ed. 1999	Conditions of Contract for Construction First edn, 1999	Conditions of Contract for Construction MDB Harmonised Edition 2010	Conditions of Contract for Plant and Design Build First edn, 1999	Conditions of Contract for EPC/ Turnkey Projects First edn, 1999	Conditions of Contract for Design, Build and Operate Projects First edn, 2008		Form of Contract for Dredging and Reclamation Works First edn, 2006
	Conditions of Contract for Construction Second edn 2017		Conditions of Contract for Plant and Design Build Second edn 2017	Conditions of Contract for EPC/ Turnkey Projects Second edn 2017		Conditions of Contract for Under-ground Works First edn, 2019	Form of Contract for Dredging and Reclamation Works Second edn 2016

DOI: 10.4324/9781003200901-1

CHAPTER 2

The FIDIC Golden Principles[1]

Dr Donald Charrett[2]

2.1 Introduction

FIDIC publishes General Conditions of contract that are widely used for international construction contracts. They are intended to be used in any legal jurisdiction. FIDIC General Conditions are explicitly based on a fair and equitable risk allocation between Employer and Contractor and are widely recognised as striking an appropriate balance between the reasonable expectations of the contracting Parties.

Arguably, a contract recognised as a fair and balanced 'FIDIC contract' has real commercial value to both Employer and Contractor, both at the tendering stage and while the Works are being performed.

General Conditions prepared for use in a wide range of projects and jurisdictions inevitably require supplementation with Particular Conditions that address the particular requirements of the Site and the unique features of the specific project. Particular Conditions may also be necessary to amend the General Conditions to comply with mandatory law that applies to the Site or the legal jurisdiction.

Provided that such modifications are limited to those necessary for the particular features of the Site and the project and do not change the essential fair and balanced character of a FIDIC Contract, the contract is recognisable as a FIDIC contract.

The essential features of a FIDIC Contract that make the risk/reward allocation fair and balanced are referred to as the **FIDIC Golden Principles (GPs)**.

This chapter outlines the development of the GPs and the reasons for them, and their application in drafting Particular Conditions.

1 This article was first published in (2018) 13(2) *Construction Law International*, and is reproduced by kind permission of the International Bar Association, London, UK © International Bar Association.

2 Principal Drafter, FIDIC Working Group TG15.

DOI: 10.4324/9781003200901-2

2.2 Fair and balanced contracts

Contract risks refer to the chance that contractual objectives will not be fulfilled. The Contract defines who bears the liability for the contract risks. The form and terms of the Contract can increase or decrease those risks from the norm. Thus, use of the appropriate form and terms of a construction contract can play a major role in minimising the risk that the contractual objectives will not be fulfilled. Conversely, use of an inappropriate form or terms of a construction contract can significantly increase the risk that the contractual objectives will not be fulfilled.

Strictly, it is incorrect to refer to contracts as 'allocating' risk, as contracts allocate obligations and confer rights.[3] A risk, being the chance of an event happening, is not 'allocated' to either Party by the Contract. A risk event may exist separate and independent of the obligations and rights of the Parties, or the risk event may be under the 'control' of one of the Parties. Whether or not one of the Parties has 'control' over a risk event, it is the obligations and rights arising as a consequence of the risk event happening that are 'allocated' by the Contract, and this is the commonly accepted usage of the term 'risk allocation'.

Many standard form contracts are based on the explicitly stated principle of balanced or fair risk allocation, eg the Australian Standard 4000 series,[4] the US ConsensusDocs,[5] the UK New Engineering Contract,[6] contracts promoted by the European Engineering Industries Association,[7] the International Chamber of Commerce,[8] the Baltic and International Marine Council[9] and the UK offshore oil and gas industry.[10] The principle is also espoused by government procurement agencies in the UK,[11] Australia[12] and the USA.[13]

Many writers suggest that adherence to the principle of balanced risk allocation enhances the prospect of successful contracts, by encouraging contractual performance

3 Report by NPWC/NBCC Joint Working Party, 'No Dispute Strategies for Improvement in the Australian Building and Construction Industry' (May 1990) 7.

4 'Standard Conditions of Contract' (2001) 4 *BDPS News* 1, 4.

5 http://www.consensusdocs.org/FooterSection_About/FooterSection_WhyConsensusDocs (accessed 18 March 2018).

6 Brian Eggleston, *The New Engineering Contract: A Commentary* (Blackwell Publishing 1996) 7.

7 Orgalime Turnkey Contract for Industrial Works.

8 International Chamber of Commerce Model Turnkey Contract for Major Projects (2007). http://www.iccbooks.com/Product/ProductInfo.aspx?id=488 (accessed 18 March 2018).)

9 https://www.bimco.org/about-us-and-our-members/about-us/our-history (accessed 18 March 2018).

10 Leading Oil and Gas Industry Competitiveness (LOGIC) http://www.logic-oil.com (accessed 18 March 2018).

11 HM Treasury, *The Green Book Appraisal and Evaluation in Central Government* http://greenbook.treasury.gov.uk/annex04.htm (accessed 26 August 2008): 'The governing principle is that risk should be allocated to whichever party from the public or private sector is best placed to manage it. The optimal allocation of risk, rather than maximising risk transfer, is the objective, and is vital to ensuring that the best solution is found.'

12 Department of Treasury and Finance Victorian Government, *Partnerships Victoria Updated Standard Commercial Principles* (2008) 99: 'Both the government and the private party should seek to ensure that cost and adequate risk transfer are balanced as far as possible to achieve the best value for money on a particular project.'

13 US Department of Transportation Federal Highway Administration, *Risk Assessment and Allocation for Highway Construction Management* (2006) § 6.1.1 http://www.international.fhwa.dot.gov/riskassess/risk_hcm06_06.cfm (accessed 26 August 2008):

> 'A fundamental tenet of risk management is to allocate the risks to the party best able to manage them. The party assuming the risk should be able to best evaluate, control, bear the risk of, and benefit from its assumption.'

that minimises adverse outcomes and thereby reduces disputation.[14] In a survey of 10 case studies of Australian projects to determine project-related factors critical to project success, Sidwell et al found that equitable risk allocation was one of the top four factors found to be critical in explaining overall project performance, and was the most significant factor related to the conditions of contract.[15]

'Non-standard' contract terms (in the sense of altering the 'normal' balanced risk allocation in standard form contracts) in either standard form contracts or bespoke contracts are usually put forward by one party to alter the risk allocation to be more favourable to it. As Employers generally put forward proposed conditions of contract with the tender documents, it is likely that non-standard terms in these contracts will involve the Contractor in accepting more risk than 'normal'.

The conditions of contract based on a standard form contract typically comprise General Conditions and Particular Conditions (or amendments to the General Conditions). The General Conditions are typically drafted by a committee representing a wide range of interests and represent a consensus of contract terms appropriate to many 'typical' projects and locations. However, these General Conditions cannot take account of the specific requirements of a particular project, or perhaps the requirements for a particular location. General Conditions typically require modification for the project.

Every project has unique circumstances, and there are many legitimate reasons for Particular Conditions that alter standard form General Conditions to suit these circumstances. For example, provisions in the General Conditions may be inconsistent with the mandatory law of the Site.

Typically, there is no formal constraint on the extent of risk transfer to the Contractor via the Particular Conditions, other than the requirements of mandatory law. However, arguably, Particular Conditions that alter the fundamental balanced risk allocation in the General Conditions change the character of the contract so that it is no longer recognisable as a contract of the type understood by the name of the General Conditions.

The consequences of inappropriately allocating excessive risk to the Contractor can actually have the opposite effect to that desired, by increasing the Employer's risks. The Japan International Cooperation Agency (JICA) commissioned the Association of Japanese Consulting Engineers to prepare a 'Check List for One Sided Contracts', to be used for the preparation of reasonable bidding documents. JICA noted that if modifications for a particular project alter the originally contemplated risk distribution in a FIDIC Red Book Contract to a large extent and the risks allocated to the Contractor become excessively high, the following problems may occur:

- Higher bid price
- Bid failure and disruption of project implementation
- Non-participation in the bid by conscientious and capable contractors
- Contract award to a bidder who failed to or was not capable of estimating the risks properly

14 NPWC/NBCC Joint Working Party, 'No Dispute Strategies for Improvement in the Australian Building and Construction Industry' (May 1990) 6–7; Sir Michael Latham, 'Constructing the Team' (July 1994) Final Report 37.

15 AC Sidwell, RJ Kennedy and APC Chan, 'Re-Engineering the Construction Delivery Process' (2002) *Construction Industry Institute Australia Report* 34.

- Poor construction quality and delay to the progress of the work due to lack of risk contingency
- Undermining the relationship of mutual trust and respect between the Employer and the Contractor
- Repetition of groundless claims from the Contractor
- Frequent disputes between the Employer and the Contractor, and
- In an extreme case, termination of the contract.[16]

2.3 The FIDIC Golden Principles

The Golden Principles were developed by FIDIC Task Group 15 (**TG15**), [17] which reported to the FIDIC Contracts Committee. Consistent with FIDIC's structured approach to developing consensus documents, drafts of TG15's report were reviewed by the Contracts Committee and a number of friendly reviewers. As noted in paragraph 1.4 above, the Emerald Book and the Second Editions of the FIDIC Red, Yellow and Silver Books recommend that the drafters of Particular Conditions take all due regard to the Golden Principles.[18]

The Golden Principles have been articulated for Works Contracts, and not Services Contracts. FIDIC has confined its attention to Particular Conditions (**PCs**) that change the General Conditions (**GCs**) to the extent that they do not comply with the GPs. It has not considered misuse of unamended GCs.

In order to promote understanding, the GPs have been formulated at a conceptual level to encapsulate the essence of a FIDIC contract. Each GP expresses a single readily understood and generally accepted concept. The GPs have been limited to the minimum number necessary for completeness. Except for GP5, the GPs are stated in broad terms, without reference to specific clauses of the GCs.

GPs function as constraints on modifications to the GCs made in the PCs. They cannot prevent misapplication of existing unamended GCs. By definition, unamended GCs are an application of the GPs.

The following overarching considerations underpin the GPs:

- The terms of the contract are comprehensive and fair to both contracting Parties.
- The legitimate interests of both contracting Parties are appropriately considered and balanced. The legitimate interests of each Party include the right to enjoy the benefits of the contractual relationship generally recognised as implicit in the GCs. For example, the Employer's legitimate interests include the right to a facility constructed to the contractually specified quality, within the time and for the price in the Contract. The Contractor's legitimate interests include the right to execute the Works in the manner contracted for, within a reasonable time and for a commercial price paid on time.
- Best practice principles of fair and balanced risk allocation between the Employer and the Contractor are put into effect in accordance with the provisions of the GCs.

16 Checklist for One Sided Contracts (Japan International Cooperation Agency 2011), 1.

17 The author was the Principal Drafter for TG15. The other members were Husni Madi (Jordan) – Team Leader, Axel Jaeger (Germany) and Dr Rafal Morek (Poland).

18 Guidance for the Preparation of Particular Conditions, 8.

- No Party shall take undue advantage of its bargaining power.
- Payments to the Contractor or Subcontractor in accordance with the Contract are adequate to maintain its cash flow.
- The Employer obtains the best value for money.
- To the extent possible, co-operation and trust between the contracting Parties is promoted, and adversarial attitudes are to be discouraged and should be avoided.
- The contract provisions can be practically put into effect.
- Disputes are avoided to the extent achievable, minimised when they do arise, and resolved efficiently.

The Golden Principles are as follows:

GP1: The duties, rights, obligations, roles and responsibilities of all the Contract Participants must be generally as implied in the General Conditions, and appropriate to the requirements of the project.
GP2: The Particular Conditions must be drafted clearly and unambiguously.
GP3: The Particular Conditions must not change the balance of risk/reward allocation provided for in the General Conditions.
GP4: All time periods specified in the Contract for Contract Participants to perform their obligations must be of reasonable duration.
GP5: Unless there is a conflict with the governing law of the Contract, all formal disputes must be referred to a Dispute Avoidance/Adjudication Board (or a Dispute Adjudication Board, if applicable) for a provisionally binding decision as a condition precedent to arbitration.

2.4 Reasons for Golden Principles

GP1: The duties, rights, obligations, roles and responsibilities of all the Contract Participants must be generally as implied in the General Conditions, and appropriate to the requirements of the project.

As with most construction contracts, FIDIC Contracts refer to a number of other persons (such as the Engineer, Dispute Adjudication Board and Subcontractors), in addition to the contracting Parties (Employer and Contractor). All the persons referred to in a FIDIC Contract (**Contract Participants**) have clearly defined roles, duties and obligations important to the efficient administration and proper functioning of the Contract. Concomitant with those roles are rights defined in the Contract.

The allocation of specific roles, duties and obligations to the various Contract Participants in FIDIC Contracts has evolved over a long period and has stood the test of time. Experience has shown that this allocation is consistent with widely accepted and understood international usage. Further, it is submitted that it provides the best opportunity for the Contract Participants to deliver a project that satisfies the Parties' reasonable performance expectations.

The delivery of a large construction project involves a complex interaction between all the Contract Participants. Each has its own roles, duties and obligations, which interface with the roles, duties and obligations of the other Contract Participants. The roles, duties and obligations defined in a FIDIC Contract have been determined to be those most appropriate to the efficient delivery of the contractual objectives, and best suited to the skills and expertise normally expected of and exercised by the Contract Participants.

A FIDIC contract is based on the Employer and the Contractor undertaking their roles, duties and obligations, and having their rights as implicit in the General Conditions. For the Employer this involves, for example, providing access to the Site at the time contracted for, and paying the Contractor. For the Contractor it involves, for example, executing and completing the Works in accordance with the Contract, and rectifying defects during the Defects Notification Period.

The roles, duties and obligations of other Contract Participants as defined in the GCs are equally important for efficiently delivering the contractual objectives (notwithstanding that, not being Parties, they are not bound by the terms of the Contract). Thus, for the Red, Pink and Yellow Books, this requires that an Engineer be appointed with appropriate authority, competence and resources to carry out the role, and that they fulfil their duties and obligations as defined in the Contract. Further, the Engineer must exercise their contractual authority and make fair determinations in accordance with the Contract, taking due regard of all relevant circumstances. This means that they must not make determinations that only suit the Employer's interests, without having due regard to the Contractor's rights under the Contract.

Similarly, for the Silver Book, the Employer's Representative must have appropriate authority to carry out the role and must carry out that role to enable the Contractor to enjoy its contractual rights.

GP2: The Particular Conditions must be drafted clearly and unambiguously.

FIDIC GCs undergo a comprehensive drafting and independent review process to ensure that they are clear and unambiguous. Clear and unambiguous drafting is fundamental to all Contract Participants understanding their roles and duties so they can fulfil their obligations and exercise their rights.

The conditions of a FIDIC Contract comprise the GCs and the PCs, which incorporate any additions or changes to the GCs. A 'FIDIC contract' will only be clearly and unambiguously drafted if the Particular Conditions are clearly and unambiguously drafted, and interface harmoniously with the GCs and the Appendix to Tender/Contract Data.

GP3: The Particular Conditions must not change the balance of risk/reward allocation provided for in the GCs.

Fair and balanced risk allocation is widely accepted as the most appropriate basis for drafting of construction contracts to minimise the prospects of disputes and enhance the likelihood of achieving successful project outcomes. It is a fundamental principle on which FIDIC contracts are based.

The **Abrahamson Principles**, well known to construction lawyers, are widely regarded as the basis of 'balanced' or 'fair' risk allocation.[19] These principles, as refined by Dr Nael Bunni, stipulate that risks should be allocated by considering:

- Which Party can best control the risk and the associated consequences?
- Which Party can best foresee the risk?

19 Max W Abrahamson, 'Risk Management' [1983] *International Construction Law Review* 241, 244.

- Which Party can best bear the risk?
- Which Party ultimately most benefits or suffers when the risk eventuates? [20]

GP4: All time periods specified in the Contract for Contract Participants to perform their obligations must be of reasonable duration.

Time periods specified in the GCs have evolved as a consensus among the international construction community as an appropriate balance between the interests of a Contract Participant required to perform a duty, and the interests of the Party whose rights are dependent on the execution of that duty. FIDIC considers they are reasonable time periods, sufficient to carry out the required duties, but without undue delay.

The consequences of reducing the time periods provided for in the GCs may result in a Contract Participant having insufficient time to perform their required duties properly or to exercise their rights. An earlier trigger of a time bar than is contemplated in the GCs is one potential consequence of reducing time periods.

Conversely, significantly extending those time periods may adversely affect the rights and entitlements of the Party for whose benefit the duties are being performed. For example, a longer period for issuing a Payment Certificate will result in the Contractor's cash flow being adversely affected.

In many provisions of the GCs, the Parties are invited to amend the 'default' time periods by agreement, using words such as 'unless otherwise agreed'. Such time periods are recognised as being determined by negotiation if appropriate, whilst providing a default option considered to be a reasonable time period.

GP5: Unless there is a conflict with the governing law of the Contract, all formal disputes must be referred to a Dispute Avoidance/Adjudication Board (or a Dispute Adjudication Board, if applicable) for a provisionally binding decision as a condition precedent to arbitration.

The Dispute Avoidance/Adjudication Board (**DAAB**) in the 2017 Red, Yellow and Silver Books, the Dispute Adjudication Board (**DAB**) in the 1999 Red Book and the Dispute Board (**DB**) in the 2010 Pink Book have evolved as important entities to help the Parties avoid disputes, and as a procedure for resolving disputes (at least provisionally) at much lower cost and in much less time than required for arbitration. The DAAB/DAB procedure provides an independent third party that assists in maintaining appropriate communication between the contracting Parties and promotes early resolution of disputes to enable the project to proceed without unnecessary disruption. The 1999 Yellow Book and the 1999 Silver Book provide for an 'ad hoc' DAB, implemented when a dispute has arisen. A DAAB or DAB resolves the conflicts of interest that formerly occurred, where the Engineer (engaged and paid by the Employer) not only certified the Contractor's entitlements under the Contract, but also had the authority to resolve disputes.

If one of the Parties is not satisfied with a DAAB/DAB decision, it can issue a Notice of Dissatisfaction and trigger the arbitration process. However, arbitration can be delayed until the project is complete, helping to prevent project personnel from

20 Nael Bunni, 'The Four Criteria of Risk Allocation in Construction Contracts' (2009) 26 *International Construction Law Review* 4, 9.

becoming distracted. In the meantime, the Parties have a decision that provides a provisional resolution of the dispute.

FIDIC considers the availability of an independent and impartial DAAB/DAB to (provisionally) resolve disputes fundamental to a fair and balanced contract. A DAAB/DAB can resolve disputes in real time, and thereby enable the Parties to plan their future activities based on the reasoned decision of experienced, independent and impartial persons who are familiar with the execution of projects and administration of construction contracts.

2.5 Guidance for drafting contract documents for consistency with the Golden Principles

Minor additions or grammatical changes to the wording of a GC sub-clause that do not alter the intent are not a breach of the GPs. However, such cosmetic changes should only be made for good reason.

In the PCs, changes to the GCs required to comply with local law are consistent with GC sub-clause 1.13 and are necessary and appropriate for the Contract to express the Parties' legal and contractual obligations properly. Such changes do not constitute a breach of the GPs.

One of the following terms in a GC generally indicates that it may be amended by the PCs without being in conflict with the GPs:

- 'or as otherwise agreed'
- 'except as otherwise agreed'
- 'unless otherwise agreed'
- 'unless otherwise agreed by both Parties'
- 'unless otherwise stated in the Particular Conditions'
- 'except as otherwise stated in these Conditions' or
- 'unless otherwise stated in the Contract' (however, this is ambiguous as it does not necessarily refer to the Particular Conditions).

It is important that the technical documents do not redefine the duties, rights, obligations, roles or responsibilities of any Contract Participants, in a manner that is inconsistent with the GCs as modified by the PCs. For example, the Engineer has a clearly defined role in the Red and Yellow Books to make determinations as required by the Contract, after consulting both Parties. It would be a breach of GP1 for a Contract to require the Engineer to seek approval from the Employer before issuing any determination under sub-clause 3.5 (1999 editions) or sub-clause 3.7 (2017 editions).

The requirements of the project include the Laws applicable to execution of the Works, as well as the applicable Laws relevant to the rights and obligations of the Contract Participants. Changes in the PCs to make the Contract compliant with the relevant legal regimes are appropriate and necessary, and not in conflict with GP1.

Compliance with GP2 requires, amongst other things, that each of the documents comprising the Contract provide a cohesive and comprehensive whole, without overlap or inconsistencies. The contents of each Contract document should be confined to its scope as generally understood. The appropriate document to amend the GCs is the PCs; the 'contractual' issues detailed in the GCs should not be amended in other documents such as the Employer's Requirements or the Specification.

The content of 'technical' documents such as the Employer's Requirements, drawings or Specifications should be confined to technical issues, consistent with the provisions of the GCs as modified by the PCs.

GP3 is a fundamental principle that should be considered in any PC amendment to the GCs. The yardstick to apply in drafting any provision that amends the roles, duties or obligations as defined in the GCs is to enquire whether risks are being allocated to the Party that is in the best position to control them and bear the consequences of a potential risk becoming a reality. If so, the amendment is compliant with GP3.

There are two alternative considerations involved in complying with GP4 in respect of providing the Contract Participants with a reasonable time to perform their obligations and exercise their rights:

- 'Fixed' timeframes (ie those that are not qualified by a phrase such as 'unless the parties agree otherwise') should not be significantly changed from their value in the GCs.
- 'Default' timeframes (ie those that are qualified by a phrase such as 'unless the parties agree otherwise') when amended should not provide unreasonably short or unreasonably long timeframes. A timeframe would be unreasonably short if it did not provide sufficient time for the Contract Participant to perform its duties properly or exercise its rights; a time frame would be unreasonably long if it significantly affects a Party's enjoyment of its rights, such as the Contractor's right to suspend or terminate the Works.

GP5 requires that the Contract provide for a DAAB or DAB to give a provisionally binding decision on any formal dispute, as a condition precedent to referring a dispute to arbitration. Compliance with GP5 (and GP1) entails retention of the GC clauses referring to the role and operation of the DAAB/DAB, and not significantly changing its role, duties, obligations and rights as defined in the GCs.

2.6 Conclusion

FIDIC's initiative in promoting the recognition and application of the GPs is intended to encourage the use of FIDIC GCs as they have always been intended: fair and balanced risk/reward allocation, clear definition of scope, duties, roles, rights and responsibilities, and contract documents that constitute a contract management manual for best practice international project execution.

The use of the GPs is endorsed in the 2017 Editions of the Red, Yellow and Silver Books and the Emerald Book in the following terms:

> FIDIC strongly recommends that the Employer, the Contractor and all drafters of the Special Provisions take all due regard of the five FIDIC Golden Principles.[21]

21 Guidance for the Preparation of Particular Conditions, 8.

CHAPTER 3

Preparation of Particular Conditions

Dr Donald Charrett

3.1 What should be in the Particular Conditions?

As noted in paragraph 1.2.3 above, the Particular Conditions in the 2017 rainbow suite comprise Part A Contract Data, and Part B Special Provisions.

3.1.1 Particular Conditions Part A – Contract Data

The Contract Data provides the specific information referred to in the General Conditions required to define the unique characteristics of the particular Contract. Most of this information will be provided by the Employer to define its requirements in the Tender documents, including the time and cost parameters of the Contract, certain risk allocation parameters, and a number of contract administration matters. The 'legal' data required is confined to the governing law of the contract; if this is not specified, the governing law of the contract will be the law of the Country. Certain parts of the Contract Data may be provided by the Contractor in its Tender.

 DOI: 10.4324/9781003200901-3

Not all of the data items will require completion, as some refer to options in the General Conditions that may not be applicable, eg, the data for the proportions of local and foreign currency (sub-clause 14.15(a)(i)) does not need to be completed if payment is to be made in one currency only. Many of the data items have default provisions specified in the relevant sub-clause that will apply if the item is not completed in the Contract Data. Table 3.1 in the Annexure to this chapter comprises the Contract Data from the 2017 Yellow Book, annotated with the default provisions in the General Conditions.

If data is not provided for some items, the data may be provided by the applicable law, eg if the number of days for the Time for Completion are not defined for sub-clause 1.1.86, the law would generally imply that the time period be reasonable.

It is strongly recommended that, to avoid ambiguity, all the items in the Contract Data be filled in, with the project specific data, reference to the default in the sub-clause if that is appropriate, or Not Applicable if the sub-clause provision does not apply. This will materially assist in the subsequent administration of the Contract, by providing all the relevant information in one location.

3.1.2 Particular Conditions Part B – Special Provisions

Particular Conditions Part B Special Provisions is the contract document where any changes or additions to the General Conditions are documented. All references in the following sections to Particular Conditions refer to Part B Special Provisions in the 2017 rainbow suite.

Special Provisions necessary for the particular requirements of the Works may comprise either modifications to the General Conditions, or additional provisions that supplement the General Conditions. Such modifications may be necessary or desirable so that:

- The Contract wording is consistent with applicable law.
- The Contract wording draws attention to relevant applicable law that must be complied with.
- Specific requirements for the Site or the Works are documented.
- The Employer's preferences are defined.

As noted in Table 1.2 of contract document hierarchy in paragraph 1.2.1 above, the Particular Conditions have precedence over the General Conditions in the event of any ambiguity. Thus, any Special Provisions that modify the General Conditions supersede the relevant parts of the General Conditions.

For clarity, the Special Provisions should comply with the following:

- A Special Provision modification to a sub-clause of the General Conditions should use the same sub-clause numbering as in the General Conditions.
- Additional Special Provisions should use sub-clause numbers that are not used in the General Conditions.
- Special Provisions may provide additional provisions to the General Conditions or may change provisions in the General Conditions.

Skilled legal advice is required to determine whether the contractual provisions of the General Conditions are incompatible with the applicable mandatory law, and to make the necessary amendments in the Special Provisions. Legal review should also determine whether it is appropriate to add Special Provisions to modify non-mandatory law that would otherwise apply. The following chapters provide guidance on the applicable law in a range of jurisdictions where FIDIC contracts are used.

3.2 Governing law

3.2.1 Governing law of the contract

The principle of freedom of contract means that, subject to any mandatory law, the Parties are free to choose the governing law of their Contract, even if this is in a different jurisdiction to where the work is carried out or to the domicile of the contracting Parties. This principle of party autonomy in selecting the governing law of a contract is widely recognised. For example, the following articles of the *2015 Principles on Choice of Law in International Commercial Contracts*[1] of the Hague Conference on Private International Law (Hague Principles) provide:

> **Article 2 Freedom of choice**
>
> 1. A contract is governed by the law chosen by the parties.
>
> ...
>
> 4. No connections required between the law chosen and the parties for their transaction.
>
> **Article 3 Rules of law**
>
> The law chosen by the parties may be rules of law that are generally accepted on an international, supranational or regional level as a neutral and balanced set of rules, unless the law of the forum provides otherwise.
>
> **Article 11 Overriding mandatory rules and public policy (*ordre public*)**
>
> 1. These Principles shall not prevent a court from applying overriding mandatory provisions of the law of the forum which apply irrespective of the law chosen by the parties.
> 2. The law of the forum determines when a court may or must apply or take into account overriding mandatory provisions of another law.
> 3. A court may exclude application of a provision of the law chosen by the parties only if and to the extent that the result of such application would be manifestly incompatible with fundamental notions of public policy (*ordre public*) of the forum.
> 4. The law of the forum determines when a court may or must apply or take into account the public policy (*ordre public*) of a State the law of which would be applicable in the absence of a choice of law.
> 5. These Principles shall not prevent an arbitral tribunal from applying or taking into account public policy (*ordre public*), or from applying or taking into account overriding mandatory provisions of a law other than the law chosen by the parties, if the arbitral tribunal is required or entitled to do so.

The nature of the Hague Principles are as follows:

> **I.8** As their title suggests, the Principles do not constitute a formally binding instrument such as a Convention that States are obliged to directly apply or incorporate into their domestic law. Nor is this instrument a model law that States are encouraged to enact.

1 https://assets.hcch.net/docs/5da3ed47-f54d-4c43-aaef-5eafc7c1f2a1.pdf (accessed 23 February 2021).

> Rather, it is a non-binding set of principles, which the Hague Conference encourages States to incorporate into their domestic choice of law regimes in a manner appropriate for the circumstances of each State. In this way, the Principles can guide the reform of domestic law on choice of law and operate alongside existing instruments on the subject (see Rome I Regulation and Mexico City Convention both of which embrace and apply the concept of party autonomy).[2]

The Hague Principles have so far only been implemented in legislation in Paraguay[3] and Uruguay.[4] However, a number of arbitration centres either have incorporated the Principles into their own institutional rules or are advertising or facilitating their use in other ways compatible with the Hague Principles. For example, in respect of the Council for National and International Commercial Arbitration in India (**CNICA**):

- The CNICA Arbitration Rules are consistent with the Hague Principles.
- The CNICA Arbitration Rules allow parties to select the applicable law (Article 2).
- Tribunals constituted under the CNICA Arbitration Rules respect the law chosen by the parties.
- Parties are free to select a non-state law under the CNICA Arbitration Rules (Article 3).
- Tribunals constituted under the CNICA Arbitration Rules respect the parties' choice of a non-state law (Article 3).[5]

The law of the forum (or *lex fori* as it is sometimes known) is the law of the place in which court or arbitral proceedings are conducted. Thus, under the Hague Principles and more generally, if the Parties have not selected the governing law of the contract, it will be determined by a judge in the jurisdiction where legal proceedings are initiated, or by an arbitral tribunal. Due to differences in conflicts of law rules, the outcome may be unpredictable.

It should be noted that the Hague Principles do not require the rules of law to be laws of a country. The UNIDROIT Principles of International Commercial Contracts would be regarded as 'an international neutral and balanced set of rules'. Such anational rules of law are also permitted by the *European Contracts Convention* (**Rome I**),[6] and the *Inter-American Convention on the Law Applicable to International Contracts.*[7]

3.2.2 Choosing the governing law of the contract

As noted in the Annexure to this chapter, if the Parties do not nominate the governing law of the contract in the Contract Data for sub-clause 1.4 in the 2017 rainbow suite, the default position in the General Conditions is that the governing law of the contract will be the law of the Country.

---

2 https://www.hcch.net/en/instruments/conventions/full-text/?cid=135 (accessed 23 February 2021).

3 *Paraguayan Law 5393 of 2015* regarding the applicable law to international contracts https://assets.hcch.net/upload/contractslaw_py.pdf (accessed 23 February 2021).

4 http://www.diputados.gub.uy/wp-content/uploads/2020/11/00130.pdf (accessed 23 February 2021).

5 https://assets.hcch.net/docs/b9627fbb-eac1–4aae-a23c-ef059e24849e.pdf (accessed 23 February 2021).

6 *Regulation (EC) No 593/2008* of the European Parliament and of the Council of 17 June 2008 on the law applicable to contractual obligations.

7 http://www.oas.org/juridico/english/treaties/b-56.html (accessed 10 July 2018).

Issues to consider in choosing the governing law if it is not to be the law of the Country:

- Are there any legal constraints on selecting the governing law in the Country or the domiciles of the contracting Parties?[8]
- Is the proposed law well known?
- Is legal advice on the proposed law readily available?
- Is the proposed law familiar to the contracting Parties, the DAAB/DAB and arbitrators?
- Is the governing law predictable?
- Are there any potential inconsistencies with the Laws of the Country?
- What is the extent of modification of FIDIC General Conditions necessary for consistency with the governing law?
- The preferences of the contracting Parties.
- Availability of reference materials (eg books, legislation, case law) in the language for communication.

3.2.3 The law governing the agreement to arbitrate

In respect of sub-clause 21.6 Arbitration, the Notes on the Preparation of Special Provisions in the 2017 rainbow suite recommend careful selection of the place or 'seat' of arbitration in a jurisdiction other than the Country:

> For major projects tendered internationally, it is desirable that the place of arbitration be situated in a country other than that of the Employer or Contractor. This country should have a modern and liberal arbitration law and should have ratified a bilateral or multilateral convention (such as the *1958 New York Convention on the Recognition and Enforcement of Foreign Arbitral Awards*), or both, that would facilitate the enforcement of an arbitral award in the states of the Parties.

The consequence of nominating the seat of arbitration is the selection of that jurisdiction's law as the *lex arbitrii* – the law governing the arbitration process. The intent of FIDIC's recommendation is to ensure that neither Party will have a 'home country' advantage in the dispute resolution process.

As discussed in paragraph 1.5.6 above, the law governing the arbitration process (*lex arbitrii*) is not necessarily the same as the governing law of the contract, or the law governing the agreement to arbitrate. Where the governing law of the contract is different to the *lex arbitrii*, there may be a question of what the governing law of the arbitration is, that is the law governing the validity and scope of the arbitration agreement. Where the Parties have not made an explicit choice of the governing law of the contract, there are arguments (and case law) in support of the law governing the arbitration agreement being either the governing law of the contract or the *lex arbitrii*.

The finely balanced arguments for either possibility were canvassed in the case of *Enka Insaat Ve Sanayi AS v OOO Insurance Company (Enka Insaat)*.[9] In this case, the central issue concerned which system of national law governed the validity and scope of the arbitration agreement when the governing law of the contract containing it differed from the law of the seat of the arbitration. The Parties had not made an

8 For example, Article 869 of the *Colombian Commercial Code* states that Contracts that are performed in Colombia will be governed by Colombian Law.

9 [2020] UKSC 38.

explicit choice of the governing law of the contract but had selected London as the seat of arbitration. The majority (Lord Hamblen and Lord Leggatt, Lord Kerr agreeing) applied English common law rules for resolving conflicts of laws and held that in the absence of the parties' choice, the law applicable to the arbitration agreement is the system of law with which the arbitration agreement is most closely connected. Where the parties have chosen a seat of arbitration, the governing law of the arbitration agreement will generally be the law of the seat, even if this differs from the governing law of the contract.[10] In dissent, Lord Burrows (with whom Lord Sales agreed) held that the 'main contract' approach should be preferred to the 'seat' approach in determining the governing law of the arbitration agreement.

Where the Parties have made a choice of governing law of the contract, the majorities' summary in *Enka Insaat* noted that under English law:

> iv) Where the law applicable to the arbitration agreement is not specified, a choice of governing law for the contract will generally apply to an arbitration agreement which forms part of the contract.
>
> v) The choice of a different country as the seat of the arbitration is not, without more, sufficient to negate an inference that a choice of law to govern the contract was intended to apply to the arbitration agreement. [11]

As the FIDIC Conditions of Contract specify the governing law of the contract either by explicit nomination or in default as the law of the Country, the issue of a different law governing the agreement to arbitrate is probably unlikely to arise except in unusual circumstances.

3.3 Special Provisions for consistency with applicable law

Irrespective of the wording of the Conditions of Contract, mandatory law will always apply, and the Parties are required to comply with it both as a matter of law, and to comply with the Contract. Such mandatory law may comprise either

(a) Provisions that are incompatible with the General Conditions, or
(b) Provisions that are not incompatible with the General Conditions, but the General Conditions do not refer to the issue within the scope of the mandatory law.

In the case of (a), it is highly desirable that Special Provisions are written to modify the General Conditions and make them consistent with the mandatory law. In addition, it is also desirable to prepare Special Provisions to incorporate mandatory law provisions of type (b), to draw attention to these obligations in a document that (hopefully) is used as a contract management manual.

Special Provisions that incorporate mandatory law of type (a) will ensure that the contract wording is accurate and not misleading; Special Provisions that incorporate mandatory law of type (b) will significantly enhance the usefulness of the Conditions of Contract as a comprehensive contract management manual.

As discussed in paragraph 1.5 above, statute law may be either mandatory or non-mandatory. If a law is not mandatory, contracting Parties may choose not to follow

10 Ibid [170].
11 Ibid.

it by incorporating specific terms in the Contract. However, unless there are such contract terms 'otherwise' the law will apply as a default option, whether or not the Parties are aware of it. In the circumstances where the Parties do not wish to apply the default law, Special Provisions will be necessary to define the contractual alternative.

Thus, the General Conditions may require modification, or it may be desirable to modify them where the governing law of the contract is that of a particular jurisdiction. The following are some examples of issues where it may be necessary or desirable to prepare Special Provisions that align the Conditions of Contract with the provisions of the governing law:

- Changed conditions:
  - Laws of economic disequilibrium, eg France, former French colonies and Turkey
  - Rules about commercial impracticability, eg USA
- Limitation period for liability, eg Brazil
- Delay damages (liquidated damages)/proof of loss
  - May be lowered if the actual damage is less in a civil law jurisdiction, eg Switzerland
  - May be nullified if it is not a genuine pre-estimate of loss in a common law jurisdiction, eg Australia, England
- Termination, eg Australia, Brazil, France
- *Force majeure*, eg China, the Philippines, Indonesia, United Arab Emirates
- Obligation to complete with a certain result, eg Peru
- Subcontractors, eg China, France
- Provisions relating to the extinguishing of liability will not apply in jurisdictions which do not allow contractual waiver of liability in the case of gross negligence or fraud, eg California
- Disputes relating to non-contractual claims may not be arbitrable, eg Pakistan and fraud
- Rights of 'set off', 'abatement' or similar rights that are inconsistent with the payment provisions in the General Conditions, eg under the common law, a right of set-off is difficult to exclude by contract language
- Valuation of Variations, eg France
- Burdensome obligations on the Contractor in the EPC Silver Book are unlikely to be upheld in France and Francophone and other countries of French civil law tradition
- The responsibility of Contractors to implement Variations instructed by the Employer, eg Germany
- The corresponding duty of Employers to pay for Variations, eg Brazil, Italy
- Principles relating to the obligations to produce a result versus the obligation to apply the means, eg Peru
- Good faith, eg Brazil, Peru
- Time bars may not be allowed under the governing law as a breach of good faith in civil law jurisdictions, eg Peru, United Arab Emirates
- Legislation dealing with unfair contract conditions eg Germany, Holland, Sweden, England, France
- Allocation of ground risk, eg Brazil, Germany.

Each of the following chapters of this book provides guidance on the application of FIDIC contracts in a particular jurisdiction and addresses the above issues where they are relevant to the jurisdiction.

3.4 Guidance for the preparation of Particular Conditions

The Guidance for the Preparation of Particular Conditions in the 2017 rainbow suite contains detailed Notes on the preparation of Special Provisions in the section titled 'Particular Conditions Part B – Special Provisions'. The Introduction to this section includes a strong recommendation 'that the Employer, the Contractor and all drafters of the Special Provisions take all due regard of the five FIDIC Golden Principles' enumerated in bold (see paragraph 1.4 above). The FIDIC Golden Principles are listed and discussed in detail in Chapter 2 above.

Some direct warnings on amending sub-clauses then follow:

> Before incorporating any new or changed sub-clauses, the wording must be carefully checked to ensure that it is wholly suitable for the particular circumstances. Unless it is considered suitable, example wording should be amended before use.
>
> Where any amendments or additions are made to the General Conditions, great care must be taken to ensure that the wording does not unintentionally alter the meaning of other clauses in the Conditions of Contract, does not inadvertently change the obligations assigned to the Parties or the balance of risks shared between them and/or does not create any new ambiguity or misunderstanding in the rest of the Contract documents.

The 'Notes on the Preparation of Special Provisions' are prefaced with the following caution prior to providing detailed suggestions for specific clauses:

> It is very important that all Employers (and all drafters of the Special Provisions) work with their professional advisers to review specific terminology in the General Conditions for compliance and consistency with accepted practice in the legal jurisdiction they are operating in.
>
> . . .
>
> The following references and examples show some of the Sub-Clauses in the General Conditions which may need amending to suit the needs of the project or the requirements of the Employer. The selected Sub-Clauses and the example wording are included as examples only. They also include, as an aide memoire, references to other documents such as the Specification and/or Drawings and the Contract Data, where particular issues may need to be addressed.
>
> The selected Sub-Clauses do not necessarily require changing and the example wording may not suit the needs of a particular project or Employer. It is the responsibility of the drafter of the Special Provisions to ensure that the selection of the Sub-Clauses and the choice of wording is appropriate to the project concerned.
>
> Furthermore, there may be other Sub-Clauses, not mentioned below, which need to be amended. Great care must be taken when amending the wording of Sub-Clauses from the General Conditions, or adding new provisions, to ensure that the balance of obligations and rights of the Parties are not unintentionally compromised.

The following sections identify four distinct types of modifications that may be required to the clauses in the General Conditions, as identified in the 2017 rainbow suite:

- Special Provisions necessary or desirable for consistency with the governing law of the contract
- Special Provisions necessary or desirable for consistency with applicable laws

- Special Provisions necessary or desirable for the Project requirements
- Special Provisions necessary or desirable for the Employer's Preferences.

The following sections are intended as a brief introduction to some of the more common and well recognised General Conditions clauses that may require modification. Although extracted from the Notes in the 2017 rainbow suite, they are not intended to provide detailed guidance, nor to suggest specific wording for particular sub-clauses – those are covered in considerable detail in the FIDIC rainbow suite.

The following tables do not provide any indication of which modifications may be necessary or desirable for a particular jurisdiction – those are covered in the following chapters, each of which address the requirements of a particular jurisdiction.

3.4.1 Special Provisions necessary or desirable for consistency with the governing law of the contract

Some of the following Special Provisions are also included in the table in paragraph 3.4.2 below, as the Laws in the Country may be applicable in some circumstances.

Yellow Book Sub-clause	*Special Provision*	*Page*[12]
1.1.XX[13] Additional Definitions	Add definition of Gross Negligence	15
1.6 Contract Agreement	Contract Agreement: If entry into a formal Contract Agreement is mandatory, delete the word 'unless they agree otherwise.'	15
4.2 Performance Security	The provisions in 4.2 in respect of Performance Securities may have to be amended to comply with applicable law.	22
8.XX Additional sub-clause for Concurrent Delay	Add a provision 8.XX to define the rules and procedures applicable to concurrent delay under the governing law of the contract.	35
11.10 Unfulfilled Obligations	It may be necessary to review the effect of 11.10 in relation to the period of liability imposed by the applicable law, and in particular the second paragraph may require amending.	36
15.2 Termination for Contractor's Default	Sub-clause 15.2 may require amendment for consistency with the governing law of the contract.	47
15.5 Termination for Employer's Convenience	Amend the wording of 15.5 if it is not permissible under the governing law of the contract for the Employer to terminate the Contract for convenience.	48
16.2 Termination by Contractor	Amend the wording of 16.2 if the General Condition provision for termination by the Contractor is not compatible with the governing law of the contract.	48

12 Page numbers are the page numbers in the Guidance for the Preparation of Particular Conditions in the 2017 Yellow Book.

13 XX denotes a new number distinct from the numbering in the General Conditions. See paragraph 3.1.2 above.

3.4.2 Special Provisions necessary or desirable for consistency with applicable laws

The following Special Provisions generally refer to applicable laws of the Site and in the Country.

Yellow Book Sub-clause	*Special Provision*	*Page*[14]
1.6 Contract Agreement	Contract Agreement: If entry into a formal Contract Agreement is mandatory, delete the word 'unless they agree otherwise.'	15
1.13 Compliance with Laws	Additional provision in 1.13 in respect of the Goods for a plant contract.	16
3.5 Engineer's Instructions	Amend 3.5 if the applicable law prevents the Contractor from complying with any Engineer's instruction that may have an adverse effect on the health and safety of the Contractor's Personnel.	21
4.2 Performance Security	The provisions in 4.2 in respect of Performance Securities may have to be amended to comply with applicable law.	22
4.16 Transport of Goods	Add a provision to 4.16 if the Contractor is required to obtain permission prior to the delivery of Goods to the Site.	25
5.2.2 Contractor's Documents - Review by Engineer	Amend 5.2.2 if there is a requirement under the applicable law for the mandatory review/checking of certain elements of design (by an authorised professional or other legally recognised individual) and/or verification that such design is in accordance with the applicable law, before such design can be implemented in the Works.	29
6.3 Recruitment of Persons	Amend or delete 6.3 if the relevant labour Laws applicable to the Contractor's Personnel and/or the Employer's Personnel do not permit any restriction on the right of any worker to seek other positions.	30
11.10 Unfulfilled Obligations	It may be necessary to review the effect of 11.10 in relation to the period of liability imposed by the applicable law, and in particular the second paragraph may require amending.	36
14.1 The Contract Price 14.XX Additional sub-clause for Import Duties	Amend 14.1 and add an additional sub-clause 14.XX if the Contractor is not required to pay import duties on Goods imported by the Contractor into the Country.	40
14.1 The Contract Price 14.XX Additional sub-clause for Expatriate Staff Income Tax	Amend 14.1 and add an additional sub-clause 14.XX if expatriate staff are exempted from paying local income tax.	40

14 Page numbers are the page numbers in the Guidance for the Preparation of Particular Conditions in the 2017 Yellow Book

3.4.3 Special Provisions necessary or desirable for the project requirements

Yellow Book Sub-clause	*Special Provision*	*Page*[15]
1.1 Definitions	Amend definitions of Country, Local Currency, add new definitions.	14
Various	Consider increasing the timescales for Notices in the General Conditions if Notices are only to be given in paper format by post. The following sub-clauses in the Yellow Book provide for specific periods of time for submitting a Notice: 1.9; 3.4; 3.5; 3.7.3; 3.7.4; 3.7.5; 4.2.2; 4.3; 4.4; 4.5.1; (4.7.2); 4.9.1; 4.12.2; 4.16; 4.17; 5.2.2; 6.12; 7.5; 8.1; 8.3; 8.12; 9.1; 9.2; 10.1; 10.3; 11.6; 11.7; 11.9; 12.1; 15.2.2; 16.1; 16.2.1; 16.2.2; 17.3; 18.2; 20.2.1; 20.2.2; 20.2.4; 21.4.4. The following sub-clauses in the Yellow Book Dispute Adjudication Agreement provide for specific periods of time for submitting a Notice: 2.2; 9.1. Rule 10 in the Yellow Book DAAB Procedural Rules provide for specific periods of time for submitting a Notice.	15
1.5(g) Priority of Documents	If the Employer's a Requirements are to comprise a number of documents, consider amending 1.5(g) by adding an order of precedence for the various documents in the Employer's Requirements.	15
1.14 Joint and Several Liability	Additional provisions in 1.14 if the Contractor is a Joint Venture.	16
2.1 Right of Access to the Site	Amend 2.1 if right of access to, and possession of, the Site cannot be granted by the Employer in the normal way.	18
3.4 Delegation by the Engineer	Amend 3.4 if it is anticipated that the Engineer's Assistants may not all be fluent in the language for communication is defined in 1.4.	20
3.5 Engineer's Instructions	Add a provision to 3.5 to allow for the giving of oral instructions by the Engineer.	21
4.2.1 Performance Security – Contractor's Obligations	If the sample forms for Performance Securities are not used, consider adding to 4.2.1 a provision to reduce the amount of the Performance Security following issue of the Taking-Over Certificate for the whole of the Works.	22
4.3 Contractor's Representative	Add provisions to 4.3 if it is necessary to stipulate that the Contractor's Representative shall be qualified, experienced and competent in a particular engineering discipline in relation to the Works, be fluent in a particular language other than the language for communications or is not required to be fluent in the language for communications.	22
4.8 Health and Safety Obligations	Amend 4.8 if the Contractor is sharing occupation of the Site with others.	24

15 Page numbers are the page numbers in the Guidance for the Preparation of Particular Conditions in the 2017 Yellow Book

4.21 Security of the Site 4.22 Contractor's Operations on Site	Amend 4.21 and 4.22 if the Contractor is sharing occupation of the Site with others.	26
6.8 Contractor's Superintendence	Amend 6.8 if it is permissible that the Contractor's superintending staff are not all fluent in the language for communications.	30
6.8 Contractor's Superintendence	Add a provision to 6.8 if it is necessary to stipulate that the Contractor's superintending staff shall be fluent in a particular language.	31
6.12 Key Personnel	Add a provision to 6.12 if it is permissible that all Key Personnel are not fluent in the language for communications.	31
6.XX Additional sub-clauses for circumstances of the Site	It may be necessary, appropriate and/or desirable to include additional sub-clauses to 6 to take account of the circumstances and locality of the Site: Foreign personnel Supply of foodstuffs Supply of water Measures against insect and pest nuisance Alcoholic liquor or drugs Arms and ammunition Festivals and religious customs Funeral arrangements Forced labour Child labour Employment records of workers Workers organisations Non-discrimination and equal opportunity	
8.3(a) – (k) Programme	For less complex projects, consider simplifying the requirements for the Contractor's programme in 8.3(a) – (k).	34

3.4.4 Special Provisions necessary or desirable for the Employer's preferences

Yellow Book Sub-clause	*Special Provision*	*Page*
1.5 Priority of Documents	Amend 1.5 if no order of precedence of documents is to be prescribed in the Contract. In the event of an ambiguity or discrepancy, the priority will be determined by the governing law of the contract.	15
1.10 Employer's Use of Contractor's Documents	Additional provisions to 1.10 may be required if all rights to particular items of eg computer software are to be assigned to the Employer.	15
1.15 Limitation of Liability	Replace 1.15 if it is required that the limitation of each Party's liability to the other Party is to include certain 'indirect or consequential loss or damage' and is also to take into account liabilities to be insured under 19.	16
2.6 Employer-Supplied Materials and Employer's Equipment	Additional provisions to 2.6 if Employer Supplied Materials or Employer's Equipment are listed in the Employer's Requirements.	18

(*Continued*)

Yellow Book Sub-clause	*Special Provision*	*Page*
3.2 Engineer's Duties and Authority	Any requirements for the Engineer to obtain the Employer's consent should be added to 3.2.	20
4.4 Subcontractors	Add a provision to 4.4 if it is appropriate or desirable to encourage the Contractor to employ local subcontractors.	23
4.4 Subcontractors	Delete the last three paragraphs of 4.4 if no consent by the Engineer to Subcontractors is required.	23
4.4 Subcontractors	Amend 4.4 if the Engineer's consent is required to the suppliers of certain Materials, or subcontracts should provide for assignment of the subcontractor to the Employer pursuant to 15.2 or after the expiry of the DNP.	23
4.4 Subcontractors	Amend 4.4 if it is anticipated that a Subcontractor that is not a Nominated Subcontractor is to be instructed under 13.3.	24
4.12 Unforeseeable Physical Conditions	If the risk of Unforeseeable physical conditions is to be shared between the Parties, amend 4.12.	25
4.17 Contractor's Equipment	Add a further provision to 4.17 if vesting of the Contractor's Equipment to the Employer is required (and consistent with the Laws of the Country).	26
4.XX Additional sub-clause for completion of certain parts of the Works	Additional sub-clause 4.XX if the Employer wishes to have certain parts of the Works completed within certain times but does not wish to take over such parts when completed (Milestones).	27
14.4 Schedule of Payments	Amend 14.4 if certain payments to the Contractor are to be made on completion of each Milestone.	28
7.7 Ownership of Plant and Materials	Add a provision to 7.7 if the Contractor is to provide high-value items of Plant and/or Materials.	33
7.XX Additional sub-clause for financing institution rules	Add a sub-clause 7.XX if the Contract is being financed by an institution whose rules or policies require a restriction on the use of its funds.	34
8.1 Commencement of Works	Amend 8.1 if the Commencement Date is not to be within 42 days after the Contractor receives the letter of Acceptance.	
8.XX Additional sub-clause for early completion incentives	Add a sub-clause 8.XX if the Contract provides incentives for early completion.	35
9.1 Contractor's Obligations	Amend 9.1 if the product produced by the Tests on Completion is to be retained by the Contractor and not the Employer.	36
11.3 Extension of Defects Notification Period	Amend the period of two years in 11.3 if the Employer requires a longer or shorter period.	36

11.XX Additional sub-clause for new or innovative technology	Add an additional sub-clause 11.XX if the Works comprise new or innovative technology in the Country and the Employer requires its permanent operating personnel to be given supervisory assistance in the operation and maintenance of the Plant during the DNP.	37
12.1 Procedure for Tests after Completion	Amend 12.1 if the provisions for Tests after Completion are to be different to those in the General Conditions.	37
13.2 Value Engineering	Add provisions for sharing of the benefit, costs and/ or delay between the Parties applying to a Value Engineering Variation instructed by the Engineer.	
13.7 Adjustments for Changes in Cost	Amend 13.7 if it would be unreasonable for the Contractor to bear the risk of escalating costs due to inflation.	38
14.XX Additional sub-clauses for exceptions to payment provisions	Add additional sub-clauses 14.XX to cover any exceptions to the provisions in 14.1 and if 14.1(a) (lump sum) is not to apply.	40
14.2 Advance Payment	Amend 14.2 if the Employer wishes to provide the advance payment in instalments.	42
14.XX Additional sub-clause for interim payments	Add an additional sub-clause 14.XX if interim payments are to be paid other than on the basis of a Schedule of Payments.	43
14.XX Additional sub-clause for simple measurement for interim valuations	If the Works consist of only a few different types of operations, a simple measurement type of approach for interim valuations may be detailed in an additional sub-clause 14.XX.	44
14.8 Delayed Payment	Amend 14.8 if payment is to be on the basis of the Contractor's actual financing Costs.	45
14.XX Additional sub-clause for guarantee instead of Retention Money	Add an additional sub-clause 14.XX if part of the Retention Money is to be released and substituted by an appropriate guarantee.	45
14.15 Currencies of Payment	Replace 14.15 if all payments are to be made in Local Currency.	45
14.XX Additional sub-clause for requirements of financing entities	Add additional sub-clauses 14.XX to cover the requirements of financing entities such as aid agencies, development banks, export credit agencies, or other international financing institutions.	46
14.XX Additional sub-clause for Contractor finance	Add an additional sub-clause 14.XX for Contractor finance.	47
15.XX Additional sub-clause for Employer-Supplied Materials	An additional sub-clause 15.XX may be appropriate if the Employer has made available any Employer-Supplied Materials and/or Employer's Equipment.	47
16.3 Contractor's Obligations after Termination	Amendment of 16.3 may be desirable if the Employer has made available any Employer Supplied Materials and/or Employer's Equipment.	48

(Continued)

17.XX Additional sub-clause for Contractor's use of Employer's facilities	Add an additional sub-clause 17.XX if the Contractor is to be allowed to use and/or occupy any of the Employer's facilities and/or accommodation temporarily during the Contract.	49
19 Insurance	Amend 19 if the Employer wishes to change the insurance provisions in the General Conditions.	49
20.1 Claims	Consider replacing the words 'within a reasonable time' in the last paragraph of 20.1 by a specified time period.	50
1.1.22 Definition of DAAB 1.1.23 Definition of DAAB Agreement 21.1 Constitution of the DAAB 21.3 Avoidance of Disputes 21.4 Obtaining DAAB's Decision	Amendments to 1.1.22, 1.1.23, 21.1 and 21.4 and deletion of 21.3 will be required if an ad-hoc Dispute Adjudication board (DAB) is to be appointed instead of a DAAB.	52
21.5 Amicable Settlement	A longer period than 28 days may be desirable under 21.5 to give the Parties an opportunity to arrive at an amicable settlement procedure.	53
Various	If Building Information Modelling (BIM) is to be adopted, a number of sub-clauses need to be thoroughly reviewed when drafting the Special Provisions.	58

3.5 Format of Conditions of Contract

As noted above, there are a number of legitimate reasons why the General Conditions may need to be modified and/or supplemented by Special Provisions.

In an endeavour to discourage users from changing the General Conditions excessively, FIDIC currently insists on use of the General Conditions in their original form, irrespective of the extent to which Particular Conditions might change them.

Before a Contract has been entered into, a tenderer needs to assess the Conditions of Contract to determine, amongst other things, the risks that are to be undertaken by the Contractor. A tenderer familiar with FIDIC General Conditions needs to assess, in particular, those Particular Conditions that alter the risk allocation under the General Conditions. From the practical perspective of assessing how far a Contract deviates from a 'FIDIC contract', a redlined markup of the FIDIC General Conditions is the most user friendly. It avoids a reviewer spending any time on assessing unaltered sub-clauses, and it draws specific attention to those sub-clauses that have been altered, and the specific way in which they have been altered. This is not necessarily straightforward if the alterations are in a separate Particular Conditions document, as this requires a close comparison of the corresponding General Conditions sub-clauses.

However, once a contract has been executed, for the purpose of complying with and administering the Contract, users generally prefer a single 'clean' document of the Conditions of Contract that incorporates the General Conditions, plus the Particular Conditions, Contract Data, the General Conditions of the Dispute Adjudication Agreement, Dispute Adjudication Agreement and Procedural Rules all using the FIDIC sub-clause numbering.

Under current arrangements, users can obtain the benefits of a single Conditions of Contract document by negotiating a licence for an electronic copy with FIDIC. This avoids the inconvenience of referring to a separate Particular Conditions document in addition to the General Conditions to understand the Contract Conditions.

Under existing arrangements FIDIC may negotiate an electronic licence on an exceptional basis as follows:

- FIDIC provides a soft copy of the General Conditions.
- The licensee may alter the text of the General Conditions.
- The final issued version of the Contract must append a markup of the amended FIDIC General Conditions that identifies the changes by redlining.
- The amended General Conditions may only be used for a single Project.
- The resulting Contract will no longer be a 'FIDIC contract' and must not be represented as one.

Thus, those preparing Conditions of Contract must weigh up the cost and convenience of having a single user-friendly document (and a red-lined version showing changes to the General Conditions), with the traditional approach of having a separate document for Particular Conditions that must be read in conjunction with the printed General Conditions to understand the Conditions of Contract.

3.6 References

- Conditions of Contract for Construction (2nd edn, 2017) Guidance Notes for the Preparation of Particular Conditions
- Conditions of Contract for Plant and Design-Build (2nd edn, 2017) Guidance Notes for the Preparation of Particular Conditions
- Conditions of Contract for EPC/Turnkey Projects (2nd edn, 2017) Guidance Notes for the Preparation of Particular Conditions

ANNEXURE

TABLE 3.1 CONTRACT DATA IN 2017 YELLOW BOOK, ANNOTATED WITH DEFAULT PROVISIONS

Sub-Clause	*Data to be given*	*Default Data*
1.1.20	Where the Contract allows for Cost Plus Profit, percentage profit to be added to the Cost:	5%
1.1.27	Defects Notification Period (DNP):	One year
1.1.30	Employer's name and address:	
1.1.35	Engineer's name and address:	
1.1.86	Time for Completion:	
1.3 (a) (ii)	Agreed methods of electronic transmission:	System(s) acceptable to the Engineer
1.3 (d)	Address of Employer for communications:	
1.3 (d)	Address of Engineer for communications:	
1.3 (d)	Address of Contractor for communications:	
1.4	Contract shall be governed by the law of:	The law of the Country.
1.4	Ruling language:	The language of these Conditions.
1.4	Language for communications:	The ruling language of the Contract.
1.8	Number of additional paper copies of Contractor's Documents:	0
1.9	Period for notification of errors, faults or other defects in the Employer's Requirements:	42 days
1.15	Total liability of the Contractor to the Employer under or in connection with the Contract:	The Accepted Contract Amount.
2.1	After receiving the Letter of Acceptance, the Contractor shall be given right of access to all or part of the Site within:	Within such times as may be required to enable the Contractor to proceed in accordance with the Programme or, if there is no Programme at that time, the initial programme submitted under-Clause 8.3 [Program].

DOI: 10.4324/9781003200901-3

2.4	Employer's financial arrangements:	
4.2	Performance Security (as percentages of the Accepted Contract Amount in Currencies): percent: currency: percent: currency:	Sub- clause 4.2 does not apply.
4.4 (a)	Maximum allowable accumulated value of work subcontracted (as a percentage of the Accepted Contract Amount):	The whole of the Works.
4.4 (b)	Parts of the Works for which subcontracting is not permitted:	
4.7.2	Period for notification of errors in the items of reference:	28 days.
4.19	Period of payment for temporary utilities:	Each month.
4.20	Number of additional paper copies of progress reports:	0
6.5	Normal working hours on the Site:	
8.3	Number of additional paper copies of programmes:	0
8.8	Delay Damages payable for each day of delay:	
8.8	Maximum amount of Delay Damages:	No limit.
13.4 (b) (ii)	Percentage rate to be applied to Provisional Sums for overhead charges and profit:	
14.2	Total amount of Advance Payment (as a percentage of Accepted Contract Amount):	Sub-clause 14.2 does not apply.
14.2	Currency or currencies of Advance Payment:	
14.2.3	Percentage deductions for the repayment of the Advance Payment:	25%
14.3	Period of payment:	After the end of each month.
14.3 (b)	Number of additional paper copies of Statements:	0
14.3 (iii)	Percentage of retention:	
14.3 (iii)	Limit of Retention Money (as a percentage of Accepted Contract Amount):	
14.5 (b) (i)	Plant and Materials for payment when shipped:	
14.5 (c) (i)	Plant and Materials for payment when delivered to the Site:	
14.6.2	Minimum amount of Interim Payment Certificate (IPC):	
14.7 (a)	Period for payment of Advance Payment to the Contractor:	21 days
14.7 (b) (i)	Period for the Employer to make interim payments to the Contractor under Sub- Clause 14.6 [*Interim Payment*]:	56 days
14.7 (b) (ii)	Period for the Employer to make final payment to the Contractor under sub-clause 14.13 [*Final Payment*]:	28 days
14.7 (c)	Period for the Employer to make final payment to the Contractor:	56 days
14.8	Financing charges for delayed payment (percentage points above the average bank short–term lending rate as referred to under sub-paragraph (a))	3% above benchmark specified in sub-clause 14.8.
14.11.1 (b)	Number of additional paper copies of draft Final Statement:	0
14.15	Currencies for payment of Contract Price:	

(*Continued*)

Sub-Clause	*Data to be given*	*Default Data*
14.15 (a) (i)	Proportions or amounts of Local and Foreign Currencies are: Local: Foreign :	
1415 (c)	Currencies and proportions for payment of Delay Damages:	
14.15 (g)	Rates of exchange	Those prevailing on the Base Date.
17.2 (d)	Forces of nature, the risks of which are allocated to the Contractor:	
19.1	Permitted deductible limits: Insurance required for the Works: Insurance required for Goods: Insurance required for liability for breach of professional duty: Insurance required against liability for fitness for purpose (if any is required): Insurance required for injury to persons and damage to property: insurance required for injury to employees Other insurances required by Laws and by local practice:	
19.2 (1) (b)	Additional amount to be insured (as a percentage of the replacement value, if less or more than 15%):	
19.2 (1) (iv)	List of Exceptional Risks which shall not be excluded from the insurance cover for the Works:	
19.2.2	Extent of insurance required for Goods:	
19.2.3 (a)	Amount of insurance required for liability for breach of professional duty:	The amount agreed with the Employer.
19.2.3 (b)	Insurance required against liability for fitness for purpose:	No insurance required against liability for fitness for purpose.
19.2.3	Period of insurance required for liability for breach of professional duty:	
19.2.4	Amount of insurance required for injury to persons and damage to property:	The amount agreed with the Employer.
19.2.6	Other insurances required by Laws and by local practice (give details):	
21.1	Time for appointment of DAAB:	28 days.
21.1	The DAAB shall comprise	3 members.
21.1	List of proposed members of DAAB: - proposed by Employer: - proposed by Contractor:	
21.2	Appointing entity (official) for DAAB members:	

CHAPTER 4

The FIDIC conditions of contract for underground works (the Emerald Book)

The Hon Peter Vickery QC

DOI: 10.4324/9781003200901-4

4.1 Introduction

The contemporary imperative for underground solutions of today for the urban environment, for transportation, water supply, sanitation, extraction of geothermal energy and hydro energy generation and transmission, has resulted in underground works becoming a growing field of engineering and contract law.

Tunnel engineering is of ancient origin.[1] The Romans, for example, were remarkable tunnel engineers. One notable illustration of the many constructed was the tunnel built in the time of Emperor Claudius in the first century (41 CE) to drain the Fucine Lake (Lacus Fucinus).[2] Its purpose was to drain the lake to create more arable land. The tunnel was on a massive scale for its day. It was 5,623 metres in length and was serviced by shafts that were up to 122 metres deep.

Moving forward 2,000 years to the contemporary context:

> The world-wide trend of increased urbanisation creates problems for expanding and newly-developing cities alike. Population increase leads to an increased demand for reliable infrastructure, nowadays combined with a need for increased energy efficiency and a higher environmental awareness of the public. The use of underground space can help cities meet these increased demands while remaining compact, or find the space needed to include new functions in an existing city landscape. In many cases, underground solutions to urban problems are only considered if all other (above ground) options have been exhausted. When underground solutions are considered and evaluated from the planning or initial project stages onwards, more optimal solutions will become possible. [3]

Dr Wout Broere's prediction as to a huge expansion of the cities of the world is borne out by contemporary analyses. An example is the PricewaterhouseCoopers pre-Covid study released in 2019.[4] Key conclusions of the study included:

- By 2050, the urban population will increase by 75% to 6.3 billion, from 3.6 billion in 2010.
- By 2025, there will be 37 'megacities', an increase from 23 today.
- 1.5 million residents a month will move to Chinese cities in this decade.

---

1 See Roberto Cudmani, 'The Development of Tunnel Construction and Tunnelling Machines'' in Werner Lang and Cornelia Hellstern (eds), *Visionaries and Unsung Heroes*, (De Gruyter 2019) 162–65.

2 ibid.

3 Wout Broere, 'Underground Space: Solving the Problems of Today's Cities' (2016) 55 *Tunnelling and Underground Space Technology* 245 https://reader.elsevier.com/reader/sd/pii/S0886779815302923?token=BEB17276F33530A941FD2C17187F60772301F81FB930004AECECF12C-B10F14C6E12324A5C0880453CE6CA79487600E74 (accessed 21 September 2020).

4 'PwC Real Estate 2020: a world-wide study: *Building the future*' www.pwc.com/sg/en/real-estate/assets/pwc-real-estate-2020-building-the-future.pdf (accessed 4 September 2020).

- The volume of urban building activity will be huge.
- Global construction output is expected to almost double to US$15 trillion by 2025.
- Emerging markets in Asia will be the fastest growing region (with Sub-Saharan Africa expected to be the second highest).

At the same time, the technical capacity to service projects which involve working underground has grown apace and continues to grow. The machines of today have the capacity to provide efficient and rapid excavation, usually by use of sophisticated tunnel boring machines (**TBMs**).[5] These combine the processes of tunnel boring at the face with tunnel lining, which transfers a large part of the load of the surrounding medium to tunnel lining fixed to the cavity wall. This is performed in a single operation as the machine advances on its laser guided course. Development of the engineering of TBMs is continuing, for example with the invention of earth pressure balance tunnelling machines (**EPBs**) which provide good control of face pressure through effective control of chamber pressure in a wide variety of ground conditions.[6] The capital cost, and hence associated commercial risk, of these bespoke machines is enormous.

However, a dominant risk factor unique to these works remains the 'known unknown'[7] of the actual subsurface conditions, particularly at the time of planning and tendering, including uncertain and unascertainable ground and groundwater conditions, often at considerable depths. The Snowy 2.0 hydro-electricity project in the Snowy Mountains of Australia, for example, will involve underground excavation and tunnelling works between dams at Tantangara and Talbingo some 27 kilometres in length to depths of up to one kilometre.[8]

Sir Harold Harding has said of the uncertainty of exploring ground conditions for tunnel projects:

> The only bore hole that can be relied upon to describe the ground conditions precisely would be one the length of the tunnel and several feet larger in diameter.[9]

It was considerations such as these which drove development of the FIDIC Conditions of Contract for Underground Works known as the Emerald Book. As its title suggests, this is a standard form contract designed specifically to manage the unique risks arising from projects which have a large component of subsurface works.

This chapter approaches the Emerald Book from the perspective of the unique contractual requirements for the construction of tunnels, irrespective of jurisdiction. Although it uses some Australian examples, the physical and commercial risks of tunnel construction generally do not depend on the Country the Site is located in, nor do the overarching requirements of maintaining a safe working environment depend on jurisdiction specific legislation. The following jurisdiction specific chapters highlight the Particular Conditions necessary for conformity with local Laws where the governing law of the contract is that of the jurisdiction, and where the Site is located in the jurisdiction. It can be seen that there are only one or two jurisdictions where the General Conditions

---

5 Cudmani (n 1).

6 RJ Mair, 'Tunnelling and geotechnics: new horizons' (2008) 58(9) *Geotechnique* 695, 710.

7 Derived from an oft-quoted observation of Donald Rumsfeld (21st United States Secretary of Defence).

8 See www.snowyhydro.com.au (accessed 7 July 2019).

9 Sir Harold Harding, 'Presidential Address' (1963) *Proceedings of the Institution of Civil Engineers*.

in the rainbow suite are incompatible or inconsistent with the Laws of the Site/Country, and the necessary Particular Conditions in these jurisdictions do not involve major departures from the FIDIC General Conditions, eg see paragraph 7.4.2 below. The following chapters detail the issues in the rainbow suite where Particular Conditions are necessary for conformity with Laws where the governing law of the contract is that of the jurisdiction, and these apply equally to an Emerald Book contract. Accordingly, this chapter does not address the issue of whether any specific Particular Conditions are necessary to use the Emerald Book in any jurisdiction.

4.2 A short history of the Emerald Book

4.2.1 ITA/AITES

The Emerald Book was the product of a truly international collaboration which spanned nearly a decade. It may be attributed in large part to the dedication of Australian lawyer and scientist (geology), Professor Arnold Dix, who was a key driver of the project. He is recognised internationally for his expertise in subsurface infrastructure[10] and in 2020 is Vice President of the International Tunnelling and Underground Space Association (**ITA-AITES**), otherwise known as 'Association Internationale des Tunnels et de L'Espace Souterrain'.

ITA-AITES is the leading international organisation promoting the use of tunnels and underground space. It achieves this through the sharing of specialist knowledge and technical advances and fostering ethical business practice. It was founded in 1974 on the initiative of nineteen nations. Headquartered in Switzerland, it has now grown to include 78 Member Nation States and 310 affiliate corporate and individual members.

Sir Alan Muir Wood (1921–2009), a British engineer and graduate from Cambridge University, is recognised as the founding father of ITA-AITES. In 1952, he joined the engineering consultancy Halcrow, where in 1958 he began work on the Channel Tunnel, a project he would repeatedly return to over the next 20 years. Muir Wood was founding president of the International Tunnelling Association in 1974 and served as honorary president until his death, an appointment which is revered to this day.[11] He imbued the organisation with the concept of innovation as a key to achieving economy and safety in tunnelling projects and the philosophy that the inherent uncertainty attending these endeavours needs to be understood and controlled so that it does not give rise to damaging consequences.

Giving practical effect to the Muir Wood founding concepts, ITA-AITES has the following aims:

- To encourage the use of the subsurface for the benefit of public, environment and sustainable development, and
- To promote advances in planning, design, construction, maintenance and safety of tunnels and underground space, by bringing together related information and studies.

10 He is Adjunct Associate Professor of Tunnel Engineering, Tokyo City University, and is Vice President of the International Tunnelling and Underground Space Association (ITA-AITES). Professor Dix is also a founding member of the international Underground Works Chambers. See www.uwchambers.com.

11 After his death in 2009, ITA introduced the Sir Alan Muir Wood Lecture, which is conducted each year.

4.2.2 ITA contractual framework checklist

As a first step towards creation of a dedicated underground works standard form contract, in April 2011 ITA-AITES published its ground-breaking report: the **ITA Contractual Framework Checklist**.[12] Professor Dix was a key initiator of the ITA Contractual Framework Checklist project and presided as Animateur (chair) in leading the twenty eminent contributors drawn from the four corners of the world towards successful completion.[13]

Written for projects involving significant underground works, the ITA Contractual Framework Checklist catalogues and explains the major contractual issues that ought to be considered to ensure a successful project. Its goal was not to specify how each issue should be resolved or present a standard form contract for adoption; rather, the object was to highlight common issues which ITA-AITES believed were fundamental to ensuring the success of subsurface construction projects and provide recommendations on how they should be addressed.

The ITA Contractual Framework Checklist was designed to be compatible with and provide guidance for reviewing standard contracts such as FIDIC and NEC. In this way it was intended to work as an aid in the drafting of bespoke contracts suitable for specialist subsurface construction. It filled a gap which was recognised at the time, namely that existing construction guidelines and standard forms and contracts did not adequately deal with the particularities of the subsurface environment.[14] The document recommended that 'the timely and appropriate consideration of all the matters raised in this publication is essential for the successful subsurface project delivery'.[15] It detailed the subject areas which, in the opinion of the ITA, should be considered and where appropriate, complied with, 'as a minimum requirement within the contracts in order to provide the most favourable legal basis for the subsurface construction process in the specific circumstances of the project'.[16]

The ITA Contractual Framework Checklist identified a series of issues that should be contractually defined. These can be summarised as follows:

- Methods for dealing with geotechnical uncertainties should be defined in the contract.
- There should be an appropriate level of geotechnical/geological investigation.
- Sufficient mobilisation periods should be allowed.
- Sufficient time should be allowed for testing and commissioning.

---

12 ITA-Working Group 3 Contractual Practices, *The ITA Contractual Framework Checklist for Subsurface Construction Contracts* (ITA Report No 006, April 2011) https://www.google.com/url?sa=t&rct=j&q=&esrc=s&source=web&cd=&ved=2ahUKEwj9rLaiivnrAhU66XMBHYWk-CIkQFjAAegQIAxAB&url=https%3A%2F%2Fabout.ita-aites.org%2Fpublications%2Fwg-publications%2Fdownload%2F82_ca1e25b526079aa7b0d24474b29143c9&usg=-AOvVaw1vmcDCQMr1fMWBt-jIBhX5 (accessed 21 September 2020).

13 Professor Arnold Dix (Animateur), Australia; Max John, Austria; Andres Marulanda, Columbia; ME Abdel Salam, Egypt; Christian Genschel, Germany; Esther Kalman, Hungary; Gyula Greschik, Hungary; Patrizio Torta, Italy; Yoshilsazu Ota, Japan; Yokoo Atsushi, Japan; Gisle Alexander Fossberg, Norway; Martin Smith (Vice Animateur), United Kingdom; Martin Knights (Tutor), United Kingdom; William Edgerton, United States of America; Erich Bako, Slovakia; Alan Hodgkinson, Switzerland; Matthias Neuenschwander, Switzerland; Chawalit Tanomtin, Thailand; Zaw Zaw Aye, Thailand; and Yücel Erdem, Turkey.

14 ITA (n 12) 4.

15 ibid.

16 ibid.

- Procedures for timely dispute resolution should clearly defined.
- Quality and performance requirements should be clearly defined and measurable.
- Provision should exist for the cost consequences of unforeseen circumstances.
- Dispute resolution processes should be clearly defined.
- Payment processes should be fair and clearly defined.
- Risk should be clearly allocated and parties should be able to bear the risks they carry.
- There should be a mechanism for adjusting payments according to conditions.
- The risk management approach should be clearly defined.
- Admeasurement or unit price approaches are recommended.
- The responsibilities of each party must be clearly defined.
- The consequences of non-performance should be clearly defined.
- The Construction Programme (Schedule) should be realistic.[17]

4.2.3 Confirmation of ITA contractual framework checklist

On completion of the Checklist, an online survey was then developed to test the Checklist's recommendations. The results were reported in an ITA paper: the Road Test Paper.[18] The object of the survey was to determine whether adhering to the ITA Contractual Framework Checklist's recommendations correlated positively to successful project outcomes.[19]

The study was performed using an online survey provided to selected industry practitioners. The respondents were requested to report on the contractual practices and project outcome of a single project with a significant subsurface component. The survey questions were detailed and comprehensive. They were grouped into 12 categories, and included 60 questions in total, and 57 multiple choice questions.[20]

The survey confirmed that the Checklist's recommendations were borne out in practice.[21] Notably, the Risk Allocation section indicated the importance of clearly and fairly allocating risk, including the ground risk. Clear definition of contractual procedures, including those for resolving disputes, changing scope, payment mechanisms, and resolving claims, were other important components seen by respondents to ensure project success, as was the technical and managerial skill and experience of the Contractor, and the capacity to generate teamwork and cooperation.

These factors were emphasised by the recommendations in the Checklist, namely that subsurface works require experienced specialists, and that contracts should clearly describe the duties and responsibilities of all parties and define procedures for resolving differences, in a manner that fosters cooperation.[22]

---

17 Alan Hodgkinson, David Caiden and Petros Fortsakis, 'Road Testing the ITA Contractual Practices Checklist' (2016) *International Tunnelling Association* https://www.google.com/url?sa=t&rct=j&q=&esrc=s&source=web&cd=&ved=2ahUKEwjy-ou3kPnrAhXg7HMBHTdQB28QFjAAegQIAxAB&url=http%3A%2F%2Fwww.softxs.ch%2Fpapers%2FITA-2016-PAPER-Hodgkinson.pdf&usg=AOvVaw3FcQe8_lPd0_o1JsfEls7P (accessed 21 September 2020). The authors were members of the ITA Working Group 3, with Professor Dix as the assigned group task leader.

18 ibid.

19 ibid 2.

20 ibid 2–3.

21 ibid 8.

22 ibid.

Conclusions reported in the Road Test Paper were that the survey results, which represented experience drawn from a wide range of projects and geographical areas, showed that the Checklist's recommendations correlated positively to project outcomes. The fact that none of the correlations and statements about project experiences and recommendations from survey respondents conflicted with anything in the Checklist added to confidence that the Checklist recommendations were accurate and useful.[23]

Overall, the Road Test Paper concluded that: 'The Contractual Framework Checklist is a useful reference when formulating contract documents for projects with substantial underground work.'[24]

4.2.4 Further studies

Following development of the ITA Contractual Framework Checklist and the Road Test work, a comparative study was then undertaken with the Swiss General Conditions of Contract for Underground Construction.[25] This ITA/SIA study was founded upon an analysis of the risk allocation for a specific subsurface construction project in Zurich, Switzerland, being the Weinberg train tunnel connecting Oerlikon in the north with Zurich's main station. A major conclusion of this study was that 'the standards according to SIA correspond generally with the recommendations of the ITA'.[26]

On the other side of the Atlantic, experience in the United States of America in the use of 'Geotechnical Baseline Reports' for subsurface construction projects became a significant influence in drawing international attention to the need for more advanced contracting practices in this specialist field. The American Society of Civil Engineers, under the committee chairmanship of Randall Essex, in 2007 produced an authoritative report on the subject.[27] Influential American supporters of the international initiative included Randall Essex, John Riley and Bill Edgerton. Then followed a period of engagement with a range of organisations well known for their work in developing standard form engineering works contracts, some of which had been used or adapted for use in underground works.

4.2.5 FIDIC involvement

The epoch of collaboration between FIDIC and ITA in formulating a standard form of contract for subsurface works began with Professor Dix meeting with representatives of organisations such as in London with the Institution of Civil Engineers (ICE), in Paris with the French Tunnelling and Underground Space Association (AFTES), and later in Barcelona with FIDIC at its 2013 Annual General Meeting.

Appreciating the need for a standard form contract which focused on underground works, the Emerald Book was to become the latest addition to FIDIC's suite of contracts. With this objective in mind, FIDIC agreed to work collaboratively in building upon ITA's earlier work to achieve a positive outcome. This was the first time in FIDIC's

23 ibid 9.

24 ibid.

25 Swiss Engineering and Architectural Association, *Underground Structures Execution* (SIA 118/198).

26 ITA/SIA Study 20.

27 American Society of Civil Engineers Technical Committee, *Geotechncial Baseline Reports for Construction – Suggested Guidelines* (2007).

distinguished history since its foundation in 1913 that the organisation agreed to participate in a joint exercise with an external organisation to produce a standard form contract. It did so in recognition of the special expertise which ITA could bring to the table in the drafting process. The association proved to be an ideal match.

And so it was that in 2014 a joint FIDIC/ITA task group known as Task Group 10 ultimately came to be. The Task Group was announced at the FIDIC International Contract Users' Conference held in London, December 2014. The conference noted that according to UNICEF forecasts,[28] from 1950 to 2050 the world's population will grow from 3 to 9 billion. Yet in the same time frame, *urban* population will grow from 1 to 7 billion. In this context, the need for a specific form of contract to service the growing market for underground works was advanced to address urban needs for energy, transportation, urban infrastructure and dealing with space shortage in cities.

Three members from FIDIC were appointed – Jim Maclure (United Kingdom), Gösta Ericson (Sweden) and Hannes Ertl (Austria), and four members from ITA-AITES were appointed on the recommendation of Professor Dix: Matthias Neuenschwander (Switzerland), Martin Smith (United Kingdom/Korea), Andres Marulanda (Colombia) and Charles Nairac (France). Matthias Neuenschwander was appointed to chair the group.

4.2.6 Drafting of the Emerald Book

Between 2014 and 2019, the joint Task Group 10 worked on developing general conditions of a standard form contract tailored to address the special risks relating to subsurface physical conditions. Ultimately, the 2017 second edition of the FIDIC Yellow Book was selected and used as the basis for the drafting process. However, in achieving the objectives of the Emerald Book, the 2017 Yellow Book had to be substantially modified to accommodate the hazards and difficulties typically encountered by Underground Works.

Much effort was devoted by the task group to carefully defining new concepts such as the Geotechnical Baseline Report **(GBR)**, apportioning responsibility for unforeseeable risks to the Employer, adjustments for Time for Completion (increased for unforeseeable conditions and decreased for conditions better than expected), clear articulation of the critical path of works and milestones, including schedules of baselines and completion schedules.

From this beginning, drafting of the Emerald Book contractual terms was subjected to continuous peer review by Professor Dix and Randall Essex on behalf of the ITA. The Emerald Book was launched on 7 May 2019 at the World Tunnel Congress 2019 in Naples, Italy. It was ultimately peer reviewed by over 70 industry experts, following the years of prior work.

Commenting on the launch of the Emerald Book, President of the International Tunnelling and Underground Space Association, Professor Tarcisio Celestino said:

> The Emerald Book will bridge an important gap. Despite all of the technological developments of equipment and techniques in the field, many underground construction projects end up unsuccessful because of contractual disputes. The book brings together the result of the expertise and respectability of ITA-AITES and FIDIC in the fields of contracts and specificities for underground constructions.

28 UNICEF, *World Urban Population 2050*.

4.3 Why the need for a specialist contract?

Or, as the great Roman engineers would have said: '*Quare non opus est*?'

In the contemporary context, tunnelling and other Underground Works carry with them a series of distinct risks which are specific to this mode of construction. In particular, risks arising from the construction of subsurface Works have origins in the following sources:

- Varied subsurface physical conditions which are not possible to assess with precision in advance of the Works Contract
- The method of excavation and ground support
- Limited access to the Works, often placing serious constraints on construction logistics and the environment
- Ownership of the land above and beneath the Works typically belonging to a number of third parties
- Substantial investment required for Contractor's Equipment and
- The complexity of Underground Works.

These factors are mirrored in the five features identified in the opening Notes to the Emerald Book which distinguish construction of Underground Works compared to other Works.[29] Three of those are said predominantly to characterise subsurface construction:

- The method of excavation and ground support are major factors for the successful realisation of the project, and therefore part of the Works
- Physical access to the Works is often limited to just a few locations or even a single location, which places serious constraints on construction logistics and the environment
- The land beneath which the Works are to be constructed, typically belongs to a number of parties.

To these are added two other important features that, while not unique to Underground Works, are characteristic of all such Works:

- They require extensive investment in contractor's equipment and
- Underground excavation and lining works are very time-consuming.

Developing the nature of these risks a little further, Underground Works risks may be divided into two principal categories of risk – the physical and the commercial.

4.3.1 Physical risks

The physical risks of tunnelling projects were well known to the ancients. Tunnels had to be regularly maintained to clear accumulated debris and deal with water leaks. Unless these were attended to, a dangerous situation could develop which could lead to the collapse of the tunnel. Vertical shafts were used to provide

29 Emerald Book, Notes.

maintenance workers with access to the tunnel for these purposes. In tunnels used for water carriage, the shafts could also be used to release air pressure when the flow of water increased dramatically. The Roman architect and engineer Vitruvius[30] in his 10-volume treatise on architecture, *De Architectura* written 30–20 BCE, describes how Roman *qanat* tunnels were constructed with vertical shafts (called *puteus* or *lumen*) dug at 35.5 m (120 foot) intervals. This was prescribed by Vitruvius in the following terms:[31]'The distance between the shafts over the tunnelled part is to be one hundred and twenty feet.'[32]

But it is during construction that physical risks, both in destruction of the tunnel fabric and risks to the life and limb of workers, becomes a matter of most immediate concern to the modern engineer.

Vitruvius asserted that there were three principles of good architecture:

- *Firmatis* (Durability)– It should stand up robustly and remain in good condition.
- *Utilitas* (Utility) – It should be useful and function well for the people using it.
- *Venustatis* (Beauty) – It should delight people and raise their spirits.

He neglected, however, to make mention of the safety of workers during construction – no doubt because the workforce was substantially sourced from an international pool of dispensable slave labour.

However, times have changed for the better, albeit at a slow pace, with the progressive international movements to abolish slavery and the post-Second World War introduction of the United Nations sponsored Universal Declaration of Human Rights[33] enshrining 'the right to life, liberty and security of person'.[34]

Nevertheless, and in spite of these momentous developments in social thinking manifested in law reform, during the course of the first Snowy Hydro Scheme project in Australia (1949–1974) officially 121 workers lost their lives in industrial accidents, with most fatalities caused by operating plant in confined spaces.[35]

Today, engineering projects are subject to a range of occupational safety and health regulations on a scale unknown in previous eras of tunnel construction. The *Guide for Tunnelling Work* published by Safe Work Australia (the WSA Guide)[36] is one example.

30 Marcus Vitruvius Pollio, commonly known as Vitruvius, was a Roman architect and civil and military engineer during the 1st century BC. He is best known for his multi-volume work entitled '*De architectura*', which he dedicated to Emperor Augustus. His discussion of perfect proportion in architecture and the human body led to the famous Renaissance drawing by Leonardo da Vinci of Vitruvian Man.

31 *De architectura*, ch VII of 'Book the Eighth', entitled 'Of conducting waters', as translated from Latin to English by Morris Hicky Morgan.

32 Even though in reality intervals could vary between 30 m to 60 m. The shafts were equipped with handholds and footholds and were covered with wooden or stone lids. Noted in Victor Labate, 'Roman Tunnels' (2016)www.ancient.eu/article/882/roman-tunnels/ (accessed 8 September 2020).

33 General Assembly Resolution 217 of 10 December 1948 at Palais de Chaillot, Paris, France https://www.un.org/en/universal-declaration-human-rights/ (accessed 21 September 2020).

34 United Nations, *Universal Declaration of Human Rights* (1948), art 3. The right to life is also enshrined in the United Nations' International Covenant on Civil and Political Rights 1966 Article 6: '1. Every human being has the inherent right to life. This right shall be protected by law. No one shall be arbitrarily deprived of his life.' http://www.un-documents.net/iccpr.htm (accessed 21 September 2020).

35 Siobhan McHugh, 'Life and Death on the Snowy' *Irish Times* (16 October 1999).

36 Safe Work Australia, *Guide for Tunnelling Work*, November 2013. Safe Work Australia (SWA), is an Australian Government statutory agency established in 2009. https://www.safeworkaustralia.gov.au/tunnelling (accessed 3 July 2019).

It describes and underscores a range of physical health and safety risks associated with tunnelling work. For this purpose, in the WSA Guide, tunnelling work is defined to include constructing a tunnel and supporting systems and associated temporary work. A supporting system means a system necessary to construct the tunnel, for example a ventilation system.

Construction work carried out in or near a tunnel or associated excavation is stated to be high risk construction work under the *WHS Regulations* administered by Comcare.[37] Risk management planning at the start of a tunnelling project is noted to be critical to preventing deaths caused by tunnelling work.[38]

The complexity of tunnelling work means there are often numbers of parties and many specialists involved. All those participating in tunnelling work are exposed to health and safety duties and risks when carrying out the work and often, more than one party and person has the same duty.[39] Table 1 of the WSA Guide[40] sets out a summary description of the health and safety duties of the major project participants in relation to tunnelling work prescribed by the *WHS Act* and *WHS Regulations*.

Section 3 of the WSA Guide describes the common physical hazards and risks associated with tunnelling work. They are said to include:

- Confined spaces with build-up of gas and fumes
- Rock falls (including those caused by the dynamic behaviour of rocks as they are disturbed and adverse reaction to the excavation and ground support processes)
- Failure of floor or roadway
- Scaling
- High water and mud inflow
- Gas inrush
- Falls from height
- Loss of electricity and lighting
- Moving plant in confined spaces
- Manual activities and tasks
- Loss of concentration through heat stress, noise, ingress of hazardous chemicals and dust and
- Fire and explosion from flammable gases and vapours.

Other sections of the WSA Guide go on to underline the physical risks associated with tunnelling work.[41] These considerations dictate that safe systems of work and effective control measures are essential to be put in place for tunnelling projects.[42]

37 Comcare is the safety, rehabilitation and compensation commission of the Commonwealth government. It administers the *Work Health and Safety Act 2011* (Cth) (*WHS Act*) and *Work Health and Safety Regulations 2011* (Cth) (*WHS Regulations*) in the Commonwealth jurisdiction. The *WHS Act* and *WHS Regulations* implement model work health and safety laws that have also been adopted in most of the Australian States and Territories.

38 ibid.

39 ibid 1.2.

40 ibid 4–5.

41 Controlling the Risks, s 4, 29–48; Air Quality and Ventilation, s 5, 49–55; Plant Use Management, s 6, 56– 60; s 7; Elimination of Fire and Explosion, 61–63 and Other Risks, 63–70.

42 WSA Guide, Controlling Risks in Tunnelling Work, s 4, 6–21.

4.3.2 Commercial risks

The commercial risks associated with Underground Works are principally sourced from significant geotechnical uncertainty combined with high project costs. Projects conducted in this sphere will generally involve uncertain subsurface conditions which will not be fully ascertainable with sufficient precision during the tendering process. Risks arising out of foreseen and unforeseen properties of the ground and obstacles in the course of construction may be expected to occur.

The impact of this level of uncertainty will be reflected in the cost of the excavation and Lining Works, which largely depend on the subsurface physical conditions and/or ground reaction(s) to such Works. Further, the time for completion of the Works, of a section or any milestone may largely depend on the subsurface physical conditions that are encountered during excavation. This in turn gives rise to the likelihood of adjustment of the Time for Completion due to the difference between the contractually agreed and the encountered subsurface physical conditions.

The typically long duration of Underground Works will also give rise to commercial risk. This will impact on the high cost of investment in specialised equipment and associated costs of depreciation, interest, leasing and maintenance. It will also bear upon the stable retention of personnel and contractors who have gained valuable project experience. The need to secure and maintain contractors with staff of sufficient specialised calibre and experience in constructing Underground Works is a critical factor in project success.

A range of environmental factors will also present themselves as commercial risks. These issues may typically include: construction logistics and physical access constraints; dealing with very large volumes of extracted spoil in often sensitive environments; and third-party interests in the surrounding land and land above and beneath the constructed Works.

4.3.3 Underground works and construction risk

Construction is inherently a risky business.[43] In his 1994 review into the construction industry's procurement and contractual arrangement practices in the United Kingdom, Sir Michael Latham remarked that '[n]o construction project is free of risk. Risk can be managed, minimised, shared, transferred or accepted. It cannot be ignored'.[44]

A similar view was expressed by the Supreme Court of Victoria in *APN DF2 Project 2 v Grocon Constructors (Victoria) & Ors (No 2)*,[45] where the managing judge[46] observed:

> It is widely accepted that each construction project is a unique endeavour. As such, each is a risky venture, and therefore is vulnerable to disputation. This is so because every construction project, whether large or small, is something of an experiment.

43 See Andrew Burr, *Delay and Disruption in Construction Contracts* (5th edn, Routledge 2016) 13 [2-001].

44 Sir Michael Latham, *Constructing the Team: Final Report of the Government/Industry Review of Procurement and Contractual Arrangements in the Construction Industry* (Her Majesty's Stationery Office 1994) 14.

45 [2014] VSC 597 [89]. This passage was cited in *WTE Co-generation v RCR (No 3)* [2016] VSC 674 [56].

46 The author Vickery J (as he then was).

As has been said:

> [t]he construction of every capital asset involves unique design, procurement and construction challenges. Different locations and site conditions, construction methods, equipment and materials, and the assembly and management of a team of people to design, procure and construct each asset invariably mean the construction process is essentially one of creating a prototype.[47]

If the level of risk is such in the usual above ground construction project, how much greater is the level of risk in one involving Underground Works?

4.3.4 Consideration of the risk

As a member of Underground Works Chambers Lord Robert Mair has written:

> At the heart of the design process for tunnelling and underground Works is the consideration of risk. The design process involves many aspects, including full appraisal of the requirements of the project to meet the objectives of the Owner, comprehensive investigation of the ground conditions, selection of tunnel alignment (both vertical and horizontal), consideration of likely construction methods and their associated risks, design of the tunnel support system, and estimation of the probable ground movements caused by the construction and their potential effects on overlying and adjacent infrastructure.
>
> Many factors influence successful construction of tunnels and underground Works. These include full consideration of suitable construction options and the attendant risks, understanding of the nature of the ground, satisfactory procurement and contractual arrangements, and effective project management.
>
> In reality for tunnelling and underground Works there is no real distinction between design and construction: successful execution of a project requires full understanding and engagement by all parties of the overall strategy, from the first consideration of a tunnelling solution right through to the operation of the completed project. [48]

4.3.5 The 'unknown' of subsurface conditions

In relation to ground conditions, Lord Mair has further written:

> Tunnelling and underground Works are characterized by an extreme dependence on the ground. Both design and construction are dominated by the ground. It is essential to predict its properties, variability, and behaviour when excavated, with as much certainty as practicable. Groundwater conditions are a vital part of the ground characterization.
>
> Every project requires satisfactory acquisition and interpretation of data relating to the ground and to the prediction of its behaviour during tunnelling. The nature of the ground in relation to possible methods of construction needs to be reliably established during the investigation stages.
>
> Ground investigation is principally part of the design process and is usually undertaken in stages: the first stage being a desk study of the site history and existing geotechnical information, including a geological appraisal; this is followed by fieldwork comprising boreholes, geophysical and insitu testing, sampling and laboratory tests. A third stage is undertaken as part of the construction project itself once the full details of the construction are known; there may well be continuous investigation of the ground ahead of an advancing tunnel.

47 See Cooperative Research Centre for Construction Innovation, *Guide to Leading Practice for Dispute Avoidance and Resolution: An overview* (2009), cited in Paula Gerber and Brennan Ong, *Best Practice in Construction Disputes Avoidance, Management and Resolution* (LexisNexis Butterworths 2013) 7.

48 https://uwchambers.com/services/ (accessed 17 September 2020).

> It is essential that the ground investigations and their proper interpretation are sufficiently comprehensive to characterize the ground conditions with reasonable accuracy – in order to minimize the risk of unforeseen problems during construction.[49]

4.4 Allocation of principal risks under the Emerald Book

4.4.1 Drafting approach to departures from the Emerald Book General Conditions

The Emerald Book comprises the documents listed in paragraph 1.3.1 above for the rainbow suite, with the addition of the following documents:

- Guidance for the Preparation of Tender Documents and Annexes
- Annexes: Example Schedule of Baselines, Example Completion Schedule, Example Schedule of Contractor's Key Equipment.

The Emerald Book is designed as a standard form and complete contract which may adopt the General Conditions as published. However, in recognition of the fact that the General Conditions of the Emerald Book may need to be departed from by the Parties to account for local requirements in arriving at the final form of their negotiated contract, a guide to the introduction of new or changed sub-clauses of the General Conditions is provided in the section Particular Conditions Part B – Special Provisions.[50]

The purpose of this section is discussed in paragraph 3.1.2 above. It contains guidance notes on all the General Conditions' sub-clauses as discussed in paragraph 3.4 above, as well as guidance on three Emerald Book specific sub-clauses:

- 3.2.2 Engineer's Specific Duties and Authority for Excavation and Lining Works
- 4.10 Use of Site Data, of the Geotechnical Baseline Report and the Geotechnical Data Report
- 13.8 Measurement of Excavation and Lining Works and Adjustment of Time for Completion and Contract Price.

Particular Conditions Part B – Special Provisions contains similar wording to the same section in the rainbow suite, warning of the dangers of modifying General Conditions with the addition of further text relevant to the Emerald Book, including the following:

> In particular, FIDIC and ITA strongly recommend that the drafter should refrain from modifying any Sub-Clause specifically referring to Underground Works.[51]

and

> As with all FIDIC standard conditions, some Sub-Clauses may require modifications due to local legal requirements or project specific considerations. Many of the guidance notes provided for the drafting of the Particular Conditions for various Sub-Clauses for

49 ibid.
50 Emerald Book, Guidance for the Preparation of Particular Conditions and Annexes, 8–9.
51 ibid 9.

> the Conditions of Contract for Plant and Design Build are applicable for the Particular Conditions for Underground Works. FIDIC and ITA recommend to avoid modifying the specific Sub-Clauses that FIDIC and ITA have adapted for Underground Works. The modified Sub-Clauses are the result of extensive deliberation and analysis by a group of international experts on the subject. Partial modification of the Sub-Clauses could result in unintended consequences or could make the proposed Contract framework ineffective.[52]

and

> FIDIC and ITA recommend that none of the definitions that refer specifically to Underground Works be amended.[53]

These recommendations against modifying General Conditions clauses specific to Underground Works are supplemented by a list of 71 sub-clauses that FIDIC and ITA particularly recommends not be amended.

4.4.2 General approach to the risks of unexpected subsurface conditions

As earlier observed, a significant, if not the dominant challenge with Underground Works is that, particularly at the early stage of a project at the time of the tender process, they will most often involve uncertain or unexpected subsurface conditions. These conditions in many cases will not be fully ascertainable, or at best will be unsatisfactorily imprecise, at this point.

As a general principle, it is desirable that the risk arising from uncertain subsurface physical conditions in a balanced regime should not be assigned entirely to the Contractor. How this is to be achieved is the challenge. A major task of the joint FIDIC–ITA task force in producing the Emerald Book was therefore to provide a balanced risk allocation to accommodate the risk factors. In rising to meet the challenge, the Emerald Book conditions include several new concepts to accommodate risks that are unique to or most predominate in Underground Works.

4.4.3 Use of a Geotechnical Baseline Report (GBR) in risk allocation

In general terms this is achieved in the Emerald Book conditions through a mechanism which incorporates the concepts of unforeseen and foreseeable site conditions. The Employer adopts the risk of unexpected subsurface conditions, thereby taking the burden of worse than predicted conditions but enjoying the benefit if conditions are better than anticipated. Whereas the Contractor bears the performance risk and therefore benefits from faster rates of production, and conversely suffers the detriment of slower rates of production.

The key mechanism used in the Emerald Book to achieve this outcome is the use of the concept called the Geotechnical Baseline Report (**GBR**). This is a document prepared by the Employer as part of the tender documents. It is the contractual source of risk allocation between the parties related to subsurface physical conditions (sub-clauses 1.1.51 and 4.10.2) and is central to the allocation of risk in the Emerald Book.

In sum, all subsurface physical conditions not addressed in the GBR will be considered Unforeseeable, with the consequence that the risk is allocated to the Employer. On the other hand, risks set out in the GBR defined as Foreseeable are

52 ibid.
53 ibid 15.

assigned to the Contractor. The Emerald Book definition of Unforeseeable adds to the rainbow suite definition of 'not reasonably foreseeable by an experienced Contractor by the Base Date' (28 days before the latest date for submission of the Tender) the following:

> Notwithstanding the foregoing, all subsurface physical conditions described in the GBR are deemed to be foreseeable, and all subsurface physical conditions outside the scope of conditions defined in the GBR are deemed to be Unforeseeable.[54]

The Emerald Book also provides valuable guidance on the drafting of contractual documents, including GBRs. The introductory Notes explain the GBR mechanism in the following terms:

> The Geotechnical Baseline Report or GBR is defined as the single contractual source of risk allocation related to subsurface physical conditions to the Parties. Equally important to the physical conditions of the ground, the GBR addresses the reaction of the ground to excavation and support under the contractually agreed construction methodology. All subsurface physical conditions not addressed in the GBR shall be considered Unforeseeable. The risks arising out of the foreseen properties of the ground, obstacles and adverse reaction to the excavation and ground support processes are assigned to the Contractor, as well as the production rates and cost of performing the Works under the same conditions. Conversely, the risks arising out of unforeseen physical conditions of the ground, obstacles, and adverse reaction to the excavation and ground support processes are allocated to the Employer, warranting extension of time and/or reimbursement of cost to the Contractor.

Guidance as to the contents and use of the GBR is also contained in the Guidelines to the Emerald Book.[55]

The GBR is to be distinguished from the Geotechnical Data Report (**GDR**), which also has work to do in the Emerald Book. If an alternative construction method for Excavation and/or Lining Works is agreed between the Parties, and if the GBR is silent on one or more parameters that are relevant to such alternative method, reference may be made by the Contractor to the GDR to integrate or amend the GBR accordingly (sub-clause 4.10.3). However, for the GDR to assume contractual force, the agreement of the Engineer is required. The GDR is recommended to be issued to tenderers as part of the invitation to Tender to enable them to make their own interpretations and assessments of the risks associated with the baseline statements in the GBR.

In this way the design concept chosen by the Employer as reflected in the GBR amounts to an interpretation of the expected subsurface physical conditions adapted to the preferred risk allocation selected by the Employer. Due to the critical importance placed on the GBR, the Emerald Book includes detailed guidance notes on its function and preparation.[56]

As to content, the GBR requires disclosure of geological and geotechnical information describing the subsurface physical conditions. This information is designed to serve as a basis for the execution of the Excavation and Lining Works, including the relevant descriptions, data, information and warnings of anticipated physical and behavioural conditions, design and construction methods, and the likely reaction of

---

54 Emerald Book, General Conditions, sub-clause 1.1.101.

55 Emerald Book, Guidance for the Preparation of Tender Documents and Annexes, s 4.2 [Geotechnical Baseline Report] 81 and Appendix A [The Geotechnical Baseline Report] 85–90.

56 Emerald Book, Guidance for the Preparation of Tender Documents and Annexes, Appendix A [The Geotechnical Baseline Report] 85–90.

the ground to such methods. The GBR is also required to include parameters that will convey and highlight key project constraints such as ground and groundwater conditions.[57]

The GBR is to be a detailed document, with the physical and behavioural statements to be described using quantitative terms to the extent practicable, and where possible, the selected baseline parameters are to be capable of being confirmed by data gathered in the field.[58] The Emerald Book Guidelines go to some length to make recommendations on GBR content,[59] which include an example table of contents of a GBR together with appendices.[60]

Critically, the GBR allocates the risk of subsurface physical conditions between the parties, and in terms that are expressed as clearly as possible in what is designed to be a practical working document embodied in the Emerald Book.[61]

The central role of the GBR in the contractual scheme is underscored by two factors.

First, it is the only contractual definition of the foreseeable subsurface physical conditions for the Underground Works and serves as the basis for the preparation of the Tender and for execution of the Works. As such and because it is provided at the tender stage, it will have a direct effect on bid prices. Pursuant to the Conditions of Contract for Underground Works, both the GBR and the GDR are to be made available to the Contractor before 28 days prior to the latest date for submission of the Tender (sub-clauses 2.5 and 1.1.4). This is part of the Employer's wider obligation to provide all relevant information in the Employer's possession on the topography of the Site, on hydrological, climatic and environmental conditions at the Site and adjacent property, and on the geological, geotechnical and hydrological data of the subsurface of the Site.

Secondly, the risk allocation in the GBR is dependent on the Employer's preferred level of risk acceptance. As such, the drafting of the GBR will directly influence allocation of risk. An overly cautious GBR may result in higher bid prices, whereas an overly simplified GBR may excuse a Contractor from otherwise foreseeable risks.

It is to be noted that the GBR falls within sub-clause 1.5(f) in the priority of documents forming part of the Contract. As such, it has a mid-range priority within the contractual regime, and priority over the General Conditions.

On the other hand, the GDR falls within sub-clause 1.5(l) 'any other documents' in the priority of documents forming part of the Contract. As such, it has the lowest priority within the contractual regime.

4.4.4 Adjustment of the Time for Completion

The Time for Completion of the Works, of a Section or any Milestone in Underground Works projects more than likely will largely depend on the subsurface physical conditions that are encountered during the excavation phase. Time for Completion needs to be adjusted by the variation of these predicted conditions within the limits defined by the GBR insofar as this variation affects the critical path of the Works, or of a Section or any Milestone. [62]

57 ibid 86.
58 ibid.
59 ibid 87–88.
60 ibid 89–90.
61 ibid 85.
62 Emerald Book, Notes.

The Emerald Book provides flexibility in its mechanism for adjusting the Time for Completion that relates directly to ground conditions. In the case where the extent of more onerous physical conditions are encountered which are greater than described in the GBR, the Time for Completion should be extended, while in the case where the extent of less onerous physical conditions encountered is greater than that described in the GBR, the Time for Completion should be reduced.[63] Accordingly, the Contractor's Tender is required to include production rates for each excavation drive or zone, based upon the conditions described in the GBR.

4.4.5 Measurement and basis of completion time, payment and adjustments

The Emerald Book also provides a flexible mechanism for remuneration geared to ground conditions. The evaluation of the time for the excavation and support depends on the expected subsurface physical conditions and on the production rates submitted by the tenderer. As the subsurface physical conditions are within the risk sphere of the Employer and the production rates are within the risk sphere of the Contractor, the time available to the Contractor for the underground Excavation and Lining Works is to be measured and adjusted against the difference between the subsurface physical conditions expected (as described in the GBR and as quantified in the Schedule of Baselines) and the subsurface conditions actually encountered.[64]

The Schedule of Baselines is to be prepared by the Employer and completed by the Contractor as attached to the Letter of Tender and included in the Contract. Included in the Schedule of Baselines are the Completion Schedule, the Schedule of Rates and Prices and the Schedule of the Contractor's Key Equipment. It may also include data, quantities, lists and Schedules of Payments and/or Schedules of Performance Guarantee (sub-clause 1.1.84).

A Completion Schedule is also required to be completed by the Contractor. This will demonstrate the Time for Completion of the Milestones, based on the sequential logical links between the Milestones with Times for Completion that are based on and consistent with the production rates provided by the Contractor in the Baseline Schedule for the excavation and Lining Works, and with the Times for Completion of the other Works (sub-clause 8.2.1).

The Schedule of Contractor's Key Equipment is also to be prepared by the Contractor. This will include those items of the Contractor's Equipment that need to be made specifically available for the execution of the Works and are deemed essential for it to carry out the Works, such as TBMs or critical components of TBMs. These items may be distinguished from other Contractor's Equipment that can be readily replaced (sub-clause 4.17).[65]

The estimated quantities of the excavation, ground support, ancillary measures and lining, as well as the corresponding production rates are required to be included in the Schedule of Baselines (sub-clause 8.2.2). This schedule sets out the anticipated activities or items of work for the Excavation and Lining Works and their corresponding quantities consistent with the conditions described in the GBR, corresponding to

63 ibid.

64 Emerald Book, Guidance for the Preparation of Tender Documents and Annexes, s 2.4 [Adjustment of Time for Completion] 78.

65 Emerald Book, Guidance for the Preparation of Tender Documents, s 2.5 [Contractor's Key Equipment] 78.

each drive and/or other area of work within the Sections and/or Milestones in the Completion Schedule.

A major portion of the costs incurred by the Contractor is related to time rather than to quantities produced, in particular, technical, commercial and administrative overheads, depreciation, leasing costs and the like. It is recommended in the Guidance section that the Bill of Quantities shall therefore provide for time related items which allow for corresponding adjustments in the Contract Price according to the adjustments in Time for Completion.

The Bill of Quantities sets out the quantities, units of measurement and applicable unit rates and prices for all Excavation and Lining Works (sub-clause 13.8.2). The quantities are to be measured in accordance with sub-clause 13.8 and the Contract Price and Time for Completion of the relevant Milestone are to be adjusted accordingly (sub-clause 13.8). The Contractor is to be responsible for the measurement, save as otherwise agreed (sub-clause 13.8.1). The measurement, with supporting material, is to be submitted to the Engineer who is then required to proceed under sub-clause 3.7 to agree or determine the measurement (sub-clause 13.8.1).

The time allowed in the Completion Schedule and/or the Programme for completion of the Works, Sections and/or Milestones comprising the Underground Works, is to be reassessed (ie reduced or extended) by the Engineer by applying the production rates provided by the Contractor to the measured quantity of each item of work or activity in the Schedule of Baselines. Based upon this assessment, an adjustment is to be calculated for the Time for Completion based on the logical sequential links provided in the Completion Schedule and/or the relevant Programme (sub-clause 13.8.3).

Correspondingly, the Contract Price is to be adjusted by the Engineer by valuing each relevant item in accordance with sub-clause 13.8.1, adjusted in accordance with sub-clause 13.8.3.

4.4.6 Adjustment of the Contractor's remuneration for time-related charges

Due to the typically long duration of Underground Works and to the high cost of investment in equipment, an important portion of the cost to the Contractor, such as depreciation of and interest for equipment, overhead charges and the like, is time-related, whilst the remainder of the cost depends on the volume or quantity of the performed Works. Hence, the adjustment of Time for Completion (if any) due to the difference between the contractually agreed and the actually encountered subsurface physical conditions should also lead to an adjustment of the Contractor's remuneration for time-related charges.

The Bill of Quantities for Excavation and Lining Works is therefore required to distinguish between time-related rate items, quantity-related rate items and fixed rate items for the performance of the Works (sub-clauses 13.8.2 and 13.8.3).

4.5 The Tender

4.5.1 Preparation of Tender documents and selection of Contractor

A feature of the Emerald Book is its inclusion of comprehensive guidance for Employers in preparing Tender documents for projects using the General Conditions. This is set out in the 'Guidance for the Preparation of Tender Documents' in the

Guidance Notes section.[66] As such, the Guidance notes are not intended to be included in the Underground Works Contract.

The Guidance notes that the Emerald Book provides internationally acceptable, comprehensive, best practice procedures 'designed to increase the probability of receiving responsive clear and competitive tenders using FIDIC forms of contract'.[67] This approach emphasises the importance placed upon the quality of the Tender documents prepared by the Employer and the likely impact of those documents in turn on the quality of the contract negotiated and on the ultimate success of the project. As is recommended, the preparation of the Tender documents requires a 'dedicated time frame, independent of the time allocated by the Employer to any previous design stages'.[68]

This section also emphasises the importance of risk allocation particulars being included in the Tender documents for Underground Works by Employers providing detailed information about the anticipated subsurface physical conditions, including expected ground and groundwater risks identified by the Employer, and the design considerations relating to these risks that the Employer has taken into consideration when formulating the Employer's reference design.[69]

In recognition of the factors underpinning Lord Mair's observations earlier referred to,[70] it is recommended in the Emerald Book that the Tender documents for Underground Works should include detailed information about the anticipated subsurface physical conditions, including expected ground and ground water risks identified by the Employer and the design considerations relating to these risks that the Employer has taken into consideration when formulating the Employer's reference design.[71]

The Guidance further recommends that sufficient investigation of the subsurface physical conditions, of access limitations to the Site and the potential influence of the Works on the surrounding ground, ground water table and on the surface should be carried out by the Employer and the results provided to tenderers in the Tender documents.

4.5.2 Employer's Requirements

The concept of the Employer's Requirements is central to defining the Works and scope to be performed by the Contractor (sub-clause 1.1.39). Being essentially a design and construct contract, the Emerald Book establishes this as the critical document which sets the parameters which the Contractor is required to design to.[72]

The Employer's Requirements is defined in sub-clause 1.1.39 to mean the document called by this description included in the Contract, and any other additions and modifications to the document made in accordance with the Contract. The document describes the purpose(s) for which the Works are intended, and specifies the Contractor's Key Personnel and required equipment (if any), the scope and any preliminary design

66 Emerald Book, Guidance for the Preparation of Tender Documents, 73–84.
67 ibid 73.
68 ibid s 2.1 [Risk Allocation Particulars in Tender Documents for Underground Works] 77.
69 ibid.
70 Mair above (n 48).
71 Emerald Book, Guidance for the Preparation of Tender Documents, s 2.1 [Risk Allocation Particulars in Tender Documents for Underground Works] 77.
72 Emerald Book, sub-clause 5.1.

carried out by or on behalf of the Employer (being the Employer's reference design), and design and/or other performance, technical and evaluation criteria for the Works.

The tendering process for Underground Works requires a high degree of preparation devoted to the Employer's reference design. It is recommended that the Employer's reference design should:

(a) Be compatible with the Employer's Requirements, and the Employer's preferred assessment of acceptable physical risks
(b) Be based on and consistent with the conclusions of the preliminary investigations in the GDR
(c) Cover the Permanent Works and the excavation and support procedure for the Underground Excavation and Lining Works and
(d) Be consistent with the GBR and the various Schedules.[73]

4.5.3 Preparation of the Tender

Accordingly, FIDIC and ITA strongly recommend that the Employer engages a team with sufficient experience in the design, procurement and management of Underground Works to undertake the necessary preparatory tasks, as well as providing the team with sufficient time for careful and thorough preparation of the Tender documents.

The tendering process must also allow for sufficient time for tenderers to prepare their proposals of appropriate quality.

4.5.4 Experience of the Contractor

Finally, the relevant experience of the Contractor is of paramount importance to the success of Underground Works. FIDIC and ITA strongly recommend that Employers take care in engaging with high quality selection processes to ensure the skill and experience of the Contractor.

4.6 Safety of the workforce

Safety of the workforce is dealt with in the Emerald Book by separate obligations imposed on the Contractor on the one hand and the Employer on the other. The Notes on the Preparation of Special Provisions in relation to sub-clause 4.8 state that if the Contractor is sharing occupation of the Site with others, it may not be appropriate for him/her to provide some of the listed items. In these circumstances:

- This Sub-Clause should be amended to specify exactly what health and safety obligations are the Contractor's under the Contract, and
- The health and safety obligations which are to be fulfilled by the Employer and/or others should be specified in the Employer's Requirements

so that it is clear which Party is responsible for what in respect of the health and safety obligations for the Site and for the Works.

73 Emerald Book, Guidance for the Preparation of Tender Documents, s 3.2 [Employer's Reference Design] 79.

Safety of the workforce is further dealt with by the mechanism of an Employer's indemnity in favour of the Contractor in sub-clause 17.5. This provides incentive for the Employer to guard against workers suffering bodily injury, sickness, disease or death which is attributable to any negligence, wilful act or breach of contract by the Employer, the Employer's Personnel, or any of their respective agents.

4.7 Design

Vitruvius said this of the importance of clarity in expression of design specifications:

> Again, in writing the specifications, careful regard is to be paid both to the employer and to the contractor. For if the specification is clearly written, either party may be released from his obligations to the other, without raising of captious [fault finding] objections.[74]

The Emerald Book strives to achieve this ideal by imposing significant obligations on the Contractor/designer.

As earlier observed, the Emerald Book was built upon the FIDIC 2017 Yellow Book which in turn was founded on the earlier 1999 edition. The basic structure of these contracts, as adopted for Underground Works, is that the Contractor designs and constructs the Works, and may provide Plant, in accordance with the Employer's Requirements, including combinations of civil, mechanical, electrical and/or construction Works. Hence, the design obligations, which fall upon the Contractor, assume importance. Sub-clauses 5.1–5.8 of the Emerald Book define the design obligations and duties.[75]

Sub-clause 5.1 describes the general design obligations, which are to be assumed by the Contactor. Important elements of the sub-clause include the following:

> The Contractor shall carry out, and be responsible for, the design of the Works to the extent specified in the Employer's Requirements, and, where applicable, in accordance with the Geotechnical Baseline Report.
>
> Design shall be prepared by designers who:
>
> (a) are engineers or other professionals, qualified, experienced and competent in the disciplines of the design for which they are responsible;
> (b) comply with the criteria (if any) stated in the Employer's Requirements; and
> (c) are qualified and entitled under applicable Laws to design the Works.

Importantly, a warranty as to competence is provided by the Contractor in the following terms:

> The Contractor warrants that the Contractor, the Contractor's designers and design Subcontractors have the experience, capability and competence necessary for the design. The Contractor undertakes that the designers and design Subcontractors shall be available to attend discussions with the Engineer and/or Employer at all reasonable times (on and off the Site), until the issue of the Performance Certificate.

A review mechanism is also put in place in sub-clause 5.2.2 which enables the Engineer to review aspects of the design specified in the Employer's Requirements. This is supported by a sanction directed against the Contractor in the following terms:

> If the Engineer instructs that further Contractor's Documents are reasonably required to demonstrate that the Contractor's design complies with the Contract, the Contractor shall prepare and submit them promptly to the Engineer at the Contractor's cost.

---

74 Vitruvius, *De Architectura*, bk 1, ch 1 '*On the training of architects*'.

75 See also: Emerald Book, Guidance for the Preparation of Particular Conditions, 28–29.

The Contractor is further obliged to provide an undertaking in sub-clause 5.3 as follows:

> The Contractor undertakes that the design, the Contractor's Documents, the execution of the Works and the completed Works will be in accordance with:
>
> (a) the Laws of the Country; and
> (b) the documents forming the Contract, as altered or modified by Variations.

Then follow obligations for the Contractor to comply with applicable technical standards and regulations (sub-clause 5.4); to undertake training of employees of the Employer as identified in the Employer's Requirements (sub-clause 5.5); to prepare and keep up-to-date a complete and precise set of 'as-built' records of the execution of the Works (sub-clause 5.6); and to prepare and keep up-to-date a complete set of operations and maintenance manuals (sub-clause 5.7).

4.8 Guidance on use of building information modelling systems (BIM)

Building information modelling (**BIM**) is described in a guidance section of the Emerald Book in terms which emphasise the importance of collaboration and teamwork:

> BIM is not a set of contract conditions; it is a mechanism to provide an environment where all parties have access to information relevant to their role in the design and construction of a project. Wherever possible, a combined (sometimes called federated or collaborative) model is developed for all parties to share, even if, as is often the case, various designers have used different computer aided design programs to develop their respective designs. Drawings and specifications are held in a common database accessible to everyone. These can be used for clash detection, coordination of designs, communication of changes and construction sequencing.
>
> Coordination of goals and effort is essential and is generally achieved by a BIM Protocol and a BIM Execution Plan, both key documents to access and understand work in this environment.
>
> BIM is founded on a team approach and successful projects utilising BIM encourage collaboration.

The Guidance Notes in the Emerald Book proceed to describe a variety of useful practical measures to achieve these objectives.[76]

4.9 Role of the Engineer

The Engineer assumes a critical role in the administration of the Emerald Book General Conditions, as incorporated into the Emerald Book in sub-clauses 3.1–3.8.

The basic Engineer's general duties and authority are conferred by sub-clause 3.2.1 which commences in the following terms:

> Except as otherwise stated in these Conditions, whenever carrying out duties or exercising authority, specified or implied by the Contract, the Engineer shall act as a skilled professional and shall be deemed to act for the Employer.

The 2017 FIDIC Yellow Book introduced a number of modifications to the role of the Engineer from the 1999 edition. These included the following changes, each of which have been incorporated into the Emerald Book in the sub-clauses referred to below:

76 Emerald Book, Guidance for the Preparation of Particular Conditions, 57–59.

4.9.1 Sub-clause 3.1 The Engineer

The Engineer must be suitably qualified and fluent in the language of the Contract.

4.9.2 Sub-clause 3.3 The Engineer's Representative

The Engineer can appoint an Engineer's Representative who shall remain on Site throughout the execution of the Works.

4.9.3 Sub-clause 3.5 Engineer's Instructions

If the Contractor believes that an Engineer's instruction constitutes a Variation though the instruction then the Contractor may issue a Notice to the Engineer to the effect that the instruction is a Variation. If the Engineer does not respond within seven days, then the Engineer is deemed to have revoked the instruction.

4.9.4 Sub-clause 3.7 Agreement or Determination

Sub-clause 3.7 provides that when carrying out his/her duties under this sub-clause, the Engineer 'shall act neutrally between the Parties and shall not be deemed to act for the Employer.' This is in contrast to sub-clause 3.2.1 which as earlier noted, provides that the Engineer otherwise is deemed to act for the Employer.

A procedure is then established which covers the position whenever the Conditions of Contract provide that the Engineer shall proceed under this sub-clause to agree or determine any matter or claim.

In this case, the Engineer is required to consult with the Parties and to encourage discussion in an attempt to reach agreement promptly within the 42-day time limit provided for seeking agreement. If agreement is reached, the Engineer must give a 'Notice of the Parties' Agreement'. If no agreement is reached, the Engineer has a further 42 days to make a fair determination of the matter or Claim. This provides a generous period to encourage a resolution of the issue in a consensual process. If the Engineer fails to make a determination in time, then that will amount to a rejection of the Claim as provided for in sub-clause 3.7.3.

4.9.5 Sub-clause 3.7.5 Dissatisfaction with Engineer's Determination

If a Party is dissatisfied with an Engineer's determination or failure to make a determination then under sub-clause 3.7.5 the Party is required to serve a 'Notice of Dissatisfaction with the Engineer's Determination' within 28 days of the determination (or when it should have been made) setting out the reasons for dissatisfaction.

If a Party fails to give this Notice then the Engineer's Determination will be deemed to have been accepted and be final and binding on the Parties.

4.10 Dispute resolution

Given the complexity and risks associated with Underground Works, issues will inevitably arise in the progress of the Works which will call to be resolved.

The Guidance section of the Emerald Book observes that:

> It is generally accepted that construction projects depend for their success on the avoidance of Disputes between the Employer and the Contractor and, if Disputes do arise, the timely resolution of such Disputes.

Therefore, the Contract should include provisions under Clause 21 which, while not discouraging the Parties from reaching their own agreement on Disputes as the Works proceed, allow them to bring contentious matters to an independent and impartial dispute avoidance/ adjudication board ('DAAB') for resolution.[77]

'Dispute' is defined in sub-clause 1.1.35 to mean any situation where:

(a) one Party makes a claim against the other Party (which may be a Claim, as defined in these Conditions, or a matter to be determined by the Engineer under these Conditions, or otherwise);
(b) the other Party (or the Engineer under Sub-Clause 3.7.2 [*Engineer's Determination*] rejects the claim in whole or in part; and
(c) the first Party does not acquiesce (by giving a NOD under Sub-Clause 3.7.5 [*Dissatisfaction with Engineer's Determination*] or otherwise),

provided however that a failure by the other Party (or the Engineer) to oppose or respond to the claim, in whole or in part, may constitute a rejection if, in the circumstances, the DAAB or the arbitrator(s), as the case may be, deem it reasonable for it to do so.

'Claim' is defined in sub-clause 1.1.6 to mean:

a request or assertion by one Party to the other Party for an entitlement or relief under any Clause of these Conditions or otherwise in connection with, or arising out of, the Contract or the execution of the Works.

The Emerald Book adopts the well-known FIDIC dispute resolution structure which is provided for in Clause 21 Disputes and Arbitration (sub-clauses 21.1–21.8). This tiered system derived from other FIDIC standard form contracts in its rainbow suite, includes the appointment of a standing Dispute Avoidance/Adjudication Board (DAAB).[78] Of note is the Guidance to Clause 21 provided in the Emerald Book[79] and a sample Dispute Avoidance/Adjudication Agreement.[80] Reference to ICC arbitration is provided for disputes not resolved at the DAAB level (sub-clauses 21.6–21.8).

The architecture of the Emerald Book dispute resolution system should be well suited to the demands of Underground Works. Indeed, the appointment of a standing Dispute Avoidance/Adjudication Board could be considered an essential contractual provision given the unusually high level of uncertainties, and hence risks, involved in Underground Works.

Further, given the extensive duration of most large-scale Underground Works and the technical disciplines involved, a three person DAAB would appear to be preferable to the appointment of a single member. This would ensure that the desired level of Underground Works technical and legal expertise is retained from the outset, and that the continuity and security in the knowledge base developed by the Board in the course of the project, is retained and is able to be passed on to any newly constituted Board, should that become necessary as the Works are managed to completion.

77 Emerald Book, Guidance for the Preparation of Particular Conditions, 50.
78 Emerald Book, sub-clauses 21.1–21.4 and APPENDIX General Conditions of DAAB Agreement, 117–25 and Annex DAAB Procedural Rules, 126–32.
79 Emerald Book, Guidance for the Preparation of Particular Conditions, 50–56.
80 Emerald Book, Forms of Letter of Tender, Letter of Acceptance, Contract Agreement and Dispute Adjudication/Avoidance Agreement, v–vi.

4.11 Conclusion

At the launch of the Emerald Book in May 2019, FIDIC contracts committee chair Zoltán Záhonyi said:

> Working together, FIDIC and ITA-AITES have created a contract that we believe, and hope will command the respect and authority of the tunnel engineering and construction sector and that both clients and Contractors can use with confidence. The new Emerald Book addresses several critical areas that should lead to the smoother running of contracts in the growing tunnelling and underground Works sector.

Indeed, it should. Underground Works projects involve managing numbers of unique risks, including the 'known unknown' of subsurface physical conditions. The Emerald Book, produced by the joint FIDIC and ITA-AITES Task Group after years of endeavour, looks to have surfaced on solid ground in achieving a balanced risk allocation for Underground Works contracts. As such, it is set to significantly enhance the prospects for positive project outcomes in these challenging enterprises.

Since its launch in 2019, the Emerald Book has been taken up for use in underground works projects amongst the 21 member APEC countries (APEC-Asia-Pacific Economic Cooperation), notably in Singapore. Within APEC, China is the major constructor of underground works. In Australia, uptake of the Emerald Book at time of writing has been slower.

For countries like Australia, which has a regular need to attract the expertise of international Contractors to execute Underground Works, working with a familiar internationally based contract such as the Emerald Book, will assist to provide comfort and encourage high quality tendering for the provision of their valuable services.

Returning to Sir Alan Muir Wood, who once said of tunnels:

> It has been said that a tunnel is a long cylindrical hole through the ground, with a geologist at one end and a group of lawyers at the other. Yet more dire is the present day phenomenon of lawyers at each end.[81]

Uncertainty is a feature that is unavoidable in tunnelling. But it can be understood and controlled so that it does not cause damaging risk. The Emerald Book will contribute significantly to understanding and managing the risk. It will provide a safer contractual space to advance the contemporary imperative for underground solutions in the built environment of today.

In sum, it may be said that FIDIC and ITA have fairly addressed the fundamental importance of certainty of contractual terms in a construction environment with inherent and complex ground risks. The Emerald Book seeks to balance the importance of Contractors meeting their promises as to time, cost and quality with the Employer's requirements of certainty. It achieves this principally by better aligning the contractual terms to actual conditions encountered in construction of the Underground Works. By this means a measure of controlled elasticity is introduced into the Contract which facilitates appropriate adjustments to accommodate what may not have been anticipated at the time of Tender and contracting.

81 This insight was attributed as having been quoted by Sir Alan Muir Wood from an 'unnamed source' by Professor John B Burland, Department of Civil Engineering, Imperial College London and Professor Lord Robert J Mair, Engineering Department, University of Cambridge writing in (2013) 59 *Biographical Memoirs*.

CHAPTER 5

JICA's perspectives on the use of FIDIC contracts

Takashi Ito and Michino Yamaguchi

5.1 JICA's development objectives

Japan International Cooperation Agency (**JICA**), an incorporated administrative agency in charge of administering Japan's Official Development Assistance (**ODA**), is one of the world's largest bilateral aid agencies supporting socioeconomic development in developing countries in different regions of the world. In accordance with Japan's *Development Cooperation Charter* (2015), JICA set out its mission in 2017 as 'to achieve Human Security and Quality Growth' and support the resolution of issues in developing countries through a flexible combination of various assistance methods, such as technical cooperation, finance and investment cooperation, and grants. It operates in approximately150 countries and regions of the world. Japan's ODA is illustrated in Figure 5.1.

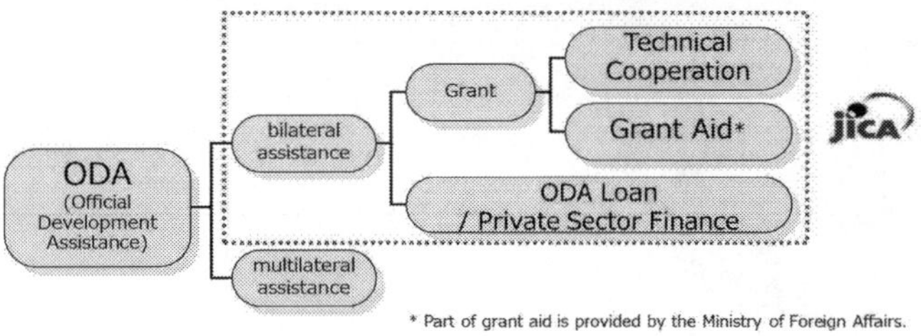

Figure 5.1 Japan's Official Development Assistance

DOI: 10.4324/9781003200901-5

Figure 5.2 below summarises JICA's operations in Japanese Fiscal Year (**JFY**) 2018. This clearly shows that finance and investment cooperation occupies the most important share, in which ODA loans represent an absolute majority (ie amounting to JPY1,253.3 billion (Japanese Yen) (US$11 billion) (commitment basis) for 34 projects), where different FIDIC contract forms are used.

5.2 Role of Japanese ODA loans in infrastructure development in the world

JICA, together with other international financial institutions, both bilateral and multilateral, has taken a leading role in the development of infrastructure in developing countries, in particular the Asian region, by providing ODA loans on concessional terms. Highways, expressways, ports, container terminals, airport, railways, power plants, water treatment plants, urban drainage systems, irrigation systems, etc., having benefited from finance by Japanese ODA loans, today serve as the 'national economic backbone' and/or social basis for local communities in many of JICA's partner countries.

Looking more closely at the geographical distribution of the accumulated committed amount of ODA loans at the end of JFY 2018 (Figure 5.3), Asia's share was very high, including a large proportion for Southeast Asia at 41 per cent and South Asia at 26 per cent.

By sector, in accordance with the trend shown in the sectoral distribution of accumulated committed amount of ODA loan as of the end of JFY 2018 (Figure 5.4), the transportation sector is the largest at 35 per cent, including railway and roads, followed by electric power and gas at 20 per cent.

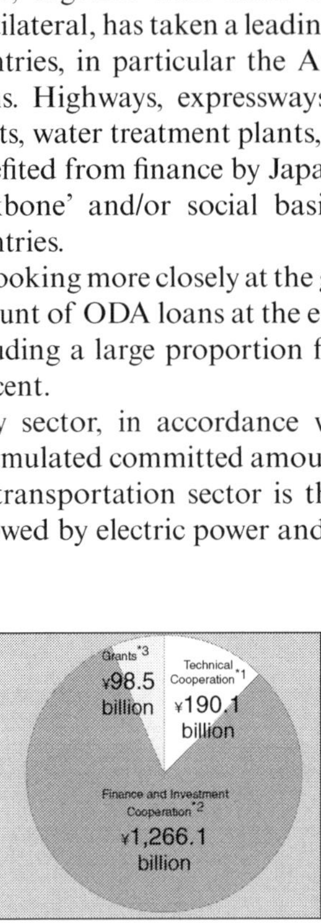

Note) Exchange rate: US$1.00 = ¥110.4 (the offical Development Assistance Committee [DAC] rate in 2018)

*1 Technical Cooperation expenses include Technical Assistance expenses managed under the Finance and Investment Account budget, but exclude administration costs.

*2 Total commitment amount of ODA Loans and Private-Sector Investment Finance.

*3 The amount is calculated based on the fiscal 2018 budget; it does not correspond to the total amount of Grant Agreements (G/As) concluded in fiscal 2018.

Figure 5.2 JICA's Scale of Operations in JFY 2018

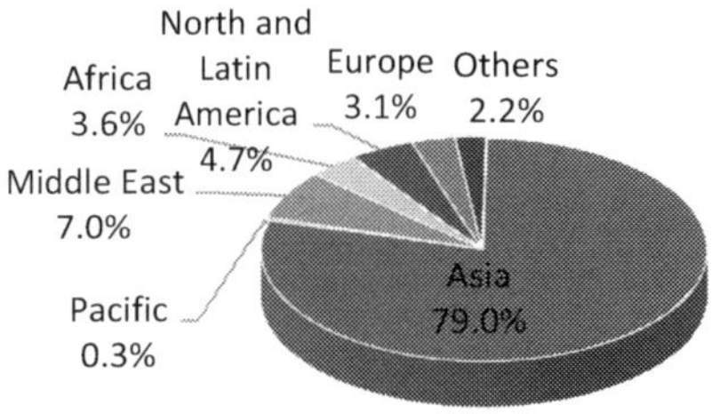

Figure 5.3 Geographical Distribution of Accumulated Committed amount of ODA loan

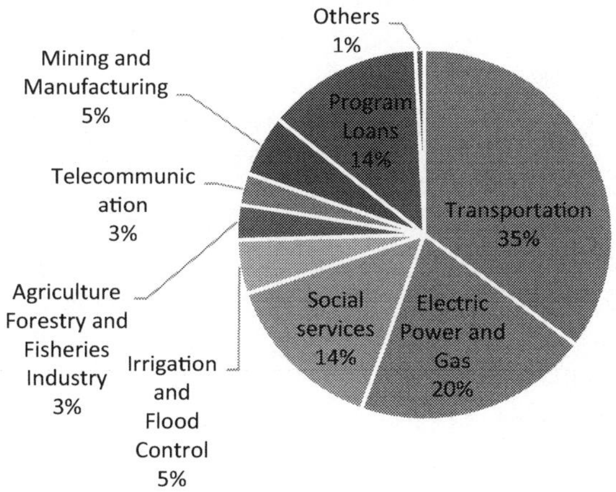

Figure 5.4 Sectoral Distribution of Accumulated committed amount of ODA loan

5.3 Procurement for a project financed by ODA loan

5.3.1 Guidelines for procurement under Japanese ODA loans

Fiduciary risk is one of the major risks in the implementation of public investment projects. To minimise the fiduciary risk in the procurement process under Japanese ODA loans, documents issued by the project executing agencies (**EAs**) (eg bidding documents, bid evaluation reports) for contracts exceeding certain threshold are subject to JICA's review and concurrence.

It is in the same context that, as in other international financial institutions, JICA requires EAs to comply with JICA's **Procurement Guidelines**, 'Guidelines for Procurement under Japanese ODA Loans'. The latest edition of the Procurement Guidelines was published in April 2012, and sets out JICA's policy and general rules to be followed by EAs.

In terms of policy, section 1.01 of the Procurement Guidelines stipulates four principles of procurement: (1) economy; (2) efficiency; (3) transparency; and (4) non-discrimination among bidders eligible for procurement contracts. Accordingly, EAs are required to conduct procurement under Japanese ODA loans in accordance with those principles of the Procurement Guidelines. To attain these essential objectives, JICA believes that, in most cases, international competitive bidding (**ICB**) is the best method for selecting the capable Contractor and satisfying the different complex requirements of large-scale investment projects.

In addition, as one of the general rules, the Procurement Guidelines require the EAs to use the latest edition of JICA's Standard Bidding Documents as one of the most essential tools to attain JICA's policy objectives.

5.3.2 Standard bidding documents under Japanese ODA loans

JICA has published seven different standard bidding documents (**SBDs**), two of which adopt FIDIC conditions of contract.

SBDs for Procurement of Works (**SBD Works**)[1] is designated for design bid build types of civil works, which includes the FIDIC MDB Harmonised Edition, June 2010 (**Pink Book**) as the standard contract form.[2] While being well aware of the latest edition of FIDIC Red Book published in 2017, JICA has decided to continue to use the Pink Book, at least for the time being, since:

(1) After more than 10 years' experience from the first edition of the Pink Book in 2005, JICA considers that its clients and other stakeholders (eg Contractors) are now very familiar with the Pink Book.
(2) Some of the improvements in the 2017 edition of the Red Book (eg many time bars at different stages/processes) appear too precise and even complicated.
(3) 'MDB's requirements' such as 'social clauses' are integrated in the General Conditions of Contract of the Pink Book, which is far more user-friendly than adding many other requirements in the Special Provisions if using the 2017 edition of the Red Book.

The decision to continue with the Pink Book in JICA's SBD, however, does not mean that JICA refuses use of the 2017 edition of the Red Book. JICA will be flexible, taking account of its clients' needs and pursue the best choice of the applicable contract form.

SBD for Design Build, Plant and Works (**SBD Design Build**) includes the 1999 FIDIC Plant and Design Build Contract (Yellow Book). Although the status of SBD Design Build has been 'trial version' since its first publication in 2015, the revised version of SBD Design Build currently under preparation (as of August 2020) will not be 'trial' to formally join the line-up of JICA's SBD.

5.4 Use of FIDIC contract conditions as standard forms

5.4.1 Fair and balanced risk allocation

JICA strongly believes that an appropriate contract form should be chosen in light of the nature and characteristics of the works to be executed, and that the right choice of contract form is one of the essential factors to attain fair and balanced risk allocation between the parties. This is why, at the time of JICA's appraisal for new projects, JICA always discusses applicable contract forms with the EAs.

JICA also has standard terms of reference for construction supervision consultants for different contract forms. When use of FIDIC contract forms (either Pink or Yellow) is agreed upon, use of standard terms of reference giving power and authority as 'the Engineer' to the consultant is also agreed upon so that there will not be any gap between the role and power of the Engineer in the construction contracts and those in the consulting contract.

Needless to say, for the readers of this book, use of SBD Design Build (Yellow Book) is justified when 'fit for purpose' is required and appropriate and uncertainties deriving from the ground conditions are limited. EAs sometimes prefer, however, to apply the SBD Design Build (Yellow Book) to conventional civil works contracts by misunderstanding that design build method will be 'cheaper, less time-consuming and

1 https://www.jica.go.jp/english/our_work/types_of_assistance/oda_loans/oda_op_info/guide/handbooks/c8h0vm0000aoeux8-att/201204_chapter2_en.pdf (accessed 2 October 2020).

2 https://www.jica.go.jp/english/our_work/types_of_assistance/oda_loans/oda_op_info/guide/tender/c8h0vm0000aoesst-att/works_2019.pdf (accessed 2 October 2020).

risk free for the Employer (in particular, free from design responsibility)'. In this regard, JICA believes that the role of FIDIC is extremely important for further dissemination and training for FIDIC users on appropriate use of the FIDIC rainbow suite in line with the FIDIC Golden Principles. JICA is eager to collaborate with FIDIC and other like-minded international financiers for this purpose.

5.4.2 FIDIC Golden Principles and procurement guidelines

JICA fully supports the FIDIC Golden Principles. Accordingly, section 4.01 of the Procurement Guidelines stipulates: 'Borrowers shall use the appropriate SBD of the latest version issued by JICA *with minimum changes acceptable to JICA, as necessary to address project-specific conditions*.'

Unfortunately, it is not very rare to see cases violating those principles. Typical examples are:

- Dozens of specific provisions which don't really have anything to do with project specific situations
- Provisions affecting balanced risk allocations, eg no price adjustment, domestic arbitration institution as appointing agency of DB member and/or as arbitration institution, restriction to the Engineer's power and authority, etc.
- 'Copy and paste' of those bad examples.

Again, JICA has high expectations on the role of FIDIC to train users of FIDIC contract forms for proper use in accordance with the FIDIC Golden Principles. A clear message has to be passed to all users that unfair risk allocation may result in unfortunate situations for all the project stakeholders, eg high bid price, bid failure and rebidding, non-participation of capable competitors in the bidding process, poor construction quality and delay of the works. As detailed in the discussion of fair and balanced contracts in paragraph 2.2 above, JICA has published the 'Check List for One Sided Contracts' that identifies the types of problems that arise from unfair risk allocation.

5.4.3 Dispute Boards for dispute avoidance and resolution

Dispute resolution has been one of the most important themes in contract management, and this is also the case in the projects funded by Japanese ODA loans. JICA and other international financiers are very interested in Dispute Boards (DBs), for their uniqueness serving not only dispute resolution but also dispute prevention. This is why JICA has been very much devoted to promotion of DBs for a long time. In addition to a series of dissemination seminars organised in Asian countries in the beginning of 2010s, JICA contributed to setting up a National List of Adjudicators in Japan, all in collaboration with a number of reputed FIDIC experts. JICA actively participates in FIDIC's gatherings, in particular User's Conferences organised in Asian countries where JICA's experience of the promotion of DBs is shared.

It is also noteworthy that a Dispute Board Manual has been available since 2012 on JICA's website for practitioners.[3] This manual has been prepared to assist all the stakeholders by giving concise and practical guidance on how to set up and manage a DB.

3 https://www.jica.go.jp/activities/schemes/finance_co/procedure/guideline/pdf/DisputeBoard-Manual_201203_e.pdf (accessed 2 October 2020).

Recognising the DB as a mechanism for sound contract management rather than conflict settlement procedures, it is JICA's conviction that a standing DB should be established for a contract whose amount exceeds a certain threshold, since an ad-hoc DB doesn't have a standing DB's unique advantage, ie the dispute avoidance function.

5.5 Challenges for implementing a standing Dispute Board

The promotion of a DB sometimes faces difficulties. Unwillingness to set up DB prevails among the stakeholders due to lack of experiences and knowledge of DBs. In this regard, JICA conducted a survey 'Application of Dispute Board for Project Funded under Japanese ODA Loan' in the JFY 2017–2018. One of remarkable findings is that almost all Employers and Contractors who had experience of DB were largely satisfied with its function, with special appreciation to the dispute avoidance function, even though the number of contracts with actual establishment of DB is limited. Encouraged by the findings of the survey, JICA will continue to disseminate the advantage of a standing DB so that the Parties to the Contract will benefit from this very useful tool of sound contract management.

5.6 Lessons learned for proper contract management and smooth implementation of the project

Sound contract management is enhanced by a sound working environment. It is JICA's conviction that the role of the Employer is of paramount importance in this respect: allowing a reasonable time for completion, sufficient working area, use of suitable contract form, coordination with other public authorities, etc. are very basic frameworks that only the Employer can establish. The role of engineering consultants who assist the Employer in project formulation/preparation is also essential.

Harmonisation between the applicable construction contract and consulting contract for supervision constitute another 'must-have': Terms of reference covering functions of the Engineer together with decent quantities of person-months allow the consultant to exercise his/her professional skill fully to manage FIDIC conditions of contract.

FIDIC Golden Principles are a guiding light to be followed.

Finally, use of a standing DB in accordance with FIDIC Conditions of Contract, including setting it up immediately after the start of construction work, is recommended to serve not only dispute resolution but also provide a dispute avoidance mechanism.

5.7 Internet references

The following documents referred to in the text above are available on JICA's website:

- Procurement Guidelines and SBDs under Japanese ODA loan

https://www.jica.go.jp/english/our_work/types_of_assistance/oda_loans/oda_op_info/guide/index.html

- Dispute Board Manual

https://www.jica.go.jp/activities/schemes/finance_co/procedure/guideline/pdf/DisputeBoardManual_201203_e.pdf

CHAPTER 6

Applying FIDIC contracts in Australia

Dr Donald Charrett[1]

1 I thank Professor John Sharkey for reviewing this chapter and providing constructive comments.

DOI: 10.4324/9781003200901-6

6.1 Outline of the legal environment in Australia

6.1.1 The constitutional structure of Australia

Australia is a constitutional monarchy with a federal system of government. The formal Head of State is the Queen of Australia, who is also the Queen of the United Kingdom and of 14 other Commonwealth realms. In practice, the Queen's representatives, the Governor-General (Commonwealth) and Governors (States), exercise her formal powers on a day-to-day basis. Nowadays, despite the formal constitutional structure, Australia effectively functions more like a republic than a monarchy. Since the *Australia Act 1986* (the name given to two separate Acts that eliminated the remaining associations between the laws and judiciary of Australia and their counterparts in the United Kingdom), the United Kingdom Parliament does not even have a theoretical legislative role to play in Australian affairs.

Since 1 January 1901, the fundamental law of the Commonwealth of Australia is in a written *Constitution*, comprising 128 articles in eight chapters. These articles cover: The Parliament, the Executive Government, the Judicature, Finance and Trade, the States, New States, Miscellaneous and Alteration of the Constitution. The High Court of Australia is the supreme judicial authority for Australian law. In the event of a challenge to the constitutionality of any Act of Parliament, the High Court of Australia is the sole authority.

The Commonwealth of Australia is a federation of six States and two Territories. The Commonwealth and each of the States and Territories have Parliaments that pass laws. The *Constitution* grants the Commonwealth Parliament 39 heads of legislative power 'to make laws for the peace, order, and good government of the Commonwealth', and exclusive power to make laws with respect to the Commonwealth government and public service. In respect of powers shared with the States, if the Commonwealth legislation 'covers the field', then any State legislation is void to the extent of any inconsistency.[2] Matters which do not come under these 39 heads of power are generally the province of the State and Territory Parliaments, unless these Parliament refer their powers to the Commonwealth. The responsibility for private law generally rests with the States and Territories, except where the Commonwealth relies on its heads of power in the *Constitution*.

6.1.2 The common law of Australia[3]

Australia is a common law country, and in contrast to the USA, with a single common law applicable to all States and Territories.[4] Much of Australia's common law does not substantially differ from the common law of England where it originated. Whilst Australia is a federation of six States and two Territories, the High Court of Australia, the country's final court of appeal, has held that not only is there a 'common law of Australia' but also that it is 'a single and unified one'.[5] However, as in any common law jurisdiction, the legislators of the nine Australian jurisdictions (including the Federal Parliament) have intervened to supplement or replace the common law in many areas. The inevitable result of this is that there are sometimes nine separate (and sometimes very different) laws dealing with the same issue.

The Commonwealth, States and Territories do, however, have uniform laws on some matters. On some matters the States have ceded their legislative power to the Commonwealth which has passed a single Australian law; in other cases, the various governments have agreed to pass uniform legislation. Thus, there is a single law applying to companies,[6] whereas each of the States and the Territories have *Arbitration Acts* based on the UNCITRAL Model Law that is similar to the *International Arbitration Act 1974* (Cth).

6.1.3 The court system in Australia[7]

There are typically three levels of courts in the Australian States: Magistrates' Courts, County (or District) Courts and Supreme Courts. In addition, there are Tribunals that have jurisdiction over certain defined controversies, typically consumer type disputes.

Each State and Territory has a Supreme Court, which has appellate jurisdiction to hear all matters within its jurisdiction. State Supreme Courts are also vested with Federal jurisdiction to hear actions arising under the laws of the Commonwealth of Australia.[8]

2 *Constitution* section 109.

3 Donald Charrett and Matthew Bell, 'Statutory intervention into the common construction law of Australia – progress or regress?' (2011) 137 *Australian Construction Law Newsletter* 6; (2012) *Journal of the Canadian College of Construction Lawyers* 11.

4 *Farah Constructions Pty Ltd v Say-Dee Pty Ltd* (2007) 230 CLR 89, 151-2.

5 *Farah Constructions Pty Ltd v Say-Dee Pty Ltd* (2007) 230 CLR 89, 151-2.

6 *Corporations Act 2001* (Cth).

7 Donald Charrett and Matthew Bell, 'Statutory intervention into the common construction law of Australia – progress or regress?' (2011) 137 *Australian Construction Law Newsletter* 6; (2012) *Journal of the Canadian College of Construction Lawyers* 11.

8 See, primarily, *Jurisdiction of Courts (Cross-Vesting) Act 1987* (Cth).

Thus, a single controversy involving matters arising under the common law, State law and Federal law can be heard by a State Supreme Court. There is also a Federal Court which has jurisdiction to hear actions arising under Federal law. Subject to the provisions of the *Judiciary Act 1903* (Cth), the Federal Court also has delegated jurisdiction to hear matters arising under State law. The High Court of Australia is the ultimate court of appeal from both State and Territory Supreme Courts, and the Federal Court.

In principle, judgments in other common law jurisdictions (particularly England, New Zealand and Canada, but also other ex-English colonies such as the USA, South Africa and Singapore) may be consistent with the common law in Australia, and relied upon by Australian judges if the factual circumstances are sufficiently similar: as Justice Paul Finn has put it, the High Court has viewed such foreign materials as being 'persuasive to the extent they could persuade'.[9] However, any judgment from an extraneous jurisdiction (including another State of Australia) must be carefully reviewed for any relevant differences in the applicable statutory framework, or whether it has been overruled by a relevant court in the applicable jurisdiction.[10]

6.2 The construction industry in Australia

6.2.1 Overview

In 2019, the construction industry was the third largest employer in Australia, employing nearly 1.2 million people (9.5 per cent of the workforce). It contributed AU$134 billion (US$100 billion) (8 per cent) to GDP, the third largest contributor by volume of output, behind mining (10 per cent) and finance (9 per cent).[11] In addition to this direct contribution to GDP, construction activity supports a large upstream and downstream supply chain – the manufacture of building materials and accessories, sale, management and financing of property, engineering and architectural design services and transport and wholesaling of building materials. Collectively, these upstream and downstream activities extend the reach of construction-related activity to around 20 per cent of the economy, in output (value added) terms.[12]

Prior to the 2020 Covid-19 pandemic, Australia's population growth rate was around 1.6 per cent, nearly two-thirds as a result of immigration. This population is concentrated in urban areas – 50 per cent of the population live in one of the 11 major cities, with 40 per cent in Sydney and Melbourne. Population growth requires substantial new construction each year for dwellings and commercial structures, as well as expanding and upgrading infrastructure. The resources industry (minerals and oil and gas) is a major contributor to Australia's economy; however, construction for this industry tends to be cyclical from boom to bust.

There are approximately 338,000 businesses in the industry nationwide. The supply chain for construction is complex and strongly interrelated, encompassing

9 Paul Finn, 'Internationalization or isolation: the Australian *cul de sac*? The case of contract law' in Elise Bant and Matthew Harding (eds), *Exploring Private Law* (Cambridge University Press 2010) 45.

10 See eg *Farah Constructions Pty Ltd v Say-Dee Pty Ltd* (2007) 230 CLR 89 [135].

11 https://www.rba.gov.au/education/resources/snapshots/economy-composition-snapshot/ (accessed 9 February 2020).

12 http://cdn.aigroup.com.au/Economic_Indicators/Construction_Survey/2015/Construction_industry_profile_and_Outlook.pdf (accessed 9 February 2020).

manufacturing (materials, equipment components), services (engineering, design, surveying, consulting, lease management) and traditional construction trades.

The Australian Industry Group describes the construction industry in the following terms:

> [t]he industry is overwhelmingly comprised of small businesses with fewer than 20 employees (98.6 per cent of construction businesses). Indeed, 60 per cent of construction businesses are sole operators with no employees. The majority (82.2 per cent) of these small businesses operate in the trade services sector of the building industry that includes plumbers, electricians, plasterers and a myriad of other specialist building trades. Medium sized businesses (employing between 20 and 200 employees) made up 1.3 per cent of the total number of businesses while medium to large businesses (employing 200 or more persons) accounted for just 0.1 per cent of the total. Whilst the majority of companies participating in the industry are Australian-owned, the majority of tier one contractors are foreign-owned, if not foreign controlled.
>
> Only 5.9 per cent of construction businesses generated more than AU$2 million of revenue in 2013–14, while the majority (60.8 per cent) generated revenue of less than AU$200,000.[13]

The construction industry operates in both the private and public sectors, across three broad areas of activity:

- Engineering construction (major infrastructure, mining and heavy industrial resource based projects
- Non-residential building (including offices, shops, hotels, industrial premises, hospitals, entertainment facilities), and
- Residential building (houses, flats, home units, townhouses).[14]

6.2.2 Regulation

Australia's construction industry is highly regulated. The States and Territories register some or all of architects, engineers, building practitioners and surveyors. State or Territory licences or permits may be required for the following trades:

- Building licences
- Plumbing licences
- Gas fitting licences
- Electrical licences
- Development applications
- Zoning approvals
- Heavy vehicle licences
- Obtaining a white card
- Water usage or constructing a bore or well
- Connection or work on sewerage/drain
- Carrying out high risk work
- Protecting trees and wildlife
- Fire management and safety

13 http://cdn.aigroup.com.au/Economic_Indicators/Construction_Survey/2015/Construction_industry_profile_and_Outlook.pdf (accessed 9 February 2020).

14 http://cdn.aigroup.com.au/Economic_Indicators/Construction_Survey/2015/Construction_industry_profile_and_Outlook.pdf (accessed 9 February 2020).

- Use of blasting explosives
- Removal of asbestos
- Use of public land
- Work on heritage properties
- Building energy efficiency
- Disposal of waste
- Handling, storage and use of chemicals or dangerous substances.[15]

The Australian government maintains the Australian Business Licence and Information Service (**ABLIS**) which provides an online search facility to find information about licences, regulations, council approvals and compliance requirements.[16] The Australian government also maintains a website that provides information for businesses in the construction industry on:

- Businesses in the construction industry
- Legislation, standards and initiatives
- Taxation
- Finance
- Grants
- Employment
- Workplace health and safety (**WHS**)
- Environment
- Insurance
- List of government organisations relevant to the building and construction industry.[17]

A white card is a mandatory requirement for all construction workers in Australia. White card is the common name for the 'Prepare to Work Safely in the Construction Industry CPCCWHS1001' training course. A white card is obtained by completing an official, certified general construction induction training with a registered organisation within Australia. Courses typically take one day. The following site personnel require a white card:

- Construction labourers
- Tradespeople
- Site managers
- Supervisors
- Surveyors
- People who access operational construction zones unaccompanied or unsupervised
- Workers who routinely enter operational construction zones (which may include Dispute Board members).

15 https://www.business.gov.au/Planning/Industry-information/Building-and-construction-industry#licences-and-permits (accessed 18 December 2020).
16 https://ablis.business.gov.au (accessed 18 December 2020).
17 https://www.business.gov.au/Planning/Industry-information/Building-and-construction-industry (accessed 23 February 2021).

In addition to a white card, workers in some specialisations require additional certification. For example, rail network operators require workers to maintain a Rail Industry Worker card to demonstrate competency to undertake rail safety work on their networks.

Details of the regulatory environment for business in Australia is included in the IBA publication *Doing Business in Asia Pacific Guidebook.*[18] This includes issues relevant to the construction industry such as business and corporate structures, foreign investment, employment industrial relations and work health and safety, tax law, intellectual property and privacy laws and data protection.

6.2.3 Labour relations

Australia's workplace relations system is established by the *Fair Work Act 2009* (Cth) and other laws and covers the majority of private sector employees and employers in Australia. The *Fair Work Act* is lengthy and highly prescriptive of the regulation of labour relations, containing over 800 sections. The key elements of the workplace relations framework set out in the *Fair Work Act* and other workplace legislation, are:

- A safety net of minimum terms and conditions of employment.
- A system of enterprise-level collective bargaining underpinned by bargaining obligations and rules governing industrial action.
- Provision for individual flexibility arrangements as a way to allow an individual worker and an employer to make flexible work arrangements that meet their genuine needs, provided that the employee is better off overall.
- Protections against unfair or unlawful termination of employment.
- Protection of the freedom of both employers and employees to choose whether or not to be represented by a third party in workplace matters and the provision of rules governing the rights and responsibilities of employer and employee representatives.[19]

The practical application of the *Fair Work Act* in workplaces is overseen by the Fair Work Commission and the Fair Work Ombudsman. The practical application of the *Fair Work (Registered Organisations) Act 2009* (Cth) is overseen by the Fair Work Commission and the Registered Organisations Commission.[20] In 2016, the Commonwealth Government established the Australian Building and Construction Commission (**ABCC**) 'to uphold the law and change behaviour to make the building and construction industry fair, efficient and productive'.[21]

Notwithstanding the freedom not to join a union enshrined in the *Fair Work Act*, powerful militant unions have forced many contractors to operate their sites as a closed shop where every construction worker (including self-employed subcontractors) is required to join a union. Certain union officials have engaged in blatantly unlawful conduct by intimidating site staff and officials and breaching the provisions of the *Fair*

18 Australia https://www.ibanet.org/Regional_Fora/Regional_Fora/Asia_Pacific_Forum/Doing-business.aspx (accessed 11 February 2021).

19 https://www.ag.gov.au/industrial-relations/australias-national-workplace-relations-system/Pages/default.aspx (accessed 18 December 2020).

20 ibid.

21 https://www.abcc.gov.au/about/who-we-are/overview (accessed 18 December 2020).

Work Act. The resulting substantial fines paid by the union and its officials totalling millions of dollars have not been effective in eliminating illegal behaviour.[22]

Recently there have been a large number of reported instances of 'wage theft' in Australia, in which employees have not been paid the wages they are legally entitled to. In May 2020 the ABCC reported that it had recouped more than AU$2 million (US$1.5 million) in unpaid wages since 2016. In response to a number of recent, high-profile cases of underpayment by large companies (and law firms), the Victorian parliament recently passed a law creating new criminal offences relating to the underpayment of employment entitlements and failures in record keeping.[23] The Commonwealth Government is considering similar legislation with penalties of up to four years jail and fines of AU$1.1 million (US$800,000).[24]

6.2.4 Safety culture

There is increasing emphasis on workplace health and safety on construction sites. Each jurisdiction has detailed WHS laws that place a significantly higher burden of responsibility and compliance on organisations working in the construction industry than previously. One of the significant recent developments is the formalisation of higher WHS obligations on organisations that design, manufacture, import or supply products. Many contracts let by government instrumentalities and resource companies include stringent reporting provisions in an endeavour to improve site safety. Notwithstanding this increased focus on safety, construction still has the fourth highest rate of fatalities in Australia.[25] Queensland, [26] the ACT[27] and Victoria[28] have industrial manslaughter laws that apply to negligent conduct causing death. Maximum penalties are up to 20 years' imprisonment and/or a fine of AU$320,000

22 An example of such illegal behaviour by the Construction, Forestry, Mining, Maritime and Energy Union (CFMEU) was reported in the Financial Review on 5 April 2019:

> In 2019 the CFMEU forced the shutdown of the Lendlease Barangaroo site in Sydney in support of a union delegate who had been suspended from employment after throwing a punch at a site manager and threatening to 'kill' him. Justice Geoffrey Flick imposed the original record fine $1.33 million on the CFMEU, and almost $200,000 on nine union officials in a scathing judgment that declared maximum fines were no longer enough to deter the militant union.
>
> He said the CFMEU "has repeatedly sought to place itself above the law' and its officials have shown a 'total contempt for the rights of occupiers and a total contempt for the constraints imposed by the law'.
>
> 'It is, with respect, not possible to envisage worse union behaviour. The CFMEU assumes a prominent role in the industrial affairs of this country and had consistently exhibited a contempt for compliance with the law.'
>
> A full court on appeal reduced the maximum penalty against the CFMEU to 75 per cent of the maximum, or US$1 million, and slashed fines against the NSW branch from 75 per cent to 40 per cent, or US$510,000, after considering its history of recidivism was not as bad as that of the national union.

23 *Wage Theft Act 2020* (Vic).

24 https://www.theguardian.com/australia-news/2020/dec/07/coalition-proposes-four-year-jail-sentence-and-11m-penalty-in-wage-theft-crackdown (accessed 18 December 2020).

25 https://www.safeworkaustralia.gov.au/statistics-and-research/statistics/fatalities/fatality-statistics-industry#figure-1-worker-fatalities-proportion (accessed 9 February 2020).

26 *Work Health and Safety Act 2011* (Qld) Pt 2A Industrial Manslaughter.

27 *Crimes Act 1900* (ACT) Pt 2A Industrial Manslaughter.

28 *Occupational Health and Safety Act 2004* (Vic) Pt 5A Workplace Manslaughter.

(US$240,000) for senior officers and AU$10 million (US$7.6 million) for bodies corporate.[29]

6.2.5 *Innovation*

Most construction in Australia is site based. There is limited use of modular construction in the cities using units fabricated offsite in factories. Modular construction is, however, extensively used for resource projects in remote locations, particularly for offshore oil and gas projects.

The Australian construction industry is slow to embrace innovation. Based on Australian Bureau of Statistics data for 2014–2015, the construction industry is the third least innovative industry in the country (ahead of agriculture and transport) in embracing digital technologies and innovation.[30] Building Information Management (BIM) has not yet been widely adopted, and governments have not developed any coherent policies to encourage and accelerate its uptake. However, one notable Australian innovation is the widely used Aconex project management software, bought by Oracle in 2017.

6.2.6 *Government procurement*

All Australian governments have guidelines or legislation for procurement of government construction projects. These policies may disentitle a contractor from bidding for government work if it does not comply with all of its legal obligations. For example, the rationale for the NSW Building and Construction Guidelines is as follows:

> The Guidelines reflect the NSW government's commitment to greater productivity within the State's building and construction industry, and are designed to ensure that the NSW government maximises value for money on its spending on infrastructure projects.
>
> In particular, the Guidelines are directed to supporting outcomes associated with compliance with the law, productivity, safety and freedom of association.[31]

6.2.7 *Insurance*

In addition to mandatory workers compensation insurance and vehicle insurance, most construction contracts contain provisions on some or all of the following insurances:

- Professional indemnity insurance
- Public liability insurance
- Structural defects/builders' indemnity insurance
- Vehicle and heavy machinery insurance
- Tools, plant and equipment insurance for tradespeople
- Loss or damage to property in the course of construction.

29 https://www.nortonrosefulbright.com/en-au/knowledge/publications/9f55ad77/industrial-manslaughter---do-you-have-a-culture-of-compliance (accessed 4 December 2020).

30 https://backtobasics.edu.au/2019/03/construction-industry-facts/ (accessed 9 February 2020).

31 https://www.industrialrelations.nsw.gov.au/industries/key-industries-in-nsw/building-and-construction/ (accessed 9 February 2020).

6.2.8 Common forms of contract

Government procurement is usually based on the use of government contracts, eg GC21 is used for projects valued at more than AU$1 million in NSW.[32] Private sector contracts may be modified standard forms of contract or bespoke contracts. The most common standard forms are based on Australian Standard forms, even though they have not been updated for over 20 years. Modifications to standard forms are the norm: a survey in 2014 found that 84 per cent of standard form contracts were modified.[33] Resource companies generally use their own bespoke contracts. Design and construct contracts are widely used. Australia has developed a particular expertise in the use of alliance contracts for public infrastructure, although these types of contracts have not been used as much in recent years.

6.2.9 Dispute resolution

Disputes arising from construction contracts are resolved by one or more of mediation, expert determination, arbitration or litigation. Dispute Boards are used in NSW and Queensland for large government infrastructure projects. They have been very successful in assisting the parties to avoid disputes – many Dispute Boards have not been required to adjudicate on formal disputes. Mediation is widely used and is generally a mandatory precondition to a court hearing. NSW and Victoria have specialist superior court lists for technology and construction cases.

Disputes over payment in many construction projects are provisionally determined under mandatory *Security of Payment legislation* applying in all States and Territories. These *Acts* mandate procedures for submission of payment claims and provide for a rapid adjudication of disputes over payment to facilitate the Contractor's and the Subcontractor's cash flow. The decision of an adjudicator determines which party holds the claimed money and is binding unless a different outcome is ultimately determined in arbitration or litigation.

6.2.10 Current challenges

The most significant challenge facing the Australian construction industry in 2020 is to improve the quality of construction. There are many hundreds of high-rise buildings around Australia with combustible cladding that does not comply with the *Building Regulations*. Remediation or replacement of such cladding will be very expensive and result in substantial litigation.[34] The quality of construction of high-rise buildings has also been under the spotlight following the evacuation or residents from two NSW buildings because of structural defects.[35] A 2018 report

32 https://www.procurepoint.nsw.gov.au/before-you-buy/construction/construction-contracts/gc21-edition-2 (accessed 9 February 2020).

33 Professor John Sharkey and others, 'Standard Forms of Contract in the Australian Construction Industry' (2014) University of Melbourne Research Report, 4

https://law.unimelb.edu.au/__data/assets/pdf_file/0007/1686265/Research-Report-Standard-forms-of-contract-in-the-Australian-construction-industry.pdf (accessed 9 February 2020).

34 The first case determined in the Victorian Civil and Administrative Tribunal found the Building Surveyor, the Architect and the Fire Engineer liable for approximately AU$12 million: *Owners Corporation No 1 of PS613436T v LU Simon Builders Pty Ltd (Building and Property)* [2019] VCAT 286.

35 John Carter, Mark Hoffman and Stephen Foster, *Opal Tower Investigation Final Report* (2019) *Unisearch* https://www.planning.nsw.gov.au/-/media/Files/DPE/Reports/opal-tower-investigation-final-report-2018-02-22.pdf?la=en (accessed 23 February 2021).

recommended a number of measures to improve the effectiveness of compliance and enforcement systems for the building and construction industry across Australia.[36] Recent legislative measures to improve the quality of design and construction include registration of engineers in Victoria,[37] registration of design and building practitioners in NSW[38] and introduction of a mandatory code of conduct for Building Surveyors in Victoria.[39]

In 2017, the government ministers responsible for construction commissioned a report on improving the effectiveness of compliance and enforcement systems for the building and construction industry. The report made 24 recommendations on measures to improve the quality of construction in Australia on:

- Registration and training of practitioners
- Roles and responsibilities of Regulators
- Role of fire authorities
- Integrity of private Building Surveyors
- Collecting and sharing building information and intelligence
- Adequacy of documentation and record keeping
- Inspection regimes
- Post-construction information management
- Building product safety.[40]

There are a number of other challenges facing the Australian construction industry including:

- Prompt payment of contractors and subcontractors
- Time and cost overruns
- Lack of productivity – construction lags behind other key industries such as agribusiness, mining and health
- Skill shortages – both in building and engineering professions and building and engineering trades.[41]

A recent University of Melbourne report on the health of the Australian construction industry made the following key findings from a survey of industry participants:[42]

36 Peter Shergold and Bronwyn Weir, *Building Confidence: Improving the effectiveness of compliance and enforcement systems for the building and construction industry across Australia* (2018) https://aibs.com.au/Public/News/2018/ShergoldWeir.aspx (accessed 4 December 2020).

37 *Professional Engineers Registration Act 2019* (Vic).

38 *Design and Building Practitioners Act 2020* (NSW).

39 https://www.vba.vic.gov.au/__data/assets/pdf_file/0015/114351/VBA-Code-of-Conduct-for-Building-Surveyors.pdf (accessed 4 December 2020).

40 Above n36.

41 https://www.employment.gov.au/occupational-skill-shortages-information (accessed 9 February 2020).

42 Professor John Sharkey AM, Phillip Greenham and others, *The Health of the Australian Construction Industry* (University of Melbourne September, 2020) https://law.unimelb.edu.au/__data/assets/pdf_file/0005/3501086/Health-of-the-Australian-Construction-Industry-Research-Report.pdf (accessed 16 December 2020).

	Tender Phase	*Contract Phase*	*Contract Administration Phase*
Top three challenges named by survey participants	1. Quality of information provided in the request for tender 2. Time for tender response 3. Tender conditions	1. Absence of capped liability provision 2. Exposure to consequential loss 3. Narrow entitlement to extra money	1. Decisions in relation to claims 2. Delayed administration of claims 3. Lack of explanation in relation to decisions on claims
Source of disincentives	• Risk allocation • Documentation • Project scope • Tendering costs • Price competition	• Risk allocation • Performance evaluation • Contractual provisions • Contract administration	• Lack of impartiality • Assessment of claims • Emphasis on technicality

6.3 The impact of Covid-19 in Australia

The first case of Covid-19 in Australia arrived via a traveller from Wuhan who was hospitalised on 24 January 2020. The Victorian Infectious Diseases Reference Laboratory was the first organisation worldwide to cultivate the virus and on 30 January shipped frozen samples of the virus around the world.[43] The Australian government closed its border to travellers who had been in China on 1 February 2020 and declared Covid-19 to be a pandemic on 27 February 2020. The World Health Organisation declared a health emergency of international concern on 30 January 2020 but did not declare Covid-19 a pandemic until 11 March 2020.

6.3.1 The impact of Covid-19 on the execution of construction projects in Australia

6.3.1.1 Government measures

As a consequence of the federal nature of Australia, both the Commonwealth Government and the governments of the States and Territories passed laws implementing temporary measures to deal with the impacts of Covid-19. The majority of these laws related to the States' and Territories' heads of power under the *Constitution*. State public health laws were used to impose a range of coercive measures, such as mandatory quarantine, compulsory wearing of face masks, restrictions on people's movements and gatherings, the closure of businesses and border closures between states. The Commonwealth Government used the *Biosecurity Act 2015* (Cth) to impose overseas travel bans (including a cap on the number of returning travellers per week), restricted travel and other emergency procedures for remote communities, and enforced quarantine of returning travellers.

A National Cabinet was implemented to coordinate an Australia wide response comprising the Prime Minister, Premiers of the states and Chief Ministers of the

43 'How Australia Led the Global Virus Battle' *The Australian Financial Review* (25–26 January 2021) 16.

territories, however this proved singularly ineffective in achieving national uniformity on measures such as the closure of borders. Each state and territory passed legislation based on the perceived needs of its own citizens, irrespective of the impact in other parts of Australia. Notwithstanding a national definition of a 'Covid hot spot', each state and territory applied different (and in some cases very stringent) criteria to close their borders to visitors from other parts of Australia even where there were no 'Covid hot spots'. Some states aimed for elimination of the virus and required no community transmission in another state for more than 28 days before allowing visitors from that state. After a small outbreak of Covid-19 in Sydney in late 2020, Victoria closed its borders to all visitors from NSW, including residents of Victoria. The impact of such border closures inevitably caused labour shortages in some parts of the country.[44]

6.3.1.2 Impacts in Victoria

In view of the extensive reach of the legislative responses to Covid-19 and the differences between states and territories, the following discussion on actions that impacted the execution of construction projects is mainly confined to Victoria.

Although 'non-essential' businesses were required to close for the period 23 March to 13 April, the construction industry was not classified as non-essential. Accordingly, although impacted by other WHS requirements arising out of Covid-19, the construction industry in Victoria continued to work through the first wave of the pandemic. The stay-at-home directions issued for the period 31 March to 11 May 2020 permitted persons to leave home for the purposes of work, whereas those who could work at home were required to do so. In recognition of the additional inefficiencies from working in the Covid-19 environment, New South Wales permitted construction sites to operate on weekends and public holidays irrespective of what consents might otherwise allow.

The health authorities mandated additional WHS measures to reduce the risk and slow the spread of infection in workplaces and elsewhere, including physical distancing of 1.5 m, and detailed cleaning and disinfection procedures. Employers were required to keep records of employee work locations to assist in tracking contacts of infected persons. In the event of a person becoming infected at the workplace in Victoria, Worksafe had to be informed, and health authorities gave directions on deep cleaning and disinfection, and whether the workplace was required to close. The CEO of one of Australia's major construction companies estimated the cost of the extra burden of Covid measures such as temperature checking equipment, on-site Covid-19 marshals and providing extra space for distancing: 'It's fair to say on most jobs the cost of implementing that sort of equipment and labour associated with controlling Covid conditions is something between 0.5 and 1 per cent of the project cost.'[45]

From early July 2020 Melbourne suffered a more severe second wave of infections, arising from failures in the management of returned travellers in hotel quarantine. This was the most severe outbreak of Covid-19 in Australia and triggered a second Stage 3 lockdown and the compulsory wearing of masks outside the home. Three weeks of Stage 3 lockdown did not noticeably reduce the number of infections, and in early August the Victorian government implemented severe Stage 4 restrictions that

44 'Skill Shortages Threaten Infrastructure Boom', *The Australian Financial Review* (Sydney Australia), 25 January 2021.

45 'Builders count the cost of COVID compliance', *The Australian Financial Review* (Sydney Australia), 22 January 2021, 31.

shut down substantial parts of the economy for 112 days, including architectural, engineering and technical services.

The operation of construction projects was restricted as follows:

- Large-scale construction comprising any project of more than three stories was limited to a maximum of 25 per cent of normal employees onsite compared to normal operations, a high risk Covid-19 safe plan was required, and workers could only work at one site in a discrete shift.
- Small-scale construction comprising any building project of three stories or less was limited to a maximum of five workers (including supervisors), a universal Covid-19 safe plan was required, and workers could only work at one site in a discrete shift.
- State and civil construction projects were exempt from reduction targets but were required to implement a high risk Covid-19 safe plan.

6.3.1.3 Constraints on travel

From 20 March 2020, the borders of Australia were closed except for Australian citizens, residents and immediate family members. All arrivals into Australia were required to self-isolate for 14 days, either at a hotel or a designated facility. Travel from Australia was severely curtailed and the number of flights in and out of Australia dropped to a fraction of normal volume. At various times (sometimes with less than 24 hours' notice) certain States closed their borders to most persons arriving from other States and imposed a mandatory 14-day quarantine on all persons allowed to enter for a permitted purpose. Some employees were required to temporarily relocate their residence for the duration of the border closures. At the time of writing (February 2021) the international border was still closed, and was expected to remain so for all of 2021, notwithstanding the start of the vaccination programme in mid-February 2021.

6.3.1.4 Changes to normal employment

In recognition of the severe economic impact resulting from the mandatory restrictions, the Commonwealth government provided a 'Jobkeeper' payment of AU$1,500 per fortnight for employees in businesses that had suffered a 30 per cent drop in turnover as a result of Covid-19 (50 per cent for businesses with turnover of greater than AU$1 billion). This programme ran for six months, followed by another six months at reduced rates of payment.

Where an employer received payments for an employee under the Jobkeeper scheme it could give the employee three new kinds of 'jobkeeper enabling directions' pursuant to the *Fair Work Act 2009* (Cth):

- A 'job keeper enabling stand down' (s 789GDC)
- A direction to an employee to perform other duties (s 789GE)
- A direction to work at a different place (s 789GF).

Other temporary changes to Australia's very restrictive employment laws enabled an employer to request an employee to work on days or at times different from normal (s 789GG), or to take paid annual leave (s 789GJ(1)); an employee could not unreasonably refuse such a request. Temporary changes were also made to 99 employment awards to give workers access to two weeks' unpaid 'pandemic leave' and also to enable them to take annual leave at half pay.

Governments also provided other financial support such as a temporary cash flow boost for employers, additional tax deductions, wage subsidies for apprentices, government guarantees of loans from lenders and waiver of a range of licenses and permits for 12 months. To discourage workers with Covid-19 symptoms from attending work the Victorian Government provided for immediate payments of AU$300 during self-isolation after testing, and AU$1,500 for persons who tested positive or were a close contact of confirmed case.

6.3.2 The impact of Covid-19 on the operation of construction contracts in Australia

Australian governments did not pass any Covid-19 specific legislation that changed the 'normal' operation of construction contracts. The Honourable Peter Vickery QC wrote a paper highlighting contractual issues likely to arise where parties have not made adequate provision for *force majeure*, and advocated for a new piece of legislation introducing a statutory *force majeure* clause to:

- Define Covid-19 or like epidemic or pandemic diseases as triggering events for the operation of the statutory *force majeure* clause
- Provide in the statutory *force majeure* clause that the duration of such an event of *force majeure* which causes delay to the project or part thereof, any clause in the contract which provides for liquidated damages to apply will be suspended.[46]

This proposal was not taken up in Australia, unlike Singapore which passed the *Covid-19 (Temporary Measures) Act 2020* on 7 April 2020, which legislation provided for, inter alia, suspension of the period for calculation of liquidated damages (see paragraph 19.3.2 below). Contracting parties were therefore reliant on contractual provisions for any relief for the additional time and costs arising in a construction contract as a consequence of Covid-19. Although three states have laws relating to frustration of contracts (see paragraph 6.7.2 below), this legislation is unlikely to provide any relief as the Covid-19 pandemic would not generally surmount the high threshold of making the performance of contractual obligations impossible.

Australia did, however, pass temporary insolvency and corporate governance legislation that may assist construction businesses indirectly. The temporary insolvency provisions applying for six months included a temporary 'safe harbour' for directors by providing relief from personal liability if trading while insolvent, the statutory demand threshold and timeframe to pay were increased and the bankruptcy threshold and timeframe to pay were increased. Some corporate governance requirements were temporarily relaxed, including the ability to conduct virtual annual general meetings, and allowing electronic execution of documents by companies.

Australian courts adjusted rapidly to online hearings for the majority of ongoing cases, for example the Federal Court ceased all face-to-face hearings in Melbourne during the second wave. Only bail, family violence, remand, child protection, warrants and urgent guardianships, human rights or residential tenancy issues were classified as urgent and permitted court hearings. Some superior courts conducted directions hearing

46 The Hon Peter Vickery QC, 'Payments – No liquidated damages due to COVID-19' (May 2020) Submission to the Senate Select Committee on Covid-19 and the government's response as part of the Australian Construction Industry Forum's contribution https://www.petervickeryqc.com/s/COVID-19-Liquidated-Damages-Statutory-Force-Majeure-8-May-2020-2.docx (accessed 31 July 2020).

by telephone, and conducted virtual trials comprised only of evidence with legal issues determined on the papers. Many cases proceeded via online hearings even where one of the parties sought an adjournment pending an in-person hearing.[47] Some trials were, however, adjourned where personal evidence was required to assess issues such as the credit of witnesses[48] or where there were security issues with an electronic platform.[49]

6.4 Australian governing law of the contract[50]

6.4.1 Constraints on the governing law of a construction contract

The common law of Australia recognises the parties' freedom of contract to choose the law governing their contract.[51] It is doubtful whether it recognises their right to choose non-State rules of law.[52] Australia has not implemented the *Hague Principles*, and accordingly has not enshrined in legislation the ability of parties to choose 'rules of law that are generally accepted on an international, supranational or regional level as a neutral and balanced set of rules'.[53]

However, the situation is different if the parties submit their dispute to international arbitration. If the seat of an international arbitration is in Australia, the *International Arbitration Act 1974* (Cth) (***IAA***) will apply to the proceedings. The *IAA* incorporates the *UNCITRAL Model Law* as the law governing the procedure of an arbitration held in Australia. Article 28 (1) provides:

> The arbitral tribunal shall decide the dispute in accordance with such rules of law as are chosen by the parties as applicable to the substance of the dispute. Any designation of the law or legal system of a given State shall be construed, unless otherwise expressed, as directly referring to the substantive law of that State and not to its conflict of laws rules.

In *Musawi v RE International (UK) Ltd*, [54] the High Court of England affirmed that section 46(1)(b) of the *Arbitration Act 1996* (UK) 'allows parties the freedom to apply a set of rules or principles which do not in themselves constitute a legal system' and that 'such a choice may include a non-national set of legal principles (such as the 1994 UNIDROIT Principles of International Commercial Contracts) or, more broadly, general principles of commercial law or the *lex mercatoria*.

Section 46(1)(b) of the *Arbitration Act 1996* (UK) is in similar terms to Article 28(1) of the UNCITRAL Model Law, and there is no reason to expect that an Australian court would come to a different conclusion in respect of the parties' autonomy to choose a non-national set of legal principles such as the UNIDROIT Principles under the *IAA*.

If the seat of a domestic arbitration is in Australia, the relevant State or Territory *Commercial Arbitration Act* will apply to the proceedings. The *Commercial Arbitration Act* of each State and Territory also incorporate the UNCITRAL Model Law as the law governing the procedure of an arbitration held in Australia. Accordingly, it is submitted that where the Contract has an arbitration clause, the parties are free to

---

47 See eg *Capic v Ford Motor Company of Australia Limited* [2020] FCA 486.

48 See eg *Porter v Mulcahy & Co Accounting Services Pty Ltd (Ruling)* [2020] VSC 430.

49 *Roberts-Smith v Fairfax Media Publications Pty Limited* [2020] FCA 614.

50 Residential building contracts are outside the scope of this book and accordingly there is no reference in this chapter to Australian Acts on the special contractual requirements for residential building works.

51 *Dubbee Ltd v Gilman & Co Pty Ltd* (1968) 70 SR (NSW) 219.

52 Ian Govey AM, 'Australia and Unidroit' in *The Age of Uniform Law Essays in honour of Michael Joachim Bonnell to celebrate his 70th birthday* (UNIDROIT 2016) 331.

53 *Hague Principles on Choice of Law in International Commercial Contracts* (2015) art 3.

54 [2007] EWHC 2981 (Ch).

choose a non-State set of rules of law as the governing law of their contract, such as the UNIDROIT Principles, which choice would be expected to be implemented by an arbitral tribunal in the absence of countervailing considerations.

The parties' choice of the governing law of their contract is not unlimited, as a court or an arbitral tribunal may decline to give effect to the parties' choice of law if it lacks bona fides, legality or is contrary to public policy on an issue of overriding concern.[55] There is an argument that parties' choice of governing law for a building contract different to the jurisdiction of the Site lacks bona fides, because the subject matter of the contract has its closest and most real connection with the laws of the Site.[56] Clearly, the choice could be overturned in whole or in part if it was contrary to a statutory requirement; see below for a Queensland statute that restricts the parties' choice of aspects of the governing law for a 'building contract'.

There is also an argument that the parties' choice of governing law different to the law of the Site may be contrary to public policy in respect of building contracts. Each State and Territory is entitled to regulate conduct within its borders (subject to the provisions of the *Constitution*), [57] and has a *Building Act* or its equivalent.[58] These *Acts* prescribe many and varied requirements for the regulation of building work, including inter alia, requirements for carrying out building work, registration of contractors and professionals involved in building work, limitation period for liability of building actions, certification of building work, owners' building manual, bushfire prone land and negation of joint and several liability in certain cases. The prescriptive provisions of these *Acts* are the State and Territory Parliaments' concerted efforts to regulate building in the public interest. There is a strong argument that parties' choice of a governing law for a building contract other than that of the Site would be contrary to the public policy given effect to by the relevant *Act*, and accordingly may not be given effect to by a court or an arbitral tribunal. It should be noted that there is no universally accepted definition of what constitutes 'building work'. In some jurisdictions it includes the design or certification of a building, whereas it is confined to the physical construction of a building in other jurisdictions. Further the types of construction work that are excluded from building work vary between jurisdictions.

6.4.1.1 Building contracts in Queensland

There is a specific statutory limitation to the freedom to choose the governing law of the contract for a 'building contract' in Queensland. The *Queensland Building and Construction Commission Act 1991* (Qld) provides that a building contractor commits an offence if it enters into a building contract not put into writing (s 67G) which must include mandatory conditions prescribed by regulation (s 67GA). A contractor must not enter into a building contract that includes a prohibited condition prescribed by regulation (s 67GB). Further, a building contract is void to the extent that it incorporates a prohibited condition or may reasonably be construed as an attempt to enforce a prohibited condition (s 67GB). There are various other prescribed and

55 *Vita Foods Products Inc v Unus Shipping Co Ltd* [1939] ACC 277, 290 (Lord Wright).

56 ibid.

57 '[i]t is clear that the Constitution intended each State to have primary legislative responsibility, subject to the Commonwealth's enumerated powers, for occurrences within its borders' *Sweedman v Transport Accident Commission* (2006) 226 CLR 362 [123] (Heydon J).

58 The statute regulating building work in NSW is the *Environmental Planning and Assessment Act 1979* (NSW), and in SA is the *Development Act 1993 (SA)*.

proscribed conditions for a building contract in Part 4A [Building contract other than domestic building contracts]. A building contract is a contract for 'building work' as defined (Schedule 2) but does not include work excluded in the *Queensland Building and Construction Commission Regulation 2003* (Qld) (Schedule 1AA). 'Construction work' as broadly defined in the *Building Industry Fairness (Security of Payment) Act 2017* (Qld) includes building work, but also includes other types of infrastructure construction that are not building work, including roadworks, powerlines, telecommunications apparatus, aircraft runways, docks and harbours, railways, inland waterways, pipelines, reservoirs, water mains, wells, sewers, industrial plant and installations for land drainage or coast protection.[59]

The provisions of Part 4A of the *Queensland Building and Construction Commission Act 1991* (Qld) apply to a building contract even if it was entered into outside Queensland or the Parties have chosen the governing law of the contract to be a jurisdiction other than Queensland (s 67E). The consequences are that, irrespective of the governing law of the contract, for building work carried out in Queensland, any provisions of the contract that are contrary to the requirements of the *Queensland Building and Construction Commission Act 1991* (Qld) are void to the extent of the inconsistency.

6.4.2 Formal requirements for a construction contract

The requirements for a valid contract in Australia are those of common law: the parties are legal persons who intend to create a legal relationship, an agreement constituted by offer and acceptance, supported by consideration (except for contracts executed under seal) with terms that are clear and certain.

Australian law recognises two forms of contracts: a simple contract and a contract under seal, sometimes referred to as a **specialty**. A simple contract does not need to be in writing but requires consideration to pass in exchange for a contractual promise. However, a contract under seal requires no consideration.

Construction contracts are classified as contracts for the provision of work and labour, and not for the sale of goods, and accordingly the State and Territory *Sale of Goods Acts* do not apply. Construction contracts are typically simple contracts, and there is no particular form required. With the exception of 'building contracts' in Queensland, a construction contract does not have to be in writing.

The other significant difference between a simple contract and a contract under seal is the limitation period within which an action for breach of contract can be commenced. The statutory provisions in each Australian jurisdiction prescribe that an action on a simple contract shall not be brought after the expiry of six years from the date on which the cause of action accrued.[60] For contracts under seal, the limitation periods are 12 years in New South Wales, Queensland, Tasmania, Western Australia and the ACT.[61] The period in Victoria and South Australia is 15 years.[62] The limitation period in the ACT may be extended to 15 years for latent damage to property and economic loss.[63]

59 See s 65.

60 *Limitation Act 1985* (ACT) s 13; *Limitation Act 1969* (NSW) s 16; *Limitation Act* (NT) s 12; *Limitations of Actions 1974* (Qld) s 10(3); *Limitation of Actions Act 1936* (SA) s 35(a); *Limitation Act 1974* (Tas) s 4(3); *Limitations of Actions Act 1958* (Vic) s 5(1)(a); *Limitation Act 1974* (WA) s 18.

61 *Limitation Act 1985* (ACT) s 11(1); *Limitation Act 1969* (NSW) s 14(1); *Limitation Act* (NT) s 12; *Limitations of Actions 1974* (Qld) s 10; *Limitation Act 1974* (Tas) s 4(1)(a); *Limitation Act 1974* (WA) s 13.

62 *Limitation of Actions Act 1936* (SA) s 34; *Limitations of Actions Act 1958* (Vic) s 5.

63 *Limitation Act 1985* (ACT) s 40(1).

These limitation periods are, however, subject to a limitation period of 10 years for 'building actions' after the date of issue of either the relevant occupancy permit or the certificate of final inspection of the building work in ACT, [64] New South Wales, [65] Northern Territory, [66] South Australia, [67] Tasmania[68] and Victoria.[69]

6.5 What Special Provisions in the Particular Conditions are necessary for consistency with applicable laws in Australia?

6.5.1 FIDIC General Conditions are incompatible or inconsistent with Australian governing law of the contract

If the Contract is for 'building work' in Queensland, the General Conditions should be reviewed to determine whether any Special Provision is required to comply with section 67G of the *Queensland Building and Construction Commission Act 1991* (Qld).

6.5.2 FIDIC General Conditions are incompatible or inconsistent with the law of the Site / Country

No Special Provisions in the Particular Conditions are necessary for consistency with applicable laws of the Site in Australia.

6.5.3 FIDIC General Conditions are incompatible or inconsistent with the relevant laws on dispute determination in Australia

No Special Provisions in the Particular Conditions are necessary for consistency with applicable laws on dispute determination in Australia.

6.6 What Special Provisions in the Particular Conditions are desirable for consistency with applicable laws in Australia?

6.6.1 Security of payment[70]

The various *Security of Payment Acts* in the States and Territories all set up a system of progress payments, rapid adjudication of payment disputes and contract reform. The first *Act* (NSW) included similar adjudication provisions to the *Housing Grants, Construction and Regeneration Act 1996* (UK), and formed the model upon which other Australian jurisdictions, to varying degrees, based their legislation. Unlike the UK *Act*, however, statutory adjudication in Australia is confined to payment disputes. Not only are there significant differences in detail between the individual Australian *Acts*, but there are also conceptual differences between the NT Act (**West Coast model**) and the Acts in the other jurisdictions (**East Coast model**).[71]

64 *Building Act 2004* (ACT) s 142.

65 *Environmental Planning and Assessment Act 1979* (NSW) s 6.20.

66 *Building Act* (NT) s 160.

67 *Development Act 1993* (SA) s 73.

68 *Building Act 2000* (Tas) s 327.

69 *Building Act 1993* (Vic) s 134.

70 Donald Charrett, 'Statutory Adjudication in Australia' in Lukas Klee *International Construction Contracts* (2nd edn, John Wiley & Sons 2018) 475–81.

71 The Australian Government appointed John Murray AM to carry out a review of Security of Payment Laws to identify legislative best practice, with a view to improving consistency in security of payment legislation and the level of protection afforded to construction industry subcontractors to ensure they obtain payment for work they have completed or for goods and services they have supplied. His report dated December 2017 made

The significant differences between the *Security of Payment Acts* and between the East Coast and West Coast models means that there is no 'Australian adjudication' as such. As space here does not permit further comparison of the differences between the various Acts, the following description refers to the operation of the *Building and Construction Industry Security of Payment Act 1999* (NSW) (***BCISPA***).

The *BCISPA* provides various statutory entitlements that operate in addition to (or in substitution for inconsistent) contractual provisions. Operation of the *BCISPA* is mandatory for any 'construction contract', covering both 'construction work' and 'related goods and services' as broadly defined. However, there are significant carve-outs for eg extraction of oil and gas or minerals and residential construction, with the consequence that it does not apply to a substantial part of construction work in NSW. The *BCISPA* provides an entitlement to progress payments, either in accordance with the provisions of the Contract, or at monthly intervals if the interval is not specified in the Contract.

The *BCISPA* fetters freedom of contract in several ways. Thus, 'pay when paid', or 'pay if paid' provisions in a contract are of no effect. Further, in the event that the agreed amount of a progress claim or the adjudicated amount is not paid, the claimant may stop working under the contract after giving two business days' notice. These provisions may not be contracted out of.

The *BCISPA* specifies a formal procedure that must be followed to recover progress payments, and details the consequences if payment is not made. In the event of a dispute over payment, the claimant can initiate an adjudication process that is intended to be speedy and cost-effective. Adjudication is carried out by an adjudicator who is formally accredited by an 'authorised nominating authority'. There is an expedited process for a claimant to obtain a debt judgment in court of a progress payment or the adjudicated amount of a progress payment.

It is important to note that the *BCISPA* is directed to maintaining cash flow in relation to progress payments and does not override other legal rights that either party has under the contract or the law. An adjudication determines the amount of a progress payment on account only and does not provide a final determination of the parties' legal rights. A respondent that is required to pay an adjudicated amount may therefore seek to recover that amount in subsequent court or arbitration proceedings, if the respondent can prove its legal entitlement pursuant to, eg defect rectification or liquidated damages for late performance. Nevertheless, in practice the adjudicated amount frequently becomes a final payment, as few payment disputes proceed to an ultimate determination of legal rights in arbitration or litigation.

As the statutory entitlements under the *BCISPA* are additional to the provisions of the relevant construction contract, certain formalities must be complied with to invoke its operation. Thus, a 'payment claim' must identify the construction work carried out or the relevant goods and services supplied, and the amount of the claim. A payment claim must be made within the time provided for in the contract, but no more than 12 months after the relevant work was carried out or the goods and services supplied. Only one payment claim may be made in respect of each 'reference date'.

---

a number of recommendations, including the use of a legislative model which is based on what is commonly known as the East Coast model of security of payment laws, most notably that existing in the State of NSW, and the establishment of a system of statutory trusts to apply throughout the contractual payment chain and to certain construction projects and monies. See J Murray AM, 'Review of Security of Payment Laws Building Trust and Harmony' (2017) *Australian Government* https://docs.jobs.gov.au/system/files/doc/other/review_of_security_of_payment_laws_-_final_report_published.pdf (accessed 26 August 2018).

The person from whom payment is claimed (the respondent) may respond by providing a 'payment schedule' detailing the amount the respondent proposes to pay and must specify the reasons for any difference between that amount and the amount claimed. If the respondent does not serve a payment schedule within the time provided by the contract, or a maximum of 10 business days, it becomes liable to pay the amount of the payment claim in full. In that event, the claimant may either recover the amount claimed as a debt in court or make application for adjudication.

Similarly, if the respondent does not pay the full amount in its payment schedule by the due date, the claimant may either recover the amount claimed as a debt in court or make application for adjudication. If the claimant seeks to recover the amount claimed in court, the respondent may not bring any cross claim or raise any defence in relation to matters arising under the construction contract. Amendments made to the *BCISPA* in 2013 mandate payment periods for progress payments, irrespective of the provisions of the contract.

Details of the prescriptive process for adjudication are beyond the scope of this book; for further details see Donald Charrett, 'Statutory Adjudication in Australia' in Lukas Klee, *International Construction Contracts.*[72]

The right to make a claim for progress payment pursuant to the relevant *Security of Payment Act* is a statutory right in addition to the rights to payment defined in the Contract. If the type of work in the Contract comes within the ambit of the relevant *Act*, the statutory rights cannot be contracted out of. Whilst those statutory rights are generally not inconsistent with the contractual rights to payment defined in the FIDIC General Conditions, it is desirable to add Special Provisions in the Particular Conditions to align the payment provisions in the Contract with the relevant *Security of Payment Act*. Competent advice should be sought as to the wording of the relevant Special Provisions appropriate for the specific jurisdiction and the Employer's preferences for the particular project.

6.6.2 Frustrated contracts

New South Wales, South Australia and Victoria have legislation that applies to frustrated contracts. If the governing law of the contract is one of these jurisdictions, clause 18 of the General Conditions should be reviewed to determine whether it is appropriate in the light of this legislation.

6.6.3 Contracting out of proportionate liability

Legislation for the proportionate liability of 'concurrent wrongdoers' is discussed in paragraph 6.10.2 below. This legislation provides that where a plaintiff has suffered loss due to the failure of more than one person to take reasonable care, the court may apportion liability between concurrent wrongdoers. If the Employer wishes to hold the Contractor wholly liable for all damages resulting from breach of contract, a Special Provision should be inserted to contract out of the relevant proportional liability legislation (except in Queensland where contracting out is prohibited). Referring all disputes to arbitration (as provided for in the FIDIC General Conditions) may achieve the same result.[73]

72 (2nd edn, John Wiley & Sons 2018) 475–81.

73 David Levin, 'Proportionate Liability in Arbitrations in Australia?' (2009) 25 *Building and Construction Law* 298. See also *Aquagenics Pty Ltd v Break O'Day Council (No 2)* [2009] TASSC 89.

6.7 Summary of applicable legislation for Australian governing law of the contract

	Australian Capital Territory	***New South Wales***	***Northern Territory***	***Queensland***	***South Australia***	***Tasmania***	***Victoria***	***Western Australia***
6.7.1 Entry into a construction contract								
Contracts generally	*Australian Consumer Law*[74]	*Australian Consumer Law*	*Australian Consumer Law*	*Australian Consumer Law*	*Australian Consumer Law*	*Australian Consumer Law*	*Australian Consumer Law*	*Australian Consumer Law*
Construction contracts				For building contracts: *Queensland Building and Construction Commission Act 1991* (Qld)				

74 The *Australian Consumer Law* comprises a schedule to the *Competition and Consumer Act 2010* (Cth), which is the harmonised re-enactment of the *Trade Practices Act 1974* (Cth).

6.7.2 *Termination of a construction contract*

Frustration		*Frustrated Contracts Act 1978* (NSW)			*Frustrated Contracts Act 1988* (SA)		*Australian Consumer Law and Fair Trading Act 2012* (Vic) Pt 3.2	
Bankruptcy, insolvency, liquidation	*Bankruptcy Act 1996* (Cth) *Cross Border Insolvency Act 2008* (Cth) *Corporations Act 2001* (Cth)	*Bankruptcy Act 1996* (Cth) *Cross Border Insolvency Act 2008* (Cth) *Corporations Act 2001* (Cth)	*Bankruptcy Act 1996* (Cth) *Cross Border Insolvency Act 2008* (Cth) *Corporations Act 2001* (Cth)	*Bankruptcy Act 1996* (Cth) *Cross Border Insolvency Act 2008* (Cth) *Corporations Act 2001* (Cth)	*Bankruptcy Act 1996* (Cth) *Cross Border Insolvency Act 2008* (Cth) *Corporations Act 2001* (Cth)	*Bankruptcy Act 1996* (Cth) *Cross Border Insolvency Act 2008* (Cth) *Corporations Act 2001* (Cth)	*Bankruptcy Act 1996* (Cth) *Cross Border Insolvency Act 2008* (Cth) *Corporations Act 2001* (Cth)	*Bankruptcy Act 1996* (Cth) *Cross Border Insolvency Act 2008* (Cth) *Corporations Act 2001* (Cth)
Guarantees under forms of Security (Tender Security, Demand Guarantee, Surety Bond, Advance Payment Guarantee, Retention Money Guarantee, Payment Guarantee by Employer)	*Civil Law (Property) Act 2006* (ACT) s 205	*Conveyancing Act 1919* (NSW) s 12 Assignment of debts and choses in action	*Statute of Frauds 1677* s 4	*Property Law Act 1974* (Qld) s 56 Guarantees to be in writing	*Law of Property Act 1936* (SA) s 15 Assignment of debts and choses in action	*Conveyancing and Law of Property Act 1884* (Tas) s 86 Legal assignments of things in action *Mercantile Law Act 1935* (Tas)	*Property Law Act 1958* (Vic) s 134 Legal assignment of things in action *Instruments Act 1958* (Vic) s 126	*Property Law Act 1969* (WA) s 20

6.7.3 *Dispute resolution*

Limitation periods	*Limitation Act 1985* (ACT) s 11; s 13; s 40 *Building Act 2004* (ACT) s 142	*Limitation Act 1969* (NSW) s 14(1); s 16 *Environmental Planning and Assessment Act 1979* (NSW) s 6.20	*Limitation Act* (NT) s 12 *Building Act* (NT) s 160	*Limitations of Actions 1974* (Qld) s 10	*Limitation of Actions Act 1936* (SA) s 34; s 35 *Development Act 1993* (SA) s 73	*Limitation Act 1974* (Tas) s 4 *Building Act 2000* (Tas) s 327	*Limitations of Actions Act 1958* (Vic) s 5 *Building Act 1993* (Vic) s 134	*Limitation Act 1974* (WA) s 13; s 38

	Australian Capital Territory	***New South Wales***	***Northern Territory***	***Queensland***	***South Australia***	***Tasmania***	***Victoria***	***Western Australia***
Liability	*Civil Law (Wrongs) Act 2002* (ACT) Ch 7A Proportionate liability	*Civil Liability Act 2002* (NSW) Pt 4 Proportionate liability	*Proportionate Liability Act* (NT)	*Civil Liability Act 2003* (Qld) Ch 2 Pt 2 Proportionate liability	*Law Reform (Contributory Negligence and Apportionment of Liability) 2001* (SA) Pt 3 Apportionable liability *Development Act 1993* (SA) s 72 Negation of joint and several liability in certain cases	*Civil Liability Act 2002* (Tas) Pt 9A Proportionate liability	*Wrongs Act 1958* (Vic) Pt IVAA Proportionate liability	*Civil Liability Act 2002* (WA) Pt 1F Proportionate liability
Adjudication	*Building and Construction Industry (Security of Payment Act) 2009* (ACT)	*Building and Construction Industry Security of Payment Act 1999* (NSW)	*Construction Contracts (Security of Payments) Act* (NT)	*Building Industry Fairness (Security of Payment) Act 2017* (Qld)	*Building and Construction Industry Security of Payment Act 2009* (SA)	*Building and Construction Industry Security of Payment Act 2009* (Tas)	*Building and Construction Industry Security of Payment Act 2002* (Vic)	*Building and Construction Industry (Security of Payment) Act 2021* (WA)
Arbitration	*International Arbitration Act 1974* (Cth) *Commercial Arbitration Act 2017* (ACT)	*International Arbitration Act 1974* (Cth) *Commercial Arbitration Act 2010* (NSW)	*International Arbitration Act 1974* (Cth) *Commercial Arbitration (National Uniform Legislation) Act 2011* (NT)	*International Arbitration Act 1974* (Cth) *Commercial Arbitration Act 2013* (Qld)	*International Arbitration Act 1974* (Cth) *Commercial Arbitration Act 2011* (SA)	*International Arbitration Act 1974* (Cth) *Commercial Arbitration Act 2011* (Tas)	*International Arbitration Act 1974* (Cth) *Commercial Arbitration Act 2011* (Vic)	*International Arbitration Act 1974* (Cth) *Commercial Arbitration Act 2012* (WA)

6.8 Summary of applicable legislation if the Site/Country is in Australia

	Australian Capital Territory	**New South Wales**	**Northern Territory**	**Queensland**	**South Australia**	**Tasmania**	**Victoria**	**Western Australia**
6.8.1 Operation of a construction contract								
Registration and administration of professionals – engineers, architects, quantity surveyors, certifiers, building surveyors, surveyors	*Architects Act 2004* (ACT) *Building Act 2004* (ACT) (Div 3.2) *Construction Occupations (Licensing) Act 2004* (ACT) *Surveyors Act 2007* (ACT)	*Architects Act 2003* (NSW) *Building Professionals Act 2005* (NSW) *Professional Standards Act 1994* (NSW) *Surveying and Spatial Information Act 2002* (NSW) *Design and Building Practitioners Act 2020* (NSW) *Building and Development Certifiers Act 2018* (NSW)	*Architects Act* (NT) *Professional Standards Act* (NT) *Licenced Surveyors Act* (NT) *Building Act 1993*	*Architects Act 2002* (Qld) *Professional Engineers Act 2002* (Qld)[75] *Professional Standards Act 2004* (Qld) *Surveyors Act 2003* (Qld)	*Architectural Practice Act 2009* (SA) *Professional Standards Act 2004* (SA) *Surveying Act 1992* (SA)	*Architects Act 1929* (Tas) *Professional Standards Act 2005* (Tas) *Surveyors Act 2002* (Tas) [Registration *Occupational Licencing Act 2005* (Tas)]	*Architects Act 1991* (Vic) *Building Act 1993* (Vic) Pt 11 *Professional Engineers Professional Engineers Registration Act 2019* (Vic) *Professional Standards Act 2003* (Vic) *Surveying Act 2004* (Vic)	*Architects Act 2004* (WA) *Professional Standards Act 1997* (WA) *Licenced Surveyors Act 1909* (WA) [Regulations to be amended to require registration of Engineers in the building sector (May 2020)]
Registration/ licencing of contractors and subcontractors	*Construction Occupations (Licensing) Act 2004* (ACT)		*Electrical Workers and Contractors Act* (NT) *Plumbers and Drainers Licensing Act* (NT)	*Queensland Building and Construction Commission Act 1991* (Qld) Pt 3 *Plumbing and Drainage Act 2002* (Qld)	*Building Work Contractors Act 1995* (SA)	*Occupational Licensing Act 2005* (Tas)	*Building Act 1993* (Vic) Pt 11	*Builders Registration Act 1939* (WA)

75 Queensland has had statutory registration of engineers since 1929.

(*Continued*)

	Australian Capital Territory	**New South Wales**	**Northern Territory**	**Queensland**	**South Australia**	**Tasmania**	**Victoria**	**Western Australia**
Use of liens / Assignment of debts	*Civil Law (Property) Act 2006* (ACT) s 205	*Contractors' Debts Act 1997* (NSW) *Conveyancing Act 1919* (NSW) s 12	*Statute of Frauds 1677 s 4*	*Building Industry Fairness (Security of Payment) Act 2017* (Qld) *Property Law Act 1974* (Qld) s 56	*Workers Liens Act 1893* (SA) *Law of Property Act 1936* (SA) s 15	*Conveyancing and Law of Property Act 1884* (Tas) s 86 *Mercantile Law Act 1935* (Tas)	*Property Law Act 1958* (Vic) s 134	*Property Law Act 1969* (WA) s 20
Labour	*Fair Work Act 2009* (Cth)	*Fair Work Act 2009* (Cth) *Industrial Relations Act 1996* (NSW)	*Fair Work Act 2009* (Cth)	*Fair Work Act 2009* (Cth)	*Fair Work Act 2009* (Cth) *Fair Work Act 1994* (SA)	*Fair Work Act 2009* (Cth) *Industrial Relations Act 1984* (Tas)	*Fair Work Act 2009* (Cth)	*Fair Work Act 2009* (Cth) *Industrial Relations Act 1979* (WA)
Design / Moral Rights	*Work Health and Safety Act 2011* (ACT) *Designs Act 2003* (Cth) [76] *Copyright Act 1968* (Cth) Pt IX	*Work Health and Safety Act 2011* (NSW) *Designs Act 2003* (Cth) *Copyright Act 1968* (Cth) Pt IX	*Work Health and Safety (National Uniform Legislation) Act* (NT) *Designs Act 2003* (Cth) *Copyright Act 1968* (Cth) Pt IX	*Work Health and Safety Act 2011* (Qld) *Designs Act 2003* (Cth) *Copyright Act 1968* (Cth) Pt IX	*Work Health and Safety Act 2012* (SA) *Designs Act 2003* (Cth) *Copyright Act 1968* (Cth) Pt IX	*Work Health and Safety Act 2012* (Tas) *Designs Act 2003* (Cth) *Copyright Act 1968* (Cth) Pt IX	*Designs Act 2003* (Cth) *Copyright Act 1968* (Cth) Pt IX	*Designs Act 2003* (Cth) *Copyright Act 1968* (Cth) Pt IX
Copyright	*Copyright Act 1968* (Cth)	*Copyright Act 1968* (Cth)	*Copyright Act 1968* (Cth)	*Copyright Act 1968* (Cth)	*Copyright Act 1968* (Cth)	*Copyright Act 1968* (Cth)	*Copyright Act 1968* (Cth)	*Copyright Act 1968* (Cth)

76 This legislation may not apply to design of construction Works as its scope is the registered design of (industrial) products.

The product being produced from the Works	*Dangerous Substances Act 2004* (ACT)	*Environmentally Hazardous Chemicals Act 1985* (NSW)	*Dangerous Goods Act* (NT) *National Electricity (Northern Territory) (National Uniform Legislation) Act* (NT)		*Dangerous Substances Act 1979* (SA)	*Electricity Supply Industry Act 1995* (Tas) *Water and Sewerage Industry Act 2008* (Tas)	*Dangerous Goods Act 1985* (Vic)	*Dangerous Goods Safety 2004* (WA) *Rail Safety National Law (WA) Act 2015* (WA) *Water Services Act 2012* (WA)
First nation people's land rights	*Native Title Act 1993* (Cth)	*Native Title Act 1993* (Cth)	*Native Title Act 1993* (Cth)	*Native Title Act 1993* (Cth)	*Native Title Act 1993* (Cth)	*Native Title Act 1993* (Cth)	*Native Title Act 1993* (Cth)	*Native Title Act 1993* (Cth)
Planning	*Planning and Development Act 2007* (ACT)	*Environmental Planning and Assessment Act 1979* (NSW)	*Planning Act* (NT)	*Planning Act 2006* (Qld)	*Planning, Development and Infrastructure Act 2016* (SA)	*Land Use Planning and Approvals Act 1993* (Tas)	*Planning and Environment Act 1987* (Vic)	*Planning and Development Act 2005* (WA)
Work affecting adjacent property to the Site		*Access to Neighbouring Land Act 2000* (NSW) *Real Property Act 1900* (NSW) s 46A	*Law of Property Act* (NT) Pt 9 Div 2, Div 3		*Real Property Act 1886* (SA) Pt 8	*Conveyancing and Law of Property Act 1884* (Tas) Pt VIA *Land Titles Act 1980* (Tas) Pt 6 Div 9		
Heritage	*Aboriginal and Torres Strait Islander Heritage Protection Act 1984* (Cth) *Heritage Act 2004* (ACT)	*Aboriginal and Torres Strait Islander Heritage Protection Act 1984* (Cth) *Heritage Act 1977* (NSW)	*Aboriginal and Torres Strait Islander Heritage Protection Act 1984* (Cth) *Heritage Act* (NT)	*Aboriginal and Torres Strait Islander Heritage Protection Act 1984* (Cth) *Queensland Heritage Act 1992* (Qld)	*Aboriginal and Torres Strait Islander Heritage Protection Act 1984* (Cth) *Heritage Places Act 1993* (SA)	*Aboriginal and Torres Strait Islander Heritage Protection Act 1984* (Cth) *Historic Cultural Heritage Act 1995* (Tas)	*Aboriginal and Torres Strait Islander Heritage Protection Act 1984* (Cth) *Heritage Act 2017* (Vic)	*Aboriginal and Torres Strait Islander Heritage Protection Act 1984* (Cth) *Heritage of Western Australia Act 1990* (WA)

(*Continued*)

	Australian Capital Territory	New South Wales	Northern Territory	Queensland	South Australia	Tasmania	Victoria	Western Australia
Environment	*Environmental Protection and Biodiversity Conservation Act 1999* (Cth) *Environment Protection Act 1997* (ACT)	*Environmental Protection and Biodiversity Conservation Act 1999* (Cth) *Protection of the Environment Operations Act 1997* (NSW)	*Environmental Protection and Biodiversity Conservation Act 1999* (Cth) *Environmental Assessment Act* (NT)	*Environmental Protection and Biodiversity Conservation Act 1999* (Cth) *Environmental Protection Act 1994* (Qld)	*Environmental Protection and Biodiversity Conservation Act 1999* (Cth) *Environmental Protection Act 1993* (SA)	*Environmental Protection and Biodiversity Conservation Act 1999* (Cth) *Environmental Management and Pollution Control Act 1994* (Tas)	*Environmental Protection and Biodiversity Conservation Act 1999* (Cth) *Environmental Protection Act 1970* (Vic)This	*Environmental Protection and Biodiversity Conservation Act 1999* (Cth) *Environment Protection 1986* (WA)
Building and construction permits, Execution of construction work, Standard of construction work	*Building Act 2004* (ACT) *Water and Sewerage Act 2000* (ACT) *National Construction Code (Building Code of Australia 2019)*	*Environmental Planning and Assessment Act 1979* (NSW) *Plumbing and Drainage Act 2011* (NSW) *National Construction Code (Building Code of Australia 2019)*	*Building Act* (NT) *National Construction Code (Building Code of Australia 2019)*	*Building Act 1975* (Qld) *Plumbing and Drainage Act 2002* (Qld) *National Construction Code (Building Code of Australia 2019)*	*Development Act 1993* (SA) *National Construction Code (Building Code of Australia 2019)*	*Building Act 2000* (Tas) *National Construction Code (Building Code of Australia 2019)*	*Building Act 1993* (Vic) *National Construction Code (Building Code of Australia 2019)*	*Building Act 2011* (WA) *National Construction Code (Building Code of Australia 2019)*
Health and safety	*Work Health and Safety Act 2011* (ACT) *Electricity Safety Act 1971* (ACT) *Gas Safety Act 2000* (ACT)	*Work Health and Safety Act 2011* (NSW) *Work Health and Safety Act (Mines and Petroleum Sites) 2013* (NSW) *Gas and Electricity (Consumer Safety) Act 2017* (NSW) *Electricity Supply Act 1995* (NSW) *Explosives Act 2003* (NSW)	*Work Health and Safety (National Uniform Legislation) Act* (NT)	*Work Health and Safety Act 2011* (Qld) *Electrical Safety Act 2002* (Qld) *Explosives Act 1999* (Qld)	*Work Health and Safety Act 2012* (SA) *Electricity Act 1996* (SA) *Explosives Act 1936* (SA)	*Work Health and Safety Act 2012* (Tas) *Explosives Act 2012* (Tas)	*Occupational Health and Safety Act 2004* (Vic) *Electrical Safety Act 1998* (Vic) *Gas Safety Act 1997* (Vic) *Radiation Safety Act 1975* (WA)	*Occupational Safety and Health Act 1984* (WA)

Employer's sale of Contractor's Equipment, surplus material, wreckage and Temporary Works	*Personal Properties Security Act 2009* (Cth)	*Personal Properties Security Act 2009* (Cth)	*Personal Properties Security Act 2009* (Cth)	*Personal Properties Security Act 2009* (Cth)	*Personal Properties Security Act 2009* (Cth)	*Personal Properties Security Act 2009* (Cth)	*Personal Properties Security Act 2009* (Cth)	*Personal Properties Security Act 2009* (Cth)
Insurance	*Workers Compensation Act 1951* (ACT)	*Workers Compensation Act 1987* (NSW)	*Return to Work Act* (NT)	*Workers Compensation and Rehabilitation Act 2003* (Qld)	*Return to Work Act 2014* (SA)	*Workers Rehabilitation and Compensation Act 1988* (Tas)	*Workers Compensation Act 1958* (Vic)	*Workers Compensation and Injury Management Act 1981* (WA)
Statutory rights that coexist with contractual rights	*Australian Consumer Law* *Fair Trading (Australian Consumer Law) Act 1992* (ACT) *Building and Construction Industry (Security of Payment Act) 2009* (ACT) Pt 3	*Australian Consumer Law* *Building and Construction Industry Security of Payment Act 1999* (NSW) Pt 2	*Australian Consumer Law* *Construction Contracts (Security of Payments) Act* (NT) Pt 2	*Australian Consumer Law* *Building Industry Fairness (Security of Payment) Act 2017* (Qld)	*Australian Consumer Law* *Building and Construction Industry Security of Payment Act 2009* (SA) Pt 2	*Australian Consumer Law* *Building and Construction Industry Security of Payment Act 2009* (Tas) Pt 3	*Australian Consumer Law* *Building and Construction Industry Security of Payment Act 2002* (Vic) Pt 2	*Australian Consumer Law* *Building and Construction Industry (Security of Payment) Act 2021* (WA)
Liability for defective work	*Building Act 2004* (ACT) (ss140–142) *Civil Law (Wrongs) Act 2002* (ACT) (Ch 7A)	*Environmental Planning and Assessment Act 1979* (NSW) Pt 6 Div 6.6 *Civil Liability Act 2002* (NSW) Pt 4	*Proportionate Liability Act* (NT)	*Queensland Building and Construction Commission Act 1991* (Qld) Pt 6 *Civil Liability Act 2003* (Qld) Ch 2 Pt 2	*Development Act 1993* (SA)Pt 6 Div 7 *Law Reform (Contributory Negligence and Apportionment of Liability) 2001* (SA) Pt 3	*Building Act 2000* (Tas) Pt 15 *Civil Liability Act 2002* (Tas) Pt 9A	*Building Act 1993* (Vic) Pt 7; Pt 9 *Wrongs Act 1958* (Vic) Pt IVAA	*Civil Liability Act 2002* (WA) Pt 11
Liability for nuisance				*Environmental Protection Act 1994* (Qld) s 15; s 440			*Water Act 1989* (Vic) s 16	

(Continued)

	Australian Capital Territory	New South Wales	Northern Territory	Queensland	South Australia	Tasmania	Victoria	Western Australia
Construction for Government Employer Commonwealth: *Building Code 2013*[77]	*Government Procurement Act 2001* (ACT) *Government Procurement Regulation 2007* (ACT) Government Procurement[78]	NSW Building and Construction Guidelines[79]	Northern Territory Procurement Code 2011[80] NPWC Conditions of Contract and Tendering[81]	Building Construction and Maintenance[82]	Construction Procurement Policy Project Implementation Process 2015[83]	Buying for Government[84]	Instructions for Public Construction in Victoria (mandatory)[85] Guidance for Public Construction in Victoria (non-mandatory)[86]	Procurement Practice Guide[87]
Other issues							*Crimes Act 1958* (Vic) S254 Destruction of evidence; s 255 corporate criminal responsibility for offence against s 254	

77 https://www.abcc.gov.au/building-code (accessed 23 February 2021).

78 https://www.procurement.act.gov.au/policy-and-resources/factsheets-and-policies (accessed 23 February 2021).

79 https://www.industrialrelations.nsw.gov.au/industries/key-industries-in-nsw/building-and-construction/ (accessed 23 February 2021).

80 https://nt.gov.au/industry/government/what-you-need-to-know-about-procurement/procurement-code (accessed 23 February 2021).

81 https://nt.gov.au/industry/government/what-you-need-to-know-about-procurement/terms-and-conditions/conditions-contract/construction/national-public-works-council (accessed 23 February 2021)

82 https://www.forgov.qld.gov.au/building-construction-maintenance (accessed 23 February 2021).

83 https://dpc.sa.gov.au/documents/rendition/B17988 (accessed 23 February 2021).

84 https://www.purchasing.tas.gov.au/buying-for-government/resource-library/publications (accessed 23 February 2021).

85 https://www.dtf.vic.gov.au/public-construction-policy-and-resources/ministerial-directions-and-instructions-public-construction-procurement (accessed 23 February 2021).

86 https://www.dtf.vic.gov.au/practitioners-toolkit/practitioners-toolkit-guidance-public-construction-procurement (accessed 23 February 2021).

87 http://www.finance.wa.gov.au/cms/uploadedFiles/Government_Procurement/Guidelines_and_templates/Goods_and_service_procurement_practice_guide.pdf (accessed 23 February 2021).

6.8.2 Termination of a construction contract

Bankruptcy, insolvency, liquidation	*Bankruptcy Act 1996* (Cth)	*Bankruptcy Act 1996* (Cth)	*Bankruptcy Act 1996* (Cth)	*Bankruptcy Act 1996* (Cth)	*Bankruptcy Act 1996* (Cth)	*Bankruptcy Act 1996* (Cth)	*Bankruptcy Act 1996* (Cth)	*Bankruptcy Act 1996* (Cth)
Stay on enforcing rights against an entity that has publicly announced it will be making an application to avoid being wound up in insolvency	ss415D – 415G, 434J *Corporations Act 2001* (Cth)	ss415D – 415G, 434J *Corporations Act 2001* (Cth)	ss415D – 415G, 434J *Corporations Act 2001* (Cth)	ss415D – 415G, 434J *Corporations Act 2001* (Cth)	ss415D – 415G, 434J *Corporations Act 2001* (Cth)	ss415D – 415G, 434J *Corporations Act 2001* (Cth)	ss415D – 415G, 434J *Corporations Act 2001* (Cth)	ss415D – 415G, 434J *Corporations Act 2001* (Cth)

6.8.3 Dispute resolution

Dispute before a local board / Adjudication	*Building and Construction Industry (Security of Payment Act) 2009* (ACT)	*Building and Construction Industry Security of Payment Act 1999* (NSW)	*Construction Contracts (Security of Payments) Act* (NT)	*Building Industry Fairness (Security of Payment) Act 2017* (Qld)	*Payment Act 2009* (SA)	*Building and Construction Industry Security of Payment Act 2009* (Tas)	*Building and Construction Industry Security of Payment Act 2002* (Vic)	*Building and Construction Industry (Security of Payment) Act 2021* (WA)
Limitation periods	*Limitation Act 1985* (ACT) s 11; s 13; s 40 *Building Act 2004* (ACT) s 142	*Limitation Act 1969* (NSW) s 14(1); s 16 *Environmental Planning and Assessment Act 1979* (NSW) s 6.20	*Limitation Act* (NT) s 12 *Building Act* (NT) s 160	*Limitations of Actions 1974* (Qld) s 10	*Limitation of Actions Act 1936* (SA) s 34; s 35 *Development Act 1993* (SA) s 73	*Limitation Act 1974* (Tas) s 4 *Building Act 2000* (Tas) s 327	*Limitations of Actions Act 1958* (Vic) s 5 *Building Act 1993* (Vic) s 134	*Limitation Act 1974* (WA) s 13; s 38

6.9 Summary of applicable legislation if the 'seat' of the dispute determination is in Australia

	Australian Capital Territory	**New South Wales**	**Northern Territory**	**Queensland**	**South Australia**	**Tasmania**	**Victoria**	**Western Australia**
Limitation periods	*Limitation Act 1985* (ACT) s 11; s 13; s 40 *Building Act 2004* (ACT) s 142	*Limitation Act 1969* (NSW) s 14(1); s 16 *Environmental Planning and Assessment Act 1979* (NSW) s 6.20	*Limitation Act* (NT) s 12 *Building Act* (NT) s 160	*Limitations of Actions 1974* (Qld) s 10	*Limitation of Actions Act 1936* (SA) s 34; s 35 *Development Act 1993* (SA) s 73	*Limitation Act 1974* (Tas) s 4 *Building Act 2000* (Tas) s 327	*Limitations of Actions Act 1958* (Vic) s 5 *Building Act 1993* (Vic) s 134	*Limitation Act 1974* (WA) s 13; s 38
Adjudication	*Building and Construction Industry (Security of Payment Act) 2009* (ACT)	*Building and Construction Industry Security of Payment Act 1999* (NSW)	*Construction Contracts (Security of Payments) Act* (NT)	*Building Industry Fairness (Security of Payment) Act 2017* (Qld)	*Payment Act 2009* (SA)	*Building and Construction Industry Security of Payment Act 2009* (Tas)	*Building and Construction Industry Security of Payment Act 2002* (Vic)	*Building and Construction Industry (Security of Payment) Act 2021* (WA)
Arbitration	*International Arbitration Act 1974* (Cth) *Commercial Arbitration Act 2017* (ACT)	*International Arbitration Act 1974* (Cth)	*International Arbitration Act 1974* (Cth)	*International Arbitration Act 1974* (Cth)	*International Arbitration Act 1974* (Cth)	*International Arbitration Act 1974* (Cth)	*International Arbitration Act 1974* (Cth)	*International Arbitration Act 1974* (Cth)

6.10 Issues that a court or arbitrator may construe differently to that expected from the words of the contract, because of local law or custom

6.10.1 Misleading or deceptive conduct[88]

Section 18 of the *Australian Consumer Law* (*ACL*) states simply and broadly: 'A person shall not, in trade or commerce, engage in conduct that is misleading or deceptive or is likely to mislead or deceive'.[89] The use of 'person' extends its reach to individuals and unincorporated associations as well as corporations.

This is a comprehensive provision of wide impact, designed to do no less than change behaviour in the business community. The prohibition on misleading or deceptive conduct is not confined to a dispute involving a 'consumer' as defined in the *ACL*, and applies where a person (which, for these purposes, might be a sole trading subcontractor or a multinational company) alleges it has suffered loss through misleading or deceptive conduct. An intention to mislead or deceive is not necessary for a contravention of the provision, and a firm or individual which acts honestly and reasonably and takes reasonable care may nevertheless engage in misleading or deceptive conduct in breach of the *ACL*.

The provision does not of itself create liability for misleading or deceptive conduct, but establishes a norm of conduct, breach of which has the consequences provided for in Chapter 4 – offences and Part 5 – enforcement and remedies of the *ACL*. It should be noted that, although the provision does not adopt the language of the common law, it creates a statutory cause of action which a party can sue on in addition to other causes of action such as breach of contract or negligence in tort.

Warranties contained in contracts are 'conduct' within the ambit of the *ACL* and will breach the prohibition if they are false or misleading.[90] Further, silence may also be 'conduct', and therefore constitute misleading or deceptive conduct, where there is a duty to reveal relevant facts, [91] or where in all the relevant circumstances, it constitutes misleading or deceptive conduct.[92]

Decisions in case law have developed to the stage where section 18 applies across the spectrum of conduct from that directed to the public at large to private negotiations between two parties.[93] An expression of expert opinion could constitute misleading or deceptive conduct if it was not honestly held on rational grounds involving an application of relevant expertise.[94]

The strong policy underpinnings of the prohibition on misleading and deceptive conduct mean that the parties' freedom to contract out of it, or to modify the statutory liabilities flowing from such conduct, are severely curtailed. This not only impacts the significance of behaviour prior to entering into a contract, it also limits the effect of certain types of contract clauses. For example, exemption clauses in contracts may not

88 Donald Charrett and Matthew Bell, 'Statutory intervention into the common construction law of Australia – progress or regress?' (2011) 137 *Australian Construction Law Newsletter* 6; (2012) *Journal of the Canadian College of Construction Lawyers* 11.

89 Previously s 52 of the *Trade Practices Act 1974* (Cth).

90 *Accounting Systems 2000 (Developments) Pty Ltd v CCH Australia Ltd* (1993) 42 FCR 470.

91 *Henjo Investments Pty Ltd v Collins Marrickville Pty Ltd (No 1)* (1988) 39 FCR 546.

92 *Demagogue Pty Ltd v Ramensky* (1992) 39 FCR 31.

93 Russell V Miller, *Miller's Australian Competition and Consumer Law Annotated* (33rd edn, Thomson Reuters 2011) 491.

94 *Bateman v Slatyer* (1987) 71 ALR 553, 559.

operate so as to negate the effects of misleading or deceptive conduct. As Sheppard J observed:

> [T]he remedy conferred by s 52 of the *Trade Practices Act* will not be lost whatever the parties may provide in their agreement. If a vendor of goods has engaged in misleading or deceptive conduct, the law makes that person accountable for loss and damage suffered as a result of the unlawful conduct. That conduct will usually have been committed, as in this case, prior to the signing of any contract. If, as a result of the conduct, a person is induced to enter into a contract and suffers loss, an action to recover it lies. The terms of the contract are irrelevant.[95]

The same principle may apply to a clause in a contract in which one party warrants that it has not relied on any statements by the other party to enter into the contract: such an exclusion clause cannot operate as a defence to a claim for damages if there has been misleading or deceptive conduct in contravention of the *ACL*.[96] There have been many and varied attempts to draft around the prohibition over the past 45 years. However, whether the relevant mechanism is an 'entire agreement' clause, disclaimer or acknowledgement (or a combination of these), the only effective counter to the prohibition is if the relevant conduct could not, in all circumstances, be characterised as misleading or deceptive, or the claimant did not reasonably rely upon the conduct.

The intrusion of the misleading or deceptive conduct provisions of the *ACL* into freedom of contract was aptly summed up by Gummow J in respect of a contract of sale:

> [I]t is well to bear in mind that whilst contractual rights subsisted between the parties their relationship is not governed simply by the general law as to vendor and purchaser. The legislation regulates the existence and exercise of what would otherwise be the rights at general law and, in addition, itself creates new rights and remedies.[97]

The remedies provided for misleading or deceptive conduct in the *ACL* include compensation for damages caused by the misleading conduct, as broad -ranging orders:

- Declaring the whole or part of a contract void from the beginning
- Varying contracts or arrangements
- Refusing to enforce a contract
- Directing a person who engaged in contravening conduct to refund money or return property
- For the payment of compensation
- To undertake repairs or supply parts
- To provide specified services, or
- To terminate leases and mortgages or require land to be transferred.

6.10.2 Proportionate liability[98]

Where a party has breached the contract, the normal position is that the innocent party may recover damages caused by the breach of contract from the contract breaker.

95 *Clark Equipment Australia Ltd v Covcat Pty Ltd* (1987) 71 ALR 367, 371.
96 *Waltip Pty Ltd v Capalaba Park Shopping Centre Pty Ltd* (1989) ATPR paras 40-975, 50-661.
97 *Demagogue Pty Ltd v Ramensky* (1992) 39 FCR 31, 37.
98 Philip Loots and Donald Charrett, *Practical Guide to Engineering and Construction Contracts* (CCH 2009) 64–66.

Such damages are calculated as the amount required to put the innocent party in the position it would have been in if the contract had not been breached. The common law position in respect of damages for breach of contract in Australia follows the well-known English case of *Hadley v Baxendale*.[99]

In situations where a person has suffered loss caused by the actions of more than one person, the traditional common law position has been that a plaintiff can choose to act against one or more of the wrongdoers and execute judgment for the entire amount of the damages against any one of the defendants found to be jointly and severally liable. For example, in a design and construct contract where the design was negligently prepared by the Contractor's subcontractor resulting in loss to the Employer, the Employer plaintiff could seek to recover all of the damages from the Contractor's breach of contract, notwithstanding that the Employer may also have a cause of action against the negligent designer.

This principle of joint and several liability can result in a person being legally liable for 100 per cent of the damages, even though that person's causal contribution to the damage was very minor. One of the consequences of joint and several liability in respect of building actions was that the legal burden of paying damages for defective building work was suffered disproportionately by those parties with insurance (because these were the parties a plaintiff elected to sue).

However, in circumstances where a plaintiff has suffered loss due to a failure of more than one person to take reasonable care (concurrent wrongdoers), the common law position has been changed by proportionate liability legislation. Since 1993, six Australian jurisdictions endeavoured to lower the insurance burden by legislating for 'proportionate liability' in respect of 'building actions'.[100]

The concept of proportionate liability involves the apportionment by the court of liability between defendants or third parties for a plaintiff's loss or damage, which reflects the responsibility for that loss or damage. Following the 'insurance crisis' after the collapse of HIH in 2002, all Australian jurisdictions widened the scope of proportionate liability more generally to encompass claims for damages for economic loss or damage to property arising from a failure to take reasonable care, and for breaches of the *Trade Practices Act* (now the *Australian Consumer* Law) and *Fair Trading Acts*.[101] With the exception of South Australia, [102] the specific proportionate liability legislation in respect of building actions was subsumed by the more general legislation. Proportionate liability does not apply to claims involving fraud or personal injury, nor does it affect the operation of contributory negligence, agency or vicarious liability.

A defendant to proceedings in relation to a building or construction dispute may plead the defence of proportionate liability in order to minimise the amount of damages it

99 (1854) 9 Ex 341.

100 Donald Charrett and Matthew Bell, 'Statutory intervention into the common construction law of Australia – progress or regress?' (2011) 137 *Australian Construction Law Newsletter* 6, 16; (2012) *Journal of the Canadian College of Construction Lawyers* 11, 32.

101 *Wrongs Act 1958* (Vic) Pt IVAA Proportionate liability; *Civil Liability Act 2002* (NSW) Pt 4 Proportionate liability; *Civil Liability Act 2003* (Qld) Ch 2 Pt 2 Proportionate liability; *Law Reform (Contributory Negligence And Apportionment of Liability) Act 2001* (SA) Pt 3 Apportionable liability; *Civil Liability Act 2002* (WA) Pt 1F Proportionate liability; *Civil Liability Act 2002* (Tas) Pt 9A Proportionate liability; *Civil Law (Wrongs) Act 2002* (ACT) Ch 7A; *Proportionate Liability Act 2005* (NT).

102 *Development Act 1993* (SA) Division 7.

may be liable for. In order to successfully invoke the defence of proportionate liability, the following elements must be present and proved:

(a) There is a claim for damages for economic loss or damage to property caused by either:

  (i) a failure to take reasonable care – whether in tort, contract, under statute or otherwise; or
  (ii) misleading or deceptive conduct in contravention of the *Australian Consumer Law*.

(b) There is a 'concurrent wrongdoer' – that is a person who is one of two or more persons whose acts or omissions caused (independently of each other or jointly) the loss or damage suffered by the plaintiff.

Whilst there are some differences between the proportionate liability legislation enacted by the States, Territories and the Commonwealth, the legislation in Victoria is unique in Australia. In Victoria, proportionate liability legislation differs from other jurisdictions in the following manner:

- When determining liability, the court will not consider the liability of wrongdoers who are not parties to the proceeding.[103]
- There is no obligation on a defendant to inform the plaintiff of the identity of other concurrent wrongdoers; however, unless it joins those other concurrent wrongdoers to the proceeding, it will not derive any benefit from the proportionate liability legislation.

Since the court will not assign liability to a non-party to an action in Victoria, it is in the interests of a defendant to join other concurrent wrongdoers to the action, even over the objections of the plaintiff. In contrast, in other jurisdictions in Australia, proportionate liability legislation shifts the decisions of joinder to the plaintiff because the court can consider the liability of non-parties. It is in the interests of the plaintiff in those jurisdictions to join all likely concurrent wrongdoers to ensure one proceeding, minimise cost and ensure the fullest possible recovery of damages.

A plaintiff to proceedings in Victoria should therefore be aware that a defendant may seek to utilise the statutory provisions for proportionate liability and join any other wrongdoers to the proceeding, in order for the court to apportion liability among a greater number of parties. This may pose some difficulty for the plaintiff in recovering damages, as there may be a number of judgment debtors against whom the judgment will need to be enforced.

The application of proportionate liability legislation in complex construction disputes can introduce substantial additional complexity in the proceedings and make an out of court settlement much more difficult to achieve. Because of this complexity, and the significant differences between legislation in different jurisdictions, a plaintiff should be aware of the relevant proportionate liability legislation that applies in the particular jurisdiction which governs the dispute. The relevant legislation in NSW, [104]

103 *Wrongs Act 1958* (Vic) s 24AI(3).
104 *Civil Liability Act 2002* (NSW) s 3A(2).

Western Australia[105] and Tasmania[106] expressly permit parties to exclude, modify or restrict the operation of proportionate liability. The Queensland legislation specifically prohibits contracting out of its provisions.[107] There is no express provision, either way, as to contracting out of the proportionate liability legislation in the Australian Capital Territory, the Northern Territory, South Australia or Victoria, nor in respect of the Commonwealth provisions contained in the *Australian Consumer Law*.

As noted in paragraph 6.6.3 above, in jurisdictions other than Queensland, an Employer may consider it appropriate to include in the Contract a provision to contract out of the application of the proportionate liability legislation. Further, although the issue has not been decided by a superior court, there are good arguments that in all States and Territories the relevant proportional liability legislation does not apply to arbitrations conducted under the applicable *Commercial Arbitration Act*.[108]

6.11 References

6.11.1 Books

John Dorter & John Sharkey AM, *Building and Construction Contracts in Australia Law and Practice* (Thomson Reuters, looseleaf)

Damien Cremean, Michael Whitten and Michael Sharkey, *Brooking on Building Contracts* (6th edn, LexisNexis Butterworths 2020)

Ian Bailey, *Construction Law in Australia* (4th edn, Thomson Reuters Australia 2019)

Sharon Christensen, *The Construction and Performance of Commercial Contracts* (Federation Press 2018)

Jeremy Coggins, Tom Davie, Tony Earl & Phil Evans, *Understanding Construction Law* (LexisNexis Butterworths 2016)

Marcus Jacobs, *Security of Payment in the Australian Building and Construction Industry* (Lawbook Co 2014)

Sir Kim Lewison and David Hughes, *The Interpretation of Contracts in Australia* (Thomson Reuters 2012)

Doug Jones, *Commercial Arbitration in Australia* (Thomson Reuters 2011)

Rashda Rana and Michelle Sanson, *International Commercial Arbitration* (Thomson Reuters 2011)

JR Cooke, *Architects, Engineers and the Law* (4th edn, Federation Press 2010)

Philip Loots and Donald Charrett, *Practical Guide to Engineering and Construction Contracts* (CCH 2009)

Ian Bailey and Matthew Bell, *Understanding Australian Construction Contracts* (Thomson Lawbook Co 2008)

6.11.2 Journals

Australian Construction Law Bulletin
Australian Construction Law Newsletter
Building and Construction Law Journal

105 *Civil Liability Act 2002* (WA) s 4A.
106 *Civil Liability Act 2002* (Tas) s 3A(3).
107 *Civil Liability Act 2003* (Qld) s 7(3).
108 David Levin, ' Proportionate Liability in Arbitrations in Australia?' (2009) 25 *Building and Construction Law* 298. See also *Aquagenics Pty Ltd v Break O'Day Council (No 2)* [2009] TASSC 89.

Jonathan Kay Hoyle, 'The Rainbow Down Under Part 1' (2002) 19(1) *International Construction Law Review* 5.

Jonathan Kay Hoyle, The Rainbow Down Under Part 1 [2001] 18.1 *International Construction Law Review* 5.

6.11.3 Internet

All Australian jurisdictions case law and legislation: http://www.austlii.edu.au

6.11.3.1 Legislation

Australian Capital Territory: https://www.legislation.act.gov.au/
New South Wales: https://www.legislation.nsw.gov.au/#/
Northern Territory: http://www.legislation.nt.gov.au
Queensland: https://www.legislation.qld.gov.au
South Australia: https://www.legislation.sa.gov.au/index.aspx
Tasmania legislation: https://www.legislation.tas.gov.au/
Victoria: http://www.legislation.vic.gov.au/
Western Australia: https://www.legislation.wa.gov.au/

6.11.3.2 Case law

Australian Capital Territory: https://www.courts.act.gov.au/supreme
New South Wales: https://www.caselaw.nsw.gov.au/
Northern Territory: http://www.supremecourt.nt.gov.au/index.htm
Queensland: https://sclqld.org.au/
South Australia: http://www.courts.sa.gov.au/Pages/default.aspx
Victoria: https://www.courts.vic.gov.au/
Western Australia: https://ecourts.justice.wa.gov.au/eCourtsPortal/

6.11.4 ADR

Andrew Stephenson, 'ADR in Construction: Australia' (May 2014), IBA International Construction Projects Committee. https://www.ibanet.org/Article/NewDetail.aspx?ArticleUid=AC86FC65-E413-4D55-B2A9-952F30F1655F#arbitrationinconstructionguides (accessed 21 March 2019).

CHAPTER 7

Applying FIDIC contracts in China

Sun Yiwen

DOI: 10.4324/9781003200901-7

7.1 Outline of the legal environment in China

7.1.1 The constitutional structure of China

The *Constitution of China* was first created on 20 September 1954. On 4 December 1982, it was promulgated for a fourth time and has served as a stable constitution since then with amendments in 1988, 1993, 1999, 2004 and 2018. The current *Constitution* comprise 143 articles in four chapters, stipulating the basis system,[1] the fundamental rights and duties of citizens,[2] the structure of the state,[3] etc.

According to the *Constitution*, China is a socialist state. All power vested in state organs belongs to the people of China.[4] The National People's Congress and the Local People's Congresses with their respective Standing Committees at various levels are the organs through which the people exercise state power, especially legislative power.[5] The President of China, who is elected by the National People's Congress, is the head of state with limited powers.[6] The State Council of the People's Republic of China, which is the Central People's Government, is the executive body of the highest organ of state power, with the Premier assuming overall responsibility.[7]

The highest judicial branch consists of the Supreme People's Court and the Supreme People's Procuratorate, which are responsible to the National People's Congress and its Standing Committee.

1 *Constitution* ch I.
2 ibid ch II.
3 ibid ch III.
4 ibid ch 2.
5 ibid arts 57, 58.
6 ibid arts 79–84.
7 ibid arts 85, 86.

There are 34 provincial-level administrative divisions in China, including 23 provinces, four municipalities, five autonomous regions and two Special Administrative Regions: Hong Kong and Macau. Every province except Hong Kong, Macau and Taiwan has a Communist Party Committee. The committees are headed by a Secretary, who over-ranks the nominal Governor of the provincial government.[8]

Under the principle of 'one country, two systems', Hong Kong and Macau, as two Special Administrative Regions, are highly autonomous and self-governing with legislative, executive and judicial powers.[9] However, the State Council retains control over foreign policy and military defence.

7.1.2 The legal system of China

The legal system of China is officially referred to as the socialist legal system with Chinese characteristics,[10] with four separate legal systems of Mainland China, Hong Kong, Macau and Taiwan.

From an academic point of view, Mainland China's legal system stems from a civil law system. Under this legal system, statutory laws are the primary and formal source of law, and include law, administrative regulations, local regulations, autonomous regulations, separate regulations and rules. Another formal source of law is interpretations of laws. There are three kinds of interpretations of laws: legislative interpretations, executive interpretations and judicial interpretations, among which judicial interpretations play the most important role.[11] Judicial interpretations are made by the Supreme People's Court to interpret laws and regulations based on the actual demands of trial work. Since the 1980s, judicial interpretations have been developed to an unprecedented extent due to multiple reasons, such as legislation technology, judges' ability of logical thinking, etc.[12] The Supreme People's Court, with relatively weak power, has the broadest power to interpret laws, and the legislation trend is becoming a basic characteristic of judicial interpretations.[13] Furthermore, judicial interpretations are listed as a formal source of international private law by some scholars.[14]

In Mainland China, judicial decisions are not legally binding, although the Supreme People's Court, as the highest-level court, issues 'guiding cases' from time to time.[15] These guiding cases are meant to help the People's Court at all levels to 'further improve the quality and efficiency of case trial, ensure the unity of the legal and social effects of adjudications'.[16] If there is any doubt and ambiguity during the application of laws, these guiding cases are the ones judges will turn to. In addition, legal opinions

---

8 ibid art 105.

9 *Basic Law of the Hong Kong Special Administration Region*; *Basic Law of the Macao Special Administrative Region* art 2.

10 The first part of *Decision of the CPC Central Committee on Major Issues Pertaining to Comprehensively Promoting the Rule of Law 2014*.

11 Shu Guoying, *Introduction to Jurisprudence* (2nd edn, Peking University Press 2012) 235.

12 Dong Hao, *On Judicial Interpretation* (China University of Political Science and Law Press 1999) 140.

13 Yuan Shengming, 'On the Legislation Trend of Judicial Interpretation' (2009) 2 *Study in Law and Business* 86.

14 Yu Fei, 'Judicial Interpretations on Conflicts of Laws in China' (2003) 6 *Ascent* 74.

15 https://www.chinacourt.org/article/subjectdetail/type/more/id/MzAwNEiqNACSYAAA.shtml (accessed 23 April 2019).

16 *Notice of the Supreme People's Court on Issuing the First Set of Guiding Cases* No 354 [2011] of the Supreme People's Court.

from superior courts exert great influence on decision-making. Sometimes, if judges do not know how to decide a certain issue, they may submit an application to the superior court for instructions. The superior court will issue an official reply, which will be obeyed by the judge.

Under the principle of 'one country, two systems', Hong Kong and Macau have their own legal systems separate from Mainland China, respectively based on English common law and Portuguese civil law. The legal system of Taiwan is based on civil law and codified into the six Codes.

Generally speaking, if a contract appoints Chinese law to be the governing law, it refers to the law of Mainland China, not including the law of Hong Kong, Macau or Taiwan.

7.1.3 The court system of China

The Supreme People's Court is the highest court in China, of which there are six Circuit Courts. There are two branches of courts under the Supreme People's Court. One is the local People's Courts at various levels, which are divided into basic People's Courts, intermediate People's Courts and higher People's Courts.[17] The other branch is the special People's Courts, which include military courts, railway transport courts, maritime courts, intellectual property courts and the Hangzhou Internet Court.[18]

7.2 The construction industry in China

7.2.1 Overview

In 2019, the construction industry in Mainland China contributed 7,090 billion RMB (US$1,056 billion) to GDP, an increase of 5.6 per cent over 2018.[19] The proportion of the added value of the construction industry in GDP has remained above 6.6 per cent since 2010, indicating that the construction industry has been a stable pillar industry of the national economy.

The construction industry continues to play a significant role in absorbing employment of the rural migrant population, promoting the construction of new urbanisation and maintaining social stability. At the end of 2019, the construction industry employed 54.27 million people, accounting for 7.01 per cent of the total labour force.[20]

The construction industry has led to the development and prosperity of related industries. The construction industry consumes a large amount of materials and products from various sectors of the national economy. The most obvious industries directly and indirectly driven by the construction industry are the manufacturing industry of metal products, mechanical equipment and building materials, as well as the mining industry, chemical industry, transportation, post and telecommunications industries.

The most distinct feature of the construction industry in Mainland China is the large proportion of railway construction. In 2019 alone, the investment scale in railway was 800 billion RMB (US$119 billion).[21] This is due to multiple reasons. The first is a large

17 *Organic Law of the People's Courts (2018 Amendment)* ch II.
18 ibid art 15.
19 http://www.zgjzy.org.cn/menu20/newsDetail/8344.html (accessed 27 October 2020).
20 http://www.zgjzy.org.cn/menu20/newsDetail/8344.html (accessed 27 October 2020).
21 https://www.sohu.com/a/366960387_482010 (accessed 27 October 2020).

territory with a relatively high population density. Although China has a huge land area, the population density is 148.35 person/km^2, much higher than other countries with a similar land area, such as the United States, Canada and Russia. This provides fundamental conditions for the profitable and sustainable operation of railways. The second reason is that different provinces in China are under the unified leadership of the Central Government, which makes construction of railways across provinces much easier. Benefiting from the above two main reasons, railway construction has become the biggest sector in the construction industry.

Construction of water and environmental protection has developed rapidly. In 2019, notwithstanding the background of slow growth in infrastructure investment, the construction of water and environmental protection maintained a high growth trend. According to the Report on the Development of China's Environmental Protection Industry (2018) released by the China Environmental Protection Industry Association, the total business income of the environmental protection industry is expected to exceed 2 trillion RMB (US$298 billion) in 2020.

The construction industry is very centralised. There are approximately 103,814 businesses in the construction industry. The number is not as large as in other similar countries, and even smaller than countries with a small-sized construction industry. Chinese construction businesses have become very internationalised. Seventy-four Chinese enterprises were listed in ENR's 2020 Top 250 International Contractors in 2020; the number decreased by one compared with the previous year but continued to rank first among other countries.

According to China's National Economic Industry Classification Standard (GB/T 4754-2002), the construction industry is subdivided into:

1. The housing and civil engineering construction industry
2. The installation industry
3. The building decoration industry and
4. Other construction industry.

Regulations on Administration of Foreign-Invested Construction Enterprises and Measures for the Implementation of Qualification Management of Foreign-Invested Construction Enterprises used to provide that if foreign construction enterprises want to participate in the construction business in China, they have to set up a subsidiary in China, wholly-owned or in a joint venture, which is called a foreign-invested construction enterprise. Wholly foreign-owned construction enterprises may only undertake specific types of projects within the scope of their qualifications, such as projects funded totally by foreign investments, foreign grants or foreign investments and grants, projects financed by international financial organisations and awarded through international tendering processes in accordance with the provisions of the loan agreement, etc. However, these limitations do not apply to sino-foreign construction enterprises, who only have to undertake construction projects within the permitted scope of their grades of qualifications.

These two rules provided details on how international contractors take part in the Chinese construction industry; however, they were abolished in January 2020, and there are no new rules, so it is not clear for now what international contractors should do if they want to enter this industry. The competition in China's construction industry is very fierce, the profit margin is getting smaller and smaller and the specialisation trend of the division of labour is more and more obvious. Therefore, in order to save costs, subcontracting is a common practice in the construction industry. In order to manage the subcontracting and ensure the quality of projects, China has taken a series of measures, such as the introduction of a number of regulations on subcontracting, and the Ministry of Housing and Urban Rural Development inspects the subcontracting from time to time, etc.

7.2.2 Regulation of individuals

The construction industry in China is highly regulated. People or enterprises who want to be engaged in certain activities in the construction industry need to obtain specific licenses, certificates or qualifications first. There are nine kinds of certificates for individuals:

1. National Certified Constructor: it includes Constructor (Level One) and Associate Constructor (Level Two), certified by the Ministry of Human Resources and Social Security and Ministry of Housing and Urban-Rural Development of the People's Republic of China.
2. Certified Cost Engineer: it is certified by the Ministry of Housing and Urban-Rural Development, Ministry of Transport and Ministry of Water Resources of the People's Republic of China.
3. Certified Supervision Engineer: it is certified by the Ministry of Housing and Urban-Rural Development, Ministry of Transport and Ministry of Water Resources of the People's Republic of China.
4. Registered Civil Engineer: it consists of the specialties of geotechnical engineering, water conservancy and hydropower, as well as ports and waterways.
5. Registered Electrical Engineer: it includes the specialties of power distribution as well as power generation and transmission.
6. Registered Utility Engineer: it includes the specialties of HVAC, water supply and drainage, and power.
7. Registered Architect: it consists of Class 1 Registered Architect and Class 2 Registered Architect.
8. Registered Structural Engineer: it consists of Class 1 Registered Structural Engineer and Class 2 Registered Structural Engineer.
9. Certified Safety Engineer: it is certified by the Ministry of Human Resources and Social Security and Ministry of Emergency Management of the People's Republic of China.

7.2.3 Regulation of construction enterprises

The qualification standards for general contracting construction enterprises include 12 categories, namely:

- Construction engineering
- Highway construction
- Railway construction
- Port and waterway construction
- Water resources and hydropower engineering construction
- Power engineering construction

- Mine engineering construction
- Metallurgical engineering construction
- Petrochemical engineering construction
- Municipal public works
- Communication engineering construction and
- Mechanical and electrical engineering construction.

Each of these categories of general contracting is generally divided into four classes: special class, first class, second class and third class. Generally speaking, the special grade and first grade of the general contractor qualification are subject to licensing by the housing and urban-rural development department under the State Council. The second grade of the general contractor qualification is subject to licensing by the housing and urban-rural development departments of the People's Governments of the provinces, autonomous regions or municipalities at places where they are located. The third grade are subject to licensing by the housing and urban-rural development departments of the People's Governments of the district cities at the place of industrial and commercial registration of the enterprise concerned. There are no limits on the size of projects that can be undertaken in each class according to law, but there will be requirements in tender documents.

The qualification standards for specialised contracting enterprises, including consulting engineers who prepare designs and contractors/subcontractors who carry out construction, consist of 36 categories, namely:

- Foundation engineering
- Crane installation engineering
- Ready-mixed concrete
- Electronic and intelligent engineering
- Fire-fighting facilities engineering
- Waterproof, anti-corrosion and thermal insulation engineering
- Contracting qualification of bridge engineering
- Tunnel engineering
- Steel structure engineering
- Formwork and scaffolding
- Building decoration engineering
- Construction electromechanical installation engineering, building curtain wall engineering
- Ancient architectural engineering
- Urban and road lighting engineering
- Highway and pavement engineering
- Highway subgrades engineering
- Highway traffic engineering
- Railway electrical engineering
- Railway track laying and beam erecting engineering
- Railway electrification engineering
- Airport field engineering
- Air traffic management engineering and airport minor systems engineering
- Airport visual aids engineering

- Port and coastal engineering
- Waterway engineering
- Navigation structure engineering
- Port and shipping equipment installation and water traffic management engineering
- Hydraulic metal structure production and installation engineering
- Electromechanical installation of water resources and hydropower engineering
- River and lake treatment engineering
- Power transmission and transformation project
- Nuclear engineering
- Offshore oil engineering contracting
- Environmental protection engineering
- Specialist engineering.

These categories of specialised contracting enterprises are generally divided into three classes first class, second class and third class. Generally speaking, the first grade qualification are subject to licensing by the housing and urban-rural development department under the State Council. The second grade qualification are subject to licensing by the housing and urban-rural development departments of the People's Governments of the provinces, autonomous regions or municipalities at places where they are located. The third grade are subject to licensing by the housing and urban-rural development departments of the People's Governments of the district cities at the place of industrial and commercial registration of the enterprise concerned. There are no limits on the size of projects that can be undertaken in each class according to laws, but there will be requirements in tender documents.

7.2.4 Labour

Qualifications of labour subcontracting companies are not divided into categories or classes. These companies provide subcontract labour to general contracting and specialised contracting enterprises.

There are many migrant workers in the construction industry. Migrant workers mean the workers who are farmers but come to cities to engage in non-agricultural labour. In the *Regulation on Ensuring Wage Payment to Migrant Workers*, Article 2 provides that 'migrant worker' means any rural resident who provides labour for an employer. This *Regulation* is implemented for the purposes of regulating wage payments to migrant workers and ensuring that migrant workers receive their wages on time and in full.[22] This is because payment of wages in arrears in the construction industry is common and serious.

The government takes serious measures to make sure payments to migrant workers are made on time and in full. In 2019, the General Office of the State Council established a specific task force fundamentally to solve the problem of wage arrears of migrant workers. On 12 July 2018, Qiu Xiaoping, Vice Minister of the Ministry of human resources and social security, announced the first batch of 'blacklist' of wage arrears of migrant workers, involving 14 illegal enterprises and six illegal personnel; this has been followed by five batches to date. The *Regulation* is a part of these measures.

22 *Regulation on Ensuring Wage Payment to Migrant Workers* art 1.

Chapter 4 of the *Regulation* provides several special provisions regarding wage payments in the construction industry. According to Articles 23 and 24, the Employer needs to arrange proper wage funding to obtain a construction permit and shall provide a guarantee for the payment of project funds to the construction contractor to ensure payments of wages from the Contractor to its migrant workers. When negotiating a written contract for construction of a project, the Employer and the Contractor must agree on the calculation cycle of project payments, the measures for progress payments and the allocation cycle of labour costs, and specify labour costs according to the requirements for ensuring the payment of migrant workers' wages in full and on time. The allocation cycle of labour costs shall not exceed one month. During the construction of a project, the Contractor must open special accounts for migrant workers' wages, which are used exclusively for payment of the wages of migrant workers.

7.2.5 Safety culture

In order to strengthen the supervision over and administration of safety on construction projects, The *Administrative Regulations on the Safety of Construction Projects* have been formulated. They provide 'safety first, precaution crucial' as the fundamental principle and allocate the responsibilities between Employer, Contractor and Subcontractor. Whoever violates these provisions is subject to severe punishment.

7.2.6 Government/private sector procurement

In the *Government Procurement Law*, government procurement refers to the procurement of goods, projects and services within the lawfully made centralised procurement lists or above the procurement limits by the state organs, public institutions and bodies with public fiscal funds. The procurement of projects by government apply the method of bidding and the *Bidding Laws* are applicable. However, private sector procurement of projects is not required to use this method of bidding.

7.2.7 Insurance requirements

There are no mandatory provisions on insurance requirements in legislation, but all Employers require the Contractor to buy certain types of insurance, such as all risks insurance, third party liability insurance, etc. This is the usual practice in the international construction industry.

7.2.8 Common forms of contract

The Ministry of Housing and Urban Rural Development formulated a series of common forms of contract, such as the construction contract, subcontracting contrast, etc. These forms of contract are derived from FIDIC contracts and combine specific requirements due to the particular conditions in China. Employers and Contractors are encouraged to use these forms but are not required to do so. For now, these forms are popular to some extent.

7.2.9 Dispute resolution – litigation, arbitration, Dispute Boards

The most common methods of dispute resolution are litigation and arbitration. If two parties submit the dispute to litigation, the local People's Court of the project has jurisdiction. For arbitration, the China International Economic and Trade Arbitration Commission (**CIETAC**) and Beijing Arbitration Commission are the popular choices among Employers and Contractors.

7.3 The impact of Covid-19 in China

7.3.1 The impact of Covid-19 on the execution of construction projects in China

The outbreak of the coronavirus epidemic coincided with the Spring Festival holiday in China. The Spring Festival holiday lasted for seven days, from 24 January to 31 January. On 26 January, the Central Committee of the Task Force on Coronavirus held a meeting and made it clear that the epidemic prevention and control arrangements should be implemented after the Spring Festival holiday, and the Spring Festival holiday should be extended appropriately. Shortly after this meeting, the General Office of State Council issued an announcement that in order to prevent and control the spread of the coronavirus epidemic, effectively reduce the infection numbers and better protect the peoples' lives and health, the State Council had approved the extension of the Spring Festival holiday by three days, to 2 February 2020.

In the next day or two, most provincial governments issued notices to postpone the resumption of work of enterprises and the opening of schools, which clearly stipulated that all kinds of enterprises should return to work no earlier than 24:00 on 9 February. There were exceptions for those enterprises related to the national economy and the peoples' livelihood that were necessary to protect the epidemic prevention and control areas and the peoples' livelihood.

As a consequence of the direction to postpone the resumption of work, as of 8 March, there were a total of 192,500 housing construction and municipal infrastructure projects under construction in China, of which only 111,900 (58.15 per cent) had been started and resumed. Therefore, on 18 March, the General Office of State Council put forward the Implementation of Measures to Strengthen the Stable Employment in the Light of the Coronavirus Epidemic (*Guobanfa* [2020] 6) and made clear provisions for resuming work and resuming production during the epidemic period. It provided that the whole country would speed up the resumption of major engineering projects and key export enterprises, taking manufacturing, construction, logistics, public service and agricultural production as breakthrough points, and gradually promote employment in other industries and regions.

Various Ministries and Commissions of the State Council also directed certain measures to reduce the burden of the losses suffered by the construction industry due to the epidemic. For example, before the end of June 2020, construction projects were allowed to suspend the payment of migrant workers' wage deposits, and enterprises with good payment records could be exempted from the deposit. For the enterprise qualifications of survey and design, construction, engineering supervision, etc., whose validity period expired before 30 June, it was automatically extended to 31 July. During this period, those enterprises continued to participate in construction, bidding and other activities. At the same time, banks were encouraged to support construction enterprises with good credit in terms of credit lines and loan interest rates. The government vigorously promoted the whole process of online approval of construction projects and adopted the mode of online applications and online approvals.

On construction sites, various measures were taken to make sure that the coronavirus was under control. The information of the personnel who returned to work was double checked in advance to ensure safety, such as name, body temperature, cities visited and whether they had contacted other coronavirus patients. Contractors were required to reserve enough qualified epidemic protective masks, thermometers, disinfectants, medical alcohol, emergency drugs, etc., to provide material support for epidemic control. Employees were required to wear masks and keep enough distance apart on the site. Meetings were held through the internet. Face to face meetings were not encouraged unless necessary. When having meals, employees were separated to avoid face-to-face dining, speaking and eating in groups.

7.3.2 The impact of Covid-19 on the operation of construction contracts in China

Under China's contract law, the Covid-19 epidemic could possibly constitute *force majeure*, which is an excuse for both parties to escape from the responsibility for breach of contract. In addition, the Supreme People's Court issued a series of guidance notes on how to accurately apply laws and balance the interests of the parties when hearing civil cases concerning the pandemic. On 16 April, the Supreme People's Court issued the Guiding Opinions (Part I) on Several Issues of Properly Hearing Civil Cases concerning the Covid-19 pandemic. There are three parts of the Guiding Opinion in total, with Part II issued on 15 May and Part III issued on 16 June. In these Guiding Opinions, the Supreme People's Court make its position clear about the extension of time limits such as the period of litigation[23] and the time limit for presenting evidence.[24]

Part II stipulates specific provisions on construction contracts. It provides that if the Contractor fails to complete the construction within the agreed construction period due to the epidemic or the epidemic prevention and control measures, the Employer is not entitled to require the Contractor to be responsible for the breach of contract, and the Contractor is entitled to ask for an extension of time for the construction period in light of the impact of the epidemic, or the impact of epidemic prevention and control measures on the performance of the contract.[25] If a sharp increase in labour costs and building materials costs or losses in labour costs or equipment leasing costs occurred due to the epidemic or the epidemic prevention and control measures, which makes it obviously unfair for the Contractor to continue to perform the contract, the Contractor has the right to require an adjustment of the price, and the People's Courts shall adjust the price in accordance with the principle of fairness.[26]

---

23 Part I art 7.
24 Part III art 2.
25 Part II art I.7.
26 Part II art I.8.

7.4 Chinese governing law of the contract

7.4.1 Constraints on the governing law of a construction contract

In Mainland China, the Parties are free to choose the laws to govern their contracts.[27] If the Parties choose the laws of a country as the governing law, and the country has different law districts, the law of the district which has the closest relation with this civil relation shall apply.[28] As for any international treaty chosen by Parties but not yet binding upon China, if such international treaty does not contradict the social public interests or mandatory provisions in the laws and regulations of China, the People's Court may exercise its discretion to decide whether to try the case in accordance with such international treaty.[29]

There are three main constraints on the choice of the governing law of a construction contract.

The first constraint is that the agreement on choice of law shall be explicit.[30] In some countries, judges can rely on implications to determine the choice of law by the Parties. For example, judges could presume the intention of the Parties on choice of law through other expressions made by the Parties, such as an arbitration clause. They believe that the choice of judges is equivalent to a choice of law. However, Chinese law does not recognise implications on choice of law.[31] The Parties can explicitly choose the governing law in a construction contract. But if the Parties did not choose the governing law before any dispute arises, and they invoke the laws of another country and neither of them has raised any objection to the applicable law during the process of the trial, the People's Court may determine that the laws of the selected country are the governing law.[32]

The second constraint is that forum public policy shall prevail if the governing law chosen by Parties violates the forum public policy.[33] The Supreme People's Court applies strict interpretations to the public policy principle. In several cases concerning the recognition and enforcement of a foreign arbitration award, the Supreme People's Court considered that public policy is deemed to maintain the fundamental legal order,[34] which can only be invoked if Chinese sovereignty is violated.[35] Although these considerations were applied at the stage of recognition and enforcement of a foreign arbitration award, there is discussion as to whether the applications of public policy at the stage of choice of governing law shall be the same. Some scholars believe that the Supreme People's Court standpoint on the strict interpretation of public

27 *Law on Choice of Law for Foreign-related Civil Relationships* art 14.

28 ibid art 6.

29 *Interpretations of the Supreme People's Court on Several Issues Concerning Application of the Law of the People's Republic of China on Choice of Law for Foreign-Related Civil Relationships* art 9.

30 ibid art 3.

31 Zhao Xianglin, *Private International Law* (China University of Political Science And Law Press 2007) 161.

32 *Interpretations of the Supreme People's Court on Several Issues Concerning Application of the Law of the People's Republic of China on Choice of Law for Foreign-Related Civil Relationships* art 8.

33 ibid art 5.

34 *Letter of Reply of the Supreme People's Court on Request for Instructions on Enforcement of Arbitration Award (2003) Mao Zhong Cai Zi No 138* ([2005] Min Si Ta Zi No 45).

35 *Letter of Reply of the Supreme People's Court to a Request for Instructions on the Non-Recognition and Non-Enforcement of an Arbitration Award of the ICC International Court of Arbitration* ([2008] Min Si Ta Zi No 11).

policy will be maintained.[36] This means that the Supreme People's Court adopts a 'narrow' interpretation of public policy – only violation of Chinese sovereignty can be interpreted to violate public policy.

The third constraint is that if there are mandatory rules on foreign-related civil relations in the Chinese laws, these Chinese mandatory rules shall directly apply.[37] Directly applied Chinese mandatory rules includes provisions relating to the protection of labour, food, public health, environmental safety, financial safety and anti-monopoly and anti-dumping.[38]

As for international projects, the Country where the construction project is located usually has mandatory rules regarding construction activities. Then another issue arises. If the Parties to an international construction contract choose the law of another country to be the governing law, and the seat of a lawsuit or an arbitration of international construction is in Mainland China, should the judges or arbitrators be obliged to apply the mandatory rules of the ***lex loci solutionis***?[39]

Article 7 of *Convention on the Law Applicable to Contractual Obligations* (*Rome I*) provides:

> When applying under this Convention the law of a country, effect may be given to the mandatory rules of the law of another country with which the situation has a close connection, if and in so far as, under the law of the latter country, THOSE rules must be applied whatever the law applicable to the contract.

Some countries incorporate this provision into their conflict of laws. For example, Article 19 of *Switzerland's Federal Code on Private International Law* stipulates that a mandatory provision of a third country may apply if close connections with that law exist.[40] The earlier draft of *Law of the People's Republic of China on Choice of Law for Foreign-related Civil Relationships* included a similar provision, which, however, was deleted in the later draft and the final version.[41] This leaves a gap in the legislation regarding the application of mandatory rules of *lex loci solutionis*. Some Chinese scholars believe that choice of the law of another country instead of *lex loci solutionis* constitutes evasion of *lex loci solutionis*, which will result in the direct application of *lex loci solutionis*. However, private international law in Mainland China does not even incorporate any provision relating to evasion of law, not to say evasion of *lex loci solutionis*. Some countries give the effect of *lex loci solutionis* through interpreting the principle of public policy and bona fides. For example, an English court held in *Foster v Driscoll*[42] that to ignore the mandatory rules of the USA:

> would furnish a just cause for complaint by the United States Government against our Government (of which the partners are subjects), and would be contrary to our obligation of international comity as now understood and recognized, and therefore would offend against our notions of public morality.

36 Xiao Yongping, Long Weidi, 'On Mandatory Rules in Private International Law' (2012) 10 *Social Sciences in China* 119.

37 *Law on Choice of Law for Foreign-related Civil Relationships* art 4.

38 *Interpretations of the Supreme People's Court on Several Issues Concerning Application of the Law of the People's Republic of China on Choice of Law for Foreign-Related Civil Relationships* art 10.

39 The Latin term for 'law of the place where relevant performance occurs'.

40 *Switzerland's Federal Code on Private International Law* art 19.

41 Xiao Yongping, Long Weidi, 'On Mandatory Rules in Private International Law' (2012) 10 *Social Sciences in China* 114.

42 [1929] 1 KB 470.

In Mainland China, there has been no such interpretation in judicial practice. Some scholars believe the gap in law and judicial practice would not affect the application of *lex loci solutionis* by judges.[43] Furthermore, some scholars infer that, in *Hai Ga Mu Pu Co Ltd v Moraglis SA*,[44] the judges left some room for the application of mandatory rules of *lex loci solutions* by interpreting the mandatory provisions in Article 4 of *Law of the People's Republic of China on Choice of Law for Foreign-related Civil Relationships* including foreign mandatory provisions.[45] However, the mainstream opinion holds that the judges mis-comprehended Article 4. Although Article 4 confuses domestic mandatory provisions with international mandatory provisions, it is the international mandatory provisions not domestic mandatory provisions that shall directly apply;[46] the legislation leaves no opportunity for application of *lex loci solutionis*.[47]

To sum up, the mandatory provisions of *lex loci solutionis* exert no constraint on the choice of the governing law. If the Parties choose the law of another country as the governing law of a construction contract, and the seat of the arbitration is in Mainland China, the mandatory provisions of *lex loci solutionis* will not be considered.

7.4.2 Formal requirements for a construction contract

According to Chinese *Contract Law*, once an agreement has been reached, the contract is concluded. In some circumstances, offer and acceptance analysis is used to inform when and where the contract was concluded. The contract becomes effective upon its conclusion,[48] with three main exceptions:

(a) Some contracts' effectiveness are subject to approval or registration as stipulated by relevant laws or administrative regulations.[49]
(b) A contract concluded by a person with limited legal capacity shall be effective after being ratified afterwards by the person's statutory agent.[50]
(c) A contract whose effectiveness is subject to certain conditions, which may be agreed upon by the Parties, shall become effective when such conditions are accomplished.[51]

In Mainland China, the Parties may use written, oral or other forms in entering into a contract. A contract shall be in written form if the laws or administrative regulations so provide.[52] Article 270 of *Contract Law* provides that a contract for a construction project shall be in written form, or otherwise the construction contract will not be deemed to be valid.

43 Xiao Yongping, Long Weidi, 'On Mandatory Rules in Private International Law' (2012) 10 *Social Sciences in China* 117.
44 (2012) Hu Gao Min Er (Shang) Zhong Zi No 4.
45 Lin Yanping, 'On the Purpose of Article 4 of *Law on Choice of Law for Foreign-related Civil Relationships and Related Interpretations*' (2003) 11 *Law Science* 72.
46 Liu Renshan, 'The Application of Directly applicable law in China' (2013) 3 *Study in Law and Business* 77.
47 Dong Jinxin, *On the Application of Third Country Mandatory Rules in Forum* (China Renmin University Press 2016) 104-108.
48 *Contract Law* art 44.
49 ibid.
50 ibid art 47.
51 ibid art 46.
52 ibid art 10.

7.5 What Special Provisions in the Particular Conditions are necessary for consistency with applicable laws in China?

7.5.1 FIDIC General Conditions are incompatible or inconsistent with Chinese governing law of the contract

In order to ensure the quality and safety of construction projects, Chinese law puts great value on the registration and licensing of contractors. Construction activity is deemed to be exclusive to the Contractor and can only be carried out by the Contractor. However, in practice some Contractors intend to make a profit by assigning the whole Works or to subcontract the main Works to another non-licensed contractor, resulting in cheating on workmanship and materials. So *Contract Law* and *Construction Law* do not allow the Contractor to assign the whole Works to any third party.[53] Dividing the whole contracted construction project into several parts and separately subcontracting each part to a third party under the guise of sub-contracting is considered to be assigning the whole Works in a disguised form, which is forbidden.[54] Where a Contractor assigns the construction contract or illegally subcontracts the main structure of the project, such assignment and subcontracting are invalid. From this perspective, sub-clause 1.7 of FIDIC General Conditions needs modification if the governing law is Chinese law. Sub-clause 1.7 of FIDIC General Conditions provides that the Contractor may assign the whole or any part of the Contract with the prior agreement of the Employer. However, if the governing law is Chinese law, the Contractor shall not assign the whole Contract with or without the prior agreement of the Employer.

Although the Contractor is allowed to subcontract some parts of the construction Works, the main structure of the construction project must be carried out by the Contractor itself.[55] Therefore, the Particular Conditions should contain a provision referring to sub-clause 5.1 of the Red Book or sub-clause 4.4 of the Yellow and Silver Books that subcontracting the main structure is not permitted.

7.5.2 FIDIC General Conditions are incompatible or inconsistent with the laws of the Site/Country

7.5.2.1 Construction contract cannot materially change the bidding documents and proposals

If the Site of the project is in Mainland China, and the Contractor is chosen by a bidding process, the Chinese *Bidding Law* and the *Regulation on the Implementation of the Bidding Law* shall be applied.[56] In order to protect the competition result of the bidding process, Article 57 of *Regulation on the Implementation of the Bidding Law* provides:

> The tenderee and the bid winner shall sign a written contract according to the provisions of the Bidding Law and this Regulation, and the main clauses such as subject matter of the contract, payment, quality and time limit for the performance of the contract shall be consistent with the content in the bid invitation documents and the bidding documents of the bid winner.

53 ibid art 272.
54 ibid.
55 ibid.
56 *Bidding Law (2017 Amendment)* art 2.

In other words, any sub-clauses in FIDIC General Conditions which deviate from any main clause of the bid invitation documents and the proposal shall be deemed to be incompatible or inconsistent with Chinese law. Generally speaking, price, liability for breach of contract, dispute resolution, etc., are the main clauses of the Contract in addition to those listed in Article 57. However, some available judicial decisions show that judges do not strictly stick to the nature of clauses when deciding whether there is a deviation. For example, in one case, the price was modified in the Contract and different from the bidding proposal.[57] Judges held that the Parties agreed to the modified price, and the new price, which was lower than that of the proposal, did not damage other tenderers' interests. Therefore, such modification was not regarded as a material change. In another case,[58] the quantities of the project were reduced, and the construction duration and price were reduced proportionally. Judges considered such modifications did not harm other tenderers' interests, so such material change was allowed. If the price was raised while other conditions remained the same, such modification would be regarded as a material change because it harmed other bidders' interests.[59]

To sum up, Article 57 of *Regulation on the Implementation of the Bidding Law* is meant to maintain competition, to guarantee the fairness of the bidding process, and to protect the interest of all other tenderers. Whether there is a material change from the bidding documents and the proposal depends on whether the modification damages other tenderers' interest. Therefore, some changes are permitted in the construction contract, but any modification that interferes with competition will be invalid under Chinese law.

It is desirable to examine the General Conditions whether there is any provision materially changing the bidding invitation documents and the proposal. If there is any provision deviating from the bidding invitation documents and the proposal, it should be modified in Particular Conditions in accordance with the bidding invitation documents.

7.5.2.2 Defects notification period and retention money

If the Site of the project is in Mainland China, several provisions about the Defects Notification Period and retention money need to be followed.

In order to lighten the burden on construction enterprises, and shorten the length of the defect liability period, (equivalent to the Defects Notification Period defined in the FIDIC General Conditions), Article 2 of *Measures for the Management of Construction Project Quality Deposits 2018 (the Measures)* provides:

> The defect liability period shall generally be one year, shall not exceed two years at maximum, and shall be agreed to by the contract-issuing party and the contractor in the contract.

Article 7 stipulates:

> A contract-issuing party shall reserve deposits [*which is called retention money in FIDIC contract conditions*] by the method as agreed to in the contract and the total proportion of deposits reserved shall not be higher than 5% of the total project settlement price. Where

57 (2013) Nei Min Yi Zhong Zi No 168.
58 (2011) Wu Zhong Min Si Zhong Zi No 68.
59 (2011) Yu Fa Min Zai Zi No 60.

> a contractor is required to replace a reserved deposit with a bank letter of guarantee as agreed to in the contract, the amount of letter of guarantee shall not be higher than 5% of the total project settlement price.

Accordingly, if the Defects Notification Period is longer than two years, or the retention money is higher than 5 per cent of the total Contract Price, the proportion which exceeds the above-mentioned amounts is invalid, for which the Contractor bears no liability.

7.5.2.3 The time when the defects notification period commences

In FIDIC General Conditions, the Defects Notification Period is calculated from the Date of Completion of the Works (or Section or Part). Under the premise that taking-over conditions are met, if the Employer does not issue the Taking-Over Certificate nor reject the Contractor's application within 28 days after the Employer receives the Contractor's Notice to apply for the Taking-Over Certificate, the Taking-Over Certificate shall be deemed to have been issued on the fourteenth day after the Employer receives the Notice, and the Defect Notification Period commences.

However, Article 8 of the *Measures* stipulates:

> The defect liability period shall be calculated from the date when the project passes the test on completion . . . Where the test on completion of the project is unable to be conducted within the prescribed time limit due to reasons attributable to the employer, the project shall automatically enter the defect liability period on the 90th day after the contractor submits the application for the test on completion to the employer.

There are two main differences between these two provisions. First, the preconditions for the Taking-Over Certificate to be deemed to be issued in the FIDIC rainbow suite are that the project has passed the Tests on Completion, while the *Measures* do not require such conditions. This leaves a loophole. There may be a possibility that the project has not been completed in accordance with the Contract and has some defects, however, if the Employer is remiss in carrying out the Tests on Completion, the *Measures* permit the project to enter the Defects Notification Period and be put into use, which may be extremely dangerous. Unfortunately, this is a legal requisite which cannot be contracted out of.

Secondly, the number of days from when the Employer receives the Notice to the date the Defects Notification Period starts to be calculated are different. The *Measures* stipulate 90 days, while the FIDIC General Conditions provide for 14 days. This also cannot be contracted out if the Site of the project is in Mainland China.

Therefore, it is desirable to make sure that the commencement date of the Defects Notification Period are in accordance with the Measures in Particular Conditions.

7.5.2.4 Brief introduction to Chinese *Construction Law* (2019 Amendment)

The *Construction Law* applies to construction activities and supervision of construction activities conducted in Mainland China.[60] This means if the Employer and the Contractor choose Chinese law as the governing law of a construction contract

60 *Construction Law (2019 Amendment)* art 2.

relating to a project in another country, the *Construction Law* is not applicable. As to construction activities, the *Construction Law* adopts a narrow definition, which refers to construction of all kinds of buildings and the ancillary facilities and the installation of the supporting lines, pipes and equipment.[61] The construction of civil engineering projects is not deemed to be construction activities under the *Construction law*. The *Construction law* does not apply to civil engineering projects.

The *Construction Law* lists provisions on construction licences, contracting and subcontracting of construction projects, supervision of construction projects, management of safety and quality. Some of the provisions may determine the validity of a contract. For example, the prohibitive provisions on subcontracting[62] may cause the provisions in a construction contract relating to assignment of the whole or part of the project to be void. Some of the provisions may impact the commencement date of the project. For example, according to the *Construction Law*, the Employer needs to get construction licences from construction administrative departments.[63] The construction activities need to start within three months after construction licences are issued. Therefore, if the *Construction Law* applies, it is necessary to refer to Chinese construction lawyers for professional advice.

7.5.3 FIDIC General Conditions are incompatible or inconsistent with the relevant laws on dispute determination in China

No Special Provisions in the Particular Conditions are necessary for consistency with applicable law if the seat of the arbitration is in Mainland China.

7.6 What Special Provisions in the Particular Conditions are desirable for consistency with applicable laws in China?

7.6.1 The time when the constructions contract comes into full force and effect

In Mainland China, controversies exist on the time when the construction contract comes into full force and effect if the Contractor is chosen through a tender process. There are three main perspectives. The first is that the construction contract become effective when the Contractor receives the letter of award.[64] People who support this perspective consider that Tender documents issued by the Employer constitutes an invitation to treat, the Contractor's proposal constitutes its offer, and the Employer's letter of award constitutes acceptance. According to *Contract Law*, when the acceptance reaches the Contractor, the acceptance becomes effective; that is when the construction contract is concluded, upon which the Contract becomes effective.

The second point of view is that when the letter of award reaches the Contractor, the Contract is established, but does not become effective.[65] When the Employer and the Contractor execute the contract agreement, the Contract comes into force.

61 ibid.
62 *Construction Law (2019 Amendment)* arts 28 and 29.
63 ibid art 7.
64 Zheng Lijun, Liu Yi, 'On the Improvement on the Bidding Law' (2013) 7 *China Construction Law Review* 240.
65 ibid 241.

The third perspective is that the effectiveness of the letter of award marks a preliminary agreement becoming effective between the Contractor and the Employer.[66] The construction contract becomes effective upon the execution by the Parties. The new interpretation made by the Supreme People's Court on issues concerning the application of law for the trial of cases of dispute over contracts on undertaking construction projects seems to end these controversies,[67] but so far, there is no consensus.

As to whether the liability undertaken by the Party who does not sign the contract after the letter of award is effective, judges hold different opinions in judicial decisions. Some judges, who believe that the construction contract becomes effective when the letter of award reaches the Contractor, hold that the Party who does not sign the contract shall be liable for breach of contract.[68] Some judges hold the third point of view aforementioned, and determine that the Party who does not sign the contract undertakes precontractual liability according to Article 42 of *Contract Law*.[69] Generally speaking, most judges hold that the construction contract comes into full force when the letter of award reaches the Contractor.

Clause 5 of the Contract Agreement in the 2017 FIDIC Silver Book stipulates:

> The Contract shall come into full force and effect on the date when the following conditions are satisfied.

This clause should be deleted if the governing law is Chinese law, because it will not change the time when the Contract becomes effective according to the law.

7.6.2 Construction lien

In order to secure payment to contractors, Article 286 of Chinese *Contract Law* provides:

> If the employer failed to pay the price in accordance with the contract, the contractor may demand payment from the employer within a reasonable period. Where the employer fails to pay the price at the end of such period, the contractor may enter into an agreement with the employer to liquidate the project, and may also petition the People's Court to auction the project in accordance with the law, unless such project is not fit for liquidation or auction in light of its nature. The construction project price shall be paid in priority out of proceeds from the liquidation or auction of the project.

This provision leaves many issues unclear; for example, whether the Contractor's profits are covered by the lien, whether the construction project should be completed for the Contractor to exercise the lien, how to define the 'reasonable period', and so on. To clarify the uncertainties, the Supreme People's Court issued a series of interpretations and official replies, including *Interpretation I 2004 and II 2019 on Issues Concerning*

66 ibid.

67 Article 10 of *Interpretation II* provides that if the main clauses of the construction contract materially change the clauses of invitation to bidding, bidding documents and the letter of award, such changes are invalid.

68 *Hebei Construction Group Co Ltd v Chongqing Cloud Computing Investment and Operation Co Ltd* [2017] Yu Min Zhong No 22); *Xinjiang Zhongxin Resource Co Ltd v Daqing Oilfield Engineering Co Ltd* [2016] Supreme People's Court Zai No 11; *Guangxia Construction Group Co Ltd v Fuzhou Taijiang Real Estate Co Ltd* [2014] Min Yi Zhong Zi No 155.

69 *Linzhou Caisang Construction Labor Co Ltd v Tianjin Xiqing Dasi Ni Huang Zhuang Village Committee* [2014] Min Shen Zi No 952; *Wuhu Guangye Construction Co Ltd v Wuhu Jiujiang Construction and Investment Co Ltd* Anhui Higher People's Court [2016] Wan Min Zhong No 700.

the Application of Law for the Trial of Cases of Dispute over Contracts on Undertaking Construction Projects (the *Interpretation I* and the *Interpretation II*, respectively), *Official Reply on Issues Concerning the Construction Lien 2002*,[70] and *Official Reply on Whether Payment for a Renovation and Decoration Project Is Entitled to Construction Lien 2004*.[71]

7.6.2.1 Whether the profits are covered by the lien

According to Article 3 of the *Official Reply on Issues Concerning the Construction Lien*, the 'project price' in Article 286 includes due payment for labour, materials and other actual costs, not including the damage suffered by the Contractor due to the Employer's breach of contract. Whether the profits are covered by the lien remains unclear. Article 5 of the *Interim Regulations concerning Administration on Contract and Contracting Prices in Project Construction Work* provides that the project price shall consist of direct cost, indirect cost, tax and profits. Based on this provision and commercial practice, the consensus has been reached that, although the *Official Reply* does not incorporate the profit in its context, profits, as a part of the project price, can definitely be covered by the construction lien.[72]

7.6.2.2 Whether the construction project should be completed for the Contractor to exercise the lien

As to whether the construction project should be completed for the Contractor to exercise the lien, *Interpretation II 2019* offers an answer, Article 20 of which provides:

> If the uncompleted construction work meets the quality requirements, the people's court of all levels shall support the contractor's claim of the construction lien over the cash equivalent or auction price of the uncompleted project.

Combined with Article 19, which provides that if the completed project meets the quality requirements, the People's Court shall support the Contractor's claim of the construction lien, the basic element of construction lien is not that the project shall be completed, but the quality of the project is satisfactory. However, what if the uncompleted project cannot be auctioned? This situation is addressed by Article 286 of *Contract Law*. If the project, whether it is completed or not, is not fit for liquidation or auction in light of its nature, there is no construction lien.

7.6.2.3 The commencement date of construction lien

As to the 'reasonable period', in accordance with Article 4 of *Official Reply on Issues Concerning the Construction Lien 2002*, the period is six months, commencing from the date of actual completion or the completion date stipulated in the construction contract. However, in practice, many projects are not able to be completed due to various reasons. Some projects are suspended and cannot be resumed in the predictable future, while some contracts are terminated. In these circumstances, as the projects cannot be completed there is no completion date, then Article 4 is not applicable.

---

70 Fa Shi [2002] No 16.

71 [2004] Min Yi Ta Zi No 14.

72 Du Wanhua, *China Trial Guide Reference and Guide to Civil Trial* (People's Court Press, Vol. 38, 2009) 306-307.

Mechanically sticking to the provisions of *Official Reply on Issues Concerning the Construction Lien 2002* in judicial decisions will result in a detrimental effect on the interest of Contractors. Before the issuance of *Interpretation II 2019*, judges applied this provision flexibly and diversely based on the facts of cases. In some cases, judges decided that the period for exercising the construction lien starts from the date when the Employer ought to make the payment, not the completion date.[73] In one case, judges held that if the construction contract had been terminated, the Contractor could exercise the construction lien from the date on which the Contract was terminated.[74] This decision is listed by the Supreme People's Court as Guiding Case No. 73. In one case,[75] judges in the Higher People's Court of Zhejiang Province considered the suspension date as the commencement date of the construction lien. In these cases, the judges did not apply Article 4 of *Official Reply on Issues Concerning the Construction Lien 2002* rigidly. They skipped Article 4 and interpreted the Article 4 of *Official Reply on Issues Concerning the Construction Lien 2002* and Article 286 of *Contract Law* following the mischief rule, breaking through the limit of these two provisions and eventually protecting the interests of the Contractors in each case.

To adapt this judicial trend, *Interpretation II 2019* modified the commencement date, Article 22 of which provides that the period of six months shall start from the date when the Employer should make the payment to the Contractor.

7.6.2.4 Whether the Contractor can exercise the construction lien if the construction contract is invalid

No article of the law or interpretations stipulates whether the Contractor can exercise the construction lien if the construction contract is invalid. However, based on some cases and some rules issued by Higher People's Courts of several provinces, a valid construction contract is not a prerequisite for the Contractor to exercise the construction lien. Article 17 of *Opinions on Issues Concerning the Application of Law for the Trial of Cases of Dispute over Contracts on Undertaking Construction Projects* issued by Anhui Higher People's Court provides:

> If the construction contract is invalid, but the project is qualified, the contractor's request for the exercising the construction lien shall be sustained.

The 2010 version of *Guidance on the Trial of Cases of Dispute over Construction Contracts* issued by Jiangsu Higher People's Court provides:

> If the construction contract is invalid, the contractor's request for exercising the construction lien shall not be sustained.

However, after the issuance of this guidance, there are still some cases decided by the Jiangsu Higher People's Court where the Contractor's request for exercising the construction lien was sustained even when the construction contract was invalid. In 2018, the Jiangsu Higher People's Court issued *Replies to Issues on the Trial of Cases of Dispute over Contracts on Undertaking Construction Projects*, Article 15 of which changes the above provision, stipulating:

73 *Er Shen* (2016) Supreme People's Court Min Zhong No 602; (2014) Su Min Zhong Zi No 2089.
74 (2014) Wan Min Yi Zhong Zi No 54.
75 (2013) Zhe Min Ti Zi No 72.

> The effectiveness does not affect the contractors' right to exercise the construction lien. Contractors are still entitled to construction lien even if the construction contract is invalid.

In *Zhejiang Dongyang Construction Group Co Ltd v Xi'an Kangfu Real Estate Development Co Ltd*, [76] the judges in the Supreme People's Court held that Article 286 is intended to protect Contractors so that they can get payment in time. An invalid construction contract cannot exclude the application of this provision.

Some scholars support the above opinion. They believe that the process of construction fixes the labour and materials in the project, which is the basis of the construction lien. Even if the construction contract is invalid, the basis remains the same.[77] Therefore, a valid contract is not a prerequisite for the construction lien.

7.6.2.5 Whether the Subcontractor or the actual contractor is entitled to the construction lien

Article 286 of *Contract Law* entitles Contractors to the construction lien. This is in accordance with the doctrine of privity of contract. It is the Contractor who signed the construction contract, so it is the Contractor who has the right to exercise the construction lien. However, in practice, some Contractors subcontract the whole or part of project to others, with the consequence that the actual contractors are not the ones who signed the construction contract with the Employer. Whether the actual contractors are entitled to the construction lien remains unclear. The Higher People's Court of different provinces and different judges in the Supreme People's Court hold opposite opinions. The Higher People's Court of Anhui and Zhejiang Province issued *Guidance on the Trial of Cases of Dispute over Construction Contracts*, stipulating that if the Subcontractors or the actual contractors complete the project in accordance with the construction contract and the project is qualified, but the Contractors are indolent in exercising the construction lien, the Subcontractors or the actual contractors are entitled to the construction lien over their due payments.

Unlike the above courts, the Higher People's Court of Guangdong Province set up a few preconditions for the Subcontractors to exercise the construction lien.[78] The first is that the general construction contract and the subcontract shall be valid. The second is that only the Subcontractors can exercise the construction lien, while actual contractors are not entitled to this right. The last one is that the Contractors' reluctance to exercise the right damages the interests of the Subcontractors.

In the Supreme People's Court, some judges held that as long as the project is of qualified quality, the actual contractor has the right to exercise the construction lien, as in *Zhuhai Baohui Biological Technology Co Ltd v Wu Changqing*, [79] and *SABIC Innovative Plastics (China) Co Ltd v Fujian Xinyuan Construction Development Co Ltd*.[80] However, in *Wang Chunlin v Liaoning Wantai Real Estate Development Co Ltd*

---

76 [2014] Min Yi Zhong Zi No 108.

77 Li Houlong, Pan Junfeng, 'On Difficult Issues of Construction Lien' (2016) 10 *Journal of Law Application* 63.

78 *Guidance on the Application of Article 286 of Contract Law in Trial by Guangdong Higher People's Court* art 2.

79 (2013) Min Shen Zi No 283.

80 (2013) Min Shen Zi No 39.

and *He Shichang, Liaoyuan Harmony Real Estate Development Co Ltd v Liaoyuan Rural Commercial Bank Co Ltd*, the judges in the Supreme People's Court held that the Subcontractor and the actual contractor are not party to the general construction contract, and do not have the right to the construction lien under Article 286 of the *Contract Law*.

To sum up, whether the Subcontractor or the actual contractor is entitled to the construction lien will lead to different decisions in different courts.

7.6.2.6 How to exercise the construction lien?

Article 286 of *Contract Law* stipulates two ways to exercise the construction lien. One is that the Contractor and the Employer negotiate to convert the project into money, and the other is that the Contractor files a petition to the People's Court to auction the project. What is unknown from this article is that whether there needs to be litigation to confirm the amount of the due payment. In practice, there are two different opinions.

In *Li Rusen v Sanshui Fuyang West Roofing Tile Co Ltd*[81] the judges in the Intermediate People's Court of Guangdong Foshan held that the Contractor can directly file the enforcement petition to auction the project, as long as the Contractor and the Employer reach a consensus on the amount of the due payment. However, some scholars believe that only a suit can confirm whether the Contractor has the right to exercise the construction lien.[82] Exercising the construction lien directly through an enforcement procedure may result in mistakes.[83]

The Higher People's Court of Zhejiang Province issued the *Official Reply to Issues on the Enforcement of Construction Lien*,[84] section 2 of which stipulates that the Contractor can exercise the construction lien by filing an enforcement petition to auction the project. A suit for declaration over the construction lien is not a necessity. The Higher People's Court of Guangdong Province is of the same opinion.[85]

However, the Jiangsu Higher People's Court have the opposite view. They believe that the Contractor can only exercise the construction lien by launching a suit or an arbitration for declaration, while an enforcement procedure is not acceptable.[86]

There is no consensus on this issue. Whether the way to exercise the construction lien is effective depends on the judges and where the forum is.

7.6.2.7 Whether the parties can contract out the construction lien?

According to Article 23 of *Interpretation II*, the Employer and the Contractor can contract out or place restrictions on the construction lien. However, if contracting out or the restriction damages the interest of construction workers, such contracting out or the restriction shall not be sustained by the People's Court.

81 (2003) Fo Zhong Fa Min Yi Zhong Zi No 1181.

82 Zhang Wei, 'On Construction Lien' (2005) 7 *Peking University Law Review* 259.

83 Lei Yunlong, Huang Feng, 'On Construction Lien' (2005) 10 *Journal of Law Application* 59, 60.

84 Zhe Gao Fa Zhi [2012] No 2.

85 *Replies on Difficult Issues on Dispute over Construction Contract by Guangdong Higher People's Court.*

86 *Replies on Difficult Issues on Dispute over Construction Contract by Jiangsu Higher People's Court.*

7.7 Summary of applicable legislation for Chinese governing law of the contract

	Legislation	Interpretation
7.7.1 Entry into a construction contract		
Contracts generally	*Contract Law 1999* *General Provisions of the Civil Law 2017*	*Interpretation I, II and III of the Supreme People's Court of Several Issues concerning the Application of the Contract Law*
Construction contracts		*Interpretation I and II of the Supreme People's Court on Issues Concerning the Application of Law for the Trial of Cases of Dispute over Contracts on Undertaking Construction Projects*
7.7.2 Termination of a construction contract		
Fundamental change of circumstances		*Interpretation II of the Supreme People's Court of Several Issues Concerning the Application of The Contract Law*
Bankruptcy, insolvency, liquidation	*Enterprise Bankruptcy Law*	*Provisions I, II and III of the Supreme People's Court on Several Issues concerning the Application of the Enterprise Bankruptcy Law*
Rescission of a construction contract		*Interpretation I and II of the Supreme People's Court on Issues Concerning the Application of Law for the Trial of Cases of Dispute over Contracts on Undertaking Construction Projects*
7.7.3 Dispute resolution		
Limitation period	*General Provisions of the Civil Law 2017* *Opinion of the Legislative Affairs Commission of the Standing Committee of the National People's Congress on Issues concerning the Limitation of Prosecution for the Illegal Act of Construction or Design in Violation of the Planning Permission or the Compulsory Construction Standards*	*Interpretation of the Supreme People's Court on Several Issues concerning the Application of the Extinctive Prescription Rules in the General Provisions of the Civil Law*

Liability	*Contract Law 1999* *Construction Law (2019 Amendment)*		
Arbitration	*Arbitration Law of the People's Republic of China (2017 Amendment)*	*Interpretation of the Supreme People's Court concerning Some Issues on Application of the Arbitration Law of the People's Republic of China (2008 Adjustment)*	

7.8 Summary of applicable legislation if the Site/Country is in China

	Legislation	Interpretation	Others
7.8.1 Operation of a construction contract			
Registration and administration of professionals – *Jian Li*,[87] certified constructors[88]	*Construction Law (2019 Amendment)* *Administrative Provisions on the Qualifications of Project Supervising Enterprises (2016 Amendment)* *Administrative Provisions on Certified Jian Li (2016 Amendment)* *Provisions on the Administration of Certified Constructors (2016 Amendment)*		
Licensing of Contractors and Subcontractors	*Administration of Qualifications of Enterprises in the Construction Industry (2018 Amendment)*	*Interpretation I and II of the Supreme People's Court on Issues Concerning the Application of Law for the Trial of Cases of Dispute over Contracts on Undertaking Construction Projects*	

87 Supervising engineer with contractual authority as Employer's agent, and statutory duties and obligations in respect of safety, quality, project management, cost control and coordination between Employer and Contractor. Jian Li is discussed in detail in para 7.9.1 below.

88 The 'certified constructors' mentioned in these legislations refers to the professional technicians who have obtained the certified qualification after passing assessment or examination, have obtained a registration certificate and a practicing seal after making registration according to these provisions, and are acting as the project managers of Contractors and engaging in relevant activities.

(Continued)

	Legislation	Interpretation	Others
Subcontracting	*Measures for the Administration on the Construction by Subcontract of House-building and Municipal Infrastructure Projects (2014 Amendment)*	*Interpretation I and II of the Supreme People's Court on Issues Concerning the Application of Law for the Trial of Cases of Dispute over Contracts on Undertaking Construction Projects*	*Notice of the Ministry of Housing and Urban-Rural Development on Issuing the Measures for the Administration of the Determination and the Investigation and Punishment of Assignment of Contract, Illegal Subcontracting and Other Illegal Acts in the Construction of Building Projects (for Trial Implementation)*
Construction lien	*Contract Law 1999*		*Letter of Reply of the Supreme People's Court on Whether Payment for a Renovation and Decoration Project Is Entitled to Priority in Compensation as Provided for in Article 286 of the Contract Law 2004* *Reply of the Supreme People's Court on Construction Lien 2002*
Retention money			*Measures for the Management of Construction Project Quality Deposits*
Labour	*Labour Law (2018 Amendment)* *Labour Contract Law (2012 Amendment)*	*Interpretation, II, III and IV of the Supreme People's Court of Several Issues on the Application of Law in the Trial of Labour Dispute Cases*	
Design/Moral rights	*Regulation on the Administration of Survey and Design of Construction Projects (2017 Amendment)*		
Copyright	*Copyright Law (2010 Amendment)* *Regulation for the Implementation of the Copyright Law (2013 Amendment)* *Patent Law (2008 Amendment)* *Detailed Rules for the Implementation of the Patent Law (2010 Amendment)* *Regulations on Construction Technology (2014 Amendment)*	*Interpretation I and II of the Supreme People's Court on Several Issues concerning the Application of Law in the Trial of Patent Infringement Dispute Cases*	

Environment	*Law of the People's Republic of China on Prevention and Control of Pollution from Environmental Noise (2018 Amendment)* *Law of the People's Republic of China on Environmental Impact Assessment (2018 Amendment)*		
Planning	*Urban and Rural Planning Law(2015 Amendment)*		
Work affecting adjacent property to the Site	*General Provisions of the Civil Law 2017*		
Heritage	*Cultural Relics Protection Law (2017 Amendment)*		
Building and construction permits	*Measures for the Administration of Construction Permits for Construction Projects (2018 Amendment)*		*Notice of the Ministry of Housing and Urban-Rural Development on Further Strengthening the Administration of Construction Permits for Construction Projects (2018 Amendment)*
Standard of construction work	*Regulations on the Quality Management of Construction Projects*		
Health and safety	*Regulations on the Safety Management of Construction Projects*		
Ownership of plant and materials	*Property Law*		
Insurance	*Social Insurance Law of the People's Republic of China (2018 Amendment)*	*Provisions of the Supreme People's Court on Several Issues concerning the Trial of Administrative Cases on Work-Related Injury Insurance*	

(*Continued*)

	Legislation	Interpretation	Others
Statutory rights that coexist with contractual rights	*Contract Law 1999* *Construction Law (2019 Amendment)*	*Interpretation I and II of the Supreme People's Court on Issues Concerning the Application of Law for the Trial of Cases of Dispute over Contracts on Undertaking Construction Projects*	
Liability for defective work	*Construction Law (2019 Amendment)* *Regulations on the Quality Management of Construction Projects*		
Other issues	*Criminal Law*		

7.8.2 Termination of a construction contract

Bankruptcy, insolvency, liquidation	*Enterprise Bankruptcy Law*	*Provisions I, II and III of the Supreme People's Court on Several Issues concerning the Application of the Enterprise Bankruptcy Law*	

7.8.3 Dispute resolution

Limitation period	*General Provisions of the Civil Law 2017* *Opinion of the Legislative Affairs Commission of the Standing Committee of the National People's Congress on Issues concerning the Limitation of Prosecution for the Illegal Act of Construction or Design in Violation of the Planning Permission or the Compulsory Construction Standards*	*Interpretation of the Supreme People's Court on Several Issues concerning the Application of the Extinctive Prescription Rules in the General Provisions of the Civil Law*	

7.9 Summary of applicable legislation if the 'seat' of the dispute determination is in China

	Legislation	Interpretation
Limitation period	*General Provisions of the Civil Law 2017* *Opinion of the Legislative Affairs Commission of the Standing Committee of the National People's Congress on Issues concerning the Limitation of Prosecution for the Illegal Act of Construction or Design in Violation of the Planning Permission or the Compulsory Construction Standards*	*Interpretation of the Supreme People's Court on Several Issues concerning the Application of the Extinctive Prescription Rules in the General Provisions of the Civil Law*
Suit	*The Civil Procedure Law (2017 Amendment)*	*Interpretation of the Supreme People's Court on the Application of the Civil Procedure Law*
Arbitration	*Arbitration Law of the People's Republic of China (2017 Amendment)*	*Interpretation of the Supreme People's Court concerning Some Issues on Application of the Arbitration Law of the People's Republic of China (2008 Adjustment)*

7.10 Issues that a court or arbitrator may construe differently to that expected from the words of the Contract, because of local law or custom

7.10.1 Chinese engineer – Jian Li (the project supervisor)

In FIDIC contract conditions, the Engineer plays a very important role. In the Red Book, for example, the duties of the Engineer depend on the duties assigned to it in the construction contract by the Employer. Generally speaking, the duties of the Engineer under the Red Book include the following. First, the Engineer has the right to review or approve specific documents submitted by the Contractor, such as the designs which are part of the Permanent Works,[89] the Contractors' application for payment,[90] etc. Secondly, the Engineer may exercise the authority to issue instructions and clarifications to the Contractor. For example, if the Contractor finds an ambiguity or discrepancy in the Contract documents, and sends a Notice to the Engineer, the Engineer shall issue the necessary clarification or instruction.[91] Thirdly, the General Conditions of the 2017 Red Book stipulates that when it comes to determination, the Engineer is to consult with both Parties and encourage them to reach agreement, failing which the Engineer is required to make a determination. This is one of the major changes of the 2017 edition. Instead of acting for the Employer, when performing this duty, the Engineer is required to be neutral between both Parties. Fourthly, the

89 Red Book 2017 sub-clause 4.1.
90 ibid sub-clauses 14.2 and 14.3.
91 ibid sub-clause 1.5.

Engineer may hold meetings to discuss matters relating to the execution of the project. By and large, the Engineer works on behalf of the Employer as Employer's Personnel, except when it comes to making a determination.

In 1984, the Chinese Employer of the Lubuge Reservoir Project engaged with an international consulting company to manage the execution of the project. This is the first time Engineers were engaged in Mainland China, and with great success. Some years later, the government introduced *Jian Li* into Mainland China and began to implement a unique system of construction supervision. In a Chinese construction contract, the word 'engineer' means *Jian Li*. Although the concept of Jian li stems from the engineer, there is one distinct difference between the *Jian Li* and the Engineer. The origins of these two concepts are quite different. The role of the Engineer in the FIDIC Contract Conditions is the result of a spontaneous process, which is a bottom-up process, while the Chinese government take a top-down approach to implement the concept of the *Jian Li*. This is due to a certain pattern in Mainland China that Chinese governments tend to set up a supervisory body when problems occur. 'If someone or somebody is not doing a job well, the answer is to let someone else to watch over them'.[92] This top-down tendency leads to a statutory characteristic of the *Jian Li*. *Contract Law* recognises the principle of the autonomy of the will as to the authority of the *Jian Li*. Article 276 of the *Contract Law* provides that:

> Where the employer engages with a *Jian Li*, the employer shall enter into a consulting agreement with a *Jian Li* in writing. The rights, obligations and associated legal liabilities of the employer and *Jian Li* shall be prescribed in accordance with the provisions in the Contract Law concerning contracts for commission.

In accordance with this provision, the Employer and the *Jian Li* have a principal–agent relationship. The authority of the *Jian Li* is vested by the Employer. From this perspective, the *Jian Li* performs a contractual obligation in the execution of the project. However, in other laws and regulations, several obligations are imposed on the *Jian Li*.

Article 8 of the *Ordinance on Construction Supervision* lists several kinds of construction projects where the appointment of a *Jian Li* is a necessity, for example, infrastructure, projects funded by the government or international agencies, etc. Article 9 prescribes the main duties of the *Jian Li*, which are to ensure that the project is carried out safely and meets the quality standards, to manage the whole execution process of the project, to keep the cost down and control the investment, and to coordinate the relationship between the Employer and the Contractor. *Construction Law* restates these duties of *Jian Li*.

Regulations on the Quality Management of Construction Projects and the Regulations on the Safety Management of Construction Projects apply more duties on the *Jian Li* regarding the quality and safety management of projects.

The first half of Article 14 of *Regulations on the Safety Management of Construction Projects* provides that:

> The *Jian Li* shall examine whether the safety technologies and measures in the construction designs or the special construction program are in line with the mandatory standards on the construction of projects.

---

92 Jie Tang, *Managers and Mandarins in Contemporary China: the Building of an International Business Alliance* (Routledge 2005) 48.

This provision puts emphasis on the obligation of the *Jian Li* to ensure the safety of the project. If the *Jian Li* fails to perform these obligations, his/her licence will be revoked, and s/he will face huge fines or be criminally responsible.[93]

Along with many obligations regarding supervision on the quality and safety of the project, these laws and regulations also give the *Jian Li* considerable power.

Article 37 of the *Regulations on the Quality Management of Construction Projects* provides that:

> Without signature of the *Jian Li*, no construction materials, components, fittings or equipment may be used or installed in the project, and the construction entity may not undertake the construction of the next process. Without signature of the chief *Jian Li*, the employer shall not appropriate the project fund, nor conduct completion- based check and acceptance.

In accordance with this provision, the *Jian Li* has a lot of power during the execution of the project. The *Jian Li* has the power to approve the use of all the materials and the application of all the payments. The second sentence of this article seems to put the *Jian Li* in a position higher than the Employer. If the *Jian Li* does not sign the application of payment or issuance of the completion certificate, the Employer cannot make the payment or issue the certificate even if it wants to.

Article 14 of *Regulations on the Safety Management of Construction Projects* provides that:

> Where the *Jian Li* discovers any potential risk of safety accident in the course of conducting supervision, it shall demand the contractor to correct; if the circumstance is serious, it shall demand the contractor to suspend the work, and report to the employer. If the contractor refuses to correct or suspend, the *Jian Li* shall report to relevant administrative departments in time.

In accordance with this provision, the *Jian Li* has the power to instruct the Contractor to suspend the Works, and to report to the government agency to impose administrative penalties on the Contractor.

Jian Li has the above-mentioned rights and obligations, which are stipulated by the law, with or without the approval of the Employer. As a result of the administrative effort, *Jian Li* is also subject to the supervision of a government agency. Articles 12 and 13 of *Construction Law* stipulate that the *Jian Li* companies are rated into different classes according to their registered capital, professionals and technicians, technical equipment and performance record of completed construction projects, etc. Only when they pass qualification examinations and obtain appropriate qualification certificates, may they engage in construction activities commensurate with the scope of their qualification classes.

With all these administrative characteristic, *Jian Li* and its authorities are mainly mandatory, which result in the statutory role of *Jian Li* being similar to that of an independent checker of projects in many countries,[94] with considerably more authority and duties than the Engineer in FIDIC General Conditions.

The second difference between *Jian Li* and the Engineer is that the Engineer acts on behalf of the Employer and is only required to be neutral when an agreement

93 *Regulations on the Quality Management of Construction Projects;* art 57 of *Regulations on the Safety Management of Construction Projects* arts 61–62.

94 Hew Kian Heong, *The Foreign Project Consultant as Jian Li* http://kluwerconstructionblog.com/2009/12/06/the-foreign-project-consultant-as-jian-li/ (accessed 2 April 2019).

needs to be reached or a determination needs to be made, whereas the *Jian Li* has to be objective and fair all the time, even though s/he is employed by the Employer. The requirement to be neutral is set out in Article 34 of *Construction Law*, which provides that:

> The *Jian Li* shall carry out construction supervision in an objective and fair manner in accordance with the entrustment by the employers.

Whether the *Jian Li* can be neutral and independent remains uncertain in practice, because the *Jian Li* is hired by the Employer and is paid by the Employer. Considering this background, requiring the *Jian Li* to act fairly between Employer and the Contractor may be expecting too much.[95]

To sum up, the Chinese engineer, the *Jian Li*, has some distinguishing characteristics from the Engineer in the FIDIC General Conditions. To obtain a better understanding of the concept of the Chinese *Jian Li*, it is recommended to obtain professional advice from Chinese lawyers.

7.10.2 Exceptional Events

In the FIDIC 2017 editions, *Force Majeure* has been renamed as Exceptional Events. In Mainland China, Exceptional Events not only include *force majeure*, but also **Fundamental Change in Circumstances**. Fundamental Change in Circumstances is a principle implemented in civil law countries, which is similar to the principle of frustration of contract in common law countries. If the circumstances change fundamentally after the execution of a contract so that performance of the Contract would be onerous for one Party, that Party has the right to terminate the Contract or to modify some articles of the Contract. As this principle grants Parties the right not to perform a valid contract, legislators in many countries are quite cautious about including this principle in statutory law.[96] In Germany, this principle was not provided in the *Civil Code* at the beginning.[97] Along with the theoretical and practical promotion, the 2002 edition *Civil Code* in Germany has finally included this principle. Like Germany, in Mainland China, this principle was not stipulated in *Contract Law* due to different opinions in 1999, but is provided in the later-issued *Interpretation II of the Supreme People's Court of Several Issues concerning the Application of the Contract Law of the People's Republic of China*, Article 26 of which provides that:

> Where any major change which is unforeseeable, is not a business risk and is not caused by a *force majeure* occurs after the formation of a contract, if the continuous performance of the contract is obviously unfair to the other party or cannot realize the purposes of the contract and a party files a request for the modification or rescission of the contract with the people's court, the people's court shall decide whether to modify or rescind the contract under the principle of fairness and in light of the actualities of the case.

95 Yang Yanyan, *Research on the Legal System of the Construction Supervision in China* (Zhengzhou University 2011) 35. Editor's note. This echoes the concerns expressed in common law countries as to whether the Engineer, engaged by the Employer, can realistically be expected to act neutrally between Employer and Contractor. See Philip Loots and Donald Charrett, *Practical Guide to Engineering and Construction Contracts* (CCH 2009) 6.1.

96 Han Qiang, 'Study on Classification of the Principle of the Fundamental Change of Circumstances' (2010) 4 *Chinese Journal of Law* 58.

97 Du jinglin, 'Codification of the Basic Obstacles to the German System of Legal Acts and New Debt Law' (2005) 3 *Journal of Comparative Law* 53.

In judicial practice, the key to apply this principle properly is to distinguish the fundamental change of circumstances and the business risk correctly. As for disputes arising from construction contracts, price fluctuation of materials and labour and changes in government policies are two main concerns regarding to the fundamental change of circumstances. Primarily, the change in government policies has to be the only and direct reason why the continuous performance is obviously unfair.[98] If an obstacle of performance exists before the change of policies, and one Party wants to terminate the Contract due to this obstacle based on the Fundamental Change in Circumstances, such petition will not be sustained by the courts.[99] As to the price fluctuation of materials and labour, the judges tend to consider the price fluctuation simply due to market factors to be the business risk, which shall be taken into account by Parties when executing the Contract and shall be borne by the Parties.[100]

As can be seen, the standard of the principle of Fundamental Change in Circumstances is quite hard to meet. Judges of all levels tend to be cautious when deciding whether or not the principle can apply. Furthermore, the Supreme People's Court issued the *Notice of the Supreme People's Court on Correctly Applying the Interpretation II of Several Issues concerning the Contract Law of the People's Republic of China so as to Serve the Primary Objectives of the Party and the State* in 2009, which stipulates that judges must prudently apply this principle, and application of this principle shall be subject to the scrutiny of the Higher People's Court, and be submitted to the Supreme People's Court for review when necessary.

7.11 References

7.11.1 Books

Shu Guoying, *Introduction to Jurisprudence* (2nd edn, Peking University Press 2012)

Dong Hao, *On Judicial Interpretation* (China University of Political Science and Law Press 1999)

Zhao Xianglin, *Private International Law* (China University of Political Science and Law Press 2007)

Dong Jinxin, *On the Application of Third Country Mandatory Rules in Forum* (China Renmin University Press 2016)

Du Wanhua, *China Trial Guide Reference and Guide to Civil Trial, vol 38* (People's Court Press 2009)

Jie Tang, *Managers and Mandarins in Contemporary China – the Building of An International Business Alliance* (Routledge 2005)

7.11.2 Journals

Study in Law and Business

Ascent

Social Sciences in China

98 *Dazong Group Co Ltd Zong Xijin v Huaibei Shenghuo Mine Co Ltd, Huaibei Shenghuo Real Estate Development Co Ltd* (2015) Min Er Zhong Zi No 236.

99 *Chongqing Changhong Plastic Factory v Chongqing Tianlong Real Estate Development Co Ltd* (2016) Supreme People's Court Min Zhong No 203.

100 *Guangdong Dian Bai Construction Co Ltd v Dongguan Changan Zhen Real Estate Development Co Ltd* (2013) Min Shen Zi No 1099.

Law Science
China Construction Law Review
Journal of Law Application
Peking University Law Review
Chinese Journal of Law
Journal of Comparative Law

7.11.3 Internet

http://www.bjac.org.cn/news/view?id=2821
http://kluwerconstructionblog.com/2009/12/06/the-foreign-project-consultant-as-jian-li/
http://www.pkulaw.cn/
https://www.itslaw.com/

CHAPTER 8

Applying FIDIC contracts in Fiji

Nicholas Barnes, Melvin Chand and Komal Singh

DOI: 10.4324/9781003200901-8

8.1 Outline of the legal environment in Fiji

8.1.1 The constitutional structure of Fiji

Fiji is a constitutional democracy. It gained colonial independence from the United Kingdom in 1970 and established a republic. There were three subsequent constitutions establishing the executive, legislative and judicial branches of government, together with a bill of rights. The most recent constitution, *Constitution of the Republic of Fiji 2013*, declares Fiji as a sovereign democratic state. The head of state is the President of Fiji, who has a ceremonial function in the governance of the country (assent is required to formalise Acts of Parliament). The executive consists of the President, the Prime Minister and cabinet. Fiji's Parliament consists of a single House of Representatives with 51 seats on a multi-member open list system of proportional representation with a single national constituency.

The *Constitution* is divided into 12 chapters containing 174 articles. The articles cover inter alia: the Bill of Rights, the State, the Parliament, the executive (comprising the President and cabinet), the judiciary, state services, revenue and expenditure, and amendment of the *Constitution*. The Supreme Court of Fiji is the final appellate court and has original jurisdiction to hear and determine constitutional questions referred to it (up until 1987 the Privy Council of the United Kingdom was the final appellate court). Fiji has a *Bill of Rights* providing civil and political rights, as well as social and economic rights such as the right to food, water and education, the social and economic rights are subject to the state's best endeavours.

The authority and power to make laws for the state is vested in Parliament consisting of the Members of Parliament (MPs) and the President, through the enactment and passing of bills assented to by the President. The entire country is a single state and daily affairs are run by government ministries assisted by (so far) unelected, local municipal councils.

8.1.2 The common law of Fiji

Fiji is a common law country, and the courts recognise a distinct common law of Fiji. In *Hassan v Transport Workers Union*[1] the Supreme Court of Fiji declared that the common law of Fiji is ultimately that declared by the Supreme Court. As much of Fiji's common law originated from the common law of England, Fiji aligns its common law very closely to the common laws of England and Wales, Australia, New Zealand and Canada, which are also highly persuasive. These jurisdictions are frequently cited in argument. The common laws of South Africa, Singapore and India also carry persuasive value. In *Hassan* the Supreme Court said that '[a] conservative principle should be applied to maintain, so far as possible, a degree of certainty and

1 [2006] FJSC 11, CBV0006U.2005S (19 October 2006).

predictability about the judge-made law', which results in Fiji courts often adopting English and Australian principles adjusted to the Fijian context.

Fiji is a member state of the United Nations and has ratified a number of international conventions (which the *Constitution* recognises). In the context of construction contracts and dispute resolution, the most current adoption has been the *UNCITRAL Model Law on International Commercial Arbitration* adopted by the United Nations Commission on International Trade Law on 21 June 1985 and as amended by the United Nations Commission on International Trade Law on 7 July 2006, through the *International Arbitration Act 2017* of Fiji.

8.1.3 The court system in Fiji

The judicial power and authority of the state is vested in the Supreme Court (the final appellate court), the Court of Appeal, the High Court, the magistrates' court, and other courts and tribunals created by legislation. The judiciary is headed by the Chief Justice, who is also the President of the Supreme Court. The Supreme Court has exclusive jurisdiction to hear and determine appeals from all final judgments of the Court of Appeal and has original jurisdiction to hear and determine constitutional questions referred to it. The Supreme Court is the Fiji equivalent to the Supreme Court of the United Kingdom and the High Court of Australia.

The High Court has unlimited original jurisdiction to hear and determine any civil or criminal proceedings under any law and has original jurisdiction in any matter arising under the *Constitution* or its interpretation. The High Court exercises its common law and equity jurisdictions concurrently.

In the context of construction law, Australian and New Zealand decisions are highly relevant and persuasive.

8.2 The construction industry in Fiji

The construction industry has played a key role in Fiji's socio-economic development and with increased investments in infrastructure projects, the building and construction industry in Fiji is operating at capacity.[2] With some major local construction companies, high-quality construction services are provided, often using local materials and labour.

The Fiji Construction Industry Council (**CIC**) comprises all the major builders, sub-contractors, architects, engineers, quantity surveyors, hardware suppliers, developers, project managers and key government representatives. The CIC addresses major concerns affecting the construction industry and regulates the education, licensing, insurance, cyclone certification, building code review, occupational health and safety and authority approvals for constructions projects. The CIC also recommends the actions taken to resolve disagreements in the industry under their 'dispute resolutions' function.

The FIJI *National Building Code* forms the basis for the Fiji Standard Form of Building Contract, which is widely used and preferred in domestic construction transactions. It is presently subject to review. Apart from the Fiji Standard Form

2 Building and construction to Fiji, Trends and opportunities https://www.austrade.gov.au/australian/export/export-markets/countries/fiji/industries/Building-and-construction (accessed 9 February 2021).

of Building Contract, domestic transactions are contracted under model contracts from Australia and New Zealand. FIDIC contracts are less common under private transactions.

FIDIC contracts have become more frequent in the public space with the advent of government engaging overseas contractors for capital developments. Public enterprises and government owned companies have started adopting the FIDIC contracts in line with the Asian Development Bank triggered reforms. The Water Authority of Fiji, Energy Fiji Limited and the Fiji Roads Authority, for example, have as standard practice adopted FIDIC contracts from about 2015.[3]

8.3 The impact of Covid-19 in Fiji

8.3.1 The impact of Covid-19 on the execution of construction projects in Fiji

Fiji placed governmental restrictions on overseas travel, movement and large gatherings in the early stages of the pandemic. Domestically, the government responded by imposing a nationwide curfew, restricting large gatherings and closing down schools and non-essential services over a period of 14 days.

Lockdown of both Suva and Lautoka resulted in significant business interruptions. There were no government directions to lockdown construction sites; a 20-person limit was applied to all non-essential services including construction sites.[4]

There was no strict requirement of using face masks; however, there were compulsory health requirements such as physical distancing, compulsory temperature checks before entry at venues and sites and washing or sanitising hands thoroughly and regularly. These requirements continue to be in place at the time of writing (February 2021). A contact tracing app named careFIJI was also developed to assist medical services in Fiji to speed up contact tracing efforts and help stop the spread of Covid-19. These health measures applied to everyone including workers on a construction site.[5]

The only Covid-19 specific legislation that was passed was the *Employment Relations (Amendment) Act 2020*, an Act to amend the primary legislation governing employment laws in Fiji.[6] The amendment defined the pandemic as an act of God, a statutory exemption from the duty to provide work and pay to an employee.[7] There are no decided cases on this point.

Banks and financial institutions in Fiji have introduced relief packages to their customers affected by Covid-19 by providing principal and interest holidays for up to six months, thus relaxing repayments.

Many employers, including employers in the construction industry reduced pay and work hours requirements after consultation with their employees in an effort to reduce the impact of the challenges faced by both the employer and employees.

3 http://www.parliament.gov.fj/wp-content/uploads/2018/05/PAC-Commentary-for-Special-Projects-report-FINAL.pdf;https://www.adb.org/sites/default/files/linked-documents/48141-001-sd-02.pdf (accessed 13 May 2019).

4 Ministry of Health and Medical Services Appendix 1: Information on restrictions http://www.health.gov.fj/wp-content/uploads/2020/04/Appendix-1-Information-on-restrictions.pdf (accessed 9 February 2021).

5 https://carefiji.digitalfiji.gov.fj/ (accessed 9 February 2021).

6 *Employment Relations Act 2007*.

7 ibid s 24.

8.3.2 The impact of Covid-19 on the operation of construction contracts in Fiji

The only specific legislation passed in response to Covid-19 was the *Employment Relations (Amendment) Act 2020* which only relates to employment contracts.

Unless the individual construction contracts expressly account for pandemics, making the performance of a contract impossible, the contracts have to be performed, despite the difficulties due to Covid-19. The effect of the *force majeure* clauses remains to be judicially determined under the existing common law rules.

8.4 Fijian governing law of the contract

8.4.1 Constraints on the governing law of a construction contract

In Fiji, there is no specific law that deals with construction contracts and the courts apply common law principles in determining construction contract disputes. Damages are awarded pursuant to traditional common law principles of contract and construction law. In construction contract cases, three categories of damages may be claimed: (1) damages for defective workmanship; (2) schedule/ contractual related damages (special damages); and (3) damages for failure to perform.[8]

The common law of Fiji recognises the Parties' freedom of contract to choose the law governing their contract. Fiji has not ratified the *Hague Principles on Choice of Law in International Commercial Contracts* and does not have any legislative provisions affecting the Parties' ability to choose 'rules of law that are generally accepted on an international, supranational or regional level as a neutral and balanced set of rules'.

Governing law and the choice of jurisdiction in a contract are distinct matters.

Fiji courts have generally accepted the governing law of the contract as the Parties agreed to.[9] However, if the construction site is in Fiji, various pieces of legislation require compliance, such as the *Environment Management Act 2005*, *Public Health Act 1935* and occupational health and safety requirements along with various municipal council bye-laws requiring special permits and approvals for construction, as well as the validity of completion. It would not be unusual for a Fiji court, to the extent necessary, to override the parties' choice of governing law to ensure compliance with Fiji laws and provide available remedies to aggrieved parties on the grounds of public policy. In *Khans Shipping Company Ltd v High Commission for the Government of Tuvalu*[10] (although not a construction contract matter), the High Court held that:

> The principles to be derived from the series of cases cited by the plaintiff and defendant is that the proper law of the contract could be determined by reference to that with which the transaction has its closest and most real connexion ... In *Coast Lines Ltd v Hudig & Veder Chartering NV* (supra) Lord Denning MR stated that the shipowners were English was as important as the circumstances that the charterparty was signed in Rotterdam by Dutch charterers for performance in the Netherlands. Megaw LJ (op cit at page 458) stated the charterparty was only in 'that somewhat technical sense ... "made" there. The fact that the freight and demurrage were expressed in sterling deserves slightly greater weight, although again, it is not a strong factor in the light of the evidence ... I would go so far as to say that in a charterparty case the flag of the vessel is likely normally to be important. But it

8 *Raju v Chetty* [2018] FJHC 553, HBC102.2017 (26 June 2018).

9 *Herbert Construction Company (Fiji) Ltd v Malolo Development Company (Fiji) Ltd* [2008] FJHC 302, HBC336.2007 (12 September 2008).

10 [2011] FJHC 260, Civil Action 158.2002 (12 May 2011).

> must be considered along with the other relevant factors ...' The Court held that English law was the proper law of the contract. The form and place of payment were also held to be matters of 'very considerable importance' by Singleton L.J. in *The Assunzione* 1954 (1) AER, at page 291. The charter agreement in the matter before the Court was signed in Fiji. The ship was a Fijian ship. The agreement provided that the charter rate of the vessel was to be paid in Fijian currency. The contract was performed in Tuvalu. In my judgment, on a consideration of all aspects of the transaction, the system of law with which the transaction had its closest and most real connection are the laws of Fiji.

The Fiji courts have held that:

> Fiji Courts have a solemn obligation to uphold a litigant's right to invoke their jurisdiction in a case properly within their jurisdiction and that [a]t common law, it is also settled that a contract which ousters the jurisdiction of a court is contrary to public policy.[11]

In *Atkinson v Namale West Inc* the High Court adopted LJ Denning's ratio in *The Fehmarn*,[12] where he said:

> One of the rules they apply is that a stipulation that all disputes shall be judged by the tribunals of a particular country is not absolutely binding. It is a matter to which the Courts of this country will pay much regard and to which they will normally give effect but it is subject to the overriding principle that no one by his private stipulation, can oust these Courts of their jurisdiction in a matter that properly belongs to them ... I do not regard the choice of law in a contract as decisive. I prefer to look to see with what country the dispute is most closely concerned.

The situation is different if the parties submit their dispute to international arbitration. Under the *International Arbitration Act 2017*, an arbitration is international if inter alia the parties have expressly agreed that the subject matter of the arbitration agreement relates to more than one state. An arbitration agreement must be in writing. A court before which an action is brought where the parties are subject to an arbitration agreement, on the request of a party, may refer the parties to arbitration unless the court finds the agreement is null and void. The parties are free to agree on the procedure to be followed by the arbitral tribunal in conducting the proceedings. The parties are also free to agree on the place and language of arbitration. The *International Arbitration Act 2017* adopted the *UNCITRAL Model Law on International Commercial Arbitration* adopted by the United Nations Commission on International Trade Law on 21 June 1985 and as amended by the United Nations Commission on International Trade Law on 7 July 2006 as the law governing the procedure of an arbitration held in Fiji. Section 46(1) and (2) of the *Act* provides:

> (1) The arbitral tribunal shall decide the dispute in accordance with such rules of law as are chosen by the parties as applicable to the substance of the dispute. Any designation of the law or legal system of a given State shall be construed, unless otherwise expressed, as directly referring to the substantive law of that State and not to its conflict of laws rules.
> (2) Failing any designation by the parties, the arbitral tribunal shall apply the law determined by the conflict of laws rules which it considers applicable.

The Fiji courts, unless there are differentiating circumstances, accept the parties' choice of law under a contract as well as at arbitration. In *Raghwan v Fiji National Provident Fund*[13] the Court of Appeal upheld an arbitrator's ruling where the choice of law for

11 *Atkinson v Namale West Inc* [2010] FJHC 10, HBC166.2008 (22 January 2010).
12 [1958] 1 All ER 33.
13 [2016] FJCA 74, ABU0063.2013 (27 May 2016).

the arbitration under the memorandum of agreement for arbitration was the New Zealand *Arbitration Act* supplemented by the Fiji *Arbitration Act*. The aggrieved party applied to set aside the arbitrator's ruling. The court held that the arbitration legislation of either New Zealand or Fiji did not allow the court to replace or supplement the arbitrator's ruling unless the arbitrator's ruling was legally 'incomplete' (the common law test of the arbitrator's jurisdiction); the findings of facts by the arbitrator in *Raghwan* were undisturbed by the High Court and the Court of Appeal.

8.4.2 Formal requirements for a construction contract

The requirements for a valid contract in Fiji are those of common law: the parties are legally sound persons who intend to create a legal relationship, an agreement constituted by offer and acceptance, supported by consideration with terms that are clear and certain. Fijian law recognises both simple contracts and contracts under seal or specialty, although a specialty is uncommon, if not unused.

A construction contract does not need to be in writing in Fiji, although this is never the case in practice. Construction contracts in Fiji have a close link to the *Fijian Competition and Consumer Commission Act 2010*, which regulates the provision of services (as well as goods) and which includes the provision of work and labour. 'Services' under the *Act* includes rights, benefits, privileges and facilities that are, or are to be, provided, granted or conferred under a contract for or in relation to the performance of work including building work and work of a professional nature.

The actual design and construction need to comply with building specifications and standards under legislation such as the public health and local government legislation. The *Public Health Act 1935*, which has its roots in the English *Building Regulations 1935*, prescribes a Fiji *National Building Code*. The *Code* itself mirrors the Australian and New Zealand standards from around 1990. Australian and New Zealand stakeholders were instrumental in contributing to the content of the Fijian *Building Code*.

The limitation period for bringing any action founded on simple contract is within six years from when the cause of action arises and for a specialty 12 years, in accordance with section 4 of the *Limitation Act 1971*.

8.5 What Special Provisions in the Particular Conditions are necessary for consistency with applicable laws in Fiji?

8.5.1 FIDIC General Conditions are incompatible or inconsistent with Fijian governing law of the contract

If the governing law is the law of Fiji then no Special Provisions in the Particular Conditions are necessary for consistency with the applicable laws in Fiji, although attention should be paid to limitation periods (six years for simple contracts and tort claims from the date the cause of action arises) and environmental compliance laws. Provisions relating to restrictive trade practices such as misrepresentation are governed by the provisions of the Fijian *Competition and Consumer Commission Act 2010*, which override the provisions of the contract. That is not to say that the respective FIDIC General Conditions are incompatible or inconsistent with Fijian law; however, Parties may wish to take the legislative provisions as a cue to obtain independent legal advice on the practical effects of conditions and warranties (which are regarded as representations) provided in the FIDIC contracts.

The parties to construction contracts which deal with native land (**iTaukei land**) and or state leases should ensure that the required statutory consents are obtained as a condition precedent to the Contract. To deal with *iTaukei* land (dealing includes leasing and sub-leasing), consent is required from the iTaukei Land Trust Board under the *iTaukei Land Trust Act 1940* and to deal with State land, the consent of the Director of Land is required under the *State Lands Act 1945*. A contract is deemed void *ab initio* without the statutory consents, although equitable reliefs such as restitution (for deposit monies) are available in limited circumstances.

8.5.2 FIDIC General Conditions are incompatible or inconsistent with the law of the Site/country

If the Site is in Fiji then no Special Provisions in the Particular Conditions are necessary for consistency with the applicable laws in Fiji, although attention should be paid to limitation periods and environmental compliance laws.

Common law principles apply in relation to Employer-independent Contractor/Subcontractor relationships. Parties should ensure by means of Special Provisions that the conditions of contract comply with *Hadley v Baxendale*[14] principles of attributing liability as intended.

It should be made clear by Special Provisions whether or not the Employer can sue Subcontractors and if the Contractor can exclude liability for the actions of its Subcontractors.

Proper indemnity clauses should be included in the Particular Conditions for statutory liabilities. It is also important to clarify these liabilities and limits of responsibility as these have respective labour law and health and safety implications, as well as environmental law implications.

8.5.3 FIDIC General Conditions are incompatible or inconsistent with the relevant laws on dispute determination in Fiji

If the governing law is the law of Fiji then no Special Provisions in the Particular Conditions are necessary for consistency with the applicable laws in Fiji, although attention should be paid to limitation periods, and note paragraphs 8.5.1 and 8.5.2, if applicable.

8.6 What Special Provisions in the Particular Conditions are desirable for consistency with applicable laws in Fiji?

Construction contracts in Fiji are regulated by the common law principles of contract law, more often guided by the common law developments in England and Australia, as applicable, based on the facts. The courts generally respect the parties' freedom to contract and the terms and conditions agreed upon, subject to laws and public policy. Having no legislative guide for the 'management' of construction contracts, disputing parties are unfortunately forced into invoking dispute resolution clauses or making applications for interim measures in court, which can delay projects. Contracting parties should obtain proper legal advice on appropriate Special Provisions aiming to streamline the dispute resolution clauses in the General Conditions to suit Fiji needs

14 (1854) 9 Ex 341.

in terms of fast-tracking dispute resolution and avoiding protracted litigation (which is almost always the case).

There is no security of payment or frustrated contracts legislation in Fiji.

In terms of proportionate liability, a plaintiff party can claim common law contractual damages from any one offending party, for example, a principal Contractor for the actions of a Subcontractor in a building contract, and a principal Contractor for the negligence of designing engineers in a design and build contract. Naturally, insured parties are made defendants to actions. In Fiji, it is up to the defendant to join other parties which it thinks fault should be attributed to or who had a greater role, and thus responsibility for liability, in the causal connection to the resulting damage. The Fiji *High Court Rules 1988* issued under the *High Court Act* regulate the process for issuing joinder or third/fourth party proceedings to achieve this. The common law principles for joint and several liability apply in Fiji. It is highly unlikely, based on public policy and/or the laws under the Fijian *Competition and Consumer Commission Act 2010* such as unconscionability and fair trade practices, that parties can contract out of principles relating to joint and several liability by inserting Special Provisions under the Particular Conditions.

8.7 Summary of applicable legislation for Fijian governing law of the contract

8.7.1 Entry into a construction contract

Contracts generally	*Public Health Act 1935* *Fijian Competition and Consumer Commission Act 2010*
Construction contracts	*Public Health Act 1935* *Fijian Competition and Consumer Commission Act 2010*

8.7.2 Termination of a construction contract

Bankruptcy, insolvency, liquidation	*Companies Act 2015* *Bankruptcy Act 1944*
Guarantees under forms of security (tender security, demand guarantee, surety bond, advance payment guarantee, retention money guarantee, payment guarantee by employer)	*Property Law Act 1971*

8.7.3 Dispute resolution

Limitation periods	*Limitation Act 1971*
Liability	*Law Reform (Contributory Negligence and Tortfeasors) Act 1946* *Limitation Act 1971*
Arbitration	*Arbitration Act 1965* *International Arbitration Act 2017*

8.8 Summary of applicable legislation if the Site/Country is in Fiji

8.8.1 Operation of a construction contract	
Registration and administration of professionals: engineers, architects, quantity surveyors, certifiers, building surveyors, surveyors	*Public Health Act 1935*
Registration/licensing of contractors	*Public Health Act 1935*
Use of liens/Assignment of debt	*Property Law Act 1971*
Labour	*Employment Relations Act 2007* *Accident Compensation Act 2017*
Design/Moral rights	*Copyright Act 1999* *Trade-Marks Act 1933* *Health and Safety at Work Act 1996*
Copyright	*Copyright Act 1999*
The product being produced from the Works	*Health and Safety at Work Act 1996* *Public Health Act 1935* *Environment Management Act 2005*
First nation people's land rights	*iTaukei Land Trust Act 1940*
Planning	*Town Planning Act 1946* *Local Government Act 1972* *Public Health Act 1935*
Work affecting adjacent property to the Site	*Local Government Act 1972* *Environment Management Act 2005*
Heritage	*National Trust of Fiji Act 1970*
Environment	*Environment Management Act 2005*
Building and construction permits, execution of construction work, standard of construction work	*Local Government Act 1972* *Electricity Act 1966* *Public Health Act 1935*
Health and safety	*Health and Safety at Work Act 1996* *Accident Compensation Act 2017*
Employer's sale of Contractor's Equipment, surplus material, wreckage and Temporary Works	*Personal Property Securities Act 2017*
Insurance	*Accident Compensation Act 2017*
Statutory rights that coexist with contractual rights	*Fijian Competition and Consumer Commission Act 2010*
Liability for defective work	*Fijian Competition and Consumer Commission Act 2010*
Liability for nuisance	*Fijian Competition and Consumer Commission Act 2010*
Other issues	*Financial Transactions Reporting Act 2004*
8.8.2 Termination of a construction contract	
Bankruptcy, insolvency, liquidation	*Companies Act 2015* *Bankruptcy Act 1944*
8.8.3 Dispute resolution	
Limitation periods	*Limitation Act 1971*

8.9 Summary of applicable legislation if the 'seat' of the dispute determination is in Fiji

Limitation periods	*Limitation Act 1971*
Arbitration	*Arbitration Act 1965* *International Arbitration Act 2017*

8.10 Issues that a court or arbitrator may construe differently to that expected from the words of the Contract, because of local law or custom

As discussed in this chapter, construction contracts in Fiji are regulated by the common law principles of Fiji, which mirror the common law principles of England and Australia. More often an aggrieved plaintiff formalises its claim in common law, supplemented by damages accruing pursuant to legislative rights, such as damages under the Fijian *Competition and Consumer Commission Act 2010* for unfair trade practices; for example, misrepresentation.

Generally, offences under legislation carry strict liability and intention may only go so far as mitigation or in the case of a civil claim based on a statutory offence, to mitigating quantum. Section 75 of the Fijian *Competition and Consumer Commission Act 2010* stipulates that:

> (1) A person shall not, in trade or commerce engage in conduct that is misleading or deceptive or is likely to mislead or deceive;
> (2) Nothing in this Division shall be taken as limiting by implication the generality of subsection

A 'person' includes all legally recognised persons, natural or by statute. An intention to mislead or deceive is not a necessary ingredient in establishing the offence and, arguably, liability. Like in Australia, warranties in a construction contract would be tantamount to 'conduct' under the *Act*. The result is that it is difficult to contract out of such statutory compliance and possible liability through exclusion clauses, which places a limit on the parties' freedom to contract on negotiated terms. Remedies for damages flowing from statutory breaches may well be the same damages an aggrieved plaintiff would recover under common law.

The Fijian *Competition and Consumer Commission Act 2010* has close parallels to the *Australian Competition and Consumer Act 2010*. The Australian *Act* forms a baseline guide on interpreting the provisions of the Fijian *Act*. The Fijian courts, adjusting to the Fijian context, have cited Australian cases. For example, the Fiji Court of Appeal in *McGoon v Ali*,[15] while discussing the concept of unconscionable conduct, said at [28]:

> The first requirement was considered in *Australian Competition and Consumer Commission –v- C.G. Berbatis Holdings Pty Limited and Others* (2003) 214 CLR 51 at pages 62 and 63 where the High Court (per Gleeson CJ) considered that the disability or disadvantage must be a special disadvantage in the form of a disabling circumstance that seriously affected a party's ability to make a judgment in his own best interests. In the same decision the view was expressed that inequality of bargaining power alone does not establish a position of relevant disadvantage. At page 64 it was noted that: 'Many, perhaps even most, contracts are made between parties of unequal bargaining power and good conscience does not require parties to contractual negotiations to forfeit their advantage or neglect their own interests'.

15 FJCA 31, ABU16.2007 (27 February 2015).

The Australian and Fijian *Acts* are similar, and Fiji courts certainly take interpretational guide from the Australian jurisprudence.

There are no strict proportionate liability defences available in Fiji, although a defendant who is not fully responsible in the causal chain may issue joinder or third/fourth party actions under common law to include other parties to share liability. A defendant may also claim contribution post-judgment under the *Law Reform (Contributory Negligence and Tortfeasors) Act 1946*; however, the *Limitation Act 1971* limits such an action to two years from the date on which a right to seek contribution arises.

8.11 References

8.11.1 Internet

Legislation
https://www.laws.gov.fj/
Case law
http://www.paclii.org/
Articles
www.parliament.gov.fj

CHAPTER 9

Applying FIDIC contracts in Hong Kong

Ben Bury and Julie-Anne Mallis

DOI: 10.4324/9781003200901-9

9.1 Outline of the legal environment in Hong Kong

9.1.1 The constitutional structure of Hong Kong

Hong Kong is a Special Administrative Region of the People's Republic of China. Its legal system is very much embedded within the legal system of Mainland China[1] and Hong Kong comes directly under the Central People's Government. Nonetheless, China has granted Hong Kong a high degree of autonomy through the *Basic Law of the Hong Kong Special Administrative Region of the People's Republic of China* (the *Basic Law*).[2] The *Basic Law* is a quasi-constitutional document (sometimes described as a 'mini-constitution') and derives its authority from Article 31 of the *Constitution of the People's Republic of China*, which empowers the Chinese State to establish Special Administrative Regions when necessary.

The constitutional framework for Hong Kong is governed by the *Basic Law*. The *Basic Law* maintains 'the laws previously in force in Hong Kong'.[3] This is a reference to

1 Lo Pui Yin, *The Judicial Construction of Hong Kong's Basic Law* (Hong Kong University Press 2014) 4.

2 Adopted at the Third Session of the Seventh National People's Congress on 4 April 1990; promulgated by Order No 26 of the President of the People's Republic of China on 4 April 1990, 29 ILM 1511–1548 (1990).

3 *Basic Law*, art 8.

the common law, rules of equity, ordinances, subordinate legislation and customary law implemented between 1842 and 1997, when Hong Kong was a British colony. During that period, Hong Kong's legal system was based on the common law of England and Wales 'except where the same shall be inapplicable to the local circumstances of [Hong Kong], or of its inhabitants'.[4]

On 19 December 1984, Britain and China signed the Sino-British Joint Declaration,[5] whereby the nations agreed Hong Kong would be returned to China on or before 1 July 1997. Several essential policies were agreed relating to the governing of Hong Kong from 1 July 1997. Those policies formed the basis for the *Basic Law*. The primary policy was the adoption of the principle of 'one country, two systems', whereby Hong Kong retains its system of common law and capitalism for a period of 50 years from 1 July 1997, despite being an inalienable part of China, which has its own socialist system and policies. The expression 'one country, two systems' is found in Article 2 of the *Basic Law*. The laws of Mainland China are not applied in Hong Kong except for laws relating to defence and foreign affairs, as well as other matters outside the limits of the autonomy of Hong Kong as a Special Administrative Region.[6]

The *Basic Law* comprises 160 Articles in nine chapters.[7] The chapters cover: general principles; the relationship between the Chinese government and Hong Kong; fundamental rights and duties of the residents; the structure and functions of the branches of government including the political structure, the economy, education, science, culture, sports, religion, labour and social services, and external affairs; and interpretation and amendment of the *Basic Law*.[8] There are three annexures to the *Basic Law*, which cover: the method for selection of the Chief Executive; the method of formation of the Legislative Council and its voting procedures; and the Mainland Chinese laws to be applied in Hong Kong, which relate to defence and foreign affairs.

Other central principles include: 'Hong Kong People administering Hong Kong', which provides that the executive authorities and legislature of Hong Kong shall be composed of permanent residents of Hong Kong;[9] and the special status afforded to the Hong Kong *Bill of Rights Ordinance* (Cap 383), which applies the provisions of the *International Covenant on Civil and Political Rights*.[10]

9.1.2 The common law of Hong Kong

Whilst the common law of Hong Kong is derived from the common law of England and Wales and does not differ substantially from it, the courts in Hong Kong are not bound to follow the decisions of English courts. The courts may nonetheless refer to English precedents and precedents of other common law jurisdictions.[11]

4 Yash P Ghai, *Hong Kong's New Constitutional Order – the Resumption of Chinese Sovereignty and the Basic Law* (2nd edn, Hong Kong University Press 2011) 22–23; *Supreme Court Ordinance 1844*. In circumstances where the law of England and Wales was not suitable, Chinese law and customs would apply.

5 The Sino-British Joint Declaration was later ratified on 27 May 1985.

6 *Basic Law*, art 18.

7 Ghai (n 4) 137.

8 ibid.

9 *Basic Law*, art 3.

10 ibid art 39.

11 ibid art 84. Decisions from the United Kingdom Supreme Court (or the House of Lords as it was previously known) and the Privy Council are treated with great respect: *A Solicitor v The Law Society of Hong Kong* [2008] 2 HKLRD 576 [6]–[17].

9.1.3 The court system of Hong Kong

Hong Kong enjoys executive, legislative and independent judicial power, including that of final adjudication.[12] The power of final adjudication is vested in the Court of Final Appeal,[13] which replaced the judicial committee of the Privy Council in London prior to the resumption of Chinese sovereignty. The Court of Final Appeal is unique in that it is staffed not only by judges from Hong Kong, but also by judges from other common law jurisdictions including England and Wales, Australia and Canada.[14]

Other than the establishment of the Court of Final Appeal, Hong Kong has maintained the same court system practiced under British rule.[15] The lower courts consist of the High Court, District Court, magistrates' courts and other special courts. The High Court comprises the Court of Appeal and the Court of First Instance.

The Court of Final Appeal is the ultimate appellate court in Hong Kong. Therefore, notwithstanding that Hong Kong is an inalienable part of China, there is no right of appeal to the Supreme People's Court if a party is dissatisfied with the Court of Final Appeal's judgment. In addition, the courts of Hong Kong are permitted to exercise judicial power independently, free from any interference (including from Mainland China).[16] The courts of Hong Kong are permitted to interpret on their own, in adjudicating cases, the provisions of the *Basic Law* which are within the limits of the autonomy of Hong Kong, notwithstanding the fact that the *Basic Law* derives from the *Constitution of the People's Republic of China*.[17]

The exceptions to the court's power to interpret the *Basic Law* is where a matter concerns (a) the affairs which are the responsibility of the Chinese government; or (b) the relationship between the Chinese government and Hong Kong. In these instances, the court must seek an interpretation of the *Basic Law* from the Standing Committee of the National People's Congress (**NPCSC**).[18]

Interpretations from the NPCSC do not have retrospective effect and only bind future judgments. Interpretations are relatively infrequent. There is only one instance in which the Hong Kong courts have sought an interpretation of the *Basic Law* from the NPCSC.[19] The NPCSC has also issued four further interpretations on its own volition or at the instigation of the Chief Executive.[20]

12 *Basic Law*, art 2.

13 ibid art 82.

14 As permitted by ibid art 82.

15 ibid art 81.

16 ibid art 85.

17 ibid art 158.

18 ibid art 158. The NPCSC has the power to interpret the *Basic Law* under art 158.

19 *Democratic Republic of Congo v FG Hemisphere Associates LLC* [2011] 5 HKC 151. The interpretation sought by the Hong Kong courts related to diplomatic immunity.

20 Devin Lin, Valentin Günther and Mathias Honer, 'Interpreting Article 104: The Way, the How, the Timing' (2007) 47 *Hong Kong Law Journal* 475. The interpretations issued by the NPCSC are: (i) in 1999 an interpretation in relation to the right of abode; (ii) in 2004 an interpretation in relation to the election of the Chief Executive; (iii) in 2005 an interpretation in relation to replacing the Chief Executive; and (iv) in 2016 an interpretation in relation to taking the oath for office.

9.2 The construction industry in Hong Kong

9.2.1 Overview

During the 1980s and 1990s, the construction industry in Hong Kong experienced significant economic growth due to strong public demand for residential investment and the implementation of several major infrastructure projects such as the Mass Transit Railway (**MTR**) network and the Airport Core Programme.[21] Since then, the construction industry has continued to experience rapid growth.[22] In the last decade alone, the gross value of construction works in nominal terms rose from HK$100.94 billion (US$13 billion) in 2009 to HK$236.49 billion (US$30.5 billion) in 2019.[23]

Consistently the second highest contributor to the GDP behind the services industry, the construction industry accounted for 5.2 per cent of Hong Kong's GDP in 2016, 5.1 per cent in 2017, 4.5 per cent in 2018 and 4.1 per cent in 2019.[24] In addition to its direct contribution to GDP, the construction industry also contributes to the GDP of inter-related industries including real estate, professional services (such as engineering and design services), and transport and storage. Whilst the construction industry experienced a mild slowdown in 2019, continuing and positive growth (albeit, on a lower scale than what was previously predicted due to the impact of Covid-19 pandemic) is forecast for public and private construction expenditure in Hong Kong until the end of 2030.[25] In the 2020 Policy Address, the Chief Executive, Carrie Lam, noted that it is expected that capital works expenditure will continue to grow from 2021–2022 onwards and exceed HK$100 billion (US$12.9 billion) per annum in coming years.

In addition to its economic significance, the construction industry – comprising a diverse range of individuals from architects, surveyors and engineers, management personnel and administrative staff to technical and skilled workers and site labour – is a major employer in Hong Kong. The industry consistently employs between 6 per cent and 9 per cent of the total workforce in Hong Kong, with approximately 309,300 persons employed in the first quarter of 2020.[26]

The construction industry in Hong Kong operates within two main sectors: the private sector and the public sector. Construction works – which include new construction, repair, maintenance, alteration and additional works, civil engineering works and electrical and mechanical works – commonly carried out by the private

21 The Core Airport Programme comprised several infrastructure projects centred on the development of the new Hong Kong International Airport.

22 'Review of Construction Industry in Hong Kong' (Census and Statistics Department, January 2000) https://www.censtatd.gov.hk/hkstat/sub/sp330.jsp?productCode=FA100218 (accessed 30 November 2020).

23 'Table 106: Gross value of construction works performed by main contractors analysed by broad trade group (in nominal terms)' (Census and Statistics Department 2019) https://www.censtatd.gov.hk/hkstat/sub/sp330.jsp?tableID=106&ID=0&productType=8 (accessed 30 November 2020).

24 'Table 036: Gross Domestic Product (GDP) by major economic activity - percentage contribution to GDP at basic prices' (Census and Statistics Department 2019) https://www.censtatd.gov.hk/hkstat/sub/sp250.jsp?tableID=036&ID=0&productType=8 (accessed 30 November 2020). Note that the figure for 2019 is a preliminary figure.

25 'Construction Expenditure Forecast' (Hong Kong Construction Industry Council 2020) http://www.cic.hk/common/Fore/Fore.aspx?lang=en-US&year=2020_21 (accessed 30 November 2020).

26 'Employment distribution by industry section' (Census and Statistics Department https://www.censtatd.gov.hk/hkstat/sub/sp452.jsp?productCode=D5250016 (accessed 30 November 2020). See also 'Quarterly Report on General Household Survey - January to March 2020' (Census and Statistics Department (accessed on 27 November 2020).

sector include residential, industrial and commercial works. Construction works commonly carried out by the public sector comprise:

- Infrastructure works commissioned by the Hong Kong government[27]
- Infrastructure works carried out by quasi-government statutory bodies including the MTR, the Airport Authority Hong Kong and the Hospital Authority
- Extensive public housing works carried out by the Hong Kong Housing Authority.[28]

Recent public sector infrastructure works include the Guangzhou-Shenzhen-Hong Kong Express Rail Link (a high-speed rail link connecting Guangzhou and Shenzhen in Mainland China to Hong Kong) completed in September 2018; the Hong Kong-Zhuhai-Macau Bridge (the longest bridge-cum-tunnel sea crossing in the world connecting the Hong Kong Port, Zhuhai Port in Mainland China and Macau Port) completed in October 2018; and phase 1 of the Tuen Ma MTR line completed in February 2020. There are several major public sector infrastructure works currently underway including the Hong Kong International Airport third runway expansion, the 10-Year Hospital Development Plan (which includes the construction of a New Acute Hospital at Kai Tak Development Area and the redevelopment and expansion of 11 existing hospitals), the Liantang/Heung Yuen Wai Boundary Control Point and the Central Kowloon Route linking West Kowloon with the road network on Kai Tak Development and Kowloon Bay in East Kowloon. In addition, the Housing Authority has five major developments underway in Kai Tak, Yuen Long South, Kwu Tung North/Fanling North, Tung Chung New Town Extension and Hung Shui Kiu/Ha Tsuen which are expected to produce a total of 277,950 new public housing units.

9.2.2 Recent developments

An aging population,[29] rise in the demand for manpower, and lack of uptake for vocational training has resulted in Hong Kong experiencing a skilled labour shortage of approximately 10,000 skilled workers across 26 trades including plastering, concreting, carpentry, plumbing, welding and metal works, and electrical and mechanical works.[30] With several major public sector infrastructure projects currently in the pipeline, the demand for construction labour is predicted to grow at an annual rate of 0.5 per cent.[31]

27 Such works are usually commissioned by the government Works Departments including the Architectural Services Departments, Buildings Department, Civil Engineering and Development Department, Drainage Services Department, Electrical and Mechanical Services Department and Water Supplies Department under the overall supervision of the Development Bureau, and the Highways Department under the supervision of the Transport and Housing Bureau. Other departments and statutory bodes including the Environmental Protection Department, Home Affairs Department and Urban Renewal Authority may also commission construction works.

28 The Housing Department which is also under the supervision of the Transport and Housing Bureau provides executive services to the Housing Authority.

29 As at 31 March 2019, approximately 43.8% of registered construction workers were aged over 50 years old compared with 14.7% of registered construction workers aged below 30 years old.

30 'Skilled Construction Workers Forecast (2018-2022)' (Construction Industry Council) http://www.cic.hk/cic_data/files/CICMF_en_17w.pdf (accessed 30 November 2020).

31 The Report on Manpower projection to 2027 (Government of the Hong Kong Special Administrative Region in December 2019 predicts that the demand for construction works will grow at a rate of 0.5% between the years 2017 and 2027.

To add to the problem, construction activities in Hong Kong are labour intensive and, occasionally, inefficient.[32]

To help mitigate the skilled labour shortage, the Hong Kong government has introduced several measures aimed at increasing manpower and improving productivity and efficiency in the construction industry. These measures include: (1) providing funding support to initiatives aimed at enhancing vocational training and attracting young local talent to join the construction industry;[33] (2) implementing expedited procedures for the Supplementary Labour Scheme so that contractors are able to access certain imported labour; and (3) promoting the adoption of construction information technology such as Building Information Modelling (**BIM**) and Digital Works Supervision Systems (**DWSS**).[34]

BIM technology is increasingly used on construction projects in Hong Kong. Since 2013, the Construction Industry Council, a statutory body established under the *Construction Industry Council Ordinance* (Cap 587), has carried out several initiatives aimed at promoting and developing the use of BIM in Hong Kong. Such initiatives include establishing the Task Group on BIM Implementation, publishing of the 'Roadmap for Building Modelling Strategic Implementation in Hong Kong's Construction Industry' and the 'BIM Standards (Phase One)' and establishing the BIM Innovation and Development Centre which provides basic training and an in-depth management course. There has also been a push by the Hong Kong government to adopt BIM on public works projects. On 1 December 2017, the Development Bureau issued Technical Circular (Works) No. 7/2017 on the Adoption of Building Information Modelling for Capital Works Projects mandating the use of BIM for capital works projects with an estimated project value of more than HK$30 million (US$3.8 million).[35] The Technical Circular has been superseded by Technical Circular (Works) No. 18 of 2018 which enhanced the implementation requirements, and later Technical Circular (Works) No. 9 of 2019 which expanded the scope to certain applications in investigation, feasibility and planning stage, design for digital fabrication as well as sustainability evaluation.[36]

In addition to the use of BIM, there has been an increase in the use of innovative construction methods as such Modular Integrated Construction (**MiC**) and smart construction. Whilst most construction in Hong Kong is still site based, the move towards using MiC is gaining traction. The first pilot project in Hong Kong to adopt MiC is the Disciplined Services Quarters for the Fire Services Department at Pak Shing Kok, which was commissioned by the Architectural Services Department of

32 James Wong, Judy Zhang and Julian Lee, 'A Vision of the Future Construction Industry of Hong Kong' (Construction Industry Council, June 2015) http://www.iaarc.org/publications/fulltext/FFACE-ISARC15-3061494.pdf (accessed 30 November 2020).

33 In 2018, the Construction Industry Council established the Hong Kong Institute of Construction which offers various accredited training programmes and courses including a full-time Diploma in Construction.

34 Under Technical Circular (Works) No 3/2020 on Digital Works Supervision System (Ref: DEVB(PSGO)/38/2) from 1 April 2020 capital works contracts with a pre-tender estimate exceeding HK$300 million (US$38.7 million) must adopt a Digital Works Supervision System with the aim of enhancing the standard and efficiency of works supervision as well as the quality and safety of works.

35 Technical Circular (Works) No 7/2017 on the Adoption of Building Information Modelling for Capital Works Projects (Ref: DEVB(W) 430/80/01).

36 Technical Circular (Works) No 18/2018 on the Adoption of Building Information Modelling for Capital Works Projects (Ref: DEVB(W) 430/80/01) and Technical Circular (Works) No 9/2019 on the Adoption of Building Information Modelling for Capital Works Projects (Ref: DEVB(W) 430/80/01).

the Hong Kong government. The Hong Kong government also used MiC to build quarantine facilities and a temporary hospital in response to the Covid-19 outbreak. On 31 March 2020, the Development Bureau issued Technical Circular (Works) No. 2/2020 on Modular Integrated Construction (MiC) mandating that MiC be adopted for designated government buildings with a total construction floor area larger than 300m^2 under capital works projects tendered on or after 1 April 2020.[37] In addition, to help facilitate the wider use of MiC for private building developments, the Buildings Department has established a pre-acceptance arrangement for granting in-principle acceptance to MiC systems and components. Relevant design considerations and compliance requirements are set out in Practice Notice PNAP ADV-36.[38] A MiC Display Centre was also opened by the Development Bureau and Construction Industry Council in November 2018.

Whilst modular integrated construction offers improved productivity, safety and quality control, the challenge for Hong Kong will be implementation and logistics given its high-density urban environment and limited space. In October 2018, the Hong Kong government launched a HK$1 billion (US$130 million) Construction Innovation and Technology Fund (**CITF**) to encourage the use of innovation and advanced technology in the construction industry with a view to promoting productivity, uplifting built quality, improving site safety and enhancing environmental performance. As at October 2020, the CITF has approved more than 1,200 applications and subsidised over 700 enterprises for the adoption of innovative construction technologies such as BIM and MiC.

9.2.3 Public procurement

Public procurement of construction and engineering works by the Hong Kong government[39] is guided by twin policy objectives of: (1) achieving the best value for money; and (2) maintaining fair and open competition.[40] These complementary objectives are premised on encouraging participation through open, fair and transparent procurement procedures and practices so that the Hong Kong government can obtain responsive and competitive tenders from which the Hong Kong government can determine the most advantageous one which serves the public interest of Hong Kong.[41]

The legal framework for the public procurement process in Hong Kong is governed by the *Stores and Procurement Regulations* (***SPR***) issued by the Financial Secretary under the *Public Finance Ordinance* (Cap 2).[42] The *SPR* applies to: (1) purchases or

37 Technical Circular (Works) No 2/2020 on Modular Integrated Construction (MiC) (Ref: DEVB(PSGO)38/1).

38 Practice Note or Authorized Persons, Registered Structural Engineers and Registered Geotechnical Engineers ADV-36 issued by the Buildings Department in December 2017 and revised September 2019 https://www.bd.gov.hk/en/resources/codes-and-references/modular-integrated-construction/index.html (accessed 30 November 2020).

39 *Chapter III of the Stores and Procurement Regulations*, s 300. See n 27 above for a list of government departments that procure construction and engineering works.

40 'Guide to Procurement' (Financial Services and Treasury Bureau, Treasury Branch, 2020) https://www.fstb.gov.hk/tb/en/guide-to-procurement.htm (accessed 30 November 2020).

41 ibid.

42 The *Stores and Procurement Regulations* is supplemented by Financial Circulars and Financial Services and Treasury Bureau Circular Memoranda issued from time to time. In relation to Works Departments supervised by the Development Bureau, the Development Bureau also issues Technical Circulars from time to time and advises on tendering procedures and contract administration in respect of public works contracts.

acquisitions made on behalf of the Hong Kong government (except in respect of land or buildings); (2) services performed by the private sector for, or on behalf of, the Hong Kong government; and (3) revenue contracts which generate revenue for, or on behalf of, the Hong Kong government. Notably, the *SPR* only applies to procurement by the Hong Kong government. Quasi-government statutory bodies such as the MTR, the Airport Authority Hong Kong and the Hospital Authority have their own procurement policies in place.

The tendering procedures for public procurement in Hong Kong are set out in Chapter III of the *SPR*. In selecting the main Contractor for public infrastructure works, the *SPR* provides that government departments should adopt open competitive tendering for invitation of tenders (where the tender is advertised and all interested contractors are free to submit their tenders) and use alternative tendering methods in 'special circumstances' only.[43] Such alternative tendering methods include:

- Selective competitive tendering (which is a two-stage process – (1) stage one seeks to limit the number of competing contractors; and (2) stage two provides for the final selection of a Contractor (usually determined on the criteria of price))[44]
- Single and restricted tendering (where tenders are invited from only one or a limited number of contractors)[45]
- Prequalified tendering (where prequalification is provided to a list of tenderers that are financially and technically capable of undertaking a particular project).[46]

The *SPR* also provides for direct engagement (where a Contractor is directly engaged without recourse to tendering procedures) but only in circumstances where open tendering, selective tendering, single and restricted tendering would not be an effective means of procurement.[47] Such an approach, however, must be supported with very strong justification.[48]

An invitation to tender should consist of the following standard contract forms: (1) terms of tender; (2) general conditions of contract;[49] (3) special conditions of contract; (4) offer to be bound or form of tender; (5) bills of quantities or quantities required of the contract (where applicable); and (6) tender specifications and detailed

43 *Chapter III of the Stores and Procurement Regulations*, ss 315 and 316. The Guide to Procurement (Financial Services and Treasury Bureau (Treasury Branch) provides that government procurement exceeding HK$1.4 million (US$180,000) (for goods and services), HK$3 million (US$387,000) (for consultancy services) and HK$7 million (US$903,000) (for construction and engineering works) in value is normally done by open and competitive tendering procedures so as to obtain the best value for money.

44 *Chapter III of the Stores and Procurement Regulations*, section 320.

45 ibid s 325.

46 ibid s 330.

47 ibid s 331.

48 ibid s 331.

49 The Hong Kong government tenders for new infrastructure projects using its own standard forms of general conditions of contract, which were originally modelled on the Institution of Civil Engineers standard form contracts and now frequently adopt provisions from the New Engineering Contracts (NEC) suite of contracts, including the recently published NEC4 suite of contracts. Quasi-government statutory authorities such as the MTRC and Airport Authority Hong Kong have developed their own standard forms of general conditions.

price schedules or schedule of rates (where applicable).[50] All tenderers must receive identical sets of the tender documents, with any addenda provided to each tenderer. The *SPR* also prescribes guidelines for the submission,[51] and evaluation,[52] of tenders. Unless authority has been delegated to government departments or tender boards, the Permanent Secretary for Financial Services and the Treasury is the approving authority for acceptance of successful tenders.[53] In the 2020 Policy Address, the Chief Executive, Carrie Lam announced that the Hong Kong government would introduce parallel tendering and shorten the tender evaluation process with the aim to expedite the tendering process of works projects (where appropriate) and speed up infrastructure development.

In addition to the legal framework, the public procurement process is also subject to international protocols and free trade agreements.[54] As Hong Kong is a signatory to the World Trade Organization Agreement on Government Procurement (**WTO GPA**), any procurement which comes within the minimum threshold set out in the WTO GPA is subject to additional requirements.[55]

To be eligible to carry out public infrastructure works in Hong Kong, contractors and suppliers must be on the List of Approved Contractors for Public Works or List of Approved Suppliers of Materials and Specialist Contractors for Public Works maintained by the Development Bureau.[56] The lists comprise five major categories of contractors approved to carry out public works, namely: (1) Buildings; (2) Port Works; (3) Roads and Drainage; (4) Site Formation; and (5) Waterwork and is further subdivided into Group A, B or C according to the value of contracts for which contractors are normally eligible to tender.[57] Contractors applying to be admitted to the lists must satisfy certain financial, technical and management criteria.[58]

---

50 *Chapter III of the Stores and Procurement Regulations*, s 345.

51 Tenderers must submit their tenders and deposit them into the prescribed tender box before the tender closing date and time stipulated in the tender documents. Tenders must be submitted in two separate sealed envelopes – one containing technical information and the other containing price information. Normally, the price information will not be opened until the technical assessment is completed.

52 Tender evaluations (which determine whether a tender meets the conditions and specifications laid down in the tender documents) are normally conducted by a tender assessment panel which consists of not less than two people established by the relevant government departments in accordance with *Chapter III of the Stores and Procurement Regulations*, s 370. Government departments shall then prepare a tender report containing a clear recommendation in accordance with *Chapter III of the Stores and Procurement Regulations*, s 375.

53 *Chapter III of the Stores and Procurement Regulations*, s 390.

54 For example, the Free Trade Agreement between Hong Kong, China and Chile and the Free Trade Agreement between Hong Kong, China and Australia.

55 See eg *Chapter III of the Stores and Procurement Regulations*, ss 340(c)–(f) and 390(c). Subject to meeting the minimum threshold set out in the WTO GPA, the WTO GPA applies to all government bureau and departments (the minimum threshold being 130,000 SDR for the procurement of goods and services and 5,000,000 for the procurement of construction services) and quasi-government statutory bodies including the MTRC and Airport Authority Hong Kong (the minimum threshold being 400,000 SDR for the procurement of goods and services and 5,000,000 for the procurement of construction services). **SDR** are Special Drawing Rights https://www.imf.org/en/About/Factsheets/Sheets/2016/08/01/14/51/Special-Drawing-Right-SDR (accessed 30 November 2020).

56 Contractor Management Handbook: Revision B-15 (20 July 2018), s 2.

57 ibid. Contractors in Group A may tender for contracts up to the value of HK$100 million (US$12.9 million), contractors in Group B may tender for contracts up to the value of HK$300 million (US$38.7 million) and contractors in Group C may tender for contracts exceeding the value of HK$300 million (US$38.7 million). Contractors in Group C are generally not permitted to tender for contracts below HK$300 million unless there is an inadequate number of eligible contractors.

58 Contractor Management Handbook: Revision B-14 (1 December 2016), Apps 2A, 2B, 2C, 3B and 3C.

The Construction Industry Council also maintains its own General Vendor List of contractors and suppliers for the issuance of procurement notifications in relation to certain categories of goods and services. Subject to satisfying certain verification requirements, any contractor or supplier can apply to the Procurement Department of the Construction Industry Council to be included on the General Vendor List, although continued inclusion is dependent on the contractor or supplier demonstrating an ability to offer competitive quotes and on their performance in connection with any contracts or orders they are awarded.

9.2.4 Regulatory environment

Hong Kong has strict building, and licensing and registration controls as explained at paragraphs 9.6.4 and 9.6.5.

A Green Card, which is the common name for the certificate issued on completion of the 'Mandatory Basic Training Course', is a mandatory requirement for construction workers in Hong Kong. Valid for between one and three years, a Green Card is obtained by completing a safety training recognised by the Commissioner for Labour. Save for when falling within the arrangement under the *Construction Workers Registration Ordinance* (Cap 583), construction workers must carry a Green Card whilst at work on a construction site and produce it upon demand by the proprietor or an Occupational Safety Officer of the Labour Department.

The primary legislation governing Hong Kong's workplace relations is the *Employment Ordinance* (Cap 57). Subject to limited exceptions, the *Ordinance* applies to all employees in Hong Kong regardless of their nationality and guarantees certain minimum rights and entitlements including paid annual leave, sick leave and maternity and paternity leave, and minimum notice of termination and the right to make a payment in lieu of notice on resignation or termination of an employment contract. Most employees are guaranteed a minimum wage under the *Minimum Wage Ordinance* (Cap 608) and are provided with compulsory insurance under the *Employees' Compensation Ordinance* (Cap 282).

Monetary claims arising from the failure to comply with the provisions of the *Employment Ordinance* (Cap 57), *Minimum Wage Ordinance* (Cap 608) or *Apprenticeship Ordinance* (Cap 47), for example, in relation to unpaid entitlements, are usually overseen by the Labour Tribunal, which offers a quick, informal and inexpensive way of settling monetary disputes between employees and employers.[59] In addition to the Labour Tribunal, minor monetary claims can be adjudicated the Minor Employment Claims Adjudication Board. Aggrieved parties can also refer private sector employment disputes to the conciliation service of the Labour Relations Division of the Labour Department.

Save for employees under 18 years old, who are not permitted to work in excess of 48 hours per week, there are no restriction on working hours in Hong Kong. Following the submission of a report by the Standard Working Hours Committee on working hours policy direction, the Hong Kong government announced that it would introduce working-hour guidelines which address working hours arrangements and

59 The Labour Tribunal hears claims of HK$8,000 (US$1,030) or more whereas the Minor Employment Claims Adjudication Board hears claims involving not more than 10 claimants and not exceeding HK$8,000 (US$1,030) per claimant. Claims that arose more than 6 years ago may be statute barred under the *Limitations Ordinance* (Cap 347).

overtime compensation methods for 11 sectors including construction, warehouse and cargo transport and cement and concrete. The guidelines are expected to be published in 2020.

Hong Kong residents have the right to join and form trade unions.[60] There are a number of construction specific trade unions presently operating in Hong Kong, although participation is relatively low. Trade disputes are governed by the *Labour Relations Ordinance* (Cap 55).

There are strict anti-corruption laws governing the public and private sectors in Hong Kong. The primary legislation, the *Prevention of Bribery Ordinance* (Cap 201), is enforced by the Independent Commission Against Corruption (**ICAC**), a statutory body tasked with investigating acts of corruption and bribery. The Ordinance establishes various offences for persons engaging in corrupt conduct and bribery in connection with public procurement, tenders and auctions, and illicit enrichment by public officials. Regarded as one of the most vigorous and effective law enforcement bodies in the world, the ICAC is vested with broad law enforcement powers including the power to search and seize, arrest, detain and grant bail. In addition to the statutory controls under the Ordinance, all Hong Kong government standard form contracts contain provisions preventing corruption and bribery.

9.2.5 Resolution of disputes

Disputes arising from construction contracts are resolved by one or more of mediation, expert determination, arbitration or litigation. Mediation is widely used as a voluntary resolution process and is frequently mandated as part of the dispute resolution procedure in contracts with government and quasi-government entities. Whilst mediation is not generally a precondition to a hearing in court proceedings, the court will take into account all relevant circumstances when exercising its discretion to award costs and has the power to make an adverse costs order against a party where it unreasonably fails to engage in mediation. The main arbitration institutions in Hong Kong are the Hong Kong International Arbitration Centre (**HKIAC**), the International Court of Arbitration of the International Chamber of Commerce (**ICC**) and the China International Economic and Trade Arbitration Commission (**CIETAC**). The HKIAC and ICC are also able to appoint a mediator and have their own institutional mediation rules.

There has been various recent reform in Hong Kong relevant to the resolution of disputes in the construction industry. On 14 June 2017, the Legislative Council passed the *Arbitration and Mediation Legislation (Third Party Funding) (Amendment) Ordinance 2017* which amended sections 98K and 98L of the *Arbitration Ordinance* (Cap 609) to permit third party funding of arbitrations seated in Hong Kong and related litigation and mediation. Historically, third party funding was prohibited in Hong Kong except in limited circumstances by the common law offences of maintenance and champerty. The *Code of Practice for Third Party Funding of Arbitration and Mediation*, which came into force on 1 February 2019, sets out the practices and standards that litigation funders are ordinarily expected to comply with in carrying on activities in connection with third party funding of arbitration and mediation in Hong Kong including in relation to the scope of funding agreements, termination of funding agreements,

60 Trade unions must be registered under the *Trade Union Ordinance* (Cap 332).

capital adequacy, conflicts of interest, control of proceedings and liability for adverse costs. A third-party funder can now provide arbitration funding to a party under a funding agreement in exchange for a financial benefit but only when the arbitration is successful within the meaning of the funding agreement. This reform is a positive development for Hong Kong as an arbitration friendly seat.

On 1 October 2019, the *Arrangement Concerning Mutual Assistance in Court-ordered Interim Measures in Aid of Arbitral Proceedings by the Courts of the Mainland and of the HKSAR* came into effect. Under the reciprocal arrangement, parties (irrespective of their nationality) to Hong Kong and Mainland China seated arbitrations administered by qualified institutions can apply directly to the courts in each other's jurisdiction for interim measures. Therefore, in the case of Hong Kong seated arbitrations, parties can seek property, asset or conduct preservation orders in the Intermediate People's Court in Mainland China. Typically, such measures are only available in respect of domestic arbitrations in Mainland China. Reciprocal arrangements between Hong Kong and Mainland China concerning arbitration are not new. The mutual recognition and enforcement of arbitral awards between Hong Kong and Mainland China has been in place since 1999 under the Arrangement Concerning Mutual Enforcement of Arbitral Award Between the Mainland and Hong Kong (**1999 Arrangement**). On 27 November 2020, the 1999 Arrangement was amended by the Supplemental Arrangement Concerning Mutual Enforcement of Arbitral Awards between the Mainland and Hong Kong, which seeks to further enhance the ease of enforcement of arbitral awards between Hong Kong and Mainland China. Under the new amendments: (1) a reference to 'enforcement' of arbitral awards in the 1999 Arrangement is a reference to 'recognition and enforcement'; (2) the scope of application has been clarified, namely, that Mainland awards are those issued under the Arbitration Law of the People's Republic of China; (3) parties are permitted to make simultaneous applications for enforcement to the Hong Kong and Mainland courts; and (4) where an application is made (and pursuant to the law of the place of enforcement) an enforcing court may issue preservation or mandatory measures before or after its acceptance of an application for the enforcement of an arbitral award.[61]

The most significant pending reform remains the security of payment legislation. The proposed regime is discussed in detail at paragraph 9.6.1 below.

9.2.6 Future opportunities and challenges

In addition to domestic construction opportunities, on 1 July 2017 the National Development and Reform Commission, the Hong Kong government and governments of Macau and Guangdong signed the Framework Agreement on Deepening Guangdong-Hong Kong-Macau Cooperation Development in the 'Greater Bay Area'. The Greater Bay Area comprises of two special administrative regions – Hong Kong and Macau – and nine municipalities – Guangzhou, Shenzhen, Zhuhai, Foshan, Huizhou, Dongguan, Zhongshan, Jiangmen and Zhaoqing in Guangdong Province. The stated objective of the Greater Bay Area Initiative is to leverage the integrated advantages of the Guangdong, Hong Kong and Macau region fully and deepen cooperation and take forward the development of the Greater Bay Area and promote

61 Amendments 1 and 4 came into effect on 27 November 2020. The date for the commencement of amendments 2 and 3 will be announced after the completion of the relevant procedures in Hong Kong.

coordinated regional economic development, to develop an international first-class bay area ideal for living, work and travelling. This presents a number of opportunities for the construction sector in the region, including in Hong Kong.

On 18 February 2019, the National Development and Reform Commission, the Hong Kong government and governments of Macau and Guangdong signed an Outline Development Plan for the Guangdong-Hong Kong-Macau Greater Bay Area, which contemplates inter alia the development of a world class airport cluster comprising the Hong Kong International Airport third runway expansion, reconstruction and expansion projects in Macau, Guangzhou and Shenzen and a batch of feeder airports; extensive regional transport infrastructure including the construction of various road and rail links to improve connectivity between the Greater Bay area and Mainland China; modern freight and logistic services; and social infrastructure including sporting facilities, convention and exhibition spaces, cultural centres and museums, and amusement parks.

Recently, the Hong Kong government collaborated with Mainland Chinese Authorities to establish a new registration system that enables architectural and engineering related consultant firms on the Hong Kong government's approved list of Contractors and Consultants and related registered professionals to provide professional services for development projects in the Greater Bay Area.

In terms of future challenges, in addition to the skilled labour shortage, one of the most significant challenges for the Hong Kong construction industry is the cost of carrying out construction works and the growing demand for better safety, innovation, quality and environmental friendliness. Hong Kong is one of the most expensive cities in the world to carry out construction works. The situation is further hindered by the stretched labour supply and increasing volume of construction work. Whilst Hong Kong is consistently recognised as a global leader as regards the quality of its infrastructure, there has been some recent concern as to quality in relation to both project delivery and the quality of completed works on mega public infrastructure projects and safety. To help address these challenges, the Hong Kong government has launched the 'Construction 2.0' initiative which is predicated on the core pillars of innovation, professionalisation and revitalisation and aims to upgrade the construction industry with the wider adoption of information technology.[62]

9.3 The impact of Covid-19 in Hong Kong

9.3.1 The impact of Covid-19 on the execution of construction projects in Hong Kong

Hong Kong was one of the first places to introduce protection measures in relation to Covid-19. On 30 January 2020 and 4 February 2020, the Hong Kong government enforced a series of partial border closures between Hong Kong and Mainland China including a suspension of all cross-border rail links and ferries, a suspension of a number of border checkpoints, and the reduction of cross-border flights and buses. On 8 February 2020, the Hong Kong government implemented compulsory quarantine for all people who entered Hong Kong from Mainland China or who had been in

62 Report titled 'Construction 2.0' https://home.kpmg/cn/en/home/insights/2018/10/construction-2-0-time-to-change.html (accessed 30 November 2020).

Mainland China in the 14 days preceding their arrival to Hong Kong. From 25 March 2020, Hong Kong closed its borders to all inbound travellers except for Hong Kong residents, spouses of Hong Kong residents and certain exempt persons (for example, transiting passengers, government officials on official business and sea and air crew). All arrivals into Hong Kong were required to undertake a Covid-19 test and mandatory 14-day quarantine.[63]

On 29 April 2020, the *Prevention and Control of Disease Ordinance* (Cap 599) – the primary legal framework used by the Hong Kong government to introduce border control, social distancing and health and safety regulations – was amended to include Covid-19 to the Scheduled Infectious Diseases.[64] The *Ordinance* grants the Hong Kong government wide powers to prevent the introduction, spread and transmission of diseases during a public health emergency.

Notwithstanding the significant protection measures adopted, there has been no official government 'lockdown' in Hong Kong.[65] Work in the construction industry has largely continued during the pandemic, and very few construction sites have had to close due to construction workers contracting Covid-19.[66]

Nevertheless, it is projected that there will be a decline in Hong Kong's GDP for 2020 due to the impact of Covid-19 and declines in contributions by the construction industry will contribute to this. In the first quarter of 2020, expenditure on building and construction in terms of gross domestic fixed capital formation (**GDFCF**) was HK$72.124 billion (US$9.4 billion), representing a drop of 9.1 per cent in real terms against the same period in 2019 and a drop of 6.5 per cent against the fourth quarter of 2019.[67] Whilst the situation improved in the second quarter of 2020 (with the GDFCF dropping 3.6 per cent in real terms against the same period in 2019), it deteriorated in the third quarter of 2020 (with the GDCFC dropping of 10.4 per cent in real terms against the same period in 2019).[68]

The unemployment rate has also risen to a high of 10 per cent. The Hong Kong government has not enacted any employment specific laws in response to Covid-19. Therefore, employment relationships including in relation to termination, unpaid leave, medical leave and compensation thereof continue to be governed by individual employment contracts and the *Employment Ordinance* (Cap 57). Any variation to an employee's employment contract, for example, in relation to unpaid leave or

63 There is an exception for 'exempt persons' under the *Compulsory Quarantine of Certain Persons Arriving at Hong Kong Regulation* (Cap 599C).

64 *Prevention and Control of Disease Ordinance* (Cap 599), sch 1.

65 The Hong Kong government has implemented social distancing regulations under the *Prevention and Control of Disease Ordinance* (Cap 599) including limiting the number of people in public gatherings, limiting the number of people dining at restaurants and the closure from time to time of certain nightlife, entertainment, recreation and leisure venues and beauty parlours.

66 For example, in July 2020 a construction site on the Peak on Hong Kong Island closed following a large-scale cluster outbreak.

67 'Gross Domestic Product – First Quarter 2020' (Census and Statistics Department, 15 May 2020) https://www.censtatd.gov.hk/hkstat/sub/sp250.jsp?productCode=B1030001 (accessed 30 November 2020) with figures revised in 'Gross Domestic Product - Third Quarter 2020' (Census and Statistics Department on 13 November 2020 https://www.censtatd.gov.hk/hkstat/sub/sp250.jsp?productCode=B1030001 (accessed 30 November 2020).

68 'Gross Domestic Product – Second Quarter 2020' (Census and Statistics Department, 14 August 2020) https://www.censtatd.gov.hk/hkstat/sub/sp250.jsp?productCode=B1030001 (accessed 30 November 2020) and 'Gross Domestic Product - Third Quarter 2020' (Census and Statistics Department, 13 November 2020) https://www.censtatd.gov.hk/hkstat/sub/sp250.jsp?productCode=B1030001 (accessed 30 November 2020).

remuneration, must be by consent.[69] An employer can direct employees to take annual leave providing they give a minimum of 14 days' written notice.[70] If an employee is diagnosed with Covid-19 and is quarantined, or is prevented from reporting to work due to mandatory government requirements (for example, the employee is under medical surveillance due to close contact with a confirmed Covid-19 patient), the employee will be entitled to sickness allowance provided the conditions under the *Ordinance* are met. The Labour Department has issued a guidance note for employers and employees titled 'Obligations and rights of employers and employees under the Employment Ordinance relating to the Coronavirus Disease 2019'.

Employers also have legal obligations under the *Employees' Compensation Ordinance* (Cap 282) (for example, if an employee contracts Covid-19 by an accident arising out of and in the course of their employment they may be entitled to compensation)[71] and *Disability Discrimination Ordinance* (Cap 487) (for example, an employer cannot treat an employee who is infected or suspected of being infected with Covid-19 or associated with a person infected with Covid-19 less favourably). Employers should also take care not to breach the *Personal Data (Privacy) Ordinance* (Cap 468) or the data protection principles when collecting employees' travel and medical history, including any results obtained during medical examinations and temperature testing.

Further, employers have a common law and statutory duty under the *Occupational Safety and Health Ordinance* (Cap 509) to take reasonable care of the health and safety of their employees' and to provide and maintain a safe workplace. This duty – which includes inter alia the provision of a clean and adequately ventilated workplace – applies to both industrial and non-industrial workplace environments. The Centre for Health Protection of the Department for Health has published advice titled 'Health Advice on Prevention of Coronavirus disease (Covid-19) in Workplace' which recommends that employers undertake regular temperature testing and maintain environment hygiene including maintaining good ventilation, clean environment and toilet hygiene, and that employees wear masks and maintain good personal hygiene and a distance of 1.5 metres from others.[72] The advice also provides guidance for the cleaning and disinfecting of an environment which has been exposed to a confirmed

69 Generally, unilateral variations to employment contracts are not permitted.

70 *Employment Ordinance* (Cap 57), s 41AA.

71 Whilst Covid-19 is not listed as an 'occupational disease' under sch 2 of the *Employees' Compensation Ordinance* (Cap 282), an employee may still be entitled to compensation under ss 5 and 36 of the *Employees' Compensation Ordinance* (Cap 282). See clarification issued by the Labour Department on 10 February 2020 in a press release titled 'Protection under the Employees' Compensation Ordinance for Employees Contracting the Severe Respiratory Disease Associated with a Novel Infectious Agent in the Course of Work' https://www.info.gov.hk/gia/general/202002/10/P2020021000730.htm?fontSize=1 (accessed 30 November 2020).

72 See advice published by Centre for Health Protection - Infection Control Branch of the Health Department titled 'Health Advice on Prevention of Coronavirus Disease (Covid-19) in Workplace' last reviewed on 16 October 2020 https://www.chp.gov.hk/files/pdf/nid_guideline_workplace_eng.pdf (accessed 30 November 2020). Whilst initially facemasks were not mandatory in Hong Kong, most people elected to wear face masks during the early stages of the outbreak. In July 2020, the Legislative Council passed the *Prevention and Control of Disease (Wearing of Mask) Regulation* (Cap 599I), which made wearing masks mandatory when taking public transport. Shortly after, the requirement to wear face masks was extended to enclosed public spaces, followed by outdoor public spaces. These requirements continue to remain in effect at the time of writing (November 2020). Although, under the *Regulation* a person has a reasonable excuse to not comply with the requirement as regards outdoor public spaces if they are engaged in any physical activity that may reasonably be regarded as strenuous. Whilst this is likely to include construction labour, construction workers will still need to comply with occupational health and safety policies imposed by their employer.

case of Covid-19. Whilst it is not workplace specific, the Department of Health has also published 'Guidelines on Prevention of Coronavirus Disease 2019 for the General Public', which encourages inter alia reduced social interactions, social distancing and good hygiene measures.

The Hong Kong government has established an Anti-Epidemic Fund (**Fund**) to help relieve financial burdens on the construction industry caused by Covid-19. The Fund, which is administered by the Construction Industry Council, was initially split into two rounds with the first round taking effect in April 2020 and the second round taking effect in June 2020.[73] A third round was announced in September 2020; however, the measures are not directly aimed to benefit the construction industry. During the first-round subsidies of:

- HK$50,000 and HK$20,000 (US$6,450 and US$2,580) were offered to eligible: (i) contractors, subcontractors and consultants; and (ii) small and medium-sized consultants, respectively, to help cover expenses associated with anti-epidemic equipment such body temperature measuring equipment
- HK$1,500 and HK$1,000 (US$195 and US$130) were offered to eligible: (i) registered construction workers; (ii) non-registered construction workers carrying out small-scale works, respectively, to help cover the cost of personal protective and antiseptic equipment such as hand sanitiser.

During the second round, subsidies were offered to certain categories that did not qualify during the first round, namely:

- HK$20,000 (US$2,580) was offered to eligible contractors, specialist contractors and suppliers, and company members of major construction-related trade associations
- HK$10,000 (US$1,290) was offered to eligible registered minor works contractors, various registered trade contractors and suppliers of construction-related machineries and equipment rental.

In addition, a further subsidy of HK$7,500 (US$970) was offered to eligible registered construction workers who had already received HK$1,500 (US$195) as part of the first round of the Fund.

The Hong Kong government also introduced other relief measures during the second round of the Fund, namely:

- A new wage subsidy Employment Support Scheme (**ESS**) to eligible employers, which includes contractors. The subsidy, which is calculated at 50 per cent of the employee's monthly wage, is capped at an eligible salary of HK$18,000 (US$2,320) for six months and maximum monthly subsidy of HK$9,000 (US$1,160) per employee. Employers who receive the subsidy are required to undertake not to make employees redundant for the subsidy period and to spend the full amount of the subsidy on paying wages to their workers.

73 In order to seek relief, eligible individuals and companies are required to submit an application to the Construction Industry Council.

- A one-off subsidy of HK$36,000 (US$4,650) per a 'qualified employee' to employers in the construction industry who have employed casual employees on a long-term basis to supplement the ESS and help reduce the rising unemployment rate in the construction industry.[74] The same undertakings also apply.
- A training subsidy of HK$50,000 (US$6,450) to eligible consulting firms to assist with furthering employee skill development and enhancing technology.

9.3.2 The impact of Covid-19 on the operation of construction contracts in Hong Kong

Covid-19 has presented several challenges for contractors and subcontractors. For example, in the initial stages, there were delays in the supply chain due to closures of factories and manufacturing plants in Mainland China and elsewhere. Whilst factories in Mainland China have mostly reopened, there continues to be delays in the shipment and delivery of materials, plant and equipment from outside Hong Kong due to the various restrictions globally on transportation, flights and shipping. However, Hong Kong has not in general experienced any surge in extension of time and additional cost claims from Contractors experiencing delays and losses associated with Covid-19.

The Hong Kong government has not passed any Covid-19 specific legislation changing the 'normal' operation of construction contracts. Whilst there has been no legislative change, the Hong Kong government has introduced certain facilitation measures with the view to providing greater flexibility in handling government works and non-works contracts and other project developments, easing cash flow difficulties for government contractors and addressing the challenges timely completion of development projects during the pandemic. Under the current facilitation measures, the Hong Kong government will:[75]

- In relation to public works contracts, forgo liquidated damages arising from the outbreak of Covid-19 and grant an extension of time of up to six months under the relevant contractual mechanism upon receipt of an application from a Contractor, save for contracts which provide for general damages. The Hong Kong government will also shorten payment processing time with a view to expediting payment to Contractors and consultants.
- In relation to non-works contracts, handle contract payment schedules in a compassionate manner. The Hong Kong government has also encouraged procuring departments to provide more frequent payments to Contractors (from 30 days to 7–14 days), break up milestones in payment schedules into more deliverables to enable more frequent payments, and provide larger sums for upfront/milestone payments.
- In relation to other development projects, provide (through the Lands Department) a free extension of time of the Building Covenant period of up to six months in land leases.

74 To be a 'qualified employee' an employer must have made contributions for a 'casual employee' under the Mandatory Provident Fund (MPF) Industry Schemes for at least 15 days in the calendar month of March 2020.

75 Enclosure J to Item for Finance Committee FCR(2020–21) 2.

It is predicted that around 1,000 contractors, consultants and lessees will benefit from the above measures.

The Hong Kong government also introduced various significant financial measures to help businesses cope with the Covid-19 pandemic. In addition to the Fund, the Hong Kong government guaranteed concessionary low interest rate loans to small and medium enterprises. Further, the Hong Kong Monetary Authority instructed all banks in Hong Kong to grant a loan repayment holiday until 30 April 2021 for all small to medium enterprises with an annual turnover of less than HK$800 million (US$103 million).[76]

9.4 Hong Kong governing law of the contract

9.4.1 Constraints on the governing law of a construction contract

Hong Kong has not implemented the *Hague Convention on Choice of Law in International Commercial Contracts*. Therefore, there is no statutory right for parties to choose 'rules of law that are generally accepted on an international, supranational or regional level as a neutral and balanced set of rules'.

Nevertheless, subject to a few narrow exceptions set out below, the courts in Hong Kong recognise a party's right to choose the applicable law governing their contract. Parties can elect to be bound by any law, even one that has no apparent connection to the underlying contract.[77]

If there is no clause expressly stating the parties' choice of law, Hong Kong courts will seek to infer this from all of the relevant circumstances including the contractual terms (particularly the jurisdiction clause if there is one).[78] In the absence of an express or implied agreement as to the governing law, Hong Kong courts will generally apply (by considering the surrounding circumstances) the law with the '*closest and most real connection*' to the contract.[79] While there is no hard rule, factors which have been found to suggest a '*closest and most real connection*' include: (1) the subject matter of the contract (if the place of the subject matter is relevant, this will be taken into account); (2) the place of negotiation and execution of the contract; (3) the domicile of the parties; (4) references to a particular currency in the agreement; and (5) any related transactions. The position is different for non-contractual claims. For example, where the claim is based in tort, Hong Kong courts will apply a rule of double actionability.[80]

Where a dispute is submitted to arbitration, the *Arbitration Ordinance* (Cap 609) applies.[81] The *Ordinance* establishes a unitary procedural framework for domestic and international arbitrations seated in Hong Kong principally based on the UNCITRAL

76 The loan holiday was initially in place for a period of six months until 31 October 2020, but was extended in September 2020 to 12 months until 31 April 2021.

77 While the law of a "civilised society" of a non-recognised state may be permitted, other non-recognised states' laws may not be permitted.

78 The Hong Kong courts will only draw an inference if the matter is a substantive one. If the matter is procedural, the Hong Kong courts will apply the law of Hong Kong. Characterising substantive and procedural law matters is often a difficult and complex task.

79 See eg *Waxman v Li Fei Yu* [2013] 3 HKLRD 711. Note, however, the recent reiteration of the test by the English Supreme Court in *Enka Insaat Ve Sanayi AS v OOO Insurance Company Chubb* [2020] UKSC 38.

80 Under the rule of double actionability, the claim must be actionable under both the law of the place where events constituting the tort occurred and under Hong Kong law unless the application of the rule would cause injustice.

81 *Arbitration Ordinance* (Cap 609).

Model Law (as adopted on 21 June 1985 and amended on 7 July 2006) with specific Hong Kong modifications and supplementary provisions.

The *Arbitration Ordinance* incorporates Article 28(1) of the UNCITRAL Model Law, which provides that:

> The arbitral tribunal shall decide the dispute in accordance with such rules of law as are chosen by the parties as applicable to the substance of the dispute. Any designation of the law or legal system of a given State shall be construed, unless otherwise expressed, as directly referring to the substantive law of that State and not to its conflict of laws rules.

Pursuant to subsection 56(7) of the *Arbitration Ordinance*, unless the parties agree otherwise, the tribunal may adopt either an adversarial or inquisitorial approach to the arbitral proceeding. This decision will impact the manner in which evidence is gathered, the appointment of expert witnesses, examination of witnesses, disclosure of documents in support of a party's case, the way in which the oral hearing is conducted and whether a decision is based on the parties' evidence or inquiries of the arbitral tribunal. Therefore, if the parties are minded that the arbitration be conducted in a certain manner, this should be agreed in their arbitration agreement.

The parties' right to choose the law applicable to their contract is not unlimited. Hong Kong courts are unlikely to give effect to an applicable law clause in circumstances where it is not bona fide or legal, or it is in violation of public policy of the place in which the contract is performed.

9.4.2 Formal requirements for a construction contract

The formal requirements for a construction contract in Hong Kong are the same as the requirements for most contracts under the common law: (1) an agreement constituted by offer and acceptance; (2) sufficient consideration (this requirement does not apply to contracts made under seal); (3) an intention by the parties to be legally bound; (4) certainty of the terms of the agreement; and (5) each of the parties has the legal capacity to enter into an agreement.

A construction contract can be in writing or it can be oral provided that the formal requirements are present. It should be noted, however, that the *Arbitration Ordinance* applies only to an arbitration agreement that is in writing[82] and therefore oral arbitration agreements may not be binding.

As is the position in England and Wales (and other similar common law jurisdictions), Hong Kong law recognises two forms of contract, a simple contract and a contract made under seal (that is, by deed). The main differences between a simple contract and contract made under seal are the signature requirements[83] and the limitation period within which an action can be commenced. A claim for breach of a simple contract must be commenced within 6 years from the date on which the action accrued, whereas a claim for breach of a contract made under seal must be commenced within 12 years.[84]

82 ibid s 19, which contains a broad definition of what constitutes an arbitration agreement in writing.

83 Signature requirements for companies executing deeds are found in the *Companies Ordinance* (Cap 622), s 128.

84 *Limitation Ordinance* (Cap 347), s 4(1) and 4(3).

9.5 What Special Provisions in the Particular Conditions are necessary for consistency with applicable laws in Hong Kong?

9.5.1 FIDIC General Conditions are incompatible or inconsistent with Hong Kong governing law of the contract

The FIDIC suite of standard form contracts have not enjoyed wide domestic use in Hong Kong. However, this is not due to any particular incompatibilities or inconsistencies with Hong Kong law. Generally speaking, no Special Provisions in the Particular Conditions are necessary to ensure that the FIDIC General Conditions are compatible or consistent with Hong Kong law if it is the governing law of the contract.

9.5.2 FIDIC General Conditions are incompatible or inconsistent with the law of the Site country

No Special Provisions in the Particular Conditions are necessary for consistency with applicable laws in Hong Kong if it is the law of the Site/Country.

9.5.3 FIDIC General Conditions are incompatible or inconsistent with the relevant laws on dispute determination in Hong Kong

No Special Provisions in the Particular Conditions are necessary for consistency with applicable laws in Hong Kong in the event that it is the law of the arbitral seat.

9.6 What Special Provisions in the Particular Conditions are desirable for consistency with applicable laws in Hong Kong?

9.6.1 Security of payment

Unlike some other common law jurisdictions, the Hong Kong Legislative Council has not passed any security of payment legislation. Disputes are generally resolved by reference to the contract and the procedural rules of court or arbitration, depending on which is chosen.

It is likely that security of payment legislation will be passed in Hong Kong in the not too distant future. A statutory regime for security of payment for construction activities conducted in Hong Kong has been debated within the government since at least 2011, and a comprehensive survey undertaken by the government confirmed that payment delays, disputes and unfair contract terms adversely affect many in the construction industry.[85]

It is expected that any security of payment legislation that is passed in Hong Kong will provide for the prohibition of 'pay when paid' and conditional payment provisions, and a statutory entitlement for either party to refer disputes arising in relation to payment claims to adjudication for a decision within a short period of time. It is anticipated that the legislation will provide for adjudicators' decisions to be enforced in the same way as court judgments, without set off or deduction, whilst allowing paying parties the right to challenge the enforceability of a decision.

85 Development Bureau of Hong Kong, *Report on Public Consultation on Proposed Security of Payment Legislation for the Construction Industry* (April 2016).

Since there is, at present, no security of payment legislation in Hong Kong, it is not necessary to add Special Provisions in the Particular Conditions to align the payment provisions in the Contract with the relevant security of payment legislation. Nevertheless, the government has stated that it intends to proceed with the legislation[86] and therefore advice should be sought prior to executing any construction contract in Hong Kong as to whether the legislation has been enacted and, if so, whether the wording of the relevant Special Provisions are appropriate.

9.6.2 Frustrated contracts

Hong Kong has legislation that applies to frustrated contracts: the *Law Amendment and Reform (Consolidation) Ordinance* (Cap 23). In particular, section 16(2) and 16(3) of the *Ordinance* seek to address circumstances where a contract has been brought to an end by frustration and: (a) money has been paid or is owing prior to the frustrating event; or (b) one party has conferred a valuable benefit on the other prior to the frustrating event. These sections of the *Ordinance* confer a wide discretion on Hong Kong courts and tribunals to determine what it considers to be a 'just sum'; however, it cannot exceed the expenses incurred or the value of the benefit conferred. Clause 18 of the FIDIC General Conditions should be reviewed to determine whether it is appropriate in light of this legislation.[87]

9.6.3 Rights of third parties

In 2016, the *Contracts (Rights of Third Parties) Ordinance* (Cap 623) was enacted in Hong Kong, which created an exception to the long standing doctrine of privity of contract.[88] Pursuant to the *Ordinance*, a third party may enforce a term of a contract (including a term that excludes or limits liability) if the contract expressly provides that the third party may do so or the term purports to confirm a benefit on third party.[89] The third party must be expressly identified in the contract by name, as a member of a class or as answering a particular description.[90] The *Ordinance* applies to all contracts executed from 1 January 2016.[91]

Contracting parties can 'opt-out' of the application of the *Ordinance* by express agreement. Parties should therefore seek competent advice before executing contracts in Hong Kong to ensure that the desired effect is achieved as regards to third parties.

9.6.4 Building controls

Hong Kong has strict statutory controls relating to the approval and construction of new buildings or new building works (including supply of construction materials, site preparation, design parameters, loads and stresses, structural requirements, layout,

86 Development Bureau of Hong Kong, *Report on Public Consultation on Proposed Security of Payment Legislation for the Construction Industry* (April 2016), para 145.

87 2017 FIDIC Yellow Book, 2017 FIDIC Red Book and 2017 FIDIC Silver Book.

88 The *Contracts (Rights of Third Parties) Ordinance* (Cap 623) largely mirrored the *Contracts (Rights of Third Parties) Act 1999* (UK).

89 *Contracts (Rights of Third Parties) Ordinance* (Cap 623), section 4(1).

90 ibid s 4(2).

91 However, it applies to new contracts or amendment agreements to existing contracts.

methods of construction, fire safety and demolition works),[92] and the monitoring and maintenance of existing buildings.[93] Parties should seek competent advice on these statutory controls, especially in connection with Sub-Clause 1.13 of the FIDIC General Conditions,[94] and sub-clause 4.8 in connection with health and safety in the carrying out building works.

The *Buildings Ordinance* (Cap 123) is the primary statutory control for buildings works in Hong Kong.[95] Its objective is to provide for the planning, design and construction of buildings and associated works and to make provision for the rendering safe of dangerous buildings and land, and for regular inspections of buildings and the associated repairs to prevent the buildings from becoming unsafe.[96]

The *Buildings Ordinance* has a wide application and will apply to most, if not all, building, construction and infrastructure projects in Hong Kong.[97] For example, the term 'building works' includes any kind of building or construction works (large scale or otherwise), site formation works, ground investigation, foundations works, drainage works, street works, repairs, demolition, alteration, addition and every other kind of building operation.

In relation to new buildings and/or new building works, the *Buildings Ordinance* establishes system of vetting, building plan approvals,[98] building consents,[99] compliance requirements,[100] and the use of Authorised Persons and registered construction professionals[101] to carry out the works, to ensure that the works meet the required building standards.

Building works are overseen by the Building Authority, a statutory body created under the *Buildings Ordinance* with responsibility to undertake detailed supervision, compliance and reporting works for building works in Hong Kong.[102] Subject to

92 TWY Cheng and GKLSoo, *Construction Law and Practice in Hong Kong* (3rd edn, Sweet & Maxwell 2017) [10.016], [10.019].

93 Arthur McInnis, *Emden's Construction Law Hong Kong* (Lexis Nexis Butterworths, looseleaf), ch XV [254].

94 The sub-clause identified applies to 2017 FIDIC Red Book and 2017 FIDIC Yellow Book. Sub-clause 1.12 is the relevant sub-clause in the 2017 FIDIC Silver Book.

95 Subsidiary legislation includes, but is not limited to, the following: *Buildings (Administration) Regulations* (Cap 123A), *Buildings (Construction Works) Regulations* (Cap 123B), *Buildings (Demolition Works) Regulations* (Cap 123C), *Buildings (Planning) Regulations* (Cap 123F), *Buildings (Private Streets and Access Roads) Regulations* (Cap 123G), *Building (Planning Streets and Access Roads) Regulations* (Cap 123G), *Buildings (Refuse Storage and Material Recovery Chambers and Refuse Chutes) Regulations* (Cap 123H), *Buildings (Standards of Sanitary Fitments, Plumbing, Drainage Works and Latrines) Regulations* (Cap 123I), *Buildings (Ventilating Systems) Regulations* (Cap 123J), *Buildings (Oil Storage Ventilations) Regulations* (Cap 123K), *Building (Appeal) Regulations* (Cap 123L), *Building (Energy Efficiency) Regulations* (Cap 123M), *Buildings (Minor Works) Regulations* (Cap 123N), *Buildings (Minor Works) (Fees) Regulations* (Cap 123O) and *Buildings (Inspection and Repair) Regulations* (Cap 123P).

96 *Buildings Ordinance* (Cap 123), Foreword.

97 Cheng and Soo (n 92) [10.018].

98 This includes obtaining approval from the Building Authority for building plans prior to the commencement and carrying out of the works. Approval of building plans takes approximately two months.

99 Consent to commence building works takes approximately 28 days.

100 Once building and construction works commence, statutory agents (amongst others) will routinely supervise and inspect the Site and the building works and identify any irregularities or compliance issues.

101 An **Authorised Person** is an architect, engineer or surveyor registered under the *Buildings Ordinance* (Cap 123). All consultants (ie engineers, surveyors and architects) and Contractors carrying out building works in Hong Kong must be registered with the Building Authority and on the Hong Kong government's approved lists of Contractors and Consultants.

102 *Buildings Ordinance* (Cap 123), pt 1.

minimal exceptions,[103] building works cannot commence until the Building Authority has approved building plans and granted consents, and the relevant permits have been issued.[104] The Building Authority can refuse consent on specified grounds or impose conditions on the granting of its consent.[105] There are severe consequences for failing to comply with these requirements.[106] In the event that building works are being carried out in contravention of the *Ordinance* or materially deviated from the approved plans, the Building Authority can direct the cessation of works.[107]

In relation to the continued monitoring of buildings, the *Buildings Ordinance* establishes a system for ongoing monitoring, inspection and enforcement after the completion of building works to ensure that buildings are properly maintained and to prevent unauthorised modifications to buildings which do not accord with approved building plans (for example, unauthorised building works).[108]

Any person intending to carry out building works is required under the *Buildings Ordinance* to appoint an Authorised Person (that is an architect, engineer or surveyor registered under the *Ordinance*), and where necessary a registered Structural Engineer, and use construction professionals and Contractors that are registered on the Hong Kong government's approved list of Contractors and Consultants.[109] If the building works involve geotechnical elements, a registered Geotechnical Engineer must also be appointed to prepare and submit plans for the approval of Building Authority.

On completion of the building works, it is necessary to obtain an occupation permit from the Building Authority before the building can be occupied.[110]

9.6.5 Development controls

Hong Kong has long suffered from issues of overcrowding and land shortage. The result is a highly regulated legislative framework for planning and land development.[111]

The *Town Planning Ordinance* (Cap 131)[112] regulates planning and land use in urban areas. Applications for planning permission are regulated by section 16 of the *Ordinance*.[113] Applications to the Town Planning Board for 'rezoning' of a particular site or area in which the site is located are regulated by section 12A of the *Ordinance*. Applications can be lengthy processes, undergoing public consultations. Appeals are determined by the Appeal Board and applications for appeals are regulated by section 17 of the *Ordinance*. If the applicant is still aggrieved by the decision of the Appeal Board, it can seek judicial review of the matter in the Hong Kong courts.

---

103 For instance, minor works, urgent works or works which are in a building but do not involve a building's structure.
104 *Buildings Ordinance* (Cap 123), s 14.
105 ibid ss 16 and 17. Examples of relevant permits include hoarding permits and excavation permits.
106 ibid s 40.
107 ibid s 23.
108 ibid ss 25, 26, 26A, 27, 27A, 27B, 27C, 28, 29, 29A.
109 ibid pt 1. The list of consultants is maintained by the Architectural and Associated Consultants Selection Board. It comprises of the following categories: architectural, building services, building surveying, landscape architectural, quantity surveying and structural engineering. Contractors must be registered with the Building Authority and obtain certain consents while conducting the building works.
110 ibid s 21.
111 ibid [101].
112 Which includes the following subsidiary legislation: *Town Planning Regulations* (Cap 131A), *Town Planning (Appeals) Regulations* (Cap 131B) and *Town Planning (Taking Possession and Disposal of Property) Regulations* (Cap 131C).
113 *Town Planning Ordinance* (Cap 131), s 16.

Additional complexities apply to applications for planning permission to build within country parks, marine parks and other special areas, which are regulated by the *Country Parks Ordinance* (Cap 208).

9.6.6 Environmental controls

Hong Kong has also implemented extensive environmental protection legislation. This includes (a) the *Air Pollution Control Ordinance* (Cap 311), which controls the emission of air pollution from stationary sources including construction activities under a licensing system; and (b) the *Noise Control Ordinance* (Cap 400), which controls noise pollution, including from construction activities. There is also legislation concerning waste disposal and water pollution, which would apply to construction sites.[114]

Contractors should also be aware of the requirements of the *Environmental Impact Assessment Ordinance* (Cap 499), which provides for the assessment of the environmental impact of certain projects and proposals prior to permissions and consents being granted. An environmental permit is required for any project that causes adverse environmental impact, which is a risk on almost all reasonably sized construction projects in a high-density area such as Hong Kong.

There has also been a recent focus on promoting energy efficiency and sustainability. Under the *Buildings Energy Efficiency Ordinance* (Cap 610) a developer or owner of a prescribed newly constructed building must ensure that building services installation – namely – air-conditioning installation, lighting installation, electrical installation and lift and escalator installation – complies with the design standards of the Building Energy Code. Similarly, if specified works to be carried out in an existing prescribed building involve the installation or replacement of building services, the owner must ensure that the building services installation complies with the Building Energy Code. An energy audit in respect of central building services installation must be carried out in accordance with the *Ordinance* every 10 years.

In addition, developers who obtain a Green Building Certification Label from the Green Building Council by proposing sustainable developments may be granted additional gross floor area for the development from the Buildings Authority.

9.6.7 Requirements under Hong Kong law to hire local labour

Parties should give due consideration to how they will resource their building, construction and infrastructure works carried out in Hong Kong and make appropriate provision for the time it may take to source an appropriate work force. Hong Kong has legislated so as to encourage companies to employ local workers on construction projects. Contractors must apply for approval to fill vacancies with foreign workers, and this is provided on a case by case basis. If an employer successfully obtains approval, they must pay a levy for each foreign worker to the Employees Retraining Board. Foreign workers must also obtain an appropriate visa and/or entry permit and Hong Kong identity card[115] in order to work in Hong Kong. In light of the current skilled labour shortage, Contractors involved in public infrastructure works who are experiencing difficulties in resourcing their works can refer to the expedited procedures for the Supplementary Labour Scheme.[116]

114 See *Waste Disposal Ordinance* (Cap 354) and *Water Pollution Control Ordinance* (Cap 358).

115 A Hong Kong identity card is required for any worker admitted for employment in Hong Kong for a period more than six months. See the *Registration of Persons Ordinance* (Cap 177).

116 As explained at para 9.2.2 above.

9.6.8 Mandatory insurance

The *Employees' Compensation Ordinance* (Cap 282) sets out the rights and obligations of employers and employees with respect to injuries or death caused by (a) accidents arising out of and in the course of employment; or (b) prescribed occupational diseases. It is mandatory that each Consultant and Contractors' employee on a building, construction or infrastructure project be insured in accordance with the *Ordinance*.

Parties may wish to bear in mind the compulsory obligations considered above in relation to insurance against injuries in the drafting sub-clause 19.2.5 [Injury to employees] of the FIDIC General Conditions and consider incorporating Special Provisions generally that set out their respective obligations with reference to the legislation referred to above.[117]

9.6.9 Gross negligence

Sub-clauses 1.15, 8.8, 11.10 and 14.14 of the FIDIC General Conditions[118] refer to the term 'gross negligence' as an exception to the application of the limitation of liability. Hong Kong does not recognise a concept of 'gross negligence' as distinct from negligence. While Hong Kong courts may follow the English courts' willingness to interpret the use of the phrase,[119] parties should consider whether it is appropriate.

9.7 Summary of applicable legislation for Hong Kong governing law of the contract

9.7.1 Entry into a construction contract

Contracts generally	*Unconscionable Contracts Ordinance* (Cap 458) *Misrepresentation Ordinance* (Cap 284)
Construction contracts	-

9.7.2 Termination of a construction contract

Frustration	*Law Amendment and Reform (Consolidation) Ordinance* (Cap 23)
Bankruptcy, insolvency, liquidation	*Bankruptcy Ordinance* (Cap 6) *Companies Ordinance* (Cap 622) *Companies (Winding Up and Miscellaneous Provisions) Ordinance* (Cap 32)
Guarantees under forms of Security (Tender Security, Demand Guarantee, Surety Bond, Advance Payment Guarantee, Retention Money Guarantee, Payment Guarantee by Employer	*Conveyancing and Property Ordinance* (Cap 219)

117 2017 FIDIC Yellow Book, 2017 FIDIC Red Book and 2017 FIDIC Silver Book.
118 The sub-clauses identified apply to 2017 FIDIC Red Book and 2017 FIDIC Yellow Book. Sub-clauses 1.14, 8.8, 11.10 and 14.4 are the relevant sub-clauses in the 2017 FIDIC Silver Book.
119 See Moore-Bick LJ in *Tradigrain SA v Intertek Testing Systems (ITS) Canada Limited* [2007] EWCA Civ 154 and Aikens LJ in *Springwell Navigation Corporation v JP Morgan Chase Bank* [2010] EWCA Civ 1221.

9.7.3 Dispute resolution

Limitation periods	*Limitation Ordinance* (Cap 347)
Liability	*Civil Liability (Contribution) Ordinance* (Cap 377) *Occupiers Liability Ordinance* (Cap 314) *Law Amendment and Reform (Consolidation) Ordinance* (Cap 23)
Adjudication	There is no adjudication legislation in Hong Kong
Arbitration	*Arbitration Ordinance* (Cap 609)

9.8 Summary of applicable legislation if the Site/Country is in Hong Kong

9.8.1 Operation of a construction contract

Registration and administration of professionals – Engineers, Architects, Quantity Surveyors, Certifiers, Building Surveyors, Surveyors	*Buildings Ordinance* (Cap 123) *Architects Registration Ordinance* (Cap 408) *Engineers Registration Ordinance* (Cap 409) *Surveyors Registration Ordinance* (Cap 417)
Registration/licencing of Contractors and subcontractors	*Buildings Ordinance* (Cap 123) *Construction Workers Registration Ordinance* (Cap 583)
Subcontractors	*Contracts (Rights of Third Parties) Ordinance* (Cap 623)
Use of liens /Assignment of debts	*Law Amendment and Reform (Consolidation) Ordinance* (Cap 23)
Labour	*Employment Ordinance* (Cap 57) *Minimum Wage Ordinance* (Cap 608) *Employees' Compensation Ordinance* (Cap 282) *Contracts for Employment Outside Hong Kong Ordinance* (Cap 78) *Immigration Ordinance* (Cap 115) *Construction Workers Registration Ordinance* (Cap 583) *Mandatory Provident Fund Schemes Ordinance* (Cap 485) *Trade Unions Ordinance* (Cap 332) *Industrial Relations Ordinance* (Cap 55) *Personal Data (Privacy) Ordinance* (Cap 468) *Disability Discrimination Ordinance* (Cap 487) *Sex Discrimination Ordinance* (Cap 480) *Family Status Discrimination Ordinance* (Cap 527) *Race Discrimination Ordinance* (Cap 602)
Copyright	*Copyright Ordinance* (Cap 528) *Patents Ordinance* (Cap 514)
The product being produced from the Works	*Air Pollution Control Ordinance* (Cap 311) *Waste Disposal Ordinance* (Cap 354) *Water Pollution Control Ordinance* (Cap 358) *Noise Control Ordinance* (Cap 400) *Ozone Zone Layer Protection Ordinance* (Cap 403) *Dumping at Sea Ordinance* (Cap 466) *Environmental Impact Assessment Ordinance* (Cap 499) *Hazardous Chemicals Control Ordinance* (Cap 595)
Planning	*Town Planning Ordinance* (Cap 131) and its regulations *Country Parks Ordinance* (Cap 208)

(*Continued*)

Work affecting adjacent property to the Site	*Buildings Ordinance* (Cap 123)
Heritage	*Antiquities and Monuments Ordinance* (Cap 53) *Environmental Impact Assessment Ordinance* (Cap 499) *Country Parks Ordinance* (Cap 208)
Environment	*Air Pollution Control Ordinance* (Cap 311) *Waste Disposal Ordinance* (Cap 354) *Water Pollution Control Ordinance* (Cap 358) *Noise Control Ordinance* (Cap 400) *Dumping at Sea Ordinance* (Cap 466) *Environmental Impact Assessment Ordinance* (Cap 499) *Buildings Energy Efficiency Ordinance* (Cap 610) *Buildings Ordinance* (Cap 123)
Building and construction permits, execution of construction work, Standard of Construction Work	*Buildings Ordinance* (Cap 123) and its regulations
Health and safety	*Occupational Safety and Health Ordinance* (Cap 509) and its regulations *Factories and Industrial Undertakings Ordinance* (Cap 59) and its regulations *Builders, Lifts and Tower Working Platforms (Safety) Ordinance* (Cap 470) *Boilers and Pressure Vessels Ordinance* (Cap 56) *Buildings Ordinance* (Cap 123)
Calibration of testing apparatus, equipment and Instruments	No applicable legislation
Ownership of Plant and Materials	No applicable legislation
Employer's sale of Contractor's Equipment, surplus material, wreckage and Temporary Works	*Bills of Sale Ordinance* (20) *Companies Ordinance* (Cap 622)
Insurance	*Employees' Compensation Insurance Ordinance* (Cap 282)
Statutory rights that coexist with contractual Rights	*Trade Descriptions* (Cap 362) *Misrepresentation Ordinance* (Cap 284) *Sale of Goods Ordinance* (Cap 26) *Control of Exemption Clauses Ordinance* (Cap 71) *Supply of Services (Implied Terms) Ordinance* (Cap 457)
Liability for defective work	*Supply of Services (Implied Terms) Ordinance* (Cap 457) *Sale of Goods Ordinance* (Cap 26)
Liability for nuisance	*Public Health and Municipal Services Ordinance* (Cap 132) *Noise Control Ordinance* (Cap 400)
Other issues	*Basic Law* *Hong Kong Bill of Rights Ordinance* (Cap 383) *Interpretation and General Clause Ordinance* (Cap 1) *Building Management Ordinance* (Cap 344)

9.8.2 Termination of a construction contract

Bankruptcy, insolvency, liquidation	*Bankruptcy Ordinance* (Cap 6) *Companies Ordinance* (Cap 622) *Companies (Winding Up and Miscellaneous Provisions) Ordinance* (Cap 32)

9.8.3 Dispute resolution

Dispute before a local board/ Adjudication	There is no statutory adjudication regime in Hong Kong
Limitation periods	*Limitation Ordinance* (Cap 347)

9.9 Summary of applicable legislation if the 'seat' of the dispute determination is in Hong Kong

9.9.1 Dispute resolution

Limitation periods	*Limitation Ordinance* (Cap 347)
Adjudication	There is no statutory adjudication regime in Hong Kong
Arbitration	*Arbitration Ordinance* (Cap 609)
Limitation periods	*Limitation Ordinance* (Cap 347)

9.10 Issues that a court or arbitrator may construe differently to that expected from the words of the Contract because of local law or custom

9.10.1 Misleading and deceptive conduct

Parties to construction contracts occasionally make pre-contractual statements during the negotiation stage which are intended to encourage the other party to enter into the contract. It is therefore important to understand what impact a false statement may have (where it was made innocently, deliberately or recklessly) on the validity of a construction contract.

Under the *Misrepresentation Ordinance* (Cap 284), and at law, a party who has been induced to enter into a contract by a false statement of past or present fact or law is entitled to rescind the contract and/or, depending on the circumstances, claim damages for any loss or damage suffered. A misrepresentation may be innocent, fraudulent or negligent and may constituted by conduct, words and even silence.[120]

In the case of an innocent misrepresentation, the *Ordinance* confers a broad discretion on the court or tribunal to declare that a contract is subsisting, award damages in lieu of rescission and to do what is equitable.[121] In exercising this discretion the court or tribunal may consider a number of factors including the nature of the misrepresentation, the loss caused if the contract is not rescinded and the loss caused to the person who made the innocent misrepresentation if the contract is rescinded.

9.10.2 Proportionate liability

Unlike some other common law jurisdictions, Hong Kong has not legislated in favour of a proportionate liability scheme. It may nonetheless be relevant to mention that, pursuant to the *Civil Liability (Contribution) Ordinance* (Cap 377), each defendant(s)

120 In Hong Kong, mere silence or inaction does not constitute a representation at law unless the person making the representation has a duty to disclose or intentionally withholds part of the truth.

121 *Misrepresentation Ordinance* (Cap 284), s 3(2). See also *Green Park Properties Ltd v Dorku Ltd* [2001] 1 HKLRD 139.

responsible for a single, indivisible loss suffered by a plaintiff is potentially liable for the entire loss.[122]

9.10.3 Implied terms

As with other common law jurisdictions, in addition to the express terms, certain terms may be implied under Hong Kong law into construction contracts depending on the court or tribunal's interpretation of sub-clause 1.15 of the FIDIC General Conditions (which limits either party's liability for loss and damage to breaches of specific clauses in the contract).[123]

Hong Kong law follows general common law principles in relation to implication of terms. There is a five-fold test for determining whether a term is capable of being implied into a contract: (1) the term must be reasonable and equitable; (2) the term must be necessary to give 'business efficacy' to the contract; (3) the term must be so obvious it goes without saying; (4) it must be capable of clear expression; and (5) the term must not contradict any express terms of the contract.[124]

Terms might also be implied by statute. Of potential relevance to construction projects is the *Supply of Services (Implied Terms) Ordinance* (Cap 457). By this *Ordinance*, the following terms are implied into a contract for supply of services, specifically, that:

- The supplier will carry out the service with reasonable care and skill and within a reasonable time[125]
- The recipient of the services will pay a reasonable charge.[126]

The *Sales of Goods Ordinance* (Cap 26) might also apply where the obligations under the construction contract include the sale of equipment or supplies. This *Ordinance* implies the following conditions, inter alia, into a contract:

- The seller has a right to sell the goods[127]
- The goods are free from encumbrances[128]
- The goods are of merchantable quality (including that the goods are free from defects, safe and durable) [129]
- The goods are reasonably fit for purpose[130] and
- The goods correspond with the description or sample.[131]

Parties should be aware of the general application of implied terms and seek competent advice on the potential risks.

122 *Civil Liability (Contribution) Ordinance* (Cap 377), s 3.

123 The sub-clause identified applies to 2017 FIDIC Red Book and 2017 FIDIC Yellow Book. Sub-clause 1.14 is the relevant sub-clause in the 2017 FIDIC Silver Book.

124 *Shirlaw v Southern Foundries (1926) Ltd* [1939] 2 KB 206 at 227; *Kensland Realty Ltd v Whale View Investment Ltd* (2001) 4 HKCFAR 381 at 391.

125 *Supply of Services (Implied Terms) Ordinance* (Cap 457), ss 5 and 6.

126 ibid s 7.

127 *Sales of Goods Ordinance* (Cap 26), s 14.

128 ibid.

129 ibid s 16.

130 ibid.

131 ibid ss 15 and 17.

9.11 References

9.11.1 Books

McInnis, *Emden's Construction Law Hong Kong* (Lexis Nexis Butterworths, looseleaf)
Cheng and Soo, *Construction Law and Practice in Hong Kong* (3rd edn, Sweet & Maxwell 2017)
Choong and Weeramantry, *The Hong Kong Arbitration Ordinance, Commentary and Annotations* (Sweet & Maxwell 2011)
Yash P Ghai, *Hong Kong's New Constitutional Order – the Resumption of Chinese Sovereignty and the Basic Law* (2nd edn, Hong Kong University Press 2011)
Lo Pui Yin, *The Judicial Construction of Hong Kong' Basic Law* (Hong Kong University Press 2014)
Geoffrey Ma, *Arbitration in Hong Kong, A Practical Guide* (4th edn, Sweet & Maxwell 2017)
Ellis Baker, Ben Mellors, Scott Chalmers and Anthony Lavers, *FIDIC Contracts: Law and Practice* (Informa 2013)
Sergeant and Wieliczko, *Construction Contract Variations* (Informa 2014)
Robert Clay (ed), *Hudson's Building and Engineering Contracts* (13th edn, Sweet & Maxwell 2018)
The Hon Sir Vivian Ramsey and Stephen Furst, *Keating on Construction Contracts* (10th edn, Sweet & Maxwell 2018)

9.11.2 Journals

Hong Kong Law Journal
Hong Kong Lawyer
The International Construction Law Review
Construction Law Journal

9.11.3 Internet

Hong Kong case law, legislation and the *Basic Law*: www.hklii.org
Legislation: https://www.elegislation.gov.hk/
Case law: https://www.judiciary.hk/en/home/index.html

CHAPTER 10

Applying FIDIC contracts in India

Shri Venkatesh, Kanika Chugh, Ashutosh Kumar Srivastava, Aditya Vardhan Sharma, Aditya Ajay

 DOI: 10.4324/9781003200901-10

10.1 Outline of the legal environment in India

10.1.1 The constitutional structure of India

The *Constitution of India* lays foundation to the new Indian renaissance. It is an elaborate written *grund norm* comprising of 441 articles and 12 Schedules,[1] which act(s) as the fundamental law of the land. The conscience of the *Constitution of India* speaks through its preamble,[2] and its subtleties are defined in Article 38.[3] The preamble is a solemn resolution by the people of India to create a sovereign, socialist, secular, democratic republic, and to secure certain indispensable rights to 'all its citizens'.

Even though the *Constitution of India* does not describe the country as 'federal', it establishes a federal Union of 28 states and nine Union territories. However, the pragmatic federalism which, while distributing legislative powers and specifying the spheres of governmental powers of central and state governments, is overlaid by strongly 'unitary' features buttressed by the dominance of the centre over states.[4] Thus, it would not be remiss to say that India is federal in form, but unitary in spirit.

The President of India is the constitutional head of the Union, commander-in-chief of the armed forces and head of the government in a 'nodal' capacity, as the 'actual' executive power is vested with the Prime Minister (and his/her council of ministers), whose 'aid and advice'[5] is binding on the President. Similarly, at the state level, while

1 Originally, the *Constitution of India* consisted of 395 Articles arranged under 22 Parts and eight Schedules. It has undergone 104 amendments as at January 2020.

2 UN Gupta, 'Legal Realism and Indian Constitutional Interpretations' (1975) 17 *Journal of the Indian Law Institute* 212.

3 (1) The State shall strive to promote the welfare of the people by securing and protecting as effectively as it may a social order in which justice, social, economic and political, shall inform all the institutions of the national life. (2) The State shall, in particular, strive to minimise the inequalities in income, and endeavour to eliminate inequalities in status, facilities and opportunities, not only amongst individuals but also amongst groups of people residing in different areas or engaged in different vocations.

4 *SR Bommai v Union of India* (1994) 3 SCC 1.

5 *Constitution of India*, art 74.

governors are the nodal head of the states, executive powers are vested with the chief ministers (and their respective Council of Ministers).[6]

The *Constitution of India* adopts a bicameral form of legislature at the Centre.[7] The Parliament consists of two Houses:

- **Lok Sabha** (House of the People): The political party (or a coalition of political parties) with majority in the Lok Sabha forms the government. The members of Lok Sabha are elected by the people of the country from their respective local constituencies.[8]
- **Rajya Sabha** (Council of States): The members of the Rajya Sabha are elected indirectly from state Assemblies.[9]

At the state level, the state legislature comprises the Legislative Assembly (similar to the Lok Sabha).[10] States may also have a second House (ie the Legislative Council).[11] The area of operation of the Parliament vis-*à*-vis the state legislatures is envisaged in Schedule VII of the *Constitution of India*, which essentially consists of three lists. List I defines the Union List, wherein the Parliament has the sole authority to frame laws. List II defines the state list, which falls within the exclusive domain of state legislatures. Finally, List III is the concurrent list, wherein both the Parliament and state legislatures are empowered to frame laws. However, through various precedents of the Supreme Court, it has now been held that within the concurrent list, the laws framed by the Parliament would have supremacy.[12]

India adheres to a Montesquieuan system of 'separation of powers'.[13] Although the doctrine of 'separation of powers' has not been recognised under the *Constitution of India* in its absolute rigidity, the framers have meticulously defined the functions of various organs of the state.[14] The legislature, the executive and the judiciary, being the three pillars of the Indian democracy, have to function within their own spheres demarcated under the *Constitution of India*.

10.1.2 The legal system of India

The Indian legal system follows a common law structure which is based on various judicial precedents inherited from the British colonial legacy. The judiciary guarantees that all the organs of the state function within their individual constitutional limits.

Criminal law in India is governed by the provisions of the *Indian Penal Code* 1860 and the *Criminal Procedure Code 1973*. Similarly, civil law is governed by the provisions of the *Code of Civil Procedure* 1908. There is no codified statute dealing with tort law in India. However, most cases of tort are governed by the principles of common law.

6 HM Seervai, *Constitutional Law of India* (4th edn, Universal Law Publishing Co Ltd India 2005) 2021.
7 *Constitution of India*, art 79.
8 ibid art 81.
9 ibid art 80.
10 ibid art 168.
11 Currently, only seven of the 28 states have a Legislative Council.
12 *M Karunanidhi v Union of India* (1979) 3 SCC 431.
13 *Fertilizer Corpn Kamgarh Union v Union of India* (1981) 1 SCC 568.
14 *Asif Hameed v State of J&K* 1989 Supp (2) SCC 364.

10.1.3 The court system of India

The structure of courts within India is divided into a three-tier system:

- The Supreme Court of India is the Apex Court of the country. It is the court of record and its directions are binding on all subordinate courts. The Supreme Court of India derives overarching powers to adjudicate on the functions of the legislature and executive from Article 142 of the *Constitution of India*. This power is vested in the Apex Court to bring about complete justice. This power is supplemented by Article 141 which provides that the law declared by the Supreme Court of India shall be binding on all courts within the territory of India.[15] Additionally, Articles 32[16] and Article 136[17] add to the inherent power of the Apex Court to protect the people of India from violation of fundamental rights and grave injustice. The Chief Justice of India is the head of the judges of the Supreme Court. The present strength of the Supreme Court of India includes 34 judges. Article 132 of the *Constitution of India* allows the Supreme Court to hear constitutional, civil and criminal appeals against orders and judgments of High Courts.
- High Courts are the highest courts of the concerned state. The High Courts are vested with the supervisory powers over all subordinate courts and tribunals, situated within the territorial limits of the concerned High Court, as envisaged under Article 227[18] of the *Constitution of India*. The judgment of a High Court is binding upon the subordinate courts within the High Court's territorial jurisdiction. However, a decision of a High Court is not binding upon other High Courts, and at best can only have a persuasive value. Further, Article 226[19] gives discretionary power to the High Courts to issue appropriate directions, orders, and writs to any person or the government, to secure the fundamental rights of the citizens. The High Courts, in their original and appellate jurisdictions, adjudicate upon matters arising out of both central as well as state laws. There are 25 High Courts in India. Out of these, six High Courts exercise their powers over more than one state/Union Territory.
- Subordinate courts are also known as the 'People's Court' because these are the courts where litigation generally begins. These are classified as civil courts and criminal courts. These courts are headed by judicial officers of the concerned area.

Apart from the above, there are tribunals and local *panchayat* which have been created by an Act of Parliament or state legislatures, and are vested with certain specific functions as per the statutes under which they are created. The introduction of Tribunals to the Judicial system of India was through an Act of Parliament, by amending the *Constitution*

15 Dr Durga Das Basu, *Commentary on the Constitution of India* (9th edn, LexisNexis 2014) 9826, 9827.

16 Power to issue appropriate writs in order to secure fundamental rights of the citizens.

17 Special leave to appeal from any judgment, decree, determination, sentence or order in any cause or matter passed or made by any court or tribunal in the territory of India.

18 Power of superintendence over all courts by the High Court.

19 Power of High Courts to issue certain writs.

of India.[20] This was primarily done to bring specialisation in justice dispensation, and to reduce burdens from the existing judicial system.[21] These also ensure the citizens' right to fair and speedy trial, which is an inherent part of the right to life and personal liberty enshrined under Article 21[22] of the *Constitution of India*.

10.2 The construction industry in India

10.2.1 Overview

The construction industry in India is one of the oldest and largest industries, primarily in the unorganised sector, and has provided employment to a large number of people from every class of the society. Prior to independence, construction activity in India was restricted to places of worship or individual residences. The construction industry in India, like most other developing nations, was initially driven by the government and has witnessed subsequent participation by private players.[23]

The Indian government identified infrastructure/construction as one of the primary drivers of economic development, and in this regard, various policies and laws were enacted. Investment in infrastructure witnessed a substantial increase from about 5 per cent of the gross domestic product (GDP) in the 10th Five Year Plan period (2002–2007), to about 9 per cent in the 11th Five Year Plan period (2007–2012).[24]

As of 2019, the construction industry is the second largest industry in India after agriculture, and employs nearly 50 million people in the country.[25] While 42.39 per cent of the workforce in India were employed through agriculture in the year 2019, the other half was evenly distributed among other industries and services.[26] The construction industry contributed about 11 per cent of total GDP in India.[27] Construction, being the second largest economic activity in the country, contributes 55 per cent share in the cement and steel industry, 15 per cent in the paint industry and 30 per cent in the glass industry.[28] The gross value added (GVA) at current prices by the construction industry in India is estimated to be about US$192 billion in 2019–2020, as compared to US$183.5 billion in 2018–2019.[29]

The construction industry, with its forward and backward linkages with associated industries like cement, steel, bricks, etc. has proliferated employment generation in India. With the progression of the construction sector in India, employment and

20 Article 323-A and 323-B were inserted by the *42nd Amendment Act 1976*.

21 *L Chandra Kumar v Union of India* (1997) 3 SCC 261.

22 Protection of life and personal liberty.

23 PC Markanda, *Building and Engineering Contracts: Law and Practice* (4th edn, LexisNexis 2013) 47.

24 Annual Report the GVA figure of US$192 billion below2019-2020, Ministry of Commerce and Industry, Department for Promotion of Industry & Internal Trade https://dipp.gov.in/sites/default/files/annualReport_English2019-20.pdf (accessed 14 October 2020).

25 Indian Construction Industry.com, Indian Construction Industry Overview https://www.indianconstructionindustry.com/overview.html (accessed 10 October 2020).

26 Statista, India: Distribution of the workforce across economic sectors from 2009 to 2019 https://www.statista.com/statistics/271320/distribution-of-the-workforce-across-economic-sectors-in-india/ (accessed 10 October 2020).

27 Statista, Contribution of construction sector to India's GDP from January 2016 to January 2019 https://www.statista.com/statistics/1069818/india-gdp-contribution-by-construction/ (accessed 10 October 2020).

28 Press Information Bureau, First Advance Estimates of National Income, 2019–2020 https://pib.gov.in/Pressreleaseshare.aspx?PRID=1598643 (accessed 10 October 2020).

29 ibid.

investment opportunities have also picked up a substantial pace. This is also bolstered by the fact that both central and state governments act as catalysts in undertaking large infrastructure projects at both the national and state levels. With space available in the private as well as the public domain, the construction industry, in terms of value, is expected to record a compound annual growth rate of 15.7 per cent to reach US$738.5 billion by the year 2022.[30] India, with its current growth rate, is set to become the third largest construction industry in the world by 2025.[31]

According to the Indian census conducted in the year 2011, only 31 per cent of the population of India lives in urban areas.[32] Urbanisation in India has increased the construction industry, the growth of which is backed by dynamic policies propelling both local and foreign investments.

The construction industry in India consists of following three categories, involving players from both private and public sectors:[33]

- Industrial construction (consists of oil and gas refineries, power plants, pipelines, textiles, etc.)
- Urban development or infrastructure building (broadly consists of sub-segments such as water supply, sanitation, urban transport, education, healthcare, etc.)
- Real estate (consists of residential buildings, offices, hotels, leisure parks, etc.).

The construction sector in India is highly fragmented, with a number of unorganised players working on a subcontracting basis. However, with respect to more technology and capital-intensive projects, the government has been encouraging bidding processes to ensure competitive prices and avoiding monopolistic practices. These large-scale infrastructure projects are usually a carried out through a public private partnership (**PPP**). PPP employs models such as Build-Operate-Transfer (**BOT**), Build-Own-Operate (**BOO**), Build-Own-Operate-Transfer (**BOOT**) and other similar arrangements.

10.2.2 Laws governing construction activities

The construction sector in India is highly regulated and monitored at various levels through numerous legislations and bye-laws. Laws governing construction activities are enacted by both the Parliament, as well as state legislatures due to the federal structure envisaged under Schedule VII of the *Constitution of India*.

10.2.2.1 Contract

At the very threshold, a construction contract, to be legally enforceable, must comply with the basic requirements of a 'contract' as provided under the *Indian Contract Act 1872*.[34]

30 See n 25 above.

31 'India to become 3rd largest construction market by 2025' *Financial Express* https://www.financialexpress.com/industry/india-to-become-3rd-largest-construction-market-by-2025-kpmg/377794/ (accessed 10 October 2020).

32 Ministry of Housing and Urban Affairs, 'Urban Growth' http://mohua.gov.in/cms/urban-growth.php (accessed 10 October 2020).

33 Invest India, 'Building a Sustainable Future' https://www.investindia.gov.in/sector/construction (accessed 10 October 2020).

34 *Indian Contract Act 1872*, s 2(h) and s 10.

10.2.2.2 Labour

India has a strict and robust labour regime in place which every Employer and Contractor must comply with. Following are the noteworthy legislation which aims to protect the rights of workmen:

- The *Industrial Disputes Act 1947* provides legal recognition to the laborers/workers by defining the word 'workmen'[35] and entitles them to several statutory benefits and fair treatment by the Employer/Contractor.
- Any principal Employer/Contractor which hires 20 or more contract laborers for an 'establishment' must comply with the *Contract Labour (Regulation and Abolition) Act* 1970. To comply with its terms, the establishment must be registered in accordance with the legislation, and all such Contractors must obtain a licence from the authorised authority specified therein.
- Regarding the condition of service of interstate laborers, the *Inter-State Migrant Workmen (Regulation of Employment and Conditions of Services) Act 1979* mandates that all Contractors employing five or more inter-state migrant workmen must register themselves.
- The *Workmen's Compensation Act 1973* requires that compensation be paid to workers that become injured in the course of employment.
- The *Code on Wages* 2019, which is pending enforcement, seeks to amend and consolidate the laws relating to wages, bonus and matters connected or incidental thereto, and subsumes the provisions of the *Payment of Wages Act 1936*, the *Minimum Wages Act 1948*, the *Payment of Bonus Act 1965* and the *Equal Remuneration Act 1976*.[36] It extends to all establishments, employees, employers, unless specifically exempted. The code, inter alia, provides for a national floor rate of wages which is to be determined by the central government after taking into account minimum living standards. The code further provides a review of the minimum wages at intervals not exceeding five years.

10.2.2.3 Taxation

Payment of any sum to a Contractor attracts deduction of tax commonly known as Tax Deducted at Source (**TDS**) in terms of section 194C of the *Income Tax Act* 1961. Under the Goods and Services Tax (GST), work contracts in relation to immovable property and consultancy services are treated as 'services' to be taxed at the current tax slab range ie 12 per cent to 18 per cent.[37] Under the *Building and Other Construction Workers Welfare Cess Act* 1996 which is applicable if there are 10 or more building workers, a cess (tax) of 1 per cent is collected from the Employer/Contractor on the total cost of construction.[38]

35 *Industrial Disputes Act 1947*, s 2(s).

36 PRS Legislative Research, 'The Code on Wages' (2019) https://www.prsindia.org/billtrack/code-wages-2019 (accessed 10 October 2020).

37 *Central Goods and Service Tax Act 2017*, s 2 (119), read with para 6A of sch 2.

38 *Building and Other Construction Workers Welfare Cess Act 1996*, s 3.

10.2.2.4 Insurance

Legislation including the *Employees' State Insurance Act 1948*,[39] *Payment of Gratuity Act 1972*[40] and the *Public Liability Insurance Act 1991*[41] requires every business (which includes players involved in construction business) to comply with their relevant provisions. In addition, most construction contracts mandate a developer to put in place a Contractors' All Risk (**CAR**) policy which provides coverage for damage to property and third-party claims.

10.2.2.5 Environment

Environmental clearances for construction projects are obtained from the state government and/or the central government depending upon the nature and size of the project. The objective behind such clearances is to ensure that the least damage is caused to natural resources and to incorporate suitable remedial measures from the stage of project formulation. The *Environmental Impact Assessment Notification 2006* (***EIA***) issued by Ministry of Environment and Forest (**MoEF**) under the *Environment (Protection) Act 1986* is applicable to public and private sector projects specified within the Schedule of the *EIA Notification* and a developer must obtain the specified necessary clearances before commencement of work. The draft *EIA Notification 2020*, which is pending enactment, also seeks to make the process more transparent and expedient by implementing an online system, further delegation, rationalisation and standardisation of the process for specified activities as defined in the Schedule. In addition to the above statutory requirements, construction projects are also subject to regulatory oversight by the National Green Tribunal (**NGT**), a specialised body under the *National Green Tribunal Act 2010*. The NGT has been set up as an environment regulatory body to monitor the environmental impact of projects in India. The NGT has been vested with both original as well as appellate jurisdiction. An affected party can challenge the environment clearance granted in terms of *EIA Notification* before the NGT, and even original disputes *qua* pollution by the operation/construction of industry can be brought before the NGT. However, in certain cases, it has been found that public agitation and protracted disputes before the NGT leads to avoidable delay in the execution of projects.

10.2.2.6 Limitation period

The limitation period applicable to claims arising out of a construction contract before any court of law is governed by the *Limitation Act 1963*. Accordingly, a party claiming breach of contract must institute a suit before the competent court within three years from the date on which the cause of action arises.

10.2.2.7 No objection certificates

Further, there are numerous state and project specific legislations which the Employer/Contractor must comply with before undertaking a project. The Employer/Contractor is required to obtain a no objection certificate (**NOC**) from various departments specified under relevant legislation before undertaking a project:

39 *Employees' State Insurance Act 1948*, s 39.
40 *Payment of Gratuity Act 1972*, s 4A.
41 *Public Liability Insurance Act 1991*, s 4.

- Airport Authority where the construction is taking place near airport zone
- Telecom Authority
- Electricity Board
- Water Supply and Sewage Board
- State Pollution Control Board
- Environmental clearances (for projects above 20,000 square metres of built-up area and for activities as specified in the *EIA Notification*)
- Fire Department (where the height of the building is beyond five floors or 15 metres)
- State Development Authority (for development beyond five acres of land or in authority zones and for the master plan and layout sanction plan)
- Local Municipal Corporation (for seeking final building plan approvals)
- Railway/Drainage/Sewage/Natural Gas Authority (if a project is being constructed near a railway line, drainage system, gas pipeline, etc.).

10.2.3 Other approvals

The central and state governments, through their ministries, maintain various portals that provide information about regulations, permissions, clearances and other statutory requirements related to construction.[42] There are several initiatives being taken up at various levels of the government to provide a one-window clearance to construction projects and ease of access to project developers. Further, various government websites provide information to project developers regarding:

- Foreign direct investment (**FDI**) in construction business in India
- Regulatory compliances
- Environmental compliances
- Company law related compliances
- Labour and workforce related information
- Subsidies, grants and exemptions
- Corporate social responsibility.

10.2.4 Government initiatives

In recent years, the Indian government has aligned its focus towards growth of the construction industry through policies such as open FDI norms, large budget allocations to the infrastructure sector, Smart Cities mission, etc.[43] Some more notable initiatives taken up by the government are:

42 Ministry of Commerce and Industry, Construction and Related Engineering Services https://www.indiaservices.in/construction (accessed 10 October 2020).

43 India Services Portal, Department of Commerce, Ministry of Commerce & Industry, Sector Overview: Construction and Related Engineering Services https://www.indiaservices.in/construction (accessed 10 October 2020).

- An investment amounting to US$31.7 billion has been proposed under the Smart City mission.[44]
- *Pradhan Mantri Awas Yojna* – The 'Housing for All by 2022' scheme which was launched in June 2015, aims to build nearly 20 million urban homes and about 30 million rural houses by 2022.
- FDI limit for real estate projects within Special Economic Zones (**SEZs**) and industrial parks under the automatic entry route has been raised to 100 per cent.[45] 100 per cent FDI through the automatic route is permitted for the following construction (development) projects:[46]
  - Development of townships
  - Construction of residential/commercial premises
  - Construction of roads or bridges
  - Construction of hotels, resorts
  - Construction of hospitals, educational institutions
  - Construction of recreational facilities
  - Construction of city and regional level infrastructure.

Post 2000, the Indian government has placed heavy reliance on procurement of construction material and services in infrastructure projects through a transparent competitive bidding process. The government has issued competitive bidding guidelines for public projects, which must be followed by project proponents in the selection of Contractors. The employment of a competitive bidding process has not only increased private participation but also introduced a fair price mechanism.[47]

10.2.5 Challenges

Notwithstanding the projected growth of the construction industry in India, there are multiple challenges faced by the Employer/Contractor such as socio-economic stress, resource shortage, lack of technical workforce and institutional weaknesses.[48] Some of the major challenges are:

- Work force considerations: While undertaking technology intensive projects, India is largely dependent on equipment and technical workforce from China, USA and Japan which leads to a substantial increase in project cost, thereby restricting infrastructure augmentation.[49]

44 Ministry of Housing and Urban Affairs, Schemes/ Programmes, Smart Cities http://mohua.gov.in/cms/smart-cities.php (accessed 10 October 2020).

45 Department for Promotion of Industry and Internal Trade, Consolidated FDI Policy https://dipp.gov.in/sites/default/files/CFPC_2017_FINAL_RELEASED_28.8.17_1.pdf (accessed 10 October 2020).

46 Department for Promotion of Industry and Internal Trade, Consolidated FDI Policy https://dipp.gov.in/sites/default/files/CFPC_2017_FINAL_RELEASED_28.8.17_1.pdf (accessed 10 October 2020).

47 P Raju, P Jayeshkumar P and J Jaydev J, 'A Review on Competitive Bidding Procedure and Strategy of Bidding' (2015) 2 *Journal of International Academic Research for Multidisciplinary* 84.

48 Arghadeep Laskar and others, 'Challenges before Construction Industry in India' (Department of Civil Engineering, Indian Institute of Technology, Kanpur 2009) https://www.iitk.ac.in/nicee/RP/2004_Challenges_Construction_Industry_Proceedings.pdf (accessed 10 October 2020).

49 A Sawhney, R Agnihotri and KV Paul, 'Grand Challenges for the Indian Construction Industry' (2014) 4(4) *Built Environment Project and Asset Management* 317 https://doi.org/10.1108/BEPAM-10-2013-0055 (accessed 10 October 2020).

- Safety: Safety remains an ongoing concern for construction managers. Any untoward incident is associated with concomitant increase in cost, loss of efficiency and other complications which may be difficult to quantify.[50]

Construction contracts involve many risks and consequently requires effective risk allocation amongst the parties involved. Further, due to various challenges faced in project execution, the construction industry witnesses numerous disputes between the parties. While disputes may crop up from the initial stage of formation of the contract, the major issues that arise are on account of delays, Variations and recovery of additional cost.

10.2.6 Dispute resolution

Due to the absence of a dedicated statutory enactment to refer a payment/contractual dispute to adjudication, the process of adjudication is subject to the agreement between the parties. In most cases, arbitration is the preferred method of dispute resolution. However, in the absence of an arbitration agreement, parties are relegated to legal proceedings, either under the *Civil Procedure Code 1908*, or any other statutory relief such as the *Insolvency and Bankruptcy Code 2016*, for example.

A dispute arising out of a construction contract may relate to non-performance of a financial obligation incurred by one of the contracting parties. The *Insolvency and Bankruptcy Code 2016* was enacted by the Parliament, inter alia, to consolidate and amend the laws relating to reorganisation and insolvency resolution of corporate persons, partnership firms and individuals, in a time bound manner. Following the enactment of the *Insolvency and Bankruptcy Code 2016*, financial and operational creditors can initiate the Corporate Insolvency Resolution Process (**CIRP**)[51] against a corporate debtor, for an amount which, until 24 March 2020, had to be above INR 100,000 (one lakh) (US$1,360).[52] The strict mandate of the *Insolvency and Bankruptcy Code 2016* has acted as a word of caution for parties entering any construction contract, and such contracting parties have become mindful of the timely discharge of the financial obligations contained in and agreed upon in the contract.

10.2.7 Dispute Boards

In a construction project, saving time and cost is of the utmost importance. Any disruption due to a dispute leads to cost and time overruns which is not in the best interest of either party. Disputes in an ongoing project may be adjudicated by a Dispute Board, such as a DAB[53] or DRB.[54] In India, such Dispute Boards were first implemented post liberalisation, when they were mandated for all projects financed by the World Bank having a value above US$50 million. Their importance has again been

50 E. Shrishail Shirur and others, 'Indian Construction Industry: Challenges for the Construction Managers' (2014) 16(4) *IOSR Journal of Business and Management* 65.

51 *Insolvency and Bankruptcy Code 2016*, ss 7–10, read with Pt 3.

52 Notification dated 24 March 2020 of the government of India, the minimum threshold for filing an application for initiation of CIRP was revised to INR 10 million (**one crore**).

53 Clause 20.2, FIDIC Red Book (1999 Edition).

54 World Bank Standard Bidding Documents 1990.

revived and Dispute Boards have recently been employed in several large construction projects.[55]

However, Dispute Boards have not proved to be an effective dispute resolution forum in India due to their lack of enforceability. The parties are supposed to promptly comply with the decision of a Dispute Board. However, to seek a strict enforcement of such decision, the dispute has to be referred to arbitration.[56]

10.2.8 Arbitration

The *Arbitration and Conciliation Act 1996* is the governing law of arbitration in India which is essentially based on the *UNCITRAL Model Law 1985* and *UNCITRAL Model Arbitration Rules 1976*. Broadly, the *Act* is divided in two parts. Part I is applicable for all arbitrations seated in India (domestic or international arbitrations). Part II pertains to enforcement of foreign awards. India, to a great extent, is an arbitration-friendly jurisdiction with a pro-arbitration *Act*. However, the process of arbitration in India is plagued with judicial interventions, concomitant delays and cost. Under the unamended *Arbitration and Conciliation Act* 1996, a challenge to an arbitration award would make the award unenforceable in the interim due to operation of an automatic stay on the execution of the award.[57] Further, under the unamended *Arbitration and Conciliation Act* 1996, there was no mandatory time limit prescribed for making an arbitral award resulting in long drawn out proceedings.

In order to address the above concerns, Parliament enacted the *Arbitration and Conciliation (Amendment) Act 2015*. This amendment brought in various changes to:

- Facilitate international arbitration[58]
- Limit courts' intervention in arbitration proceedings by restricting challenges to an award to those plagued with fraud or corruption, in contravention with the fundamental policy of Indian law; or in conflict with the most basic notions of morality or justice[59]
- Widen the powers of an arbitral tribunal for effective and speedy adjudication of disputes[60]
- Introduce a mandatory time limit of 12 months for making an arbitral award.[61]

Furthermore, to make India a pro-arbitration nation and to bolster the faith of foreign investors in Indian arbitration, Parliament passed the *Arbitration and Conciliation (Amendment) Act* 2019. By way of the amendment, the Arbitration Council of India (**ACI**) was introduced with the objective to promote and encourage alternative dispute

55 Bid Document, Dedicated Freight Corridor, Civil and Structures Contract Package, June 27 2018 https://dfccil.com/upload/Bid_Doc_BRKN-DER_RFO_Pt_1-4.pdf (accessed 10 October 2020).

56 1999 FIDIC rainbow suite sub-clause 20.7; Indian Council of Arbitration, New Delhi, 'Improving the Functioning of Dispute Review Boards (DRB) in India', World Bank, in Standard Operating Procedures for Dispute Boards in India, (April 2016) 2 http://www.icaindia.co.in/DB-ica/Final-SOP.pdf (accessed 20 October 2020).

57 *Arbitration and Conciliation Act 1996* s 34.

58 Amendment to section 2(2) of the *Arbitration and Conciliation Act 1996*.

59 Amendment to section 9 and 34 of the *Arbitration and Conciliation Act 1996*.

60 Amendment to section 17 of the *Arbitration and Conciliation Act 1996*.

61 *Arbitration and Conciliation (Amendment) Act 2015*, s 29(a).

resolution, grade the arbitral institutions and arbitrators in the country, and boost institutional arbitration.

10.2.9 Summary

India continues to be an upcoming and growing market for construction contracts. However, there are key concerns *qua* workforce and environmental compliance (pre and post approval by the appropriate authority) that remain challenges which are beyond the control of the contracting parties. However, the Parliament has taken some concrete steps by introducing the *Insolvency and Bankruptcy Code 2016* to ensure financial discipline, and the amendments to the *Arbitration and Conciliation Act* 1996 to ensure judicial discipline while dealing with contracts between parties.

10.3 The impact of Covid-19 in India

10.3.1 The impact of Covid-19 on the execution of construction projects in India

The impact of Covid-19 on the construction industry has been extensive and damaging. After being declared as a pandemic by the World Health Organization (**WHO**) the government of India, in order to break the chain of Covid-19, decided to treat this as a notified disaster.[62]

Immediately after the outbreak and the declaration of the pandemic by WHO, the government of India and local/municipal bodies imposed strict preventive measures to contain the spread of Covid-19. These measures, inter alia, included restrictions on transport, international and domestic travel, etc. The Order dated 24 March 2020[63] issued by Ministry of Home Affairs, Government of India (**MHA**) directing a lockdown of 21 days and its subsequent order dated 17 May 2020,[64] extending the lockdown until 31 May 2020 has had a significant impact on the entire Indian economy, including the construction industry.

The Indian construction sector, which was already struggling with multiple challenges on account of lack of capital and credit funding due to insolvencies, various frauds and regulatory burdens, is now marred by the effects of the measures taken by the government to contain Covid-19.

Due to such restrictions, the construction sector in India was impaired as, inter alia, the supply chain was completely disrupted. In addition, the MHA issued the National Directive for Covid-19 Management which included:[65]

- Wearing of face cover in all public and workplaces was made compulsory
- Adherence to the social distancing norms (minimum 1.8m distance)
- Frequent sanitisation of entire workplace and
- Curfews from 07:00 PM to 07:00 AM.

62 *Disaster Management Act 2005* s 3(1)(a)[i] read with s 6(2)(i).
63 Ministry of Home Affairs Order No 40-3/2020-D dated 24 March 2020.
64 Ministry of Home Affairs Order No 40-3/2020-DM-I(A) (17 May 2020).
65 Annexure to Ministry of Home Affairs Order No 40-3/2020-D (24 March 2020).

In the Indian construction ecosystem, migrant workers comprise a large part of the workforce and are typically stationed in labour colonies in and around the construction site. Prior to the restrictions, there were about 20,000 ongoing construction projects across India which involved a workforce of approximately 8.5 million labourers.[66] However, the lockdown led to reverse migration and it is estimated that more than two million workers left the construction sites.[67] Further, transportation of construction material came to a complete halt as Indian states closed their borders, bringing construction work to a standstill. The cumulative effect of these measures has been detrimental to the entire sector.

In fact, even after the lockdown being lifted, there are severe challenges such as re-mobilisation of the workforce and associated cost increases that are being faced by project developers.

10.3.2 The impact of Covid-19 on the operation of construction contracts in India

The impact of Covid-19 on construction contracts is varied and largely depends on the on-going stage of a concerned project. For example, projects in the power, real estate and transport sectors are expected to witness a steep increase in the overall project cost on account of increases in manpower, cost of compliance with the National Directive for Covid-19 Management and increases in plant and machinery cost.

In a survey conducted by KPMG[68] regarding the effect of Covid-19, it was observed that:

> The actual impact would depend on multiple factors, including the cost-benefit analysis of alternative supply chains identified for the risks mapped against tier one and tier two suppliers across the world. For firms whose supply chain is significantly dependent on countries like the U.S., Europe, China, South Korea and Japan, an impact on the cost of the supply due to delays or due to the costs of switching on a new supply chain exists.[69]

With this backdrop, delay, suspension and termination of projects along with concomitant losses, increases in cost and expenses are inevitable. Parties are likely to invoke respective contractual provisions for extension of time and/or recovery of additional costs. However, such entitlement would depend on the terms of the Contract executed between the parties as there is no umbrella legislation to determine such disputes specific to Covid-19. In India, various EPC and other infrastructure related contracts are based on the 1999 FIDIC forms of contract, particularly the Silver Book. Following are the claims which either party would seek to address:

- *Force majeure*: In certain scenarios, the Contract exhaustively lists events that shall be construed as *force majeure* events, and any event which falls outside the list cannot trigger the *force majeure* clause. Per contra, certain *force majeure* clauses, such as Clause 19 of FIDIC 1999, provide a non-exhaustive list of events that could fall within the definition of *force majeure*, however, with the

66 Ministry of Statistics and Programme Implementation – 409th Flash Report dated December 2019.

67 Affidavit filed by government of India before the Supreme Court in April 2020.

68 KPMG is a global network of professional firms providing audit, tax and advisory services.

69 KPMG – COVID-19: Assessment of economic impact on construction sector in India, May 2020 https://home.kpmg/content/dam/kpmg/in/pdf/2020/05/covid-19-assessment-economic-impact-construction-sector.pdf?r (accessed 10 October 2020).

qualification that the event has to be exceptional, beyond the affected Party's control, not foreseeable and which is not substantially attributable to the affected Party.[70] These conditions form part of most construction contracts.

- In the case where a contract does not have an express *force majeure* clause, the Contract will then be governed by the *Indian Contract Act 1872*.[71] Relief is only available where the party is 'prevented' from performing its obligations by reason of an event that satisfies all of the above conditions for *force majeure*. In most contracts, a party claiming relief of *force majeure* has mandatorily to inform the other party of the occurrence of such an event and its likely effect on performance of the contract.[72] It is noteworthy that *force majeure* clauses in most contracts do not include 'pandemic' in the categories of event and, therefore, to establish Covid-19 as a *force majeure* event, these conditions necessarily have to be satisfied.
- Change in law: A party may be entitled to an extension of time or recovery of additional cost if such delay or cost is a result of a change in law or change in interpretation of such laws. Any legislation or decree of a court which affects the execution of the project may qualify as a 'change in law' and a party may claim relief under it. In India, the National Directive for Covid-19 Management dated 24 March 2020 issued by MHA is sought to be considered as a 'change in law' which directed a lockdown/embargo in ongoing construction activity. In certain cases, the enhanced cost of construction, especially increased Interest During Construction (IDC) due to the Order dated 24 March 2020, is sought as change in law.

In addition, there will be situations, depending on the stage of the project, where parties may resort to re-negotiating contractual terms or terminate the Contract if the damages payable are less than the loss likely to be caused to the project developer in execution of the project. Another aspect emerging from *force majeure* is that certain contracting parties are seeking the relief of 'frustration', when in such contracts time was of the essence. However, at the time of writing (October 2020) such disputes are still at a nascent stage and no conclusive decision has been rendered by the Supreme Court of India on such disputes.

The government of India has taken robust steps to restore the balance through various packages and notifications. Unlike a few other common law jurisdictions, India is yet to come up with umbrella legislation which deals with the implication of Covid-19 on businesses, particularly the construction sector. However, the government of India, in order to tackle the economic slowdown associated with a robust lockdown, has notified certain measures which includes relief to Contractors by way of an extension of up to six months for completion of contractual obligations, including in respect of EPC and concession agreements.[73] In addition, the retention money in lieu

70 FIDIC Conditions of Contract for EPC/Turnkey Projects 1999.

71 *Indian Contract Act 1872*, s 32 and s 56.

72 FIDIC Conditions of Contract for EPC/Turnkey Projects 1999.

73 Press Information Bureau, 'Announcement of Stimulus Package by the Ministry of Finance, Government of India' (13 May 2020) https://pib.gov.in/PressReleseDetailm.aspx?PRID=1623601 (accessed 10 October 2020).

of performance guarantee was released to Contractors involved in construction of roads and highways along with certain exemptions and waivers.[74]

The Covid-19 pandemic has impacted businesses, financial markets and economies all over the world, including India, and created uncertainty and stress for businesses.[75] Accordingly, on 5 June 2020, the *Insolvency and Bankruptcy Code (Amendment) Ordinance* 2020 was promulgated which inserted a new section 10A in the *Insolvency and Bankruptcy Code* 2016. According to section 10A, no application shall be filed for initiation of CIRP for any default arising after 25 March 2020 for a period of six months to one year. The aforesaid provision was rightly inserted to prevent corporate persons which are experiencing distress on account of the unprecedented situation, being pushed into insolvency proceedings under the *Insolvency and Bankruptcy Code 2016* for some time, and provides a fair chance to the contracting parties to perform contracts, including construction contracts.

Disputes due to impact of Covid-19 have already reached the courts and in the absence of any specific legislation governing the effects of Covid-19, courts have taken a divergent view depending on the nature of breach, terms of contracts and the circumstances surrounding the breach.[76]

The full impact of Covid-19 is nearly impossible to predict, but as India is a major importer of materials, any prolonged slowdown in the global economy is likely to have significant ramifications on overall project cost whether in the development or conceptual stage.

10.4 Indian governing law of the contract

10.4.1 Constraints on the governing law of a construction contract

The Indian law governing contracts has been codified by the Parliament as *The Indian Contract Act 1872*. Section 10 of the *Indian Contract Act 1872* provides several prerequisites[77] that must be observed for a valid and binding contract to come into existence. Subject to satisfaction of these prerequisites, parties have the autonomy to agree upon such terms as they deem fit in their contracts. Therefore, construction contracts do not warrant a distinct set of legal rules. The law relevant to such contracts would be akin to the general legal principles governing contracts in India.

One must not misjudge the importance of construction contracts in the economic prosperity of the country, considering the influx of capital from foreign multinationals in the field of building and infrastructure. Accordingly, it is necessary to evaluate the law applicable to such contracts as well as the disputes arising therefrom. While courts in India acknowledge international contracts specifying the jurisdiction of foreign

74 Ministry of Road Transport and Highways, Order dated 3 June 2020 passed by the Ministry of Road Transport and Highways https://morth.nic.in/sites/default/files/circulars_document/COVID%20relief%20atmanirbhar%20Order%20030620.pdf (accessed 10 October 2020).

75 *Statement of Objects of Insolvency and Bankruptcy Code (Amendment) Ordinance 2020*.

76 *M/s Halliburn Offshore Services Inc. v Vedanta Limited* (O.M.P. (I)(COMM) & I.A. 3697/2020) Delhi High Court; *Standard Retail Pvt Ltd v Gs Global Corp*, Commercial Arbitration Petition (Lodging) No 404 of 2020 Bombay High Court; and *Ramanand and Ors v Dr Girish Soni and Anor*, CM APPL. 10848/2020 & CM APPL 10847/2020 in RC REV 447/2017 Delhi High Court.

77 The prerequisites include competence of parties to contract, valid offer and acceptance thereof, lawful consideration and object, and free consent.

courts, there is uncertainty surrounding the legitimacy of clauses that stipulate a foreign jurisdiction in case of contracts governing Indian parties.

Courts in India have promulgated the principle that 'the expressed intention of the parties is generally decisive in determining the proper law of contract'.[78] The only limitation to this rule is that the intention of parties must be expressed *bona fide* and it should not be opposed to public policy.[79] In *Rhodia Ltd v Neon Laboratories Ltd*, [80] while adjudicating on the issue of exclusion of jurisdiction of Indian courts, the Bombay High Court held that the purpose and intent of the clause granting exclusive jurisdiction will have to be viewed in accordance with the 'proper law' of the contract. If proper law of the contract (ie the English law in *Rhodia*) grants exclusive jurisdiction in favour of courts in England, then the competent Indian court will be ousted of jurisdiction. However, it is noteworthy that such ouster of jurisdiction has been allowed by courts only when parties are involved in international trade and commerce. A similar avenue may not be available to two Indian parties that wish to circumvent the jurisdiction of Indian courts, as such contracts will be subject to restrictions prescribed by section 28[81] of the *Indian Contract Act 1872*.

Contracts for construction of roads and buildings present certain special features from a legal perspective. Large scale construction contracts also entail involvement of geo-political interventions depending on the location of the project. It has been observed that often, large-scale contracts face opposition from project affected persons (PAPs) in so far as acquisition of land as well as construction of the project is concerned. Therefore, it is often seen that project developers are faced with disputes emanating outside their contract, in the form of public interest litigation (PIL) and/or proceedings before the NGT.

Arbitration has evolved as an effective and efficient method of dispute resolution in construction-related disputes. The principle of party autonomy allows parties to choose the proper law that governs their dispute. Parties that submit their disputes to arbitration are free to decide procedural aspects such as the nature of arbitration, seat and venue, number of arbitrators, and their qualifications. This flexibility is particularly important for disputes arising out of construction or building contracts as these, being essentially technical in nature, require a degree of subject-matter expertise.

The *Arbitration and Conciliation Act* 1996 provides an efficient framework for an ad-hoc arbitration of disputes arising out of domestic contracts. Nevertheless, in the case of international transactions, parties favor institutional arbitration under rules formed by universally recognised institutions such as the Singapore International Arbitration Centre, the International Chamber of Commerce or the London Court of International Arbitration. Courts in India have upheld party autonomy and seek to implement a pro-arbitration approach to keep judicial interference to a minimum especially after the amendments to the *Arbitration and Conciliation Act 1996*. It has been maintained that party autonomy 'being the brooding and guiding spirit in arbitration, the parties are free to agree on application of three different laws governing their entire contract: (1) proper law of contract, (2) proper law of arbitration agreement, and (3)

78 *National Thermal Power Corporation v Singer Company* (1992) 3 SCC 551.

79 *Vita Food Products Inc v Unus Shipping Co Ltd* (1939) AC 277, 290.

80 AIR 2002 Bom 502.

81 Agreements which restrict parties from enforcing rights by way of legal proceedings as well as those which limit the time within which the contractual rights may be enforced are void.

proper law of the conduct of arbitration, which is popularly and in legal parlance known as "curial law"'.[82]

This approach is seemingly consistent with the statutory concession under section 28 of the *Indian Contract Act 1872,* which provides:

> Exception 1: Saving of contract to refer to arbitration dispute that may arise - This section shall not render illegal a contract, by which two or more persons agree that any dispute which may arise between them in respect of any subject or class of subjects shall be referred to arbitration, and that only the amount awarded in such arbitration shall be recoverable in respect of the dispute so referred.

In further consideration of construction contracts, section 20A of the *Specific Relief Act 1963* as amended in 2018 provides that no injunctions shall be granted by a court in a suit involving a contract relating to an infrastructure project.

10.4.2 Formal requirements for a construction contract

In the context of building and construction, there are no specific formalities that need to be fulfilled by parties while executing a construction contract. Nevertheless, a contract must satisfy certain conditions before it is recognised by the law as valid and binding. There must be at least two parties to a contract, a party under obligation and another entitled to enforce such obligation. The parties must be competent and willing to enter into the contract. They must also be *ad idem* with the object and purpose of the contract.[83] Lastly, a valid contract must be in lieu of a lawful consideration and a lawful object.[84]

It is particularly important that an agreement to refer disputes to arbitration must be in, or substantiated by, writing. The *Arbitration and Conciliation Act* 1996 requires all arbitration agreements to be in writing for them to be enforced in accordance with the statutory regime.[85] Likewise, this requirement is maintained by several jurisdictions internationally.

In the case of contracts between the government and any other person, the *Constitution of India* provides a particular format in which such contracts are to be executed. Article 299 of the *Constitution of India* states that all contracts made in exercise of the executive power of the Union or of a state shall be expressed to be made by the President, or the governor of the state, as the case may be, by such persons and in such manner as he may direct or authorise.

Provided that a contract satisfies the requirements stated above, parties are free to agree upon such terms as they choose befitting their purpose.

10.5 What Special Provisions in the Particular Conditions are necessary for consistency with applicable laws in India?

The FIDIC suite of contracts are prevalent in India and have been successfully adopted in various EPC and large-scale projects. As such, FIDIC contracts, by their very nature, adhere to the essential elements of a valid contract as per the provisions

82 *Bharat Aluminium Co v Kaiser Aluminium Technical Services Inc* (2016) 4 SCC 126.
83 *Mahanagar Telephone Nigam Ltd v Canara Bank* 2019 SCC OnLine SC 995.
84 *Chitty on Contracts, Volume I, General Principles* (31st edn, Sweet & Maxwell 2012) 3-001.
85 *Arbitration and Conciliation Act 1996*, s 7.

of the *Indian Contract Act 1872*.[86] Accordingly, no Special Provisions in the Particular Conditions are necessary for consistency with the applicable laws of India.

10.6 What Special Provisions in the Particular Conditions are desirable for consistency with applicable laws in India?

10.6.1 Performance guarantee

As a way of practice, construction contracts necessitate that the Contractor must furnish an unconditional performance bank guarantee as security to ensure that it fulfills its contractual obligations adequately and in a timely manner. This performance bank guarantee must be kept valid by the Contractor until expiry of the defects liability period (FIDIC – Defects Notification Period). In this regard, the FIDIC General Conditions provides that the Contractor shall obtain (at its cost) a performance security for proper performance, in the amount and currencies stated in the Particular Conditions, if the condition is specified in the Contract.

Courts in India have held that a performance bank guarantee is a distinct contract, which is independent of any dispute between the parties.[87] Therefore, unless otherwise provided, invocation of a performance bank guarantee must be honoured unconditionally as and when called upon by the Employer. Further, the Supreme Court of India has held that injunction on the invocation of bank guarantees may only be granted in exceptional cases such as that of fraud, irretrievable loss or injury and special equity.[88]

10.6.2 Force majeure

Force majeure has been defined as 'an event or effect that can be neither anticipated nor controlled'.[89] This concept has been recognised under the doctrine of frustration of contracts as per section 56 of the *Indian Contract Act 1872*. Accordingly, a contract is said to be frustrated if performance of obligations contained therein become impossible or illegal. Frustration of a contract discharges the parties of all underlying obligations. However, this principle is not applicable to cases of mere inconvenience, economic unfeasibility, or in case performance of contractual obligations has become burdensome, but not impossible.[90]

Further, in contracts which stipulate a specific clause dealing with *force majeure*, the provisions of *The Indian Contract Act 1872* would not be attracted.

10.6.3 Extension of time

Typically, time is of an essence in a construction contract and such contracts provide for a fixed timeline that must be adhered to by the Contractor. There is a fixed date of commissioning by which the entire scope of construction must be completed. Accordingly, courts in India have held that in cases concerning building and engineering,

86 *Indian Contract Act 1872*, s 10.
87 *Himadri Chemicals Industries Ltd v Coal Tar Refining Co* (2007) 8 SCC 110.
88 *UP Co-op Federation Ltd v Singh Consultants and Engineers (P) Ltd* (1988) 1 SCC 174.
89 Bryan Garner, *Black's Law Dictionary* (7th edn, West Publishing Co USA 1999).
90 *Energy Watchdog v Central Electricity Regulatory Commission* (2017) 14 SCC 80.

'time is the essence' of the contract.[91] The completion of work by a specified date may be a condition precedent to the Contractor's right to claim full payment.[92]

In order to ensure adherence to specific timelines, contracts impose an obligation on the Contractor to pay liquidated damages (**LDs**) occasioned by a delay which deters execution of the project. As far as concurrent delays on the part of both the Employer and Contractor are concerned, an Employer may substitute payment of damages to a Contractor by granting an extension of time. Conversely, a Contractor may cite such delay to avoid its responsibility to pay liquidated damages. Therefore, for concurrent delays, a Contractor may be granted an extension of time, and not compensation for any loss that it may have suffered on account of delays.[93] A Contractor would be entitled to an extension of time for the period of delay caused by the relevant event notwithstanding the concurrent effect of another event.[94]

A clause stipulating extension of time is generally provided in construction contracts to mitigate the effect of events that would delay the completion of the work. The FIDIC General Conditions also provide that the Contractor shall be entitled to an extension of time for completion, subject to conditions stated therein.

10.6.4 Variations

Variations may be made by the Employer in the scope of work to be executed under a construction contract. In case of such Variations, a Contractor has the right to request additional payments and/or novation of contract, given that the variations have been duly sanctioned by the Employer. However, in certain contracts Variations to the scope of work should not substantially modify the Contract and should be executable by the Contractor.

Further, as contracts for are generally 'fixed time and cost' contracts, it is preferable to set a threshold to variations (10 per cent to 20 per cent of the contractual value).

10.6.5 Suspension

Suspension clauses in a contract are quite similar to the provisions dealing with termination. A Contractor may suspend the execution of work due to an alleged breach of contract by the Employer. Similarly, an Employer may suspend payments owed to the Contractor on grounds of delay.

It would be difficult for either party to enforce a right to suspend in the absence of express provisions in the contract. Courts in India have frequently refused to enforce such a right. Thus, a suspension clause which adequately addresses the practical consequences of suspension of work is desirable in construction contracts.

10.6.6 Limitation period for claims

The time period for filing a claim arising out of a contract before any court of law is governed by *The Limitation Act 1963*. Accordingly, proceedings must be instituted by a party claiming breach of contract within three years from the date on which the

91 *Hind Construction Contractors v State of Maharashtra* (1979) 2 SCC 70.
92 *Halsbury's Laws of England Vol 4* (4th edn, LexisNexis Butterworths 2002) [1179].
93 *De Beers UK Ltd v Atos Origin IT Services UK Ltd* [2010] EWHC 3276 (TCC).
94 *Walter Lilly & Co Ltd v Mackay* [2012] EWHC 1773 (TCC).

cause of action arises. It is pertinent to note that the *Arbitration and Conciliation Act 1996* does not provide any provisions vis-*à*-vis limitation. Thus, the provisions of *The Limitation Act 1963* would be applicable to proceedings under the *Arbitration and Conciliation Act 1996*.

10.6.7 Termination

The provisions of *The Indian Contract Act 1872* permit a party to terminate a contract on an instance of breach by the other party. In addition, parties may agree upon contractual stipulations recognising events which would amount to breach of contract and entitle the injured party to terminate the contract.

Specific performance is the foremost remedy available to a party alleging breach of contract. Accordingly, specific performance of a contractual obligation may be directed in cases where awarding damages may not be considered an appropriate remedy. As to whether or not such specific performance would be directed by a court or arbitral tribunal largely depends on the intention of the parties to the Contract, the conduct of the parties, and other applicable considerations.

Section 10 of the *Specific Relief Act 1963* details certain circumstances in which specific performance of a contract can be enforced. Previously, even if a contract fell within the category of those that are specifically enforceable, a court may have refused to grant relief on the basis of the facts and circumstances of the case, conduct of the parties, etc. However, the recent amendment[95] to the *Specific Relief Act 1963* has sought to take away the wide discretion of courts in granting specific performance, and to make specific performance of contracts a general rule. The amended section 10 of the *Specific Relief Act 1963* states that the specific performance of a contract shall be enforced by a court, subject to the provisions contained in sections 11, 14 and 16.

Conversely, determinable contracts are derived from the termination clause provided within the contract.[96] A contract which provides for termination at convenience, allowing a party to terminate the Contract without prior notice or assigning any reason, are said to be determinable in nature. A contract can be terminated due to a certain action or omission by a party which was an essential condition on which the Contract was premised. Lastly, a contract can also be terminated in case the performance of the act on which the Contract was contingent has exceeded the prescribed time limit. Section 14 of the *Specific Relief Act 1963*, inter alia, states that a contract may not be specifically enforceable if it is determinable in nature.[97]

Further, a contract may be terminated by a party if the contractual terms provide for termination of the Contract upon commencement of insolvency or bankruptcy process against the other party. However, initiation of the such proceedings does not result in *ipso facto* termination of all pending contracts, and the party is free to perform its obligations under the existing contract if the situation so permits.

10.7 Summary of applicable legislation for Indian governing law of the contract

All of the legislation listed below was passed by the Parliament.

95 *Specific Relief (Amendment) Act 2018*.
96 Anirudh Wadwha, *Mulla The Indian Contract Act* (16th edn, LexisNexis India, 2021) 2016, 2017.
97 *Indian Oil Corporation Ltd v Amritsar Gas Service* (1991) 1 SCC 533.

10.7.1 Entry into a construction contract

Contracts generally	*The Indian Contract Act 1872* *Specific Relief Act 1963*

10.7.2 Termination of a construction contract

Frustration	*Indian Contract Act 1872*
Bankruptcy, insolvency, liquidation	*Insolvency and Bankruptcy Code 2016*
Guarantees under forms of Security (Tender Security, Demand Guarantee, Surety Bond, Advance Payment Guarantee, Retention Money Guarantee, Payment Guarantee by Employer)	*Indian Contract Act 1872* *Specific Relief Act 1963*

10.7.3 Dispute resolution

Limitation periods	*Limitation Act 1963*
Liability	*Indian Contract Act 1872*
Adjudication	*Arbitration and Conciliation Act 1996* *Industrial Disputes Act 1947*
Arbitration	*Arbitration and Conciliation Act 1996*

10.8 Summary of applicable legislation if the Site/Country is in India

10.8.1 Operation of a construction contract

Registration and administration of professionals – Architects and Certifiers	*Architects Act 1972* *Insurance Regulatory and Development Authority Act 1999*
Registration/licencing of Contractors and subcontractors	*Contract Labour (Regulation & Abolition) Act 1970*
Subcontractors	*Contract Labour (Regulation & Abolition) Act 1970*
Use of liens/Assignment of debts	*Securitisation and Reconstruction of Financial Assets and Enforcement of Security Interest Act 2002*
Labour	*Industrial Disputes Act 1947* *Factories Act 1948* *Contract Labour Act 1970* *Inter-State Migrant Workers Act 1979* *Trade Union Act 1926* *Code on Wages 2019*[98]
Design/Moral rights	*Patents Act 1970* *Trade Marks Act 1999*
Copyright	*Copyright Act 1957*

(*Continued*)

98 The Code on Wages 2019 is pending enactment.

The product being produced from the Works	*Environment (Protection) Act 1986*
First nation people's land rights	*Constitution of India*
Planning	*Model Regional & Town Planning & Development Law 1985*
Work affecting adjacent property to the Site	*Indian Easements Act 1882*
Heritage	*Ancient Monuments and Archaeological Sites and Remains Act 1958*
Environment	*Environment (Protection) Act 1986* *Air (Prevention and Control of Pollution) Act 1981* *Water (Prevention and Control of Pollution) Act 1974* *Wildlife Protection Act 1972* *Forest Conservation Act 1980* *Biological Diversity Act 2002* *National Green Tribunal Act 2010*
Local procurement	*Indian Contract Act 1872* *Sale of Goods Act 1930*
Building and construction permits, Execution of construction work, Standard of construction work	*National Building Code 2005*
Health and safety	*Factories Act 1948* *Employees Compensation Act 2009* *Maternity Benefit Act 1961* *Payment of Gratuity Act 1972.* *Employees Provident Fund and Miscellaneous Provisions Act 1952.* *Building and Other Construction Workers Welfare Cess Act 1996.* *Sexual Harassment at Workplace (Prohibition, Prevention and Redressal) Act 2013*
Calibration of testing apparatus, equipment and instruments	*Bureau of Indian Standards Act 2016*
Ownership of Plant and Materials	*Transfer of Property Act 1882* *Indian Registration Act 1908*
Employer's sale of Contractor's Equipment, surplus material, wreckage and Temporary Works	*Sale of Goods Act 1930* *Indian Contract Act 1872*
Insurance	*Insurance Act 1938* *Employees' State Insurance Act 1948* *Life Insurance Corporation Act 1956* *Marine Insurance Act 1963* *Motor Vehicles Act 1988*
Statutory rights that coexist with contractual rights	*Constitution of India*
Liability for defective work	*Indian Contract Act 1872*
Liability for nuisance	*Indian Penal Code 1860* *Code of Criminal Procedure 1973*
Other issues	*Constitution of India* *Indian Contract Act 1872* *Indian Penal Code 1860* *Code of Criminal Procedure 1973*

10.8.2 Termination of a construction contract

Bankruptcy, insolvency, liquidation	*Insolvency and Bankruptcy Code 2016*

10.8.3 Dispute resolution

Dispute before a local board/ Adjudication	*Arbitration and Conciliation Act 1996* *Industrial Disputes Act 1947*
Limitation periods	*Limitation Act 1963*

10.9 Summary of applicable legislation if the 'seat' of the dispute determination is in India

Dispute resolution	*Arbitration and Conciliation Act 1996* *Industrial Disputes Act 1947*
Limitation periods	*Limitation Act 1963*
Adjudication	*Arbitration and Conciliation Act 1996* *Industrial Disputes Act 1947*
Arbitration	*Arbitration and Conciliation Act 1996* *Industrial Disputes Act 1947*

10.10 Issues that a court or arbitrator may construe differently to that expected from the words of the Contract, because of local law or custom

10.10.1 Subject matter arbitrability

Every civil and commercial dispute arising out of a contract is capable of being adjudicated by arbitration unless the jurisdiction of an arbitral tribunal is expressly barred by law. The *Arbitration and Conciliation Act 1996* does not specifically exclude any particular category of disputes from arbitrability.

Section 8 of the *Arbitration and Conciliation Act 1996* mandates that where an action is brought before a judicial authority in a matter, which is the subject of an arbitration agreement, the parties shall be referred to arbitration. However, courts in India have refused to refer disputes pertaining to certain subject-matters to arbitration.

The question of subject-matter arbitrability of disputes in India was first dealt by the Supreme Court in the case of *Booz Allen and Hamilton v SBI Home Finance Limited.*[99] The Supreme Court, in its attempt to define the true scope of subject matters arbitrable by a private adjudicator, held that: 'Every commercial or civil dispute, either contractual or non-contractual which can be decided by a court, is capable of being adjudicated and resolved by arbitration unless it is excluded either expressly or by legal sanction.' Consequently, 'rights in rem' exercisable against the world at large were excluded from the scope of arbitrable disputes.

99 (2011) 5 SCC 532.

Although the Apex Court has not enunciated an exhaustive list of subject matters outside the ambit of arbitrability, some examples of non-arbitrable disputes in India are:

- Disputes relating to rights and liabilities which give rise to or arise out of criminal offences
- Matrimonial disputes relating to divorce, judicial separation, restitution of conjugal rights
- Disputes involving anti-trust/competition law
- Disputes related to intellectual property rights
- Matters pertaining to Guardianship
- Matters related to insolvency and winding up
- Testamentary matters (grant of probate, letters of administration and succession certificate)
- Eviction or tenancy matters governed by special statutes
- Matters related to mortgages
- Cases arising out of a Trust Deed and the *Trust Act*
- Matters relating to fraudulent practices.

Thus, ensuring the objective arbitrability becomes pivotal since courts in India, under section 34[100] of the *Arbitration and Conciliation Act 1996*, are empowered to set aside an arbitral award on the ground that the subject-matter of the dispute was not capable of resolution by arbitration. Parties to a construction contract must ensure that the provisions agreed upon do not fall within a subject-matter which may be excluded from the scope of arbitrability.

10.10.2 Enforcement of foreign judgments

In contracts that specify jurisdiction of foreign courts, the enforcement of foreign judgments is subject to certain limitations. The procedure for enforcement of foreign judgments in India differs on the basis of reciprocating and non-reciprocating territories. In the case of 'reciprocating territories', [101] judgments may be enforced directly as a decree and an execution decree may be obtained to this effect from an Indian Court. Conversely, judgments from 'non-reciprocating' territories are not executed directly by a court of law. A fresh lawsuit must be filed within three years for enforcement of such foreign judgments.

10.10.3 Claims by third parties

Construction contracts in India are generally supervised by third parties such as engineers, architects and designers that may be appointed by an Employer. The scope of their functions and duties are contractually defined.

100 Application for setting aside of an arbitral award.

101 United Arab Emirates, United Kingdom, Singapore, Bangladesh, Malaysia, Trinidad and Tobago, New Zealand, the Cook Islands (including Niue) and the Trust Territories of Western Samoa, Hong Kong, Papua New Guinea, Fiji, Aden are reciprocating territories of India.

Third parties cannot bring claims or enforce terms of a contract against a party to a contract. This principle emanates from the doctrine of 'privity of contract', which confers rights and obligations arising out of a contract only upon parties to a contract. Hence, in the landscape of construction law, a Contractor cannot be subjected to claims from third parties to a construction contract. However, third parties are entitled to a remedy under tort law for injury suffered due to negligent acts of a Contractor.

10.11 References

10.11.1 Books

Chitty on Contracts, Volume I, General Principles (31st edn, Sweet & Maxwell 2012)

Dr Durga Das Basu, *Commentary on the Constitution of India* (9th edn, LexisNexis 2014)

HM Seervai, *Constitutional Law of India* (4th edn, Universal Law Publishing Co Ltd 2005)

PC Markanda, *Building and Engineering Contracts: Law and Practice* (4th edn, LexisNexis India 2013)

Anirudh Wadhwa, *Mulla The Indian Contract Act* (16th edn, LexisNexis 2021)

10.11.2 Internet

Ministry of Commerce and Industry, Department for Promotion of Industry & Internal Trade: https://dipp.gov.in

Indian Construction Industry.com: https://www.indianconstructionindustry.com

Invest India, Building a sustainable future: https://www.investindia.gov.in/sector/construction

Ministry of Commerce and Industry, Construction and Related Engineering Services: https://www.indiaservices.in/construction

Ministry of Housing and Urban Affairs, Schemes/ Programmes, Smart Cities: http://mohua.gov.in/cms/smart-cities.php

Ministry of Housing and Urban Affairs, Urban Growth: http://mohua.gov.in/cms/urban-growth.php

Ministry of Road Transport and Highways: https://morth.nic.in

PRS Legislative Research, The Code on Wages, 2019: https://www.prsindia.org/billtrack/code-wages-2019.

11

Applying FIDIC contracts in Indonesia

Prof Dr Sarwono Hardjomuljadi, Ir Dona Alisyah Siregar, Henrico Hariandja, Dr Peni Jati Setyowati, Ir Enni M Soetanto, Reynaldo Albertiny

 DOI: 10.4324/9781003200901-11

11.1 Outline of the legal environment in Indonesia

11.1.1 The constitutional structure of Indonesia

The *Constitution* is a legal instrument that is very important and must exist in a country, where it will serve as a guideline or basis for every implementation of state life and as a limitation on the power held by the authorities in carrying out their duties in the country. Indonesia's *1945 Constitution* is the State Constitution which was officially ratified on 18 August 1945 and has been amended four times in which there have been many changes to the constitutional structure in order to achieve a more effective presidential system.

A very basic change to the *1945 Constitution* is the rules for drafting laws and regulations. Initially, the President had full rights to formulate a law in accordance with Article 5 paragraph 1 of the *1945 Constitution*: 'The President holds the power to establish the laws with the approval of People's Representative Council'. However, after the amendment to the *1945 Constitution*, the provisions in Article 5 paragraph 1 were changed to: 'The President has the right to submit a draft law to the People's Representative Council.'

Amendments to the power to form or establish a law are currently under the authority of the People's Representative Council according to the amendment to the *1945 Constitution* which has been regulated in Article 20 paragraph (1) and (2), which states:

1. The People's Representative Council has the power to form laws; and
2. Every draft law is discussed by the People's Representative Council and the President for joint approval.

Furthermore, further rules in the formulation of legislation are contained in *Law No 12 of 2011 regarding The Formation of Statutory Regulations* and *Law No 15 of 2019* and amendments to *Law No 12 of 2011*.

11.1.2 The legal system in Indonesia

The Indonesian State is a constitutional state as stated in Article 1 paragraph 3 of the *1945 Constitution*: 'The Indonesian State is a state of law' where the legal system in Indonesia is a mixture of European, Islamic and the customary legal system. In general, the legal system adopted in Indonesia is dominated by the influence of European law, both criminal and civil; this comes from the historical aspect of Indonesia which was a colony of the Netherlands.

Islamic law regulates only a small part of the Indonesian legal system such as marriage, kinship and inheritance. The influence of customary law is also insignificant on the legal system in Indonesia; it is only absorbed into laws and regulations or jurisprudence where the transmission of local community rules on culture or customs has been carried out since long ago and this view also overrides the standard rules of law.

The influence of European Continental law or what is usually called civil law greatly affects the Indonesian legal system, be it from history, politics, law, legal sources or the law enforcement system. The main characteristics of this legal system are (1) the existence of a codified system, and (2) judges are not bound by jurisprudential decisions. Therefore, the law becomes the main legal reference (3). The judicial system is inquisitorial (4); the main principle is that the law gains binding strength (5). The purpose of law is to provide legal certainty. At first, law was only classified into two categories, namely public law (constitutional law, state administration, criminal law) and private law (civil and commercial law), but along with the times, the boundaries between public and private law are increasingly blurred along with the harmonisation of the common law legal system.

In principle, the common law system is the same as customary law which adheres to a decision as its source of law. Harmonisation of the civil law and common law systems in Indonesia is due to the development of civilisation with the progress and connectivity of information and trade that crosses borders and forces changes to the legal system. As an example, international trade law applies where an international trade contract must be defined in a broad sense, which is not only limited to trading activities in goods, but also includes trade in services, including contracts related to investment, finance, construction, transportation, and even contracts made in electronic form. This is also what makes the legal system in Indonesia diverse.

11.1.3 The court system in Indonesia

The judicial system in Indonesia can be interpreted as an orderly and interconnected structure, which relates to the activities of examining and terminating cases carried out by courts, be they courts located within the general courts, religious courts, military courts, and state administrative courts which are based on the views, theories, and principles in the field of justice prevailing in Indonesia. The initial rules for the judicial system were stipulated in Article 24 paragraph 2 of the *1945 Constitution*:

> Judicial power is exercised by a Supreme Court and judicial bodies under it in the General Court, Religious Courts, Military Courts, State Administrative Courts, and by a Constitutional Court.

The explanation of paragraph 2 above concludes that the Supreme Court is the highest State Court and the judicial bodies below are regulated in law. Article 25 paragraph 1 of *Law No 48 of 2009 regarding Judicial Power* states that:

> The judiciary which is under the scope of the Supreme Court includes the judiciary within the General Court, Religious Court, Military Court, and State Administrative Court.

Each judiciary has its own powers and authorities which can be described as follows:

1. The General Court handles criminal and civil cases in general. The board that implements it consists of the District Court as the first instance court and the High Court as the court of appeal.
2. The Religious Courts only handle certain civil cases for the Muslim community. The board that implements it consists of the Religious Courts as the first instance courts and the High Religious Courts as courts of appeal.
3. The State Administrative Court only handles cases of lawsuits against state administrative officials as a result of a written ruling that is detrimental to a person or a civil legal entity. The board that implements it consists of the State Administrative Court as the first instance court and the High State Administrative Court as the court of appeal.
4. The Military Court only handles cases within the armed services. The board that implements it consists of the Military Courts, the High Military Courts and the Major Military Courts.

The General Court is the court with the broadest scope, in which can be formed special courts such as the Juvenile Court, Corruption, Fisheries, Human Rights, Commerce and Industrial Relations. Contract disputes or construction projects that fall within the realm of civil law are resolved through the General Court.

11.2 The construction industry in Indonesia

11.2.1 Overview

Based on data from the official website of Directorate General of Construction,[1] there are 129,221 national contractors which consist of 127,061 general contractors and 2,160 specialist contractors. For construction consultants, there are 9,702 national consultants. There are two forms of foreign construction service business entities in Indonesia, namely **BUJKA** (foreign construction services), which forms a representative office and **PT PMA,** which forms a joint venture with a local contractor. Based on existing data, there are 200 foreign contractors and 46 foreign construction consultants in Indonesia. For construction workers, as of July 2020 there were 267,868 with a construction expert certificate, including 103,790 at the qualification level of young experts, 149,681 at the intermediate expert qualification level, and 14,215 at the level of master expert qualification.

The construction industry in Indonesia is regulated through *Law No 02 of 2017*, along with the amendments listed in *Law 11 of 2020 regarding Job Creation*. To be able to do construction works and construction consultancy services, every business entity is required to have a Construction Service Business License (**IUJK**) and a Business

1 http://binakonstruksi.pu.go.id (accessed 5 March 2021).

Entity Certificate (**SBU**). IUJK is issued through an online single submission, where a business entity only needs to register its details online in an information system. After registering online, business entities need to meet the requirements submitted to the Regency/City government to obtain an effective Construction Service Business License. For Business Entity Certificates, business entities are subject to verification and validation by the Association of Business Entities, and the certification process is then carried out by the business entity certification unit assigned by the Construction Development Board (**LPJK**). The government has issued *Government Regulation No 14 of 2021 revision of Government Regulation No 22 of 2020 the implementation of Law No 2 of 2017*. This regulation issued by the government harmonised with *Law No 11 of 2020 regarding Job Creation* and also with *Government Regulation No 05 of 2021 regarding Implementation of Risk-Based Business Licensing*. Those regulations issued by the government provide convenience for doing business, including in the construction service sector.

11.3 The impact of Covid-19 in Indonesia

11.3.1 The impact of Covid-19 on the execution of construction projects in Indonesia

Covid-19 has proven to be an obstacle for parties involved in construction projects. However, the FIDIC Covid-19 Guidance Memorandum[2] gave clear guidance on how to proceed during this tough time especially by building and maintaining good communication between parties.

In Indonesia, the government took related action by issuing *Presidential Decree KEPPRES No 12 of 2020*[3] on 13 April 2020. *KEPPRES No 12 of 2020* provides that on making policy and regulations in their respective regions, governors, regents, and mayors as chairpersons of the Task Force for Acceleration in Handling Coronavirus Disease 2019 (Covid-19) in the regions must be based on the policy of the central government. Various regulations and decisions in respect of Covid-19 were enacted by governors for regions and cities in the provinces. In Indonesia, in order to apply *force majeure*, there is a regulation requiring that an event considered as *force majeure* should be based on the decree of the local government. On this occasion, some of the local governments hesitated to release that statement for Covid-19.

KEPPRES No 12 of 2020 together with other regulations enacted by the President, governors, regents and mayors in respect of Covid-19, such as social distancing and quarantine inside and outside of the area, have undoubtedly impacted the performance of Works by Contractors. However, in some provinces the governors issued certain regulations exempting projects of national strategic importance as well as construction projects in general from some of the more onerous constraints imposed by such regulations and ensured that the execution of construction projects in Indonesia did not stop. Indonesian Law requires the parties to a contract to perform their obligations in good faith, so some projects still continued during the Covid-19

2 https://fidic.org/sites/default/files/FIDIC%20Guidance%20Memorandum%20to%20Users%20of%20the%201999%20Conditions%20of%20Contract%20dated%201st%20April%202013.pdf (accessed 30 July 2020).

3 Determination of Natural Disaster of the Spreading of Coronavirus Disease 2019 (Covid-19) as National Disaster.

outbreak with the Contractor using all reasonable efforts to mitigate the impact of Covid-19, with some compensation.

However, after the Covid-19 outbreak, the Indonesian government closed all areas to people from other countries. Foreigners were required to obtain a special permit to come to Indonesia. Thus, some construction projects which require foreign operators either to operate the machinery or to give training to local operators faced delay.

For example, power plant construction project in Indonesia requires the first-year inspection to be done in order the for the contract to be completed. First year inspection is an inspection of the power plant conducted by a foreign operator after the first year of maintenance since taking over was signed by the parties. Because of the Covid-19 outbreak and new regulations in Indonesia, the foreign operator was required to undertake an extra administration process to enter Indonesia which caused delay in the first year inspection. In one project, the Employer did not want to complete the contract without the first-year inspection, while the Contractor did not want to extend the bank guarantee which is very large since this is a power plant contract. After a series of discussions between the parties, they both agreed that the first-year inspection would be delayed by three months from the initial plan, however the Contractor changed the bank guarantee with another guarantee which cost it less.

11.3.2 The impact of Covid-19 on the operation of construction contracts in Indonesia

Covid-19 has two types of potential impact on the operation of construction contracts in Indonesia. The first potential impact is the performance of Employers, for example related to late payments to Contractors as a result of reallocating funds or budgets for payments to Contractors in the current fiscal year. The second is the impact on Contractor performance, for an example due to the application of health protocols or due to handling of Covid-19 cases at work during work implementation or due to constraints in mobilising materials, tools or labour due to large-scale social restrictions.

With all the efforts from Contractors, Employers typically granted extensions of time for projects. However, Contractors have had to support their claims with all reasonable evidence. For example, unforeseeable shortages in the availability of personnel or Goods because of governmental actions such as social distancing and no entry or exit from an area caused delays in material transportation. Also the implementation of the new regulations that everyone must wear a mask and use hand sanitiser, are grounds for the Contractor to claim for additional cost because of changes in regulations.

There were no specific regulatory provisions that generally govern the resolution of issues arising from the impact of Covid-19 on the operation of construction contracts in Indonesia. However, there were policies issued by government agencies to regulate the settlement of the impact of Covid-19 on contract implementation using government budget funding sources, such as policies issued by the Government Procurement Policy Agency (**LKPP**) and the Ministry of Internal Affairs through a Joint Circular Letter No 119/3039/SJ and No 11 of 2020.[4] With the issuance of this policy, Employers who are local governments can optimise contracts by adjusting the

---

4 Concerning Follow-up on Goods/Services Procurement Contracts on Adjustments to the 2020 Regional Revenue and Expenditure Budget as an Impact of Public Health Emergencies as the 2019 Corona Virus Disease National Disaster (Covid-19).

scope of work to the available budget in 2020, permanently terminating contracts for work that can be delayed, or temporarily suspending the contract only for work where completion may be postponed.

The Ministry of Public Works and Public Housing issued a new policy through the Circular Letter No 26/SE/ M/2020.[5] In this policy, the owner of the project can extend the contract period for construction works affected by Covid-19 from a single year contract to a multi-year contract. In addition, the Employer can adjust the contract price or adjust the handover mechanism. This policy only applies to projects managed by Ministry of Public Works and Housing.

11.4 Indonesian governing law of the contract

11.4.1 Constraints on the governing law of a construction contract

In Indonesia, in general, the regulation of choice of law in the *Civil Code* provides that the parties to a contract may choose for themselves which laws to apply to the contract, subject to some restrictions. These restrictions are that the choice of law does not violate public order and may not be transformed into illegal action while still paying attention to the legal conditions of an agreement.[6]

Thus, the main basis of a contract for construction works is an agreement for the parties in accordance with the principle of freedom of contract and *pacta sunt servanda* as referred to in Article 1338 paragraph 1 of the *Civil Code* which states that: 'All agreements made legally act as laws for those who make them.'

However, it is emphasised that the choice of law for a Construction Work Contact must comply with the applicable law in Indonesia which specifically regulates Construction Work Contracts. In particular, the Construction Work Contract is regulated in *Law No 2 of 2017 Construction Services*. Chapter 1 Article 1 paragraph 8 states:

> Construction Work Contracts are all contract documents that regulate the legal relationship between the Employer and the Contractor in the implementation of Construction Services.

More details on its implementing rules are in Article 75 paragraph 2 of *Government Regulation No 22 of 2020* which states:

> Construction Work Contracts are subject to applicable laws in Indonesia.

Accordingly, it can be interpreted that the governing law of a Construction Work Contract is Indonesian law, where the governing law that applies for the contract is used to determine or explain the terms of the contract or the law that will determine and regulate the contract, determine the legal certainty that applies to the contract during the performance of the parties' contractual obligations, and as a source of law for a situation that is not regulated in the Construction Work Contract.

The choice of law made in a Construction Work Contract is separate from the choice of jurisdiction for the determination for disputes. Jurisdiction is defined as the power or authority of a court to decide a dispute or it is also called the authority of a

---

5 Concerning Adjustments to Construction Service Work Packages Affected by Refocussing activities and Budget Reallocation in the 2020 Fiscal Year Due to Handling of the 2019 Corona Virus Disease Pandemic.

6 *Civil Code*, art 1320.

court of competent jurisdiction.[7] In the preparation of a Construction Work Contract where one of the parties is a foreign party, in general the choice of jurisdiction in the event of a dispute is usually determined to be arbitration. The choice of arbitration for contracts with foreign parties is strongly influenced by the existence of provisions in Indonesian civil procedural law. Article 436 *Reglement op de Burgerlijke rechtvordering* (Rv) states that the execution of decisions of foreign domestic courts cannot be carried out, unless a law regulates otherwise, or at least in order to be enforceable it is necessary to submit a new lawsuit using the decision of the foreign district court as evidence for reconsideration by the competent court.

11.4.2 Formal requirements for a construction contract

In making a Construction Work Contract, attention must be paid to the existing provisions according to the law and not conflict with the provisions stipulated by law so that problems do not arise in the future. There are four conditions for the validity of an agreement in Article 1320 of the *Civil Code*, namely:

> In order to be valid, an agreement must satisfy the following four conditions:
>
> 1. There must be consent of the individuals who are bound thereby; (Bw.28, 1321v.)
> 2. There must be capacity to enter into an obligation; (Bw. 1329v.)
> 3. There must be a specific subject matter; (Bw. 1332v.)
> 4. There must be a lawful cause. (Bw.1335v.; Civ. 1108).

The first and second terms are called subjective requirements because they are related to the subject of agreement. The third and fourth requirements, which are related to the object of agreement, are called objective requirements.

In a Construction Work Contract, the requirements in Article 1320 of the *Civil Code* are satisfied where the Employer and the Contractor responsible for mutually agreeing are stated in a contract document. The agreement is formed because of the bargaining process where the parties mutually propose their intention. What is stated by each party in the *Civil (Agreement) Law* is commonly referred to as a statement of intention. To reach agreement, two elements must always be met cumulatively. On the one hand, there is no agreement without a bid; on the other hand, there is no agreement without acceptance. The validity of a contract depends on the legality of agreement, and to determine whether the agreement is binding on the parties, an assessment must be made of the process of forming it. Likewise, matters regarding the implications of cancellation or revocation of either offer or acceptance. Therefore, in trying to understand agreement, one must understand these two elements. With an understanding of these two elements, the agreement between the parties in a construction contract can be reached both from the Employer and from the Contractor. Furthermore, the results of the agreement will be stated in a contract document known as a Construction Work Contract.

As explained in the previous section Construction Work Contracts in Indonesia are specifically regulated in *Law No 2 of 2017 Construction Services*. In Chapter V Third Paragraph, Article 47 paragraph 1 of the *Law* states:

> (1) The Construction Work Contract must at least include a description of:
>
> a. The Parties;
> b. Work Formulation;

7 Huala Adolf, *Dasar-Dasar, Prinsip & Filosofi Arbitrase* (1st edn, Keni Media 2014) 141.

c. Coverage Period;
d. Equal Rights and Obligations;
e. Use of construction labor;
f. Payment method;
g. Default;
h. Dispute resolution;
i. Termination of construction work contracts;
j. *Force Majeure;*
k. Building failure;
l. Worker protection;
m. Protection of Third Parties;
n. Environmental aspects;
o. Guarantee for risks and legal liability; and
p. Construction dispute resolution options.

Further provisions for a Construction Work Contract are regulated in *Government Regulation No 22 of 2020 the Implementation Rules of Law No 2 of 2017 Construction Services* in Article 76, which explains that a Construction Work Contract contains several documents that are inter-related and contain at least:

a. An Agreement Letter signed by the Employer and the Contractor, which at least contains:
    1) Description of the parties;
    2) Consideration;
    3) Scope of work;
    4) Principal matters such as the contract price, the contract performance period/time for completion; and
    5) List of binding documents along with the sequence
    6) Hierarchy.
b. Particular Condition of Contract containing work information data and terms of changes permitted by the general condition of contract based on the specific characteristics of the work;
c. General Condition of Contract which contains general provisions governing the engagement based on the administration system, scope of work, method of payment and system for calculating the results of the work;
d. Employer Requirement/Employer Document which is part of the selection/bidding document which is the basis for Contractor to compile the offer/bidding, which contains the scope of duties and requirements, including the requirements for work specifications, drawings, list of output/quantity and price;
e. Proposals or Offering Letter, which are prepared by the Contractor based on a selection/bidding document containing the method, bid price, time schedule, and resources;
f. Minutes/Certificate containing the agreement between the Employer and the Contractor during the evaluation process of a proposal or offer by the Employer in the form of clarification on matters that raise doubts;
g. Statement Letter from the Employer which states that he has accepted or approved the proposal or offer from the Contractor; and
h. Statement Letter from the Contractor stating the ability to carry out the work.

The documents listed above are the minimum documents that must be available to prepare a Construction Work Contract in accordance with the definition of a Construction Work Contract in Article 1 paragraph 8 referred to in paragraph 11.4.1 above.

Another issue that is an important concern in the preparation of a Construction Work Contract is the implementation of the good faith principle which is based on mutual trust. At first, the principle of good faith was understood to apply at the time of contract execution, but in its development this principle is now understood to have started from the pre-contract stage, namely during the negotiation process where there was an offer and acceptance to reach an agreement. Failure to apply the principle of good faith can cause losses to either party, which can lead to new legal problems such as a statement of accountability before the Construction Work Contract is executed.

In the *Civil Code*, there is no limit to good faith, but for a Construction Work Contract, the implementation of good faith has been regulated at the time of implementation as stated in the Construction Work Contract Standard in *Ministerial Regulation No 14 of 2020 Standards and Guidelines for the Procurement of Construction Services by Service Providers* as mentioned in Article 80 of the General Conditions of Contracts in paragraphs 1 and 2:

(1) The parties act on the basis of mutual trust in accordance with the rights contained in the Contract.
(2) The parties agree to carry out the agreement honestly without highlighting the interests of each party. If during the Contract, one of the parties feels aggrieved, then the best action is sought to resolve the situation.

11.5 What Special Provisions in the Particular Conditions are necessary for consistency with applicable laws in Indonesia?

11.5.1 FIDIC General Conditions are incompatible or inconsistent with Indonesian governing law of the contract

11.5.1.1 Addendum of construction contract

The terms addendum and amendment are documents that are normatively implemented in the contracting process in Indonesia. Basically, both an addendum and a contract amendment are also agreements. Therefore, in the event of any change in contract implementation the process of administering the change must also fulfil the four conditions for the validity of an agreement in Article 1320 of the *Civil Code* listed in paragraph 11.4.2, namely:

1. There must be consent of the individuals who are bound thereby; (Bw.28, 1321v.)
2. There must be capacity to enter into an obligation; (Bw. 1329v.)
3. There must be a specific subject matter; (Bw. 1332v.)
4. There must be a lawful cause. (Bw.1335v.; Civ. 1108).

Changes to the implementation of a contract in this case must meet the requirements of Article 1320 of the *Civil Code*, namely the existence of an agreement or consent and the authority to act from the party making changes in the said change agreement (conditions 1 and 2 above).

The agreement in the *Civil Code* does not require a written agreement, but also includes an agreement made orally. However, an agreement made in writing will provide proof if a dispute occurs in an arbitration or court process. Also, contract changes must also be agreed upon by the competent parties in the contract, therefore any changes to the implementation of the contract made in writing in the form of a contract amendment or addendum must be signed by the competent parties in the contract. After the execution of the written change agreement in the form of addendum or amendment it will become a ground for any following action by the parties bound to it, among others to make a payment for the changes.

Under FIDIC General Conditions there are no specific clauses that regulate amendment/addendum of the Contract. Referring to sub-clause 1.5 [Priority of Documents] the Contract Agreement is the highest priority contract document. According to the definition of Contract, sub-clause 1.1.1.2 [Definition of the Contract Agreement], and sub-clause 1.6 [Contract Agreement] in the FIDIC General Conditions, there are no requirements to make an addendum or amendment in the event of any changes in the technical, financial or administrative aspects during the contract period which shall become the agreement with the highest enforceability of the contract documents binding the parties.

Further, according to sub-clause 13.3 [Variation Procedure] there is also no provision that requires the Parties to make any addendum or amendment to the Contract or to the Contract Agreement after a Variation is approved. Under the Red Book and the Yellow Book the administrator of such Variations works is the Engineer who in legal terms is not a party to the Contract. On this view, any determination of additional costs or time due to a Variation made by the Engineer cannot fulfil the four conditions of the *Civil Code* Article 1320 for the validity of an agreement to bind the Contractor and the Employer.

This legal position also will be same for the implementation of sub-clause 14.3 [Application for Interim Payments] where any estimated contract value of the Works executed by the Contractor including Variations can be included in the application for interim payments, and for payment according to sub-clause 14.6 [Interim Payments] and sub-clause 14.7 [Timing of Payments] without any written legal agreement between the Employer and the Contractor. The application of these sub-clauses will therefore not meet the conditions of validity of an agreement based on Article 1320 of the *Civil Code*.

Hence, attention needs to be given in drafting the Particular Conditions to include the requirement to make a contract addendum or amendment in the event of any change to costs or time during execution of the project. This requirement is necessary for consistency with applicable laws in Indonesia to ensure the validity of the changes agreed between the Parties.

11.5.1.2 Termination of a construction contract

In principle, Article 1266 of the *Civil Code* provides an obligation that although the parties regulate a cause for the termination of the agreement either unilaterally or mutually (das Sein), if it is related to the cancellation of the agreement as a result of default, the agreement must be subject to the provisions of Article 1266 KUHPer (das Sollen) itself, when the cancellation of the agreement must be requested from the court. As stated in Article 1266 of the *Civil Code*:

> The condition for cancelling is considered always included in a reciprocal agreement, if one of the parties does not fulfill its obligations. In such a case the agreement is not null and void, but the cancellation must be requested to the Court. This request must also be made, although the cancellation conditions non-fulfillment of obligations are stated in the agreement. If the conditions for cancellation are not stated in the agreement, the Judge by observing the circumstances, at the request of the defendant, is free to give a period of time to fulfill the obligations, but that period cannot be more than one month.

The legal consequence of the aforementioned Article is that although there are FIDIC General Conditions that contain conditions for termination or cancellation of the contract as stipulated in sub-clause 15.2 [Termination by Employer], 16.2 [Termination by the Contractor] and 19.6 [Optional Termination, Payment and Release],[8] if later the regulated conditions are fulfilled, then in Indonesia the cancellation still has to be submitted to the court to be decided by the judge.

As the termination or cancellation of agreement through the courts is inefficient, in the practice of drafting business contracts in Indonesia, there are many contracts containing an article or provision that state that the parties agree that Article 1266 of *Civil Code* is waived in the event of termination of the contract. With this waiver the parties intend that if the conditions for termination are fulfilled, the agreement is terminated or cancelled between the parties according to the termination conditions provided in the contract without a decision of any judicial body.

However, the consequence of this waiver is that termination or cancellation may be misused by one of the parties, including the consequences for a third party to the agreement or contract. The legal consequences of the waiver of Article 1266 of Indonesian *Civil Code* are discussed by Kartini Muljadi and Gunawan Widjaja in their book *General Engagement*:

> In an agreement or contract terminated by the parties, the parties cannot abolish or eliminate the rights of the third party that have been issued in connection with the agreement that they cancelled (for this, see the provisions of Article 1340 jo. Article 1341 *Civil Code*). What can be done away with by such cancellation are only the consequences that may occur in the future between the parties. As for the agreement cancelled by judge, the cancellation returns the position of all parties and materials to their original state, as if the agreement had never occurred, with the exception of certain rights which are retained by law for the benefit of certain parties.[9]

The cancellation according to Article 1266 does not cause the agreement/contract to be null and void. Article 1267 enables a request for cancellation to also include reimbursement of costs, losses, and expenses. Thus, Article 1267 provides that the consequences of cancellation by a judge under article 1266 shall not merely consider that the parties are returned to their original state as if the contract had never been entered into, but also consider any costs, losses and expenses including any consequences to related third party.

It can therefore be concluded that the legal consequence of waiver of *Civil Code* Article 1266 are as follows. Where the termination/cancellation can be carried out unilaterally by one of the parties based on the fulfilment of the termination requirements, such termination does not cause the legal relationship of the parties to return to their original state as if there was no agreement between them. Rather it terminates the engagement and agreement between them at the time of termination so that they are not bound to continue the contract, nor bound by any consequences that may occur in the future between them as agreed in the contract for the period after termination. Thus, the interests of third parties that have been incurred as a result of the agreement must still be borne by the parties.

However, for a cancellation with the result that the agreement had never occurred (null and void), based on the law it must still be requested from the Court to be determined by a judge as regulated in Article 1266.

8 1999 Red Book and Yellow Book.

9 Kartini Muljadi and Gunawan Widjaja, *Perikatan pada Umumnya* (Raja_Grafindo Persada, 2003) 138.

Therefore, to ensure consistency of waiving Article 1266, additional provisions should be included in the Particular Conditions for the purpose of termination. Care must be taken in the contract drafting to distinguish between the legal consequences and the intentions mandated in *Civil Code* Articles 1266 and 1267 which constitute the cancellation of the contract to become null and void as if it had never existed between the parties.

11.5.2 FIDIC General Conditions are incompatible or inconsistent with the law of the Site/Country

11.5.2.1 Limit of liability for building failure

In relation to the Contractor's liability for remedying defects during the Defects Notification Period in Indonesia, the Contractor cannot avoid responsibility for the possibility/risk of building failure. Building failure is regulated in *Law No 2 of 2017, Construction Services* Article 47(1)(k), which contains provisions on the obligations of the Contractor and/or the Employer for building failure and the period of responsibility for building failure. In *Law No 2 of 2017*, building failure is given the following meaning: 'A condition of building collapse and/or non-functioning of the building after the final handover of the completed construction services.'

In Article 60(1) of *Law No 2 of 2017 Construction Services*, both the Contractor and the Employer are deemed to be responsible in the event of a building failure caused by the implementation of construction services that do not fulfil the security, safety, health and sustainability standards stipulated in *Law No 2 of 2017 Construction Services*. According to Article 65(1) and (2), in the event that the planned construction age is more than 10 years, the Contractor is only responsible for the failure of the building for a maximum period of 10 years from the date of the final handover of construction services on the issuance of the Performance Certificate. The Employer also bears responsibility for building failures that occur after the Contractor's insurance period has passed for the building failure as regulated in Article 65(3).

Furthermore, in accordance with the provisions of Article 65(4) the period of coverage for building failure which is the responsibility of the Contractor as referred to in Article 65(1) and (2) must be set out in the Construction Work Contract which refers to the construction life plan. Accordingly, with the enforcement of public law on the responsibility for building failure as stated in Article 60(1) in *Law No 2 of 2017 Construction Services*, both the Contractor and the Employer are responsible for the building failure risks to the public during the limitation period of liability for building failure which is enforced in accordance with *Law No 2 of 2017, Construction Services.*

The limitation period of the parties' obligations to the public for the risk of building failure as stipulated by law is binding and is not limited to the duration of the contract or its extension (including the extension of the Defects Notification Period) as detailed in the FIDIC General Conditions. Therefore it should be included in Special Conditions that the Contractor is obliged to be responsible for building failure within the specified period in accordance with the construction age plan for maximum of ten years from the date of the issuance of the Performance Certificate. The Employer is then responsible after the Contractor's liability period is over.

In view of the inconsistencies between the FIDIC General Conditions and the provisions of Article 65 of *Law No 2 of 2017, Construction Services*, the following must be included in the Particular Conditions:

a. An exception to the limit of liability of the Contractor's obligations under sub-clause 11.9 [Performance Certificate] in the case of building failure based on Indonesian law;
b. An additional provision to the sub-clause on limitation of liability[10] that the liability of both the Employer and the Contractor shall not limited in any case of building failure according to *Law No 2 Year 2017, Construction Services.*

11.5.3 FIDIC General Conditions are incompatible or inconsistent with the relevant laws on dispute determination in Indonesia

11.5.3.1 Stages of dispute resolution in construction contracts

FIDIC General Conditions provide for dispute resolution by a stepped process: DAB or DAAB, amicable settlement, and finally arbitration. If one party is dissatisfied with the Engineer's determination it can submit a Notice of Dissatisfaction and proceed to obtain the DAB/DAAB's decision. If either Party does not accept that the DAB/DAAB's decision settled the dispute, then the Parties can proceed to amicable settlement before commencing arbitration.

FIDIC's approach in solving disputes under the General Conditions is different to the three-step process under *Indonesian Law No 2 Year 2017 Construction Services* in Article 88. The stages of efforts to resolve construction disputes according to *Law No 2 of 2017* are regulated in the provisions in Chapter XI Article 88 which provides:

> (1) Disputes that occur in a Construction Work Contract shall be settled on the basic principle of amicability to reach a consensus.
> (2) In the event that the parties amicable settlement as referred to in paragraph (1) cannot reach an agreement, the parties shall take the stages to resolve the dispute as stated in the Construction Work Contract.
> (3) If the parties have not determined the dispute settlement provisions, the disputing parties will make a written agreement on the procedure to be chosen for resolving the dispute.
> (4) Stages of dispute resolution efforts include:
>
> a. mediation;
> b. conciliation; and
> c. arbitration.
>
> (5) In addition to dispute resolution efforts as referred to in paragraph (4) letters a and b, the parties can appoint a Dispute Board.

The first and second stages in paragraph (4) can be replaced by using a Dispute Board (as an option for the Parties) in the form of a DAB/DAAB under a FIDIC Contract. Paragraph (1) encourages the implementation of prior amicable settlement between the parties before a dispute settlement involves a third party which starts from the mediation process.

10 2017 Red Book sub-clause 1.14, Yellow and Silver Books sub-clause 1.15; 1999 Red, Yellow and Silver Books sub-clause 17.6.

Accordingly, an appropriate Special Provision is required to consider the settlement stages according to the law in relation to the DAB/DAAB process in the dispute resolution provisions stated in the FIDIC General Conditions for construction contracts in Indonesia.

11.5.3.2 Government projects

In Indonesia there is another law applied to government projects that requires special attention, related to the involvement of the State Auditor, namely the Financial and Development Supervisory Agency (**BPKP**) according to *Presidential Regulation No 192 Year 2014.* The Financial and Development Supervisory Agency comprises a Secretariat and a Number of Deputies with various responsibilities. The Deputy for Investigation's duties, regulated under section 8 clause 27, are to prevent corruption, audits of price adjustments, audits of claims, investigative audits of irregularities that indicate losses to state finances, audits of state financial losses, and providing expert statements.

Under *Presidential Regulation 192*, most government projects in Indonesia first come to the Deputy for Investigation to settle a dispute through a mediation process by BPKP as the first stage of the dispute settlement according to *Law No 2 of 2017*.

Accordingly, an appropriate Special Provision is required to consider this *Regulation* and the settlement stages according to the law in relation to the DAB/DAAB process in the dispute resolution provisions stated in the FIDIC General Conditions for government projects.

11.6 What Special Provisions in the Particular Conditions are desirable for consistency with applicable laws in Indonesia?

It is desirable to modify some clauses in the FIDIC GCs for consistency with Indonesian law, including for the following issues:

a. Subcontractors
b. Local Plant and Materials (local content)
c. Variations (including Silver and Yellow Books)
d. Key Personnel
e. Financial arrangements
f. Incentives for early completion
g. Additional contract documents such as:
    - Minutes of clarification or clarification report containing an agreement between the Employer and the Contractor during the evaluation process of a proposal or offer by the Contractor in the form of clarification of matters that raise doubts
    - A statement letter from the Contractor which states that it has accepted or approved the proposal or offer from the Service Provider and
    - A statement letter from the Contractor stating its ability to carry out the work.

Some of these issues are briefly discussed in the sections below to provide an overview of some of provisions that are appropriate to be included in the Particular Conditions.

11.6.1 Requirements for the use of Subcontractors

In a construction contract the provisions for the use of a Subcontractor must be regulated, as stated in *Law No 2 of 2017 Construction Services*, Article 48(b), which reads:

> [F]or construction service implementation activities, [the contract] may contain provisions on sub-service providers as well as suppliers of materials, building components, and/or equipment that must meet applicable standards.

Furthermore, in the implementation of construction services, the Contractor can assign some part of the main work to a Subcontractor. According to the elucidation of *Law No 2 of 2017 Construction Services* Article 53, the 'main work is a series of activities in a Construction Services process which have the greatest risk level in causing delays in the completion of Construction Services'. The assignment of the Main Work can only be given to specialist Subcontractors. *Law No 2 of 2017 regarding Construction Services* Article 53 states:

> (1) In the implementation of Construction Services, the main work can only be assigned to the Service Sub-Service Provider who is a specialist as referred to in Article 13 and Article 14.
> (2) The granting of primary work to a Service Sub-Service Provider who is a specialist as referred to in paragraph (1) must be approved by the Employer.

According to this Article, the participation of the Sub-Service Provider is limited for works requirements that need special expertise.

Government Regulation No 22 of 2020 Implementation Rules of Law No 2 of 2017 Construction Services requires Employers in the preparation of selection documents for Contractors to outline a list of jobs with specialist classifications and specialist sub-classifications so that the Contractor in its bid can take the work into account. If the Contractor does not have these qualifications, this work can be done by operating cooperatively with specialist Subcontractors or by nominating specialist Sub-Service Providers as stated in Article 60 of *Government Regulation No 22 of 2020* as follows:

> (5) In preparing the Service Provider selection document, the Employer must describe a list of jobs for the specialist classification and specialist sub-classification.
> (6) Service Providers that do not have specialist sub-classification on:
>
> a. Classification of special construction and/or construction 'pre-fabrication must carry out joint operations; and
> b. Classifications other than those referred to in letter a must be carried out by the Sub-Service Provider who is nominated in the Service Provider selection process.

Other provisions can be seen in *Government Regulation No 22 of 2020*, Article 71 on specialist work:

> (1) Specialist construction work must be included in the document for selecting Service Providers.
> (2) Construction work that is specialist in nature as referred to in paragraph (1) must be carried out by the specialist business entity Service Provider.

Based on the provisions above, the Contractor may only subcontract specialist work if the work in the procurement documents/Tender documents and in the Contract is permitted to be subcontracted.

Thus, in Indonesia *Law No 2 of 2017* Article 53 requires that the main work allocated to subcontractors must obtain the Employer's approval, while in the Red and Yellow Book General Conditions, subcontracting can be carried out simply with the approval of the Engineer.[11]

Accordingly, the FIDIC Red and Yellow Book sub-clause on Subcontractors needs to be supplemented by an additional Special Provision in the Particular Conditions for the use of Subcontractors in construction projects in Indonesia. The additional Special Provisions should provide that the conditions for the use of Subcontractors include, among other things:

a. Permit and approval granted by the Employer and has been complied with and
b. That the subcontracted work is a specialist work as evidenced by the existence of a Specialist Business Entity Certificate.

11.6.2 Engagement of staff and labour and labour laws

In general, in Indonesia every foreign labour provider is obliged to prioritise local labour in all available positions as per *Presidential Regulation No 20 of 2018 on the Use of Foreign Workers* Article 4:

> (1) Every TKA Employer must prioritize the use of Indonesian labour in all types of positions available.
> (2) In the event that the position as referred to in paragraph (1) has not been occupied by Indonesian labour, such position may be occupied by TKA.

Specifically related to construction projects in Indonesia, in *Law No 2 of 2017 Construction Services* there is no clear definition of construction labour, it only states the obligation of each construction worker to have a work competency certificate in accordance with Article 70(1) which reads: 'Every construction worker who works in the field of Construction Services is required to have a Work Competency Certificate.'

The construction workforce itself can come from local and foreign workers, who must fulfil several required terms and conditions to obtain a work competency certificate. In the formation of a foreign construction service business entity that establishes a representative office in Indonesia, it is required to use more local workers than foreign workers. This is stipulated in *Law No 2 of 2017 Construction Services* Article 33(1)(d), which requires that it 'employs more Indonesian workers than foreign workers'. However, in relation to the use of construction labour, there are no clear rules on the comparison value between local workers and foreign workers or a limit on the number of foreign workers.

Previously, the use of foreign construction workers was regulated in *Law No 2 of 2017 Construction Services* Article 74, which states:

> (1) An employer of foreign construction workers is required to have a plan to employ foreign workers and a permit to employ foreign workers.
> (2) A foreign construction worker may perform work in the field of construction services in Indonesia only in certain positions in accordance with the provisions of laws and regulations.

11 Red Book sub-clause 5.1; Yellow Book sub-clause 4.4.

(3) Foreign construction workers in an expert position in the field of Construction Services who are to be employed by the employer must have a registration certificate from the Minister.
(4) The registration certificate as intended in paragraph (3) shall be issued based on a certificate of competence for foreign construction workers according to the laws of the country.
(5) Foreign construction workers in expert positions are required to transfer knowledge and transfer technology to accompanying workers in accordance with the provisions of laws and regulations.
(6) Supervision of the use of foreign construction workers shall be carried out by labour inspectors in accordance with the provisions of laws and regulations.
(7) Further provisions for the registration procedure for foreign construction workers as referred to in paragraph (4) shall be regulated in a Ministerial Regulation.

If viewed from the provisions of this article, it can be interpreted that the ratio of the number of foreign and local workers will be determined and measured for a certain position, a certain time, or included in the Employment Plan of Foreign Workers (**RPTKA**) of the employing company. However, the rules in *Law No 2 of 2020* Article 74 have been abolished in the *Omnibus Law No 11 of 2020 Job Creation*, where it is stipulated that further regulation of the use of foreign workers in the construction service sector will refer to the regulations stipulated by Minister of Manpower and Transmigration of the Republic of Indonesia.

The regulations that have been enforced refer to the *Minister of Manpower and Transmigration Decree No KEP.247/MEN/X/2011 regarding Positions That Foreign Workers Can Hold in the Construction Category*. This *Ministerial Decree* regulates positions that can be held by foreign workers for the construction sector, namely at the level of Commissioners, Directors, Managers and Engineers. If the position to be occupied by foreign workers is not included in the attachment to this *Decree*, the employer must obtain permission from the relevant Minister after receiving a recommendation from the Minister in charge of construction. The term of office occupied by foreign workers is a maximum of five years and cannot be extended except for the position of Commissioner or Director of a capital owner, as stated in points 2 and 3 of this *Ministerial Decree*.

Therefore, it is desirable that this specific provision be added as Particular Conditions of sub-clause 6.4 [Labour Laws], 6.8 [Contractor's Superintendence] and 6.9 [Contractors Personnel.

11.6.3 Local Plant and Materials (local content)

The Indonesian government is promoting an increase in the domestic industrial sector, and to support this matter it needs support from the construction service sector for the use of domestic materials or services. This is regulated in *Law No 2 of 2017 Construction Services*, Article 17 which reads:

(1) Construction Services business activities are supported by the supply chain business of construction resources.
(2) The construction resources as meant in paragraph (1) shall be prioritized from domestic production.

It is also stated in *Government Regulation No 2 of 2020 Implementation Regulations of Law No 2 of 2017* in Article 25 that construction resources should preferably be from domestic production, as well as optimising the use of domestic production for superior and environmentally friendly materials and equipment, technology and human resources. Article 26 of this *Government Regulation* stipulates qualifications and requirements that must be met for the use of material resources and construction equipment originating from domestic production as referred to in Article 25 paragraph (2).

The government of Indonesia encourages the use of more domestic materials and services, especially in government construction projects. The use of domestic products required in the laws and regulations mentioned above is usually stipulated in a Domestic Component Level (**TKDN**) where the procurement of machines and tools whose raw materials and components still come from abroad are assembled domestically.

The application of the use of the TKDN factor or the Increased Use of Domestic Products (**P3DN**) is a requirement which is also regulated in *Presidential Regulation No 16 of 2018 Government Procurement of Goods and Services*. Articles 66 and 67 stipulate that the Ministry/Institution/Regional Apparatus is required to use domestic products, including national design and build and national engineering.

The provisions for minimum value of use are regulated by the relevant *Ministry Regulation*. The procedure for calculating the TKDN is regulated in *Regulation of the Minister of Industry No 16/M-IND/PER/2/2011 Provisions and Procedures for Calculating Domestic Component Levels*, Article 2 paragraph (6) which states:

> Determination of domestic components for work tools/work facilities as referred to in paragraph (4) letter b, provided that:
> (f) working tools produced abroad and owned by goods/services providers in cooperation between domestic companies and foreign companies, their domestic components are assessed in proportion to the composition (comparison) of shares of domestic companies.

The requirements on the limit of TKDN value, specifications and requirements for Plant and Materials using domestic products used in a project should be specified in the Particular Conditions in relation to General Condition sub-clause 7.1 [Manner of Execution] by referring to compliance with applicable Indonesian Laws and Regulations on the minimum use of local content of Plant and Materials.

11.6.4 Government projects: evaluation of unit price contract

For government projects in Indonesia which are implemented according to *Presidential Regulation No 16 of 2018 Government Procurement of Goods/Services*, there are provisions on measurement and evaluation that are different from the provisions in the FIDIC Red Book sub-clause 12.3, which applies to re-measurement types of contracts.

In an Indonesian government project, based on *Presidential Regulation No 16 of 2018 Government Procurement of Goods/Services*, clarification must be made in the tender process against the unit price bid for each payment item. This is further regulated in the *Government Goods/Services Procurement Policy Institute Regulation (LKPP) No 9 of 2018* which contains the implementing rules of *Presidential Regulation No 16 of 2018 Government Procurement of Goods/Services*. The Appendix page on the Evaluation of Unequal Prices in points 4.2.7 letter d number 3) regulates the following:

a. For Unit Price Contracts or Combined Accumulation Contracts and Unit Prices, clarification must be made to the unit price bid which is greater than 110% (one hundred and ten percent) of the unit price stated in the estimated/estimated price from the Employer which is called Self-estimated Price (**HPS**).

b. If after clarification, it turns out that the unit price can be accounted for or is in accordance with the market price, the unit price is declared non-unequal and will become the contract unit price.
c. If after clarification, it turns out that the unit price is declared unequal against the market price, then the item of payment is stated as an item with an Unequal Unit Price in an Official Report of Clarification of Unbalanced Unit Prices and becomes part of the Contract.

According to *Presidential Regulation No 16 of 2018 Government Procurement of Goods/ Services*, when the Unequal Unit Price has been agreed to be part of the Contract, the unequal price is consolidated into the Contract Unit Price but for any items of works with that Unequal Unit Price some special provisions related to its measurement and evaluation will be applied in the implementation of the Contract.

Based on the *Regulation of the Government Procurement Policy Institute (LKPP) No 9 of 2018* which is the implementing rules of *Presidential Regulation No 16 of 2018 regarding Government Procurement of Goods/Services*, on the Appendix page on the Evaluation of Unequal Prices in point 4.2.7 letter d number 3) c) the Unequal Unit Price only applies to volumes in accordance with the List of Quantities and Prices of the initial contract. If there is an additional volume in the item of payment, the additional volume in the item of payment is paid at the unit price stated in the HPS.

When FIDIC Red Book General Conditions are used for an Indonesian government project, then Special Provisions related to Unequal Unit Prices need to be included in the Particular Conditions by revising the provisions of General Conditions sub-clause 12.2 [Method of Measurement] and sub-clause 12.3 [Evaluation/Valuation of the Works] for consistency with applicable Regulations for Government projects as explained above.

11.6.5 Government projects: right to vary, variation procedure and payment for variations

Variations are very common in construction work in Indonesia and Variations in construction work contracts are referred to in the highest regulations in Indonesia for construction services, namely *Law No 2 of 2017 Construction Services*, which applies to any construction actor in Indonesia.

However, in the implementation of construction work contracts carried out with the government, as a form of control over the government's expenditure budget, the government of Indonesia will impose a maximum value on construction changes, which is ten percent of the value of the initial work. This is regulated in *Presidential Regulation No 16 of 2018 Government Procurement of Goods/Services*, Article 54, which states:

> (2) In the event that the change in contract as referred to in paragraph (1) results in an increase in the contract value, the change in contract shall be carried out provided that the addition of the final contract value does not exceed 10% (ten percent) of the price stated in the initial Contract.

This regulation is then detailed by the *Government Goods/Services Procurement Policy Institute (LKPP)* (which is directly responsible to the President), in *LKPP Regulation No 9 of 2018 Guidelines for the Implementation of the Procurement of Goods/Services through Providers*. Appendix page point 7.13.1, adds provisions for available budgets for additional work. This needs to be known by prospective Contractors in order to anticipate work delays due to the unavailability of the budget when carrying out additional work instructed by the Employer.

For this reason, General Condition sub-clause 13.1 [Right to Vary] needs to be supplemented by a Particular Condition on the Variation value limits and how the limitations of Engineer's and Employer's rights are related to giving Variation instructions within the maximum value limit.

In addition, this provision is also needed to fulfil the involvement of the state auditor, namely the Financial and Development Supervisory Agency (BPKP) so that there are no indications of misappropriation in the construction work. BPKP's functions are listed in *Presidential Regulation No 192 of 2014 regarding the Financial and Development Supervisory Agency* Article 3(b), which states the state auditor's role as:

> b. [P]erforming audits, reviews, evaluations, monitoring, and other supervisory activities on planning, implementation and accountability for state/regional revenue accountability and accountability for state/regional financial expenditures as well as national development and/or other activities whose finances are wholly or partly financed by the state/regional budget and/or subsidies including business entities and other entities in which there are financial interests or other interests of the Central Government and/or Regional Governments as well as accountability for state/regional financial financing;

As a consequence of the BPKP's role in government projects, for the additional costs of any Variation which is valued by an Engineer's Determination, the additional costs shall be audited and evaluated by the BPKP before the Employer (who is a government body) can make any payment for it. Therefore, for a government project this requirement needs to be added as a Particular Condition for sub-clause 14.3 [Application for Interim Payment] and sub-clause 14.7 [Payment] of the FIDIC General Conditions.

As for the Variations referred to in sub-clause 13.1 [Right to Vary], if they occur in government projects in Indonesia, the implementation will also be subject to *Presidential Regulation No 16 of 2018*, Article 54 paragraph (1), where each Variation includes conditions that are required to make changes/addendum to the Contract. For government projects that refer to *Presidential Regulation No 16 of 2018*, changes/addendum to the contracts are also required for the payment of these Variations. This is regulated in the *Minister of Finance Regulation No 190/PMK.05/2012 regarding Payment Methods in the Context of Implementing the State Revenue and Expenditure Budget*, Article 40 paragraph (2). Variations that need to be followed up with an addendum/contract amendment are also regulated in the General Terms of Contracts Article 37.4 which is an attachment to the *Regulation of the Minister of Public Works and Public Housing (PUPR) No 14 of 2020 regarding Standards and Guidelines for the Procurement of Construction Services through Providers*.

As discussed in paragraph 11.5.1.1 above, the contract addendum requirement is not found in the provisions of the FIDIC General Conditions in the certification process and payment for Variations that have been approved by the Engineer under sub-clause 14.3 [Application for Interim Payment]. To make the payment, it is necessary to supplement General Condition sub-clause 13.3 [Variation Procedure] by adding a Particular Condition in relation to the terms of payment for the additional costs of the Variations by the requirement of a written contract amendment. The Particular Condition should address the mandatory requirement of effecting an amendment/

addendum to the Contract as a follow-up to agreement of any Variation between the Employer and Contractor.

For the Red and Yellow Books it is also necessary to supplement sub-clause 14.3 [Application for Interim Payment] by a Special Provision that the valuation of additional costs due to Variations can only be certified in an Interim Payment Certificate as well as can only be paid as an Interim Payment after the Variation has become part of an amendment/addendum to the Contract.

11.6.6 Government projects: adjustment for changes in cost

Price adjustment (escalation/de-escalation) is one of the minimum contents that must be regulated in the specific terms of a Construction Work Contract in Indonesia, both the status of its enforcement and the procedure for calculation and payment. This is stipulated in *Government Regulation No 22 of 2020 regarding the Implementation Regulations of Law No 2 of 2017 Construction Services*, part of the elucidation of *Law No 2 of 2017 Construction Services* Article 76(b), which this regulation applies to any construction actor in Indonesia.

In the FIDIC General Conditions price escalation or adjustment for changes in cost starts from the first month of the project.[12] Sub-clause 14.3 Application for Interim Payment Certificates in the Red and Yellow Books requires the Contractor to submit a monthly[13] statement to the Engineer including any amounts to be added and deducted for changes in cost, in accordance with sub-clause 13.7/13.8 [Adjustments for Changes in Cost].

For a Construction Work Contract conducted with the government, there is a provision that the new price adjustment will only take effect from the thirteenth month since the commencement of the work, and only apply to a multi-year contract whose implementation period is more than eighteen months. This is regulated in *Presidential Regulation No 16 of 2016 Government Procurement of Goods/Services*, Article 37 paragraph (2), which states:

> a. Price adjustments are applied to a Multi-Year Contract with an implementation period of more than 18 (eighteen) months;
> b. The price adjustment as referred to in letter a shall take effect from the 13th (thirteenth) month since the execution of the work;

This provision is also listed in the *Government Goods/Services Procurement Policy Institute (LKPP) No 9 of 2018 regarding Guidelines for the Implementation of the Procurement of Goods/Services through Providers*, in the Appendix paragraph 2.3.2.8 b 1) and 2).

The special conditions outlined above are not regulated in the FIDIC General Conditions sub-clause 13.7/13.8 [Adjustments for Changes in Costs].[14] Accordingly, a Special Provision in relation to sub-clause 13.7/13.8 that the value of period 'n' will only begin on the thirteenth month since the commencement of the work needs to be detailed in the adjustment formulas stated in the Particular Conditions. In this case, it is necessary to pay attention to the certainty of the date when the commencement of the 'work implementation' is meant, whether it is the same as the date of contract

12 2017 Red, Yellow and Silver Books sub-clause 13.7; 1999 Red and Yellow Books sub-clause 13.8.

13 In the 2017 editions the interval between statements is stated in the Contract Data. Monthly intervals are the default if no period is stated.

14 2017 Red, Yellow and Silver Books sub-clause 13.7; 1999 Red and Yellow Books sub-clause 13.8.

signing or the intended Commencement Date. This provision should be added in the Contract Data or in the Particular Conditions for sub-clause 13.7/13.8 [Adjustments for Changes in Cost].

In addition, if the Contractor fails to complete the work within the Time for Completion in the initial contract programme, then based on *Presidential Regulation No 16 of 2016* and *LKPP Regulation No 9 of 2018*, the index used is the lowest index determined for either the completion date in the contract programme or the actual date of completion of the Works. This provision also needs to be added in a Particular Condition to change the conditions in the General Conditions sub-clause 13.7/13.8 [Adjustments for Changes in Cost].

Another provision that needs to be added to the Particular Conditions is that price adjustments do not apply to items of Unequal Unit Price, as regulated in *Presidential Regulation No 16 of 2016* Article 37 paragraph (2)(c), which states:

> c. Unit price adjustments apply to all payment activities/items, except for the profit component, indirect costs (overhead cost), and unequal unit price as stated in the offer;

Thus, the definition of Unequal Unit Prices and the special provisions that apply to Unequal Unit Prices related to the calculation and formulation of adjustments for changes in cost as discussed in paragraph 11.6.4 above need to be added to the Particular Conditions in relation to sub-clause 13.7/13.8 [Adjustments for Changes in Costs].

As discussed in paragraph 11.6.5 above, it is important to note that in Indonesia the value of the price adjustment to be paid on a Construction Work Contract with the government is required to be audited by the Financial and Development Supervisory Agency (BPKP), as regulated in *Presidential Regulation No 192 of 2014 regarding BPKP*, Article 3(e). Special Provisions also need to be added to the Particular Conditions in respect of sub-clause 13.7/13.8 [Adjustments for Changes in Costs] and sub-clause 14.3[15] for the requirements to be able to enter escalation values so that the Service Provider can assist the Service User to prepare the required documentation at the time of the implementation of the audit by the BPKP.

11.7 Applicable legislation for Indonesian governing law of the contract

11.7.1 Entry into a construction contract

The construction contract as a form of agreement is a legal product and therefore, as a legal product, it must follow legal principles. In this case the Construction Work Contract is inseparable from the principle of the engagement, namely the occurrence of a legal event that binds the parties. The juridical principles for construction contracts are contained in in Book III of the *Civil Code of Indonesia* re: Agreement, Articles 1233 to Article 1864.

Specific obligations related to Construction Work Contract agreements are regulated in *Law No 2 of 2017 Construction Services* in Articles 46–51. Article 46 states that the arrangement of work relations between Employer/Owner and Service Providers must be set forth in a written Construction Work Contract. According to *Law No 2 of*

15 2017 Red and Yellow Book sub-clause 14.3(ii); 1999 Red and Yellow Books sub-clause 14.3(b).

2017 Article 1(8), Construction Work Contracts are defined as all contract documents that regulate the legal relationship between Employer/Owner and Service Providers in the provision of Construction Services. Article 49 states that the provisions of the Construction Work Contract as referred to in Article 47 also apply to the Construction Work Contract between service providers and sub-service providers.

More details on the implementation of *Law No 2 of 2017* are provided in the rules in Article 75 paragraph 2 of *Government Regulation No 22 of 2020*, which states that Construction Work Contracts are subject to applicable laws in Indonesia. Therefore, as discussed in paragraph 11.4.1 above, it is mandatory to use Indonesian law as the governing law of a construction contract in Indonesia.

Another important provision related to the validity of construction contracts in Indonesia that must be considered relates to the ruling language of the contract used in construction contracts, especially for contracts made with foreign parties. Since the enactment of *Law No 24 of 2009 regarding Flag, Language, National Emblems and the National Anthem* (*UU Bahasa Indonesia*), there have been many court decisions related to the use of a foreign language (English) in agreements made between Indonesian citizens or Indonesian legal entities with foreigners or foreign legal entities. One of the most well-known verdicts was the verdict that cancelled the loan agreement between PT Bangun Karya Pertama Lestasri and Nine AM for violating *UU Bahasa Indonesia* Article 31 paragraph (1). Related to this dispute, in June 2013, the West Jakarta District Court issued a decision which declared that a contract not drafted in the Indonesian language was null and void.[16] After that case, a number of private contract cases have been resolved by the State Court, the High Court and the Supreme Court, where almost all of the decisions cancelled the agreements written in foreign languages. It has influenced industries in Indonesia to use governing language clauses and translation clauses into foreign language agreements based on freedom of contract and *pacta sunt servanda*.

The language for Construction Work Contracts in Indonesia is regulated in Article 50 of *Law No 2 of 2017 Construction Services*. This article can be interpreted that it requires Construction Work Contracts to be made in Indonesian and enforces Indonesian as the applicable language in any dispute over a bilingual Construction Work Contract.[17] In this regard, *Government Regulation No 22 of 2020* stipulates that the documents comprising a Construction Work Contract are: (i) a letter of agreement signed by the parties; (ii) particular conditions of contract; (iii) general condition of contract; (iv) Employer documents (Employer requirement); (v) proposals or offers; (vi) minutes or certificate containing agreements between the Employer and Contractor during the evaluation of proposals or offers; (vii) a statement from the Employer who agrees to the Contractor's proposal; and (viii) a letter of commitment from the Contractor. This matter leads to an interpretation that all documents which are part of a Construction Work Contract need to be made in Indonesian or enforce Indonesian as the applicable language if there is a dispute over a bilingual Construction Work Contract. Therefore, it is important for foreign entities, which plan to enter into

16 The West Jakarta District Court Decision No 451/Pdt.G/2012/PN. Jkt.Bar dated 10 July 2013.

17 Under art 50 of the New Construction Services Law, construction work contracts are made in Indonesian. However, the Construction Work Contract carried out with a foreign party must be made in Indonesian and English, where in the event of a dispute with a foreign party, the Indonesian version is used.

a contract with an Indonesian party to have the Indonesian draft of the agreement ready prior to signing.

11.7.2 Termination of a construction contract

As discussed in paragraph 11.5.1.2 above, applicable legislation for Indonesian governing law of the contract related to termination of a contract in general are in Article 1266 and Article 1267 of the *Civil Code*. For a construction contract in Indonesia, specific regulations are in *Law No 2 of 2017 Construction Services*.

There is no detailed provision regarding the termination of a construction contract in *Law No 2 of 2017 Construction Services* nor in *Government Regulation No 22 of 2020 regarding Implementation Regulation of Law No 2 of 2017*. *Law No 2 of 2017* Article 47 only requires that a construction contract at a minimum shall include a provision regarding the termination of the contract:

> (i) [T]ermination of the Construction Work Contract, contains provisions regarding termination of the Construction Work Contract arising from failure to fulfill the obligations of one of the parties.

This provision is in line with clauses 15 and 16 of the FIDIC rainbow suite which contain provisions concerning matters that can lead to termination of the contract by one party due to default of the other party. There are no other detailed provisions found in *Government Regulation No 22 of 2020*.

However, other regulations that are enforced in the event of a contract termination due to the circumstances of one of the parties 'becomes bankrupt or insolvent, goes into liquidation, has a receiving or administration order made against him, compounds with his creditors, or carries on business under a receiver, trustee or manager for the benefit of his creditors, or if any act is done or event occurs which (under applicable Laws) has a similar effect to any of these acts or events',[18] are regulated under *Law No 37 of 2004 regarding Bankruptcy and Delay of Payment Obligation j.o Constitutional Court Decision number 071/PUU-II/2004;001–002/PUU-III/2005 j.o Law No 40 of 2014*. Care should be taken to ensure that the provisions of sub-clauses 15.4 and 16.4 relating to the details of the process and the terms of payment after termination are consistent with the provisions of this law.

11.7.3 Dispute resolution of construction contracts

In Indonesia, for commercial contracts including construction contracts, the available steps in dispute resolution can be through the courts (litigation) and institutions outside the court (non-litigation) or alternative dispute resolution (ADR). In general, the arrangements for the implementation of arbitration and ADR out of court (non-litigation) are regulated in *Law No 30 of 1999 Arbitration and Alternative Dispute Resolution*. Specifically, dispute settlement mechanisms outside the court (ADR) for a construction contract are regulated in more detail in *Law No 2 of 2017 Construction Services* and *Government Regulation No 22 of 2020*

18 1999 Red and Yellow Book sub-clauses 15.2(e) and 16.2(g) and Silver Book sub-clauses 15.2(e) and 16.2(f). Similar provisions are in 2017 Red and Yellow Book sub-clauses 15.2.1(g) and 16.2.1(i) and Silver Book sub-clauses 15.2.1(g) and 16.2.1(h).

regarding Implementation Regulations of Law No 2 of 2017. The stages of the dispute settlement of a construction contract are regulated in *Law No 2 of 2017 Article 88* as explained in paragraph 11.5.3.1 above.

11.7.3.1 Execution of foreign arbitration awards

The majority of FIDIC contracts in Indonesia are carried out with foreign parties, where the parties may agree on the choice of arbitration seats in foreign arbitration institutions. In this case the enforceability of a foreign arbitration award in Indonesia is an important matter for the parties.

Based on *Law No 30 of 1999 Arbitration and Alternative Dispute Resolution*, Article 66 states that international arbitration awards are only recognised and can be implemented in the jurisdiction of the Republic of Indonesia, if they meet the following requirements:

a. International arbitration awards are issued by an arbitrator or an arbitral tribunal in a country with which Indonesia is bound by an agreement, either bilaterally or multilaterally, for the recognition and implementation of an international arbitration award, and the country of the seat of arbitration is a signatory to the *New York Convention*, and recognised and enforced awards rendered in Indonesia.
b. International arbitration awards are limited to decisions which according to the provisions of Indonesian law fall within the scope of commercial law and are limited to decisions that do not conflict with public order based on Indonesian laws and regulations. Therefore, any disputes that include any fraud, criminal act or corruption for example cannot be decided by arbitration.
c. International arbitration awards can only be implemented after obtaining executor approval from the Supreme Court of the Republic of Indonesia which has been delegated to the Central Jakarta District Court.
d. International arbitration awards can be implemented in Indonesia after obtaining execution decision from the Head of the Central Jakarta District Court.

Further according to Article 67 of *Law No 30 of 1999*, the application for implementation of the international arbitration award shall be made after the decision has been submitted and registered by the arbitrator or the recipient of his power of attorney to the Registrar of the Central Jakarta District Court.

If the Head of the Central Jakarta District Court decides to recognise and implement an international arbitration award, the decision cannot be appealed. However, if the Head of the Central Jakarta District Court refuses to implement an international arbitration award, an appeal or cassation may be filed against the decision of the Central Jakarta District Court which refuses pursuant to Article 68 paragraph (1) and (2) of *Law No 30 of 1999*. After the Head of the Central Jakarta Court issues an execution order, the further execution will be delegated to the Head of the District Court who is authorised to carry it out the decision.

The process of executing international arbitration awards and the implementing regulations are detailed in the *Supreme Court Regulation No 1 of 1990 regarding Procedures for Implementing Foreign Arbitration Awards*.

11.8 Summary of applicable legislation for Indonesian governing law of the contract

11.8.1 Entry into a construction contract

Contracts generally	*Book III of Civil Code of Indonesia re: Agreement, Articles 1233–1864*
Construction contracts	*Law No 2 of 2017 Re: Construction Services*

11.8.2 Operation of a construction contract

Guarantees under forms of Security	*Law No 2 of 2017 Construction Services* *Government Regulation No 22 of 2020 j.o No 14 Of 2021 Re: Implementation of Law No 2 of 2017*

11.8.3 Termination of a construction contract

Termination under the law	*Civil Code Articles 1265–1267*
Bankruptcy, insolvency, liquidation	*Law No 37 of 2004 Re: Bankruptcy and Delay Of Payment Obligation j.o Constitutional Court Decision number 071/PUU-II/2004;001–002/PUU-III/2005 j.o Law No 40 of 2014*

11.8.4 Dispute resolution

Limitation periods	*Civil Code Article 1946–1996*
Arbitration	*Law No 30 of 1999 Arbitration and Alternative Dispute Resolution* *Supreme Court Regulation No 1 of 1990 Re:Procedures for Implementing Foreign Arbitration Awards.*

11.9 Summary of applicable legislation if the Site/Country is in Indonesia

11.9.1 Operation of a construction contract

Registration and administration of professionals – Engineers, Architects, Quantity Surveyors, Certifiers, Building Surveyors, Surveyors	*Law No 11 Year 2020 Re: Job Creation* *Law No 02 Year 2017 Re: Construction Services* *Law No 11 Year 2014 Re: Engineering* *Law No 06 Year 2017 Re: Architect* *Government Regulation No 25 Year 2019 Re: Implementation of Law No 11 Year 2014* *Government Regulation No 22 Year 2020 Re: Implementation of Law No 02 Year 2017*
Registration/licencing of Contractors and subcontractors	*Law No 02 Year 2017 Re: Construction Services* *Government Regulation No 22 Year 2020 Re: Implementation of Law No 02 Year 2017*
Labour	*Law No 13 Year 2003 Re: Labour*
Copyright	*Law No 28 Year 2014 Re: Copyright*

The product being produced from the Works	Port and Harbour (Terminal Operation): *Law No 17 Year 2008 Re: Shipping* *Government Regulation No 61 Year 2009 Re: Harbour* *Government Regulation No 20 Year 2010 Re: Transportation in territorial sea* Railway Infrastructure (Rail, Station and other Railway facilities): *Law No 23 Year 2007 Re: Railways* *Government Regulation No 50 Year 2009 Re: Railways operation.* *Government Regulation No 72 Year 2007 Re: Traffic and Railway Transportation.* Airport: *Law No 1 Year 2009 Re: Air Transportation* Electricity (Power Plant, Transmission and Distribution): *Law No 30 Re: Electricity* *Law No 27 Year 2003 Re: Geothermal* *Government Regulation No 59 Year 2007 Re: Geothermal Operation and Business* *Government Regulation No 3 Year 2005 Re: Changing of Government Regulation No 10 Year 1989 Re: Utilization of Geothermal for Electricity Business* Water Supply (Water processing, Transmission and Distribution): *Law No 17 Year 2019 Re: Water Resources* Road and Toll Road: *Law No 38 Year 2004 Re: Road* *Government Regulation No 15 Year 2005 Re; toll Road* *Government Regulation No 44 Year 2009 Re: Changing on Government Regulation No 15 Year 2005* *Law No 22 Year 2009 Re: Traffic and Road Transportation*
Land Acquisition	*Law No 2 Of 2012 Re: Land Acquisition* *Presidential Regulation No 102 Of 2016 Re: Funding for Land Acquisition for Development for Public Interest in the Context of Implementing National Strategic Projects* *Presidential Regulation No 148 Of 2015 Re: Fourth Amendment to Presidential Regulation No 71 of 2012 concerning Implementation of Land Acquisition for Development for Public Interest*
Planning	*Law No 17 Year 2007 Re: National Long Term Development Plan Year 2005–2025* *Government Regulation No 17 Year 2017 Re: Synchronization of Planning and Budgeting Process for Government Projects*
Heritage	*Law No 11 Of 2010 Re: Cultural Heritage*
Environment	*Law No 32 of 2009 Re: Protection and Management of Environment j.o Constitutional Court Decision No 18/PUU-XII/2014*
Local procurement	*Presidential Regulation No 16 Of 2018 Re: Government Procurement j.o Presidential Regulation No 12 Year 2021*
Building and construction permits, Execution of construction work, Standard of construction work	*Law No 28 Year 2002 Re: Building*
Health and safety	*Ministry of Public Works and Housing No 02/PRT/M/2018 Re: Guidelines for Occupational Safety and Health Management Systems*
Insurance	*Law No 40 Of Year 2014 Re: Insurance*

(*Continued*)

11.9.2 Termination of a construction contract

Bankruptcy, insolvency, liquidation	*Law No 37 of 2004 Re: Bankruptcy and Delay Of Payment Obligation j.o Constitutional Court Decision number 071/ PUU-II/2004;001–002/PUU-III/2005 j.o Law No 40 of 2014*
Decennial liability and liability generally for the total or partial collapse of structures	*Law No 02 Year 2017 Re: Construction Services* *Government Regulation No 22 Year 2020 Re: Implementation of Law No 02 Year 2017*

11.9.3 Dispute resolution

Dispute before a local board/Adjudication	*Law No 02 Year 2017 Re: Construction Services* *Government Regulation No 22 Year 2020 Re: Implementation of Law No 02 Year 2017 Article 93–96*
Limitation periods	*Civil Code Article 1946–1996*

11.10 Applicable legislation if the 'seat' of the dispute determination in Indonesia

11.10.1 Dispute resolution for a construction works contract

In general, the arrangements for the implementation of Arbitration and ADR out of court (non-litigation) are regulated in *Law No 30 of 1999 Arbitration and Alternative Dispute Resolution*, with the exception of the use of a Dispute Board, which is regulated in *Government Regulation No 22 of 2020, Implementation Regulations of Law No 2 of 2017* Articles 93–96.

Law No 2 Year 2017 provides for a three-step process of dispute resolution for a Construction Works Contract: first mediation, second conciliation and third arbitration. The first and second step can be replaced by using ***Dewan Sengketa*** or a DAB/DAAB under a FIDIC Contract.

A construction dispute is first resolved by way of deliberation (negotiation) to reach a consensus; if it cannot be resolved through deliberation the next stage emphasises settlement outside the court (non-litigation). In this *Law*, the settlement of litigation by a court is no longer included in the stages of dispute resolution efforts, except in cases involving general crimes, corruption, or crimes related to building failure in project work.

The stages of efforts to resolve construction disputes according to *Law No 2 of 2017* are regulated in the provisions in Chapter XI Article 88 as explained under paragraph 11.5.3.1. Article 88 provides that the stages of dispute resolution efforts include mediation, conciliation, and arbitration. As an alternative to the dispute resolution efforts for the stages of mediation and conciliation, the parties can appoint a Dispute Board.

11.11 Summary of applicable legislation if the 'seat' of the dispute determination is in Indonesia

Lawsuit	*Indonesian Civil Code Article 1338* *Indonesian Procedure of Civil Law*

Dispute of Construction Services	*Law No 2 Year 2017, Re: Construction Services* *Government Regulation No 22 Year 2020, Re: Implementation Regulations of Law No 2 of 2017*
Dispute of Construction Services Especially for Government Construction Project	*President Decree No 16 Year 2018 Re: Government Procurement of Goods and Services* *Regulation of the National Public Procurement Agency (NPPA) (LKPP) No 9 Year 2018* *Ministry of Housing and Public Works Regulation No 14 Year 2020 Standards and Guidelines for Procurement of Construction Services Using Services Providers*
Arbitration and Alternative Dispute Resolution	*Law No 30 Year 1999, Re: Arbitration and Alternative Dispute Resolution* *Law No 48 Year 2009, Re: Judicial Power* *Regulation of the Supreme Court of the Republic of Indonesia No 1 Year 2016, Re: Mediation Procedures in Courts*

11.12 Issues that a court or arbitrator may construe differently to that expected from the words of the Contract, because of local law or custom

Sub-clause 20.1 [Contractor's Claims] of the 1999 FIDIC General Conditions sets out the detailed requirements for the Contractor to submit a claim, that is a notice of a claim which must be submitted by the Contractor to the Engineer 'as soon as practicable, and not later than 28 days after the Contractor became aware, or should have become aware, of the event or circumstance'. If the Contractor fails to give notice of a claim within such period of 28 days, the Time for Completion shall not be extended, the Contractor shall not be entitled to additional payment, and the Employer shall be discharged from all liability in connection with the claim.

Sub-clause 2.5 [Employer's Claims] of the 1999 FIDIC General Conditions sets out the detailed requirements for the Employer to submit a claim to the Contractor 'as soon as practicable after the Employer became aware of the event or circumstances giving rise to the claim.' There is no specific provision for a time-bar or time limitation of the claim submission nor is there any consequence for the failure of the Employer or the Engineer to do so 'as soon as practicable'.

Comparing sub-clauses 2.5 and 20.1, there are unbalanced provisions and consequences between the Contractor and the Employer related to their rights on applying for a claim. The Contractor, besides being bound to a stricter time frame is also obligated to a due care requirement in identifying its claim by the words: 'or should become aware', where such requirement is not imposed on the Employer nor the Engineer. The consequence of the Contractor's failure to comply with the provisions of sub-clause 20.1 result in loss of the fundamental right to make a claim. However, this harsh consequence is not forced upon the Employer, another imbalance between the Employer and the Contractor. It is also necessary to consider the absence of a definition or meaning of phrase 'as soon as practicable' as well as the phrase 'event or circumstances'. Considering the complexity of a construction project, the circumstances itself will depend on verifiable facts or conditions. Clearly, there is a room for debate on the interpretation of those phrases.

This comparison could be viewed as an unduly imbalanced provision in the favour of the Employer by judges in judicial proceedings. A judge in Indonesia has the power to decide a case on the principle of ***ex aequo et bono***,[19] as judges have the freedom to decide disputes not only on rigid legal provisions but also on the principle of justice. On this basis, a judge or arbitrator who is requested to decide based on this principle may not apply the strict consequences of article 20.1, on the basis of fairness standards based on the law. The principle of fairness and balance are mentioned in the *Law No 2 of 2017 Construction Services* in Article 2 that regulate the principles in Construction Services in Indonesia; all construction contracts shall comply with these principles.

Other provisions in the Indonesian *Civil Code* that need attention are related to the enforceability of Article 20.1, namely Article 1967 which regulates Past Time/ Expiration (*Verjaring*), that all lawsuits, both material and individual are nullified due to the passing of an elapsed time of 30 years. The Time Limit/Expiration (expiry date) according to Article 1967 is the deadline for filing all claims or lawsuits against other parties, a right both material and individual in nature. Once the time limit has passed, one or more parties will be unable to file claims against a right, and one of the parties will be released from responsibility.

More specific provisions on the duration of the Time Limit/Expiration (expiry date) for construction work contracts are referred to in *Civil Code* Article 1971 which states that:

> [T]he demands of carpenters, masons and other masons for payment of the materials they provide and their wages; this demand only concerns to the work and delivery that does not concern the debtor's permanent job; all of that is past time with the passage of five years.

Thus, in that provision, the time limit for filing and waiving a claim is within a period of five years.

Based on consideration of an unduly imbalanced provision in the favour of one party, the time limit based on the applicable laws explained above and the principle of equity before the law, a judge or arbitrator may not enforce the 28 day time-bar provision stipulated in sub-clause 20.1 of the 1999 rainbow suite.

11.13 Additional references for Indonesia

11.13.1 Legislation

Legislation referred to in this chapter are found in the Indonesian language. Unofficial translations into English have been used for the purposes of drafting this chapter in English.

11.13.2 Journals

Sarwono Hardjomuljadi, 'Use of Dispute Avoidance and Adjudication Boards' [2020] *Journal of Legal Affairs and Dispute Resolution in Engineering and Construction, American Society of Civil Engineers.*

11.13.3 Internet

Supreme Court of Indonesia: www.mahkamahagung.go.id
Indonesia legal documentation and information network: www.jdihn.go.id

19 A Latin phrase meaning according to the right and good.

CHAPTER 12

Applying FIDIC contracts in Japan

Naoki Iguchi and Kaori Sugimoto

DOI: 10.4324/9781003200901-12

12.1 Outline of the legal environment in Japan

12.1.1 The constitutional structure of Japan

The *Constitution* (3 May 1947) adopted the parliamentary cabinet system. The *Constitution* also established the Supreme Court as the ultimate judicial authority to interpret and apply the national and local laws as well as the *Constitution* (Article 76(1)).

The Cabinet undertakes public administrative functions, unless otherwise set out in the *Constitution*. The central government consists of Ministerial Departments. The Prime Minister designates heads of the Ministerial Departments from the Cabinet members. As to the construction industry, the Ministry of Land, Infrastructure, Transport and Tourism (**MLIT**), headed by the Minister of the MLIT (**MLIT Minister**), is in charge of the regulation of the construction industry and the procurement and management of national infrastructure projects.

The *Constitution* also adopts the principle of local autonomy (Article 92). The *Local Autonomy Act* (Act No 67 of 1947[1]) sets out further details of the organisation and operation of the local governments. As of 2020, there are 47 Prefectures and more than 1800 Municipalities. Each tier of local government is given authority by law for (i) the regulation of the construction industry, and (ii) the procurement and management of local infrastructure.

12.1.2 The legal system of Japan

When Japan introduced European systems in the 19th century, it adopted a civil law system. The fundamental law applicable to commercial transaction is the *Civil Code* (Act No 89 of 1896). Japan also adopted the principle of freedom of contract, which is restricted by 'public policy and morals' (*Civil Code*, Article 90); however, in practice, it is quite rare that the courts vacate a contract due to the violation of public policy and morals. The *Civil Code* provides that a party's representation of its intent prevails over the law unless it conflicts with mandatory provisions (*Civil Code*, Article 91).

The *Civil Code*, when first enacted in 1896, modelled the French and the draft German *Civil Codes*. Recently, in light of developments of common law in international transactions, Japan introduced some common law perspectives in the *Civil Code* revision project in 2017. The newly revised *Civil Code* came into force from April 2020.

Local public governments may legislate their local laws (***jorei***) in accordance with the national law framework. In the context of construction business, most local laws are concerned with environmental and city planning regulations.

12.1.3 The court system of Japan

The Supreme Court is the ultimate judicial organ. As inferior courts, there are eight High Courts, 50 District Courts (with their 100 branches) and over 430 Summary Courts.

The *Code of Civil Procedures* (Act No 109 of 1996) (***CCP***) applies to civil procedure in court. The first instance courts are the District Courts and the Summary Courts. An appeal may be made to the High Courts or the District Courts.

1 We usually use refer to codes and statutes by the year of its first enactment, while almost all codes and statutes have been amended from time to time.

Japan does not have the doctrine of *stare decisis*; however, the Supreme Court's judgment or decision is *de facto* binding on the subordinate courts. If the Supreme Court finds it necessary to change its precedents, it carefully reviews the case and declares that it alters the precedent.

12.2 The construction industry in Japan

12.2.1 Structure

In 2019, investment in the construction industry was valued at JPY 62.1 trillion, (US$600 billion) consisting of approximately 11.2 per cent of the whole GDP (by reference to expenditure).[2] The industry employs more than 4 million employees,[3] working in more than 460,000 licensed companies. There are about 40 construction companies listed on the Tokyo Stock Exchange.

12.2.2 Licensing/registration

12.2.2.1 Requirement to obtain a construction business licence

The *Construction Business Act* (Act No 100 of 1949) (***CBA***) requires a contractor who intends to operate a construction business in Japan, regardless of its nationality, to obtain a construction business licence for the types of the construction works it will undertake. The licences are given by (i) the MLIT when the contractor establishes offices (head office, branch offices or equivalent) in more than two Prefectures, or (ii) the Prefectural Governor having jurisdiction over the area where the office is located only in one Prefecture (Article 3). Contractors who only undertake small-scale construction works[4] are exempt from the aforementioned requirements.

12.2.2.2 Types of construction business licence

The licences are categorised into two types: (i) the Ordinary Licence and (ii) the Special Licence. If a contractor intends to retain subcontractor(s) and the aggregate of the contract price amount(s) to be paid to such subcontractor(s) exceeds JPY 40 million (US$384,000) (in case of architectural and construction business, JPY 60 million (US$575,000)) for a particular construction work project, the contractor is required to obtain and maintain the Special Licence. In all other cases, the contractor has to obtain and maintain the Ordinary Licence.

The licence is valid for five years. If a contractor desires to continue its licence, the contractor would need to apply for renewal of the licence no less than 30 days before the expiry date, and have such application approved.

---

2 Research Institute of Construction and Economy, 'RICE Report N0.72, April 2020' 2-3.

3 https://built.itmedia.co.jp/bt/Arts/1904/01/news026.html (accessed 10 October 2020).

4 Exemption requirements are:

(a) As to general architectural and construction work, the contract price amount is less than JPY15 million (US$145,000) or the total floor space of the wooden residence to be constructed is less than 150 square meters; or,

(b) As to construction work other than general architectural and construction work, the contract price amount is less than JPY5 million (US$48,000).

12.2.2.3 Requirements to obtain a construction business licence
In order for a contractor to obtain a licence, the contractor is required to satisfy all of the following four requirements (*CBA*, Article 7). The *CBA* also provides certain disqualification grounds (*CBA*, Article 8). The following chart shows the requirements to obtain an Ordinary Licence and a Special Licence.

	Ordinary Construction Business Licence	*Special Construction Business Licence*
1. Full-time officer being responsible for managing operations	**One full-time officer**: experience requirements (eg five years or more experience of being responsible for managing operations in relation to the construction work for which the contractor wishes to be licensed (the **Subject Works**)).	
2. Full-time engineer	A **full-time engineer** who complies with one of the items below: (i) Experience in the Subject Works (a) for not less than five years following graduation from a senior high school or a secondary school or (b) for not less than three years after graduation from a university or a college with credit in the specified subjects by the MLIT; (ii) Experience in the Subject Works of not less than ten years; or (iii) Certified by the MLIT to possess experience or qualifications equivalent to or higher than those in sub-item (i) or (ii).	(i) Passed certain technical certification or examination for the Subject Works; (ii) (a) Fulfilment of all the requirements to be a full-time engineer for an ordinary construction business licence and (b) two years or more experience of being in a supervisory position for construction work, the contract price for the performance of which is more than JPY 45 million (US$430,000); or (iii) Certified by the MLIT to possess experience or qualifications equivalent to or higher than those in sub-item (i) or (ii).
3. Not likely to commit unfair or dishonest act	The officers and the representatives of its branches or offices must not be considered likely to commit an **unfair or dishonest act** with regard to any contract.	
4. Financial Status and Credibility	(i) Having more than JPY5 million (US$48,000) in equity capital; (ii) Having the ability to raise more than JPY5 million (US$48,000) in funds; or (iii) Having operated a construction business in the past five years immediately before applying for renewal of a construction business licence	(i) The total amount of its debt obligations is less than 20 per cent of the value of its capital stock; (ii) Having current asset to current debt ratio of more than 75 per cent (iii) More than JPY20 million (US$192,000) of the capital stock and more than JPY 40 million (US$384,000) in equity capital

12.2.3 Labour relations

The *Labour Standard Act* (Act No 49 of 1947) and other labour laws strictly protects employed labourers. Furthermore, the *Employment Security Act* (Act No 141 of 1947) generally prohibits a 'labour hire' (***haken-rodo***), only allowing a labour hire business under the strict requirements set out in the *Act on the Appropriate Operation of the Worker Dispatching* (ie Labour Hire) *Business and the Protection of the Dispatched Workers* (ie *Labour Hire Employees)* (Act No 88 of 1985). The legal principle is that the labour hire employees shall not be directed nor supervised by the labour hire purchasers at the workplace; otherwise, the employer may easily escape the employee protections – the Japanese law so assumes. Such an evasion of law is known as the 'Camouflaged Contractor' (***giso-ukeoi***), which is strictly regulated by the authorities, and may be sanctioned criminally if the violation is serious.

12.2.4 Safety culture

The *Worker's Safety and Health Act* (Act No 57 of 1972) (***WSHA***) is the fundamental statute that regulates the safety conditions of construction works. The subordinate ordinances sets out detailed regulations, specifically relating to the machinery, equipment, materials and hazards used or produced in works and operations: boilers and pressure vessels, cranes, gondola, organic solvent poisoning, lead poisoning, tetra alkyl lead poisoning, ionising radiation hazards, and asbestos. The *WSHA* also requires licences and skill training to handle certain machinery and equipment.

12.2.5 Modular construction using factory fabricated components

The Japan Prefabricated Construction Suppliers and Manufacturers Association has been established as an independent certification organisation for prefabricated housing and building.

12.2.6 Technology/innovation/BIM

BIM has become popular for major building works. Furthermore, the Government also proactively promotes BIM like technologies for public civil works, calling them with a unique name as *i-construction* or CIM. In fact, the MLIT first published its Draft Guideline for the Introduction of CIM in 2016, which contains a general guideline and detailed guidelines for various types of projects, such as earth works, river works, dam construction, bridge construction and tunnelling works. The MLIT has been revising the guidelines almost every year.

12.2.7 Government/private sector procurement

12.2.7.1 Private procurement

Apart from the *Act on Prohibition of Private Monopolisation and Maintenance of Fair Trade* (Act No 54 of 1947) (*Antitrust Act)* and its subordinate orders, there are no special laws or regulations applicable to private procurement activities in the construction field. Private project Employers are free to set up their own procurement procedures and standards. Certainly, the *Antitrust Act* strictly prohibits cartels.

In practice, it is common for Contractors to form a non-incorporated joint venture to make a bid and to undertake a project. It is unfortunate that since many of the joint venture agreements are not well-drafted, there have been many joint venture disputes between Contractors.

12.2.7.2 Public procurement

The *Public Accounting Act* (Act No 35 of 1947) and *the Local Autonomy Act* (Act No 67 of 1947) deal with public procurement procedures. These laws provide for the following types of procedure for public procurement: (i) open competitive tender; (ii) restricted competitive tender; and (iii) negotiated contract. After the enactment of the *Act on Promoting Quality Assurance in Public Works* (Act No 18 of 2005), the Government adopts a comprehensive evaluation of bids, not confined to price competitiveness but also focussing on quality. Criminal sanctions apply to persons who commit serious violations of procurement procedures, eg cartel, graft, etc.

The *Act on Promotion of Private Finance Initiative Funds* (Act No 117 of 1999), ignited a boom in PFI projects. Since the PFI projects contemplated project finance debts, the project finance market developed as the PFI market expanded.

12.2.8 Insurance requirements

12.2.8.1 Compulsory insurance

It is mandatory to procure and maintain (i) labour insurance in accordance with the *Employment Insurance Act* (Act No 116 of 1974) (ie the Act setting forth the benefits for workers who are unemployed, etc.) and the *Worker's Accident Compensation Insurance Act* (Act No 50 of 1947) (ie the Act setting forth the benefits to workers who suffer from work-related injury, disease, disability or death) (***WACIA***) and (ii) social insurance in accordance with the *Health Insurance Act* (Act No 70 of 1922) (ie the Act setting forth the insurance benefits for sickness, injury or death other than work-related injury, etc.) and the *Employees' Pension Insurance Act* (Act No 115 of 1954) (ie the Act setting forth the insurance benefits for workers' old age, disability and death).

12.2.8.2 Non-compulsory insurance

In practice, Contractors are often required in a contract to purchase and maintain (i) liability insurance covering personal injury and damage to property; (ii) fire insurance; (iii) automobile insurance; and (iv) product liability insurance. Although the Contractor may purchase an insurance for a single project, a general liability insurance covering a Contractor's liability for all projects is more popular for Japanese companies.

12.2.9 Common forms of contract

12.2.9.1 Public works

For public construction works for which the basic design is provided by the Employer, the Central Government published the Public Work Standard Contract (**PWSC**) as General Conditions for public construction works. Local Governments have their own modified versions based on the PWSC.

Design and build contract forms are far less used than the PWSC. In fact, there is no published version of a design and build form for public works. The Japan Society of Civil Engineers published the General Conditions for Design and Build for Public Civil Works in 2017, however, it has not become popular.

Unfortunately, it does not seem that the FIDIC contracts are used for public work projects.

12.2.9.2 Private works

For private construction works for which the basic design is provided by the Employer, the Committee of Seven Associations of Architects and Contractors (*minkan (nanakai) rengo kyotei koji ukeoi keiyaku yakkan iinkai*) published the General Conditions for Construction Contract (last amended in April 2020) (**GCCC**), which has become quite popular.

As a design and build contract form, the Japan Federation of Construction Contractors published the General Conditions for Design/Build Contract (**GCDB**) (last amended in April 2020). A unique feature of the GCDB is that the design part and the construction part are separable. In other words, the GCDB requires both Parties to confirm continuing the works after completion of the design, which means an Employer and a Contractor may renegotiate a price for the construction works. Accordingly, it should be noted that even the concept of design and build is significantly different to that in international construction practice.

For domestic plant construction projects, the Engineering Advancement Association (**ENAA**) publishes the ENAA General Conditions for Domestic Plant Construction Work (last amended in 2020) (**ENAA-Domestic**). The ENAA-Domestic is a turnkey contract under which the Contractor undertakes design, procurement, construction and commissioning, with a lump-sum fixed price.

The ENAA also publishes the following sets of international contract forms (collectively, the **ENAA-Internationals**):

- ENAA Model Form International Contract for Process Plant Construction (2010 Edition)
- ENAA Model Form International Contract for Power Plant Construction (2010 Edition)
- ENAA Model Form International Contract for Engineering, Procurement and Supply for Plant Construction (2013 Edition).

Recently, particularly in the field of off-shore wind and wave power stations, FIDIC contracts have been used in some projects. Since foreign investors/contractors/manufacturers have some advantages in this field, they request to use the FIDIC contracts as General Conditions for design and build and/or EPC contracts. However, because the traditional domestic practice largely differs from the practice based on the FIDIC contracts, it seems that there are many misunderstandings and confusions among Japanese parties and lawyers.

For example, Japanese parties and lawyers really dislike Notices of Claims given in the middle of the execution of the Works, since they do not understand the real purpose of the Notices – sharing the information of the claim events as soon as practically possible. They just deem Contractor's frequent Claim Notices as Contractor's aggressive postures. Sometimes, inexperienced parties and lawyers fail to respond to the Claim Notices – or even ignore them. They often say that the Employer will 'take care of it' after the completion of the Works. Contractors are hesitant to go further to dispute resolution procedures. This kind of practice may exacerbate the potential magnitude of disputes and cause serious frustrations between the Parties at the end of the project.

Since most of the off-shore wind and wave power projects are still in the preliminary stages, there are almost no court precedents where the Japanese courts have set out their understanding of FIDIC contracts. It may take some time for the Japanese parties and lawyers to understand and be familiar with the framework and the concepts in the FIDIC contracts.

12.2.9.3 Most commonly used

The GCCC is the most widely used standard form contract for a domestic construction project. In addition, Japanese parties prefer to use it for projects overseas where both of the Parties are Japanese. Since the GCCC contains provisions which are not familiar to foreign parties (somewhat ambiguous terms if compared with those in the international forms), foreign parties do not easily accept the use of the GCCC. At the least, it is necessary to prepare clear and detailed Special/Particular Conditions to modify the GCCC to bring it more in line with international practice.

For international projects where Japanese parties are involved, international standard forms are often used, such as the FIDIC contracts and the ENAA-Internationals. FIDIC contracts are often used in ODA projects funded by JICA since it recommends FIDIC contracts as General Condition in its standard bidding documents for JICA-funded projects. This is discussed in more detail in paragraph 5.4 above.

12.2.10 Dispute resolution – litigation, arbitration, Dispute Boards

12.2.10.1 Litigation at court

Except for small claims, the District Courts are the first instance courts. Parties may agree to select a specific court, including foreign courts, as the court for the first instance's jurisdiction (CCP, Articles 3–7 and 11). A judgment of foreign courts will be recognised and enforced by the judgment of the Japanese courts, as long as the judgment meets specific requirements given in the CCP (Article 118).

The Japanese courts generally prefer written submissions. Following the Complaint (*sojo*) and the Answer (***tobensho***), the Parties are allowed to submit the Memorials (***jumbi-shomen***) together with Exhibits several times. An average time-period for the first instance proceedings for commercial disputes is around two years, unless the Parties amicably settle at an early stage. Although witnesses are examined by direct and cross-examination, the style of witness examination largely differs from those in the common law jurisdictions. For example, the time period given to each witness is generally two hours at the longest. Interpreters are usually limited to court-appointed interpreters from the court's house list. Usually, the quality of these interpreters is not acceptable for commercial disputes, as it is far lower than the quality of party-appointed professional interpreters in international arbitration. Party-appointed experts are rarely summoned by the courts – the courts prefer to retain their own expert from the court's house list. Document disclosure requests are rarely allowed by the courts. Considering these fundamental differences, it is strongly recommended that international parties should refer any disputes to international arbitration.

12.2.10.2 Court-sponsored mediation

Since housing defect disputes are common in urban areas, Tokyo and Osaka District Courts have the Building Dispute Department (*kenchiku-bu*) (**BDD**). If a complaint is filed at the Tokyo or Osaka District Court, even a large commercial construction dispute may be assigned to the BDD. However, it should be noted that the BDD's experience is limited to domestic building disputes, particularly for housing disputes. Most of the judges and lawyers are not familiar with the concepts commonly used in international construction practice, such as Extension of Time for Completion, Taking-Over Certificate, Claim Notices, time-bars, disruption and acceleration. Furthermore, the Japanese courts, including the Building Dispute Department, do not like to allow party-retained experts to give testimony; rather, the department has its own undisclosed list of Japanese experts, who sit as a member of the Mediation Committee (*chotei-iinkai*) together with a judge for an amicable settlement, or a kind of advisor for the judges. If either party does not wish to accept a settlement proposal arranged by the Mediation Committee, the case will be sent back to regular litigation where the same judge will preside over the procedure.

Considering the strong, deep-seated domestic nature of Japanese courts, it is highly recommended that international parties refer any disputes to international arbitration, rather than to court-sponsored mediation.

12.2.10.3 *Kensetsu-Funso-Shinsa-Kai*

The *CBA* implements the Construction Dispute Adjudication Board (*Kensetsu-Funso-Shinsa-Kai*) (**KFSK**) for Government-sponsored alternative dispute resolution (Article 25). There are 47 local KFSKs and a single central KFSK (in Tokyo). Their jurisdiction is determined by the registered office of the respondent/claimant or the construction site in question. Central and local Governments appoint a panel of mediator-arbitrators. The KFSK is not the same as a Dispute Adjudication Board in the FIDIC contracts. The KFSK is only suitable for domestic disputes.

Considering the strong, deep-seated domestic nature of Japan's courts, it is highly recommended that international parties refer their disputes to international arbitration, rather than to court-sponsored ADR.

12.2.10.4 Arbitration

Japan is a member state of the *1958 New York Convention*. Furthermore, Japan enacted the *Arbitration Act* (Act No 138 of 2003) modelled on the 1985 UNCITRAL Model Law but has not adopted its 2006 amendments. Although arbitration is not a popular dispute resolution method for domestic disputes, the courts are trying to take an arbitration-friendly position.

As explained in the preceding paragraphs, international arbitration is highly recommended for international parties.

12.2.11 Unique features of the construction industry in Japan

Japanese parties generally prefer stipulating a provision of consultation/discussion in good faith in a construction contract without specifying the specific procedure when the Parties fail to reach an agreement to resolve the issue like sub-clauses 20 [*Employer's and Contractor's Claims*] and 21 [*Disputes and Arbitration*] of the FIDIC contracts.

Also, even if a dispute arises, Japanese parties prefer to avoid referring a dispute to any kind of dispute resolution procedure, and try to resolve the dispute through negotiation, particularly when the Employer is a Government body, or a main contractor and a contractor have a long-standing business relationship.

12.2.12 Current challenges

Recently, a growing number of foreign parties have entered into the infrastructure and construction market in Japan. However, typical Japanese standard form construction contracts usually are not suitable for a construction contract between foreign and Japanese parties. Many disputes are now beginning to occur between foreign and Japanese parties, due to ambiguous provisions in typical Japanese standard form construction contracts. As such, Japanese parties have recently started to amend typical Japanese standard form construction contracts to make them acceptable for international parties; however, since the Japanese parties and lawyers are not exposed to the terms and concepts in international construction practice, there are many confusions and misunderstandings. The Japanese parties should consider using international standard forms as a basis for the contract even for domestic projects if the owner is the foreign entity.

12.3 The impact of Covid-19 in Japan

12.3.1 The impact of Covid-19 on the execution of construction projects in Japan

12.3.1.1 Prohibition on construction

On 7 April 2020, the Government proclaimed a State of Emergency (**SOE**) for major cities pursuant to the *Act on Special Measures against New Types of Influenza, etc.* (Act No 31 of 2012). On 16 April 2020, the declaration was extended to the rest of the country. In the SOE, local Governments were empowered to 'request' people not to go outside (including not to go to the office if remote work was available); however, the SOE did not give local Governments the power to 'order' it, and any breaches thereof were not subject to any penalty. However, most of the Japanese companies, including construction companies, abided by the request, and almost all of the construction works were suspended during the period of the SOE.

The SOE was cancelled in May. Soon after that, many of the construction projects were resumed.

12.3.1.2 Constraints on working on construction sites

The MLIT drafted and published a Guideline regarding the preventive measures against Covid-19 dated 14 May 2020 (**MLIT Covid-19 Guideline**)[5].

5 https://www.mlit.go.jp/common/001360076.pdf (accessed 2 December 2020). In addition to the MLIT COVID-19 Guideline, the Government encouraged each business association to prepare and publish its own guideline suitable for each kind of works and operations. Such business associations include: The National Association of Construction Businesses (*Zenkoku-Kensetsugyo-Kyokai*), The Japan Federation of Construction Contractors (*Nihon-Kensestugyo-Rengokai*), and The Association of Electricity and Telecommunication Engineering for Land and Infrastructure (*Kensetsu-Denki-Gijyutsu-Kyokai*).

The MLIT Covid-19 Guideline recommends minimising face-to-face meetings on site, staggering break times and attendance times, to avoid 'three C's' (***san-mitsu***) (ie closed spaces, crowded places, close-contact settings).

12.3.1.3 Health and safety constraints on employees

The MLIT Covid-19 Guideline recommends that the workers wear face masks or face shields while working on site.

The MLIT Covid-19 Guideline also recommends that, in order to avoid heatstroke, (i) the personnel use face shields rather than face masks during the summer period, (ii) the personnel may take off face masks if personnel are more than 2 metre distance apart outside the office, and (iii) the personnel also wear air-conditioned clothing.

12.3.1.4 Health and safety constraints on the normal operation of a construction site

The MLIT Covid-19 Guideline recommends keeping a physical distance from others of at least 2 metres, checking and recording body temperature. The MLIT Covid-19 Guideline also recommends periodic sterilisation of equipment and facilities, air ventilation, and limiting the number of workers in confined areas.

12.3.1.5 Health and safety requirements after a confirmed Covid-19 infection

The MLIT Covid-19 Guideline recommends that the Contractor's supervisor on site, after consultation with the public health centre, (i) cause the infected personnel and other personnel who had a close contact with the infected personnel to stay home and (ii) deeply sterilise the area where the infected personnel worked.

The MLIT Covid-19 Guideline does not require the immediate suspension of construction work after a confirmation of Covid-19 infection

12.3.1.6 Constraints on travel

The Ministry of Foreign Affairs has given alert and recommended not to travel to the alert Level 2[6] and the alert Level 3[7] countries.

Upon arrival from any regions, Japanese nationals are requested to fill in a questionnaire, to measure their body temperature and to take an antigen test and wait to get the result in the designated area in the airport. Japanese nationals are requested to stay home or in other accommodation for two weeks. They are requested not to use public transportation. Japanese nationals are requested to fill in and declare the place to stay and the transportation measures from the airport to the place into the questionnaire. If they violate those declarations, they may be subject to a penalty under the *Quarantine Act* (Act No 201 of 1951).

Non-Japanese residents are subject to additional requirements (eg obtaining a re-entry permit, providing a certificate of a test proving the result is negative) to enter into Japan after arrival from any regions.

---

6 Level 2 indicates that 'non-essential travels are not recommended'.

7 Level 3 indicates that 'cancel to travel is recommended'.

In late September 2020, Japan and Singapore set up the Green Lane for business travellers. In December 2020 Japan discussed extending the Green Lane with other countries such as China, South Korea, Thailand and others. The Green Lane enables travellers from the designated regions to conduct certain limited business activities during the 14 day self-quarantine period after entry into Japan.

12.3.1.7 Changes to regular employment law

There were no special regulations which changed the normal employment law. The Government enacted general subsidy programmes for companies which suffered difficulties in keeping their employees.

12.3.1.8 Financial support

Businesses facing a decrease in sales by 50 per cent or more on a year-on-year monthly basis due to the effects of Covid-19 were eligible for the subsidy program, called the Subsidy Program for Sustaining Businesses. This program did not apply to large businesses with over JPY 1 billion (US$9.6 million) of capital because the Government targeted small and mid-size businesses rather than large ones.

12.3.2 The impact of Covid-19 on the operation of construction contracts in Japan

The non-performance of obligations under a contract due to Covid-19 has been widely debated in Japan. From March to May 2020 when the SOE was declared, it may have been interpreted that Covid-19 falls within a *force majeure* event.[8] However, after the cancellation of the SOE, it became difficult to interpret that Covid-19 itself falls within *force majeure*. The MLIT Covid-19 Guideline also assumes that the construction projects continue. As of December 2020, it had not been reported that the Covid-19 pandemic occurred in construction sites. However, since Japan experienced a third wave of Covid-19 in the fall and winter of 2020, this situation may not have continued.

It is also reported that some of the major construction projects suffered delay in progress – the major one is the Hokuriku Bullet Train (*Hokuriku Shinkansen*) Extension Project. According to the news, Covid-19 is not the only reason for the delay; however, the Japan Railway Construction, Transport and Technology, the Employer for the project, is considering announcing a two-year delay to the commencement of operations. Furthermore, it is also reported that in some of the offshore wind power projects, serious delays were caused by the ceasing of operation of the offshore platform providers.

8 The remedies for force majeure under Japanese law are limited.

(i) an obligee may not demand further performance from an obligor to the extent further performance is prevented due to the events not attributable to the obligor (Civil Code, art 412-2(1));

(ii) an obligee may not demand compensation for damages from an obligor (Civil Code, art 415(1)); and

(iii) an obligee may terminate a contract if an obligor fails to perform the obligation despite a demand within a reasonable period and the non-performance is material (*Civil Code*, art 541).

12.4 Japanese governing law of the contract

12.4.1 Constraints on the governing law of a construction contract

The Parties may choose a governing law[9] other than Japanese law as the governing law of the contract for construction work carried out in Japan (Article 7 of the *Act on General Rules for Application of Laws* (Act No 78 of 2006)). However, in public procurement projects, the Government usually does not accept any foreign law as the governing law. Also, even if the Parties have chosen a foreign law as the governing law, administrative laws applicable to the construction project in Japan will apply in any event. For example, if the Contractor executes the construction work without obtaining the required licence under the *CBA*, the Contractor would be subject to the sanction under the *CBA* regardless of the governing law.

The *CBA* only empowers an authority to regulate construction businesses and sanction construction companies which breach the *CBA*. It does not invalidate any provisions of the contract; however, it takes an important role by imposing *de facto* constraints against the substance of the contract, because the authority may revoke a company's business licence for violation of the *CBA*.

For example, although pay-when-paid[10] or pay-if-paid[11] clauses are commonly used in international construction subcontracts, these clauses are restricted in Japan.

First, within one month of the main Contractor's receipt of the reward/consideration paid by the Employer for the Works, the main Contractor shall pay to a Subcontractor, as compensation for the Subcontractor's services in performing the executed works, a portion of such reward/consideration for the executed works performed by that Subcontractor, compared against the value of the total works (*CBA*, Article 24-3(1)).

Secondly, if the main Contractor is a Special Licence holder, the main Contractor shall pay the reward/consideration to a Subcontractor within 50 days after the date of application by that Subcontractor and within as short a period as possible, regardless of the Contractor's receipt of payments from an Employer (CBA, Article 24–5(1)).

Also, the *Act against Delay in Payment of Subcontract Proceeds, Etc. to Subcontractors* (Act No 120 of 1956) (***Delayed Payment Act)*** applies to subcontracts for services other than the construction work (eg design work, material manufacturing work). A main Contractor shall make payment to a Subcontractor within 60 days or earlier, from the day on which the main Contractor receives the work from that Subcontractor, regardless of whether or not the main Contractor inspects the work in detail (*Delayed Payment Act*, Article 2-2(1)).

Art 2-2(2) of the *Delayed Payment Act* further provides that:

(i) If the date of payment to a Subcontractor is not provided, the date of payment to the Subcontractor shall be the date on which the main Contractor receives the proceeds from the Employer as a consideration of the works completed by the Subcontractor, and

9 There is a controversy in Japan as to whether a 'non-state law' (such as the UNIDROIT Principles) may be chosen as the governing law.

10 A pay-when-paid clause is a clause which stipulates a payment condition that establishes a reasonable time for the main Contractor to comply with its duty to make payment to a Subcontractor upon the main Contractor's receipt of payment from the Employer.

11 A pay-if-paid clause is a clause which requires payment from the Employer as a condition precedent to the main Contractor's duty to make payments to a Subcontractor.

(ii) If the date of payment to a Subcontractor provided in the subcontract is in violation of Article 2-2(1) of the *Delayed Payment Act*, the date of payment to the Subcontractor shall be the date prior to the date on which 60 days have elapsed after the main Contractor receives the proceeds from the Employer as consideration of the works completed by the Subcontractor.

12.4.2 Formal requirements for a construction contract

The *CBA* requires the Parties to specify certain items in writing, sign or affix a registered seal and exchange documents (*CBA*, Article 19(1)). This requirement applies to any contract for construction work in Japan regardless of whether the governing law of the contract is Japanese law or not.

The following items need to be included in a construction contract.

(a) Scope of Work
(b) The amount of the contract fee
(c) The date for the commencement of and the completion for the construction work
(d) When agreements are made concerning the advance payment of all or part of the contract fee or payments based on completion, the date and the method of the payment
(e) Provisions regarding changes to the period of construction, changes to the amount of the contract fee and payment of damages and the method of calculation for the amount in the event of a request from one of the parties for design changes, extension of the commencement of construction or suspension of all or part of the construction work
(f) Provisions regarding changes to the period of construction due to natural disasters and other *force majeure* events and the payment of damages and the method for calculating the amount
(g) Changes in the amount of the contract fee or the content of the construction work based on fluctuations or changes in prices, etc
(h) Provisions regarding the payment of compensation in the event of losses or damage to a third party caused by the execution of the construction work
(i) Provisions regarding the details and method for the use when the Employer supplies material used in the construction work or leases construction equipment and other machinery
(j) The date and method for the Employer to conduct an inspection in order to confirm total or partial completion of the construction work and the date of transfer
(k) The date and method for payment of the contract fee following completion of the construction work
(l) When a guarantee and insurance agreement is concluded or other measures are stipulated regarding liability of defects in the construction work and the fulfilment of said liability, the content of the agreement or measure
(m) Interest for arrears, damages for breach of contract and other damages in the event of delays in fulfilment by either party or non-fulfilment of other obligations
(n) Method of resolution for disputes concerning the contract.

The *CBA* further requires that any changes to any of the items above must also be specified in writing and both Parties must sign or affix a registered seal and exchange documents (*CBA*, Article 19(2)). The Parties usually prepare and execute an amendment agreement to comply with this *CBA* regulation, even though many of the construction contracts including the GCCC have a change mechanism.

12.5 What Special Provisions in the Particular Conditions are necessary for consistency with applicable laws in Japan?

12.5.1 FIDIC General Conditions that are incompatible or inconsistent with Japanese governing law of the contract

12.5.1.1 Overview

Generally, the provisions of FIDIC contracts are not incompatible or inconsistent with the provisions of Japanese law, since Japanese law adopts the principle of freedom of contract. However, Japanese law may impose additional obligations on the Parties, unless it is specifically derogated from. In order to ensure that FIDIC contracts operate as they are intended and provide a comprehensive statement of the Parties' rights and obligations, it is necessary to insert certain Special Provisions in the Particular Conditions to exclude application of the non-mandatory Japanese law provisions.

As stated in paragraph 12.2.9 above, as the domestic practice in Japan largely differs from international practice, some parties and lawyers misunderstand and say that the terms and conditions adopted in FIDC contracts may not be valid under Japanese laws, which is not true. However, to avoid any further misunderstanding and confusion, it is it is highly recommended that the Parties should set out all terms and conditions clearly and in detail.

12.5.1.2 Limitation period for liability

12.5.1.2.1 STATUTE OF LIMITATIONS

It should be noted that Japan takes a unique position as to the statute of limitations (**shometsu-jiko**) (*Civil Code*, Book 1, Chapter 7).

First of all, generally Parties do not have complete freedom to deviate from the provisions in the *Civil Code*; however, the agreement of the parties on a shorter period for liability has been accepted.

Secondly, limitation periods apply to substantive rights, which means if a statute of limitations applies, a substantive right is extinguished. The *Civil Code* provides a general statute of limitations as follows (*Civil Code*, Article 166(1)[1][2]):

- Five years after an obligee becomes aware that it is entitled to exercise a right
- Ten years after an obligee becomes entitled to exercise a right.

It should be noted that, by the 2017 reformed *Civil Code*, the Japanese law abolished a short period for defect liability. In fact, the defect liability was replaced by a non-conformance (***keiyaku-futekigo***) liability in the 2017 reformed *Civil Code* (*Civil Code*, Article 562). Although the substantial meanings of defect and non-conformance are almost the same, the period for the non-conformance liability is significantly different to that for the former defect liability. In short, unless otherwise agreed by the Parties, the period for the non-conformance liability may be much longer than the Defect Notification Period or DNP set out in the FIDIC contracts (ie Clause 11 [*Defects after Taking Over*]). The period for the non-conformance liability is as follows:

- An Employer shall notify a Contractor of its awareness of the non-conformance within one year after an Employer becomes aware of the existence of non-conformance to the contract (*Civil Code*, Article 637(1)), unless the Contractor was aware of or should have been aware of the existence of non-conformance at the time of delivery (*Civil Code*, Article 637(2)).
- An Employer is also required to exercise the rights to remedies under the non-conformance liability (ie demand for remedy, compensation for damages, deduction from the Contract Price or termination) before the expiration of the long stop date (ie five years after the Employer becomes aware of the existence of non-conformance and ten years after the Works are delivered to the Employer (*Civil Code*, Article 166(1)[1][2]).

As may be clear, the period runs from the date when an Employer becomes aware of the non-conformance, not from the date of delivery/completion, which may cause a large uncertainty in the length of the period for liability.[12] The period for the non-conformance liability can be illustrated as follows in Figure 12.1:

Last but not least, the non-conformance liability is not mandatory. Parties are free to agree to different terms, including but not limited to, the defect liability terms in the FIDIC contract.[13]

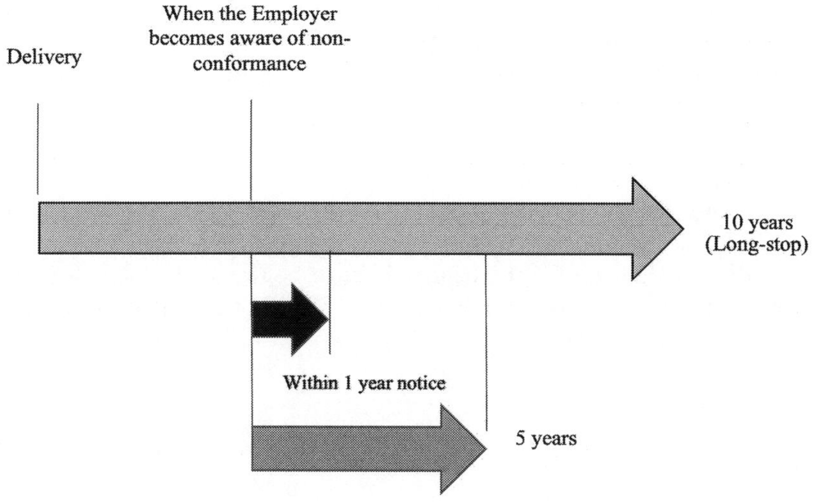

Figure 12.1 Period for the Non-Conformance Liability.

12 Even the GCCC explicitly excludes the application of art 673[1] of the *Civil Code* (GCCC, art 27-2[7]).

13 Under the *Housing Quality Assurance Act* (Act No 81 of 1999), the defect liability period for newly constructed housing is 10 years after the delivery (art 94[1]). This is a mandatory provision and the Parties are not allowed to agree to a shorter period (art 94[2]).

12.5.1.2.2 ON-CONFORMANCE LIABILITY UNDER THE *CIVIL CODE*

If non-conformance liability is simply compared with the DNP in the FIDIC contracts, it is much longer than the DNP. This is because the non-conformance liability is not a special liability originated by the contract terms. It is a general liability which generally continues for 10 years (to the long-stop date). It does not need sub-clause 11.10 [*Unfulfilled Obligations*] to make the Contractor's obligation clear, because it exists as a matter of law and continues to exist for 10 years from delivery as a consequence of the *Civil Code*. It may be a heavy burden for a Contractor.

In addition to the liability period, since the non-conformance liability is a kind of general obligation, legal consequences are much stronger than the defect liability set out in the FIDIC contracts. In case of non-conformance, an Employer may (i) request remedial works (*Civil Code*, Article 562); (ii) claim damages (*Civil Code*, Article 415); (iii) reduction of payment (*Civil Code*, Article 563); and (iii) terminate the contract (*Civil Code*, Article 541). The big difference is in the Employer's entitlement to termination. It is not clear why the lawmakers did not seriously consider any restraints to termination; however, in fact, in construction projects, it may cause a big problem if an Employer terminates the Contract after completion and/or delivery.

If the Parties intend that the non-conformance liability under the *Civil Code* applies, it is highly recommended that they set out a reasonable mechanism to (i) permit the discovery of any serious non-conformance after completion and/or delivery (ie setting up suitable check-ups, inspections, examination, testing and any other measures suitable to make sure the quality and function of the Works); and (ii) set up reasonable remedies in case of serious non-conformance. A set of the provisions of the FIDIC General Conditions also need to be excluded, because the Japanese law may conflict with, or at least may cause some confusion with, the non-conformance to the Contract (*keiyaku-futekigo*) liability under Japanese law.

Alternatively, it is also recommended to consider adopting the whole mechanism set out in FIDIC's Clause 11 as the sole remedy.

12.5.1.2.3 FIDIC'S CLAUSE 11 AS THE SOLE REMEDY

If the Parties intend that the FIDIC Clause 11 [*Defects after Taking Over*] should be the sole remedy for defect liability, it is necessary to insert a Special Provision in the Particular Conditions that the FIDIC Clause 11 is to be the sole remedy for defects, excluding the Japanese law on non-conformance liability. Since the relevant provisions of the Japanese law are not mandatory, Parties are free to agree to any form or type of defect liability.

12.5.2 FIDIC General Conditions that are incompatible or inconsistent with the law of the Site/Country

In this section, the FIDIC provisions referred to are to the 2017 FIDIC Yellow Book.

12.5.2.1 Labour

Sub-clause 6.4 [*Labour Laws*] requires the Contractor to comply with all the relevant labour laws applicable to the contractor's personnel. Certainly, this FIDIC contract's position is compatible and consistent with the Japanese law.

Applicable laws are:

- *Labour Standard Act* (Act No 49 of 1947) (*LSA*)
- *WSHA*
- *Working Environment Measurement Act* (Act No 28 of 1975) and
- *WACIA*, etc.

Most of the provisions of these laws are mandatory. These laws would apply as long as the working Site is located in Japan, regardless of whether the labourers are Japanese or non-Japanese.

FIDIC sub-clause 6.5 [*Working Hours*] provides that

> No work shall be carried out on the Site locally recognised days of rest, or outside the normal working hours stated in the Contract Data, unless:
>
> (a) otherwise stated in the Contract;
> (b) the Engineer givers consent; or
> (c) the work is unavoidable or necessary for the protection of life or property or for the safety of the Works, in which case the Contractor shall immediately give a Notice to the Engineer with reasons and describing the work required.

However, this clause will be subject to the regulations relating to the working hours under the *LSA*. In principle, the working hours must be eight hours per day and 40 hours per week (*LSA*, Article 32). If an employer and a labour union or an employee's representative enter into a labour management agreement (***roshi-kyotei***), the working hours may be extended. Under the *Act on the Arrangement of Related Acts to Promote Work Style Reform* (Act No 71 of 2018), the working hours may be extended up to 45 hours per month and 360 hours per year. However, if there is a special reason, the working hours may be extended up to 720 hours per year subject to the following requirements:

- The extension for working hours is limited to six months per year.
- The average overtime hours per month (including work on holidays) may not exceed 80 hours in any period of two months, three months, four months, five months and six months.
- Overtime hours in any month (including work on holidays) must be less than 100 hours per month.

This new Act will be applicable to the construction industry (except for a construction project for disaster restoration) from 1 April 2024. This regulation is mandatory and cannot be changed by the agreement of the parties. Accordingly, after 1 April 2024, Contractors in principle may not cause their personnel to work for hours exceeding the limitation under the new Act despite the provision of sub-clause 6.5. It would be appropriate to include a Special Provision in the Particular Conditions to the effect that the provisions of the *Act on the Arrangement of Related Acts to Promote Work Style Reform* (Act No 71 of 2018) limit working hours, notwithstanding the provisions of sub-clause 6.5.

12.5.2.2 Subcontractors

FIDIC sub-clause 4.4 [*Subcontractors*] prohibits the Contractor from subcontracting works with a total accumulated value greater than the percentage of the Accepted Contract Amount stated in the Contract Data (if not stated, the whole part of the

Works). The *Civil Code* and other private laws do not prohibit an engagement of a subcontractor.

The *CBA*, although it only empowers the authority to regulate and sanction construction companies and does not invalidate the contract provision, provides certain restrictions as to subcontracting. If a general contractor is an Ordinary Licence holder, it may subcontract the works with the value of less than JPY 40 million (US$384,000) (in case of architectural and construction business, JPY 60 million (US$575,000). On the other hand, if a general contractor is a Special Licence holder, it may also retain any subcontractor(s) for the works with the value of more than JPY 40 million (US$384,000) (in case of architectural and construction business, JPY 60 million (US$575,000)).

Also, the *CBA* prohibits a main Contractor for the construction works from subcontracting the whole Works contracted for to another operator by any means (*CBA*, Article 22(1)).[14] It is recommended to insert a Special Provision in the Particular Conditions specifically limiting the extent of subcontracting to the limits provided in the *CBA*.

In the majority of industrial plant construction projects, ie EPC, an Employer often instructs a Contractor to employ a nominated supplier and/or Subcontractor. Unlike sub-clause 4.5 [*Nominated Subcontractors*] in the FIDIC contracts, domestic parties and lawyers rarely set out any detailed provisions with respect to the nomination of the subcontractors in the contracts. As a result, in a case where such a supplier and/or Subcontractor becomes incapable of providing services or products due to the reasons uncontrollable by the Contractor, the Contractor and the Employer easily come into a dispute phase. It is highly recommended for the Parties to set out clear and detailed provisions on risk allocation between the Parties.

12.5.3 FIDIC General Conditions are incompatible or inconsistent with the laws of the seat of the arbitration or relevant laws on dispute determination

It should be noted that adjudication by a DAB or DAAB is not a known concept in Japan. Although it is allowed as a contractual dispute resolution mechanism, it is unlikely to be considered arbitration. Accordingly, it may confront difficulties at the enforcement stage.

Another practical problem is that there are very few candidates who can conduct the adjudication procedure and make a 'decision' in accordance with the FIDIC contracts. It is not a problem to appoint foreign adjudicators for projects located in Japan; however, the problem is language, unless all management documents are prepared in English.

One practical option is to make the FIDIC style adjudication waivable (and make all disputes directly referrable to arbitration), but this is not consistent with the FIDIC Golden Principles (see paragraph 2.4 above).

14 This restriction shall not apply when (i) the construction work to be subcontracted is the work other than a facility utilised by a large number of people or important construction work related to building provided for by a Cabinet order and (ii) the main Contractor has obtained the written consent of the Employer in advance (*CBA*, art 22 (3)).

12.6 What Special Provisions in the Particular Conditions are desirable for consistency with applicable laws in Japan?

12.6.1 Summary

As explained in the preceding paragraphs, there is no provision in the FIDIC contracts which is incompatible or inconsistent with mandatory provisions of Japanese law, since the Parties have freedom of contract to agree on their contract terms. However, as explained above, the domestic practice in Japan largely differs from the international practice reflected in the FIDIC General Conditions. To avoid any further misunderstanding and confusion, it is highly recommended that the Parties should set out all terms and conditions clearly and in detail as to whether they adopt the domestic practice or the international practice for each issue. We recommend that the terms and conditions generally used in international practice, including but not limited to the FIDIC contracts, be used because those terms and conditions are clear-cut. The following list highlights the most important issues in which there is a large difference between the domestic practice in Japan and international practice:

- Allocation of ground risk
- Proving entitlements to extension of time
- Variations to the Works
- Valuation of Variations.

12.6.2 Allocation of ground risk

There is no legal theory which provides a specific allocation of ground risks. Many of the typical contracts merely provide that, if any unforeseeable physical conditions are found during the execution of the Works, the Parties shall discuss it in good faith.

The GCCC treats a ground risk problem differently from the FIDIC contracts. The 'physical conditions, geological features, underground water conditions' and 'ground pollution, adverse underground obstructions, or possible buried cultural property' may entitle a Contractor to 'request the other party to change the Contract Time or the Contract Sum which is recognized as necessary'. The GCCC provides as follows:

ARTICLE 16. AMBIGUITY AND DISCREPANCY IN DRAWINGS, SPECIFICATIONS AND CONDITIONS

(1) If the Contractor discovers that any of the following events has occurred, the Contractor shall immediately so notify the Owner or the Administrative Architect in writing:

a. (omitted);
b. Any discrepancy between the actual conditions and those indicated in the Design Documents, etc. as to matters such as the physical conditions, geological features, underground water conditions or the restrictions on execution of the Work at the Site; or
c. Any obstruction to execution of the Work at the Site that was not foreseeable, such as ground pollution, adverse underground obstructions, or possible buried cultural property.

(2) (omitted)
(3) The Owner (or, if the Owner entrusts the services in this paragraph to the Administrative Architect, the Administrative Architect) will, upon receipt of

the notification provided in paragraph (1) or (2) of this Article or upon its own discovery of the facts enumerated in paragraph (1) of this Article, immediately give instructions to the Contractor in writing.

(4) In the case of paragraph (3) of this Article, the Owner or the Contractor may request the other party to change the Contract Time or the Contract Sum which is recognised as necessary.

The GCCC's solution is to refer the discovered ground risk to the change mechanism. However, the change mechanism in the GCCC is so ambiguous that two serious problems often arise. First, the change mechanism does not provide a clear and detailed method of the adjustment of the Contract Sum – it does not differentiate cost from profit. The Employer always takes a position allowing the Contractor the lowest cost possible; in the meantime, the Contractor always requests additional costs and reasonable profit. Secondly, the change mechanism, as stated in paragraph 12.6.4, does not give an immediate solution to the Parties. Unless otherwise agreed by the Parties, the problem is carried over until the time of completion. That means, the Contractor needs to continue its work without any guarantee of the additional payment of costs and profit.

The ENAA-Domestic provides a similar provision. It provides that:

Art 16(4) If any soil contamination, underground obstructions, buried cultural assets, or other unforeseeable circumstances relating to the underground conditions of the site are discovered, the Employer and the Contractor shall engage in discussion regarding the measures to be taken.

Art 16(5) If it is determined to be necessary as a result of the consultations specified in Article 16(4), either party may make a request to the other party for change of the scope of the Contractor's work, the completion date, or the contract price.

ENAA-Internationals have detailed provisions on the ground risks:

GC35 Unforeseen Conditions

35.1 If, during the execution of the Works, the Contractor shall encounter on the Site any physical conditions (other than climatic conditions) or artificial obstructions that could not have been reasonably foreseen at the date of the Agreement by an experienced contractor on the basis of reasonable examination of the data relating to the Works (including any data as to boring tests) provided by the Owner and of information the Contractor could have obtained from a visual inspection of the Site (if access thereto was available) or other data readily available to it relating to the Works, and if the Contractor determines that it will in consequence of such conditions or obstructions incur additional cost and expense or require additional time to perform its obligations under the Contract which would not have been required if such physical conditions or artificial obstructions had not been encountered, the Contractor shall promptly, and before performing additional work or using additional Materials or Construction Equipment and Facilities, notify the Owner in writing of:

(a) the physical conditions or artificial obstructions on the Site that could not have been reasonably foreseen; and
(b) the additional work, Materials, and/or Construction Equipment and Facilities required including the steps which the Contractor will or proposes to take to overcome such conditions or obstructions; and
(c) the extent of the anticipated delay; and
(d) the additional cost and expense which the Contractor is likely to incur.

35.2 Any additional cost and expense incurred by the Contractor to overcome such physical conditions or artificial obstructions referred to in GC 35.1 shall be paid by the Owner to the Contractor as an addition to the Contract Price.

35.3 If the Contractor shall be delayed or impeded in the performance of the Contract due to any such physical conditions or artificial obstructions referred to in GC 35.1, the Time for Completion shall be extended in accordance with GC 40 (Extension of Time for Completion).

If the Contract is silent or ambiguous as to the allocation of ground risk, the Japanese courts tend to interpret that the ground risk is the Contractor's responsibility. As such, it is important for the Contractor to check whether provisions exist relating to the allocation of ground risk in the construction contract and who is contemplated to undertake the ground risk.

To avoid any ambiguities, it is highly recommended that the Parties specifically agree on the allocation of the ground risks. It should be clearly stated in the Contract on what documents and Site data prepared or collected by the Employer the Contractor is undertaking the Works.

12.6.3 Proving entitlements to extension of time

There is no legal theory expressly providing Contractor's entitlements to extension of time (**EOT**). In domestic practice, the Parties and lawyers prefer to use the term 'change to the contract time', rather than the term EOT.

It should be noted that Parties are free to agree to an EOT in the contract; however, in many cases, Parties fail to set out a mechanism for an EOT, or do not agree to a workable mechanism for an EOT. The GCCC provides certain provisions regarding the 'change' of the completion date:[15]

Article 17(4)	[WORK NOT EXECUTED IN COMPLIANCE WITH CONSTRUCTION DOCUMENTS, ETC.]
Article 19(5)	[DAMAGE TO THIRD PARTY]
Article 20(2)	[DAMAGE ARISING OUT OF OR RELATING TO EXECUTION OF WORK]
Article 23-2 (6)	[STATUTORY INSPECTION]
Article 28	[CHANGES IN WORK AND CHANGES IN CONTRACT TIME]
Article 31(3)	[OWNER'S RIGHT TO SUSPEND WORK OR TERMINATE CONTRACT FOR ITS CONVENIENCE]

However, these provisions do not provide a mechanism to determine whether an EOT is allowed, and how long extension is allowed. An Employer is not obliged to respond to the Contractor's 'request'. Some Employers and lawyers even think that they can leave the Contractor's request untouched until the actual completion of the Works. In fact, the Employer is not obliged to respond to the Contractor's request within a certain period of time. In such a case, the Contractor has to continue execution of the Works without knowing when the extended time for completion would be. To make the matter worse, many of the domestic parties and lawyers understand that such provisions only allows a Contractor to commence a 're-negotiation' on the time for completion. On the other hand, Contractors sometimes fail to prepare contemporaneous records which would have been helpful for substantiating the EOT.

15 The GCCC provides that (i) the Employer may demand the change of the completion date if necessary to the reasonable extent (GCCC, art 28(1)), (ii) the Contractor may propose the change of the completion date, and upon approval of the Employer, the completion date is changed (GCCC, art 28(2)) and (iii) the Contractor may claim for the change of the completion date under certain circumstances (eg due to the event attributable to the Employer) (GCCC, art 28(6)).

There is no explicit provision under the Japanese law addressing who owes a burden of proof of the Contractor's entitlements to extension of time. In general, it is interpreted that a Party who claims for entitlements of extension of time is required to prove that it has such entitlements. Time-analysis methods have not developed, and no guidelines or protocols, such as the '*Delay and Disruption Protocol*' published by the Society of Construction Law, are published in Japan. Lacking guidelines and protocols for time-analysis, it is embarrassing that a party's re-negotiation is likely to be a bare commercial negotiation, reflecting the parties' commercial bargaining power. Contractors are often pressed by Employers to give up additional costs (and profit) in consideration of obtaining additional time. Lacking contemporaneous and powerful evidence which is prepared timeously at the time of the EOT events, the Contractors often have no other options but to accept the Employer's offer to settle.

Having said that, it is strongly recommended to set out clear and detailed terms and conditions for EOT, and to refer the dispute to international arbitration Furthermore, the Employers and the Engineers are often hesitant to unilaterally determine how many days are to be extended. Normally, both the Employer and the Contractor discuss and aim to reach an agreement regarding the extension of time. If both Parties fail to reach an agreement, the dispute will be ultimately resolved by the Japanese court, but the court does not have a standard or expertise to determine it. Again, international arbitration is strongly recommended.

12.6.4 Variations to the Works

This is one of the most important issues and area which has large gaps between international and domestic practices. This is because the Japanese parties and lawyers are often confused whether the changes are made to the whole agreement or just to the scope/volume of the Works.

The *CBA*, although it only empowers the authority to regulate and sanction construction companies and does not invalidate the contract provisions, provides formal requirements for changes. It stipulates that, (i) the Parties to a construction contract are required to stipulate certain understandings (including the amount of the Contract Price) in writing, sign or affix a registered seal impression on such written agreement, and exchange such written agreements (*CBA*, Article 19); and (ii) any changes to those understandings stipulated in the signed/sealed written agreement must also be specified in a writing which is signed or sealed by the Parties and exchanged in the same manner (*CBA*, Article 19-2).

From a private law perspective, there are no clear guidelines as to whether the Employer is entitled to issue Variations which directly contradict the Contract and the Contractor's rights; however, Parties are free to agree to a particular change/Variation mechanism in the contract. The GCCC explicitly provides that the Employer is entitled to order additional or extra works or changes in the Works and, if such order is issued, the Contractor makes a claim for a necessary adjustment to the Contract Price:

ARTICLE 28. CHANGES IN WORK AND CHANGES IN CONTRACT TIME

(1) The Owner may, if necessary, order additional or extra Work or changes in the Work.

The ENAA-Domestic provides:

Article 28: Change to the Contractor's Works and to the Completion Date

(1) In addition to the cases where otherwise provided in this Contract, the Owner may, when necessary, make a request to the Contractor to a reasonable degree for change of the Plant specifications or particulars or the Contractor's services or change of the completion date. In this case, if it is determined that commissioning preparations cannot be completed by the completion date as a result of the modification of the Contractor's services, the Contractor may request a necessary change of the completion date.

Reading this GCCC provision, it seems that an Employer may issue a Variation order with which the Contractor is required to comply. However, it should be noted that the GCCC also stipulates that a Contractor is entitled to (i) request an adjustment to the Contract Sum (GCCC, Article 29) and (ii) claim 'damages' due to the Employer's order for change from a private law perspective. It is not clear enough what 'damages' mean in a context of change to the work.

12.6.5 Valuation of Variations

There is no theory or mechanism for the valuation of Variations in the Japanese law.

In practice, if an Employer issues a Variation order, a Contractor generally complies with it. The GCCC provides that a Contractor may claim for a change of or adjustment to the Contract Sum if the original amount of the Contract Sum becomes unreasonable as a result of change to the Contractor's scope of work or the completion date (GCCC, Article 29). However, the GCCC does not provide when the additional amount of the Contract Price should be paid to the Contractor.

It is strongly recommended that the Parties agree in the Contract a valuation mechanism, such as how the varied works would be evaluated and when the additional amount would be paid to the Contractor.

12.6.6 The duty of Employers to pay for changes

First of all, if Parties agree to a mechanism for payment for changes, that mechanism will be enforceable under the Japanese law. However, in the domestic practice, Parties and lawyers usually set out ambiguous provisions such as 'parties shall discuss in case of any change to the works'. In such a case, neither the amount nor the timing of payment is clear.

Secondly, as to whether a Contractor is entitled to claim for the additional payment, the courts generally awarded an additional amount to the Contractor based on the 'implied agreement' or 'party's reasonable intent' theories, even in a case where Parties did not or could not reach an agreement on additional payment (see paragraph 12.11.3). However, the courts never presented a clear theory for calculating the adjustment.

Thirdly, the GCCC sets forth the following:

ARTICLE 29. ADJUSTMENT OF CONTRACT SUM

(1) In addition to those particularly provided in the Contract, the Owner or the Contractor may, by expressly stating the reason therefor, make a claim for a necessary adjustment to the Contract Sum due to any of the following causes:

a. If additional or extra Work or changes in the Work is ordered;
b. If the Contract Time is changed;
c. If additional or extra cost is incurred due to coordination in accordance with the provisions of Article 3 hereof;
d. If there are changes in the items, quantities, times for delivery, places of delivery, or places for return of the Furnished Materials or the Lent Articles;
e. If, during the term of the Contract, the Contract Sum has become apparently inappropriate and improper due to an enactment, revision, or abrogation of any law, ordinance, or regulation, drastic change in economic conditions, or any other unforeseeable cause;
f. If, in a long term contract, the amount of the Contract Sum corresponding to any portion of the Work that shall have been executed hereunder after the first anniversary of conclusion of the Contract is inappropriate and improper due to an enactment, revision, or abrogation of any law, ordinance, or regulation or due to any change in commodity prices, wages, and other such matters; or
g. If the amount of the Contract Sum for the Work which has been suspended or affected by disaster, becomes apparently inappropriate and improper when such Work is resumed

Item a. may work for additional payment for changes, and item b. may give a basis for an EOT; however, neither of the items provide a clear basis for additional costs and profit, and EOT, as provided in the FIDIC contracts.

The ENAA-Domestic provides:

Article 29: Adjustment of Contract Sum
In addition to the cases where otherwise provided in this Contract, if any of the following items applies, the Owner or the Contractor may make a request to the other party for a necessary adjustment of the Contract Sum.

a. If the Contract Sum is determined to be inappropriate due to the enactment, amendment, or repeal of laws and regulations which was unforeseeable by Contractor at the time of execution of this Contract, or due to a sudden change in economic circumstances, force majeure, or the like; or
b. If the Contract Sum is determined to be inappropriate as a result of modification of the particulars of the Contractor's services or change of the completion date pursuant to any paragraph of Article 28

Furthermore, neither of the items set forth any specific due date for such additional payments. It is one of the embarrassing problems of Japanese domestic practice. Accordingly, it is highly recommended for the Parties to set out a set of clear provisions to make a reasonable adjustment.

12.6.7 Burdensome obligations on the Contractor in the EPC Silver Book

It is often misunderstood even by the Parties and lawyers that, under the Japanese law, a Contractor has to take all risks. It is incorrect. It is up to the agreement of the parties as to how and which party to allocate the risks. The *Civil Code* sets out that a Contractor needs to complete the Works before requesting an Employer for payment of its remuneration (*Civil Code*, Article 632). However, this provision is not a mandatory provision. Furthermore, it is up to the agreement of the parties as to how to define the 'completion' or requirements for completion. It is also up to the agreement of the parties on how to allocate the risk which may occur during the execution of the works. Popular standard forms, ie the GCCC and the ENAA-Domestic, provide some provisions on allocation of risks. However, it is highly recommended to set out provisions on risk allocation in detail to the extent possible.

12.6.8 Principles relating to a lump sum contract

The *Civil Code* simply sets out that an Employer shall pay the remuneration upon taking delivery of the outcome of the work (*Civil Code*, Article 633). It should be noted that this is not a mandatory provision, and it is up to the agreement of the parties how to set out the nature of the Contract Price, and terms/timings of payment. Lump sum (fixed) price/payment and milestone payments are allowed under the Japanese law. In fact, they are more popular than 'measurement' contracts in Japan. 'Cost plus profit' contracts are quite rare.

The *CBA* also requires the Parties to specifically provide the amount of the Contract Price in the construction contract (*CBA*, Article 19(1)[2]). However, there is no other provision under the Japanese law as to the payment terms.

In practice, as provided in the GCCC, the Employer and the Contractor tend to agree the fixed amount which will be paid in at various times – (i) upon commencement of the work (as a kind of advance payment), (ii) milestone payments and (iii) upon taking over of the Works.

12.6.9 Design

FIDIC sub-clauses 5.1 [*General Design Obligations*], 5.2 [*Contractor's Documents*] and 5.3 [*Contractor's Undertaking*] are generally compatible and consistent with the Japanese law.

Sub-clause 5.1 requires the Contractor to carry out the design of the Works and the design shall be prepared by designers who 'are qualified and entitled under applicable Laws to design the Works'. Sub-clause 5.3(a) also requires the Contractor to undertake that the design will be in accordance with the Laws of the Country.

The *Act on Architects and Building Engineers* (Act No 202 of 1950) (***AABE***) provides that only an architect who obtains a licence under the *AABE*[16] is allowed to design the construction work for a building to be newly constructed (*AABE*, Articles 3, 3-2 and 3-3). Article 3(2) of the *AABE* also provides that any extension, rebuilding, major repair or major renovation falls within the definition of new construction and thus allows only a licensed architect to design or supervise such work.

The *Building Standards Act* (Act No 201 of 1950) (***BSA***) also requires a Contractor to execute the construction work for a building to be newly constructed (including extension, rebuilding, major repair or major renovation) based on the design prepared by an architect who has obtained a licence under the *AABE*.

Sub-clause 5.2.3 (c) allows the Contractor to modify any design which has previously been submitted for Review, by giving a Notice to the Engineer with reasons. The requirements under the *AABE* and the *BSA* apply not only to the preparation of the design but also the modification of the design. Accordingly, the Contractor is required to retain a designer who has a qualification under the *AABE* and the *BSA* to modify the design.

16 Under the *AABE*, there are three grades of licenses; a first-class architect, a second-class architect and an architect for wooden building (*AABE*, art 2). Among others, a first-class architect is the highest ranked architect and is qualified to design all size buildings. A second-class architect is only qualified to design smaller buildings such as residential wooden houses.

12.6.10 Obligation to complete with a certain result versus the obligation to apply the means

The *Civil Code* provides certain types of service contract: employment contract (*koyo*), mandate contract (***inin***) and contract for work (***ukeoi***). The obligations are deemed only to apply the means in the employment contract or the mandate contract. On the contrary, the obligation is to achieve a specific result in a contract for works. An employee or a mandatory would not be liable even if he/she does not achieve a certain result so long as he/she fulfilled a duty of care as a good manager. On the other hand, a Contractor would be liable if he/she fails to achieve the result (eg completion of the Works).

Generally, a construction contract falls within a category of 'contract for work'. Accordingly, a Contractor is deemed to have undertaken to complete with a certain result.

However, the Japanese law does not have a typical terminology such 'fit for the purpose' as used in common law jurisdictions and the FIDC contract.[17] As in in other civil law jurisdictions, 'fit for the purpose' itself cannot be a magic phrase in Japan. If the 'purpose' is specifically defined and described in the Employer's Requirements or other contract documents, a Contractor is obliged to achieve certain results specified in those attachments. On the other hand, if those attachments do not specifically define and describe the 'purpose' (as is often seen in Japan), an Employer may not require a Contractor to achieve a result which that Employer intended to achieve. When drafting a construction contract (not limited to the FIDIC contracts), it is quite important for the Parties to specifically define and describe the purpose, requirements, and functions, if any, in detail to the extent possible.

12.6.11 Force majeure

Although there is a term of *force majeure* (***fukakoryoku***) in the *Civil Code* (eg *Civil Code*, Article 419(3)), the *Civil Code* does not provide a definition of *force majeure* as in the other civil law jurisdictions.

Most of the contracts used in Japan also use the term of *force majeure* without a definition. The GCCC and the ENAA-Domestic are exceptions. The GCCC defines a *force majeure* as 'a natural or man-made event which is not attributable to either an Employer or a Contractor' (GCCC, Article 21[1]), which generally does not contradict the definition in the FIDIC contracts. However, it may be said that the GCCC's definition is not clear enough. Since the Japanese parties and lawyers may have a similar concern, there is a strange practice in Japan – listing as many potential *force majeure* events as possible as examples – sometimes more than 50. However, all the listed events are in abstract, we wonder whether such a practice is helpful. It is almost impossible to prepare an exhaustive list of the possible *force majeure* events. Rather, it is recommended to introduce a definition commonly used in the FIDIC contracts, which is much more comprehensive than those used in Japan.

17 Sub-clause 4.1 [*Contractor's General Obligations*] provides that '[w]hen completed, the Works (or Section or Part or major item of Plant, if any) shall be fit for the purpose(s) for which they are intended, as defined and described in the Employer's Requirements (or, where not purpose(s) are so defined and described, fit for their ordinary purpose(s))'.

The more important point is the consequence and remedy. The remedies for *force majeure* under the Japanese law are limited:

(i) An obligee may not demand further performance to an obligor to the extent further performance is prevented due to the events not attributable to an obligor (*Civil Code*, Article 412-2(1))[18]
(ii) An obligee may not demand compensation for damages to an obligor (*Civil Code*, Article 415(1)) and
(iii) An obligee may terminate a contract if an obligor fails to perform the obligation despite a demand within a reasonable period and the non-performance is material (*Civil Code*, Article 541).

In summary, unlike the FIDIC contracts, the Japanese law does not give a Contractor any entitlement to additional costs. However, again, Parties are free to agree to any terms and conditions with respect to *force majeure*. It is strongly recommended to set out a full set of detailed provisions on the definition, consequences and remedies of *force majeure* as in the FIDIC contracts.

12.6.12 Ownership of Plant and Materials

Sub-clause 7.7 [*Ownership of Plant and Materials*] is compatible and consistent with the Japanese law.

The *Civil Code* is silent as to when the ownership of the purchased products is transferred from a seller to a buyer. The timing of the transfer of ownership is left to the agreement of the parties. It can be read that Article 567 (1) of the *Civil Code* provides that the risk of loss is transferred to a buyer upon delivery. However, it is also recommended that the Parties agree and set out detailed provisions on the transfer of the ownership as well as the transfer of the risks.

12.6.13 Employer's sale of Contractor's Equipment, surplus material, wreckage and Temporary Works

Sub-clause 11.11 [*Clearance of Site*] is compatible and consistent with Japanese law. Sub-clause 11.11 allows the Employer to sell or dispose of any remaining items and/or may reinstate and clean the Site at the Contractor's cost if the Contractor fails to comply with certain obligations within 28 days after the issue of the Performance Certificate.

First of all, the most important statute that the Parties need to observe is the *Waste Management and Public Cleaning Act* (Act No 137 of 1970) (***WMA***). The *WMA* classifies the waste into two categories: 'Industrial Waste' and 'General Waste'. Most of the waste produced at a construction site will fall within the Industrial Waste category. The company which produced the Industrial Waste is required to dispose of it in a manner designated in the law or local laws. The company may retain a waste-disposing contractor qualified by law. The details of these regulations, including local laws applicable to the site, have to be checked before the works commences.

Secondly, from a private law perspective, Japanese law does not allow a person to sell or dispose of any remaining items that are owned by the other person; however, if

18 Although this provision does not explicitly state an entitlement of EOT, it may be interpreted that this provision gives the Contractor an entitlement for EOT.

a Contractor leaves equipment, surplus material, wreckage and temporary works, or any waste at the site, such behaviour is deemed as a waiver of ownership. It is highly recommended for the Parties to set out a clear provision by which the leftovers, as long as it is left for a certain period of time, may be disposed of by the Party which takes care of the Site.

12.6.14 Permissions

Sub-clause 1.13 [*Compliance with Laws*] requires the Employer to obtain permits, permissions, licences or approvals as required by the Employer's Requirements. This sub-clause 1.13 is compatible with the Japanese law.

It should be noted that the GCCC does not have any provisions to allocate the role of obtaining permissions. In fact, it is necessary for construction projects to obtain (i) the 'building confirmation' (***kenchiku-kakunin***) under the *BSA* and (ii) other permissions, approvals and/or licences required by the statutes. Usually, Parties arrange and obtain these permissions outside the construction contract. However, for a project in a new field such as offshore wind/wave power projects, it is recommended to set out clear and detailed provisions on the parties' responsibilities for applying and obtaining permissions. The ENAA-Domestic has a relevant provision as follows:

Article 1: Acquisition of Permits and Approvals

(1) The Owner and the Contractor shall, under their respective responsibility, acquire permits and approvals, and submit to supervisory agencies, filings necessary for the performance of the Contractor's services that should be obtained or submitted in their individual names and must provide necessary cooperation to each other.

(2) The Owner shall, under its own responsibility, acquire permits and approvals, and submit to supervisory agencies, filings necessary for operation of the Plant.

12.7 Summary of applicable legislation for Japanese governing law of the contract

12.7.1 Entry into a construction contract

Contracts generally	*Civil Code* (Act No 89 of 1896) *Commercial Code* (Act No 48 of 1899)
Construction contracts	The *Civil Code* provides sets of rules for several types of contracts, one of which is the (***ukeoi***) (Book 3, Chapter 2, section 9). Unless otherwise agreed by the Parties, construction contracts are deemed to fall within this category. The provisions are generally non-mandatory rules. Short titles of the provisions in section 8 are: - Article 632: Contracts for Work; - Article 633: Timing of Payment of Remuneration; - Articles 634: Proportional Payment in Accordance with Employer's Benefits - Article 636: Limitation to Contractor's Non-Conformance Liability;

	- Article 637: Limitation to the Period of Non-Conformance Liability as to Kind or Quality of the Object of the Contract; - Article 641: Cancellation of Contract by the Employer; - Article 642: Cancellation on Commencement of Employer's Bankruptcy Procedures *Construction Business Act* (Act No 100 of 1949)

12.7.2 Termination of a construction contract

force majeure	*Civil Code* Articles 274, 275, 348, 419(3), 609 and 610
Bankruptcy, insolvency, liquidation	*Civil Code* (Act No 89 of 1896) *Bankruptcy Act* (Act No 75 of 2004) *Civil Rehabilitation Act* (Act No 225 of 1999) *Corporate Act* (Act No 86 of 2005) *Corporate Reorganization Act* (Act No 154 of 2002)
Guarantees under forms of Security (Tender Security, Demand Guarantee, Surety Bond, Advance Payment Guarantee, Retention Money Guarantee, Payment Guarantee by Employer)	*Civil Code* (Act No 89 of 1896) *Act on the Business of Advance Payment Guarantee* (Act No 184 of 1952) - Normal practice in Japan is complex and largely different from common international practice. - First, in a context of construction of commercial or private buildings, Employers do not request Contractors to submit a tender security, advance payment guarantee, retention money guarantee nor performance guarantee, even while these types of guarantees are not prohibited under the laws. - Secondly, as for industrial plant constructions or EPC contracts, some Employers request Contractors to submit a performance guarantee. In such a case, the Contractor obtains a guarantee bond from banks or purchases a performance guarantee insurance from insurance companies. - Lastly, as for public work contracts, the Government usually requests Contractors to submit a tender security, advance payment guarantee, and performance guarantee. In addition to the banks and insurance companies, three special companies jointly established by the construction companies and banks under *the Act on the Business of Advance Payment Guarantee* (Act No 184 of 1952) provide guarantees.

12.7.3 Dispute resolution

Limitation periods	*Civil Code* (Act No 89 of 1896) - The *Civil Code* sets out statutes of limitations (Articles 144 to 161 and 166 to 169). A time-period for the statute of limitation is five years from the date when a party can enforce its right, with a longstop date of 10 years. It should be noted that Japan deems statutes of limitations as substantial laws, not procedural laws. If parties select Japanese law as the governing law, these statutes of limitation apply.
Liability	*Civil Code* (Act No 89 of 1896) *Housing Quality Assurance Act* (Act No 81 of 1999)
Adjudication	*Construction Business Act* (Act No 100 of 1949) *Civil Mediation Act* (Act No 222 of 1951)
Arbitration	*Arbitration Act* (Act No 138 of 2003)

12.8 Applicable legislation if the Site/Country is in Japan

12.8.1 Calibration of testing apparatus, equipment and instruments

Sub-clause 7.4 [*Testing by the Contractor*] is compatible and consistent with the Japanese law.

First, the *Measurement Act* (Act No 51 of 1992) sets out the standards of measurement and ensure execution of proper measurement. The *Measurement Act* specifies the measuring instruments that may be used for measurement and restricts certain instruments from being used for measurement (*Measurement Act*, Articles 16–18). The *Measurement Act* also requires a periodic inspection of the measuring instruments (*Measurement Act*, Article 19).

Article 20 of the *Measurement Act* provides that the Prefectural Governor or the head of the specified municipality may have a designated periodic inspection body execute a periodic inspection of the measuring instruments. The Japan Calibration Service System (**JCSS**) is the accreditation system for calibration laboratories or equipment under the *Measurement Act*. Since accreditation under the JCSS demands metrological traceability to the standards established by the National Metrology Institute of Japan (or at the designated institutes), calibration certificates issued by the JCSS may be used as a proof of traceability.

Secondly, after receiving notice from the Subcontractor that the contracted construction work has been completed, the main Contractor is required to make an inspection in order to confirm the completion of the work within 20 days or within as short a period as possible from the date when said notice was received (*CBA*, Article 24-4(1) and (2)).

Thirdly, the *BSA* requires the owner to pass certain statutory inspections as set forth in Article 7, 7-2, 7-3 and 7-4 of the BSA. The GCCC provides that

> At the proper time prior to any of the Statutory Inspections and any other statutory inspection described in the Design Documents, etc. to be conducted by the relevant institutions for which the Owner has applied, the Contractor shall confirm that the Work has been executed in compliance with the Design Documents, etc. and shall request the Owner for inspection.[19]

12.8.2 Bankruptcy, insolvency, liquidation

Sub-clauses 15.2 [*Termination for Contractor's Default*] and 16.2 [*Termination by Contractor*] give the Contractor or the Employer the right to terminate the Contract in the case of bankruptcy, insolvency or liquidation of the other Party. These provisions are compatible and consistent with Japanese law.

The *Civil Code* provides that if an Employer receives an order commencing bankruptcy proceedings, the Contractor or the bankruptcy trustee may terminate the Contract; provided however that this does not apply to the termination of the Contract by a Contractor after the work is completed (*Civil Code*, Article 642(1)). The Contractor's claims for compensation for loss or damage suffered as a result of the termination are permitted only for Contractors under contracts terminated by the bankruptcy trustee. In such cases, Contractors may participate in the distribution of the bankruptcy estate with respect to such compensation for loss or damage (*Civil Code*, Article 642(3)).

The *Civil Code* does not provide the Employer's termination right in the case where the Contractor receives an order commencing a bankruptcy proceeding. Thus, it can

19 GCCC, art 23-2(1).

be said that sub-clause 16.2 gives a broader right of termination to an Employer than that is given under the Japanese law.

12.8.3 Rights of set-off

As in other civil law jurisdictions, the Japanese law provides a set of provisions for set-off (*Civil Code*, Book 3, Chapter 1, section 5, subsection 2). Accordingly, unless otherwise agreed by the Parties, a Party is generally entitled to set-off its own claims against another party's counterclaims, as long as both claims have suitable conditions for set-off (**sosai-tekijo**). Details of the *sosai-tekijyo* conditions are (*Civil Code*, Article 505):

- (i) Two persons mutually owe to the other obligations
- (ii) The obligations are of the same kind and
- (iii) Both obligations are due.

Set-off is effective when one party unilaterally manifests its intention to set-off to another party. The set-off takes effect retroactively as of the time when the obligations of both parties become due and suitable for set-off (*Civil Code*, Article 506(1) and (2)).

It is normal that the GCCC and the ENAA-Domestic do not specifically provide the parties' right to set-off, which means that the Japanese popular forms accept wide set-off by either party. On the contrary, sub-clause 20.2 [*Claims for Payment and/or EOT*], inter alia, paragraph 20.2.7 [*General Requirements*], of the FIDIC contracts provides that '[t]he Employer shall only be entitled to claim any payment from the Contractor and/or to extend the DNP, or set off against or make any deduction from any amount due to the Contractor, by complying with this sub-clause 20.2'. These provisions are certainly valid and interpreted as a kind of partial prohibition of set-off.

12.8.4 Termination

First of all, Parties are free to agree which Party is entitled to terminate and under what conditions they are entitled to terminate the Contract, because the relevant provisions in the laws are not mandatory.

Secondly, as a general rule for all types of contract, either party may terminate the Contract upon another party's non-performance of the obligation (***saimu-furiko***)[20] ie breach of contract in common law terminology. Generally, a prior notice is necessary in order to give a non-performing obligor, ie breaching party, an opportunity to cure (*Civil Code*, Article 542). However, if non-performance of the obligation is caused by the grounds attributable to the obligee (ie the non-breaching party), the obligee may not terminate the Contract (*Civil Code*, Article 543).

Additionally, as a special rule for contracts for works, an Employer can terminate the Contract 'at any time whilst a Contractor has not completed the work by paying compensation for loss or damage' (*Civil Code*, Article 641). This right is given to an Employer because it would be useless to compel an Employer to receive the work that is no longer necessary for it. A Contractor, on the contrary, can terminate the Contract before completion of the work, if an Employer receives an order of commencement of bankruptcy proceedings (*Civil Code*, Article 642). The Contractor can thus avoid the risk of not being paid before completing the construction.

20 In addition to the non-performance of the obligations, 'impossibility' to perform the obligations is another cause for termination (*Civil Code*, art 541).

12.8.5 Limitation of liability

The *Consumer Contract Act* (Act No 61 of 2000) provides that the following consumer contract clauses are void: (i) clauses completely exempting a trader from liability to compensate a consumer for damages arising from default by the trader, or granting authority to the trader to determine whether or not the trader is responsible; or (ii) clauses partially exempting a trader from liability to compensate for damages arising from default by the trader, or granting authority to the trader to determine to what extent the trader is responsible (limited to default which arises due to an intentional act or gross negligence on the part of the trader, the trader's representative, or employees).

However, there are no provisions which invalidate the terms of the contract between companies providing that the limitation of liability clause does not apply in case of a breaching party's gross negligence or fraud.

12.8.6 Misrepresentation

The common law concept of misrepresentation, defined as 'an untrue statement of fact made by one party to the other which was intended and did induce the latter to enter into the contract',[21] is different to the concept in Japanese law. This is because of the difference in civil law and common law traditions. The *Civil Code* sets out that a mutual 'fictitious manifestation of intention' may be rescinded (*Civil Code*, Article 96); however, this is different from misrepresentation in common law. Instead, the tort theory embodied by a set of provisions in the *Civil Code* could be a basis of misrepresenting party's liability (*Civil Code*, Article 709). Furthermore, there is no concept equivalent to innocent misrepresentation which is recognised in common law.

12.9 Summary of applicable legislation if the Site/Country is in Japan

12.9.1 Operation of a construction contract

Registration and administration of professionals – Engineers, Architects	*Act on Architects and Building Engineers* (Act No 202 of 1950) - *Act on Architects and Building Engineers* sets out requirements, classes and regulations on Architects (***kenchiku-shi***). *Construction Business Act* (Act No 100 of 1949) - In addition to Architects, the *CBA* empowers the MLIT to stipulate technical qualifications for construction works – the managing engineer (***sekou-kanri-gishi***) and the supervising engineer (***kanri-gijiutsu-sha***). Supervising engineers shall be designated from employees who are qualified as managing engineers. Managing engineer's qualification is only admitted to experienced engineers who have expertise in certain areas and who passed the national examinations testing such expertise. *Professional Engineer Act* (Act No 25 of 1983) *Electricians Act* (Act No 139 of 1960) *Act on Ensuring Fair Electric Business Act* (Act No 96 of 1970)

21 *Misrepresentation Act 1967* (UK).

Registration/ licencing of Contractors and Subcontractors	*Construction Business Act* (Act No 100 of 1949) - The *CBA* requires all companies or person that engage in construction business to obtain a licence and register with the MLIT Minister or Prefectural Governor, depending on the territorial scope of its construction business. The *CBA* is applicable when the construction site is located in Japan. Contractors are required to make registration at the MLIT or Prefectural Governor.
Subcontractors	*Construction Business Act* (Act No 100 of 1949) - The *CBA* provides special protections for construction Subcontractors, in particular, against delayed payment. *Act against Delay in Payment of Subcontract Remuneration, Etc. to Subcontractors* (Act No120 of 1956) - This Act provides similar protections for non-construction Subcontractors.
Use of liens/ Assignment of debts	*Civil Code* (Act No 89 of 1896) *Construction Machinery Hypothecation Act* (Act No 97 of 1954)
Labour	*Labour Standard Act* (Act No 49 of 1947) *Worker's Safety and Health Act* (Act No 57 of 1972)[22] *Working Environment Measurement Act* (Act No 28 of 1975)
Design/Moral rights	*Copyright Act* (Act No 48 of 1970) *Design Act* (Act No 125 of 1959) *Unfair Competition Prevention Act* (Act No 47 of 1993)
Copyright	*Copyright Act* (Act No 48 of 1970)
The product being produced from the Works	*Civil Code* (Act No 89 of 1896) - The product being produced from the Works is called as ***dekigata*** in Japanese. - Parties have a freedom to agree on the timing and requirements of the conveyance and transfer of the ownership of the product being produced from the Works.
First nation people's land rights	*Act on Promotion of Realization of the Society Where Ainu People Can Maintain Their Pride* (Act No 16 of 2019) - This statute focuses on Ainu's cultural heritage, and it does not provide Ainu people's priority rights on land.
Planning	*National Land Use Planning Act* (Act No 92 of 1974) *Basic Act for Land* (Act No 84 of 1989) *Land Readjustment Act* (Act No 119 of 1954) *City Planning Act* (Act No 100 of 1968) *Urban Park Act* (Act No 79 of 1956) *Landscape Act* (Act No 110 of 2004) *Urban Green Area Act* (Act No 72 of 1973) *Outdoor Advertisement Act* (Act No 189 of 1949) *Act on Promotion of Smooth Transportation, etc. of Elderly Persons, Disabled Persons, etc.* (Act No 91 of 2006) *Natural Parks Act* (Act No 161 of 1957) *River Act* (Act No 167 of 1964) *Coast Act* (Act No 101 of 1956) *Flood Control Act* (Act No 193 of 1949) *Act on Reclamation of Publicly-owned Water Surface* (Act No 57 of 1921)

22 The WSHA provides certain employer's duties and preventive measures to protect the employees' health and safety, such as mandatory medical check-ups, handling of equipment and machinery, hazardous substances, training and sanitation. The Ministry of Health, Labour and Welfare issues various guidelines concerning the safety measures to be adopted in certain construction project. https://www.mhlw.go.jp/stf/seisakunitsuite/bunya/0000207439.html (accessed 3 December 2020).

	Act on Promoting the Utilization of Sea Areas for the Development of Marine Renewable Energy Power Generation Facilities (Act No 89 of 2018) - There are numerous Acts on planning and zoning urban and reserved areas. The aforementioned list of Acts is only a short list of the Acts that are frequently used for private property developments and construction projects.
Work affecting adjacent property to the Site	*Water Supply Act* (Act No 177 of 1957) *Sewerage Act* (Act No 79 of 1958) *Road Act* (Act No 180 of 1952) *Road Repair Act* (Act No 282 of 1948) *Erosion Control Act* (Act No 29 of 1897) *Landslide Prevention Act* (Act No 30 of 1958) *Act on Special Measures for Common Ducts for Utility Pies and Cables* (Act No 81 of 1963) *Act on Special Measures for Preparation, etc. of Common Use Cable Tunnel* (Act No 39 of 1995)
Heritage	*Act on Protection of Cultural Heritage* (Act No 214 of 1950) *Act on Maintenance and Improvement of Traditional Scenery in Designated Areas* (Act No 40 of 2008) *Act on Special Measures for Preservation of Historic Landscape in Ancient Capitals* (Act No 1 of 1966)
Environment	*Basic Act on Environment* (Act No 91 of 1993)[23] *Environment Impact Assessment Act* (Act No 81 of 1997)[24] *Air Pollution Control Act* (Act No 97 of 1968) *Act on Preventing Environment Pollution of Mercury* (Act No 42 of 2015) *Act on Regulation of Extraction of Groundwater for Use in Buildings* (Act No 100 of 1962) *Act on Reclamation Works of Public Water Surface* (Act No 57 of 1921) *River Act* (Act No 167 of 1964) *Construction Material Recycling Act* (Act No 104 of 2000) *Act on the Promotion of Effective Utilization of Resources* (Act No 48 of 1991)
Local procurement	*Public Accounting Act* (Act No 35 of 1947) *Local Autonomy Act* (Act No 67 of 1947) *Act on Promoting Quality Assurance in Public Works* (Act No 18 of 2005) *Act for Promoting Proper Tendering and Contracting for Public Works* (Act No 127 of 2000) *Act on Promotion of Private Finance Initiative Funds* (Act No 117 of 1999)
Building and construction permits, Execution of construction work, Standard of construction work	*Building Standard Act* (Act No 201 of 1950) *Fire Service Act* (Act No 186 of 1948) *City Planning Act* (Act No 100 of 1968) *Act on Regulation of Residential Land Development* (Act No 191 of 1961) *Water Supply Act* (Act No 177 of 1957) *Sewerage Act* (Act No 79 of 1958) *Purification Tank Act* (Act No 43 of 1983)

23 The *Basic Act on Environment* provides the fundamental framework of environmental protection.

24 The *Environment Impact Assessment Act* requires an Employer to conduct the environment impact assessments (***kankyo-eikyo-hyoka***) on a project-by-project basis (art 2).

	Act for Promoting Easily Accessible Public Transportation and Facilities for the Aged and the Disabled (Act No 91 of 2006) *Housing Quality Assurance Act* (Act No 81 of 1999) *Act on Promotion of Seismic Retrofitting of Buildings* (Act No 123 of 1995) *Act on the Improvement of Energy Consumption Performance of Buildings* (Act No 53 of 2015) *Act on Protection of Cultural Heritage (*Act No 214 of 1950) *Landscape Act* (Act No 110 of 2004) Standard of Civil Work Management and Standard Specifications (MLIT) Standard of Machinery Work Management (MLIT)
Health and safety	*Worker's Safety and Health Act* (Act No 57 of 1972) *Working Environment Measurement Act* (Act No 28 of 1975) *Act on the Promotion of Assurance of Safety and Health of Construction Workers* (Act No 111 of 2016) *Act on the Arrangement of Related Acts to Promote Work Style Reform* (Act No 71 of 2018)
Calibration of testing apparatus, equipment and instruments	*Building Standard Act* (Act No 201 of 1950) *Electricity Business Act* (Act No 170 of 1964) - There are numerous acts on calibration of testing apparatus, equipment and instruments, in accordance with the nature of the works.
Ownership of Plant and Materials	*Civil Code* (Act No 89 of 1896) - Parties have freedom to agree on the timing and requirements of the conveyance or reservation of the ownership of plants and materials.
Employer's sale of Contractor's Equipment, surplus material, wreckage and Temporary Works	*Civil Code* (Act No 89 of 1896) - Parties have freedom to agree on the terms and conditions of the Employer's entitlement to dispose of Contractor's Equipment, surplus materials and Temporary Works.
Insurance	*Civil Code* (Act No 89 of 1896)
Liability for defective work	*Civil Code* (Act No 89 of 1896)
Liability for nuisance	*Civil Code* (Act No 89 of 1896)
Other issues	*Insurance Business Act* (Act No 105 of 1995)

12.9.2 Termination of a construction contract

Bankruptcy, insolvency, liquidation	*Civil Code* (Act No 89 of 1896) *Bankruptcy Act* (Act No 75 of 2004) *Civil Rehabilitation Act* (Act No 225 of 1999) *Corporate Act* (Act No 86 of 2005) *Corporate Reorganization Act* (Act No 154 of 2002)
Liability generally for the total or partial collapse of structures	*Civil Code* (Act No 89 of 1896) - Before the 2017 amendment, the *Civil Code* set out long defect liability periods for certain types of construction works. The 2017 amendment abolished such periods and now the default period of the statutory defect liability is 1 year after notice (Articles 559 and 556). Now there is no decennial liability under the Japanese law.

12.9.3 Dispute resolution

Dispute before a local board/ Adjudication	*Construction Business Act* (Act No 100 of 1949) *Civil Mediation Act* (Act No 222 of 1951)
Limitation periods	Civil Code (Act No 89 of 1896) - The Civil Code sets out statutes of limitations (Articles 144 to 161 and 166 to 169). A time-period of the statute of limitation is five years from the date when a party can enforce its right, with a longstop date of 10 years. It should be noted that Japan deems the statutes of limitations as the substantial laws, not procedural laws. If Parties select Japanese law as the governing law, these statutes of limitation apply.

12.10 Summary of applicable legislation if the 'seat' of the dispute determination is in Japan

Dispute resolution	*Japan generally accepts the lex fori principle. Code of Civil Procedure (Act No 109 of 1996)*
Limitation periods	*Civil Code* (Act No 89 of 1896) - The *Civil Code* sets out statutes of limitations (Articles 144 to 161 and 166 to 169). A time-period for the statute of limitation is five years from the date when a party can enforce its right, with a longstop date of 10 years. It should be noted that Japan deems statutes of limitations as substantial laws, not procedural laws. If Parties select Japanese law as the governing law, these statutes of limitation apply.
Adjudication	*Construction Business Act* (Act No 100 of 1949) *Civil Mediation Act* (Act No 222 of 1951)
Arbitration	*Arbitration Act* (Act No 138 of 2003)

12.11 Issues that a court or arbitrator may construe differently to that expected from the words of the Contract, because of local law or custom

12.11.1 Construction of contract terms

It should be noted that literal interpretation is not the golden rule of interpretation in civil law jurisdictions. There is a significant risk that Japanese judges or arbitrators who are educated and practice in Japan may construe the words of the contract differently from those in common law jurisdictions. This is one of the main reasons why we recommend international arbitration as the dispute resolution for construction contracts, rather than referring a dispute to the Japanese courts or domestic alternative dispute resolution procedures (ie domestic arbitration, mediation and the KFSK).

Japanese law has developed to the situation where the Parties prefer simple and abstract wording in the contract. It was natural or even unavoidable for Japanese judges and arbitrators to unleash their creativity, interpret the contract terms without a bondage of literal meanings, to reach a suitable, sensible, fair and equitable solutions for disputes, regardless of the ambiguity and unclearness of the words of the contracts. It is true that Japanese judges and arbitrators show their respect to the contract wording; however, it may also be difficult for them to stick to literal interpretation of the words of the contract.

12.11.2 Good faith

The *Civil Code* provides that 'the exercise of rights and performance of duties must be done in good faith' (*Civil Code*, Article 1(2)). In general, Japanese courts apply the principle of good faith hesitantly, because an easy application of this principle may harm a party's reliance and foreseeability on the contract terms that they agreed. The good faith principle may be applied by the Japanese courts to a case where a socially vulnerable person needs to be protected (eg subcontractors, employees, consumers, or distributors).

There are no provisions in the FIDIC contracts that would be interpreted as invalid on its face due to violation of the good faith principle. However, we cannot totally deny the possibility that Japanese courts may deny the application of or modify the original meaning of the FIDIC contracts, depending on the circumstances. That is the reason why international arbitration is strongly recommended rather than the Japanese courts.

12.11.3 Implying terms into all contracts of a particular type

In Japan there is no 'implied terms' theory as discussed and accepted in the common law jurisdictions. Alternatively, the Japanese courts like to use a concept of implied agreement (***mokuji-no-goi***) or a party's reasonable intention (***tojisha-no-goriteki-ishi***).[25] These magic words or concepts are often used by the Japanese courts in cases where there is no evidence for an express agreement on additional changes to the Contract Price.

In a case where an Employer orders additional changes to the Works, it is more often in domestic practice that the Parties do not reach an agreement on the adjustment of the Contract Price. It may be the case that the Employer admitted that it needed to pay more than the original Contract Price, but also intended to make the additional amount lower than that which is claimed by the Contractor. Due to lack of the agreement of the parties, the Contract Price can be a subject of dispute after the work is completed. In a case before the Tokyo District Court, the court found an implied agreement, taking into consideration that the Employer continued to pay certain additional amounts without an express agreement, and that the Subcontractor repeatedly sought consent from the Contractor and the Contractor did not decline it expressly.[26]

To find an implied agreement or a party's reasonable intent, the court usually considers various factors, such as the Employer's payment of certain additional

25 If it is not possible for the court to find an 'implied agreement', the Japanese court sometimes recognises the Employer's obligation for the payment of reasonable compensation based on art 512 of the *Commercial Code* (Act No 48 of 1899). Article 512 of the *Commercial Code* provides that: 'When a merchant has conducted any act for another person within the scope of his/her business, he/she may claim a reasonable remuneration.' Under such article, a Contractor may claim 'reasonable remuneration' from the Employer if the Contractor performs work for the Employer without executing the contract.

26 Tokyo District Court, Judgment on 23 March 2016.

amounts, the Contractor's repeated request for determining the additional amount and the Employer's silence, etc. The court tries to be as fair as possible; however, it is yet unforeseeable and unreliable for commercial projects, particularly in projects where foreign parties are involved. Accordingly, it is strongly recommended that the Parties agree to the change or Variation procedures in detail, as in the FIDIC contracts, and agree to refer disputes not to the Japanese courts but to international arbitration.

12.11.4 Delay damages/penalties

First of all, it should be noted that Japan takes a unique position, in between common law and other civil law approaches.

As a general rule, when a Contractor's non-performance of obligations (***saimu-furiko***) is caused by the reasons attributable to the Contractor, the Contractor is obliged to compensate the Employer for damages incurred due to such delay (*Civil Code*, Article 415(1)). The scope of damages is determined according to the criterion of 'ordinary loss' and 'special loss' (*Civil Code*, Article 416(1)). For the latter, which amount can be larger than the former, an Employer must prove that its loss was foreseeable in order to be compensated (*Civil Code*, Article 416(2)).[27]

Regardless of this general rule, the Parties may agree that a Contractor will pay liquidated damages in the case of delay (*Civil Code*, Article 420(1)). While penalties are also allowed additionally or selectively, the *Civil Code* assumes that, unless otherwise agreed or specified in an agreement, the agreed 'penalties' are deemed to be 'liquidated damages' (*Civil Code*, Article 420(3)). There is no specific threshold as to the amount and percentage, etc. for the liquidated damages. However, an extraordinarily excessive amount or percentage of liquidated damages would be invalid and unenforceable due to a violation of public policy.

The old *Civil Code* before the 2017 reform expressly provided that the court may not increase or decrease the amount of the liquidated damages agreed between the Parties. This sentence was deleted in the 2017 *Civil Code*, because there are some arguments over whether the court has the authority at least to decrease the amount, as in the other civil law jurisdictions. The arguments could not reach a conclusion and left it to future decisions in court. In any event, it should be noted that the Japanese courts traditionally found any reason to decrease the amount of the liquidated damages, if the court saw any reason or event not attributable to the payer of the liquidated damages, by finding a payee's 'comparative negligence' (***kashitsu-sosai***) (*Civil Code*, Article 418).[28] It should be noted that the court may apply comparative negligence rules not only to tort claims, but also to contract claims including damages.

12.11.5 Appeal to a court may mean that the right to arbitration is lost

Although there is no precedent, a mainstream legal theory notes that a party who appeals to a court means will lose the right to arbitration. However, if either party's filing is not in good faith (eg one party files a lawsuit in the domestic court to evade the arbitration or files a lawsuit to the domestic court which clearly lacks the jurisdiction), the Japanese court may dismiss such a filing because of violation of good faith.

27 It is generally understood that the Japanese rule on the scope of damage is similar to the rules set out in *Hadley v Baxendale* (1854) 9 Ex 41.

28 Supreme Court, Judgment of 21 April 1942.

12.10 References

12.10.1 Books

Hiroo Sono, Luke Nottage, Andrew Pardieck and Kenji Saigusa, *Contract Law in Japan* (Kluwer Law International 2018).

Naoki Kanayama, Takashi Ogura, Naoki Iguchi and Kaori Sugimoto, 'Japan' in Phillip Greenham (ed), *The International Compendium of Construction Contracts* (Society of Construction Law Australia & De Gruyter 2020).

Study Group of the Construction Business Act (2016), *Commentary of the Construction Business Act* (12th edn, Taisei Shuppan Tokyo 2016) (only in Japanese).

12.10.2 Journals

There are many journals but unfortunately none that specialises in construction law

12.10.3 Internet

Japanese Law Translation Database System (hosted by the Ministry of Justice) http://www.japaneselawtranslation.go.jp/?re=02

The Committee of Seven Associations of Architects and Contractors (*minkan (nanakai) rengo kyotei koji ukeoi keiyaku yakkan iinkai*) http://www.gcccc.jp/ (Japanese only)

The Engineering Advancement Association http://www.enaa.or.jp/EN/about/index.html

CHAPTER 13

Applying FIDIC Contracts in Korea

Mino Han and Jennifer (Eun Kyung) Yoo[1]

1 The authors are thankful for the assistance of Boseok Kim, Junior Associate at Peter & Kim (Seoul).

 DOI: 10.4324/9781003200901-13

13.1 Outline of the legal environment in Korea

Korea (officially, the Republic of Korea; in this chapter, **Korea**) is a centralised democratic republic with three primary government branches: executive, legislative and judicial. The structure functions are based on a careful system of checks and balances between the three branches:

- The executive branch is headed by the President of Korea, who acts as the head and chief representative of the state. The President is elected directly by Korean nationals and serves for one five-year term. The executive branch also includes a range of bodies such as the Prime Minister, the State Council, individual ministries and the Board of Audit and Inspection.
- The legislative branch consists of the National Assembly of Korea, which is a unicameral structure consisting of around 300 members. The members of the National Assembly serve for four years and are responsible for a range of duties including deliberating and passing legislation, auditing the budget and ratifying treaties.
- The judicial branch can be described as a 'dual' system, the dual highest courts being the Supreme Court and the Constitutional Court. The Supreme Court is the final court of appeal for all civil and criminal cases in Korea, below which are Appellate Courts and District Courts (which serve as courts of first instance). For certain subject matters, such as patent disputes or family matters, the Korean judiciary operates specialised courts. There exists yet no specialised court for construction disputes. The Constitutional Court has jurisdiction over a limited number of issues (as further explained below), including in particular constitutional review.

The *Constitution of the Republic of Korea* serves as the foundational law for the constitutional structure of Korea. The *Constitution* was enacted with the establishment of the Republic of Korea in 1948 and has been amended eight times to date. The current *Constitution* consists of a preamble, 130 articles in 10 chapters, and supplementary provisions. It covers the rights and duties of Korean nationals (Chapter 2), the National Assembly (Chapter 3), the executive branch (Chapter 4), the courts (Chapter 5), the Constitutional Court (Chapter 6) and other matters comprising Korea's constitutional structure.

13.1.1 The legal system of Korea

The Republic of Korea is a civil law jurisdiction. It has been historically influenced by the laws of other civil law countries, such as Germany and Japan. The legal system is based on codified laws and does not adopt the principle of *stare decisis*. However, in practice, Supreme Court judgments are generally highly respected and regarded as persuasive legal authorities to be relied on for legal interpretation.

Laws in Korea can be largely classified into (1) public laws, which regulate the relations between a person(s) and the state, or between bodies of the state, and (2) private laws, which regulate the relations between private individuals. The primary examples of public laws are the *Criminal Act* and various administrative statutes, while examples of private laws include the *Civil Act* and the *Commercial Act*.

13.1.2 The court system of Korea

The Korean court system is based on a three-instance trial system composed of (1) the District Courts of the first instance, (2) the Appellate Courts (in which factual issues may be revisited), and (3) the Supreme Court (only permitted to rule on legal issues), the latter of which has the final appellate jurisdiction over all cases, except for matters overseen by the Constitutional Court. Korea does not have separate federal and provincial court systems.

The Korean court system also contains certain specialised courts, that is, the Patent Court, the Administrative Court, the Family Court and the Bankruptcy Court. With the exception of the Patent Court – which is positioned on the same level as the Appellate Courts – the specialised courts function on the same level as the District Courts (ie courts of first instance).

There is also a Constitutional Court, which exists independently from and operates on the same tier as the Supreme Court. The Constitutional Court has jurisdiction over a limited number of issues, including constitutional review, impeachment, and dissolution of a political party.

As the Korean legal system has its roots in civil law, court proceedings are based on an inquisitorial model but also exhibit certain features of the (common law style) adversarial model. The judges, in principle, play an active role in the conduct of court proceedings in Korea. For instance, they have the authority to and accordingly commonly raise questions, seek clarification on issues of fact or law, or request a party to present evidence in support of that party's pleaded case.

13.1.3 Contract law

In accordance with the principles of party autonomy and freedom of contract recognised under Korean law, all parties to a contract may freely determine in accordance with their will the contents of a contract, including whether or not to enter into a contract, choosing the counterparty to a contract and determining the method of entering into a contract.

Regarding the interpretation of contracts, the Korean *Civil Act* has no specific provisions setting out the general principles of contract interpretation. However, the Supreme Court has acknowledged in jurisprudence that the ultimate goal of contract interpretation under Korean law is to determine 'the common intent of the parties to a contract'.[2] The text of the contract is the primary and most important source to ascertain such common intent.[3] In this light, the Supreme Court has held that, in principle, Korean law does not consider inward intent – ie subjective intent – in contract interpretation.[4]

However, if the plain text of a contract is unclear or ambiguous, consideration should be further given to the context of the contract (for instance, the factual background underlying the execution of the contract) and business common sense to determine conclusively the intent of the contracting parties.[5]

13.2 The construction industry in Korea

13.2.1 Overview

Korea's construction industry has been a major contributor to the country's national economy. In 2019, the total value of domestic construction contracts entered into amounted to KRW 166 trillion (ie around US$139 billion), while the total value of overseas construction contracts entered into was around US$22.3 billion, for 669 projects in 105 countries across the world.[6]

Korea's construction industry is significantly regulated. A project owner is required to obtain various approvals and permits which are managed and issued by the relevant municipal government authorities. Failure to comply with such approval requirements can result in administrative fines and even criminal penalties.

In particular, pursuant to the Korean *Building Act*, a person who intends to construct a new building or substantially repair an existing building is required to obtain permission from the competent municipal authority.[7] However, for certain small-scale buildings, the *Building Act* provides an exception that filing a notice to the authorities (in place of obtaining a permission from the authorities) will suffice for the purposes of proceeding with constructing or substantially repairing a building.[8] In addition, a project owner who wishes to use a building after completing the construction of the building must apply for and obtain a separate 'approval for use' from the competent municipal authority.[9] The general provisions of the *Building Act* are supplemented by municipal regulations providing detailed building codes.

2 Supreme Court Judgment Case No 93*Da*2629, 2636 (26 October 1993).

3 Supreme Court Judgment Case No 2008*Da*90095, 90101 (14 May 2009); Supreme Court Judgment Case No 2010*Da*56616 (11 November 2010); Supreme Court Judgment Case No 2010*Da*26769 (11 November 2010).

4 Supreme Court Judgment Case No 2002*Da*23482 (28 June 2002); Supreme Court Judgment Case No 2005*Da*13288 (23 November 2006).

5 Supreme Court Judgment Case No 2002*Da*23482 (28 June 2002); Supreme Court Judgment Case No 2008*Da*90095, 90101 (14 May 2009); Supreme Court Judgment Case No 2010*Da*58728 (13 May 2011).

6 Constitution Association of Korea, Key Construction Statistics http://www.cak.or.kr/board/boardList.do?boardId=statistic_build&menuId=86 (accessed 21 October 2020).

7 *Building Act*, art 11.

8 ibid art 14.

9 ibid art 22.

There are various other statutes which regulate different aspects of construction and engineering projects, and the construction industry in general. For example:

- Labour relations are regulated by various statutes such as the *Labor Standards Act*, *Minimum Wage Act* and *Trade Union and Labor Relations Adjustment Act*. The *Labor Standards Act* and *Minimum Wage Act* set out the basic standards and principles which must be observed for construction workers and employees. These acts include provisions on equal treatment, protection for women and minors, maximum working hours per week and minimum wages. The *Trade Union and Labor Relations Adjustment Act* governs the rights and obligations relating to labour unions. More specific aspects of labour law in relation to construction projects are addressed in the *Act on the Employment Improvement, etc. of Construction Workers*, which particularly aims to promote employment stability in the construction industry.
- As regards health and safety, the principal law applicable to all industries is the *Occupational Safety and Health Act*. In addition, the *Housing Act*, *Building Act*, *Framework Act on the Construction Industry* and other statutes include provisions requiring construction projects to ensure compliance with applicable health and safety regulations and requirements.
- Government procurement is specifically governed by several statues, for example the *Government Procurement Act*, *Act on Contracts to Which the State is a Party*, *Act on Contracts to Which a Local Government is a Party*, and *Act on the Management of Public Institutions*. In addition, Korea is a party to the World Trade Organization Agreement on Government Procurement[10] (also known as WTO GPA), and other international instruments, including free trade agreements which address the issue of public procurement.[11]
- There are also a number of statutes that aim to ensure environmental protection in the course of a construction project, such as the *Environmental Impact Assessment Act*, *Clean Air Conservation Act*, *Noise and Vibration Control Act*, *Water Quality and Ecosystem Conservation Act*, *Sewerage Act* and *Waste Control Act*.

13.3 The impact of Covid-19 in Korea

13.3.1 The impact of Covid-19 on the execution of construction projects in Korea

There has never been an official shut-down ordered by the Korean government due to the outbreak of Covid-19. Nevertheless, various executive branches of the Korean government have issued guidelines to address the impact of Covid-19 on the execution of construction projects and more generally in the construction industry. That was

10 'The GPA is a plurilateral agreement within the framework of the WTO, meaning that not all WTO members are parties to the Agreement . . . The fundamental aim of the GPA is to mutually open government procurement markets among its parties. As a result of several rounds of negotiations, the GPA parties have opened procurement activities worth an estimated US$ 1.7 trillion annually to international competition (ie to suppliers from GPA parties offering goods, services or construction services).' https://www.wto.org/english/tratop_e/gproc_e/gp_gpa_e.htm (accessed 22 October 2020).

11 Public Procurement Service, Global Procurement Assistance (http://www.pps.go.kr/gpass/jsp/wto/wto_info.gps) (accessed 21 October 2020).

to alleviate the repercussions of Covid-19, including project delays, government or medically ordered quarantines, material and equipment shortages, labour shortages and lost productivity.

On 12 February 2020, the Korean Ministry of Economy and Finance issued the 'Guidelines for Handling Public Contracts to Respond to Covid-19' which applies to public procurement and public construction projects.[12] This guideline provides that public construction works in Korea may be temporarily suspended and that contractors should be exempted from liability on liquidated delay damages in the event of an 'inevitable delay' (the threshold of which, however, appears to be not low). Furthermore, it states that the contract price should be adjusted, should continuing construction works become difficult on site due to the spread of Covid-19. Notably, because these guidelines are aimed to address and apply to public construction contracts only, it is not fully clear whether these guidelines would also apply to private construction contracts.

With respect to labour related measures, the Ministry of Employment and Labour published on 30 January 2020 the 'Response Guidance for Businesses to prevent and control the spread of Covid-19' setting out recommendations on how businesses should act during the Covid-19 outbreak. This guidance has been updated seven times since its first publication and the latest edition (ie 8th edition) was published on 7 April 2020.[13] This guidance provides, among other things, for the following measures or remedies:

- Should the Korean government order a workplace to be shut down due to a confirmed or suspected case of Covid-19, the affected Employer will be excused from his/her obligation to pay any wages to the employees.
- Even if the workplace itself is not shut down, if an employee is unable to work due to being quarantined as a confirmed or suspected carrier of Covid-19, the Employer is not legally required to pay wages for the period during which the employee cannot work.
- Employers can also apply for a government subsidy of up to KRW 130,000 (about US$ 100) per day (per employee) to offer paid leave to those confirmed or suspected employees.

13.3.2 The impact of Covid-19 on the operation of construction contracts in Korea

The main reason the Korean government has not at the date of writing (October 2020) ordered any Covid-19-related official shut-down due to the outbreak of Covid-19, is that the impact of the virus on the operation of construction contracts can be dealt with by the already existing Korean legal regime.

Most importantly, Korea is a civil law country in which damages due to a breach of contract require the breaching party to be at 'fault' in order to be held liable.[14]

12 Ministry of Economy and Finance, 'Guidelines for Handling Public Contracts to Respond to Covid-19' (https://www.moef.go.kr/nw/nes/detailNesDtaView.do?searchBbsId1=MOSFBBS_000000000028&-searchNttId1=MOSF_000000000031992&menuNo=4010100) (accessed 21 October 2020).

13 Ministry of Employment and Labour, 'Response Guidance for Businesses to prevent and control the spread of Covid-19' (http://www.moel.go.kr/news/notice/noticeView.do?bbs_seq=20200400383) (accessed 21 October 2020).

14 *Civil Act*, art 390.

A Contractor can be exempted from liability (for liquidated delay damages or other damages) if the failure to comply with the Contract was due to a cause not attributable to the Contractor, such as the Covid-19 outbreak. In other words, there is, in principle, no *force majeure* clause needed in the Contract for a Contractor to be exempted from liability that has arisen due to Covid-19.

To avoid any confusion, however, the Korean Ministry of Land, Infrastructure and Transportation issued a public release on 28 February 2020 stating that circumstances arising from responding to the Covid-19 outbreak may qualify as 'epidemics' under a *force majeure* clause, including clause 17(1)2 of the *Standard Form Construction Contracts for Private Construction Works* (promulgated by the Ministry of Land, Infrastructure and Transportation), which expressly includes 'epidemics' as one of many *force majeure* events. This can be practically quite helpful to a Contractor because it would ease its burden of proof to seek exemption from liability.

Would any abovementioned governmental guidelines or measures qualify as 'change in law' under Korean law? Although this would primarily depend on how 'change in law' is defined in each contract, there is a good possibility that the Covid-19-related guidelines by the Korean government, or even any Covid-19-related implications on the construction industry, would not suffice to be deemed a 'change in law'. That is primarily because the measures by the Korean government have so far all been in guideline or guidance format – and not an ordinance, presidential decree or special legislation.

Absent an express clause in a contract stating that a *force majeure* event (including 'epidemics') could be relied on as a ground for termination, it is rather unlikely that a contract could be terminated based on the outbreak of Covid-19 under Korean law. For reference, there is no court precedent to date in which the Supreme Court has allowed a contracting party to terminate the contract solely on the basis of a change of circumstances (the so-called ***rebus sic stantibus*** jurisprudence). Even the global financial crisis generated by Lehman Brothers which lead to unforeseen circumstances such as a sharp increase in the exchange rate did not suffice to give rise to an entitlement to termination.[15]

13.4 Korean governing law of the contract

13.4.1 Constraints on the governing law of a construction contract

Pursuant to Article 25(1) of the Korean *Act on Private International Law*, parties to a contract have the autonomy to choose the governing law of the contract.

It must be noted, however, that under Article 25(4) of the same *Act* it states that even if all the elements of a contract are solely related to one country (eg Country A), '[i]n case . . . the parties choose the law of any other country [eg Country B], the application of the mandatory provisions of the relevant country [eg Country A] shall not be excluded'.

Whether parties to a contract are permitted to choose *lex mercatoria* as the governing law of the contract is an academic issue which has not yet been tested in the Korean courts.

15 Supreme Court Judgment Case No 2013*Da*26746 (26 September 2013).

At least in an arbitration, however, it is the authors' view that a tribunal may (and should) uphold the parties' choice of *lex mercatoria*, general principles of law, or UNIDROIT Principles as the governing law of the contract.[16] That is not only consistent with, for example, Article 21(1) of the ICC Arbitration Rules, incorporated in the FIDIC Conditions, which provides that '[t]he parties shall be free to agree upon the rules of law to be applied by the arbitral tribunal to the merits of the dispute', but also with the Korean *Arbitration Act* Article 29(1), which states that '[t]he arbitral tribunal shall decide the dispute in accordance with such rules chosen by the parties'.

13.4.2 Formal requirements for a construction contract

There are no formality requirements under Korean law, including under the *Civil Act*, for the conclusion of a construction contract so long as there is a meeting of minds of the contracting parties, normally exchanged and ascertained via valid offer and acceptance. A construction contract can even be entered into orally.

However, when a party to a construction contract is a government entity or organ, there is a special statutory requirement that a contract must be based on a statutory standard form, although deviation by the parties to individual clauses is allowed upon mutual agreement.[17] For contracts executed by an entity or organ of the Korean central government, Article 11 of the *Act on Contracts to which the State is a Party* requires that the standard form contract in Appendix 7 of the *Enforcement Decree* of this *Act* should be used. For contracts concluded by local governments or their organ, the *Act on Contracts to which a Local Government is a Party* applies, which terms are nearly identical to that of the *Act on Contracts to which the State is a Party.*

Article 49(1) and 49(3) of the *Enforcement Decree of the Act on Contracts to which the State is a Party* allows Parties, however, to deviate from the statutory standard form contract if using it is deemed undesirable in particular circumstances. Accordingly, even where the Korean government or its entities or organs are party to a construction contract, it is still possible to conclude such a contract on the basis of the FIDIC Conditions, although in such case it would be prudent to carry out, prior to signing the contract, a careful legal review and risk assessment.

13.5 What Special Provisions in the Particular Conditions are necessary for consistency with applicable laws in Korea?

13.5.1 FIDIC General Conditions are incompatible or inconsistent with Korean governing law of the contract

13.5.1.1 Payment liability of the Employer to the Contractor's personnel

Sub-clause 6.1 of the FIDIC Red, Yellow and Silver Books provides that '[e]xcept as otherwise stated in the Specification, the Contractor shall make arrangements for the engagement of all Contractor's Personnel, and for their payment, accommodation, feeding, transport and welfare'. According to this provision, unless agreed otherwise, the Employer bears no liability for making payment to the Contractor's Personnel.

16 K Suk, 'Laws Applicable to International Construction Contracts Using FIDIC Conditions and their Practical Consequences' (2014) 29(1) *Juris* 21.

17 See also art 49(2) of the *Enforcement Decree of the Act on Contracts to which the State is a Party.*

In contrast, Article 44(1) of the *Labor Standards Act* provides that, in a project that is based on several tiers of contract, '[i]f a subcontractor fails to pay wages to employees for causes attributable to the immediate upper tier contractor, the immediate upper tier contractor shall be liable for the wages jointly and severally with the subcontractor concerned'. It further sets out in the proviso of the same article that '[w]here a cause attributable to the immediate upper tier contractor occurs due to that of his/her upper tier contractor, such upper tier contractor shall also be jointly and severally responsible'. The purpose of this provision is to ensure that workers in a multi-layer contract chain are being paid properly and timely for the work they have performed. According to authoritative commentators, this provision is deemed a mandatory provision.[18]

Hence, sub-clause 6.1 of the FIDIC rainbow suite is likely be found incompatible with the above article and therefore may have to be amended by a Special Provision in the Particular Conditions in order to be consistent with mandatory Korean law.

13.5.1.2 Termination of the Contract after completion

Sub-clause 11.4(d) of the FIDIC Red, Yellow and Silver Books allows an Employer to terminate the Contract as a whole with immediate effect if the defect or damage is deemed, at the Employer's discretion, to deprive the Employer of substantially the whole benefit of the Works.

However, Article 668 of the Korean *Civil Act* states that: 'If, by reason of some defect in the finished subject-matter of the work, the purpose of the contract cannot be achieved, the person who ordered the work may rescind the contract: Provided, That this shall not apply to a building or any other structure on land.' This provision is generally construed as a mandatory one under Korean law.[19] In particular, it follows from the proviso of this article that a contract for the construction of a building or any other structure on land may not be terminated or rescinded once that building or structure is finished (or complete).

Such article is therefore likely to be deemed inconsistent with sub-clause 11.4(d) of the FIDIC rainbow suite and hence a Special Provision in the Particular Conditions may be required to address this inconsistency.

13.5.1.3 Subcontracting the entirety of the Works to a Subcontractor

Sub-clause 5.1(b) of the FIDIC Red Book and sub-clause 4.4(b) of the FIDIC Yellow and Silver Books states that the Contractor may not subcontract any part of the Works for which subcontracting is not permitted as stated in the Contract Data. Further, sub-clause 5.1(a) of the FIDIC Red Book and sub-clause 4.4(a) of the FIDIC Yellow and Silver Books provides that the Contractor is not allowed to subcontract works with a total accumulated value greater than the percentage stated in the Contract Data of the Accepted Contract Amount (under the Red and Yellow Books) or the Contract Price (under the Silver Book).

These sub-clauses, however, do not, in principle, prohibit the subcontracting of the entirety of the Works to a Subcontractor. Only in cases where no percentage is stated

18 K Suk, *Commentary on Private International Law* (PYBook 2013) 356.

19 S Kim and K Chung, 'Legal Implications related to the Application of FIDIC Contract Forms in Korea' (2016) 65(4) *Korean Lawyers Association Journal* 205.

in the Contract Data would the Contractor be prohibited from subcontracting 'the whole of the Works', pursuant to sub-clause 5.1(a) of the FIDIC Red Book and sub-clause 4.4(a) of the FIDIC Yellow and Silver Books.

On the other hand, Article 29(1) of the *Framework Act on the Construction Industry* states that: 'No constructor shall subcontract all of the construction works contracted to him/her or most of the major portions . . . of such construction works to any third constructor.' This means that the subcontracting of the entirety of the works (or even most of the major portions of the works) to a subcontractor is generally forbidden under Korean law. The same article provides an exception, which is that subcontracting the entirety of the works is permitted where the constructor plans, manages, and coordinates any construction works contracted to him/her and subcontracts to at least two persons by splitting such construction works. It is not fully settled by the Korean courts and in academia whether the above article should be deemed a mandatory provision, and what precise effect a breach of this article would have (ie whether it invalidates a contract *ab initio*, or whether it merely creates a ground for contract termination).

But even according to the view that a violation of Article 29(1) is only a ground for termination (and thus would not invalidate a contract *ab initio* unless such right of termination is exercised), the risk of violating this provision is still significant under Korean law. It would be therefore prudent to include in the Particular Conditions of a FIDIC-based contract governed by Korean law a sub-clause mirroring Article 29(1) of the *Framework Act on the Construction Industry*.

13.5.2 FIDIC General Conditions are incompatible or inconsistent with the law of the Site/Country

13.5.2.1 *Ipso facto* termination clauses

According to sub-clause 15.2.1(g) of the FIDIC rainbow suite, the Employer may terminate the Contract if the Contractor becomes bankrupt or insolvent, goes into liquidation, administration, reorganisation, winding-up or dissolution (or other equivalent cases expressly listed in the provision). Termination clauses of this type are commonly called '*ipso facto* clauses' or '*ipso facto* termination clauses'.

The Korean statutory framework governing an insolvency or rehabilitation procedure does not explicitly provide that an *ipso facto* clause is illegal or invalid. However, Article 119(1) of the *Debtor Rehabilitation and Bankruptcy Act* states that '[w]hen the debtor and the other party to a bilateral contract have yet to complete performance of the contract at the time rehabilitation procedures commence, any custodian may cancel or terminate such bilateral contract and request the debtor to meet his/her obligations and require the other party to fulfill his/her obligations'. Accordingly, a custodian has the right to elect at his/her discretion whether to terminate a mutually bilateral contract or to seek performance of it. Terminating such contract based on an *ipso facto* clause would defeat the purpose of the above article granting the custodian such statutory right of election. The Korean Supreme Court therefore ruled that an *ipso facto* clause could be deemed invalid or at least is unenforceable until the relevant insolvency proceedings are closed.[20]

20 Supreme Court Judgment Case No 2005*Da*38263 (6 September 2007).

Therefore, sub-clause 15.2.1(g) of the FIDIC rainbow suite may be deemed invalid by the Korean courts if the place in which the Contractor is incorporated is within Korea (such that Article 119(1) of the *Debtor Rehabilitation and Bankruptcy Act* would be triggered). The authors therefore recommend that this sub-clause 15.2.1(g) be deleted or at least significantly amended should the Contractor be a company incorporated in Korea.

13.5.3 FIDIC General Conditions are incompatible or inconsistent with the relevant laws on dispute determination in Korea

The FIDIC General Conditions, without being modified, are consistent with the procedural laws in Korea. In particular, the Korean *Arbitration Act*, largely following the *UNCITRAL Model Law 2006*, contains no provision that is inconsistent or incompatible with the FIDIC Conditions. However, as discussed in more detail below, the Korean Supreme Court has recognised a jurisprudence that certain arbitration agreements could be deemed invalid. Such jurisprudence therefore must be considered if the seat of arbitration is in Korea and the parties wish to modify the arbitration clause included in the FIDIC Conditions.

13.5.3.1 Optional arbitration clause

An arbitration agreement where the Parties are allowed to choose how finally to resolve the dispute under the contract is commonly referred to in Korea an 'optional arbitration agreement'.[21] For instance, a clause stating that 'the dispute shall be referred to adjudication/arbitration in accordance with the laws of the Purchaser's country' was held by the Korean courts to be an optional arbitration agreement. That was because the clause did not clearly opt for arbitration as the final and only dispute resolution mechanism but rather allowed the parties to the contract to opt for adjudication. Similarly, dispute resolution clauses under which a dispute may be finally resolved by 'arbitration or court proceedings' is also an optional arbitration clause.

The Korean Supreme Court held in 2003 that an optional arbitration agreement should in principle be deemed invalid.[22] One of the stated reasons was that an optional arbitration agreement would fall short of specificity, a condition which the Supreme Court considered as a prerequisite to oust the courts from exercising jurisdiction on the disputed matter. However, if a party wishes to challenge the validity of an optional arbitration agreement, it has to do so in a timely fashion – ie by no later than when the respondent makes its first submission on the merits, which is commonly the Answer to the Request for Arbitration. The Korean lower courts have subsequently followed this ruling.

Given the above risk, special attention should be given when modifying the arbitral clause in the FIDIC Conditions (seated in Korea) to an optional arbitration agreement. It is recommended that amending the arbitral clause (governed by Korean law and/ or where the seat of arbitration is in Korea) to an optional arbitration agreement be avoided entirely if possible.

---

21 K Kim and others, *Arbitration Law and Practice* (PYBook 2016) 69.

22 Supreme Court Judgment Case No 2003*Da*318 (22 August 2003).

13.5.3.2 Multi-tiered dispute resolution clause

Multi-tier(ed) dispute resolution clauses are clauses under which the contracting parties are required to engage in negotiation, mediation, or some other form of alternative dispute resolution method(s) before commencing an arbitration (or litigation). If a Party has failed to comply with either or all of these steps, depending on the applicable curial law, the tribunal may be deemed to have no jurisdiction over a dispute due to the non-compliance of such multi-tier dispute resolution clause.[23]

The FIDIC Conditions also adopt a multi-tier dispute resolution mechanism in that a party is in principle required to go through DAAB (or DAB) proceedings first followed by a mandatory settlement period and only after that is it allowed to initiate an arbitration. Will this dispute resolution mechanism be deemed valid and enforceable by the Korean courts?

The Korean courts consider multi-tier dispute resolution clauses valid and enforceable.[24] That is distinguishable from the Korean law position on optional arbitration clauses. That is because even if a dispute is required to be resolved in stages, a multi-tier dispute resolution clause still makes it clear how a dispute is to be finally resolved, whereas an optional arbitration clause leaves this question open and undecided until a party makes an election how to resolve a dispute finally.

There is no express Korean court precedent to date addressing the issue of whether a Tribunal has jurisdiction over a dispute where each step of a multi-tier dispute resolution clause has not been complied with. In other words, it is not entirely clear whether and to what extent the Korean courts would consider each step (eg DAB/DAAB proceedings phase, negotiation phase, etc) to be a condition precedent to initiating an arbitration. It is worth noting, however, that the Korean Supreme Court has ruled in a case where a multi-tier dispute resolution clause required the parties to first enter into negotiations before commencing an arbitration, and where the parties were in dispute whether such negotiations have been conducted, that the tribunal should be deemed to have valid jurisdiction over such dispute.[25] Hence, there is a fair chance that the Korean courts would take a more relaxed view on whether each step should be strictly construed as a condition precedent to initiating an arbitration.

13.6 What Special Provisions in the Particular Conditions are desirable for consistency with applicable laws in Korea?

13.6.1 Unfair contract terms

Article 22(5) of the *Framework Act on the Construction Industry* stipulates that the terms of a construction contract can be rendered ineffective if deemed remarkably unfair to either party to the contract. It further sets out a non-exhaustive list of circumstances where a contract could be deemed unfair:

1. Where either party to the Contract does not approve changes to the contract amount which occur due to design change or changes in economic conditions after the conclusion of the contract without good cause, or passes the burden on to the other party to the Contract;

23 Kim (n 21) 77.
24 ibid 78–79.
25 Supreme Court Judgment Case No 2005*Da*12452 (27 May 2005).

2. Where either party to the Contract does not approve the change of the contract period due to changes in the scope of work after the conclusion of the Contract without good cause, or passes the burden on to the other party to the Contract;
3. Where either party to the Contract passes responsibility for matters on to the other party to the Contract, which cannot be expected as at the time of the conclusion of the Contract in light of all the relevant conditions, such as to type of a contract for construction works and the scope of construction works;
4. When the scope of the Contract has not been specifically stipulated or a dispute exists between the parties to the Contract, where either party to the Contract infringes on a legitimate interest of the other party to the Contract by determining the scope of the Contract at his/her discretion;
5. Where either party to the Contract infringes on a legitimate interest of the other party to the Contract by determining excessively reduced or increased liability for damages of a party to the Contract due to breach of the Contract;
6. Where either party to the Contract excludes or limits the right of other party to the Contract acknowledged by related *Acts* and subordinate statutes, such as the *Civil Act*, without good cause.

None of the FIDIC Conditions appears to be inconsistent or incompatible with the above article. For instance, sub-clause 13.3.1 of the FIDIC Conditions concerning the Contractor's entitlement to an extension of time and/or additional cost following a Variation is fair and balanced, hence rather consistent with Article 22(5) of the *Framework Act*. Also, sub-clause 15.6, for instance, allows a Contractor to recover lost profits from the Employer following a termination for convenience.

However, the Parties should bear in mind that when agreeing on a deviation from the FIDIC Conditions (including by way of agreeing on Particular Conditions), and provided the Contract is governed by Korean law, Article 22(5) of the *Framework Act* should be taken into account. Otherwise, such special agreement by the Parties may run into the risk of being rendered ineffective.

13.6.2 Transfer of title

FIDIC Conditions sub-clause 7.7 provides that, to the extent that it is consistent with the Laws of the Country, Plant and Materials become the property of the Employer free from any rights of ownership or security interests of other persons from the earlier of when they are delivered to the Site or when the Contractor is entitled to payment in the event of suspension. In other words, this sub-clause presupposes the possibility that a title transfer could occur even without the delivery of the relevant Plant or Materials.

However, with respect to the transfer of title, Article 188(1) of the Korean *Civil Act* stipulates that the transfer of property rights over movables takes effect by delivery. It is possible to reach agreement with the counterparty as to when a good is deemed to be delivered. However, Korean commentators opine that the delivery element is a mandatory requirement for a title transfer and cannot be dispensed with entirely. Hence, there exists a considerable risk that the phrase in sub-clause 7.7 'or when the Contractor is entitled to payment in the event of suspension' may be construed unenforceable under Korean law.

13.6.3 Direct progress payment claims by a Subcontractor to the Employer

The FIDIC Conditions do not entitle a Subcontractor to seek progress payments directly from the Employer. This is not surprising considering the principle of privity of contract which is generally applicable in most jurisdictions (including Korea).

There are, however, special statutes in Korea enacted for the protection of suppliers and Subcontractors – one of them being the *Fair Transactions in Subcontracting Act*.[26] Article 14(1) of this *Act* sets out that 'Where a ground falling under any of the following subparagraphs occurs, [the Employer] shall pay the subcontract consideration corresponding to the completed portion of manufacturing, repair, construction, or service performance directly to the Subcontractor'. The stated grounds are as follows:

1. When the Subcontractor has requested direct payment of the subcontract consideration because the prime Contractor's payment has been suspended, the prime Contractor is bankrupt, or other similar reasons exist, or because the prime Contractor has become unable to pay the subcontract consideration due to revocation of permission, authorization, license, registration, etc. relating to the business.
2. When agreement has been made between the person placing an order, prime Contractor, and Subcontractor that the person placing an order shall pay the subcontract consideration directly to the Subcontractor.
3. When the Subcontractor has requested direct payment of the subcontract consideration where the prime Contractor has failed to pay to the relevant Subcontractor two or more instalments of the subcontract consideration to be paid by the prime Contractor as prescribed in Article 13(1) or (3).

---

26 A similar provision is provided for in art 35(2) of the *Framework Act on the Construction Industry*, which states that:

'In any of the following cases, a project owner shall make a direct payment of the subcontract price to the subcontractor for the portion of works performed by a subcontractor:

1. Where the project owner and the contractor or the project owner, the contractor, and the subcontractor have reached an agreement by specifying their intentions that the project owner pays the subcontract price directly to the subcontractor and the methods of and procedures for making such direct payments;
2. Where a final decision is rendered to order the payment of the subcontract price for the portion of works performed by the subcontractor;
3. Where the contractor delays the payment of the subcontract price referred to in Article 34 (1) on at least two occasions and the subcontractor requests a direct payment of the subcontract price to the project owner;
4. Where the contractor becomes unable to pay the subcontract price on account of the contractor's default, bankruptcy or others or the cancellation of the contractor's registration and the subcontractor requests a direct payment of the subcontract price to the project owner;
5. Where the contractor fails to issue a guarantee which certifies the payment of the subcontract price under Article 34 (2) to the subcontractor without good cause and the project owner becomes aware of such fact or the subcontractor requests a direct payment of the subcontract price to the project owner;
6. Where the contractor enters into a contract for construction works ordered by the State, a local government or a public institution prescribed by Presidential Decree at the price below the rate prescribed by Ordinance of the Ministry of Land, Infrastructure and Transport compared with the estimated price of construction works, and the subcontractor requests the project owner to directly pay the subcontract price.'

4. When the Subcontractor has requested direct payment of the subcontract consideration where the prime Contractor has failed to perform his/her obligation to guarantee the payment of subcontract consideration as prescribed in Article 13-2(1) or (2).

Although there is no need to provide for Special Provisions in the Particular Conditions that impose a duty on the Employer to make direct payment to a Subcontractor in certain circumstances, the Parties should take care that at least no Special Provisions are agreed upon that are in conflict with the above Articles of the *Fair Transactions in Subcontracting Act* or the *Framework Act on the Construction Industry*, given that those articles are generally construed mandatory provisions under Korean law.

13.6.4 Deduction of liquidated damages

Sub-clause 8.8 of the FIDIC Conditions provides for the Employer's entitlement to Delay Damages should the Contractor have failed to comply with its obligation to complete by the Time for Completion. This clause operates by way of multiplying a pre-determined amount stated in the Contract Data to every day the Contractor has been in delay. However, this sub-clause does not allow a Contractor to seek a deduction of the total liquidated damages amount due on the ground that such amount is excessive.

In contract, Article 398(2) of the Korean *Civil Act* states that '[w]here the amount of damages determined in advance is unduly excessive, the court may reduce the amount to a more reasonable and appropriate sum'. As to the meaning of 'unduly excessive', the Supreme Court ruled that the position of the creditor and the debtor, the purpose of the contract, the intent underlying the liquidated damages clause, the proportion of the liquidated damages amount as compared to the actual damages amount, the total amount of liquidated damages and transaction customs must be all considered in light of ordinary social norms. It further set out that if in light of the totality of the foregoing circumstances, it is deemed that if the bargaining powers of the Parties are imbalanced such that imposing liquidated damages on the weak party results in unfairness, the court may consider the amount of liquidated damages as 'unduly excessive'.[27] Although Article 398(2) states the 'court' may reduce the amount of liquidated damages, in practice, an arbitral tribunal seated in Korea and applying Korean law may, more often than not, exercise such power as well. Although it is still disputed in academia whether an arbitral tribunal has the power to invoke Article 398(2) of the *Civil Act*, the Korean courts have found arbitral awards enforceable where Arbitrators have deducted the amount of liquidated damages in relying on this article.

13.6.5 Act on the regulation of terms and conditions

Korean law provides for a special statute regulating standard terms and conditions – namely, the *Act on the Regulation of Terms and Conditions* (the ***ARTC***). The primary purpose of this *Act* is to protect parties with less bargaining power from having unfair standard terms and conditions in a business transaction imposed upon them.

27 Supreme Court Judgment Case No 92*Da*36212 (15 January 1993).

Article 2(1) of the *ARTC* defines 'terms and conditions' under this statute to mean 'the content of a contract that a party to a contract prepares in a specific form in advance in order to enter into a contract with multiple other parties, regardless of their name, type, or scope'. Whether the FIDIC Conditions fall under this definition is not entirely clear as the Korean courts have not yet decided on this issue. There are commentators who take the view that the FIDIC Conditions may be subject to the *ARTC*, given that this *Act* does not expressly require standard terms and conditions to have been drafted or specifically prepared by one party.[28] On the other hand, the *ARTC* contains a number of provisions that only applies to 'customers'. For instance, Article 5 states that '[t]erms and conditions shall be construed impartially in accordance with the principle of trust and good faith and shall not be construed differently depending on customers' and that '[i]f the meaning of terms and conditions is not clear, it shall be construed in favor of customers'. It is questionable whether a Contractor would qualify as customer contemplated in the *ARTC*. The applicability of the *ARTC* on contracts that are based on the FIDIC Conditions has yet to be considered in Korean courts.

Should the *ARTC* apply, any clause in the terms and conditions which is unfair and contrary to the principle of trust and good faith will be deemed null and void (see Article 6(1) of the *ARTC*). It would be therefore prudent when amending the General Conditions of the FIDIC forms (governed by Korean law) to review whether any potential risk exists that an amendment might be considered unfair under the *ARTC* such as to render the relevant clause ineffective or void.

13.7 Summary of applicable legislation for Korean governing law of the contract

13.7.1 Entry into a construction contract

Contracts generally	*Civil Act* *Commercial Act* *Act on Contracts to Which the State is a Party* *Act on Contracts to Which a Local Government is a Party*
Construction contracts	*Civil Act* *Framework Act on the Construction Industry*

13.7.2 Termination of a construction contract

Bankruptcy, insolvency, liquidation	*Civil Act* *Commercial Act* *Debtor Rehabilitation and Bankruptcy Act*
Guarantees under forms of Security (Tender Security, Demand Guarantee, Surety Bond, Advance Payment Guarantee, Retention Money Guarantee, Payment Guarantee by Employer)	*Civil Act* *Commercial Act*

28 Kim and Chun (n 19).

13.7.3 Dispute resolution

Limitation periods	*Civil Act* *Commercial Act*
Liability	*Civil Act* *Commercial Act* *Framework Act on the Construction Industry*
Arbitration	*Arbitration Act (provided that the seat of arbitration is within Korea)*

13.8 Summary of applicable legislation if the Site/Country is in Korea

13.8.1 Operation of a construction contract

Registration and administration of professionals – Engineers, Architects, Building Surveyors, Surveyors	*Building Act* *Certified Architects Act* *Construction Technology Promotion Act* *Engineering Industry Promotion Act* *Framework Act on the Construction Industry*
Registration/licencing of Contractors and subcontractors	*Building Act* *Framework Act on the Construction Industry*
Subcontractors	*Fair Transactions in Subcontracting Act* *Framework Act on the Construction Industry*
Use of liens/Assignment of debts	*Civil Act* *Commercial Act*
Labour	*Labor Standard Act* *Minimum Wage Act* *Trade Union and Labor Relations Adjustment Act*
Design/Moral rights	*Copyright Act* *Patent Act* *Trademark Act* *Utility Model Act*
Copyright	*Copyright Act* *Patent Act* *Trademark Act* *Utility Model Act*
The product being produced from the Works	*Civil Act* *Copyright Act* *Patent Act* *Trademark Act* *Utility Model Act*
Planning	*Act on the Improvement of Urban Areas and Residential Environments* *Building Act* *Landscape Act* *National Land Planning and Utilization Act* *Special Act on Promotion of and Support for Urban Regeneration* *Urban Development Act*

Work affecting adjacent property to the Site	*Civil Act* *Building Act* *Environmental Impact Assessment Act* *Clean Air Conservation Act* *Noise and Vibration Control Act* *Water Environment Conservation Act* *Sewerage Act* *Waste Control Act*
Heritage	*Cultural Heritage Protection Act*
Environment	*Environmental Impact Assessment Act* *Clean Air Conservation Act* *Noise and Vibration Control Act* *Water Environment Conservation Act* *Sewerage Act* *Waste Control Act*
Building and construction permits, Execution of construction work, Standard of construction work	*Building Act* *Framework Act on the Construction Industry*
Health and safety	*Occupational Safety and Health Act*
Ownership of Plant and Materials	*Civil Act* *Commercial Act* *Registration of Real Estate Act*
Employer's sale of Contractor's Equipment, surplus material, wreckage and Temporary Works	*Civil Act* *Commercial Act*
Insurance	*Commercial Act* *Storm and Flood Insurance Act* *National Health Insurance Act* *Employment Insurance Act* *Industrial Accident Compensation Insurance Act* *National Pension Act*
Statutory rights that coexist with contractual rights	*Fair Transactions in Subcontracting Act* *Framework Act on the Construction Industry* *Labor Standard Act*
Liability for defective work	*Civil Act* *Framework Act on the Construction Industry*
Liability for nuisance	*Civil Act, Environmental Impact Assessment Act* *Clean Air Conservation Act* *Noise and Vibration Control Act* *Water Environment Conservation Act* *Sewerage Act* *Waste Control Act*

13.8.2 Termination of a construction contract

Bankruptcy, insolvency, liquidation	*Debtor Rehabilitation and Bankruptcy Act*
Decennial liability and liability generally for the total or partial collapse of structures	*Civil Act* *Framework Act on the Construction Industry*

13.8.3 Dispute resolution

Dispute before a local board/Adjudication	*Civil Procedure Act* *Framework Act on the Construction Industry* (Article 69 – Statutory Mediation for Construction Disputes) *Enforcement Decree of the Framework Act on the Construction Industry*
Limitation periods	*Civil Act* *Commercial Act*

13.9 Summary of applicable legislation if the 'seat' of the dispute determination is Korea

Dispute resolution	*Civil Procedure Act* *Judicial Conciliation of Civil Disputes Act*
Limitation periods	*Civil Act (provided that the governing law of the contract is Korean law)* *Commercial Act (provided that the governing law of the contract is Korean law)*
Adjudication	*n/a*
Arbitration	*Arbitration Act*

13.10 Issues that a court or arbitrator may construe differently to that expected from the words of the Contract, because of local law or custom

There are terms in the FIDIC Conditions where there is no precisely corresponding term under Korean law. There are also terms in the FIDIC Conditions that may be construed differently by a Korean arbitrator (compared to an arbitrator, for instance, coming from a common law jurisdiction) because these are concepts not commonly used in the Korean construction industry.

13.10.1 Engineer

The FIDIC Conditions provide that the Engineer, on the one hand, (1) shall act as a skilled professional and shall be deemed to act for the Employer, and on the other (2) shall carry out his/her duties neutrally between the Parties. Such a concept where the Engineer may wear a dual hat (one as an agent of the Employer and one as an independent supervisor of the project) is not one commonly used in the Korean construction industry.

In Korea, a construction project is normally overseen and supervised by a third-party supervisor, also called ***Gam-Li***. *Gam-Li* under the *Construction Technology Promotion Act* applies to construction projects in which the Employer is a state, a local government, or a public institution, and *Gam-Li* of the *Building Act* applies to private construction projects. A *Gam-Li* would normally provide legal technical support and advice to the Employer, including overseeing whether the construction project is being conducted pursuant to relevant regulations or governmental restrictions (eg construction permits).

The position of *Gam-Li* is different, however, from an Engineer under the FIDIC Conditions in that (1) a Korean architect certificate is required to qualify as *Gam-Li*, (2) a *Gam-Li* would not function as certifier, and (3) a *Gam-Li* normally does not act as an agent of the Employer. *Gam-Li* is often translated into 'engineer', but the legal meaning of it is different from the meaning of an 'Engineer' as used under the FIDIC Conditions.

13.10.2 Indirect or consequential loss or damage

Pursuant to English court judgments following *Hadley v Baxendale* [1854] EWHC J70, indirect or consequential loss or damage falls within the exclusion clause in the FIDIC Conditions (see for instance sub-clause 1.14 of the FIDIC Silver Book or sub-clause 1.15 of the FIDIC Red or Yellow Book). The term 'consequential loss', however, is not a legal term used in Korean law. This expression does not appear in the *Civil Act*.

Rather, Korean law knows the term 'special loss', which are losses that are more remote than ordinary (or direct) losses or damages and are only recoverable if there was foreseeability of such loss at the time the contract was breached.[29]

It is therefore likely that Korean courts will construe indirect or consequential loss or damage, absent a special contractual definition of those, in equivalent terms to special loss under Korean law.

13.10.3 Reckless misconduct

The term 'deliberate default' in sub-clauses 1.14 and 1.15 of the FIDIC Red or Yellow Book can be construed under Korean law as 'intentional breach'.

There is, however, no legal concept in Korean law that corresponds to 'reckless misconduct'.[30] Given that reckless misconduct is generally understood to be an action expecting the possibility of harmful result without intent but wilfully taking the risk,[31] it is not precisely translatable to a grossly negligent act (under Korean law) which refers to an act by a party that was not wilfully conducted but which was easily foreseeable and avoidable and nevertheless has been conducted without even such level of care. The meaning of 'reckless misconduct' therefore will be left to the discretion of the Korean courts or a Korean arbitrator should the above phrase (alone) become an issue in a dispute.

13.11 References

13.11.1 Books

K Kim and others, *Arbitration Law and Practice* (PYBook 2016).
K Suk, Commentary on Private International Law (PYBook 2013).

29 This is distinguishable from the foreseeability requirement under English law under which consequential losses and damages are only recoverable if they were foreseeable at the time the contract was entered into.

30 S Kim and Chung, K., 'Legal Implications related to the Application of FIDIC Contract Forms in Korea' (2016) 65(4) *Korean Lawyers Association Journal* 200.

31 Bryan Garner, *Black's Law Dictionary* (9th edn, Thomson Reuters 2009) 1385 (recited from Kim and Chung (n 30), 201–202).

13.11.2 Journals

S Kim and K Chung, 'Legal Implications related to the Application of FIDIC Contract Forms in Korea' (2016) 65(4) *Korean Lawyers Association Journal* 174.
K Suk, 'Laws Applicable to International Construction Contracts Using FIDIC Conditions and their Practical Consequences' (2014) 29(1) *Juris* 3.

13.11.3 Internet

Legislation: http://www.law.go.kr/.
Case law: http://glaw.scourt.go.kr/.

CHAPTER 14

Applying FIDIC contracts in Malaysia

Ben Bury and Julie-Anne Mallis

DOI: 10.4324/9781003200901-14

14.1 Outline of the legal environment in Malaysia

14.1.1 The constitutional structure of Malaysia

Malaysia is a constitutional monarchy with a federal system of government. Having its origins in the Malay Kingdom, in the 18th century much of Malaysia was colonised by the British as part of the Straits Settlements (comprising Penang, Singapore and Malacca, and by the 19th century, states in Peninsula Malaysia).[1] In 1946, Peninsular Malaysia unified to become the Malayan Union. On 31 August 1957, the Malayan Union achieved independence from Great Britain (known as Merdeka Day) and was restructured as the Federation of Malaya.[2] In 1963, the Federation of Malaya merged

1 Following the signing of treaty of Federation 1895, four states: Perak; Selangor; Negeri Sembilan and Pahang became 'Protected States' of the British Colony (Federated Malay States). The Unfederated Malay States (Kelantan, Kedah, Perlis, Trengganu and Johore) maintained a level of autonomy over local matters, however, foreign affairs and other important aspects of government remained under British rule.

2 A number of enactments and ordinances were passed at the time as well as agreements to enable the Malayan Union to achieve its independence including the *Federation of Malay Independence Act 1957* (UK) in Britain and the Order in Council made under it, the *Federation of Malay Agreement 1957* between the British High Commissioner on behalf of Queen Elizabeth II and the traditional Malay

with Singapore, Sabah and Sarawak to form the independent state of Malaysia. On 9 August 1965, Singapore left Malaysia to become its own independent nation.

Today, Malaysia consists of 13 states and three Federal Territories separated by the South China Sea into two non-contiguous regions: Peninsular Malaysia (also known as West Malaysia) and East Malaysia. There are 11 states in West Malaysia: Kedah, Kelantan, Pahang, Penang, Perak, Perlis, Johor, Malacca, Negeri Sembilan, Selangor and Terengganu; and two federal territories: Kuala Lumpur and Putrajaya. There are two states in East Malaysia: Sabah and Sarawak; and one Federal Territory: Labuan.

Of the 13 states, nine (all located in West Malaysia) are constitutional monarchies headed by traditional Malay rulers of royal descent. The other two states in West Malaysia, Penang and Malacca, and the states in East Malaysia, Sabah and Sarawak, are headed by governors and do not have rulers of royal descent.

The constitutional framework for Malaysia is governed by the *Federal Constitution*. Each state has its own state-level constitution. Pursuant to Articles 73 to 80 of the *Federal Constitution*, the states are empowered to legislate with respect to state matters including land matters, public works, local government, agriculture and forestry, Islamic law and public holidays. The remaining powers are retained by the federal government.

The *Federal Constitution* is a higher law in the sense that any law, whether federal or state law that is inconsistent with the *Federal Constitution* will be void.[3]

Pursuant to Article 127 of the *Federal Constitution*, Malaysia enjoys a separation of powers which divides its system of governance into three distinct branches: the executive, the legislature and the judiciary.

The executive is officially headed by the Yang di-Pertuan Agong,[4] also known as the King, who is chosen on a rotational basis from the royal rulers of each state every five years or when the position becomes vacant (ie due to death, removal from office, incapacity or abdication). The Yang di-Pertuan Agong's role is largely ceremonial, however, and executive authority of Malaysia is vested in the Cabinet led by the Prime Minister.[5] The Yang di-Pertuan Agong is responsible for appointing the Prime Minister as head of government, and the Cabinet, on the advice of the Prime Minister.[6] At a state level, the executive is headed by either the Minister or the Chief Minister.

The legislature, at a federal level, consists of the Dewan Negara (the Upper House/Senate) and the Dewan Raykat (the Lower House/House of Representatives). Each state parliament consists of the State Legislative Assembly elected from single-member constituencies.

The judiciary is independent of the executive and the legislature. The composition of the judicial system is set out in paragraph 14.1.3 below.

14.1.2 The legal system of Malaysia

Malaysia is a dual legal system in which the common law and Syariah law (or Islamic law) both apply.[7]

rulers, the *Federal Constitution Ordinance 1957*, enactments in each state, and in Malacca and Penang, resolutions of the state Legislatures.

3 *Federal Constitution*, art 4.

4 ibid art 39.

5 ibid art 40.

6 ibid art 43.

7 ibid art 121 (1A). Syariah law, which mostly comprises civil laws (for example, personal laws, family law and religious observance), applies to every Muslim in Malaysia.

Malaysia inherited its common law system from England and Wales. The *Civil Law Act 1956* provides that laws of England and Wales, including the common law, equity and statutes, apply in Malaysia insofar 'as the circumstances of the States of Malaysia and their respective inhabitants permit and subject to such qualifications as local circumstances render necessary'.[8] In relation to commercial matters (including issues pertaining to the law of partnerships, corporations, banks and banking, principals and agents, carriers by air, land and sea, marine insurance, life and fire insurance and mercantile law generally) the *Act* further provides that:

- In West Malaysia (except for Malacca and Penang), in the absence of local legislation, the principles of English commercial law apply as they did on 7 April 1956[9]
- In Malacca, Penang, Sabah and Sarawak, in the absence of local legislation, the commercial law to be administered shall be the same as would be administered in England and Wales in the like case at the corresponding period, if such question or issue had arisen or had to be decided in England or Wales.[10]

In common with a number of other British colonies, Malaysia has largely codified the common law in relation to contracts in the *Contracts Act 1950.*

14.1.3 The court system in Malaysia

There is a single hierarchy of courts in Malaysia which can be separated into two categories: superior courts and subordinate courts.[11]

The superior courts comprise the High Court, the Court of Appeal, and the Federal Court, previously called the Supreme Court. The Federal Court is the final court of adjudication in Malaysia. Decisions of the Federal Court are binding on all courts inferior to it. The High Court in Kuala Lumpur (Federal Territory) and Shah Alam (in the state of Selangor) operate a specialist construction court to handle construction disputes.

The subordinate courts in Malaysia comprise the Sessions Courts, the Magistrates' Courts (which is separated into the First Class Magistrates' Court and Second Class Magistrates' Court), and other miscellaneous courts and tribunals. The subordinate courts are controlled and supervised by the superior courts, and in particular, the High Court, which has overall supervision and control over the subordinate courts.

14.2 The construction industry in Malaysia

14.2.1 Overview

Since the formation of Malaysia in 1963, the construction industry has grown exponentially – largely due to Malaysia's drive to become a developed nation,

8 *Civil Law* Act 1956 (Act 67), section 3. This provision covers West Malaysia (common law and equity as administered in England on 7 April 1957), Sabah (common law and equity together with statute as administered or in force in England on 1 December 1951) and Sarawak (common law and equity together with statute as administered or in force in England on 12 December 1949, subject to s 3(ii)). There are also similar provisions under the *Criminal Procedure Code* (1935) (Act 593) in relation to crimes.

9 *Civil Law Act 1956* (Act 67), section 5(1).

10 ibid s 5(2).

11 There is also a Syriah Court in Malaysia.

substantial investment in the development of basic infrastructure and the growing demand for affordable public housing.

In the early 1990s, former Prime Minister Mahathir Mohamad announced the 'Malaysia Vision 2020'[12] which sparked a construction boom and resulted in the construction of several mega projects including the development of the federal territory of Putrajaya, Kuala Lumpur Sentral, Petronas Twin Towers, the Kuala Lumpur International Airport and the Kuala Lumpur Integrated Transit System (Rapid KL).[13] This construction boom continued in the 2000s and early 2010s with the construction of inter alia the Express Rail Link, Stormwater Management and Tunnel Road, East Coast Expressway, the Kuala Lumpur International Airport 2 and Sultan Abdul Halim Muadzam Shah Bridge (Penang Second Bridge).[14] Recently, the construction industry has experienced steady growth due to the near completion of major infrastructure projects, the cancellation and/or suspension of several major infrastructure projects[15] and an oversupply of residential and commercial property. In 2017, the total value of construction work was MYR138.45 billion (US$34.2 billion), followed by MYR145.55 billion (US$35.9 billion) in 2018 and MYR146.37 billion (US$36.1 billion) in 2019.[16] Prior to the Covid-19 outbreak, it had been forecast that major transport and utility projects and an increase in the supply of newly planned affordable homes and industrial segments would support continued moderate economic growth in the short to medium term.[17]

Malaysia is one of the fastest growing economies amongst the Association of Southeast Asian Nations (**ASEAN**) countries.[18] Since the 1990s, the construction industry has generally accounted for 3 per cent to 5 per cent of Malaysia's Gross Domestic Product (**GDP**) (although it peaked at 8.2 per cent in 2015).[19] Recently, the construction industry accounted for 4.6 per cent of Malaysia's GDP in 2017, 4.5 per cent in 2018 and 4.7 per cent in 2019.[20] Whilst its direct contribution to Malaysia's GDP is comparatively small compared to the services, manufacturing and agriculture

---

12 The 'Malaysia Vision 2020' sought to achieve a self-sufficient, fully developed, industrialized and modernized Malaysia in all aspects of life by 2020 thereby transforming Malaysia into a prosperous, competitive, dynamic, robust and resilient country.

13 Although there was an economic downturn in the late 1990s due to the Asian Financial Crisis.

14 In addition to the 'Malaysia Vision 2020', the development of infrastructure formed an important part of the 8th, 9th and 10th Malaysia Plans (the economic development plans proposed by the federal government for 2001 to 2005, 2006 to 2010 and 2011 to 2015, respectively).

15 The federal government suspended and/or cancelled several major infrastructure projects including inter alia the suspension of the East Coast Rail Link in 2018 in order to reduce its debt, although the project has since recommenced.

16 'Quarterly Construction Statistics - Fourth Quarter 2019' (Department of Statistics Malaysia (eStatistik) 10 February 2020) https://newss.statistics.gov.my/newss-portalx/ep/epFreeDownloadContentSearch.seam?contentId=140923&actionMethod=ep%2FepFreeDownloadContentSearch.xhtml%3Acontent-Action.doDisplayContent&cid=718135 (accessed 18 January 2021).

17 See eg the Annual Report 2018 (Construction Industry Development Board) https://www.cidb.gov.my/index.php/en/about-us/publication/annual-report (accessed 18 January 2021). See para 14.2.11 below in relation to the impact of Covid-19 on the Malaysian construction industry.

18 Noranida Mokthsim and Khairulmaini Osman Salleh, 'Malaysia's Efforts towards Achieving a Sustainable Development: Issues, Challenges and Prospects' (2014) 120 *Procedia: Social and Behavioral Sciences* 299.

19 Nazirah Zainul Abidin, 'Sustainable Construction in Malaysia: Developers' Awareness' (2009) 53 *World Academy of Science, Engineering and Technology* 807, 809. See also the Economic Report Archives (Ministry of Finance Malaysia) https://www.treasury.gov.my/index.php/en/archives (accessed 18 January 2021).

20 See 'Economic Report 2020', 'Economic Report 2019' and 'Economic Report 2018' (Ministry of Finance Malaysia) https://www.treasury.gov.my/index.php/en/archives (accessed 18 January 2021).

sectors, the construction industry is a substantial economic driver for Malaysia.[21] In particular, the construction industry provides support to Malaysia's aggregate economy through forward and backward linkages with other key sectors including the manufacture of building supplies and materials (eg basic metal products), the manufacture of equipment (eg electrical equipment), real estate, professional services (for example, engineering and architectural services), financial services and transportation.[22] The construction industry also provides essential infrastructure to enable industrial growth in Malaysia.[23]

In addition to its economic significance, the construction industry – comprising a diverse range of individuals from construction professionals, management personnel and administrative staff to unskilled foreign labour – is a major employer in Malaysia. In the past five years, the construction industry has consistently employed between 8 per cent and 9 per cent of the total workforce in Malaysia, with approximately 1,273,100 persons employed in the first half of 2019.[24]

The construction industry in Malaysia operates within two main sectors: the private sector and the public sector. Historically, the public sector was the main contributor to the growth of Malaysia's construction industry; however, following the implementation of private finance initiatives by the Federal Government, there has been a shift towards a more equal contribution between the private sector and public sector.[25] For example, in the fourth quarter of 2019, the private sector accounted for a 56.1 per cent share of the value of construction work done whereas the public sector accounted for a 43.9 per cent share.[26] Construction works commonly carried out by the private sector include residential, industrial and commercial works.[27] As a developing nation, the public sector is primarily focused on the development of basic infrastructure including roads, rail links, dams, irrigation works, utilities, schools, houses, factories and other physical foundations.[28] Major public infrastructure works currently underway in Malaysia include the East Coast Rail Link (ECRL), Mass Rapid Transit 2 (MRT2), Light Rail Transit 3 (LRT3), West Coast Expressway (WCE), Bayan Lepas Light Rail Transit (LRT), Pan Borneo and Coastal Highways, Langat 2 Water Treatment Plant, Baleh Hydroelectric Dam and Sarawak Water Supply Grid Programme (Phase 1).

Whilst historically the construction industry in Malaysia has been principally domestic, following the delivery of mega projects, saturation of the domestic market

21 Raza Ali Khan, Mohd Shahir Liew and Zulkipli Bin Ghazali, 'Malaysian Construction Sector and Malaysia Vision 2020: Developed Nation Status' (2014) 109 *Procedia: Social and Behavioral Sciences* 507, 508.

22 ibid.

23 Since achieving its independence in 1965, Malaysia has transformed from an agriculture economy to a manufacturing economy.

24 'Statistical Tables: Labour Force' appended to '2020 Economic Outlook' (Ministry of Finance Malaysia, 5 November 2020 https://www.treasury.gov.my/index.php/en/archives/2020/economic-outlook-2020 (accessed 18 January 2021).

25 Mastura Jaafar and Azlan Raofuddin Nuruddin, 'The development of public and private construction procurement systems in the Malaysian construction industry' (2012) 11 *Journal of Design and Built Environment* 1, 2.

26 'Quarterly Construction Statistics: Fourth Quarter 2019' (Department of Statistics Malaysia) https://www.dosm.gov.my/v1/index.php?r=column/cthemeByCat&cat=77&bul_id=MFYyOXR-pZzR5THVKS2JxSnR6VUxWZz09&menu_id=OEY5SWtFSVVFVUpmUXEyaHppMVhEdz09 (accessed 18 January 2021).

27 Construction works in Malaysia include new construction, repair, maintenance, alteration and additional works, civil engineering works and electrical and mechanical works.

28 Nurul Alifah Jatarona, Aminah Md Yusof, Syuhaida Ismail and Chai Chaang Saar, 'Public Construction Contracts Performance in Malaysia' (2016) *Journal of Southeast Asian Research* 1, 1.

and the impact of globalisation, many Malaysian contractors began to expand their operations internationally.[29] Between 2000 and 2010, Malaysian contractors were involved in 652 projects in 49 countries including toll road projects in India, power station projects in India and Pakistan and Formula One racing circuits in the Middle East.[30] However, there has been a sharp decline in the past decade of participation in international construction projects – particularly in the Middle East.[31] This is likely due to the high risk involved with carrying out international projects.

As for foreign participation in Malaysia, whilst the Malaysian construction industry is, in theory, open to the foreign competitors, historically, only a small percentage of foreign contractors have been involved in Malaysian construction projects. The likely reason for this is the barriers to registration discussed at paragraph 14.2.3 below. Recently, there has been an influx of Chinese participation in the Malaysian construction industry either directly or through joint ventures with local contractors across both public infrastructure works (primarily rail and utility projects) and private sector works (primarily high-rise residential developments).[32] In addition, Chinese developers are actively engaged in development projects in Malaysia including in the Iskandar region (for example, Forest City) and land reclamation projects.

14.2.2 Recent developments

There have been a number of initiatives in the past 20 years aimed at modernising Malaysia's construction industry, which has long been plagued with the challenges associated with lack of education and training, productivity and efficiency, technology, safety, quality and recruitment (including labour shortages, local recruitment issues (including low wages and limited career development) and a heavy reliance on foreign labour).

In 2004, the Construction Industry Development Board (**CIDB**)[33] established the Construction Labour Exchange Centre (**CLAB**) to supply, manage and distribute manpower (including both foreign and local labour) to construction industry.

In 2006, the federal government launched the Construction Industry Master Plan (**CIMP**), a 10-year plan to transform the construction industry in Malaysia into a world class, innovative and knowledgeable global solution provider. The CIMP was based on a vision to create a dynamic, productive and resilient enabling sector, supporting sustainable wealth creation and value creation, driven by technologically-pervasive, creative and cohesive construction. It had seven 'strategic thrusts': (1) to

29 Nur Kamaliah Mustaffa, Hamimah Adnan and Mohd Zaid Zakaria, 'Entry Strategies for Malaysian Construction Related Companies Going Abroad' (2012) 6(6) *Australian Journal of Basic and Applied Sciences* 323, 323.

30 ibid.

31 Conference Paper prepared by Norliana Sarpin, Chia Yi Ling, Narimah Kasim, Hamidun Mohd Noh, Roshartini Omar and Rozlin Zainal, 'Key Strategies in Undertaking International Construction Project: Contractors' Perspective' https://www.matec-conferences.org/articles/matecconf/abs/2019/15/matecconf_iconbee2019_03019/matecconf_iconbee2019_03019.html (accessed 18 January 2021).

32 Some, but not all, Chinese participation is linked to the Belt and Road Initiative. See para 14.2.10 below.

33 The Construction Industry Development Board is a statutory body overseen by the Ministry of Works established under the *Akta Lembaga Pembangunan Industri Pembinaan Malaysia Act 1994* (Act 520). It is tasked with advising the federal government, state Governments and other stakeholders on matters affecting or connected with the construction industry in Malaysia and developing the capacity and capability of the construction industry through enhancement of quality and productivity with a particular focus on professionalism, innovation and knowledge.

integrate the construction industry value chain to enhance productivity and efficiency; (2) to strengthen the construction industry image; (3) to strive for the highest standard of quality, occupational safety and health and environment practices; (4) to develop human resource capabilities and capacities in the construction industry; (5) to innovate through research and development and adopt new construction methods; (6) to leverage on information in the construction industry; and (7) to obtain benefits from globalisation including the export of construction products and services.

Following the CIMP, in 2016 the Federal Government launched the Construction Industry Transformative Plan (**CITP**) which aimed to transform the construction industry to be highly productive, environmentally sustainable, with globally competitive players while focused on safety and quality standards.[34] As with the CIMP, the CITP was based on a number of 'strategic thrusts' – namely: (1) quality, safety and professionalism; (2) environmental sustainability; (3) productivity; and (4) internationalism and competitiveness.[35]

As part of its efforts under the CIMP and the CITP, the Malaysian construction industry has recently focused on adopting innovative construction methods including Industrialised Building System (**IBS**). IBS is a prefabrication construction method in which structural components of a structure are mass produced either in factory or at site under strict quality control and minimal onsite activities. There are a number of advantages to IBS including higher quality structural components, strict quality assurance control, flexibility in design, cleaner and safer construction sites, reduced need for onsite labour and shorter project completion (without the impact of adverse weather).

Whilst IBS was first used in Malaysia in the early 1960s, there has been a recognisable shift in the adoption of IBS in construction projects in Malaysia since its promotion under the CIMP and CITP and the introduction of several initiatives by the Federal Government and the CIDB. In 2004, new government building projects were strongly encouraged to adopt at least a 50 per cent IBS component.[36] The Federal Government then undertook in 2005 to construct 100,000 affordable housing units using IBS.[37] This was followed in 2006 by the introduction of a tax incentive for IBS manufacturers under which Acceleration Capital Allowance could be claimed for expenses incurred in the purchase of steel moulds used for precast concrete.[38] In 2008, the Treasury issued Treasury Circular SPP 7/2008 requiring all public projects with a contract value exceeding MYR10 million (US$2.5 million) adopt at least a 70 per cent IBS component as part of the contract tender.[39] The use of IBS by the public sector has

34 The Construction Industry Transformative Plan formed part of Malaysia's national agenda for 2016 to 2020. See the Construction Industry Transformative Plan website http://www.citp.my/ (accessed 18 January 2021).

35 ibid.

36 Mohd Idrus Din, Noraini Bahriand others, 'The Adoption of Industrialised Building System (IBS) Construction in Malaysia: The History, Policies, Experiences and Lessons Learned' (Paper presented at the 29th International Symposium on Automation and Robotics in Construction (ISARC), Eindhoven, Netherlands 2012) https://www.iaarc.org/publications/proceedings_of_the_29th_isarc/the_adoption_of_industrialised_building_system_ibs_construction_in_malaysia_the_history_policies_experiences_and_lesson_learned.html (accessed 18 January 2021). The IBS component is measured using an IBS Score Manual developed by the Construction Industry Development Board.

37 ibid.

38 ibid.

39 At the same time, an IBS Centre with IBS testing facilities was established by the Construction Industry Development Board.

increased significantly in recent years from 24 per cent in 2014 to 81 per cent in 2019. As of August 2019, the CIDB had registered 300 IBS manufacturers and trained 5,502 construction professionals in IBS and modular coordination. In addition, 12,315 IBS contractors and 9,076 IBS installers have registered with the CIDB.

Notwithstanding the positive developments in the adoption of IBS, Malaysia's construction industry continues to suffer from a lack of innovation and technology. Whilst Building Information Modelling (**BIM**) has been used in Malaysia since 2007 and there has been some effort by the Federal Government and CIDB to promote BIM, progress on implementing BIM on construction projects has been relatively slow. In a recent survey of 268 participants, only 13 per cent from both the public and private sectors were using BIM in their organisation.[40] To encourage the wider use of BIM, the Public Works Department has targeted the use of BIM on 50 per cent of public projects with a contract value exceeding MYR50 million (US$12.4 million) by 2021 and 80 per cent by 2025. In addition, in 2018 the CIDB introduced a mandatory requirement for the adoption of BIM on any public project with a contract value exceeding MYR100 million (US$24.7 million).

There has been a notable push in Malaysia to retain, sustain, improve and preserve the environment and promote sustainable development. Malaysia has taken several steps aimed at reducing its carbon emissions including inter alia mandating the use of palm biodiesel in diesel fuel,[41] enacting reforms including the *Renewable Energy Act 2011*[42] and *Sustainable Development Authority Act* 2011 (Act 726)[43] and ratifying the Paris Agreement.[44] Recently, the federal government announced that it intends to replace the *Environmental Quality Act 1974* with a new *Environment Protection Act* which contains comprehensive environmental protections, wider enforcement powers and stringent pollution punishments.

The CIDB has developed a number of programs and initiatives aimed at promoting sustainability in the construction industry. In particular, it has developed a 'MyCREST tool' which enables industry players to determine their carbon impact. More recently, it has developed a sustainable infrastructure rating tool 'Sustainable Infrastar' which is capable of measuring sustainable elements in the design, construction and operation of infrastructure projects. From December 2020, 50 per cent of new infrastructure projects with a contract value exceeding MYR100 million (US$24.7 million) are targeted to be certified with sustainability infrastructure tools. In addition, the CIDB has opened the Sustainable Construction Excellence Centre (**MAMPAN**) which provides operational models to develop, promote and implement innovative new sustainable options.

40 Idris Othman, Yasser Yahya Al-Ashmori, Yani Rahmawati, Y.H. Mugahed Amran, Mohammed Ali Mohammed Al-Bared, 'The level of Building Information Modelling (BIM) Implementation in Malaysia' (2020) *Ain Shams Engineering Journal* 1.

41 See the National Biofuel Policy https://policy.asiapacificenergy.org/sites/default/files/Malaysia%20Biofuel%20Policy.pdf (accessed at 18 January 2021),

42 The *Renewable Energy Act 2011* (Act 725) provides for the establishment and implementation of a special tariff system as a catalyst for the generation of renewable energy.

43 The *Sustainable Development Authority Act* 2011 (Act 726) establishes the Sustainable Energy Development Authority (**SEDA**), a statutory authority tasked with administering and managing the implementation of the special tariff system under the *Renewable Energy Act 2011* (Act 725) and promoting the use of renewable energy in power generation.

44 The Paris Agreement which was adopted on 12 December 2015 by 196 parties at the 2015 United Nations Climate Change Conference in Paris, is aimed at reducing carbon emissions by 2030.

14.2.3 Public procurement

Public procurement in Malaysia is guided by the principles of public accountability, transparency, value for money, open and fair competition and fair dealing.[45] The primary objective of public procurement is to obtain value for money through acquisition of works, supplies and services.[46] In order to meet this objective, close attention is paid to both price factors and non-price factors such as whole life cost, quality, quantity, timeliness, maintenance and warranty.[47]

The federal government has not enacted any specific legislation in respect of public procurement, although it has indicated that it will do so by 2023. The current legal framework for public procurement by the federal government, state governments and semi-government agencies comprises several statutes and instruments, namely:

- The *Government Contracts Act 1949* which empowers ministries and their delegates to enter into contracts on behalf of the federal government and state governments.
- The *Financial Procedure Act 1957* which provides for the control and management of the public finances of Malaysia and outlines financial and accounting procedures.
- Treasury Instructions which detail financial and accounting procedures and encompass regulations that must be adhered to in the management of government funds.
- Treasury Circulars which clarify, implement, improve and amend certain policies, rules and procedures whenever required by the federal government and financial authorities.
- Federal Central Contract Circulars which are issued to inform the users on the availability of common user items which are centrally purchased.

Public procurement in Malaysia is categorised into three categories: (1) works (which includes construction and engineering activities involving infrastructure including mechanical and electrical works); (2) supplies (which includes the supply of raw, intermediate or finished goods and products for any activity of users including construction materials and equipment); and (3) services (which includes the engagement of manpower, expertise and consultants in the areas of feasibility studies, research, designing, surveying, management as well as repairs, maintenance and cleaning services).

There are three modes of public procurement permitted in Malaysia. The first mode of procurement, direct purchase, is permitted for: (1) the procurement of supplies and services up to the contract value of MYR50,000 (US$12,400) and is facilitated by a Government Order; and (2) the procurement of works up to the value of MYR20,000 (US$4,936) and is facilitated by a Works Ident to a contractor who is registered with the Contractors Services Centre (**PKK**) and CIDB. The second mode of procurement, quotation, is permitted for: (1) the procurement of supplies and services with a contract value between MYR50,000 (US$12,400) and MYR500,000 (US$124,000)

45 Malaysia's Government Procurement Regime (Ministry of Finance Malaysia) https://www.treasury.gov.my/pdf/lain-lain/msia_regime.pdf (accessed 18 January 2021).
46 ibid.
47 ibid.

and requires the calling of a minimum of five quotations (with all suppliers registered with the Federal Government); and (2) the procurement of works with a contract value between MYR20,000 (US$4,936) and MYR500,000 (US$124,000) and requires the calling of a minimum of five quotations (with all contractors being registered with the PKK and CIDB). The third mode of procurement, tendering, is mandatory for all procurement with a contract value which exceeds MYR500,000 (US$124,000).

There is also no specific legislation governing tendering procedures for public procurement in Malaysia, although some guidance is provided in an authoritative paper published by the federal government titled 'Malaysia's Government Procurement Regime'.[48] Pursuant to the guidance, the relevant department and/or ministry procuring the works, supplies or services should form a technical committee to prepare the specifications. Specifications should be as detailed as possible so that tenderers have a clear idea of what is required, although tailored specifications to suit particular contractors are not permitted. The guidance also provides that tender documents should include general and specific terms and conditions, specifications, a copy of the agreement, price schedule, delivery period, objection period and the scope of works expected.

Whilst tenders can be local or international, international tenders should only be issued in circumstances where the required supplies and services are not produced locally and/or local contractors do not have the expertise and capabilities to carry out the required works. All local tenders must be advertised in at least one local daily in Malayan and state the precise date and time of closing of the tender. International tenders must be advertised in at least two local dailies – one in Malayan and one in English – and state the precise date and time of closing of the tender. Tenders may also be advertised on procuring agency websites including the My Procurement portal (http://myprocurement.treasury.gov.my) and My Government portal (www.malaysia.gov.my). Tenderers should be provided a minimum of 21 days to submit local tenders and a minimum of 56 days to submit international tenders,[49] with international tenderers also required to furnish a tender deposit with their tender.[50]

The guidance in 'Malaysia's Government Procurement Regime' also outlines the tender evaluation process.[51] The tender evaluation is normally completed by two committees – Technical Evaluation Committee and Financial Evaluation Committee.

48 'Malaysia's Government Procurement Regime' (Federal Government) www.treasury.gov.my/pdf/lain-lain/msia_regime.pdf (accessed 18 January 2021). These guidelines cover the purchase of services on behalf of the federal government and state governments including those received from consultants and advisers in the areas of engineering, technical, financial and legal.

49 The 'Malaysia's Government Procurement Regime' provides that tenders may be sent by post or dropped into designated tender boxes at a designated location. The tender should include a technical and financial proposal prepared separately in two copies and sealed in separate envelopes.

50 The tender deposit ranges from MYR60,000 (US$14,808) for tenders for supplies or services with a contract value of less than MYR5 million (US$1.234 million) and MYR1 million (US$246,792) for tenders with a contract value exceeding MYR30 million (US$7.404 million). In relation to works contracts, the tender deposit ranges from MYR60,000 (US$14,831) for tenders with a contract value of less than MYR10 million (US$2.468 million) and MYR1 million (US$246,792) for tenders with a contract value exceeding MYR100 million (US$24,679 million). Local suppliers and contractors registered with the federal government are exempt from providing a tender deposit.

51 There are no rules governing how tenders are to be evaluated. The criteria is generally based on: (1) the tenderers meeting the requirements set out in the tender document; (2) the technical capabilities of the tenderers including professional and technical staff, work experience and performance records; (3) the financial capabilities of the tenderer including capital, net worth and credit; and (4) the price of the tenders taking into account the proposed completion/ delivery period.

Following which, the tenders will be ranked and a tender evaluation report will be submitted to the Procurement Boards of Ministries/Departments (Agency Procurement Boards) who will select the successful tender. Where, however, the value of the contract exceeds MYR50 million (US$12.4 million) for supplies and services and MYR100 million (US$24.7 million) for works, the Agency Procurement Boards will provide a recommendation to the Ministry of Finance who will make the final decision as regards the successful tender.

All individuals or contractors intending to participate in public procurement must be registered with the federal government as follows:

- In relation to works contracts, individuals and contractors must be registered with the PKK, the CIDB and the Ministry of Works and
- In relation to supplies or services contracts, individuals and contractors must be registered with the Government Procurement Division, Ministry of Finance Malaysia.

This requirement enables the relevant governments to take disciplinary action and impose penalties on contractors and suppliers who do not perform according to the contract.

Malaysia is a member of the World Trade Organization (**WTO**), but not a signatory to the WTO Agreement on Government Procurement (**WTO GPA**). Whilst Malaysia is not subject to the international protocols in the WTO GPA, it is a signatory to seven bilateral Free Trade Agreements with Australia, Chile, India, Japan, New Zealand, Pakistan and Turkey and several regional Free Trade Agreements including the ASEAN Free Trade Area. Malaysia is also a member of the Asia-Pacific Economic Co-operation Forum (**APEC**), it actively participates in the Government Procurement Experts' Group and has adopted the APEC Non-Binding Principles on Government Procurement.

14.2.4 Foreign contractors

One peculiarity of the construction industry in Malaysia is that foreign contractors looking to carry out construction works in Malaysia must incorporate a local business entity (usually a limited liability company) and obtain a Registered Contractor Certificate from the CIDB. There are seven license grades for a Registered Contractor Certificate (known as a CIDB License) ranging from grade G1 (tenders not exceeding MYR200,000 (US$49,400)) to grade G7 (no limit), although the registration criteria for the higher license grades is particularly difficult for foreign contractors to satisfy.[52] As a result, foreign contractors generally bid with local contractors (who are able to contribute the CIDB License and other local qualifications) through joint ventures and consortia.

14.2.5 Standard form contracts

There is a wide range of standard form contracts in general use in construction projects in Malaysia – particularly given the relative size of the country. The federal

52 Note, that it is possible for foreign contractors to obtain a project specific license.

government and state governments usually call tenders for new building and civil engineering works using its own standard form contract, the Public Works Department of Malaysia (**PWD**) Conditions of Contract.[53] The private sector, on the other hand, commonly adopts the Pertubuhan Akitek Malaysia (**PAM**) Contract 2006 (with or without quantities) published by the Malaysian Institute of Architects[54] and the Institute of Engineers Malaysia (**IEM**) Conditions of Contract for building and civil engineering works.[55] It is expected that the recently released PAM Contract 2018 (with or without quantities) will also enjoy wide use. International standard form contracts including the FIDIC suite of standard form contracts (either in their original form or with Particular Conditions used to modify them) and Joint Contracts Tribunal suite of standard form contracts (**JCT Contracts**) are also popular in Malaysia – particularly for private projects funded by the World Bank or Asian Development Bank.[56]

14.2.6 Regulation of labour

A Green Card is the common name for the Construction Personnel Registration Card issued by CIDB for the purposes of registering and identifying construction personnel by their field and skill level. A Green Card is a mandatory requirement for all construction personnel carrying out construction work in Malaysia (including foreign labour) and must be produced before entering a construction site in Malaysia. Green Cards are obtained from CIDB on the registration of the construction personnel and the completion of the 'Safety Induction Course for Construction Workers' or equivalent.[57] Applicants must be a minimum of 18 years old, employed by the construction industry and performing construction works. In 2019, the CIDB introduced a new Green Card with a virtual ID which shows the relevant construction personnel's current registration status and enables site supervisors and/or safety officers to access the construction personnel's record attendance and prepare attendance reports. In addition, the new Green Card has an electronic payment facility which allows the construction personnel to send remittances, make payments via a QR code and in-app purchases, and reload and top-up funds.

Occupational health and safety is an ongoing concern for the Malaysian construction industry. The primary legal framework governing occupational health and safety in Malaysia is the *Occupational Safety and Health Act 1994*, *Factories and Machinery Act 1967* and *Petroleum (Safety Measures) Act 1984*.

Officers of the Department of Occupational Safety and Health (**DOSH**) have broad powers under the *Occupational Safety and Health Act 1994* to ensure the safety, health and welfare of people at work including inter alia the power to stop work if they are of the opinion that the workplace is likely to cause immediate danger to life or property[58]

53 The PWD Conditions of Contract are also often adopted by local authorities, statutory bodies and quasi-government bodies. Some state governments have developed their own standard forms. For example, in Sarawak the PWD Conditions of Contract were superseded by the JKR Sarawak Form of Contract 2006.

54 The PAM Contract 2006 is a modified version of the JCT 1963 Standard Building Contract.

55 From time to time, the PWD Conditions of Contract are used by the private sector.

56 See para 14.4 below.

57 Although applications for the registration of foreign construction workers must be made by their employer.

58 See the power to issue prohibition notices under *Occupational Safety and Health Act 1994* (Act 541), s 48.

and the power to seize property including plant and installations.[59] These powers have the potential to cause serious disruption to a construction project. Any person who contravenes any provision of the *Occupational Safety and Health Act 1994* is guilty of an offence punishable by fine or imprisonment.

Labour laws in Malaysia are particularly advantageous to employers, with employees generally not enjoying the same statutory rights and protections afforded to employees in other common law jurisdictions.[60] The primary legislation governing Malaysia's workplace relations are:

- The *Employment Act 1955* in West Malaysia and the Federal Territory of Labuan, East Malaysia.
- The *Labour Ordinance (Chapter 76)*(Sarawak) in Sarawak, East Malaysia.
- The *Labour Ordinance (Chapter 67)*(Sabah) in Sabah, East Malaysia.

Whilst the above legislation provides certain minimum rights and protections in relation to inter alia the payment of wages, sick leave, paid leave, maternity leave, working hours, overtime and termination, it is of limited effect. In particular, the legislation only applies to: (1) employees who earn a monthly salary of MYR2,000 (US$500) or less; and (2) manual labourers or supervisors of manual labourers, employees who operate or maintain any mechanically propelled vehicle for the purpose of transporting passengers or goods or for reward or commercial purposes, domestic servants, and employees in certain positions on seagoing vessels regardless of their monthly salary. The rights of all other employees are governed by their employment contracts.

Most employees (except domestic servants) are guaranteed a minimum wage under the *Minimum Wages Order 2020* (which is revised periodically) and provided with compulsory insurance.[61] The minimum retirement age is 60 years old.[62]

The Director General of the Labour Department has the power to inquire and decide any monetary claim arising from an employer's failure to comply with the provisions of the *Employment Act 1955*, *Labour Ordinance* (Chapter 76)(Sarawak) and *Labour Ordinance* (Chapter 67)(Sabah),[63] the *Wages Councils Act 1947*, and an employment contract. To start an inquiry, an employee must make a compliant to the Labour Department.[64] Disputed monetary claims will proceed to the Labour Court.

Pursuant to the *Industrial Relations Act 1967,* an employer must have 'just cause and excuse' before terminating an employee.[65] If an employee considers they have been

59 See the powers to enter into premises with and without a search warrant and seize any article, thing, book, document, plant, substance, installation or part thereof which has been used to commit or is intended to be used to commit an offence under *Occupational Safety and Health Act 1994* (Act 541), ss 40 and 41.

60 Mohammad Rizal Salim, 'Reincarnating Malaysian Airline: Labour Rights from a Malaysian Perspective' (2017) 1 *International Company and Commercial Law Review* 8, 8.

61 See para 14.5.7 below.

62 *Minimum Retirement Age Act 2012* (Act 753).

63 *Employment Act 1955*, section 69; *Labour Ordinance* (Chapter 76)(Sarawak), section 8A and *Labour Ordinance* (Chapter 67)(Sabah), section 7A.

64 The relevant procedure for such inquiry is set out in section 70 of the *Employment Act 1955*; s 7F of the *Labour Ordinance* (Chapter 67)(Sabah); and s 8F of the *Labour Ordinance* (Chapter 76)(Sarawak).

65 *Industrial Relations Act 1967* (Act 177), s 20. The *Act* applies to employees who fall within the definition of 'workmen', namely, 'any person, including an apprentice, employed by an employer under a contract of employment to work for hire or reward and for the purposes of any proceedings in relation to a trade dispute includes any such person who has been dismissed, discharged or retrenched in connection

terminated without 'just cause and excuse' (that is, they have been unfairly dismissed), the employee must lodge a representation to the Director General for Industrial Relations within 60 days from the date of dismissal.[66] Following the representation, the Industrial Relations Department will facilitate a conciliation between the employer and employee.[67] If the conciliation is not successful, the matter will be referred to the Minister of Human Resources who has a discretion to decide whether the matter be referred to the Industrial Court.[68]

Whilst trade unions – including construction worker trade unions – exist in Malaysia, they have limited influence. Trade unions are only permitted to regulate the relationship between employers and employees and cannot raise or use capital for political purposes. These restraints have resulted in trade unions holding a narrow outlook and being unable to influence national policies.[69] As such, trade unions generally have low participation.

Aside from certain protections enshrined in the *Federal Constitution* – namely, that all persons are equal before the law and there shall be no discrimination against a person on the ground only of religion, race, descent, place of birth or gender in certain prescribed circumstances[70] – there is no specific anti-discrimination legislation in Malaysia (including in relation to workplace discrimination).[71] The absence of a legal framework has resulted in certain areas that are traditionally regulated in other common law jurisdictions not being regulated in Malaysia. For example, save for employment with public authorities, employers are not prohibited from making decisions which affect a group of employees even if such decisions relate to gender or age. It is permissible for employment contracts to include clauses which are discriminatory.

14.2.7 Insurance

Save for the obligation to provide mandatory insurance under the *Employment Insurance System Act 2017*, *Employees' Social Security Act 1969*, *Workmen's Compensation Act 1952* and *Employees Provident Fund Act 1991* (see paragraph 14.6.7 below),[72] there is

with or as a consequence of that dispute or whose dismissal, discharge or retrenchment has led to that dispute.'

66 *Industrial Relations Act 1967* (Act 177), section 20 (1A).

67 ibid s 20(2).

68 ibid s 20(3). Matters conducted in the Industrial Court are similar to a civil claim – that is, there is a hearing with witness evidence. Where an award is made under s 20(3) of the *Act*, the award operates as a bar to any action for damages in any court in respect of wrongful dismissal.

69 Mohammad Rizal Salim, 'Reincarnating Malaysian Airline: Labour Rights from a Malaysian Perspective' (2017) 1 *International Company and Commercial Law Review* 8, 8.

70 *Federal Constitution*, art 8. In particular, the *Federal Constitution* provides that except as expressly authorized by this Constitution, there shall be no discrimination against citizens on the ground only of religion, race, descent, place of birth or gender in: (1) any law, appointment to any office or employment under public authority; (2) the administration of any law relating to the acquisition, holding or disposition of property; and (3) the establishing or carrying on of any trade, business, profession, vocation or employment.

71 Although, the *Employment Act 1955* (Act 265) does provide certain mechanisms for addressing complaints of sexual harassment (see sections 81A to 81G) and complaints of discrimination against foreign employees (see section 60I). In addition, persons with disabilities are provided certain rights under the *Persons with Disabilities Act 2008* (Act 685) including as regards to access to employment.

72 Many standard forms require the Contractor to maintain certain insurances until risk passes to the Employer upon the Employer retaking possession of the Works or until the expiry of the defects liability period.

no general common law or statutory requirement for parties to insure construction projects in Malaysia.[73] Nonetheless, it is common for Contractors (or Employers) in Malaysia to take out Contractors' All Risks (**CAR**) policies insuring against damage or loss to the works and damage and injuries caused to third parties by reason of the works, public liability and workman's compensation insurance. Most CAR policies exclude design defects and defective workmanship.

14.2.8 Anti-corruption

There are anti-corruption laws governing the private sector and public sector in Malaysia. The *Malaysian Anti-Corruption Commission Act 2009* establishes the Malaysian Anti-Corruption Commission (**MACC**), a government agency tasked with investigating and prosecuting offences under the *Act* including 'gratification' (which includes inter alia the soliciting or offering of pecuniary and non-pecuniary bribes, facilitation payments), deception and corruption.[74] The MACC comprises five divisions: (1) the investigation division which conducts investigations into corruption; (2) the intelligence division which gathers information through various sources, methods and techniques; (3) the legal and prosecution division which conducts trials and appeals in the Malaysian courts, and reviews, and advises in relation to, Investigation Papers prepared by the investigation division; (4) the records management and information division which inter alia receives and processes information; and (5) the Anti-Money Laundering Division which conducts investigations under the *Anti-Money Laundering, Anti-Terrorism Financing and Proceeds of Unlawful Act 2001*.

The *Act* is of general application and does not distinguish between private sector bribery and the bribery of public officials. In June 2020, new provisions came into effect which impose corporate liability on commercial organisations (including companies, corporations and partnerships and even extends to individuals including directors, controllers, officers, partners or managers of the commercial organisation if the commercial organisation is found liable)[75] where a person closely associated with it (including directors, partners and employees) corruptly gives, offers or promises any gratification to any person with an intent to obtain or retain business or a business advantage for the commercial organisation.[76]

In addition to the anti-corruption laws, there are also protections for whistleblowers who voluntarily report or reveal information on corruption activities under the *Whistleblower Protection Act of 2010*.

14.2.9 Resolution of disputes

The principal methods for resolving disputes in Malaysia arising from construction contracts is one or more of mediation, arbitration, litigation and adjudication – although traditionally such disputes are resolved by arbitration. Mediation is a

73 As there is no decennial (10-year) liability imposed by law, decennial insurance is generally not required.

74 The Malaysian Anti-Corruption Commission is modelled on the Independent Commission Against Corruption in Hong Kong and the Independent Commission Against Corruption (New South Wales) in New South Wales, Australia.

75 Individuals are liable unless they can prove that the offence was committed without their consent, and they had exercised due diligence to prevent the commission of the offence.

76 *Malaysian Anti-Corruption Commission Act 2009* (Act 694), s 17A.

voluntary process governed by the *Mediation Act 2012*.[77] Although historically not popular in Malaysia, recently there has been a push from the Malaysian courts to promote mediation with some success.[78] There are no sanctions for parties who refuse to mediate. Whilst parties are free to appoint their own mediator, they can also seek an appointment from institutions such as the Malaysian Mediation Centre (**MMC**) or Kuala Lumpur Regional Centre for Arbitration (**KLRCA**), or in the case of construction industry specific institutions, the IEM, PAM or CIDB.[79]

Both international and domestic arbitration is governed by the *Arbitration Act 2005*. There are several arbitral institutions operating in Malaysia. The main institutions are the Asian International Arbitration Centre (**AIAC**), the Malaysian Institute of Arbitrators (**MIArb**), KLRCA, and the Chartered Institute of Arbitrators (**CIArb**). There are also construction industry specific institutions such as Institute of Engineers Malaysia and PAM.

Whilst historically, Dispute Boards have not played much of a role in Asia, this is likely to change with the growing prevalence of the FIDIC suite of standard form contracts in Malaysia and the introduction of the security of payment regime in 2012.

14.2.10 Future opportunities and challenges

In 2013, President Xi Jinping of China announced the One Belt, One Road Initiative (**OBOR**), a China led and funded global infrastructure development strategy[80] modelled on the historical Silk Road which aims to connect Asia by 21st century land and maritime networks with Africa and Europe. In addition to physical networks, the OBOR has expanded over time to encompass the development of a Digital Silk Road (a digital economy) within Asia, and from Asia to Europe and Africa. The OBOR is founded on five core objectives: (1) enhanced policy coordination; (2) improved infrastructure connectivity; (3) unimpeded trade; (4) financial integration; and (5) supporting people to people bonds.

As Malaysia forms a key part of the OBOR China-Indochina Peninsula Corridor which connects Southern China through Vietnam, Laos, Thailand and Myanmar with ASEAN countries including Singapore and Indonesia (as well as the Indian Ocean and the Strait of Hormuz), the OBOR presents a number of domestic opportunities for the construction industry in Malaysia. In 2015, the federal government and China signed several memoranda of understandings and agreements relating inter alia to the development of mega projects in Malaysia. Since then, several OBOR projects have commenced including the construction of the ECRL (a 600 km rail link connecting Pahang's east-coast Kuantan Port to west-coast Port Klang). It is worth noting that FIDIC standard form contracts are being used as the starting point for a number of OBOR project construction contracts.

77 Except, for example, where mediation is mandatory under statute (for example, under the *Industrial Relations Act* 1967) or is court ordered.

78 Clive Lovatt, *Construction Law and Practice* (2nd edn, Sweet & Maxwell 2016) [7.2].

79 Each of the aforementioned institutions have their own mediation rules.

80 The OBOR development strategy includes the development of inter alia ports, roads, railways, airports, power plants and telecommunication networks spanning over 65 countries see https://www.pwc.com/gx/en/growth markets-center/assets/pdf/china-new-silk-route.pdf (accessed 18 January 2021)

In terms of challenges, notwithstanding the recent initiatives aimed at modernising the construction industry in Malaysia (see paragraph 14.2.2 above), the industry continues to lag behind in occupational health and safety, with a high number of incidents continuing to occur on construction sites. This situation is hampered by a heavy reliance on foreign labour (which is often unskilled labour), a lack of engagement in occupational health and safety issues by Contractors and poor enforcement.[81] In addition, the construction industry continues to suffer from low productivity and inefficiency (another symptom of a heavy reliance on unskilled foreign labour), deteriorating quality, lack of technology and labour intensive construction techniques.

14.3 The impact of Covid-19 in Malaysia

14.3.1 The impact of Covid-19 on the execution of construction projects in Malaysia

The *Prevention and Control of Infectious Diseases Act 1988* is the primary legislation used by the federal government to prevent the introduction and spread of infectious diseases in Malaysia. Whilst the *Act* has not been amended to refer to Covid-19, the virus squarely falls within the 'catch-all' infectious disease listed in the First Schedule to the *Act*, 'any other life-threatening microbial infection'. The Minister for Health has broad powers under the *Act* to make regulations in respect of the whole or any part of Malaysia, including as regards to the entry of persons into, and their movements within, Malaysia, and measures to prevent the introduction of any infectious disease into Malaysia from an infected area.

In response to the Covid-19 pandemic, on 17 March 2020 the Minister for Health declared that all states and Federal Territories of Malaysia were 'infected areas' of Covid-19 and announced a Movement Control Order (**MCO**) which would take effect on 18 March 2020 and restrict movement and gatherings across Malaysia including religious sports, social and cultural gatherings, and compel people to stay at home within the 'infected areas'.[82]

On 18 March 2020, the federal government gazetted the *Prevention and Control of Infectious Diseases (Measures within the Infected Local Areas) Regulations 2020* together with guidelines and frequently asked questions published by various government departments to provide further clarification to the public and affected sectors in relation to the MCO. Under the MCO, all government and private sector premises were required to close (with all operations ceased) except for those which fell within 'essential services'. 'Essential services' were defined under the *Regulations* to include inter alia electricity, energy and water services, banking and finance, fire, transportation, postal and telecommunication services, food supply and preparation services, and healthcare and medical services were permitted to open.[83] Schools, public and private higher education institutions and skills training institutions were also closed. All construction works were suspended except for 'critical works', which could be carried out during the MCO with the recommendation of the enforcement officer,

81 Lovatt (n 78) [9.2].

82 The Movement Control Order was made under the *Prevention and Control of Infectious Diseases (Declaration of Infected Local Areas) Order 2020*.

83 *Prevention and Control of Infectious Diseases (Measures within the Infected Local Areas) Regulations 2020*, sch 2.

project director or superintending officer (in respect of public works) or the resident engineer, architect or principal submitting person (in respect of private sector works).[84]

Selected construction activities approved by the Ministry of International Trade and Industry were permitted to operate from 14 April 2020 onwards subject to strict compliance with MCO protocols including physical distancing and guidelines from the Ministry of Health, police and local authorities.[85] The Ministry for Works clarified that 'critical works' were works, which if not continued with, could cause danger and harm to employees, the public or the environment.[86] Examples of 'critical works' cited by the Ministry for Works included slope failure repairs, pothole repairs, traffic management control or traffic light repairs, tunneling works, maintenance works at premises of critical services, period checks of lifts/travellators/escalators and other critical mechanical and electrical equipment.[87]

Under the MCO, Malaysia closed its borders to all inbound travelers except for Malaysian nationals and non-citizens holding certain categories of resident and employment passes or non-citizens who were granted special entry.[88] All international arrivals were required to undergo a mandatory 14-day quarantine at designated quarantine facilities and bear the costs of the quarantine themselves.[89] Malaysian nationals were only permitted to travel overseas in limited circumstances.[90] Domestic movement was also been curtailed with interstate, and even inter-district travel, prohibited during the MCO and the Conditional Movement Control Order (**CMCO**).

In addition, since 27 March 2020, areas in which a large Covid-19 cluster was detected were subject to a stricter Enhanced Movement Control Order (**EMCO**) for 14 days to allow for thorough Covid-19 testing of all residents. Under the ECMO residents were not permitted to leave their home (although adequate food supplies were provided by authorities), all businesses were required to shut, a medical base was established within the area and all roads in the area were blocked. As of December 2020, specific locations in Johor, Selangor, Kuala Lumpur, Sabah, Sarawak and Negeri Sembilan have been subject to an ECMO.

Whilst the MCO was initially in place for a two week period from 18 March 2020 until 31 March 2020, it was extended on three occasions, until 3 May 2020. On 4 May 2020, the Health Minister imposed a CMCO which sought to wind back some but not all

84 See 'Frequently Asked Questions' (Ministry of Works, 18 March 2020) http://www.kkr.gov.my/ and 'Frequently Asked Questions' (Ministry of Works, 23 March 2020) http://www.kkr.gov.my/.

85 The select construction activities encompassed projects that did not require a large number of workers on site (for example, building projects with a minimum IBS score of 70 and maintenance and construction works that have achieved more than 90% physical completion). Eligible construction companies (including architects, consultants and building material suppliers) were required to complete a compulsory registration with the Ministry of International Trade and Industry. The registration must include the scope of work and the list of employees with their personal details to be stored in a database managed by Ministry of International Trade and Industry.

86 See 'Frequently Asked Questions' (Ministry of Works, 18 March 2020) http://www.kkr.gov.my/ and 'Frequently Asked Questions' (Ministry of Works, 23 March 2020) http://www.kkr.gov.my/.

87 See 'Frequently Asked Questions' (Ministry of Works, 18 March 2020) http://www.kkr.gov.my/ and 'Frequently Asked Questions' (Ministry of Works, 23 March 2020) http://www.kkr.gov.my/.

88 As of 7 September 2020, the federal government imposed an entry ban on persons arriving from countries with more than 150,000 Covid-19 cases.

89 From 15 November 2020, all non-citizens were required to make an online payment prior to their arrival for a Covid-19 swab test and quarantine through the MySafeTravel System accessible on https://safetravel.myeg.com.my/ (accessed 18 January 2021).

90 From 15 September 2020, Malaysians who exited Malaysia during the RMCO were permitted to return to Malaysia without seeking prior approval from the Department of Immigration.

of the restrictions under the MCO.[91] The CMCO remained in place until 9 June 2020, when it was replaced by the Health Minister by a Recovery Movement Control Order (**RMCO**) which allowed for further relaxation of restrictions including the resumption of a number of businesses and social activities, the resumption of interstate travel and reopening of schools (albeit in stages). The RMCO, which was initially in place from 10 June 2020 until 31 August 2020, was extended until 31 December 2020, and then again until 31 March 2021. Notwithstanding the gradual relaxation of restrictions, a number of states were placed back under the CMCO following Covid-19 outbreaks.

On 1 May 2020, the Ministry of Works issued a Standard Operating Procedure (**SOP**) which the construction industry was required to comply with in order to operate during the CMCO.[92] Under the SOP, construction companies were required to submit a declaration of their company information and pledge compliance with the SOP to the Ministry of International Trade and Industry by 12 May 2020.[93] In addition, construction companies were also required to submit a declaration outlining their ongoing projects with the CIDB within two weeks of recommencement of their operations. Whilst there were no restrictions on operating hours or site capacity, social distancing was required to be practiced at all times. Construction companies resuming operations were required to observe all the standard operating procedures available at the websites of CIDB[94] and the National Security Council (**MKN**).[95]

The SOP also outlined protocols and safety measures in relation to inter alia the testing and health screening of workers, preparation of personal protective equipment for workers, transportation of workers, worker's movement, transportation of construction materials and supplies to construction sites, management of Covid-19 symptoms and cases, steps to be taken at the entrance of construction sites and during the execution of construction works, management of workers' break time, maintenance and cleanliness of construction site facilities and maintenance of records.

On 10 June 2020, the Ministry of Works issued a new SOP effective for the duration of the RCMO.[96] The main changes under the new SOP included: (1) construction companies were no longer required to submit a declaration to the Ministry of International Trade and Industry; (2) all foreign workers in the construction industry in the Federal Territories of Kuala Lumpur and Putrajaya, and Selangor were required to undergo mandatory Covid-19 testing; (3) employers were no longer obliged to provide workers with transportation; (4) workers were encouraged to download and register the MySejahtera mobile phone application;[97] (5) materials and/or supply delivery drivers showing Covid-19 symptoms were not permitted to enter construction sites and must seek treatment at a health facility; (6) the practice of hand cleanliness must be observed; and (7) where a worker at a Centralised Labour Quarter (**CLQ**)

91 Although not all states (namely, Kedah, Kelantan, Pahang, Sabah and Sarawak) implemented the CMCO by 4 May 2020.

92 The Standard Operating Procedure was supplemented by frequently asked questions (Ministry of Works) http://www.kkr.gov.my/.

93 Although, such declaration was not required for companies who had previously submitted an application to the Ministry of International Trade and Industry during the MCO.

94 www.cidb.gov.my (accessed 18 January 2021).

95 www.mkn.gov.my (accessed 18 January 2021).

96 As with the original Standard Operating Procedure issued by the Ministry of Works, the new Standard Operating Procedure was supplemented by frequently asked questions http://www.kkr.gov.my/.

97 The federal government launched a mobile phone application called MySejahtera to assist with contact tracing.

tested positive for Covid-19 the employer must provide alternative accommodation for close contact workers at the same CLQ.

The federal government and state governments have not enacted any employment specific laws in response to Covid-19. Therefore, employment relationships including in relation to termination, leave entitlements and compensation thereof continue to be governed by the *Employment Act 1955*, *Labour Ordinance* (Chapter 76)(Sarawak), and *Labour Ordinance* (Chapter 67)(Sabah) (to the extent that they apply see paragraph 14.2.6) and individual employment contracts. Variations to individual employment contracts, for example, salary cuts, reduced working hours and/or leave entitlements can only be made with the consent of the relevant employee.[98]

On 5 February 2020, the Ministry of Human Resources (**MHR**) issued guidelines titled 'Guidelines on Handling Issues Relating to Contagious Outbreaks Including Novel Coronavirus'.[99] The guidelines address the provision of medical examinations for employees returning from countries with confirmed Covid-19 cases, the remuneration of employees who receive quarantine orders from a medical practitioner or upon their return from business travel, unpaid and annual leave entitlements, preventing employees from attending work and restricting non-essential personal travel and business travel. Although the guidelines do not have statutory effect, the MHR has strongly encouraged employers to adhere to them. In addition, employers should take care to ensure that they comply with the requirements of the *Personal Data Protection Act 2010* when collecting personal details from employees including as regards their travel and medical history including any results obtained during medical examinations and temperature testing.

Further, employers owe both a common law and statutory duty to their employees to ensure, so far as practicable, a safe and healthy workplace.[100] This duty includes inter alia maintaining a workplace in a safe condition without risks to health and providing and maintaining a safe working environment including facilities without risks to health. In addition, under the *Occupational Safety and Health Act 1994* employers are generally required to formulate a health and safety policy at the workplace.[101] Failure to comply with this obligation will constitute an offence under the *Act*. The DOSH has published a 'Safe Work Procedure for Prevention of Covid-19 at Workplace' (**SWP**)[102] which sets out inter alia the role and responsibilities of:

- Employers including inter alia the development and implementation of a Covid-19 Risk Control Program, the provision of suitable personal protective equipment in accordance with the relevant SOP, the conduct of daily temperature checks and symptom screening and ensure employees maintain a minimum physical distance of 1 metre and
- Employees including inter alia compliance with the SWP and the required personal protective equipment, download and register with the MySejahtera

98 Or trade union (where appropriate).

99 'Guidelines on Handling Issues Relating to Contagious Outbreaks Including Novel Coronavirus' (5 February 2020) http://mpma.org.my/v4/wp-content/uploads/2020/02/Eng-Press-Release-nCov-1.pdf (accessed 18 January 2021).

100 *Occupational Safety and Health Act 1994* (Act 514), s 15.

101 ibid s 16.

102 'Safe Work Procedure for Prevention of Covid-19 at Workplace' (Department of Occupational Health and Safety) https://www.dosh.gov.my/index.php/swp-covid19-prevswp-covid19-prevention-in-workplace/file (accessed 18 January 2021).

mobile phone application, use a face shield when working in public and use face masks in public and crowded places.

In addition, the SWP outlines a procedure for every person entering a workplace including the requirement to take temperature checks, reporting to security personnel/ designated officer to record workplace attendance and attending safety briefing sessions related to control and preventative measures related to Covid-19 and specific workplace rules. The SWP also outlines general rules during work including the use of face masks, physical distancing, maintenance of good personal hygiene, cleaning and disinfecting the workplace (and in particular, common areas) and providing for staggered break times for employees. The Ministry of Health Malaysia also issued guidelines titled 'Covid-19: Management Guidelines for Workplaces' issued as part of the 'Covid-19 Management Guidelines in Malaysia No.5/2020' (**Management Guidelines**) which also lists out the steps that employers and employees should take to ensure a safe workplace.[103] There is significant overlap between the SWP and Management Guidelines.

In addition, on 30 May 2020, the Malaysian Department of Personal Data Protection issued an advisory on the collection, processing, and storage of personal data by businesses during the CMCO.[104] In summary, the advisory provided that businesses should only collect minimal personal data of customers or visitors (eg on names, contact numbers, and the date and time of attendance) and must provide a clearly visible notice detailing the purpose of the data collection. In addition, the advisory noted that personal data should only be collected for informational purposes and must be deleted 6 months after the CMCO is terminated.

The construction industry in Malaysia has been significantly impacted by the Covid-19 pandemic, and in particular, the implementation of the MCO. The CIDB Chief Executive Datuk Ir Ahmad 'Asri Abdul Hamid reported that the construction industry recorded losses of approximately MYR11 billion (US$2.72 billion) during the first phase of the MCO. Notwithstanding that construction activities were allowed to recommence on 4 May 2020, the CIDB reported that of 7,699 construction sites inspected, as of 13 June 2020, 5,528 construction sites remained closed. Reasons cited for the prolonged closures included capital and finance issues, confusion over the SOP, issues with mandatory Covid-19 testing, disruptions to the supply chain and labour shortages. It is expected that the construction industry will shrink by a total of 18.7 per cent by the end of 2020, although it is forecast to rebound by an estimated growth rate of 13.9 per cent in 2021.[105]

Whilst the federal government has not introduced construction industry specific stimulus relief, it has implemented a number of stimulus packages relevant to the construction industry[106] including the Prihatin Rakyat Economic Stimulus Package, the Prihatin SME Stimulus Package, the National Short-term Economic Recovery

103 See 'Covid-19: Management Guidelines for Workplaces' published by Ministry of Health Malaysia updated on 1 November 2020 http://covid-19.moh.gov.my/garis-panduan/garis-panduan-kkm/Annex_25_COVID_guide_for_workplaces_1_Nov_2020.pdf (accessed 18 January 2021).

104 See https://www.kkmm.gov.my/images/AdHoc/200529-ADVISORY.pdf (accessed 18 January 2021).

105 'Economic Outlook 2021: Chapter 3 Macroeconomic Outlook' (Ministry of Finance Malaysia) https://www.treasury.gov.my/index.php/en/fiscal-economy/economic-outlook-2021.html (accessed 18 January 2021).

106 The construction industry is one of the primary drivers of small or medium enterprises in Malaysia, which have been the focus of a number of stimulus packages.

Plan (***ePenjana***) and the Kita Prihatin Malaysia Economic Stimulus Package worth MYR20 billion (US$4.94 billion), MYR230 billion (US$56.85 billion), MYR10 billion (US$2.47 billion), MYR35 billion (US$8.65 billion) and MYR10 billion (US$2.47 billion), respectively. Collectively, the stimulus packages provide inter alia several:

- Tax relief measures including inter alia deductions, tax incentives and capital allowances,[107] stamp duty,[108] real property gains[109] and customs and import tax[110] exemptions and tax filing and deadline extensions.
- Employment related measures including inter alia wage subsidies for employees with a monthly income below MYR4,000 (US$987) for 9 months (capped at 200 employees per company), a 25 per cent reduction of the foreign worker levy in respect of worker permits (excluding domestic helpers) which expire between 1 April 2020 and 31 December 2020, MYR2 billion (US$494 million) in funding for reskilling and upskilling programmes aimed at enhancing the employability of the unemployed and MYR1.5 billion (US$370 million) in funding for hiring and training assistance for businesses.
- Economic stimulus measures including inter alia a grant of MYR3,000 (US$740) for qualifying micro SMEs registered with the Malaysian Inland Revenue Board, enhanced financing schemes for SMEs and a rental waiver for SME retailers renting premises owned by government-linked companies.

In addition, banks have set up new financing facilities for SMEs and introduced a decreased policy rate. The Bank Negara Malaysia (**BNM**) also issued a directive to all banks to grant an automatic six month moratorium for all loan and financing repayments between 1 April 2020 and 30 September 2020. This was extended for three months for certain targeted groups.

The Ministry of Finance has indicated in the Economic Outlook for 2021 that the stimulus packages – coupled with the reopening of most economic sectors, acceleration and revival of major infrastructure projects, civil engineering works and affordable housing projects – will be key to the gradual recovery of the construction industry from the impact of Covid-19.[111]

---

107 For example, an accelerated capital allowance (increased to 40% (current rates range from 10% to 20%) with an initial allowance of 20%) for qualifying capital expenditure incurred on machinery and equipment including Information and Communication Technology Equipment from 1 March 2020 to 31 December 2021; an annual income tax rebate of up to MYR20,000 (US$4,936) for the first three years of assessments for small or medium enterprises established and in operation between 1 July 2020 and 31 December 2021; and 100% investment tax allowance for existing companies for a period of 5 years if they relocate their overseas manufacturing facilities back into Malaysia for application submitted between 1 July 2020 and 31 December 2021.

108 For example, certain loan/financing instruments relating to restructuring or rescheduling of a business loan/financing executed between 1 March 2020 and 31 December 2020 are exempt from stamp duty. In addition, there is a stamp duty exemption on instruments executed by small or medium enterprises for mergers and acquisitions which take place between 1 July 2020 and 30 June 2021.

109 The disposal of residential property (maximum of three units) by an individual between 1 June 2020 and 31 December 2021 is exempt from real property gains tax.

110 For example, an import duty and sales tax exemption on equipment and machines for port operators (subject to conditions) for applications submitted between 1 April 2020 and 31 March 2023.

111 'Economic Outlook 2021: Chapter 3 Macroeconomic Outlook' (Ministry of Finance Malaysia) https://www.treasury.gov.my/index.php/en/fiscal-economy/economic-outlook-2021.html (accessed 18 January 2021).

14.3.2 The impact of Covid-19 on the operation of construction contracts in Malaysia

The Covid-19 pandemic has presented several challenges for Contractors and subcontractors. There has been significant disruption to supply chains including the manufacturing, shipping and delivery of materials, plant and equipment due to closures of factories and manufacturing plants in Malaysia (due to the MCO), Mainland China and elsewhere and delays to transportation, logistics and freight caused by the reduction in movement (due to the MCO and a reduction of international flights). In addition, with a significant percentage of the construction industry in Malaysia dependent on foreign labour, travel restrictions, border closures and mandatory quarantine requirements have triggered a labour shortage. This is likely to adversely impact Contractors and/or subcontractors' scheduling and other obligations on construction projects.

On 23 October 2020, the *Temporary Measures for Reducing the Impact of Coronavirus Disease 2019 (Covid-19) Act 2020* came into force providing temporary measures to contracting parties to help reduce the impact of the Covid-19 pandemic. The *Act*, which modifies certain provisions in a range of legislation,[112] will be in force for two years, or in accordance with the date or duration specified in the relevant parts of the *Act*. The operation of the *Act* can be extended by the Prime Minister at any time.

Whilst not an extensive as its Singaporean counterpart,[113] the *Act* provides some relief to contracting parties who are unable to perform their contractual obligations due to the measures taken under the *Prevention and Control of Infectious Diseases Act 1988*. In particular, section 7 of the *Act* states that:

> The inability of any party or parties to perform any contractual obligation arising from any of the categories of contracts specified in the Schedule to this Part due to the measures prescribed, made or taken under the *Prevention and Control of Infectious Diseases Act 1988* to control or prevent the spread of Covid-19 shall not give rise to the other party or parties exercising his or their rights under the contract.

The categories of contracts specified in the Schedule to Part II include inter alia (1) construction work contracts; (2) construction consultancy contracts; (3) supply contracts for construction material, equipment or workers in connection with a construction contract; (4) performance bond or equivalent that is granted pursuant to a construction contract or supply contract; and (5) professional services contracts.

The relief provided under the *Act* includes inter alia:

- An extension of the general limitation periods under the *Limitation Act 1953*, *Limitation Ordinance 1952* (Sabah), *Limitation Ordinance 1959* (Sarawak) and

112 The *Temporary Measures for Reducing the Impact of Coronavirus Disease 2019 (Covid-19) Act 2020* modifies various provisions of the *Limitation Act 1953* (Act 254), *Limitation Ordinance 1952* (Cap 72)(Sabah), *Limitation Ordinance 1959* (Cap 49)(Sarawak), *Public Authorities Protection Act 1948* (Act 198), *Insolvency Act 1967* (Act 360), *Hire-Purchase Act 1967* (Act 212), *Consumer Protection Act 1999* (Act 599), *Distress Act 1951* (Act 255), *Housing Development (Control and Licensing) Act 1966* (Act 118), *Industrial Relations Act 1967* (Act 177), *Private Employment Agencies Act 1981* (Act 246), *Land Public Transport Act 2010* (Act 715), *Commercial Vehicles Licensing Board Act 1987* (Act 334), *Courts of Judicature Act 1964* (Act 91), *Subordinate Courts Act 1948* (Act 92) and *Subordinate Courts Rules Act 1955*.

113 For example, the *Temporary Measures for Reducing the Impact of Coronavirus Disease 2019 (Covid-19) Act 2020* does not provide a statutory extension of time.

Public Authorities Protection Act 1948 which expired between 18 March 2020 and 31 August 2020 to 31 December 2020.[114]
- An increase of the minimum threshold for the presentation of a bankruptcy petition by creditor(s) against a debtor from MYR50,000 (US$12,400) to MYR100,000 (US$24,680) under the *Insolvency Act 1967*. This measure came into effect on 23 October 2020 and will remain in operation until 31 August 2021.[115]
- A prohibition on owners from exercising their powers under section 16 of the *Hire-Purchase Act 1967* to take possession of goods comprised in a hire-purchase agreement for any default of payment of installment during the period from 1 April 2020 to 30 September 2020.[116]
- A prohibition on landlords from taking action under section 5 of the *Distress Act 1951* to recover arrears of rent for the period from 18 March 2020 to 31 August 2020.[117]

Where a contract does not make adequate provision for *force majeure* (for instance, there is no *force majeure* event in the contract triggered by a 'disease', 'epidemic' or 'pandemic'), the contracting parties may still be able to seek relief pursuant to the statutory right to frustration under *Contracts Act 1950*. Section 57(2) of the *Contracts Act 1950* provides that:

> A contract to do an act which, after the contract is made, becomes impossible, or by reason of some event which the promisor could not prevent, unlawful, becomes void when the act becomes impossible or unlawful.

The threshold for establishing frustration under section 57(2) of the *Act* is high.[118] A contract will not be frustrated merely because the obligations therein are difficult or onerous to perform. The party seeking to rely on section 57(2) of the *Act* must establish that through no fault of the contracting parties, a contractual obligation has become incapable of being performed and/or the circumstances render the contract radically different from its original intention.[119] If section 57(2) of the *Act* is successfully invoked, the parties will be permanently relieved of their contractual obligations.[120]

14.4 Malaysian governing law of the contract

14.4.1 Constraints on the governing law of a construction contract

Malaysia has not implemented the *Hague Convention on Choice of Law in International Commercial Contracts*. Therefore, there is no statutory right for parties to choose 'rules

114 *Temporary Measures for Reducing the Impact of Coronavirus Disease 2019 (Covid-19) Act 2020*, Pts III to VI.
115 ibid , Pt VII.
116 ibid Pt VIII.
117 ibid Pt X.
118 Section 57(2) of the *Contracts Act 1950* (Act 136) is discussed in further detail at para 14.5.3 below.
119 *Tai Kim Yew & Ors v Sentul Raya Sdn Bhd* [2004] 4 MLJ 227; *Ramli bin Zakaria v Government of Malaysia* [1982] 2 MLJ 257.
120 The legal consequences of a frustrated contract are set out in s 66 of the *Contracts Act 1950* (Act 136) (which requires contracting parties to restore or compensate any advantage received under a void contract) and s 16 of the *Civil Law Act 1956* (Act 67) (which provides for an adjustment of rights and liabilities of parties to a frustrated contract).

of law that are generally accepted on an international, supranational or regional level as a neutral and balanced set of rules'.

Nevertheless, subject to the two exceptions set out below, the courts in Malaysia recognise a party's right to choose the applicable law governing their contract and will give effect to such a clause. If the parties do not expressly specify a choice of law, Malaysian courts will look to apply the law that the parties are presumed to have intended (ie the implied choice of law). In the absence of any express or implied choice of law, Malaysian courts will apply conflict of law rules.

Where the dispute is submitted to arbitration, the *Arbitration Act 2005* applies.[121] The *Arbitration Act* incorporates Article 28(1) of the UNCITRAL Model Law, which provides that:

> The arbitral tribunal shall decide the dispute in accordance with such rules of law as are chosen by the parties as applicable to the substance of the dispute . . . Any designation of the law or legal system of a given State shall be construed, unless otherwise expressed, as directly referring to the substantive law of that State and not to its conflict of laws rules.[122]

The *Arbitration Act 2005* also provides that:

> Failing any designation by the parties, the arbitral tribunal shall apply the law determined by the conflict of laws rules which it considers applicable . . . The arbitral tribunal shall decide according to equity and conscience only if the parties have expressly authorized it to do so.[123]

The parties' right to choose the law applicable to their contract is not unlimited. Malaysian courts are unlikely to give effect to an applicable law clause in circumstances where it infringes a rule of natural justice or it is in violation of public policy of the place in which the contract is performed.

14.4.2 Formal requirements for a construction contract

As mentioned at paragraph 14.1.2 above, Malaysia codified the law of contract in the *Contracts Act 1950*. The formal requirements for a construction contract in Malaysia are largely governed by this *Act*, except where the parties have agreed it shall not apply, in which case the common law rules apply.[124] In either case, the formal requirements generally follow the essential tenets of the English common law, which are that the

121 The *Arbitration Act 2005* (Act 646) applies to both domestic and international arbitrations and was initially principally based on the UNCITRAL Model Law (as adopted on 21 June 1985) and the New Zealand *Arbitration Act* with specific Malaysian modifications. Recently, the *Arbitration Act* was amended to bring it into line with the 7 July 2006 amendments to the UNCITRAL Model Law as well as the arbitration laws of other leading jurisdictions (including in relation to confidentiality of arbitration proceedings, awards of interest and powers of referral to the courts).

122 *Arbitration Act 2005* (Act 646), s 30. Prior to the 2018 amendment, party autonomy in respect of choice of law in domestic arbitrations was limited to circumstances where Malaysia was the seat of the arbitration.

123 ibid s 30.

124 In the Privy Council decision of *Ooi Boon Leong v Citibank NA* [1984] 1 MLJ 222 Lord Brightman held that s 1(2) of the *Contracts Act 1950* (Act 136) '[d]oes not say that the contracting parties are unable by agreement to vary the legal consequences spelt out by the *Act*. Section 1(2) has no effect on the freedom of contracting parties to decide upon what terms they desire to contract'. Although, his Lordship later observed that should the contracting parties wish to oust the application of certain provisions of the *Act*, they should do so expressly. However, notwithstanding the doctrine of freedom to contract, contracts of which the object or consideration is unlawful is void pursuant to s 24 of the *Contracts Act 1950* (Act 136).

contract: (1) must be based on an offer and acceptance;[125] (2) must be supported by lawful consideration;[126] (3) must be supported by an intention by the parties to be legally bound;[127] (4) must include terms which are certain;[128] and (5) must be executed by parties who have the legal capacity to enter into a contract.[129]

There are no specific requirements for the form of construction contracts. A construction contract can be in writing or it can be oral provided that the formal requirements are present.[130] Therefore, a letter of intent which satisfies the abovementioned formal requirements may constitute a contract, however, it must be more than an expression of a present intention to enter into a contract at a future date.[131] When signing as a company, the requirements of the *Companies Act 2016* must be followed.

A claim for breach of contract must be commenced within 6 years from the date on which the action accrued, whether in West Malaysia[132] or East Malaysia, [133] and whether in court proceedings or arbitration.[134] Unlike some other common law jurisdictions, the limitation period is the same whether the Contract is a simple contract or executed by deed. Tortious claims, except for personal injury, must be commenced within six years of the cause of action accruing in West Malaysia[135] and East Malaysia[136], except that in West Malaysia the limitation period may be extended where the damage was not discoverable prior to the expiry of the statutory limitation period.[137]

The *Limitation Act 1953* does not apply to any action or arbitration against the government.[138] Rather, the *Public Authorities Protection Act 1948* provides that the limitation period for any act done in pursuance, execution or intended execution of any written law, public duty or authority or in respect of any alleged neglect or default in the execution of any such written law, duty or authority by any person (including public servants and government agencies) is 3 years from the date on which the action accrued.[139]

14.5 What Special Provisions in the Particular Conditions are necessary for consistency with applicable laws in Malaysia?

The FIDIC 1999 suite of contracts are in general use in Malaysia, particularly the Red and Yellow Books, which are used for large scale infrastructure projects.

125 *Contracts Act 1950* (Act 136), ss 2 to 9. Acceptance of an offer must be final, absolute and unqualified.
126 *Contracts Act 1950* (Act 136), ss 8, 10 and 26.
127 Whilst this requirement is not set out in the *Contracts Act 1950* (Act 136), in relation to commercial agreements the law generally presumes that the parties intended to create legal creations see *Guthrie Waugh Bhd v Malaiappan Muthuchumaru* [1976] 2 MLJ 62. This presumption can be rebutted by adducing evidence to the contrary.
128 *Contracts Act 1950* (Act 136), s 30.
129 ibid ss 10–12.
130 This is subject to any legislative requirement that a contract be in writing.
131 *Ayer Hitam Tin Dredging Malaysia v YC Chin Enterprises* [1994] 2 MLJ 754; *Deutsche Bank (M) Sdn Bhd v MBF Holdings Bhd & Ano*r [2016] 6 MLJ 310.
132 *Limitation Act 1953* (Act 254), s 6. Other provisions of the *Limitation Act 1953* (Act 254) that apply to construction contracts include ss 3, 24 and 26 to 30.
133 *Limitation Ordinance 1952* (Cap 72) (Sabah) and *Limitation Ordinance 1959* (Cap 49) (Sarawak).
134 *Limitation Act 1953* (Act 254), s 30.
135 ibid s 6(1).
136 *Limitation Ordinance 1952* (Cap 72) (Sabah) and *Limitation Ordinance 1959* (Cap 49) (Sarawak).
137 *Limitation Act 1953* (Act 254), s 6A. See further section 1.4.5 below.
138 *Limitation Act 1953* (Act 254), ss 3 and 30; *Public Authorities Protection Act 1948* (Act 198]), s 2.
139 *Public Authorities Protection Act 1948* (Act 198), s 2.

14.5.1 FIDIC General Conditions are incompatible or inconsistent with Malaysian governing law of the contract

14.5.1.1 Copyright

Whilst copyright initially vests in the author, under the *Copyright Act 1987*, where work is commissioned under a contract of service or made in the course of the author's employment, the copyright is deemed to be transferred to the person who commissioned the work or the author's employer.[140] Accordingly, on a construction project, copyright will ultimately vest in the Employer (or Contractor (in the case of a Contractor – Subcontractor relationship in which the Contractor commissions the work)). This is inconsistent with sub-clause 1.10 of the Red Book and Yellow Book General Conditions which provide that:

> As between the Parties, the Contractor shall retain the copyright and other intellectual property rights in the Contractor's Documents and other design documents made by (or on behalf of) the Contractor.

Parties should amend their contract so that it is consistent with the *Act*.

14.5.2 FIDIC General Conditions are incompatible or inconsistent with the law of the Site/Country

No Particular Conditions are necessary for consistency with applicable laws in Malaysia if it is the law of the Site/Country.

14.5.3 FIDIC General Conditions are incompatible or inconsistent with the relevant laws on dispute determination in Malaysia

No Special Provisions in the Particular Conditions are necessary for consistency with applicable laws in Malaysia in the event that it is the law of the arbitral seat.

14.6 What Special Provisions in the Particular Conditions are desirable for consistency with applicable laws in Malaysia?

14.6.1 Liquidated damages

Under Malaysian law, liquidated damages clauses are not routinely enforced without evidence of the actual damage suffered, except where such evidence is difficult to obtain.[141] Pursuant to section 75 of the *Contracts Act 1950*, a liquidated damages clause merely entitles the claimant to 'reasonable compensation'. Furthermore, section 75 of the *Act* prohibits recovery of any sum in excess of the agreed amount in the liquidated damages clause.

Notwithstanding that in general parties have the freedom to derogate from the provisions of the *Contracts Act 1950*,[142] section 75 of the *Act* cannot be circumvented

140 *Copyright Act 1987* (Act 332), s 26.

141 *Selva Kuma all Murugiah v Thiagarajah all Retnasamy* [1995] 2 AMEJ 1097. Although see the recent decision of *Cubic Electronics Sdn. Bhd (In Liquidation) v MARS Telecommunications Sdn Bhd* Appeal No. 02(f) - 64 - 09/2016(W), where the Federal Court opined that it is not necessary for the innocent party to prove his/her actual loss or damage in every case.

142 See para 14.3.2 above.

by inserting a Special Provision in the Particular Conditions which provides that the Employer is not required to prove its actual loss and/or otherwise purport to exclude the application of section 75 of the *Act*.[143] Whilst it is settled law that parties can contract out of the *Act*, it is unlikely that they will be permitted to do so if it is inconsistent with the *Act*.[144]

Second, in light of the fact that any stipulated amount will be treated as a cap under section 75 of the *Act,* the parties should ensure that the stipulated amount is a fair estimate of the likely damages the Employer will incur in the event of delay.

14.6.2 Security of payment

In 2014, Malaysia enacted a statutory adjudication regime for security of payment under the *Construction Industry Payment and Adjudication Act 2012* which is aimed at providing a rapid and efficient mechanism for settling payment disputes in construction contracts on a provisional interim basis in order to avoid short-term cash-flow problems.[145]

The Malaysian model is a hybrid of statutory adjudication models adopted elsewhere in the world including the United Kingdom, Singapore and Australia. Key features of the Malaysian model include that it:

- Is a mandatory, statutory process and agreement of the parties is not required for the process to commence[146]
- Prohibits conditional payment (ie pay when paid) provisions[147]
- Provides default payment terms to be implied into a construction contract in the event that the construction contract does not include payment terms[148]
- Provides the parties with the power to expand the adjudicator's jurisdiction[149] and
- Provides various remedies to the successful party including an entitlement to suspend works or reduce the rate of works in the event that the adjudication determination is not paid.[150]

The *Act* applies to contracts made in writing[151] which relate to construction work including building works, infrastructure works (ie road, railway, harbour, bridge, dam,

143 See eg *Kejuruteraan Bintai Kindenko Sdn Bhd v Serdang Baru Properties Sdn Bhd* [2017] 1 LNS 693.

144 *Contracts Act 1950* (Act 136); *Isito Electronics Sdn Bhd v Teh Ah Kiam & Anor 7 MLJ 513 and PT Vision Renewable Fuels v Export-Import Bank of Malaysia Bhd* [2015] 8 MLJ 706.

145 *Construction Industry Payment and Adjudication Act 2012* (Act 746).

146 Sundra Rajoo and Harbans Singh KS, *Construction Law in Malaysia* (Sweet & Maxwell 2012) 563.

147 *Construction Industry Payment and Adjudication Act 2012* (Act 746), s 35. In *Bond M&E (KL) Sdn Bhd v Isyoda (M) Sdn Bhd (Brampton Holdings Sdn Bhd, third party)* [2017] MLJU 376 the High Court held that conditional payments are only void in relation to adjudications. This decision appears to suggest that parties may still rely on a conditional payment clause if the dispute is referred to the courts or arbitration.

148 *Construction Industry Payment and Adjudication Act 2012* (Act 746), s 36.

149 ibid s 27.

150 *Construction Industry Payment and Adjudication Act 2012* (Act 746), ss 2831.

151 The *Construction Industry Payment and Adjudication Act 2012* (Act 746) excludes oral contracts (including partly oral, partly in writing contracts) and contracts by conduct. Therefore, contracts that are not in writing are not subject to the *Construction Industry Payment and Adjudication Act 2012* (Act 746). The requirement that the contract be in writing does not mean it must be a formalised contract document signed by the parties (ie there can be an agreement contained in various letters).

pipeline, drainage and irrigation works) and utilities works (ie electrical, mechanical, water, gas, oil and telecommunication works) including preparatory (ie site clearance, soil investigation, excavation works), temporary, permanent and procurement (ie supply of equipment, materials and labour) works carried out wholly or partly within the territory of Malaysia except in relation to buildings of less than four storeys that are intended for occupation by a 'natural person' (ie residential construction contracts).[152] It also extends to consultancy agreements (including planning and feasibility studies, architectural works, engineering, surveying, exterior and interior design works, landscaping and project management services)[153] and construction contracts entered into by the various state governments in Malaysia and the federal government of Malaysia.[154]

Parties to a construction contract are not permitted to contract out of the *Act*.[155] Nevertheless, the Works Minister holds discretionary powers of exemption under the *Act*.[156] To date, there have been two categories of exemption established under the *Construction and Industry Payment and Adjudication (Exemption) Order 2014*: (i) a contract for any construction works that involve emergency, unforeseen circumstances and that relate to national security or security related facilities; and (ii) a construction contract with the government if the contract sum is MYR20 million and below. The second category of exemption only applied between from 14 April 2014 until 31 December 2015.

In relation to making a claim under the *Act,* the parties are first required to follow the payment mechanisms under the construction contract (or if the contract is silent, the default provisions under the *Act*), failing which, the *Act* specifies a pre adjudication procedure in which an unpaid party may serve a payment claim on a non-paying party.[157] The non-paying party then has 10 days to respond to the payment claim by either admitting or disputing the payment claim in whole or in part.[158] If any part of the payment claim is disputed, a payment dispute crystalises and can be referred to adjudication.[159] The *Act* imposes strict time frames for making, and responding to, an adjudication claim and requires that a determination be made by the adjudicator within 45 days of service of the adjudication response.[160]

Section 5 of the *Act* provides that 'an unpaid party may serve a payment claim on a non-paying party for payment pursuant to a construction contract'. Accordingly, a party can only make a payment claim for payment.[161] The term payment is restrictive and limited to 'payment for work done or services rendered under the express terms of a construction contract'.[162] The reference to 'work done' is in effect a reference to

152 *Construction Industry Payment and Adjudication Act 2012* (Act 746), ss 2, 3, 4. The definition of '*natural person*' does not include corporations or body corporates.

153 Rajoo and Harbans Singh (n 146) have suggested that, on a literal interpretation, the term 'consultancy agreement' should extend to conventional consultancy agreements in building, infrastructure, oil and gas, petrochemical and communications industries, including project management.

154 *Construction Industry Payment and Adjudication Act 2012* (Act 746), ss 2, 4.

155 Rajoo and Harbans Singh (n 146) 569–70.

156 *Construction Industry Payment and Adjudication Act 2012* (Act 746), s 40.

157 ibid ss 5, 36.

158 ibid s 6. Failure to respond to a payment claim is deemed as disputing the entire payment claim.

159 ibid s 7.

160 ibid. Following the Court of Appeal decision in *Bauer (Malaysia) Sdn Bhd v Jack-In-Pile (M) Sdn Bhd* (CA) Civil Appeal No. B-02(C)(A)-1187-06/2017, it is unclear whether the Act applies prospectively only or retrospectively.

161 *Construction Industry Payment and Adjudication Act 2012* (Act 746).

162 ibid ss 8 to 12.

'construction work' (which is defined under section 4 of the *Act*).[163] The reference to 'services rendered' includes consultancy services (see above) in relation to construction work.[164] This encompasses progress payments (whatever their form and frequency) and final payment, as well as Variations, diminution in value, prime cost sums, preliminaries, cost adjustments, provisional sums, contingent sums and retention sums providing these are expressly provided for under the construction contract.[165] However, payments arising by implication (ie under the common law) are excluded under the *Act*.[166]

An adjudication determination is binding unless it is set aside by the High Court on the grounds referred to in section 15 of the *Act* (ie because the adjudicator acted in excess of their jurisdiction, the adjudicator lacked independence or impartiality, there was a denial of natural justice, or the determination was procured by fraud or bribery), the payment dispute is settled in writing by the parties or the payment dispute is finally decided by arbitration or the court.[167]

In addition, a subcontractor may have a right against a Contractor or subcontractor in respect of a monetary claim arising out of labour it has provided under the relevant workplace legislation in West Malaysia and East Malaysia.[168]

Although the FIDIC General Conditions have not been amended to reflect (or refer to) security of payment legislation, parties should seek advice on the incorporation of Special Provisions that specifically cater to the operation of the *Act*. Special Provisions which seek to circumvent the operation of the *Act* will not be effective.

14.6.3 Frustrated contracts

The *Contracts Act 1950* renders contracts void in two narrow instances: (1) where the contract is to do an impossible act;[169] and (2) where a 'supervening impossibility' or 'frustration' occurs after a contract is made without default of either party which makes performance of the contract impossible, or by reason of some event which the promisor could not prevent, unlawful.[170] Notably, the word 'impossible' is not defined under the *Act*. It is clear from case law that second instance applies to circumstances where performance is radically different from what was agreed between the parties (eg there is an outbreak of war or there has been destruction of the subject matter of the Contract).[171] In either of these circumstances, an order can be made that the party who has received an advantage under the Contract restore it or otherwise make compensation for it to the other party to the Contract.[172]

163 Rajoo and Harbans Singh (n 146) 569.
164 ibid.
165 ibid 569.
166 ibid 570.
167 *Construction Industry Payment and Adjudication Act 2012* (Act 746), ss 13, 15.
168 *Employment Act 1955*, s 69(2)(ii); *Labour Ordinance* (Chapter 76)(Sarawak), s 8A(2)(b); and *Labour Ordinance* (Chapter 67)(Sabah), s 7A(2)(b). The application of these *Acts* and *Ordinances* and process for bringing a monetary claim is explained at para 14.2.4 above.
169 *Contracts Act 1950* (Act 136), s 57(1).
170 ibid s 57(2).
171 *Guan Aik Moh (KL) Sdn Bhd & Anor v Selangor Properties Bhd* [2007] 4 MLJ 201; *APT Associates Sdn Bhd v Adnan Ishak & Ors* [2016] 4 CLJ 277.
172 *Contracts Act 1950* (Act 136), s 66.

The *Civil Law Act 1956* also provides circumstances (subject to certain exceptions)[173] in which an adjustment of the parties' rights and liabilities upon the frustration of a contract may be obtained which includes (but is not limited to) the potential recoverability of monies paid under the contract prior to it being discharged (ie where a party should have performed the contract before the impossible or frustrating event occurred or performed a contract up to the occurrence of the impossible or frustrating event).[174] The *Act* also provides a mechanism to sever from the contract, and treat separately, certain parts of a contract which may otherwise frustrate the contract.[175]

Clause 18 of the FIDIC General Conditions which deals with *force majeure* (or as it is described 'exceptional events') should be reviewed to determine whether it is appropriate in light of the legislation referred to above.[176]

14.6.4 Defects

Recently, the *Limitation Act 1953* in West Malaysia was amended to introduce a new section 6A, primarily addressing tortious claims for latent defects. Under the new provision, a party which discovers a latent defect after six years from the date of occurrence of the defect has three years from the date of knowledge of such defect to commence its claim.[177] The position has not been considered in East Malaysia, and therefore a party which discovers a latent defect after six years of the date of occurrence of the defect is time-barred from bringing a tortious action. Parties carrying out projects in East Malaysia should consider whether they wish to include Special Provisions in their contracts which have the effect of entitling Employers to the same rights in respect of latent defects as they would have in West Malaysia.

14.6.5 Rights of third parties

The doctrine of privity of contract which provides that only parties to a contract can sue or be sued in relation to that contract applies in Malaysia. Therefore, a contract cannot be enforced by or against a person who is a stranger to it (ie a third party). Unlike some other common law jurisdictions, including England and Wales, Malaysia has not enacted legislation providing by way of a statutory exception that contracting parties are permitted to provide a third party with an enforceable benefit under their contract. If parties wish to confer contractual rights to a third party, they should consider naming the relevant person as a party to the contract or executing ancillary agreements, such as collateral warranties, with the third party.

14.6.6 Requirements under Malaysian law to hire local labour

Parties should give due consideration to how they will resource their project being carried out in Malaysia and make appropriate provision for the time it may take to source an appropriate work force. Malaysia has legislated to restrict the employment

173 *Civil Law Act 1956* (Act 67), s 16(5).

174 ibid ss 15 and 16. Notwithstanding these provisions, it is still debated whether sections 57 and 66 of the *Contracts Act 1950* (Act 136) apply or ss 15 and 16 of the *Civil Law Act 1956* (Act 67).

175 *Civil Law Act 1956* (Act 67), s 16(4).

176 See 2017 FIDIC Yellow Book, 2017 FIDIC Red Book and 2017 FIDIC Silver Book.

177 *Limitation Act 1953* (Act 254), s 6A.

of non-citizens in Malaysia and for the registration of non-citizens.[178] In order to work in Malaysia, non-citizens must hold a valid work permit under the *Employment (Restriction) Act 1968*.[179] It is an offence to employ non-citizens without a valid work permit.[180]

Article 153 of the *Federal Constitution* recognises the special position of native Malays and natives of Sabah and Sarawak. Consistent with this, the Malaysian government implements a policy of affirmative action to grant opportunities and, in some case, funding to companies that are majority owned by native Malays or ***Bumiputras***. One effect of this is that government-tendered projects sometimes require that companies submitting tenders be Bumiputra owned. Special Provisions are not required to take this into account, but all contractors operating in Malaysia should be cognisant of these policies.

14.6.7 Mandatory insurance

The *Employment Insurance System Act 2017* which came into force on 1 January 2018 establishes inter alia an Employment Insurance Fund, provides certain benefits for insured persons in the event that they lose their employment, and sets up a re-employment placement programme.[181] It is mandatory for both employers and employees to register under the Employment Insurance System with the Social Security Organization (**SOCSO**) and contribute to the Employment Insurance Fund at the prescribed rate (dependent on the insured person's wage) under the *Act*.[182]

The *Employees' Social Security Act 1969* establishes the Social Security Fund and sets out the rights and obligations of employers and employees with respect to injuries or death caused by (a) accidents arising out of and in the course of employment; or (b) prescribed occupational diseases.[183] Similarly, it is mandatory for both employers and employees to contribute to the Social Security Fund at the prescribed rate under the *Act*.[184] Local workmen are required to be registered under this *Act*. Similarly, there are also compulsory obligations on the employer to insure against injuries suffered in the course of employment under the *Workmen's Compensation Act 1952*.[185]

Further, the *Employees Provident Fund Act 1991* establishes the Employees Provident Fund and sets out rights and obligations of employers and employees with respect to a number of contingencies including attainment of age 55 years old, mental or physical incapacity from engaging in employment, death, and change of residence for

---

178 *Employment (Restriction) Act 1968* (Act 796), preamble.

179 ibid s 5.

180 ibid s 17.

181 The *Employment Insurance System Act 2017* (Act 800) applies to all industries having one or more employees employed under a contract of service or apprenticeship (save for those excluded under section 2 and Schedule 1 of the *Act 2017* including inter alia casual workers, domestic servants, public servants, employees of local authorities or statutory bodies, persons under 18 years old or over 60 years old and persons over 57 years old in respect of whom no contributions were payable under the *Act* before they attained the age of 57 years old).

182 ibid. The Social Security Organisation is tasked under the *Employment Insurance System Act 2017* (Act 800) with administering the Employment Insurance System including inter alia the Employment Insurance Fund.

183 *Employees' Social Security Act 1969* (Act 4).

184 ibid.

185 *Workmen's Compensation Act 1952* (Act 273).

foreign workers. Contributions under the *Act* are only mandatory for private sector works (including foreign workers who are permanent residents of Malaysia) and non-pensionable public sector employees.[186]

Parties may wish to draw attention to the compulsory obligations considered above in relation to insurance against injuries in the drafting of sub-clause 19.2.5 [*Injury to employees*] of the FIDIC General Conditions and consider incorporating Special Provisions generally that set out their respective obligations with reference to the legislation referred to above.[187]

14.6.8 Gross negligence

Sub-clauses 1.15, 8.8, 11.10 and 14.14 of the FIDIC General Conditions[188] refer to the term 'gross negligence' as an exception to the application of the limitation of liability. Malaysia does not recognise a concept of 'gross negligence' as distinct from negligence. While it is likely that the Malaysian courts will follow the English courts' willingness to interpret the use of the phrase,[189] Parties should consider whether it is appropriate.

14.7 Summary of applicable legislation for Malaysian governing law of the contract

Unless otherwise noted, all legislation in the following table (as well as the tables set out at paragraphs 14.8 and 14.9) are Federal Acts.

	West Malaysia	*East Malaysia*
14.7.1 Entry into a construction contract		
Contracts generally	*Contracts Act 1950* (Act 136) *Government Contracts Act 1949* (Act 120) *Civil Law Act 1956* (Act 67) *Consumer Protection Act 1999* (Act 599) *Competition Act 2010* (Act 712) *Specific Relief Act 1950* (Act 137)	*Contracts Act 1950* (Act 136) *Government Contracts Act* 1949 (Act 120) *Civil Law Act 1956* (Act 67) *Consumer Protection Act 1999* (Act 599) *Competition Act 2010* (Act 712) *Specific Relief Act 1950* (Act 137)
Construction contracts	*Construction Industry Payment and Adjudication Act 2012* (Act 746)	*Construction Industry Payment and Adjudication Act 2012* (Act 746)

186 *Employees Provident Fund Act 1991* (Act 452). Contributions required under the *Act* are in addition to the contributions required under the *Employment Insurance System Act 2017* (Act 800).

187 2017 FIDIC Yellow Book, 2017 FIDIC Red Book and 2017 FIDIC Silver Book.

188 The sub-clauses identified apply to 2017 FIDIC Red Book and 2017 FIDIC Yellow Book. Sub-clauses 1.14, 8.8., 11.10 and 14.4 are the relevant sub-clauses in the 2017 FIDIC Silver Book.

189 See Moore-Bick LJ in *Tradigrain SA v Intertek Testing Systems (ITS) Canada Limited* [2007] EWCA Civ 154 and Aikens LJ in *Springwell Navigation Corporation v JP Morgan Chase Bank* [2010] EWCA Civ 1221.

14.7.2 Termination of a construction contract

Frustration	*Contracts Act 1950* (Act 136) *Civil Law Act 1956* (Act 67)	*Contracts Act 1950* (Act 136) *Civil Law Act 1956* (Act 67)
Bankruptcy, insolvency, liquidation	*Insolvency Act 1967* (Act 360) *Bankruptcy Act 1967* (Act 360) *Companies Act 2016* (Act 777)	*Insolvency Act 1967* (Act 360) *Bankruptcy Act 1967* (Act 360) *Companies Act 2016 (Act 777)*
Guarantees under forms of Security (Tender Security, Demand Guarantee, Surety Bond, Advance Payment Guarantee, Retention Money Guarantee, Payment Guarantee by Employer	*Contracts Act 1950 (Act 136)* *Companies Act 2016 (Act 777)* *Loan Guarantee Act 1963* (Act 412) *Loans (International Bank) Act 1958* (Act 411)	*Contracts Act 1950 (Act 136)* *Companies Act 2016 (Act 777)* *Loan Guarantee Act 1963* (Act 412) *Loans (International Bank) Act 1958* (Act 411)

14.7.3 Dispute resolution

Limitation periods	*Limitation Act 1953* (Act 254) (Peninsular Malaysia) *Public Authorities Protection Act 1948* (Act 198)	*Limitation Ordinance 1952* (Cap 72) (Sabah) *Limitation Ordinance 1959* (Cap 49) (Sarawak) *Public Authorities Protection Act 1948* (Act 198)
Liability	*Civil Law Act 1956 (Act 67)*	*Civil Law Act 1956 (Act 67)*
Adjudication	*Construction Industry Payment and Adjudication Act 2012* (Act 746)	*Construction Industry Payment and Adjudication Act 2012* (Act 746)
Arbitration	*Arbitration Act 2005* (Act 646)	*Arbitration Act 2005* (Act 646)

14.8 Summary of applicable legislation if the Site/Country is in Malaysia

	West Malaysia	*East Malaysia*

14.8.1 Operation of a construction contract

Registration and administration of professionals – engineers, architects, quantity surveyors, surveyors	*Architects Act 1967* (Act 117) *Registration of Engineers Act 1967* (Act 138) *Quantity Surveyors Act 1967* (Act 487)	*Architects Act 1967* (Act 117) *Registration of Engineers Act 1967* (Act 138) *Quantity Surveyors Act 1967* (Act 487) *Surveyors Ordinance 1960* (Sabah)
Registration/licencing of contractors and subcontractors	*Lembaga Pembangunan Industri Pembinaan Malaysia Act 1994* (Act 520) (also known as the *Construction Industry Development Board Act 1994* (Act 520)	*Lembaga Pembangunan Industri Pembinaan Malaysia Act 1994* (Act 520) (also known as the *Construction Industry Development Board Act 1994* (Act 520)

	Industrial Co-ordination Act 1975 (Act 156)	*Industrial Co-ordination Act 1975* (Act 156)
Subcontractors	*Construction Industry Payment and Adjudication Act 2012* (Act 746)	*Construction Industry Payment and Adjudication Act 2012* (Act 746)
Use of liens /Assignment of debts	*Civil Law Act 1956* (Act 67)	*Civil Law Act 1956* (Act 67)
Labour	*Employment Act 1955* (Act 265) (Peninsular Malaysia) *Employees' Social Security Act 1969* (Act 4) *Employees Provident Fund Act 1991* (Act 452) *Workmen's Compensation Act 1952* (Act 273) *Industrial Relations Act 1967* (Act 177) *Children and Young Persons (Employment) Act 1966* (Act 350) (Peninsular Malaysia) *Minimum Retirement Age Act 2012* (Act 753) *Employment (Restriction) Act 1968* (Act 796) *Trade Union Act 1959* (Act 262)	*Employment Act 1955* (Act 265) (Federal Territory of Labuan only) *Labour Ordinance* (Chapter 76)(Sarawak) *Labour Ordinance* (Chapter 67)(Sabah) *Employees' Social Security Act 1969* (Act 4) *Employees Provident Fund Act 1991* (Act 452) *Workmen's Compensation Act 1952* (Act 273) *Industrial Relations Act 1967* (Act 177) *Minimum Retirement Age Act 2012* (Act 753) *Employment (Restriction) Act 1968* (Act 796) *Trade Union Act 1959* (Act 262)
Design/ Moral Rights	*Industrial Designs Act 1996* (Act 552)	*Industrial Designs Act 1996* (Act 552)
Copyright	*Copyright Act 1987* (Act 332) *Patents Act 1983* (Act 291)	*Copyright Act 1987* (Act 332) *Patents Act 1983* (Act 291)
The product being produced from the Works	*Environment Quality Act 1974* (Act 127)	*Environment Quality Act 1974* (Act 127)
First nation people's land rights	***Orang Asli*** enjoy customary rights in respect of lands without express legislation. The Malaysian superior courts have recognised and reaffirmed the special position of the *Orang Asli* under Article 8(5)(c) of the *Federal Constitution.*	
Planning	*Town and Country Planning Act 1976* (Act 172) *Federal Territory (Planning) Act 1982* (Act 267) *Land Development Act 1956* (Act 474) *Town Planners Act 1995* (Act 538)	*Perbadanan Labuan Act 2001* (Act 609) *Federal Territory (Planning) Act 1982* (Act 267) *Land Development Act 1956* (Act 474) *Town Planners Act 1995* (Act 538)
Work affecting adjacent property to the Site	*Street, Drainage and Building Act 1974* (Act 133) (Peninsular Malaysia)	*Building Ordinance 1994* (Chapter 8) (Sarawak) *Buildings By-Laws 1982* (Sabah)
Heritage	*National Heritage Act 2005* (Act 645)	*National Heritage Act 2005* (Act 645)

Environment	*Environment Quality Act 1974* (Act 127) *Water Services Industry Act 2006* (Act 655) (Peninsular Malaysia and the Federal Territories of Putrajaya and Labuan)	*Environment Quality Act 1974* (Act 127)
Local Procurement	*Government Contracts Act 1949* (Act 120) *Financial Procedure Act 1957* (Act 61)	*Government Contracts Act 1949* (Act 120) *Financial Procedure Act 1957* (Act 61)
Building and construction permits, execution of construction work, Standard of Construction Work	*Street, Drainage and Building Act 1974* (Act 133) (Peninsular Malaysia) *Uniform Building By-Laws 1984* (GN 5178/85) (Peninsular Malaysia) *Drainage Works Act 1954* (Act 354) (Peninsular Malaysia) *Federal Roads Act 1959* (Act 376) *Highway Authority Malaysia (Incorporation) Act 1980* (Act 231) *Federal Roads (Private Management) Act 1984* (Act 306) *Road Transport Act 1987* (Act 333) *Housing Development (Control and Licensing) Act 1966* (Act 112)	*Building Ordinance 1994* (Chapter 8) (Sarawak) *Buildings By-Laws 1982* (G.N.L 20 of 1983) (Sabah) *Federal Roads Act 1959* (Act 376) *Federal Roads (Private Management) Act 1984* (Act 306) *Malaysian Highway Authority (Incorporation) Act 1980 (Act 231)* *Road Transport Act 1987* (Act 333)
Health and safety	*Occupational Safety and Health Act 1994* (Act 541) *Factories and Machinery Act 1967* (Act 139) *Petroleum (Safety Measures) Act 1984* (Act 302)	*Occupational Safety and Health Act 1994 (Act 541)* *Factories and Machinery Act 1967* (Act 139) *Petroleum (Safety Measures) Act 1984* (Act 302)
Calibration of testing apparatus, equipment and Instruments	*Weights and Measures Act 1972* (Act 71)	*Weights and Measures Act 1972* (Act 71)
Ownership of Plant and Materials	*Hire-Purchase Act 1967* (Act 212) (relates to consumer goods and specified motor vehicles only)	*Hire-Purchase Act 1967* (Act 212) (relates to consumer goods and specified motor vehicles only)
Insurance	*Employment Insurance System Act 2017* (Act 800) *Employees Provident Fund Act 1991* (Act 452) *Employees' Social Security Act 1969* (Act 4)	*Employment Insurance System Act 2017* (Act 800) *Employees Provident Fund Act 1991* (Act 452) *Employees' Social Security Act 1969* (Act 4)

Statutory rights that coexist with contractual Rights	*Sales of Goods Act 1957* (Act 382) (Peninsular Malaysia) *Trade Descriptions Act 1972* (Act 87) *Consumer Protection Act 1999* (Act 599)	*Trade Descriptions Act 1972* (Act 87) *Consumer Protection Act 1999* (Act 599)
Liability for defective work	*Sales of Goods Act 1957* (Act 382) (Peninsular Malaysia) *Occupational Safety and Health Act 1994* (Act 541) *Street, Drainage and Building Act 1974* (Act 133) (Peninsular Malaysia) *Limitation Act 1953* (Act 254) (Peninsular Malaysia)	*Occupational Safety and Health Act 1994* (Act 541)
Liability for nuisance	*Environment Quality Act 1974* (Act 127) *Local Government Act 1976* (Act 171) (Peninsular Malaysia)	*Environment Quality Act 1974* (Act 127)
Other issues	*Federal Housing Act 1965* (Act 391) *Interpretation Acts 1948 and 1967* (Act 388) *Specific Relief Act 1950* (Act 137) *Personal Data Protection Act 2010* (Act 709)	*Federal Housing Act 1965* (Act 391) *Interpretation Acts 1948 and 1967* (Act 388) *Specific Relief Act 1950* (Act 137) *Personal Data Protection Act 2010* (Act 709)

14.8.2 Termination of a construction contract

Bankruptcy, insolvency, liquidation	*Insolvency Act 1967* (Act 360) *Bankruptcy Act 1967* (Act 360) *Companies Act 2016* (Act 777)	*Insolvency Act 1967* (Act 360) *Bankruptcy Act 1967* (Act 360) *Companies Act 2016 (Act 777)*

14.8.3 Dispute resolution

Limitation periods	*Limitation Act 1953* (Act 254) *Public Authorities Protection Act 1948* (Act 198)	*Limitation Ordinance 1952* (Cap 72) (Sabah) *Limitation Ordinance 1959* (Cap 49) (Sarawak) *Public Authorities Protection Act 1948* (Act 198)
Dispute before a local board/Adjudication	*Construction Industry Payment and Adjudication Act 2012* (Act 746)	*Construction Industry Payment and Adjudication Act 2012* (Act 746)
Arbitration	*Arbitration Act* 2005 (Act 646)	*Arbitration Act 2005* (Act 646)

14.9 Summary of applicable legislation if the 'seat' of the dispute determination is in Malaysia

	West Malaysia	*East Malaysia*
Limitation periods	*Limitation Act 1953* (Act 254) *Public Authorities Protection Act 1948* (Act 198)	*Limitation Ordinance 1952* (Cap 72) (Sabah) *Limitation Ordinance 1959* (Cap 49) (Sarawak) *Public Authorities Protection Act 1948* (Act 198)
Adjudication	*Construction Industry Payment and Adjudication Act 2012* (Act 746)	*Construction Industry Payment and Adjudication Act 2012* (Act 746)
Arbitration	*Arbitration Act* 2005 (Act 646)	*Arbitration Act 2005* (Act 646)

14.10 Issues that a court or arbitrator may construe differently to that expected from the words of the Contract because of local law or custom

14.10.1 Building and planning regulations

Malaysia has enacted a number of regulatory controls under legislation including the *Lembaga Pembangunan Industri Pembinaan Act 1994* relating to building works and the establishment of the CIDB including the approval of building plans, regulation of building materials, and the requirement for registration of Contractors, Subcontractors and other construction personnel.[190] Parties should seek competent advice on these regulatory controls, especially in connection with sub-clause 1.13 [Compliance with Laws][191], and sub-clause 4.8 [Health and Safety Obligations] of the FIDIC General Conditions.

In relation to planning, except for the Federal Territories, planning does not fall within federal jurisdiction and is dealt with at a state level. Generally speaking, planning is fairly standardised across the various local governments in each state. Planning spans across three stages: (1) land use conversion; (2) planning permission or development order approval; and (3) building plan approval.

14.10.2 Assessment of damages for breach of contract

Malaysia has codified the common law position in *Hadley v Baxendale* (1854) 9 Ex 341 in section 74(1) of the *Contracts Act 1950* which provides that:

> When a contract has been broken, the party who suffers by the breach is entitled to receive, from the party who has broken the contract, compensation for any loss or damage caused

190 *Lembaga Pembangunan Industri Pembinaan Act 1994* (Act 520) (also known as the *Construction Industry Development Board Act 1994* (Act 520)). West Malaysia has also enacted the *Street, Drainage and Building Act 1974* (Act 133). Other regulation in East Malaysia includes the *Building Ordinance 1994* (Chapter 8) (Sarawak) and the Buildings By-Laws 1982 (G.N.L 20 of 1983) (Sabah).

191 The sub-clause identified applies to the 2017 FIDIC Red Book and 2017 FIDIC Yellow Book. Sub-clause 1.12 is the relevant sub-clause in the 2017 FIDIC Silver Book.

> to him thereby, which naturally arose in the usual course of things from the breach, or which the parties knew, when they made the contract, to be likely to result from the breach of it.[192]

However, section 74(2) of the *Act* goes on to say: 'Such compensation is not to be given for any remote and indirect loss or damage sustained by reason of the breach.'

14.10.3 Misleading or deceptive conduct

Section 9 of the *Consumer Protection Act 1999* provides that:

> No person shall engage in conduct that –
>
> in relation to goods, is misleading or deceptive, or is likely to mislead or deceive, the public as to the nature, manufacturing process, characteristics, suitability for a purpose, availability or quantity, of the goods; or in relation to services, is misleading or deceptive, or is likely to mislead or deceive, the public as to the nature, characteristics, suitability for a purpose, availability or quantity, of the services.

Whilst this *Act* is intended to apply to consumer contracts, the scope of its application to contracts for the supply of construction products and services is unclear.[193]

14.10.4 Proportionate liability

Malaysia has not legislated in favour of a proportionate liability scheme. Liability in Malaysia is governed by the *Civil Law Act 1956* in which each defendant is joint and severally liable for the loss suffered by the plaintiff.[194] A defendant may, however, seek contribution from joint tortfeasors who are responsible for the same loss.[195] In determining each joint tortfeasors' contribution, the Court will consider what is just and equitable having regard to the extent of that person's responsibility for the damage.[196]

If more than one action is brought in respect of the damage suffered, the sum recoverable by way of damages under the judgments given shall not exceed in the aggregate the damages awarded by the judgement first given.[197]

14.10.5 Implied terms

As with other common law jurisdictions, in addition to express terms, Malaysia recognises implied terms into construction contracts subject to the court or tribunal's interpretation of sub-clause 1.15 [Limitation of Liability] of the FIDIC General Conditions (which limits either party's liability for loss and damage to breaches of specific clauses in the Contract).[198]

---

192 In *Toeh Kee Keong v Tambun Mining Company Ltd* [1967] 1 LNS 197 Chief Justice Azmi held that 'Section 74(1) of the Contracts Ordinance, 1950, is a statutory enunciation of the rule in *Hadley v Baxendale* [1854], 9 Exch 341'.

193 Section 9 of the *Consumer Protection Act 1999* (Act 800) refers to a 'person' engaging in misleading or deceptive conduct. Whilst the term 'person' is not defined under the Act, it should extent to corporations by virtue of sections 2 and 3 of the *Interpretation Acts 1948 and 1967* (Act 388).

194 *Civil Law Act 1956* (Act 67), s 10(1)(a).

195 ibid s 10(1)(c), subject to any indemnification that may apply.

196 ibid s 10(2).

197 ibid s 10(1)(b).

198 The sub-clause identified applies to 2017 FIDIC Red Book and 2017 FIDIC Yellow Book. Sub-clause 1.14 is the relevant sub-clause in the 2017 FIDIC Silver Book.

Malaysia follows general common law principles in relation to the implication of terms.[199] Terms commonly implied in construction contracts include terms as to non-interference; adequate possession of the Site; that require the work be completed within a reasonable time; terms that require the Employer to not hinder the Contractor from performing the Contract; and terms that oblige the Employer to cooperate or to do all that is reasonably necessary for the performance of the Contract.

Terms might also be implied by statute. Whilst the *Contracts Act 1950* is silent on implied terms (save as to distinguish between express promises and implied promises), the *Sale of Goods Act 1957* implies the following conditions, inter alia, into all contracts for the sale of goods, and this would include contracts for the sale of construction products:

- The seller has a right to sell the goods.[200]
- The goods are free from encumbrances.[201]
- The goods are of merchantable quality (including that the goods are free from defects).[202]
- The goods are reasonably fit for purpose.[203]
- The goods correspond with the description or sample. [204]

Further, as explained at paragraph 14.5.3 above, under the *Construction Industry Payment & Adjudication Act 2012*, default payment terms are implied into every construction contract that does not contain express payment terms.[205] Under the default payment terms, Contractors are entitled to issue monthly progress payments, with payment due 30 days from the date of receipt of an invoice.[206]

14.11 References

14.11.1 Books

Arjunan Krisgnan and Abdul Majid bin Nabi Baksh, *Contract Law in Malaysia* (LexisNexis 2008)

Ashgar Ali Ali Mohamed, *Malaysian Legal System* (CLJ Publication 2014)

Azizan Supardi, *Malaysian Construction Contract Law & Management* (LAP Lambert Academic Publishing 2012)

Lam Wai Loon and Ivan Y.F. Loo, *Construction Adjudication in Malaysia* (CCH 2013)

Sundra Rajoo and KS Harbans Singh, *Construction Law in Malaysia* (Sweet & Maxwell 2012)

Clive Lovatt, *Construction Law & Practice* (2nd edn, Sweet & Maxwell 2016)

199 *Dr Abdul Hamid Abdul Rashid v Jurusan Malaysia Consultants* [1997] 3 MLJ 546.

200 *Sale of Goods Act 1957* (Act 382), section 14. The *Act* applies to the Federal Territories, Johore, Kedah, Kelantan, Negeri Sembilan, Pahang, Perak, Perlis, Selangor, Terengganu, Malacca and Penang.

201 ibid.

202 *Sale of Goods Act 1957 (Act 382),* section 16. The *Act* applies to the Federal Territories, Johore, Kedah, Kelantan, Negeri Sembilan, Pahang, Perak, Perlis, Selangor, Terengganu, Malacca and Penang.

203 ibid.

204 *Sale of Goods Act 1957* (Act 382), ss 15 and 17. The *Act* applies to the Federal Territories, Johore, Kedah, Kelantan, Negeri Sembilan, Pahang, Perak, Perlis, Selangor, Terengganu, Malacca and Penang.

205 *Construction Industry Payment & Adjudication Act 2012* (Act 746), s 36.

206 ibid.

14.11.2 Journals

The University of Melbourne Southeast Asian Legal Research Guide: Introduction to Malaysia and its Legal System http://unimelb.libguides.com/c.php?g=402982&p=5823532
Current Law Journal

14.11.3 Internet

Federal Constitution: http://www.agc.gov.my/agcportal/index.php?r=portal2/left&menu_id=dDI5alZpOWFtcGl5MnZ5M1dtT1NNZz09
Legislation: http://www.agc.gov.my/agcportal/index.php?r=portal2/lom&menu_id=b21XYmExVUhFOE4wempZdE1vNUVKdz09
Federal Gazette: http://www.federalgazette.agc.gov.my/index.php
Rules of the Court: www.malaysianbar.org.my

CHAPTER 15

Applying FIDIC contracts in Nepal

Tanka Prasad Dulal and Dr Hare Ram Shrestha

DOI: 10.4324/9781003200901-15

15.1 Outline of the legal environment in Nepal

15.1.1 The constitutional structure of Nepal

The *Constitution of Nepal* comprises 308 articles in 35 chapters and 9 annexes. These articles and annexes cover the constitutional provisions of: citizenship; fundamental rights and duties of citizens including the right to enterprise, trade and profession; structure of state and distribution of state power among federal, provincial and local entities.[1] There are constitutional provisions in respect of the President and Vice President, the Federal Executive, the Federal Parliament comprising the House of Representative and the National Assembly that enacts federal law. The provincial legislature enacts the provincial law, and the local legislative bodies enact law for the local jurisdictions.[2] The *Constitution* provides the provisions for the provincial Executive and Local Executive. The judiciary exercises the power related to justice. The powers to deliver justice are vested in court and other judicial institutions in accordance with *Constitution of Nepal*, other laws and recognized principles of

1 *Constitution of Nepal* promulgated on 20 September 2015 (*3 Aswin 2072 BS*), art 57(1), (3), 109, 162(4), 197, 57(5), 109, 162(4), 197, 214(2), 221(2), 226(1) and annex 5, 7. Note: The government of Nepal officially uses the *Bikram Sambat (**BS**) calendar, which is a solar calendar based on Hindu traditions. This calendar is 56 years 8 months ahead of AD. The calendar starts with the first day of Baisakh, which usually falls on 13th or 14th of April in the Gregorian calendar.*

2 ibid art 57(2), 162(4), 231(3), 232(7), 274(4), 296(4), 57(4), 214(2), 221(2), 226(1) and annex 6, 8.

justice. The *Constitution* further provides for constitutional bodies, amendment of the *Constitution*, emergency powers, national security etc.

Nepal is a federal, democratic and republican system of government. The President is the ceremonial head of state.[3] The entire executive power of the state is vested in the Council of Ministers in accordance with the *Constitution* and the law. The President preforms his/her functions in accordance with the *Constitution* and federal laws. The major duties of the President are to abide with and protect the *Constitution*. The form of governance of Nepal is a multi-party competitive, federal democratic republican parliamentary system based on pluralism.[4] The Prime Minister is the leader of the Council of Ministers. The responsibility of issuing general directives, control and regulating the governance of Nepal is subject to the *Constitution* and law, entrusted in the Council of Ministers.[5]

The *Constitution* is the fundamental law of Nepal. All laws inconsistent with the *Constitution* are, to the extent of such inconsistency, void.[6] The *Constitution* provides power to the Supreme Court of Nepal to declare void *ab initio* any law enacted by the Federal Parliament, Provincial Parliament or local entities from the date of commencement on the basis of inconsistency with the provision of the *Constitution* and provincial laws.[7]

The basic structures of the *Constitution of Nepal* are:

> [c]ommitted to socialism based on democratic norms and values including the people's competitive multiparty democratic system of governance, civil liberties, fundamental rights, human rights, adult franchise, periodic elections, full freedom of the press, and independent, impartial and competent judiciary and concept of the rule of law, and build a prosperous nation . . . to fulfill the aspirations for sustainable peace, good governance, development and prosperity through the federal, democratic, republican, system of governance.[8]

The notion of the separation of powers and checks and balances are important features of the *Constitution*. The Federal Parliament can pass a motion of impeachment against President and Vice President on the ground of serious violation of the *Constitution* and federal laws by a two-thirds majority of the both houses of the Federal Parliament; if such a motion is passed he or she is relieved of his/her office.[9] The House of Representatives can pass a motion of impeachment against the Chief Justice and any other Justice of the Supreme Court of Nepal on the ground of his or her failure to fulfil his or her duties of office because of serious violation of the *Constitution* and the law, incompetence, misconduct, failure to discharge the duties of office honestly, or serious violation of the code of conduct. If such a motion is passed by a two-thirds majority of the total members of the House of Representative, the Justice shall be relieved of his or her office.[10]

The federal House of Representative can pass a vote of no confidence against the Prime Minister of Nepal by the existing majority to relieve him/her from his/her office.[11] The President can dissolve the House of Representatives on the recommendation of the Prime Minister if the Prime Minister fails to obtain a vote of confidence is

3 *Constitution of Nepal*, art 61.
4 ibid art 74.
5 ibid art 75.
6 ibid art 1, 133(1).
7 ibid.
8 *Constitution of Nepal*, preamble.
9 ibid art 101(1).
10 ibid art 101.
11 ibid art 100.

accordance with the article 76(5) of the *Constitution*, and the President must fix the date to conduct a fresh election within six months from such dissolution.[12] Any residuary powers not assigned to the Federation, the provinces or local entities in the annexes of the *Constitution* are vested in the Federation.[13]

The successful and proper implementation of the *Constitution* can foster the federal system of government. The democratic culture and values are the basic driving factors for the proper implementation and exercise of the constitutional power of its actors and this is one of the major challenges to implement the *Constitution* in accordance with its letter and spirit.

15.1.2 The legal system of Nepal

The Nepalese legal system is based on the Anglo-American legal system. Before 1950 (*2007 BS)* it was close to civil law system with indigenous Nepalese features. In this era the inquisitorial system was adopted for dispensing justice. The Prime Minister Junga Bahadur Rana promulgated the law code in 1853 (*Muluki Ain 1910 BS*). This *National Code 1853* was the first comprehensive law code in Nepal which was closed with the codification concept of a civil law system. This code incorporated the concepts of Hindu law and even now the concepts of Hindu law are fused in the law of succession, the law of partition, marriage law and the law of adoption.

Political change in 1950 (*2007 BS*) overthrew the Rana regime. A democratic constitution, the *Interim Government Act of Nepal 1951* (*2007 BS*) was promulgated.[14] This *Act* implemented the Westminster model of constitutional structure and after promulgation of the *Interim Government Act of Nepal 1951 (2007 BS.*, the Nepalese legal system fused with the common law system.

The *Interim Government Act of Nepal 1951(2007 BS)* was repealed by the *Constitution of the Kingdom of Nepal 1959 (2015 BS)*.[15] The British constitutional expert Sir Ivor Jennings was involved in drafting this constitution, which comprised a multi-party democratic system of governance and introduced the adversarial justice system of common law instead of the inquisitorial (civil law system) and indigenous justice system. The *Constitution of Nepal 1962 (2019 BS)* promulgated in 1962 (*2019 BS*) repealed the *Constitution of the Kingdom of Nepal 1959 (2015 BS)*, and provided for a one-party system of government including the adversarial system of justice of the common law system[16].

The enforcement of the *State Cases Act 1961* (*2017 BS)* was one of the major initiatives to convert the Nepalese legal system into the common law system. In 1974 the *Evidence Act 1974 (2031 BS)* commenced; this *Act* is entirely based on the adversarial system of justice and is still in force. The *State Cases Act 1993* (2049 BS) repealed the *State Cases Act 1961(2017 BS)* and the *State Cases Act 1993 (2049 BS)* fully converted the Nepalese legal system to the common law system. The *National Criminal Procedure Code 2017* (*2074 BS*) repealed the *States Cases Act 1993* (*2049 BS*) adopting the common law system.

12 ibid arts 76(7), 85.

13 ibid art 58.

14 Tanka Prasad Dulal and Rajesh Hamal, *Constitutional law* (Sumitra Hamal 1992) 48–49.

15 ibid 59–60.

16 Since Nepal is not a commonwealth country, Nepal has adopted only the adversarial system of justice of the common law system.

The political movement for democracy and a multiparty system of government overthrew the one-party system of government and a new constitution, the *Constitution of Kingdom of Nepal 1990 (2047 BS),* was promulgated. This constitution provided for a Westminster model of government including a multiparty democratic system and a constitutional monarchy.[17] The next political movement of 2006 to 2007 in Nepal overthrew the monarchy, and the *Interim Constitution of Nepal 2007 (2063 BS)* repealed the *Constitution of Kingdom of Nepal 1990 (2047 BS).* The *Interim Constitution of Nepal 2007(2063 BS)* was promulgated for an interim period to enable the writing of a new constitution through a constituent assembly.[18] The *Constitution of Nepal* was constructed by the constituent assembly and promulgated on 20 September 2015; this is the prevailing *Constitution of Nepal.*

The *National Code 1964* (*Muliki Ain 2020 BS*) incorporated the entire civil and criminal laws of the country, except those provided by other separate Acts. This code was a revised and advanced form of the first comprehensive code 1853 (*Mulik Ain 1910 B.S*) issued by the Prime Minister Junga Bahadur Rana. The *National Code 1964* (*Muliki Ain 2020 BS*) is repealed by the *National Civil Code 2017* (*Muliki Dewani Sanhita, 2074 BS*), *National Civil Procedure Code 2017* (*Muliki Dewanikaryabidhi Sanhita 2074 BS*), *National Criminal Code 2017* (*Muliki Aparadha Sanhita, 2074 BS*), *National Criminal Procedure Code 2017* (*Muliki Phaujdari Karyabidhi Sanhita, 2074 BS*) and *Criminal Act (Punishment Determination and Execution) Act 2017* (*Phaujdari Kasur Nirdharan Tatha Karyanwayan) Ain, 2074 BS*). These *Acts* were enacted by the Federal Parliament under the power assigned by annex 5 of the *Constitution of Nepal,*[19] and are general and uniform laws that apply all over the country.

The legal provisions on contracts including construction contracts are arranged and provided in Chapter 5 of the prevailing *National Civil Code 2017* (*2074 BS*) under the heading of 'The provisions of contract and other liabilities'.[20] This is the uniform law that applies to the Federation, entire provinces and local entities of Nepal. It is the governing law for entry into a contract, contract administration and operation including private and public sector construction contracts. The provisions of the *National Civil Code 2017 (2074 BS)*, *Public Procurement Act 2006 (2063 BS)* (***PPA***) and *Public Procurement Rules 2007 (2064 BS)* (***PPR***) are applied to public procurement construction contracts. The *PPA* and *PPR* are uniform laws and apply to the Federation, all provinces and local entities.

The *Constitution* provides a common jurisdiction to enact the laws related to contracts, insolvency, labour rights and labour dispute settlement, engineering to the Federation and provinces.[21] The *Uniform Companies Act 2006* (*2063 BS*) and the *Arbitration Act 1999 (2055 BS)* are important laws that apply to the Federation, all provinces and local entities. The *Arbitration Act 1999 (2055 BS*) is based on the UNCITRAL model law.[22]

17 Dulal and Hamal (n 14) 166.

18 *Interim Constitution of Nepal 2007 (2063 BS)*, preamble.

19 *Constitution of Nepal 2015* (*2072 BS*), arts 57(1), 109 and annex 5.

20 *National Civil Code 2017* (*2074 BS*) Chapter 5, ss 493–544.

21 *Constitution of Nepal 2015* (*2072 BS*), arts 57(4), 114(2), 221(2), 226(1) and annex 7.

22 Bharat Raj Uprety, Justice of the Supreme Court of Nepal, *Contract Law* (Legal Research and Development Forum - FREEDEL, Kathmandu Nepal, 2009) 443.

15.1.3 The court system of Nepal

The *Constitution* provides for three levels of courts in Nepal: one Supreme Court, seven High Courts including eleven extended benches, and seventy-seven District Courts.[23] The Supreme Court of Nepal is the court of record. Unless otherwise provided in the *Constitution* all other courts and judicial institutions are under the Supreme Court. The Supreme Court is the final authority to interpret the *Constitution* and the law.[24]

The power of dispensing justice is vested in the courts and other judicial institutions. Special courts and tribunals are in operation with jurisdiction on subject matter such as corruption, money laundering, organized crime, tax and elections. The precedents of the Supreme Court are binding on all. Precedents are one of the sources of law after legislation in Nepal.

15.1.3.1 Supreme Court of Nepal

The *Constitution* provides for a constitutional bench in the Supreme Court comprising 5 justices of Supreme Court including the Chief Justice of Nepal. The constitutional bench has the power of judicial review and to declare void *ab initio* any act of Federal Parliament, provincial law or laws enacted by the local entities on the ground of inconsistency with the *Constitution* and provincial laws. The Supreme Court has jurisdiction to settle disputes:

- Between the Federation and a province
- Between provinces
- Between provinces and local entities
- For election to the Federal Parliament or Provincial Assembly and
- On the eligibility of federal and provincial Parliament candidates for election.[25]

The Supreme Court can issues the writ of *habeas corpus*, *mandamus*, *certiorari*, prohibition and *quo warranto* for the enforcement of the fundamental and legal rights ensured by the *Constitution* and law.[26] It has original jurisdiction in respect of federal laws and appellate and revision jurisdiction over the verdicts of the High Court, and it can review its own previous verdicts on certain grounds as prescribed by law.[27]

The Supreme Court is the final authority to interpret the *Constitution* and any laws or judge made law to interpret the provision, terms and conditions and words of a contract in Nepal. This principle founded by the Supreme Court of Nepal under the Authority of the *Constitution of Nepal* which provides:

1. There shall be a Supreme Court in Nepal.
2. The Supreme Court shall be a court of record. All courts and judicial bodies shall, except as otherwise provided in this Constitution, be under the Supreme Court. The Supreme Court shall have the final authority to interpret this Constitution and laws.

---

23 *Constitution of Nepal 2015 (2072 BS)*, art 127.
24 ibid art 128.
25 ibid arts 1, 46, 133(1), 137.
26 ibid arts 46,133(2), (3).
27 ibid art 133(4) and *Judicial Administration Act 2016 (2073 BS)*, ss 9,10 and 11.

3. The Supreme Court may inspect, supervise and give necessary directives to, it and courts, specialized courts or other judicial bodies under its jurisdiction, in relation to matters relating to judicial administration or management.
4. All must abide by any interpretation of the Constitution or a law made by or any legal principle laid down by the Supreme Court in the course of trying a lawsuit. If anyone makes obstruction in the dispensation of justice by, or disregard any order or judgment handed down by, it or any of its subordinate courts, the Supreme Court may, in accordance with law, initiate proceedings and impose punishment for contempt. [28]

Under the provision of this article the legal principles laid down by the Supreme Court of Nepal have binding force as law and they must be abided by.

15.1.3.2 High courts

The *Constitution* provides for one High Court in each province.[29] There are seven High Courts and 11 extended benches. High courts can issue writs of *habeas corpus*, *mandamus*, *certiorari*, prohibition and *quo warranto* and injunctions for the enforcement of the fundamental and legal right ensured by the *Constitution* and law.[30] It has original jurisdiction in accordance with federal laws and the appellate jurisdiction over the verdicts of District Courts.[31] High Courts have commercial benches which have original jurisdiction on commercial cases, eg banking crime, contracts, companies and other commercial disputes.

Any party to a contract can file an application in a High Court to appoint an arbitrator in cases where the arbitrator cannot be appointed in accordance with the provision of the contract or in cases where there are no provisions to appoint an arbitrator in the contract.[32] Any party to a contract can file an application in a High Court against the award of an arbitral tribunal. High Courts can alter the decision of an arbitrator or return the file for the arbitrator to review his/her previous decision.[33] High Courts have overall jurisdiction on issues arising from the *Arbitration Act 1999 (2055 BS)*.

15.1.3.3 District Courts

There are 77 District Courts based on the administrative and geographical division of the country. Each district has one District Court. District Courts can issue writs of *habeas corpus* and injunctions for the enforcement of the fundamental and legal rights ensured by the *Constitution* and law. District Courts have original jurisdiction on the entirety of cases within their respective jurisdiction, and appellate jurisdiction on the decision of the quasi-judicial bodies[34] Construction and other contracts that do not have provision for arbitration are under the jurisdiction of the District Court.

---

28 *Constitution of Nepal 2015 (2072 BS)*, art 128.

29 ibid art 139.

30 ibid art 144(1), (2) and *Judicial Administration Act 2016 (2073 BS)*, s 8.

31 ibid art 144(3) and *Judicial Administration Act 2016 (2073 BS)*, s 8.

32 *Arbitration Act 1999 (2055 BS)*, s 7.

33 ibid s 30.

34 *Constitution of Nepal 2015 (2072 BS)*, art 148, *Judicial Administration Act 2016 (2073 BS)*, s 7, *National Civil Procedure Code 2017 (2074 BS)*, ch 3, *National Criminal Procedure Code 2017(2074 BS)*, ch 4.

15.1.3.4 Specialised courts
The *Constitution* enables the constitution and establishment of specialised courts, judicial institutions and judicial tribunals for the hearing of the special nature of the cases eg corruption, money laundering, and organized crime, tax, elections and labour disputes. However, a specialised court cannot be constituted and established for any one particular case.[35]

15.2 The construction industry in Nepal

15.2.1 Overview

Formal construction contracts in Nepal started relatively late compared to other countries. Construction companies have been registered since the early sixties. The Government of Nepal (**GoN**) established a construction company named National Construction Company of Nepal (NCCN) in 1961, liquidated later in 2010. The first *Contract Act* 1966 (*2023 BS*) was promulgated in 1966.

Construction companies formed the Contractor's Association of Nepal (**CAN**) in 1990. Later, it was reformed as the Federation of Contractor's Association of Nepal (**FCAN**) in 1997. Currently 12,408 construction companies are registered and are the members of FCAN.[36] These construction companies are registered by the Construction Business Development Council (**CBDC**), under the Ministry of Physical Infrastructure and Transport (**MoPIT**) in four categories: Class A, Class B, Class C and Class D.[37] There are 228 Class A, 282 Class B, 1,158 Class C and 10,740 class D contractors in Nepal.[38] However, no public limited construction company listed on the stock exchange has yet been established. All the construction companies are private limited companies.

The GDP contribution of the construction sector in FY 2019/2020 (*2076/2077 BS*) is NPR488.22 billion (US$4.13 billion), which is 9.59 per cent of total GDP and the fifth largest sector in GDP contribution after forest and agriculture (23.28 per cent), industry (11.88 per cent) and trade (10.95 per cent). The construction sector is the third largest lender of bank loans with 10.74 per cent of total lending from the banks after trade (20.53 per cent) and the production sector (16.58 per cent).[39]

The construction sector provides employment to about 2 million people from Nepal, India and Bangladesh and is the third largest employment sector, providing employment to 13.8 per cent of the labour force of Nepal after agriculture and forestry (21.5 per cent) and trade industry (17.5 per cent).[40] Based on the budget allocation of the current fiscal year, the annual volume of construction contracts is in the order of NPR300 billion (US$2.54 billion).[41]

The Nepalese construction sector is likely to grow with many big projects in the pipeline in the transport, energy (hydro power), and urban development and irrigation sectors. More tunnel works are needed in all sectors requiring big investments. The

35 *Constitution of Nepal 2015* (*2072 BS*), art 152.
36 FCAN website: www.fcan.org.np (accessed 23 September 2020).
37 *Construction Business Act 1999 (2055 BS*), s 8.
38 FCAN website: www.fcan.org.np (accessed 23 September 2020).
39 Nepal Economic Survey 2019/2020 (*2076/2077 BS*), Annex 5.7.
40 GoN, *Report on the Nepal Labour Force Survey 2017/18* (Central Bureau of Statistics).
41 GoN, *Red Book* (Ministry of Finance 2020).

fifteenth five-year plan envisaged investment of NPR4015.5 billion (US$34 billion) in construction of physical infrastructure, eg roads, railways, airports, energy (hydro power), irrigation, urban development etc.[42] This will put more emphasis on the use of FIDIC contracts, as more and more contracts will be let on the basis of international competitive bidding (ICB).

International construction companies are limited in Nepal. Large construction works require international competitive bidding inviting international construction companies.

15.2.2 Licensing and registration

The *Construction Business Act 1999 (2055 BS)* prohibits on carrying out a public construction contract without a licence. Section 3 of the *Act* states that:

> no person shall carry out or cause to be carried out public construction works without having obtained the license pursuant to this Act. Provided that, this Section shall not to be deemed to prevent the carrying out public construction works to be carried out through a consumers' committee or public participation to the prevailing law.

A construction company should first register in the Company Registrar's Office or the Department of Small and Cottage Industry and Department of Industries. Certificates of construction companies are in four categories – Class A, Class B, Class C and Class D based on the prescribed grounds and on the recommendation of the Construction Business Development Council pursuant to Section 8 of the *Construction Business Act 1999 (2055 BS)*. The certificates of class D construction companies are issued by local government in accordance with the *Local Government Operation Act 2017 (2074 BS)*.[43]

The minimum requirement criteria are as follows:

Class A Construction Company:

- Financial capacity: Working capital of minimum NPR10 million (US$84,500).
- Work experience: Completion of four construction contracts of more than NPR10.5 million (US$88,800) each or total of NPR60 million (US$507,000).
- Key human resources: Two full time graduate civil engineers, four technicians with certificate level, two graduate staff in any discipline, three staff with certificate level (12 class equivalent) in any discipline, one staff with graduate and one with certificate level in commerce.
- Machine and equipment: two theodolite, four level machines, two trucks or dump trucks, three water pumps, three concrete mixers, five vibrators, one set of laboratory equipment, one among backhoe, excavator or bulldozer, four among 17 types of machine/equipment (loader, bitumen distributor/ sprayer, water tanker/sprayer, motor grader, three wheeled roller, one ton roller, pneumatic roller, bitumen paver, asphalt mix plant, crane, fork lift, crusher, compactor, vibrating roller, hydraulic auger, winch and building hoist).[44]

42 GoN, *Fifteenth Periodic Plan* (National Planning Commission).
43 Section 11(2)(g)(10).
44 *Construction Business Rules 2000 (2056 BS)*, sch 10.

Class B Construction Company:

- Financial capacity: Working capital of minimum NPR5 million (US$42,300).
- Work experience: Completion of four construction contracts of more than NPR8 million (US$67,600) each or a total of NPR 20 million (US$169,100).
- Key human resources: One full time graduate civil engineer, two technicians with certificate level, two graduate staff in any discipline, two staff with certificate level (12 class equivalent) in any discipline, one staff graduated in commerce.
- Machine and equipment: One theodolite, two level machines, one truck or dump truck, two water pumps, two concrete mixtures, four vibrators, one set of laboratory equipment, one among backhoe, excavator or bulldozer, two among 17 types of machine/equipment (loader, bitumen distributor/sprayer, water tanker/sprayer, motor grader, three wheeled roller, one ton roller, pneumatic roller, bitumen paver, asphalt mix plant, crane, fork lift, crusher, compactor, vibrating roller, hydraulic auger, winch and building hoist).[45]

Class C Construction Company:

- Financial capacity: Working capital of minimum NPR2 million (US$16,900).
- Work experience: Completion of four construction contracts of more than NPR1 million each (US$8,450) or a total of NPRP 4 million (US$33,800).
- Key human resources: One full time graduate civil engineer, two technicians with certificate level, two graduate staff in any discipline, two staff with certificate level (12 class equivalent) in any discipline, one staff graduated in commerce.
- Machine and equipment: Two level machines, two water pumps, one concrete mixtures, three vibrators, one among 17 types of machine/equipment (loader, bitumen distributor/sprayer, water tanker/sprayer, motor grader, three wheeled roller, one ton roller, pneumatic roller, bitumen paver, asphalt mix plant, crane, fork lift, crusher, compactor, vibrating roller, hydraulic auger, winch and building hoist).[46]

Class D Construction Company:

- Financial capacity: Working capital of minimum NPR1 million (US$8,450).
- No work experience required.
- Key human resources: One full time technician with certificate level in civil engineering, one staff with certificate level (12 class equivalent) in any discipline, one staff with certificate level in commerce.
- Machine and equipment: One level machine, one water pump and one vibrator.[47]

The local government can issue and renew a Class D licence for a construction business in accordance with the *Local Government Operation Act 2017 (2074 BS)*.[48]

45 ibid sch 11.
46 ibid sch 12.
47 ibid sch 13.
48 Section 11(f).

15.2.3 Temporary licence for foreign construction company

A foreign construction company should obtain a temporary licence to work in Nepal. However, bidding is allowed without a licence. If a foreign company is selected for the construction contract in Nepal, the company should apply for a temporary licence.[49]

15.2.4 Labour relations

The *Labour Act 2017 (2074 BS)* and the *Child Labour (Prohibition and Regulating) Act 2000 (2056 BS)* prohibit the use of forced labour and child labour. The provisions of these *Acts* are referred to in clauses 31 and 32 of GCC of the Standard Bidding Document (SBD) prepared by PPMO. A Contractor must not employ forced or child labour.[50] The legal provisions of these *Acts* are applicable to all types of construction works. The use of SBD is mandatory to the public construction and it is optional for private constructions.

Normally labourers do not require the level of their skill to be certified. Up to now this has been based on the skill they possess which is trusted by the hiring personnel of the construction company. There is a government body the National Skill Testing Board (**NSTB**) for the certification of skill under the Council of Technical Education and Vocational Training (**CTEVT**). However, it is not legally mandatory to obtain a skill certificate to work for construction works.

15.2.5 Safety culture

Consistent with the *Labour Act 2017 (2074 BS)* Chapter 12 Article 68, occupational health and safety rules have been further specified in the Standard Bidding Document[51] that a public works contractor has to adhere to for the provision of safety, security and protection of the environment.[52] However, safety culture in wearing individual safety gear and personal protective equipment (**PPE**) is weak. The Covid-19 pandemic in 2020 reinforced the need to adhere to safety requirements.

15.2.6 Modular construction using factory fabricated components

Modular construction using factory fabricated components in Nepal is not very common, however there are some factories which produce the components of building structures. After the big Gorkha earthquake in 2015 in Nepal, prefabricated house construction was used.

15.2.7 Technology/innovation/BIM

Normally, conventional and proven construction methods are used in Nepal and use of new technology is limited in construction works. However, some new technologies have been introduced in large construction works. Recently TBM was used for the first time in Nepal in one of the multipurpose river linking projects (irrigation and

49 *Construction Business Act 1999 (2055 BS)*, s 8.

50 *Labour 2017 (2074 BS)* and *Child Labour (Prohibition and Regulating) Act 2000 (2056 BS)*.

51 SBD is prepared by PPMO for all government construction contracts, which is similar to FIDIC contracts. FIDIC contracts are used for international competitive bidding (ICB).

52 SBD, PPMO, s VIII, GCC, cl 24.

hydropower). But such cases are not common. Although BIM is not currently used in Nepal, training in the use of BIM has recently commenced.

15.2.8 Government/private sector procurement

The majority of construction projects in Nepal are government projects and hence the government is the main Employer in construction contracts. The Public Procurement Monitoring Office (**PPMO**) is the regulatory body for construction contracts provisioned under the *Public Procurement Act 2006 (2063 BS)* and is only relevant to government or semi-government institutions and public enterprises.

Recently, large construction contracts have been let by private companies also, especially in hydro power projects. Nepal has not yet developed the physical infrastructure required for the country, and many construction projects are planned in transportation, energy, urban development and various other areas. Accordingly, many large construction contracts will be let in the coming decade. A joint report published recently by the Institute for Integrated Development Studies (**IIDS**) and the Confederation of Nepalese Industries (**CNI**) estimated that physical infrastructure projects of US$203.41 billion need to be implemented during the decade 2020 to 2030- energy US$35.16 billion, transportation US$84.88 billion, water and sanitation US$31.8 billion and urban infrastructure US$51.57 billion.[53] This will require hundreds of big construction contracts to be implemented. Most of the projects will be government funded, and private funding is envisaged for the energy sector.

15.2.9 Insurance requirements

The provision of insurance is mandatory for government and semi- government construction contracts in accordance with the *PPA* and *PPR*. According to Rule 112 of the *PPR* 2007 *(2064 BS)*, SBD of GoN Section VIII GCC, clause 19.1 states the insurance requirement as

> The Contractor shall provide insurance in the joint names of the Employer and the Contractor from the Start Date to the end of the Defects Liability Period, in the amounts and deductibles stated in the SCC [Special Conditions of Contract?] for the following events which are due to the Contractor's risks:
>
> (a) loss of or damage to the Works, Plant, and Materials;
> (b) loss of or damage to Equipment;
> (c) loss of or damage to property (except the Works, Plant, Materials, and Equipment) in connection with the Contract; and
> (d) Personal injury or death.

15.2.10 Common forms of contract

Construction contracts are categorised in two types in Nepal – International Competitive Bidding (**ICB**) and National Competitive Bidding (**NCB**). FIDIC contracts are used for all ICB construction contracts. The majority of the ICB contracts are funded by MDBs and therefore the FIDIC Conditions of Contract for Construction for Building

53 Institute for Integrated Development Studies (**IIDS**) and Confederation of Nepalese Industries (**CNI**), *Nepal Infrastructure 2030: Investment and Financing Needs* (2019).

and Engineering Works Designed by the Employer, Multilateral Development Bank Edition June 2010 (Pink Book) is typically used.

The Standard Bidding Document (**SBD**) for national competitive bidding is prepared by the Public Procurement and Monitoring Office (**PPMO**) for contract amounts exceeding NPR20 million (US$170,000). This Nepalese standard form of contract is a simplified version with seven sections only with ninety-one clauses.

15.2.11 Dispute resolution – litigation, arbitration, Dispute Boards

In government and semi-government (public) construction contracts the Employer and Contractor are required to attempt to settle amicably by direct negotiation any dispute arising between them under or in connection with the Contract.[54] Any dispute arising pursuant to the Contract which cannot be settled within 30 days after the receipt by one Party of the other Party's request for such amicable settlement may be referred to adjudication or arbitration within 30 days after the expiration of the amicable settlement period. The arbitral procedure shall be in accordance with the *Arbitration Act 1999 (2055 BS), Arbitration (Court Procedure) Rules 2002 (2059 BS)* and procedure published by the Nepal Council of Arbitrations (**NEPCA**) for a dispute arising in a construction contract.[55]

Arbitrations for ICB contracts are generally referred to be administered by the Singapore International Arbitration Centre (**SIAC**) and conducted in accordance with SIAC Rules.

There is no legislative provision for Dispute Boards for NCB contracts. However, the parties to a construction contract have autonomy to appoint a Dispute Resolution Committee (**DRC**), Dispute Resolution Board (**DRB**), Dispute Board (DB) or similar dispute resolution mechanism which have the same meaning and may be used interchangeably.[56] For ICB contracts the DB has to be appointed 28 days after the commencement of the contract and appointment is generally referred to the executive committee of FIDIC if the parties do not come to a consensus to appoint the DB.[57]

15.2.12 Current challenges

Delay in construction works is very common in Nepal. Many contracts have encountered a dispute and the construction project has gone into standstill/limbo. Generally, Dispute Boards are not used for NCB contracts. In the writers' view it is desirable that Dispute Boards should be used in Nepal to minimise the complexity of disputes in construction contracts.

Another challenge is inadequate legal provisions for contract administration and weakness in execution of smooth and focussed operation of existing contracts. The government regulatory body PPMO is more concerned in the procurement process and its monitoring. If FIDIC contracts were also used for NCB, such gaps in the execution of construction contracts could be filled.

Many controversies have arisen on local and provincial procurement in construction and infrastructure development and due to these controversies, the management,

54 *Public Procurement Act 2006 (2063 BS)*, s 58.
55 SBD GCC, cl 29, consistent with Nepal *Arbitration Act 1999 (2055 BS)*.
56 Rules of Adjudication and Dispute Board, Nepal Council of Arbitration (NEPCA).
57 SBD for ICB, FIDIC MDB Harmonised Contract adopted by PPMO, GON.

operation and administration of the contracts are major challenges to construction contracts in Nepal.

The following are the current major challenges to construction contracts in Nepal:

- Facing the controversies and difficulties in the management, operation, administration of construction and infrastructure development contracts due to the delay to amend or enact new *PPA* and *PRR* aligned to the constitutional structure of the power distribution and administrative and financial autonomy of the constitutional scheme.
- Employers imposing unnecessary requirements in the SBD and contracts that are not compatible with the governing law or FIDIC standard forms of contract.
- The provision in Rule 31f of the *PPR* for the percentage allowance for preference for domestic bidders is directly inconsistent with the corresponding provision of section 12(1)(a) of the *Construction Business Act 1999 (2055 BS)*.
- Lack of provisioning an adequate budget to complete construction work within the Time for Completion causes overruns in the time and cost of the project and results in disputes.
- Delays in Site clearance by the Employer creates disputes between contracting parties.
- The legal provision of PPR prohibits the slicing and packaging of works to limit competitive bidding.[58] Construction contracts for single projects are sometimes made with more packages and vice versa. Such cases create controversies on slicing and packaging.
- Low bidding is practised due to least cost evaluation criteria. Contractors, in many cases, take risks by bidding low to win the contracts resulting in incomplete construction works and disputes.
- Procuring and entering into a contract without a strategic plan.
- Lack of good governance and proper execution of the laws for the procurement, management, operation and administration of construction contracts.
- Decreasing the decision-making power to procure and enter into a contract by the concerned authority due to the fears of a possible charge by the oversight agencies.
- The *PPA* and *PRR* provide the institutional arrangement of the Public Procurement Monitoring Office. The weak institutional structure and capacity and lack of a team of experts in the PPMO are facing difficulties in exercising the powers and performing the functions provided by section 65 of the *PPA*.[59]
- Most of the procurement units of the Employers are not effective for procurement.
- There is inadequate interaction with bidders on the terms and conditions of the construction contract.
- There is a lack of expertise in procurement, management, operation and administration of construction contracts.

58 *PPR 2007 (2064 BS)*, rule 3a.
59 Annual Report of PPMO 2018 *(2075 BS)*.

- The current single procurement Act (*PPA*) applies to all procurement, eg works, services, goods and supply. There is no separate procurement Act for construction works.
- There is a lack of knowledge on the online bidding system (e-GP) and its operation.
- There is no procedural manual or guidelines for government to government procurement.
- The design and build, EPC/turnkey, PPP, BOT and framework contract models are not effectively used in practice.
- Most of the construction contracts are based on the Employer's design that take a long time for the separate phases of design procedure and construction contracts.

15.2.13 Unique features of the construction industry in Nepal

The following are unique features of the Nepal construction industry:

- There are four classes (Class A, B, C and D) of construction industries provisioned in the law.[60]
- There is provision for domestic preference of 5 per cent while competing with international construction companies.[61]
- A contribution of 0.10 per cent is collected from the payment of contract amounts and paid into the Construction Entrepreneur's Fund in its account in the Ministry of Physical Infrastructure and Transport. This fund is utilised for various construction business activities for capacity development of the construction sector.

15.3 The impact of Covid-19 in Nepal

15.3.1 The impact of Covid-19 on the execution of construction projects in Nepal

The first case of Covid-19 in Nepal was confirmed on 23 January 2020 which was also the first case in South Asia. Nepal took measures to prevent the spread. A countrywide lock down was imposed with effect from 24 March 2020 until 21 July 2020 that prohibited the movement of all transport except vehicles carrying essential goods. After a second wave of Covid-19 cases lockdown was re-imposed from 20 August and was still in operation at the time of writing (mid-September).

15.3.1.1 Prohibition on construction

When lockdown was imposed suddenly, workers and their employers could not plan the next move as no time was given for preparation of the lock down period. They could not manage storage of food or construction material or leave the sites for a long time. Due to the rise in Covid-19 cases the first lock down was prolonged until 21 July 2020. Workers stranded at the sites had no option to move. The government was unable to

60 *Construction Business Act 1999 (2055 BS)*, s 8.
61 *Public Procurement Rules 2007 (2064 BS)*, rule 31f.

provide financial stimulus packages and Contractors were also unable to sustain their labour force at the sites. This situation created havoc due to uncertainty and workers started to leave the sites. It was reported that two hundred thousand migrant workers left the sites for their homes. They faced severe difficulties reaching their homes, and some labourers walked as far as 700 kilometres.[62] Numerous TV news, print media and online news reported the plight of these workers for many weeks.

15.3.1.2 Constraints on working on construction sites

Construction works were obstructed. Local residents obstructed the supply of construction materials. The government wanted to continue construction works by taking precautionary measures, but it did not work well.

15.3.1.3 Health and safety constraints on employees

Construction workers and employees on construction projects had to face the difficulties of increased health and safety precautions. Facemask and other safety measures were made mandatory. But on many construction sites the required PPE was not adequately supplied.

15.3.1.4 Health and safety constraints on the normal operation of a construction site

The Council of Ministers of the Central government, along with various other decisions related to Covid-19, made decisions on the construction sector as follows.

Ongoing construction projects had to limit the workforce to no more than 10 persons in one group. As most construction works in Nepal are labour intensive that has severely impacted the construction pace.

The government provided directions for a daily health check-up of workers, who were not allowed to go outside their camp. Contractors were required to arrange for the accommodation of labour within the construction area and arrange for their food.

15.3.1.5 Health and safety requirements after a confirmed Covid-19 infection

Most of the construction sites were closed after the lockdown imposed by the government. Government priority construction projects such as national pride projects were allowed to continue, following the mandatory precautionary measures in a directive issued by the Ministry of Health and Population under the authority of the law.[63]

15.3.1.6 Constraints on travel

Travel from one district to another and compulsory quarantine on arrival was imposed by the government under the authority of law.[64] This situation severely limited construction work.

---

62 The Asia Foundation, *The Impact of Covid-19 Lockdown on Nepal's Construction Sector: A Rapid Assessment* (May 2020).

63 *Infectious Diseases Act 1964 (2020 BS).*

64 ibid.

15.3.1.7 Changes to normal employment law

Companies can frame their bye laws with provisions for change of employment without breaching the legal provisions of the labour law.[65]

15.3.1.8 Financial support

No financial support was provided to the construction sector. The government issued directives to employers to provide basic wages to their workers. Under the directives issued by the government, banks rescheduled loans and extended repayment times. The government has also granted additional time for the payment of taxes in accordance with the stay order issued by the Supreme Court.[66]

15.3.2 The impact of Covid-19 on the operation of construction contracts in Nepal

The Supreme Court of Nepal issued *mandamus* to frame the comprehensive legislation for the response to the impact of Covid-19.[67] All ongoing contracts are subject to no cost time extension negotiations in accordance with the decision of the government of Nepal on *force majeure* provisions, eg suspending time bar provisions; assigning liability for cost impacts; government declaration of *force majeure*; termination of contracts.

The government allowed an extension of time on all contracts for 6 months in accordance with the decision made by the Council of Ministers, government of Nepal on 13 June 2020 *(29-03-2077)* However, there is ambiguity as to whether this is applicable to all contracts or not. FCAN has been in continuous dialogue with the government on this issue to consider this as a *force majeure*/change in law. But extensions of time will add to overhead costs. As the supply chain has been disrupted, costs have escalated. Nepali currency has already lost its value making imports more expensive. These issues could lead to claims and disputes.

15.3.2.1 Defence to breach of contract

Either *force majeure* or change in law could be applicable for the defence of breach of contract to response the Covid-19 impact. However, in the absence of appropriate contract clauses, *force majeure* may not apply in the absence of a government directive.

15.3.2.2 Commencement or continuation of court or arbitration proceedings

The Full Court of the Supreme Court of Nepal, comprising 19 justices, issued the obstacle releasing Directive *mandamus* for the time of lockdown to be treated as zero/vacuum period.[68]

---

65 *Labour Act 2017 (2074 BS).*

66 *Advocate Srijana Adhikari vs. Ministry of Finance*, GON, writ no 076 (2020)-wo-0966, SC, *Advocate Thaneshor Kafle vs. Inland Revenue Department,* GON writ no 076 (2020)-wo-974. SC.

67 *Advocate Roahani Poudyal, Advocate Saroj Krishna Ghimire v Government of Nepal, Secretariat of Prime Minister and Council of Ministers*, writ no 076 (2020)-wo-962, SC.

68 *Advocate Tika Ram Bhattarai: writ petitioner*, writ no: 076 (2020) – wo – 094 (writ of *mandamus*) Supreme Court, Case and Writ Division – Reporter, case no 076 (2020) – RE – 039.

15.3.2.3 Moratorium on calculating liquidated damages
As time extensions have been granted in accordance with the decision of the government, the six-month period will not be counted for the calculation of liquidated damages.

15.3.2.4 New dispute resolution provisions
The government decision on time extension will be applicable for resolution of disputes arising from the impact of Covid-19. Disputes will be determined as in the past.

15.3.2.5 Insolvency and bankruptcy
There has been no change to insolvency or bankruptcy law for the impact of Covid-19.

15.3.2.6 Corporate governance
There have been no changes to the provisions of the existing *Company Act* in Nepal for the impact of Covid-19.

15.4 Nepalese governing law of the contract

15.4.1 Constraints on the governing law of a construction contract

The contract law of Nepal ensures the Parties' freedom to choose the terms and conditions of their contract, including the governing law of the contract. *The National Civil Code 2017* (*2074 BS*) provides:

> Parties to be autonomous: The parties to a contract shall, subject to this Act, be autonomous to choose the form and contents of the contract, to determine terms and conditions of the contact and the nature of the remedy for its breach as well as to determine the measures for resolving disputes arising out of it.[69]

The *Arbitration Act 1999 (2055 BS)* of Nepal, based on the UNCITRAL Model Law section 18[70] provides:

> Substantive Law to be followed by Arbitrators:
>
> 1. The Nepal Law shall be the substantive law to be followed by the arbitrator, except when otherwise provided for in the agreement.
> 2. The arbitrator may settle the dispute according to the principle of justice and conscience (*ex aequo et bono*) or natural justice (*amiable compositeur*) only when explicitly authorised by the parties to do so.
> 3. Notwithstanding anything contained elsewhere in this act, the arbitrator shall settle the dispute according to the conditions stipulated in the concerned contract. While doing so, arbitrator shall also pay attention to the commercial usages applicable to the concerned transaction.

The legal provisions of section 18 of the *Arbitration Act 1999 (2055 BS)* apply for dispute resolution. In the Nepalese legal system the parties' autonomy to choose the terms and condition of the contract and the governing law is ensured by the law. In

69 Part 5 Chapter 1, s 507.
70 The corresponding provision in the UNCITRAL Model Law is s 28.

public procurement contracts the terms and conditions prescribed by the *PPA* and *PPR* have to be followed and included as per the nature of the contract. The parties' autonomy to choose the terms and condition of the contract and governing law of the contract are therefore subject to the statutory provisions that apply to bidding and entry into a contract.

In practice in NCB construction contracts generally the governing law of the contract is the contract law of Nepal, the *PPA*, *PPR* and the arbitration law of Nepal.[71] These are uniform laws that apply to the Federation, provinces and local entities. The PPMO developed and provided the SBD and standard form of construction contract for NCB. In NCB contracts the governing law for dispute settlement is generally the *Arbitration Act 1999 (2055 BS)*.

In the case of ICB contracts the parties' autonomy to choose the governing law of the contract fully applies. ICB contracts are generally based on FIDIC contracts and the governing law is that defined in the construction contract (which could be that of a country other than Nepal).

The *PPA* and *PPR* apply to public construction contracts. The largest construction contracts in Nepal are for public works. There are far fewer construction contracts in the private sector where the *PPA* and *PPR* do not apply, although the private sector can apply the process and methods of the *PPA* and *PPR* voluntarily.

The *PPA* and *PRR* were enacted before the commencement of the *Constitution of Nepal.* They will need to be amended or fully rewritten to enact new *PPA* and *PRR* in the spirit of the federal concept on the basis of the power distribution between the Federation, provinces and local entities. However, this has not yet occurred. The existing *PPA* and *PRR* do not have adequate legal provisions to cover federal procurement needs and requirements to meet the constitutional scheme of financial and development autonomy, decision making and power distribution among the Federation, provinces and local entities.

15.4.2 Formal requirements for a construction contract

The formal requirements for valid contracts in Nepal are those of the common law: the parties should be competent to conclude the contract intending to create a legal relationship; the contract should be constituted by offer and acceptances with consideration; the terms and conditions of the contract should be explicit and certain.

The concepts of contract law of Nepal are those of the common law of contract. Part 5 chapter 1 of the *National Civil Code 2017(2074 BS)* provides legal provisions on the formal requirement of a contract (including a construction contract):

Section 504 of the *National Civil Code 2017(2074 BS)* provides:

> (1) If an agreement enforceable by law is concluded between two or more persons to do or abstain from doing any act, a contract shall be deemed to be concluded.
>
> (2) For the purposes of sub-section (1), a contract shall be deemed to have been concluded once the person to whom an offer has been made by another person communicates his or her acceptance thereto.
>
> (3) Once a contract is concluded, a binding legal relationship shall be created between the parties to it.

71 See the *National Civil Code 2017 (2074 BS)* pt 5, the legal provisions on contract and other liabilities in ch 1, ss 493–544, *PPA*, *PPR* and *Arbitration Act 1999 (2055 BS)*.

- **Explanation**: For the purposes of this Chapter:

  (1) 'Offer' means an offer made by one person to another person with the intent of obtaining his or her acceptance to do or abstain from doing any act.

  (2) 'Acceptance' means the acceptance given by the person to whom the offer has been made in the same meaning in which the offer is made.

Section 505 of the *National Civil Code 2017(2074 BS)* provides:

(1) A contract concluded in fulfilment of the following conditions shall be deemed to be a contract enforceable by law:
   (a) The consent expressed by a person to a contract to bind himself or herself,
   (b) Capacity or qualification of a person to a contract to conclude the contract
   (c) Certain matter for the creation of an obligation,
   (d) Lawful obligation.

(2) A contract may be made in written or verbal form or even by conduct of the parties to it.
(3) Notwithstanding anything contained in sub-section (2), if there is a requirement that a particular contract be concluded in fulfilment of any particular procedure or formality, such a contract may not be enforceable unless such procedure or formality is completed.

Section 206 of the *National Civil Code 2017 (2074 BS)* provides:

(1) Every person other than the following persons shall be competent to conclude a contract:
   (a) One who is a minor
   (b) One who is of unsound mind.

Explanation:

(1) A person, who is usually of unsound mind, but occasionally of sound mind, may conclude a contract when he or she is of sound mind.

(2) A person, who is usually of sound mind, but occasionally of unsound mind, may not conclude a contract when he or she is of unsound mind.
(3) Notwithstanding anything contained in sub-section (1), any person who is deemed incompetent to conclude a particular contract under the law shall not be deemed to be competent to conclude such a contract.
(4) In concluding a contract on behalf of a person who is incompetent or quasi-competent, his or her guardian or curator may conclude such a contract.
(5) In concluding a contract on behalf of a legal person, it shall be concluded by a decision of the director or directors authorized for the management and operation of such a person or by a person authorized by such a director or directors.
(6) Notwithstanding anything contained elsewhere in this Section, if a person deemed to be incompetent to conclude a contract under this Chapter on any particular matter is competent by other law to conclude a contract on such a matter, such a person shall be deemed to be competent to conclude a contract on that matter.

In the case of a public procurement construction contract the following legal provisions of the *PPA* section 52 have to be compulsorily incorporated in the terms and conditions of the contract in accordance the nature of the contract:

Procurement Contract and Terms and Conditions Thereof

(1) In making procurement other than of low-value one, in accordance with this Act, the Public Entity shall have to conclude a procurement contract in accordance to this Section.

(2) The procurement contract under Sub-section (1) shall include the terms and conditions as referred to in the bidding documents, documents relating to proposal and documents relating to sealed quotation and such terms and conditions may, according to the nature of the contract be the following:-

(a) Name and address, telephone, fax number of the parties to the procurement contract and their contact person for implementation of the contract,
(b) Scope of the procurement contract,
(c) Details of the documents included in the procurement contract and their priority order,
(d) Work performance schedule,
(e) Supply time, performance time or whether time can be extended or not,
(f) Procurement contract amount or procedure of determining it,
(g) Terms and conditions for acceptance of goods, construction work or services,
(h) Terms and conditions and mode of payment including payment of foreign currency,
(i) Force majeure,
(j) If price adjustment can be made, provision thereof,
(k) If procurement contract can be amended and variation order can be issued, provision thereof,
(l) If insurance is necessary, provision relating thereto,
(m) Security required,
(n) Liquidated damages for failure of performance within the stipulated time,
(o) Provision concerning bonus to be given if work is completed before the stipulated period,
(p) Conditions in which procurement contract may be terminated,
(q) Provision whether sub-contract can be concluded or not,
(r) Mechanism for settlement of disputes,
(s) Applicable law, and
(t) Other matters as prescribed.

15.5 What Special Provisions in the Particular Conditions are necessary for consistency with applicable laws in Nepal?

15.5.1 FIDIC General Conditions are incompatible or inconsistent with Nepalese governing law of the contract

No Special Conditions in the Particular Conditions are necessary for consistency if Nepalese law is the governing law of the Contract.

15.5.2 FIDIC General Conditions are incompatible or inconsistent with the law of the Site/Country

No Special Conditions in the Particular Conditions are necessary for consistency with Nepalese law if the Site is in Nepal.

15.5.3 FIDIC General Conditions are incompatible or inconsistent with the relevant laws on dispute determination in Nepal

The applicable law for arbitration is the *Arbitration Act 1999 (2055 BS)*. Arbitrators have to take an oath of fairness, free from impartiality and sign a written oath to be sent to the High Court before the start of arbitration proceedings.[72]

72 *Arbitration Act 1999 (2055)*, s 9.

No Special Conditions in the Particular Conditions are necessary for consistency with Nepalese law if the seat of arbitration is in Nepal.

15.6 What Special Provisions in the Particular Conditions are desirable for consistency with applicable laws in Nepal?

The Public Procurement and Monitoring Office (PPMO) as a monitoring and regulating legal entity of Nepal, has prepared the SBDs for ICB and NCB. In addition to the 20 Clauses of the General Conditions of Contract of the FIDIC MDB Harmonised Contract, two additional Clauses are added in the SBD for ICB contracts for consistency with law of Nepal: Clause 21 [Customs and Tax Provisions for Contractors] and Clause 22 [Permission and Use of Explosives in the Construction Works].[73] The following description refers to the application of SBD for ICB.

15.6.1 Customs and tax provisions for Contractors[74]

SBD for ICB issued by PPMO states that:

> [w]hatsoever provisions made in the Contract shall not relieve the Contractor, its suppliers and Subcontractors from their responsibility to pay income tax that may be levied in the Employer's country on profits made by the Contractor, its suppliers and Subcontractors in respect of the Contract.

Therefore the price bid by the Contractor and its suppliers and Subcontractors should include the business taxes that may be levied in accordance with the laws and regulations in force in Nepal as of 30 days prior to the closing date for submission of Tenders on the Equipment, Plant Materials and supplies (permanent, temporary and consumables) to be acquired.

An exemption of custom duties and VAT is applicable in the event that the origin of any of the Contractor's or its Subcontractors' or the nominated Subcontractors' Plant, Equipment and Materials in India is supplied with the conditions that Contractor requests payment in Indian Currency for the Equipment and Materials imported under the 'Duty Refundable Procedures (DRP)'. The same condition applies if the Contractor requests payment in other convertible currencies for the Equipment and Materials imported under 'In Bond Transfer Procedures'. Failure to comply with these conditions will result in the application of normal customs duties and VAT in accordance with the prevailing rules and regulations of the government of Nepal.

15.6.1.1 Staff income tax

According to the *Income Tax Act 2002 (2058 BS)* it is the Contractor's duty to make a Tax Deduction at Source (**TDS**) for its staff, personnel and labourers, and those of its Subcontractors who will be liable to pay personal income taxes in the Employer's country, irrespective of whether they are local or foreign nationals. The TDS is on income earned including salaries and wages as applicable under the laws and regulations of Nepal and must be submitted to the Inland Revenue Office.

73 Standard Bidding Document, ICB, Single Stage, Two Envelope Bidding Procedure, PPMO.
74 *Income Tax Act 2002 (2058 BS)*.

15.6.1.2 Import Licence

The Contractor is required to inform the Employer and the Engineer in writing of the details of the Equipment and Materials to be imported into Nepal for use on the Works at least 45 days prior to arrival of a shipment at the disembarkation port, and shall submit a formal written request for assistance from the Employer for importation processing.

15.6.1.3 Duties on Equipment, Plant, Materials and supplies of re-exportable items

The Contractor's Plant and Equipment, including their essential tools, imported for the sole purpose of executing the Contract on condition of re-export upon completion of the Works, are exempt from payment of customs duties, VAT and other applicable taxes. The Contractor is required to deposit the amount or provide a Bank Guarantee to the Customs Office equal to the amount of customs duties and other taxes for those imported items of Equipment, Plant, Materials and supplies at the time of import. Such deposited amounts are refunded, or the Bank Guarantee cancelled by the Employer after submission of evidence to the Employer of the re-export of such Equipment, Plant and Materials. Plant, Materials or supplies imported by the Contractor and used in the Works shall be removed from Nepal within 90 days of the completion of the Works. If the Contractor disposes of or consumes any such Equipment, spare parts, unused Materials or supplies within Nepal, it shall pay all customs duties, VAT and income tax on the sales proceeds and taxes applicable on such items under the laws and regulations of Nepal in force.

15.6.1.4 Duties on Equipment, Plant, Materials and supplies of consumable items

Consumable Equipment, Plant, Materials and supplies, imported by the Contractor for execution of and incorporation in the Works, are subject to payment of customs duty at a special rate of one per cent of CIF or Customs entry point value. This customs duty is paid by the Contractor at the time of import and will be reimbursed by the Employer to the Contractor upon submission of the original receipt issued by the Customs Department.

Customs Duties at the rate of one per cent are imposed on the spare parts of the Contractor's Equipment and Plant which are imported for the execution of the Works, up to the amount of 10 per cent of the CIF or Customs entry point value of each item of Plant and Equipment. If the value of imported spare parts exceeds 10 per cent of the value of each item of Equipment and Plant, the Contractor must pay taxes and duties and the Employer will not reimburse such expenses exceeding the 10 per cent ceiling.

The Contractor is required to maintain records documenting the use of all Plant, Materials and supplies imported into Nepal and/or procured for the performance of the Works. If any of such Plant, Materials and/or supplies, imported into Nepal or otherwise supplied to the project at a special or preferential rate of customs duties or taxes are misused or found to be used or appropriated for any purposes other than the project, the Contractor is held responsible, and liable to pay customs duties, VAT and other taxes and/or any penalties in accordance with the prevailing laws and regulations of Nepal.

15.6.1.5 Duties and taxation on goods

VAT is imposed according to the prevailing laws and regulations of Nepal, on all materials and equipment purchased for the use in the Works. The Contractor is required to submit request with VAT bills to the VAT office of GoN for reimbursement of the paid VAT within the prescribed time.

15.6.1.6 Income tax

Income tax assessed in accordance with the prevailing *Income Tax Act* and as per the provisions of any applicable Double Taxation Agreement, applies to the Contractor, its Subcontractors and nominated Subcontractors. An advance income tax as per the prevailing *Income Tax Act and Finance Act* is deducted from the monthly progress payments of the Contractor.

15.6.1.7 Duties, taxes regulations, etc.

The Contractor is required to pay all duties, taxes, fees and contributions levied in Nepal in Nepalese Rupees as directed by the relevant governmental department or office or any other local statutory agency or body in accordance with the relevant rules and regulations. This provision is equally applicable to foreign Subcontractors or nominated Subcontractors of the Contractor employed for the Works.

The Contractor and all foreign Subcontractors or nominated Subcontractors employed on the Works, if not already registered in Nepal, are required to be registered with the Inland Revenue Department (**IRD**) for the purpose of the Contract within 30 days after signing of the Contract Agreement. The Contractor, Subcontractors and nominated Subcontractors are required to submit certified copies of the Registration Certificate(s) to the Engineer within 14 days of registration.

15.6.1.8 Royalties for extraction of aggregates, etc. from river bed

The Contractor is required to pay the costs of all charges and royalties levied by local governments in connection with the extraction of aggregates such as sand, stone/boulders, gravel, etc. from the river beds or from quarry sites or borrow pits and in connection with the winning of borrow material.

15.6.2 Use of explosives

Very strict procedures are followed in Nepal for the use of explosives and blasting for any purpose including construction. The Nepal Army is mandated to provide explosives and monitor the use of explosives.[75]

Compliance with Regulations for Explosives: The Contractor is required to comply with all relevant ordinances, instructions and regulations which the government, or other person or persons having due authority, may issue from time to time regarding the handling, transportation, storage and use of explosives.

Permission for blasting: The Contractor is required at all times to maintain full liaison with and inform well in advance and obtain such permission as is required from

75 *Explosive Substance Act 1961 (2018 BS).*

all government authorities, public bodies and private parties whatsoever concerned or affected, or likely to be concerned or affected by blasting operations.

Engineers approval for use of explosives: The Contractor should obtain the prior consent of the Engineer in writing for any kind of use of explosives and the Contractor should provide, supply, handle, store and transport all explosives, ancillary materials and stores and all other things of every kind whatsoever required for blasting operation, in a manner approved in writing by the Engineer and acceptable to the police and military authorities.

Records of explosive: Throughout the execution of the Contract, the Contractor is required to account, on a continuous basis, to the satisfaction of the Engineer and the police and military authorities for all explosives brought on to the Site and for all explosives consumed in the Works. The Contractor is required to remove all unused explosives from the Site on completion of the Works or shall dispose of such explosives in a manner acceptable to the police and military authorities.

15.7 Summary of applicable legislation for Nepalese governing law of the contract

15.7.1 Entry into a construction contract

Contracts generally	*National Civil Code 2017 (2074 BS)* part 5 [legal provisions relating to contracts and other liabilities], chapter 4 [procedure for preparation of the contracts documents and other deeds] *Public Procurement Act 2007(2063 BS)* *Public Procurement Rules 2008 (2064 BS)* Rules framed by the public Authority exercising the power provided by section 74 (2) of the *Public Procurement Act 2007 (2063 BS)* Rules framed by Provincial governments and local entities exercising the power provided by section 74 (3) of the *Public Procurement Act 2007(2063 BS)*
Construction contracts	*Private Financing in Build and Operation of Infrastructures Act 2006 (2062 BS)* *Public Procurement Act 2007(2063 BS)* *Public Procurement Rules 2008 (2064 BS)* *Public Private Partnership and Investment Act 2019 (2076 BS)* *Public Private Partnership and Investment Rules 2020 (2076 BS)* *Electricity Act 1992* *Electricity Rules 1993* *Construction Business Act 1999(2055 BS)* *Construction Business Rules 2000 (2056 BS)*

15.7.2 Termination of a construction contract

Termination/ Frustration	*National Civil Code 2017 (2074 BS)* [part 5 legal provisions relating to contracts, sections 502, 525, 526, 527, 531, 533, 535, 536, 538]
Bankruptcy, insolvency, liquidation	*Insolvency Act 2006 (2063 BS)* *Company Act 2007(2064 BS)* *National Civil Code, 2017(2074 BS)* [chapter 3 sections 54, 55, 57–65 – insolvency of a natural person]

(*Continued*)

Guarantees under forms of Security	*National Civil Code 2017 (2074 BS)* part 5 *Public Procurement Act 2006 (2063 BS)* *Public Procurement Rules 2007 (2064 BS)*
Public procurement	*PPA* Article 59 subsection 2: (a) Ground that the public entity may terminate the procurement contract if the supplier, consultant, service provider or construction entrepreneur fails to perform the work in accordance with the procurement contract, fails to observe the conduct pursuant to sub-section (2) of Section 62 or misuses the advance. (b) Ground that the public entity may terminate the procurement contract by convenience (termination by convenience) for public interest, (c) Ground that a supplier, consultant, service provider or construction entrepreneur may terminate the procurement contract, and (d) Ground that procurement contract may be terminated in the event of force majeure. Under the rules framed by the public Authority exercising the power provided by section 74 (2) of the *Public Procurement Act 2007(2063 BS)* Under the rules framed by Provincial governments and local entities exercising the power provided by the section 74(3) of the *Public Procurement Act 2007(2063 BS)*

15.7.3 Dispute resolution

Limitation periods	*National Civil Code 2017(2074 BS)* [part 5 legal provisions relating to contracts, sections 503, 516, 520, 534, 544, 574, 623; chapter 5 legal provisions on limitations, sections 47–62; chapter 3 legal provision of the insolvency of a natural person section 66]
Liability	*National Civil Code 2017 (2074 BS)* [part 5 legal provisions in relation to contracts sections 493–502] District Courts have jurisdiction except jurisdiction for arbitration and mediation.
Public procurement	*PPA* section 58: (1) any dispute arising between the public entity and the construction entrepreneur, supplier, service provider or consultant in connection with the implementation of the procurement contract shall be settled through mutual consent. (1a) the procurement contract shall provide that if a dispute cannot be settled through mutual consent in accordance with sub-section (1), the dispute shall be settled by arbitration under the prevailing law.
Mediation	*Mediation Act 2011 (2068 BS):* Dispute may be settled through mediation: (1) In case, any agreement provides for the settlement of dispute through mediation, the dispute concerned with that agreement or a dispute arisen under that agreement shall be settled according to the procedure prescribed in the agreement, if any. (2) Notwithstanding anything contained in Sub-section (1), in case, parties intend to settle a dispute through mediation which is sub judice or not filed in any adjudicating body and such dispute may be settled through compromise (*Milapatra*) pursuant to prevailing law, the aforesaid dispute may be settled through mediation by following the procedure pursuant to this Act.

	(3) In case, parties intend to settle a case which is sub-judice in an adjudicating body through mediation pursuant to Sub-section (2), the parties may submit an application to the concerned adjudicating body at any time, and upon the receipt of such application the adjudicating body shall issue an order to settle the dispute through mediation whether such case is sub-judice at any level. (4) Where in any case sub-judice in an adjudicating body, the aforesaid body considers it appropriate to settle through mediation and the concerned parties are agreed, the adjudicating body may issue an order to settle such dispute through mediation. (5) Notwithstanding anything contained in Sub-section (3) and (4), in case, it is deemed necessary to pronounce a decision on any issue which cannot be settled through mediation together with an issue which can be resolved through mediation the adjudicative body shall not issue an order to settle such dispute through mediation.
Arbitration	*Arbitration Act 1999 (2055 BS)* section 3: Disputes to be Settled through Arbitration: (1) In case any agreement provides for the settlement of disputes through arbitration, the disputes connected with that agreement or with issues coming under that agreement shall be settled through arbitration according to the procedure prescribed in that agreement, if any, and if not, according to this Act. (2) Notwithstanding anything contained in Sub-section (1), in case of concerned parties to a civil suit of a commercial nature which has been filed in a court and which may be settled through arbitration according to prevailing laws, file an application for its settlement through arbitration, such dispute shall also be settled through arbitration.

15.8 Summary of applicable legislation if the Site/Country is in Nepal

15.8.1 Operation of a construction contract

Registration and administration of professionals – Engineers, Architects	*Nepal Engineering Council Act 1999 (2055 BS)* *Nepal Engineering Council Rules 2001 (2057 BS)*
Registration/ licencing/permission of Contractors and Subcontractors	*Construction Business Act 1999 (2055 BS)* *Construction Business Rules 2000 (2056 BS)* *Local Government Operation Act 2017 (2074 BS)* *Investment Board Act 2012(2069 BS)* *Foreign Investment and Technology Transform Act 2019 (2076 BS)* *Electricity Act 1992 (2048 BS)* *Electricity Rules 1993 (2049 BS)*
Use of liens/ Assignment of debts	*Bank and Financial Institution Act 2017(2074 BS)* *National Civil Code of Nepal 2017 (2074 BS)* part 4 chapter 15 *Public Procurement Act 2006 (2063 BS)* *Public Procurement Rules 2007 (2064 BS)*

Labour	*Labour Act 2017 (2074 BS)* *Labour Rules 2018 (2075 BS)* *Child Labour (Prohibition and Regulating) Act 2000 (2056 BS).* *Trade Union Act 1992 (2049 BS)* *Trade Union Rules 1993 (2050 BS)*
Design/Moral rights	*Patent Design and Trademark Act 1965 (2022 BS)*
Copyright	*Copyright Act 2002 (2059 BS)*
Planning	*Town Development Act 1998 (2054 BS)* *Kathmandu Valley Development Authority Act 1989 (2045BS)* *Kathmandu Valley Development Authority Rule 2011 (2068 BS)*
Heritage	*Ancient Monument Protection Act 1956 (2013 BS)*
Environment	*Environment Protection Act 2019 (2076 BS)* *Environment Protection Rule 2020 (2077 BS)*
Domestic Preference[Note the inconsistency between s12 of the *Construction Business Act 1999 (2055 BS)* and Rule 31f in the *PPA*]	Section 12 of the *Construction Business Act 1999 (2055 BS)*: Procurement of public construction works from native construction Entrepreneur and construction entrepreneur in joint venture: (1) Notwithstanding anything contained in the prevailing law, any public Construction works mentioned in an international competitive bidding may be procured from the following construction entrepreneur in the following Circumstances: (a) Despite that the total contract price quoted in the bidding by a construction entrepreneur wholly owned by a Nepalese citizen or by a construction entrepreneur licensed under joint venture with a foreign construction entrepreneur with at least fifty per cent of share owned by the Nepalese citizen or by a construction entrepreneur making a joint venture agreement with a foreign construction entrepreneur with at least fifty per cent of share owned by the Nepalese citizen is higher by a maximum of seven and half per cent than the total contract price quoted in the bidding by a foreign construction entrepreneur, the entrepreneur making such bidding. (b) Despite that the total contract price quoted in the bidding by a construction entrepreneur licensed under joint venture with a foreign construction entrepreneur with at least twenty five per cent of share owned by the Nepalese citizen or by a construction entrepreneur making a joint venture agreement with a foreign construction entrepreneur with at least twenty five per cent of share owned by the Nepalese citizen is higher by a maximum of five per cent than the total contract price quoted in the bidding by a foreign construction entrepreneur, the entrepreneur making such bidding. The domestic preference in s12 of the *Construction Business Act 1999 (2055 BS*) has been reduced by Rule 31f the *Public Procurement Rules 2007 (2064 BS)* to 5 per cent: Preference to be given to domestic bidders: (1) Domestic preference shall be given to the domestic firms, organizations or companies that participate solely or in joint venture with domestic firms, organizations or companies in the case of an international bidding (2) In giving preference pursuant to sub-rule (1), the proposal of a domestic firm, organization or company whose bid price exceeds by up to five per cent of the bid price offered by a foreign firm, organization or company that offers the lowest price may be accepted.

Building and construction permits, Execution of construction work, Standard of construction work	*Building Act 1999 (2055 BS)* *Building Rules 2009 (2066 BS)* *Public Procurement Act 2007 (2063 BS)* *Public Procurement rules 2008 (2064 BS)* *Local Government Operation Act 2017 (2074 BS)* *Building Code*
Health and safety	*Labour Act 2017 (2074 BS)*
Insurance	*Insurance Act 1992 (2049 BS)* *Public Procurement Act 2006 (2063 BS)* *Public Procurement Rules 2007 (2064)*
Liability for defective work	*Building Act 1999 (2055 BS)* *National Criminal Code 2017 (2074 BS)* part 2 chapter 21 section 250 *Consumer Protection Act 2018 (2075 BS)* *Public Procurement Act 2006 (2063 BS)* *Public Procurement Rules 2007 (2064 BS)*
Construction for Government Employer	*Public Procurement Act 2006 (2063 BS)* *Public Procurement Rules 2007 (2064 BS)*
Explosives	*Explosive Substance Act 1961 (2018 BS)*

15.8.2 Termination of a construction contract

Termination	*National Civil Code 2017 (2074 BS)* part 5 chapter 1 *Company Act 2007(2064 BS):* Stay on enforcing right s against an entity that has publicly announced it will be making an application to avoid being wound up in insolvency
Bankruptcy, insolvency, liquidation	*Insolvency Act 2006 (2063 BS)* *Company Act 2007 (2063 BS)*
Public procurement	*PPA* Article 59 subsection 2: (a) Ground that the public entity may terminate the procurement contract if the supplier, consultant, service provider or construction entrepreneur fails to perform the work in accordance with the procurement contract, fails to observe the conduct pursuant to sub-section (2) of Section 62 or misuses the advance. (b) Ground that the public entity may terminate the procurement contract by convenience (termination by convenience) for public interest, (c) Ground that a supplier, consultant, service provider or construction entrepreneur may terminate the procurement contract, and (d) Ground that procurement contract may be terminated in the event of force majeure. Under the rules framed by the public Authority exercising the power provided by section 74 (2) of the *Public Procurement Act 2007(2063 BS)* Under the rules framed by Provincial governments and local entities exercising the power provided by the section 74 (3) of the *Public Procurement Act 2007 (2064.BS)*

(*Continued*)

15.8.3 Dispute resolution

Limitation periods	*National Civil Code 2017 (2074 BS)* [part 5 legal provisions relating to contracts, sections 503, 516, 520, 534, 544, 574, 623; chapter 5 legal provisions on limitations, sections 47–62; chapter 3 legal provision of the insolvency of a natural person section 66]
Liability	*National Civil Code 2017(2074 BS)* [part 5 legal provisions in relation to contracts sections 493–502] District Courts have jurisdiction except jurisdiction for arbitration and mediation.
Public procurement	*PPA* section 58: (1) any dispute arising between the public entity and the construction entrepreneur, supplier, service provider or consultant in connection with the implementation of the procurement contract shall be settled through mutual consent. (1a) the procurement contract shall provide that if a dispute cannot be settled through mutual consent in accordance with sub-section (1), the dispute shall be settled by arbitration under the prevailing law.
Mediation	*Mediation Act 2011 (2068 BS):* Dispute may be settled through mediation: (1) In case, any agreement provides for the settlement of dispute through mediation, the dispute concerned with that agreement or a dispute arisen under that agreement shall be settled according to the procedure prescribed in the agreement, if any. (2) Notwithstanding anything contained in Sub-section (1), in case, parties intend to settle a dispute through mediation which is sub judice or not filed in any adjudicating body and such dispute may be settled through compromise (*Milapatra*) pursuant to prevailing law, the aforesaid dispute may be settled through mediation by following the procedure pursuant to this Act. (3) In case, parties intend to settle a case which is sub-judice in an adjudicating body through mediation pursuant to Sub-section (2), the parties may submit an application to the concerned adjudicating body at any time, and upon the receipt of such application the adjudicating body shall issue an order to settle the dispute through mediation whether such case is sub-judice at any level. (4) Where in any case sub-judice in an adjudicating body, the aforesaid body considers it appropriate to settle through mediation and the concerned parties are agreed, the adjudicating body may issue an order to settle such dispute through mediation. (5) Notwithstanding anything contained in Sub-section (3) and (4), in case, it is deemed necessary to pronounce a decision on any issue which cannot be settled through mediation together with an issue which can be resolved through mediation the adjudicative body shall not issue an order to settle such dispute through mediation.

15.9 Summary of applicable legislation if the 'seat' of the dispute determination is in Nepal

Limitation periods	*National Civil Code 2017 (2074 BS)* [part 5 legal provisions relating to contracts, sections 503, 516, 520, 534, 544, 574, 623; chapter 5 legal provisions on limitations, sections 47–62; chapter 3 legal provision of the insolvency of a natural person section 66]

Mediation	*Mediation Act 2011(2068 BS)* *Mediation Rules 2014 (2070 BS)*
Arbitration	*Arbitration Act 1999 (2055 BS)* *Arbitration (Court Procedure) Rules 2002 (2059 B.S)*

15.10 Issues that a court or arbitrator may construe differently to that expected from the words of the Contract, because of the local law or custom

The Supreme Court of Nepal has observed that if arbitrators construe a contract beyond its terms and condition or provisions, this is a question of law whether the interpretation of arbitrators is within the domain of contract law or not and this matter is justiciable.[76] Thus, if an arbitrators made a mistake of law in the award in his/her construction of the contract the Court could correct it.

Section 30 of *Arbitration Act 1999 (2055 BS)* provides;

30. Circumstances in which decision may be invalidated:

(1) Any party dissatisfied with the decision taken by the arbitrator may, if one wishes to invalidate the decision file a petition to the High Court along with the related documents and a copy of the decision within 35 days from the date the decision heard or notice received thereof under this Act. Petition shall also supply a copy of that petition to the arbitrator and the other party.

(2) In case a petition is filed pursuant Sub-section (1) the High Court may, in case the petitioner proves that the arbitration decision contains any of the following matters, invalidate that decision or issue an order to have a fresh decision taken as per necessity:

(a) In case any party to the agreement was incompetent for any reason to sign the agreement at the time of signing the agreement, or in case the agreement is not valid under the law of that the nation which governs jurisdiction over the parties, or in case such law is not clear and agreement is not valid under the laws of Nepal.

(b) In case the due petition was not given a notice to appoint an arbitrator or about the arbitration proceedings in time.

(c) In case the decision has been taken on a disputed matter which had not been referred to the arbitrator, or in a manner contrary to the conditions prescribed for the arbitrator, or by acting beyond the jurisdiction prescribed for the arbitrator.

(d) Except when an agreement has been signed contrary to the laws of Nepal, in case the procedure of designation of arbitrators or their functions and actions do not conform to the agreement signed between the parties, or in case there is no such agreement it has not been done as per this Act.

(3) Notwithstanding anything contained in Sub-section (2), the High Court may invalidate the decision of the arbitrator in the following circumstances in case a petition is filed pursuant to Sub-section (1):

(a) In case the dispute settled by the arbitrator cannot be settled through arbitration under the laws of Nepal.

(b) In case the decision taken by the arbitrator is likely to be prove detrimental to the public interests or policies.

76 *Agriculture Inputs Co Ltd v Appellate Court Lalitpur* (2007) *Nepal Law Journal* 11, SC verdict no 7905.

In accordance with the precedents of the Supreme Court of Nepal, a court or arbitrator must construe a contract in accordance with the terms and conditions and words of the contract. In a case where necessary terms and conditions or words in the contract are absent, a court or arbitrator may take into consideration the background of the contract, previous exchanges of letters or correspondence, general principles of contract law, international practices on the interpretation of contract law and court practices and precedents for the interpretation of the contract. Only on matters not written in the contract can it be interpreted on the basis of the prevailing law, recognized principles of contract law, international practices or local law or custom.

15.11 References

15.11.1 Books

Bharat Raj Uprety (Justice of the Supreme Court of Nepal), *Contract Law* (3rd edn, Legal Research and Development Forum: FREEDEL 2009)

Tanka Prasad Dulal and Rajesh Hamal, *Constitutional law* (Sumitra Hamal 1992)

15.11.2 Journals

Nepal Law Journal (Supreme Court of Nepal 2007) (11), SC.

15.11.3 Internet

FCAN website: www.fcan.org.np (English and Nepalese)

Nepal Law Commission website: www.lawcommission.gov.np (English and Nepalese)

(All Legislation /Acts, Rule, Regulations of Government of Nepal are in the website of Nepal Law Commission)

Supreme Court of Nepal website: www.supremecourt.gov.np (English and Nepalese)

(All case law is available in the website of Supreme Court of Nepal)

Public Procurement Monitoring Office (PPMO) website: www.ppmo.gov.np (English and Nepalese)

15.11.4 Case law

Supreme Court of Nepal website: www.supremecourt.gov.np (English and Nepalese

(All case laws are available in the website of Supreme Court of Nepal)

15.11.5 Reports

PPMO *Annual Report 2018* (All information on the SBD for ICB and NCB, standard forms of contract, legislation, procurement procedures, guidelines, and data related to public procurement are available io the PPMO website: www.ppmo.gov.np (English and Nepalese)).

Institute for Integrated Development Studies (IIDS) and Confederation of Nepalese Industries, *Nepal Infrastructure 2030: Investment and Financing Needs* (2019).

The Asia Foundation, The Impact of Covid-19 Lockdown on Nepal's Construction Sector: A Rapid Assessment (May 2020).

Ministry of Finance, GON, Nepal Economic Survey 2019/2020 (2076/77 BS),

Central Bureau of Statistics, GON *Report on the Nepal Labour Force Survey (*2017/18).

Ministry of Finance, GON, *Red Book* (2020).

National Planning Commission, GON, *Fifteenth Periodic Plan.*

CHAPTER 16

Pakistan

Khawaja Hamid Mushtaq

DOI: 10.4324/9781003200901-16

16.1 Outline of the legal environment in Pakistan

16.1.1 The constitutional structure of Pakistan

Pakistan is a federation of units namely the provinces of Sind, Balochistan, Punjab, Khyber Pakhtunkhawa, and the federating units of Islamabad Capital Territory and Federally Administered Tribal areas (**FATA**).[1] In the 25th constitutional amendment, seven districts of the FATA along the Afghanistan border were merged with the Khyber Pakhtunkhawa Province, which reduced the number of federating units to five.

Kashmir is a disputed region between Pakistan and India. Gilgit-Baltistan, often known as Northern Areas, is a part of greater Kashmir on the Pakistani side. On 1 November 2020, the Prime Minister of Pakistan, on the occasion of the 73rd Independence Day of Gilgit-Baltistan, made an announcement to accord provisional provincial status to Gilgit-Baltistan making it the fifth province.[2] A complete provincial status will be accorded in future through a constitutional amendment which will make it the sixth federating unit of Pakistan.

The country has a multi-party parliamentary form of government quite similar to that of the United Kingdom. The legislature consists of two houses ie the upper house and the lower house. The upper house is called the Senate and it has equal representation from all the provinces/federating units. The lower house is called the National Assembly and has representation based on the population size in provinces/

1 1973 *Constitution*, Article 1.
2 https://en.wikipedia.org/wiki/Gilgit-Baltistan#cite_note-25

federating units. Thus, Punjab having the largest population has the largest number of seats in the National Assembly followed by Sind, Khyber Pakhtunkhawa, Balochistan, FATA and Islamabad.

Since 14 August 1973, the fundamental law of the Islamic Republic of Pakistan is the 1973 *Constitution*. It is the third constitution of the country since independence in 1947 and comprises 280 articles, seven schedules and a number of amendments. These articles cover fundamental rights, the role of federation, provinces and their relationship with the federation, the judicature, finance, property, contracts, elections, Islamic provisions, emergency provisions and miscellaneous provisions. As of June 2020, 25 amendments have been made in the 1973 *Constitution* of which the eighteenth amendment is the most famous one.

After the eighteenth amendment, the Prime Minister emerged as the Chief Executive of the country whereas the President became the ceremonial head of State. The office tenure of both the President and the Prime Minister is five years. The executive heads of the provinces are called Chief Ministers, whereas governors in the provinces are representatives of the federal government. The provinces have wide autonomy and exclusive authority to legislate on many more subjects than the federal government such as health, education, the environment, agriculture, industries, local government, labour, revenue, etc.

The Supreme Court of Pakistan is the apex court and judicial authority for interpretation of the *Constitution* and in all legal matters. It is the sole authority to decide in the event of challenge to any constitutional Act of Parliament.

The Council of Islamic Ideology was established under Article 230 of the *1973 Constitution* and was entrusted to make recommendations to the federal and provincial Parliaments to introduce new laws and modify the existing ones in conformity with the injunctions of Islam. Some of the recommendations of the Islamic Ideological Council which were enacted, mostly in criminal matters, include:[3]

- *The Offences against Property (Enforcement of Hudood) Ordinance 1979.*
- *The Offence of Zina(Enforcement of Hudood) Ordinance 1979.*
- *The Offence at Qazf (Enforcement at Hadd) Ordinance 1979.*
- *The Prohibition (Enforcement) of Hadd) Order 1979.*
- *The Qanun-e-Shahadat Order 1984.*
- *The Zakat and Ushr, Ordinance 1980.*
- *The Criminal Law (Amendment) Act 1997(Qanun-e-Qisas and Diyat).*
- *The Ehtram-e- Ramzan Ordinance 1984.*
- *The Enforcement of Shariat Act 1991*(adopted with certain modifications).

16.1.2 The legal system of Pakistan

Pakistan has a colonial past and as with many other things, the country inherited the legal system from British. Most of the pre-independence legislation has been adopted without much change such as the *Contract Act 1870, Limitation Act 1908, Arbitration Act 1940, Stamp Act 1899* and *Registration Act 1908* to name a few. The substantive laws of the country are very similar to the English common law in civil matters but significantly differ in criminal matters. The *1973 Constitution* in Part V, Chapter 1, Articles 141 and 142 provide details about the legislative powers of the federal

3 http://www.cii.gov.pk/MajorAchievements.aspx.

government and the provinces. The *Constitution* provides exclusive powers to both the governments to legislate in accordance with their respective federal or provincial legislative list. Pakistan is an Islamic Country and one of the prime examples of the influence of Islamic Law on common law is the enactment of the *Qanoon-e-Shahadat Ordinance 1984* which repealed the *Evidence Act 1872*. The intention of this enactment was to complement the provisions of the *Evidence Act 1872* with the injunctions of Islam. This ordinance applies to the whole of Pakistan in all civil and criminal proceedings except for arbitration.[4]

16.1.3 The court system of Pakistan

The 1973 *Constitution* of Pakistan comprehensively addresses almost all matters relating to the higher judiciary and contains express provisions on the establishment, functioning, hierarchy, powers and jurisdiction of courts.[5] In the 1973 *Constitution*, Part VII-Judicature from section 175–212 deals with all these matters.

Typically, there are three levels of courts in Pakistan. The Supreme Court is the apex court of the country and its Chief Justice is known as the Chief Justice of Pakistan.[6] The Supreme Court has original,[7] appellate[8] and advisory jurisdiction[9] and its decisions are binding on all subordinate courts.[10] The original jurisdiction is in all matters of a dispute between two or more governments ie federal and provincial governments. Similarly, Article 184(3) of the *1973 Constitution* expressly empowers the Supreme Court to take *Suo Moto* action in matters of fundamental rights. The relevant part is as follows

> (3) Without prejudice to the provisions of Article 199, the Supreme Court shall, if it considers that a question of public importance with reference to the enforcement of any of the Fundamental Rights conferred by Chapter I of Part II is involved have the power to make an order of the nature mentioned in the said Article.

The provincial High Courts are not conferred with such powers.[11] The appellate jurisdiction of the Supreme Court comes from Article 185 (1) of the *1973 Constitution* which empowers them to 'hear and determine appeals from judgements, decrees, final orders or sentences of a High Court'. The Supreme Court's advisory function comes under Article 186 (1) of the *1973 Constitution* wherein the Supreme Court gives its opinion on a question of law referred to it by the President of Pakistan.

Every province and the Islamabad Capital Territory have their own High Courts which supervise the functions of subordinate courts. The High Courts have original jurisdiction in matters of fundamental rights[12] and also act as appellate courts

4 *Qanoon-e-Shahdat Order 1984*, art 1(2) http://pakistancode.gov.pk/english/UY2FqaJw1-apaUY2Fqa-apaUY2FwbJs%3D-sg-jjjjjjjjjjjj

5 Dr Faqir Hussain, 'The Judicial System of Pakistan' https://www.supremecourt.gov.pk/downloads_judgements/all_downloads/Judicial_System_of_Pakistan/thejudicialsystemofPakistan.pdf (accessed 2 November 2020).

6 *1973 Constitution,* Article 176.

7 ibid art 184.

8 ibid art 185.

9 ibid art 186.

10 ibid art 189.

11 ibid art 175(2).

12 ibid art 199(2).

against the decisions of subordinate civil or criminal courts.[13] Article 199 of the *1973 Constitution* empowers High Courts to review any matter including any federal or provincial legislation.[14] A recent example is the challenge of *Islands Development Authority Ordinance 2020*[15] in the Sind High Court.[16]

The federal Shariat Court was constituted under the article 203C of the *1973 Constitution*. The Court may through its own motion or through a petition by any person or Government take up the question and decide whether or not any law or any provision is in contradiction to the teachings of Islam.[17] In *Muhammad Riaz etc. vs Federal Government* etc,[18] the federal Shariat Court declared 'certain provisions of the Pakistan Penal Code as well as the *Criminal Procedure Code* as repugnant to the Injunctions of Islam'.[19] This decision was upheld by the Shariat Appellate Bench of the Honourable Supreme Court of Pakistan in the case *Federation of Pakistan vs. Gul Hassan Khan*,[20] thus the said provisions, declared repugnant to the Injunctions of Islam, ceased to have effect.[21] These decisions led to substitution of sections 299 to 338 of the *Pakistan Penal Code* by the *Criminal Law (amendment) Act (II of 1997)*, commonly known as the *Qisas and Diyat Act*.[22]

The subordinate judiciary, like many other common law jurisdictions, comprises civil and criminal courts at district level. These courts are supervised by provincial High Courts which hold appellate jurisdiction against the decisions of these lower courts. There are other courts and tribunals[23] which perform special functions eg Revenue Courts, Military Courts, Banking Courts, Custom and Taxation Courts, Accountability Courts and Service Tribunals.

16.2 The construction industry in Pakistan

16.2.1 Overview

Pakistan is currently passing through an economic expansion phase and therefore witnessing huge investments in the construction sector. As per Economic Survey of Pakistan, the contribution of the construction sector in the country's GNP in the year 2019–2020 remained Rs.794,739 million (US$5 billion)[24] whereas it had about 2.53 per cent share in the country's GDP during the same period.[25] The construction

13 ibid art 203.

14 https://courtingthelaw.com/2020/05/22/commentary/judicial-review-in-pakistan/.

15 http://moma.gov.pk/SiteImage/Misc/files/Ordinance%20to%20Istablish%20President's%20Island%20Development%20Authority.pdf.

16 https://nation.com.pk/09-Oct-2020/islands-development-authority-ordinance-challenged-in-shc-notices-issued?show=preview.

17 *1973 Constitution* art 203 D(1).

18 *Muhammad Riaz etc. v Federal Government etc.*, PLD 1980 FSC-1.

19 http://www.ljcp.gov.pk/Menu%20Items/Annual%20Reports/Courts/2003/FederalShariatCourt2003.pdf [41] (accessed 15 November 2020).

20 *Federation of Pakistan v Gul Hassan Khan*, PLD 1989 Supreme Court 633.

21 http://www.ljcp.gov.pk/Menu%20Items/Annual%20Reports/Courts/2003/FederalShariatCourt2003.pdf [42].

22 http://www.ljcp.gov.pk/Menu%20Items/Annual%20Reports/Courts/2003/FederalShariatCourt2003.pdf [42] (accessed 15 November 2020).

23 *1973 Constitution* art 175.

24Economic Survey of Pakistan, Economic and Social Indicators, Table 1.5 [15] http://www.finance.gov.pk/survey/chapter_20/PES_2019_20.pdf (accessed 11 April 2020).

25 Economic Survey of Pakistan, Economic and Social Indicators, Table 1.2 [12] http://www.finance.gov.pk/survey/chapter_20/PES_2019_20.pdf (accessed 11 April 2020).

sector growth rate in Pakistan during FY 2019–20 remained 8.06 per cent.[26] During the current financial year 2020–21, the government has increased the allocation of its public sector development programme to Rs701 billion (US$4.4 billion) from Rs561.7 billion (US$3.5 billion) in financial year 2019–20.[27] These trends suggest that in the upcoming years, the outlook for the construction sector in Pakistan looks strong.

In order to reduce unemployment and poverty, the government deems it important to facilitate and support the construction sector. One of the reasons is that it employs about 7.61 per cent of the total work force, making it the fourth largest employer in Pakistan behind agriculture, manufacturing, wholesale and retail trade sectors.[28]

Pakistan is a strategic partner of China and has started an ambitious multi-sectoral development program of regional connectivity under the umbrella of China Pakistan Economic Corridor (**CPEC**), which is the part of China's One Belt One Road initiative (**OBOR**).[29] Infrastructure development is a major part of this program which is being sponsored by both China and Pakistan. It includes mega projects such as motorways, hydropower projects, airports, Gwadar sea port, special economic zones and many more. For the past few years, many large Chinese companies have started working on different infrastructure projects in Pakistan, which has also helped the local companies to grow and enhance their capacity. In some mega projects such as the Havelian-Thakot Motorway, the work was carried out under Chinese specifications. Various other infrastructure development programs are in progress with the assistance of international financial institutions and indigenous resources.

Post Covid-19, the other turnaround in Pakistan's construction sector is the investor friendly policy announced by the government of Pakistan in the housing sector. It has started an ambitious affordable housing program called the 'Naya Pakistan Housing' program to construct five million houses in five years[30] and has established a high powered task force called the Naya Pakistan Housing Task Force to oversee this program.[31] One of the jobs of this Task Force is to suggest the regulatory regime necessary to undertake this mega project.

The government is specially emphasising the development of infrastructure projects using the PPP model. Since the enactment of *Public Private Partnership Authority Act (VIII of 2017)*, the government has mandated various agencies/departments to develop infrastructure projects in PPP mode. This *Act* was amended by promulgation of *Ordinance No VIII of 2020.*[32] Among some of the notable amendments, the *Ordinance* now defines a private party as an entity in which there is no direct or indirect equity interest of the government. It means that State owned enterprises cannot bid in any PPP project at present.[33] The government's emphasis on developing future infrastructure projects using a PPP model is evident as it initiated the bidding process

26 Economic Survey of Pakistan, Economic and Social Indicators, Table 1.3 page 13 http://www.finance.gov.pk/survey/chapter_20/PES_2019_20.pdf (accessed 11 April 2020).
27 Economic Survey of Pakistan, Overview of the Economy page iii http://www.finance.gov.pk/survey/chapter_20/PES_2019_20.pdf (accessed 2 November 2020).
28 Economic Survey of Pakistan, Economic and Social Indicators, Table 12.12 [146] http://www.finance.gov.pk/survey/chapter_20/PES_2019_20.pdf (accessed 11 April 2020).
29 http://cpec.gov.pk/index (accessed 15 May 2020).
30 Economic Survey of Pakistan, Overview of the Economy, [iii] http://www.finance.gov.pk/survey/chapter_20/PES_2019_20.pdf.
31 http://nphp.com.pk/chairman-intro/ (Naya= new).
32 http://www.senate.gov.pk/1web/ordinance/ordVIIIof2020.pdf (accessed 25 May 2020).
33 https://www.dawn.com/news/1567511 (accessed 23 July 2020).

for construction of the 300 km Sukkur Hyderabad Motorway Project.[34] Some other PPP projects especially in the road infrastructure sector are in the stage of feasibility studies at the time of writing (October 2020).

In Pakistan, the construction sector can be divided into two main categories:

- Public sector construction
- Private sector construction.

Public sector construction involves projects where funds are arranged by the government or it has an equity share or has some level of supervisory control. Public sector construction projects observe certain regulations, procedures and rules during planning, procurement, execution and completion stages. On the other hand, private sector construction is less regulated in terms of rules.

The procurement process in government and private sector projects is entirely different. The government procurement is regulated by the rules of the Public Procurement Regulatory Authority (**PPRA**). These are also called *Public Procurement Rules 2004* and are applied to the procurement of all government departments whether construction related or not. These *Rules* provide details of the procurement process from advertisement through to the award of works, services and goods procurements. However, there is no requirement to follow public procurement rules in the private sector.

16.2.2 Licensing in the construction sector

The Pakistan Engineering Council (**PEC**) is the regulator in the country's construction sector. The Council was formed under the *Pakistan Engineering Council Act 1975*.[35] The objective was to establish an apex body to regulate the engineering profession in the country both in the industry and academic sectors.[36] The functions of the PEC can be broadly subdivided into the following groups:[37]

i.) Academic function
ii.) Licensing/registration of professionals and firms
iii.) Development of engineering services across industries
iv.) Dispute appointment service.

The PEC grants accreditation to all the engineering programs taught in various universities across Pakistan. The Council actively maintains a register for the information of the general public about all the accredited programs offered by both public and private sector universities.[38] The PEC recently signed the Washington Accord wherein the degrees in some of the engineering programs offered by the local universities are recognised as equivalent to the degrees awarded by universities in developed countries.[39] The Council has an accreditation committee which runs

34 ibid.
35 *Pakistan Engineering Council Act 1975*, s 1.
36 https://pec.org.pk/downloads/pec_act/PEC%20Act%20(UPDATED%20VERSION%20DEC%202016).pdf (accessed 5 April 2020).
37 *Pakistan Engineering Council Act 1975*, s 8.
38 https://www.pec.org.pk/schedule_first.aspx (accessed 22 April 2020).
39 https://www.pec.org.pk/schedule_first_level_II.aspx (accessed 22 April 2020)

comprehensive programs for the accreditation of universities and affiliated colleges.[40] The accreditation committee is empowered to withdraw the accreditation of any university or any program after fulfilment of due procedure.[41]

The Pakistan Engineering Council actively maintains a register/record of all the registered engineers, professional engineers, chartered engineers, consulting engineers, constructors and operators in Pakistan.[42] A fresh graduate is registered with the Council as a registered engineer and can be elevated to the title of professional engineer after gaining five years' experience and passing an engineering practice exam.[43] The registration process for consulting engineers/firms is also well defined.[44] Whether it is the registration of firms or individuals engineers, the PEC has the exclusive authority under the *Pakistan Engineering Council Act 1975*.

The PEC registers contractors (constructors) in eight categories starting from C-6, C-5, C-4, C-3, C-2, C-1, C-B and C-A.[45] These categories represent the maximum monetary limit up to which a contractor can submit its bid. A contractor in C-6 category can bid for a work of Rs25 million (US$150,000), whereas there is no limit on a contractor in C-A category.[46] Any engineer, having professional experience up to five years, who wants to register a firm as an owner is directly registered in C-5 category.[47] Categories of operators, eg toll operators, service area operators, bus bay operators, etc. are also similar to that of contractors. The PEC assigns different codes to contractors based on their specific works sectors such as roads, buildings, bridges, marine structures, etc.

However, for registration of foreign firms in the country, the PEC uses different criteria. Both consulting and contracting foreign firms are eligible to work in Pakistan on public and private sector projects, even if the technology is available locally. It is required that a foreign firm shall enter into a joint venture agreement with a local firm of appropriate category. The firm will employ 70 per cent of local engineers and 30 per cent of foreign engineers.[48] The only exemption to this condition is in Public Procurement Rule 5, which states that:

> Whenever these rules are in conflict with an obligation or commitment of the Federal Government arising out of an international treaty or an agreement with a State or States, or any international financial institution the provisions of such international treaty or agreement shall prevail to the extent of such conflict.

It has been observed that some of the infrastructure projects under CPEC were solely completed by Chinese firms because of the framework agreement signed between Pakistan and China. Local manpower was employed by the Chinese contractors.

The PEC plays an important role in providing training and engineering services across multiple industries. During the Covid-19 pandemic, the PEC in collaboration with the Ministry of Science and Technology played a leading role by offering technical

40 *Pakistan Engineering Council Act*, s 14(1)(2).

41 ibid s 15(1)(2).

42 ibid s 16.

43 https://www.pec.org.pk/faq.aspx#:~:text=What%20is%20the%20difference%20between,engineering%20practice%20examination%20(EPE). (accessed 22 April 2020).

44 https://www.pec.org.pk/downloads/BYELAWS%201986%20(APRIL%2023,%202013).pdf (accessed 22 April 2020).

45 https://www.pec.org.pk/downloads/supervision/guidelines.pdf (accessed 23 April 2020).

46 ibid.

47 ibid.

48 ibid.

assistance to the government in manufacturing of critical bio medical equipment. The PEC vetted and approved designs for ventilators[49] and the first batch of ventilators was handed over to the National Disaster Management Authority on 6 July 2020.

The PEC is also among the leaders of institutionalised arbitration and conciliation in Pakistan and has also developed its own rules for arbitration and conciliation. Similar to PEC, the Centre for International Investment and Commercial Arbitration (**CIICA**) is another institution which promotes all forms of ADR including arbitration.

16.2.3 Contracts

In Pakistan, FIDIC forms are the most popular standard forms used on construction projects especially in the public sector. These forms are an integral part of the bidding documents prepared by the PEC for public sector projects and are available as open source on their website.[50] The Council has so far prepared six types of bidding documents which have been approved by the federal government.[51] Moreover, the Planning and Development Division of the federal government issued a directive (available on the PEC website[52]), advising all federal secretaries that the following PEC approved bidding documents must be used on public sector projects:

i. Standard Form of Bidding Documents (Civil Work)[53] – incorporates FIDIC General Conditions of Contract Part-I (1987 reprinted in 1992 with further amendments).
ii. Standard Form of Bidding Docs for Procurement of Works (E & M)[54]– incorporates FIDIC General Conditions of Contract for Electrical and Mechanical Works (1987 Edition reprinted 1988 with editorial amendments).
iii. Standard Form of Bidding Documents for Procurement of Works for Smaller Contracts.[55]
iv. Standard Form of Contract for Engineering Consultancy Services (Time Based Assignments).[56]
v. Standard Form of Contract for Engineering Consultancy Services (Lump Sum Assignment).[57]
vi. Standard Form of Contract for Engineering Consultancy Services for Smaller Projects.[58]

49 *PEC News Letter* https://pec.org.pk/Downloadables/PEC%20Newsletter_Mar2020.pdf (accessed 25 April 2020).
50 https://www.pec.org.pk/bidding_docs_implementation.aspx (accessed 25 April 2020).
51 https://www.pec.org.pk/pec_bid_docs.aspx (accessed 25 April 2020).
52 ibid.
53 https://www.pec.org.pk/downloads/PEC_Bidding_Docs/(1)%20Std%20Form%20of%20Bidding%20Docs%20(Civil%20%20Work).pdf (accessed 4 November 2020).
54 https://www.pec.org.pk/downloads/PEC_Bidding_Docs/(2)%20Std%20Form%20of%20Bidding%20Docs%20for%20Procurement%20of%20Works%20(E&M).pdf (accessed 4 November 2020).
55https://www.pec.org.pk/downloads/PEC_Bidding_Docs/(3)%20Std%20Form%20of%20Bidding%20Docs%20for%20Proc%20of%20Works(Smaller%20Contracts).pdf (accessed 4 November 2020).
56 https://www.pec.org.pk/downloads/PEC_Bidding_Docs/(4)%20Std%20Form%20of%-20Contract%20-%20Engg%20Consultancy%20Services%20(Time%20based%20Assigns).pdf (accessed 4 November 2020).
57 https://www.pec.org.pk/downloads/PEC_Bidding_Docs/(5)%20Std%20Form%20of%20Contract%20-%20Engg%20Consultancy%20Services(Lump%20Sum%20Assigns).pdf (accessed 4 November 2020).
58 https://www.pec.org.pk/downloads/PEC_Bidding_Docs/(6)%20Std%20Form%20of%20Contract%20-Engg%20Consultancy%20Services%20for%20Smaller%20Projects.pdf (accessed 4 November 2020).

FIDIC Conditions of Contract 1987 (Red book) is the most popular standard form and is used in government sector projects. All public sector infrastructure projects sponsored by donor agencies including but not limited to the Asian Development Bank and the World Bank use FIDIC Pink Book 2010. The FIDIC Silver Book 1999 and Yellow Book 1999 are also used on both government and private sector projects.

In 2011, the PEC governing body approved a further set of 13 documents which includes rules, procedures, bidding documents and sample agreements.[59]

The most popular project delivery model in the public infrastructure development sector is the construct only model. The recently awarded Bhasha Dam project is an example of this model. The construction on this mega project started in 2020 and will take more than six years to complete. The exception to the popular construct only project delivery model can be seen on small scale housing projects completed by the private sector. Bahria Town, a real estate development organisation in the private sector, is a good example which offers turnkey solutions. In the private sector, there has been a strong demand to find all solutions under one arrangement which has led the builders and real estate developers to offer turnkey solutions to the new house owners.

16.2.4 Regulation of the construction industry

The construction industry in the country is regulated to some extent. Licenses or No Objection Certificates may be required for the following:

- Development application in urban areas
- Housing schemes
- Infrastructure projects
- Construction of houses in cities
- Heavy vehicle licences
- Construction of storm water drains on public land
- Cutting of trees
- Use of explosives
- Gas connection licence
- Electricity connection licence
- Connection to sewerage drain
- Construction on public land
- Construction on heritage land
- Handling and storage of dangerous chemicals
- Construction of high rise near airports.

These certificates/licences/permits are issued by respective federal, provincial or district level authorities. For example, a No Objection Certificate (**NOC**) for construction of high-rise buildings near airports is issued by the Civil Aviation Authority which is a federal agency whereas NOC for a residential development will be issued by a District level agency such as the Capital Development Authority, Islamabad. Similarly, NOC for use of explosives will be issued by a provincial agency.

59 https://pec.org.pk/pec_bid_docs.aspx (accessed 14 November 2020).

16.2.5 Labour

In Pakistan, the legislation covering labour laws is provincial and not federal. A number of different *Acts* exist which cover areas such as work hours, working conditions, employer's liability, employees' old age benefits, disabled persons employment, children employment, worker's welfare, workmen compensation, etc.[60] The federal and the provincial governments, however, announce the minimum wages at the time of the annual budget. Effective from 1 July 2019, the minimum wage in Sindh Province for unskilled labour is Rs17,500 (US$100) per month. It varies slightly in Punjab and other provinces.

Currently, there are no specific occupational health and safety regulations in Pakistan at the federal level. The most relevant legislation which covers some aspects of occupational health and safety is in Chapter-III of the *Factories Act 1934*. However, at the provincial level, *The Punjab Occupational Health and Safety Act 2019* is the main legislation which covers almost every aspect of occupational health and safety in great detail. Comprehensive and up to date occupational health and safety legislation at the federal level is a pressing need.

16.2.6 Innovation

The government sector has been very slow in introducing new regulations or innovations in the construction sector. In Pakistan's construction industry, BIM is still a distant idea. Most of the construction in the country is site based. Modular construction is still not very common. Similarly, use of planning software such as Primavera P6 or Asta power project for preparing work programs is not a mandatory requirement. The prime example is the FIDIC Red Book 1987, amended by Pakistan Engineering Council, which lays no such requirement. Despite this, almost all engineering institutions in Pakistan offer training in computer programmes including Autocad, STAAD Pro, Primavera, BIM and other engineering software.

16.2.7 Insurance

The insurance sector in Pakistan is regulated by *Insurance Ordinance 2000* which divides insurance contracts into two categories ie life and non-life insurance.[61]Almost all insurance companies provide all types of insurances as required by FIDIC contracts. The PEC bidding documents however specify in its amended FIDIC form 1987, under clause 25.5 (in Particular Conditions)[62] that the insurance shall be either from the National Insurance Company or any other insurance company operating in Pakistan having an AA rating.

16.2.8 Disputes

In the construction sector, disputes arising between the Parties are resolved through the standard dispute resolution mechanisms in the Contract, which include a combination

60 https://www.riaabarkergillette.com/usa/wp-content/uploads/Labour-law-in-Pakistan.pdf (accessed 15 May 2020).

61 *Insurance Ordinance 2000*, s 3.

62 https://www.pec.org.pk/downloads/PEC_Bidding_Docs/(1)%20Std%20Form%20of%20Bidding%20Docs%20(Civil%20%20Work).pdf (accessed 15 May 2020).

of Engineer's decision, amicable settlement, Dispute Boards and arbitration. Since the public sector construction projects only use FIDIC standard forms, these processes are widely adopted. ADR methods such as mediation, conciliation and expert determination are not so frequently used in the local industry. Since ADR is a private mechanism for dispute resolution, the relevant data is not publicly available.

16.2.9 Key challenges

Some of the key challenges, the construction sector is facing in 2020 include but are not limited to:

- Absence of regulations and rules
- Time and cost overruns
- Quality issues
- Workplace safety
- Trade licences.

16.3 Impact of Covid-19 in Pakistan

16.3.1 Impact of Covid-19 on the execution of construction projects in Pakistan

The first case of Covid-19 in Pakistan was confirmed in Karachi by the Ministry of Health on 26 February 2020.[63] The federal government announced the national action plan in March 2020 and set up a National Command and Control Centre[64] under the leadership of the Special Advisor to the Prime Minister to implement an organised and coherent response to the pandemic at the national level. Despite pressure from different segments of society, the federal government did not impose a full lockdown due to the weak economic condition of the country, but rather opted for a smart lockdown. The government closed Pakistan's airspace[65] for regular commercial air traffic but managed to operate flights to bring back the Pakistanis stranded abroad by following a strict protocol. However, the provinces made their own decisions and opted for more strict measures.

The federal government announced a historic Rs1.2 trillion (US$7.5 billion) economic relief package on 24 March 2020, which included accelerated crop procurement, cash and food distribution to the poor, subsidies in utility stores for the general public, relief from utility bills such as gas and electricity etc.[66] The construction sector remained open in the post Covid-19 period. On 3 April 2020, the federal government announced a massive package for the construction sector which included tax breaks, subsidies and other incentives inviting people to invest in the real estate sector. One of the main ideas was to mitigate the economic impacts of Covid-19

63 https://www.ncbi.nlm.nih.gov/pmc/articles/PMC7240311/ (accessed 21 September 2020).

64 https://www.nih.org.pk/wp-content/uploads/2020/03/COVID-19-NAP-V2-13-March-2020.pdf (accessed 21 September 2020).

65 https://www.caapakistan.com.pk/ (accessed 28 September 2020).

66 https://www.icmap.com.pk/images/covid19/EconomicImpact_of_COVID19_on_Pakistant.pdf (accessed 29 September 2020).

and provide employment opportunities especially to laborers.[67]The government also decided that all industries which form part of the construction supply chain would remain open even during lockdown.

The government issued necessary guidelines, [68] established a dedicated website and a national helpline No 1166. For all workplaces, wearing masks was made mandatory and stay at home instructions were issued to public sector employees suffering from Covid-19 related symptoms such as fever, cough, etc. Where suitable, work from home arrangements were also made. The government enforced restrictions, wherever required, under the *Epidemic Disease Act 1958* which allows the government to take necessary measures to control the spread of the disease.

16.3.2 Impact of Covid-19 on the operation of construction contracts in Pakistan

The Pakistan government did not enact any new Covid-19 specific legislation that affected the usual operation of construction contracts.

Thus, the Parties to a construction contract are confined to their normal contractual remedies to address issues such as additional costs and delays caused by the Covid-19 pandemic. The possible approaches to claims arising from Covid-19 under FIDIC contracts are discussed in paragraph 1.6.6 above. It is anticipated that there will be a significant number of disputes arising from the additional time and cost of construction projects as a result of Covid-19 pandemic.

16.4 Pakistani governing law of the contract

16.4.1 Constraints on the governing law of a construction contract

In Pakistan, the parties are free to choose any foreign law governing their contract for which the performance is required in the country and no law restricts their freedom. The courts have not objected to the parties' choice of the law of the forum either; rather they have applied the doctrine of *forum non-conveniens* in such cases and upheld the choice of the parties.

It was often argued that choice of governing law clauses is in contravention to section 28 of the *Contract Act 1870*, which invalidates any agreement that impedes the enforcement of party's legal rights through usual legal proceedings in ordinary tribunals. The relevant part of section 28 is:

> Every agreement, by which any party thereto is restricted absolutely from enforcing his rights under or in respect of any contract, by the usual legal proceedings in the ordinary tribunals, or which limits the time within which he may thus enforce his rights, is void to that extent.

However, the courts have not endorsed such arguments, rather they have taken a liberal approach and consistently upheld the choice of the parties. The Supreme Court of Pakistan in *MA Chowdhury v Messrs Mitsuoi OSK Lines Ltd and Others*[69] held that choosing a governing law is the right of contracting parties. The Honourable Supreme

---

67 ibid.

68 http://covid.gov.pk/ (accessed 29 September 2020).

69 *MA Chowdhury v Messrs Mitsuoi OSK Lines Ltd and Others* 1970 PLD 373.

Court held that the nature of such clauses is equivalent to the arbitration agreements where consent of the parties is the heart of the process. The Supreme Court observed:

> [i]n order to preserve the sanctity of contracts, it ought also to be held, as was done in the earlier cases in Great Britain, that such foreign jurisdiction clauses, even when they purport to give jurisdiction to a Court in a foreign country, are really in the nature of arbitration clauses which within the exception of section 28 of the *Contract Act* and, therefore, should be dealt in the same manner as other arbitration clauses. In the case of arbitration, it has to be remembered that jurisdiction of the courts is not altogether ousted, for, the courts merely stay their hands to allow the parties to resort to the form to which they have previously agreed.

The position of law in this area has not changed over the past fifty years. Most recently, the Sind High Court in *Global Quality Foods Pvt Ltd v Hardee's Food Systems Inc*[70] observed that:

> 18-The exclusive jurisdiction clause in an agreement cannot be ignored lightly merely at the whims of one of the parties to the contract and unless there is a 'strong cause' to displace the forum that the parties have agreed to resolve their dispute.

The court further observed on a choice of forum clause:[71]

> 20. The doctrine of *forum non conveniens* means some other forum is more proper in sense of more suitable ends of justice. At the same time, the choice of forum selection clause is made in an arm's length negotiation by experienced and sophisticated businessman, and, absent some compelling and countervailing reasons it should be honoured by the parties and enforced by the courts. These clauses cannot be objected being improper because it tends to oust a court of jurisdiction is hardly more than a vestigial legal fiction.

A similar position was taken by the Islamabad High Court in *Telecom Services and Consultants (Pvt) Ltd v OOREDOO QSC and Others.*[72] Justice Athar Minallah not only stressed that the sanctity of commercial contracts should be preserved, and the promises made by the parties at the time of entering into the contract be enforced, but also explained that section 28 of the *Contract Act 1870* is not violated in these conditions. He observed that:

> It is, therefore, obvious that upholding the sanctity of commercial bargain is pivotal. Courts will give effect to exclusive jurisdiction clauses unless the plaintiff is able to discharge the heavy burden of satisfying the Court, that circumstances exist, not foreseen at the time of execution of the contract containing such a clause that the proceedings be allowed in a non contractual forum.

In the same case, Justice Athar Minallah observed:

> Next is the effect of Section 28 of *Contract Act, 1872*. It is by now settled law that the said provision do not create a bar in enforcing forum selection clauses mutually agreed by the parties . . . it is noted that mutually agreed forum selection clauses could neither be considered contrary to public policy nor contravened the provisions of Section 28 of the *Contract Act, 1872*.
>
> 16. In the instant case, the plain language of the forum selection clause is precise, unambiguous and clear and there is no doubt that the parties have intended jurisdiction

70 *Global Quality Foods Pvt Ltd v Hardee's Food Systems Inc* PLD 2016 Sind 169, [18].

71 Editor's note: As discussed in para 3.2 above, the law of the forum (or *lex fori* as it is sometimes known) is the law of the place in which court or arbitral proceedings are conducted. If the Parties have not selected the governing law of the contract, it will be determined by a judge in the jurisdiction where legal proceedings are initiated, or by an arbitral tribunal.

72 *Telecom Services and Consultants (Pvt) Ltd v OOREDOO QSC and Others*, 2019 CLC 887 [14,15,16].

> of English Courts to be 'exclusive'. The clause covers the adjudication of grievances or cause of action disclosed and asserted in the plaint. The refusal of the instant application would indeed tantamount to enable the plaintiff to circumvent the binding obligation, which it had undertaken at the time of accepting the two process letters including the forum selection clause contained therein. Moreover, the parties had also chosen English Law as the governing law. The plaintiff has not raised any ground so as to justify refusal in giving effect to the exclusive jurisdiction clause. The plaintiff had accepted the exclusive jurisdiction clause voluntarily and out of free will. In the circumstances, it would be just and proper to give effect to the exclusive clause contained in the respective process letters.

However, in all public sector construction contracts, it has been observed that the domestic contractors are not given a choice by the public procuring agencies to choose any governing law of the contract other than that of Pakistan. The main reason is the default position adopted by Pakistan Engineering Council in its bidding documents for civil works based on FIDIC Standard Forms 1987; Particular Condition Clause 5.1(b) states that: 'Law of Islamic Republic of Pakistan shall be the Law of the Contract.' The situation however may be different in the case of a project sponsored by donor agencies or projects executed under Public Private Partnerships or under framework agreements with foreign countries or under other project delivery models; as noted above, choosing a foreign law governing the contract is not illegal.

16.4.2 Formal requirements for a construction contract

The formal requirements for a valid construction contract in Pakistan are no different from the requirements for any commercial contract formed under the *Contract Act 1872,* and these requirements are consistent with almost all the common law jurisdictions.

A legally enforceable contract is formed between the parties through offer and acceptance, against some consideration with clear and certain terms. The formation of a contract should be with the free consent of the parties and should not result from undue influence, coercion, fraud or misrepresentation. The *Contract Act 1872* also differentiates between void contracts and voidable contracts. Void contracts are illegal and voidable contracts can be termed illegal on the choice of the innocent party.

Pakistan law recognises oral contracts as well,[73] although in certain circumstances, the specific legislation may require otherwise as is in the case of section 54 of the *Transfer of Property Act 1882*. In the case titled *Government of Punjab and Others v Khyber International Printer*,[74] the plaintiff, Khyber International Printers, provided advertisement materials relating to AIDS and malaria prevention on the verbal order of the defendant, the government of Punjab. The advertisement materials, in the form of banners were delivered but the government of Punjab never paid. The plaintiff sought a remedy from the court for breach of contract. The defendant argued that no contract in writing was made and as such oral contracts are not enforceable. The court held that oral contracts are enforceable as there is no legal restraint, however, 'clearest and more satisfactory evidence would be demanded by the Court'.

73 *Contract Act 1872*, s 10.

74 *Government of Punjab and Others v Khyber International Printer*, 2009 PLD 18[8].

Similarly, in a case titled *Muhammad Nawaz through LRs v Haji Muhammad Baran Khan through LRs and Others*[75] regarding enforcement of an oral contract, the Supreme Court of Pakistan judgment laid down that the burden to satisfy the court will be higher on the petitioner and observed:

> We also hold that although it is not the requirement of law that an agreement or contract of sale of immovable property should only be in writing, however, in a case where party comes forward to seek a decree for specific performance of contract of sale of immovable property on the basis of an oral agreement alone, heavy burden lies on the party to prove that there was consensus *ad idem* between both the parties for a concluded oral agreement by which the parties intended to be bound is valid and enforceable, however, it requires for it to prove clearest and most satisfactory evidence.

According to the *Public Procurement Rules 2004*[76] for the public sector contracts, it is the discretion of the procuring agency whether it requires formal signing of the contract or otherwise. However, according to the Instruction to Bidders Clause 33 of the PEC Standard Bidding Documents, formal signing of the Contract is necessary. In the private sector, there is no such requirement for construction contracts to be in writing.

Pakistan law also recognises a contract under seal, sometimes referred to as a deed especially in cases of contracts for sale of immovable property eg sale deed, mortgage deed. Consideration is not required if the agreement is in writing and registered under law. For a sale/transfer deed of immovable property, registration is mandatory under the Article 17 of the *Registration Act 1908*. Article 25 of the *Contract Act 1872* states:

> 25. An agreement made without consideration is void, unless–
> (1) it is expressed in writing and registered under the law for the time being in force for the registration of documents.

However, the concept of a deed is quite similar to English Law. One of the major differences between a simple contract and a contract under seal (deed) is the limitation period to institute a suit for breach of contract. The limitation period for suit against breach of a simple contract in most of the circumstances as defined under *Limitation Act* is three years whereas for a title deed, it is twelve years.[77]

16.5 What Special Provisions in the Particular Conditions are necessary for consistency with applicable laws in Pakistan?

16.5.1 FIDIC General Conditions are incompatible or inconsistent with Pakistani governing law of the contract

The following are examples of FIDIC General Conditions that may be incompatible or inconsistent with the governing law of the Contract in Pakistani jurisdiction.

16.5.1.1 Employer's sale of Contractor's equipment, surplus material, wreckage and Temporary Works (11.11)

In respect of the Employer's sale of Contractor's Equipment, surplus material, wreckage and temporary works in sub-clause 11.11 of the 1999 and 2017 FIDIC

75 *Muhammad Nawaz through LRs v Haji Muhammad Baran Khan through LRs and Others*, 2013 SCMR 1300 [10].

76 *Public Procurement Regularity Authority Rules 2004*, rule 44 (a) and (b).

77 *Limitation Act Pakistan*, s 132(c).

rainbow suites, amendment may be required in the Particular Conditions. The relevant law is contained in the in the section dealing with Bailment of Pledges, sections 172 to 181 in the *Contract Act 1872*:

> **'Pledge', 'Pawnor' and 'Pawnee' defined**
>
> 172. The bailment of goods as security for payment of a debt or performance of a promise is called 'pledge'. The bailor is in this case called the 'pawnor'. The bailee is called the 'pawnee'.
>
> **Pawnee's right where pawnor makes default**
>
> 176. If the pawnor makes default in payment of the debt, or performance, at the stipulated time of the promise, in respect of which the goods were pledged, the pawnee may bring a suit against the pawnor upon the debt or promise, and retain the goods pledged as a collateral security; or he may sell the thing pledged, on giving the pawnor reasonable notice of the sale.'

General Condition sub-clause 11.11 of the FIDIC 1999 and 2017 rainbow suites entitles the Employer to sell the Contractor's Equipment, surplus material, wreckage, rubbish and Temporary Works if the Contractor fails to remove them from Site after receiving the Performance Certificate from the Employer. However, the governing law only allows such sale in circumstances where the Contractor has exclusively pledged the Goods or machinery.

It has been observed that the Employers, which are in most cases public sector agencies, tend to retain or confiscate the Contractor's Equipment on account of its default, merely on the basis of contractual entitlement. Such an action does not satisfy the requirement of section 172, of the *Contract Act 1872* because at the time of entering into the Contract, the Contractor had not intended to pledge its equipment as a security against future performance or default. The law does not give absolute rights to the Employer to retain the Contractor's Equipment and then sell it. Instead, the Contractor submits an unconditional Performance Security and the Employer's entitlement is limited to claim against the Performance Security in case of Contractor's default. In order to bring the law of pledge into action, sub-clause 11.11 must be clarified in the Particular Conditions.

Moreover, under the provincial motor vehicle registration rules, most earthmoving and construction machinery is registered as a moveable property under the motor vehicle registration laws. Therefore, a Party cannot sell someone else's registered moveable property on the basis of contractual entitlement only. In such cases, the Employer may bring a recovery suit against the Contractor and seek specific performance or damages against the Contractor for not clearing the Site in time.

It is advisable that the consent of the Contractor is obtained at the time of entering into the Contract and the Particular Conditions address how the law on bailment of pledges will apply in such circumstances.

16.5.1.2 Right of 'set-off', 'is inconsistent with the payment provisions in the General Conditions

In the FIDIC Red Book 1987, adopted by the Pakistan Engineering Council in their bidding documents, set-off is mentioned in clause 59.5, Payment to Nominated Subcontractors, wherein the Employer can pay to the Nominated Subcontractors directly upon receiving the certificate of the Engineer and can settle it by way of set-off from any of the due payment of the head Contractor. However, it has not been expressly described in payment clause 60 that outstanding payment obligations of the Parties can be discharged by way of set-off. The rights of set-off available to an aggrieved party under Pakistani Law are in addition to the payment provisions under FIDIC General Conditions. This is expressly mentioned in the *Code of Civil Procedure* in Order VIII Rule 6(2) and applied by courts in different judgments. In the case titled *Muhammad Khalid v Muhammad Adnan Qureshi*,[78] the Islamabad High Court double bench referred to the *Code of Civil Procedure 1908*, Order 8 Rule 6, which is reproduced here:

> 6.-(1) Where in suit for the recovery of money the defendant claims to set-off against the plaintiff's demand any ascertained sum of money legally recoverable by him from the plaintiff, not exceeding the pecuniary limits of the jurisdiction of the Court, and both parties fill the same character as they fill in the plaintiff's suit, the defendant may, at the first hearing of the suit, but not afterwards unless permitted by the Court, present a written statement containing the particulars of the debt sought to be set-off.
>
> (2) The written statement shall have the same effect as a plaint in a cross-suit so as to enable the Court to pronounce a final judgment in respect both of the original claim and of the set-off: but this shall not affect the lien, upon the amount decreed, of any pleader in respect of the costs payable to him under the decree.
>
> (3) The rules relating to a written statement by a defendant apply to a written statement in answer to a claim of set-off.

The Islamabad High Court in its judgment also relied on the judgment of the Supreme Court in *Civil Aviation Authority, Quaid-i-Azam International Airport, Karachi v JAPAK International, Lahore*,[79] where the Honourable Supreme Court laid down the following conditions for legal set-off:

> The essential conditions of legal set-off are as follows:
>
> i.) The suit must be one for recovery of money.
> ii.) As regards the amount claimed to be set-off:-
>   a) it must be an ascertained sum of money
>   b) such sum must be legally recoverable.

The Honourable Court further held that:

> The principles of setoff are clear in understanding as it is a counter claim for a specific amount and the same can be claimed where defendant and plaintiff are debtors of each other.

16.5.2 FIDIC General Conditions are incompatible or inconsistent with the law of the Site/Country

No Special Provisions in the Particular Conditions are necessary for consistency with the applicable laws.

16.5.3 FIDIC General Conditions are incompatible or inconsistent with the relevant laws on dispute determination in Pakistan

No Special Provisions in the Particular Conditions are necessary for consistency with the applicable laws.

---

78 *Muhammad Khalid v Muhammad Adnan Qureshi*, 2018 CLC 585.

79 *Civil Aviation Authority, Quaid-i-Azam International Airport, Karachi v JAPAK International, Lahore*, 2009 SMR 666[13].

16.6 What Special Provisions in the Particular Conditions are desirable for consistency with applicable laws in Pakistan?

16.6.1 Employer's use of Contractor's goods after termination

The concept of termination of the Contractor's employment under the Contract, in case of the Contractor's default and subsequent action by the Employer is referred in sub-clause 63.1of the 1987 FIDIC Red Book. Sub-clause 63.1 'Default of Contractor' can be loosely subdivided into two parts. The first part comprises all the reasons for the Contractor's default and the Engineer's opinion, whereas the second part comprises the actions to be carried out by the Employer. The second part is not harmonised with the local Laws. The relevant part of sub-clause 63.1 is as follows:

> . . .then the Employer may, after giving 14 days' notice to the Contractor, enter upon the Site and the Works and terminate the employment of the Contractor without thereby releasing the Contractor from any of his obligations or liabilities under the Contract, or affecting the rights and authorities conferred on the Employer or Engineer by the Contact, and may himself complete the Works or may employ any other contractor to complete the Works. The Employer or such other contractor may use for such completion so much of the Contractor's Equipment, Temporary Works and materials as he or they may think proper.

The last part of this clause, which is reproduced above, is based on the concept of bailment. It has been observed that most of the Employers from public sector agencies use this clause and after giving notice to the Contractor under sub-clause 63.1, retains its equipment at the Site. The law on bailment is in sections 148 to 171 of the *Contract Act 1872*. This law creates a legal relationship between the parties with regards to the goods bailed. It puts certain duties and liabilities on the parties to take care of goods, which in the case of FIDIC sub-clause, 63.1 are missing. In order to make this sub-clause in harmony with the governing law, it is desirable to introduce certain amendments in the Particular Conditions of contract specifically addressing the issues of:

i. Care of goods bailed under section 151 of the *Contract Act 1872*
ii. Return of goods to bailor under section 160 of the *Contract Act 1872*.

Sub-clause 15.2 of the 1999 and 2017 rainbow suites contain similar provisions to sub-clause 63.1 of the 1987 Red Book, and accordingly a similar Particular Condition is desirable for consistency with local law.

16.7 Summary of applicable legislation for Pakistani governing law of the contract

Unless otherwise noted, all of the following legislation is federal legislation.

16.7.1 Entry into a construction contract

Contracts generally	*Contract Act 1872*[80]
Construction contracts	*Public Private Partnership (Amendment) Ordinance 2020*[81] *Public Procurement Regularity Authority Rules 2004*,[82] Rule 44 (a) and (b)

80 https://www.ma-law.org.pk/pdflaw/Contract%20Act,%201872.pdf (accessed 17 November 2020).
81 http://www.senate.gov.pk/1web/ordinance/ordVIIIof2020.pdf (accessed 5 November 2020).
82 https://www.ppra.org.pk/Rules.asp (accessed 5 November 2020).

16.7.2 Termination of a construction contract

Frustration	*Contract Act 1872 section 56*
Bankruptcy, insolvency, liquidation	*The Provincial Insolvency Act 1920*
Guarantees under forms of Security (Tender Security, Demand Guarantee, Surety Bond, Advance Payment Guarantee, Retention Money Guarantee, Payment Guarantee by Employer)	*Contract Act 1872*

16.7.3 Dispute resolution

Limitation periods	*Limitation Act 1908*[83]
ADR	*Alternate Dispute Resolution Act 2017*[84] (Applies in Islamabad Capital Territory) *The Punjab Alternate Dispute Resolution Act 2019*[85] (Applies in Punjab Province) *Khyber Pakhtunkhawa Police (Amendment) Order 2015* (Applies in Khyber Pakhtunkhawa Province)
Arbitration	*The Arbitration Act 1940* *Recognition and Enforcement (Arbitration Agreements and Foreign Arbitral Awards) Act 2011* (***Foreign Awards Act***).

16.8 Summary of applicable legislation if the Site/Country is in Pakistan

16.8.1 Operation of a construction contract

Registration and administration of professionals – Engineers, Architects, Town Planers	*Pakistan Engineering Council Act 1975*[86] *Pakistan Council of Architects and Town Planners Ordinance 1983*
Registration/licensing of Contractors and subcontractors	*Pakistan Engineering Council Act 1975*
Subcontractors	*Pakistan Engineering Council Act 1975*
Labour	*The Payment of Wages Act 1936*
Copyright	*Copyright Ordinance 1962*
Work affecting adjacent property to the Site	*The Easement Act 1882*
Heritage	*The Antiquities Act 1975*
Environment	*Pakistan Environmental Protection Act 1997*
Local procurement	*Pakistan Public Procurement Regulatory Authority Ordinance 2002*
Building and construction permits, Execution of construction work, Standard of construction work	Obtained from relevant agency which holds land. Construction permits are usually the responsibility of the local municipality or district administration. Municipal, provincial and federal agencies have prepared their own building regulations.
Health and safety	*Factories Act 1974*

83 https://www.ma-law.org.pk/pdflaw/Limitation%20%20Act%20-%201908.pdf (accessed 5 November 2020).

84 http://www.na.gov.pk/uploads/documents/1486554463_506.pdf (accessed 5 November 2020).

85 http://punjablaws.gov.pk/laws/2739.html (accessed 5 November 2020).

86 https://www.pec.org.pk/downloadables/PEC%20ACT%201976%20_LATEST_.pdf (accessed 5 November 2020).

Calibration of testing apparatus, equipment and instruments	*Pakistan Council of Scientific and Industrial Research Act 1973*
Ownership of Plant and Materials	*Sale of Goods Act 1930*
Employer's sale of Contractor's Equipment, surplus material, wreckage and Temporary Works	*Contract Act 1872* (Pledge) sections 172–179
Insurance	*Insurance Ordinance 2000*[87]
Statutory rights that coexist with contractual rights	*Constitution of Pakistan 1973*[88]
Liability for defective work	*Contract Act 1872*

16.8.2 Termination of a construction contract

Bankruptcy, insolvency, liquidation	*Provincial Insolvency Act 1920* (Punjab)

16.8.3 Dispute resolution

Dispute before a local board/Adjudication	*Alternate Dispute Resolution Act 2017*[89] (Applies in Islamabad Capital Territory) *The Punjab Alternate Dispute Resolution Act 2019*[90] (Applies in Punjab Province) *Code of Civil Procedure (Sindh Amendment) Act 2018* *Khyber Pakhtunkhawa Police (Amendment) Order 2015* (Applies in Khyber Pakhtunkhawa Province)
Limitation periods	*Limitation Act 1908*

16.9 Summary of applicable legislation if the 'seat' of the dispute determination is in Pakistan

Dispute resolution	*Alternate Dispute Resolution Act 2017* (Applies in Islamabad Capital Territory) *The Punjab Alternate Dispute Resolution Act 2019*[91] (Applies in Punjab Province) *Khyber Pakhtunkhawa Police (Amendment) Order 2015* (Applies in Khyber Pakhtunkhawa Province)
Limitation periods	*Limitation Act 1908*
Arbitration	*Arbitration Act 1940*

16.10 Issues that a court or arbitrator may construe differently to that expected from the words of the Contract, because of local law or custom

16.10.1 Limitation period for liability

Limitation Act 1908 specifies the time period in which parties remain liable to each other and file any suit, appeal or application in the court. Courts in Pakistan have

87 http://pakistancode.gov.pk/english/UY2FqaJw1-apaUY2Fqa-apaUY2FobJw%3D-sg-jjjjjjjjjjjj (accessed 5 November 2020).

88 http://www.na.gov.pk/uploads/documents/1333523681_951.pdf (accessed 5 November 2020).

89 http://www.na.gov.pk/uploads/documents/1486554463_506.pdf (accessed 5 November 2020).

90 http://punjablaws.gov.pk/laws/2739.html (accessed 5 November 2020).

91 ibid.

conservatively enforced the limitation period because section 3 of the *Limitation Act* expressly provides for dismissal of the suit which is filed after the period of limitation. Section 3 is reproduced:

> **3. Dismissal of suit, etc. instituted, etc. after period of limitation.**
>
> Subject to the provisions contained in sections 4 to 25 (inclusive), every suit instituted, appeal preferred, and application made after the period of limitation prescribed therefore by the First Schedule shall be dismissed although limitation has not been set up as a defense.

The exception to this rule is contained in section 5 of the *Limitation Act 1908*, which is also reproduced here:

> **5. Extension of period in certain case.**
>
> Any appeal or application for [a revision or] a review of judgment or for leave to appeal or any other application to which this section may be made applicable [by or under any enactment] for the time being in force may be admitted after the period of limitation prescribed therefore, when the appellant or applicant satisfies the Court that he had sufficient cause for not preferring the appeal or making the application within such period.

Generally, FIDIC contracts contain time bar provisions and expressly state that a party's entitlement to claim additional payment may be lost if it fails to notify the other party within the time period specified in the Contract. This time period is generally 28 days. Since under the *Limitation Act 1908*, the time period to bring a suit for breach of contract is three years, it will be interesting to see how the courts will treat Notice provisions and Party's entitlement to claim additional amounts in time barred claims.

16.10.2 Joint and several liability under Partnership Act

The concept of proportionate liability is alien to local law. It invariably means that the traditional common law position of joint and several liabilities is relevant wherein the aggrieved party can choose to sue against all or one of the wrongdoers. This position is further elaborated in the *Partnership Act 1932*, the relevant portion of which is reproduced here:

> **25. Liability of partner for acts of a partner.**
>
> Every partner is liable, jointly with all the other partners and also severally, for all acts of the firm done while he is a partner.
>
> **26. Liability of the firm for wrongful acts of a partner.**
>
> Where, by the wrongful act or omission of a partner acting in the ordinary course of the business of a firm, or with the authority of his partners, loss or injury is caused to any third party, or any penalty is incurred, the firm is liable therefore to the same extent as the partner.

Clause 77.1 in the 1987 FIDIC Red Book Particular Conditions promulgated by the Pakistan Engineering Council, expressly states that every party in a joint venture is jointly and severally liable. So irrespective of the project delivery model, if a joint venture in a construction contract defaults, the aggrieved party can bring action against any or all partners. The same holds true in the case of Design and Build or EPC contracts.

16.10.3 Delay damages/penalties

FIDIC General Conditions entitle the Employer to deduct liquidated damages (referred to as delay damages in the 1999 rainbow suite and Delay Damages in the 2017 rainbow suite) at a rate specified in the Particular Conditions (2017 rainbow suite and 1999 Silver Book)/Appendix to Tender (1999 Red and Yellow Books) for a delay period attributed to the Contractor. In PEC approved Standard Contract Documents, the maximum amount of liquidated damages is capped at 10 per cent of the Contract Price. Delay damages or penalties in the contract are one area of law where FIDIC General Conditions are inconsistent with the governing law. The relevant law, section 74 of the *Contract Act 1872*, is as follows:

> **74. Compensation for breach of contract where penalty stipulated for**
>
> When a contract has been broken, if a sum is named in the contract as the amount to be paid in case of such breach, or if the contract contains any other stipulation by way of penalty, the party complaining of the breach is entitled, whether or not actual damage or loss is proved to have been caused thereby, to receive from the party who has broken the contract reasonable compensation not exceeding the amount so named or, as the case may be, the penalty stipulated for.

Section 74 entitles the aggrieved party to enforce stipulated damages in the Contract whether in the form of liquidated damages or penalties. It does not require proof of damage or actual loss. However, the courts have interpreted this section differently and introduced an additional test that the aggrieved party must prove evidence of its actual loss and then the court will award damages which it deems reasonable but by no means exceeding the amount already specified in the Contract. The manner in which section 74 has been drafted confirms that Pakistani law treats liquidated damages and penalties similarly. The case law developed by the apex courts reaffirms this understanding.

In *Syed Sibte Raza and Another v Habib Bank Limited*,[92] the judge observed:

> Since the amount is stipulated in the present cases, by whatever name it may be described, whether liquidated damages, penalty, recompense or, earnest money, the respondent Bank, on breach of contract by the appellants, was entitled to receive reasonable compensation.
>
> Section 74 provides for cases where a sum is named in the contract itself as the amount to be paid in the case of the breach of the contract, or if the contract contains any other stipulation by way of penalty, the party complaining of the breach has to be compensated.

In *Aslam Saeed and Co v Trading Corporation of Pakistan Ltd*, [93] the court held:

> The above section (Section 74, The Contract Act, 1872) does not recognise the difference that exists in the English law between the liquidated damages and penalty.

In *Major Aziz Ahmed Mohammad v Manzoor Ahmed Sahi*[94] the High Court of Sindh discussed section 74 of the *Act* and held as follows:

> Section 74 seeks to resolve the difficulties in the common law doctrine of damages. It dispenses with fine distinctions between the claim of damages based on the principle of liquidated damages and those imposed by way of penalty. It makes provision for both and the principle laid down is that where a sum is named or a penalty is stipulated the

92 *Syed Sibte Raza and Another v Habib Bank Limited*, PLD 1971 SC 743.

93 *Aslam Saeed and Co v Trading Corporation of Pakistan Ltd*, PLD 1985 SC 69.

94 *Major Aziz Ahmed Mohammad v Manzoor Ahmed Sahi*, PLD 1961 (WP) Karachi 305, 315C and D.

party complaining of the breach is entitled to reasonable compensation not exceeding the amount so named or penalty so stipulated.

In *Messrs United Bank Limited v Messrs M Ismail and Company (Pvt) Limited*,[95] the apex court reaffirmed that proof of actual loss is imperative to claim stipulated damages. The Courts held as follows:

> In another judgment passed in the case of *Saudi Pak Industrial and Commercial Investment Company (Pvt) Ltd v Allied Bank Limited* 2003 CLD 596 earlier case-law on the subject was again thoroughly examined by the Honourable Supreme Court of Pakistan and it was held that the liquidated damages required positive evidence to show that such actual loss was suffered by the party claiming the damages and a mere fixed amount stipulated as liquidated damages would not be recoverable if the quantum of actual loss was not proved.

In *Investment Corporation of Pakistan v Sheikhapura Textile Mills*, [96] the Sind High Court held as follows:

> By now it is well-settled that liquidated damages can be recovered only if party claiming the same, can prove the same.

In *National Bank of Pakistan v West Pakistan Tanks Terminal*, [97] the Sind High Court, while explaining the application of section 74, held as follows:

> Further, under section 74 of the Contract Act, 1872, in case of breach of contract the person complaining of the breach is entitled to claim from the party who has committed the breach reasonable compensation not exceeding the amount specified in the agreement between the parties. What is reasonable compensation is a question of fact. The plaintiff has neither shown nor indicated in any document as to how the liquidated damages have been calculated at 20 percent or offered to prove that the liquidated damages claimed are reasonable compensation in the present circumstances. The claim of liquidated damages is, thus, contrary to the provisions of the Contract Act and the law laid down by the superior Courts and is, therefore, rejected.

A review of case law shows that courts in Pakistan regard both liquidated damages and penalties as compensation for breach of contract but require proof of actual loss from the aggrieved party. It is therefore imperative that the liquidated damages or penalty mentioned in the Contract must be a genuine estimate of anticipated loss which can satisfy the requirements of the court. Therefore, while negotiating contracts at the time of bidding, the Employer may consider making the estimate of anticipated loss a part of contract documents. Mere stipulation of the amount of liquidated damages in the Particular Conditions is not maintainable in the eyes of law.

16.10.4 Force majeure

Force majeure clauses in contracts define multiple events which affect the performance of one or both the parties to the contract where neither of the parties have any control over these events. These events may include but not limited to acts of God, floods, abnormal weather conditions, epidemics, war, riots, terrorist activities etc.[98] In the

95 *Messrs United Bank Limited v Messrs M Ismail and Company (Pvt) Limited*, 2006 CLD 394.

96 *Investment Corporation of Pakistan v. Sheikhapura Textile Mills*, 2004 CLD 1396.

97 *National Bank of Pakistan v West Pakistan Tanks Terminal*, 2000 CLC 896.

98 http://www.rmaco.com.pk/covid-19-force-majeure-frustration-of-contracts (accessed 5 November 2020).

1999 FIDIC rainbow suite, clause 19 is specifically titled *Force Majeure* and it deals with two distinct issues:

i. *Force majeure* and
ii. Release from performance.

The term *force majeure* is replaced by Exceptional Event in clause 18 of the 2017 rainbow suite, but the concept is unchanged.

In Pakistani law, the term *force majeure* is not specifically defined. However, the closest in relevance to *force majeure* is section 56 of the *Contract Act 1872* which is based on the common law doctrine of frustration. When a contract is frustrated, parties can release each other from performance. Section 56 of the *Contract Act 1872* states as follows:

> **Agreement to do impossible act**
>
> 56. An agreement to do an act impossible in itself is void.
>
> **Contract to do act afterwards becoming impossible or unlawful**
>
> A contract to do an act which, after the contract is made, becomes impossible, or, by reason of some event which the promissor could not prevent, unlawful, becomes void when the act becomes impossible or unlawful.

For a matter that makes performance impossible but not specially defined as a *force majeure event*, parties can rely on section 56 of the *Contract Act 1872*.

16.10.5 Misrepresentation

Misrepresentation is defined in *the Contract Act 1872*, section 18 as:

> 18. Misrepresentation' means and includes– (1) the positive assertion, in a manner not warranted by the information of the person making it, of that which is not true, though he believes it to be true; (2) any breach of duty which, without an intent to deceive, gains an advantage to the person committing it, or any one claiming under him, by misleading another to his prejudice or to the prejudice of any one claiming under him; (3) causing, however innocently, a party to an agreement to make a mistake as to the substance of the thing which is the subject of the agreement.

If a contract is formed by misrepresentation, it is voidable at the option of the other party. Section 19 provides:

> 19. When consent to an agreement is caused by coercion, fraud or misrepresentation, the agreement is a contract voidable at the option of the party whose consent was so caused.

The Pakistan Engineering Council in its Standard Bidding Documents[99] has introduced a declaration of fees, commissions and brokerage etc. in Appendix L to Bid, known as the Integrity Pact. In this declaration the Bidder undertakes to take full responsibility and liability, including but not limited to any misrepresentation or false declaration to defeat the purpose of the Integrity Pact. Any such misrepresentation or false declaration makes the Contract voidable at the option of the government.

99 https://www.pec.org.pk/downloads/PEC_Bidding_Docs/(2)%20Std%20Form%20of%20Bidding%20Docs%20for%20Procurement%20of%20Works%20(E&M).pdf.

16.10.6 Appeal to a court does not mean that the right to arbitration is lost

Typically, in all construction contracts in Pakistan, arbitration is the preferred method of dispute resolution. Section 34 of the *Arbitration Act 1940* gives the court powers to stay proceedings and refer the Parties to resolve their dispute by arbitration. Section 34 of the *Arbitration Act 1940* is self-explanatory:

> **34. Power to stay legal proceedings where there is an arbitration agreement**
>
> Where any party to an arbitration agreement or any person claiming under him commences any legal proceedings against any other party to the agreement or any person claiming under him in respect of any matter agreed to be referred, any party to such legal proceedings may, at any time before filing a written statement or taking any other steps in proceedings, apply to the judicial authority before which the proceedings are pending to stay the proceedings; and if satisfied that there is no sufficient reason why the matter should not be referred in accordance with the arbitration agreement and that the applicant was, at the time when the proceedings were commenced, and still remains, ready and willing to do all things necessary to the proper conduct of the arbitration such authority, may make an order staying the proceedings.

16.10.7 Alternative dispute resolution

In 2017, the government of Pakistan passed the *Alternate Dispute Resolution Act 2017* with the objective to 'facilitate settlement of disputes without resort to formal litigation'.[100] This *Act* is applicable in Islamabad Capital Territory.[101] The Punjab Province[102] has also introduced their own legislation for ADR whereas in Sind, amendments have been introduced in the *Code of Civil Procedure 1908* regarding ADR.[103] In Khyber Pakhtunkhawa province, ADR has been introduced in the *Khyber Pakhtunkhawa Police (Amendment) Order 2015* by establishing a Dispute Resolution Committee (**DRC**) and emphasis is on community involvement for amicable settlement of disputes.

This federal ADR *Act* formally defines[104] alternate dispute resolution as a process wherein the parties can settle their disputes outside of court and this process includes arbitration, mediation, conciliation, neutral evaluation and dispute resolution through *Panchayat*. Except for dispute resolution through *Panchayat*, all other alternate dispute resolution methods are world renowned. The reference to ADR under this *Act* can only be made by a court of competent jurisdiction in any civil matter.

Panchayat is a traditional method of dispute resolution in this part of the world. In some areas of Pakistan, this arrangement of dispute resolution is sometimes called a *Jirga*. The function of *Panchayat* and *Jirga* is much the same as that of dispute resolution. The *Panchayat* comprises elders of a village or community who carry the trust and respect of both the parties in dispute. It has been observed that the approach and focus of *Panchayat* is to resolve disputes amicably. In case of disagreement, the *Panchayat* usually adjudicates as per traditional customs. Since it is a traditional method for more than a hundred years, the system has been successful in resolving disputes of both civil and commercial nature.

100 *Alternate Dispute Resolution Act 2017.*
101 ibid s 1(2).
102 *Punjab Alternate Dispute Resolution Act 2019.*
103 http://www.pas.gov.pk/uploads/acts/Sindh%20Act%20No.IV%20of%202019.pdf.
104 *Alternate Dispute Resolution Act 2017*, s 2(a).

In Pakistan's legal system, arbitration is the most commonly used method of alternative dispute resolution in the construction sector. Arbitration is supported by legislation, the *Arbitration Act 1940*. The Pakistan Engineering Council's Standard Bidding documents (which include the 1987 FIDIC Redbook) refers to domestic arbitration under the *Arbitration Act 1940*.

The law on enforceability of arbitral awards is settled in Pakistan, and the courts tend to enforce arbitration awards. In a case titled *National Highway Authority v Messrs China Petroleum Corporation*,[105] the Islamabad High Court reaffirmed this position. The learned Judge, Mian Gul Hassan Aurangzeb, in his judgment noted:

> There is nothing apparent on the surface of the record to indicate any misconduct on the part of the learned arbitrator. It is settled law that a court while examining the validity of an award does not sit as a court of appeal. It cannot undertake reappraisal of evidence. For a court to interfere in an arbitration award, there has to be an error on the face of it and discoverable by reading the award itself. The learned Trial Court has been mindful not to scrutinize the arbitration award dated 25.06.2007 by applying the yardstick of an appeal.

Unlike the UK and Australia, currently there is no equivalent legislation for statutory adjudication such as the *Housing, Grants, Construction and Regeneration Act 1996* (UK) or Australian *Security of Payment Acts* enacted in Pakistan. Nor is there any statutory support for Dispute Boards. Accordingly, the decisions of Dispute Boards formed under contractual agreements between the Parties are not as easily enforceable through courts as arbitral awards.

16.11 References

16.11.1 Internet

Dr Faqir Hussain, 'The Judicial System of Pakistan'https://www.supremecourt.gov.pk/downloads_judgements/all_downloads/Judicial_System_of_Pakistan/thejudicialsystemofPakistan.pdf.

'Economic Survey of Pakistan, Economic and Social Indicators' http://www.finance.gov.pk/survey/chapter_20/PES_2019_20.pdf

'China Pakistan Economic Corridor' http://cpec.gov.pk/index

Naya Pakistan Housing Program http://nphp.com.pk/chairman-intro/*DAWN News* https://www.dawn.com

https://www.pec.org.pk/schedule_first.aspx

https://www.pec.org.pk/faq.aspx#:~:text=What%20is%20the%20difference%20between,engineering%20practice%20examination%20(EPE)

https://www.pec.org.pk/bidding_docs_implementation.aspx

https://www.pec.org.pk/downloads/BYELAWS%201986%20(APRIL%2023,%202013).pdf

https://www.pec.org.pk/downloads/supervision/guidelines.pdf

PEC News Letter https://pec.org.pk/Downloadables/PEC%20Newsletter_Mar2020.pdf

https://www.pec.org.pk/bidding_docs_implementation.aspx

https://www.riaabarkergillette.com/usa/wp-content/uploads/Labour-law-in-Pakistan.pdf

https://www.pec.org.pk/downloads/PEC_Bidding_Docs/(1)%20Std%20Form%20of%20Bidding%20Docs%20(Civil%20%20Work).pdf

https://www.ncbi.nlm.nih.gov/pmc/articles/PMC7240311/

105 *National Highway Authority v Messrs China Petroleum Corporation, 2017 PLD 1 Islamabad-High-Court [32]*

https://www.nih.org.pk/wp-content/uploads/2020/03/Covid-19-NAP-V2-13-March-2020.pdf
https://www.caapakistan.com.pk/
https://www.icmap.com.pk/images/covid19/EconomicImpact_of_Covid19_on_Pakistant.pdf
http://covid.gov.pk/
http://www.rmaco.com.pk/covid-19-force-majeure-frustration-of-contracts
https://www.pec.org.pk/downloads/PEC_Bidding_Docs/(2)%20Std%20Form%20of%20Bidding%20Docs%20for%20Procurement%20of%20Works%20(E&M).pdf

16.11.2 Legislation

Pakistan Law Site www.pakistanlawsite.com
Pakistan Code http://pakistancode.gov.pk/
Commlii http://www.commonlii.org/links/3062.html
Pakistan Case Law http://pakcaselaw.com

16.11.3 Case law

http://pakcaselaw.com.

CHAPTER 17

Applying FIDIC contracts in Papua New Guinea

Joseph Barbaro, Andrew McCormack, Nick Thorne, Ryan Warokra and Kenneth Imako

DOI: 10.4324/9781003200901-17

17.1 Outline of the legal environment in Papua New Guinea

17.1.1 The constitutional and government structure in Papua New Guinea

17.1.1.1 Overview

The Independent State of Papua New Guinea (**PNG**) gained its independence in 1975 and has since been governed democratically in accordance with its *Constitution*. It is a member of the Commonwealth of Nations and has a Westminster system of government. The formal head of state of PNG is the Queen of the United Kingdom and is represented by the Governor General, who is nominated by the national Parliament, and serves a term of six years.

Under the *Constitution*, the power and authority of the people is vested in the state of PNG. Most of those powers are exercised by the national government, which consists of three principal arms: the national Parliament/legislature, the national executive and the national judiciary.[1]

The Prime Minister of PNG is the head of the national executive and is appointed by the Governor General, acting in accordance with a decision of the Parliament.[2]

1 *Constitution*, Part VI.
2 ibid s 142(2).

Within PNG there are 22 provinces (inclusive of the National Capital District and the autonomous region of Bougainville). PNG's capital is Port Moresby, which is situated in the National Capital District. Each province (except the National Capital District[3] and the autonomous region of Bougainville)[4] has a provincial and local-level government.

The provincial and local-level governments may exercise certain law-making powers delegated to them by the national Parliament.[5]

17.1.1.2 Key issues/comments

The legislation that applies to Contractors and Employers, and business more generally, will almost always be that enacted by the national Parliament and administered by the national executive and its various agencies.

There are very few (if any) provincial government or local-level government laws that are relevant to a construction contract or project in PNG. This is because provincial governments and local-level governments have very limited jurisdiction to legislate on matters generally, particularly where the matter is expressed by the national legislature to be of 'national interest' – these are matters that affect the country as a whole. Most areas/subject matters relevant to construction projects and business generally are matters of national interest and fall within the exclusive jurisdiction of the national government: for instance, the regulation of corporate entities, foreign investment, property, natural resources, the environment and conservation, building, and town planning and zoning.[6]

17.1.2 The legal system of Papua New Guinea

17.1.2.1 Overview

PNG's *Constitution* sets out the laws of PNG in a hierarchical list. The laws consist of the *Constitution*, the *Organic Laws* (which are akin to regulations forming part of the *Constitution*), Acts of the national Parliament, emergency regulations, provincial laws, laws made under or adopted by the *Constitution* and the 'underlying law'.[7]

At independence in 1975, the rules of common law and equity of England were adopted by PNG, and these rules, together with customary law, form the underlying law of the country. The underlying law can be best described as a system of rules, practices and laws analogous to the common law but developed domestically.

17.1.2.2 Key issues/comments

In relation to public procurement/tenders, Contractors should be aware that there are a number of laws that regulate the supply of works and services to the state of PNG and its various arms. A construction contract would be a supply of services.

---

3 The government system of the National Capital District is regulated by the *National Capital District Commission Act 2001*. The *Act* establishes the National Capital District Commission (a corporate-styled body), which performs certain regulatory and municipal functions within the National Capital District.

4 Bougainville is governed by the autonomous Bougainville government, which is separate and distinct from the provincial and local-level government system in PNG. The establishment of the autonomous Bougainville government was permitted by amendments to the PNG *Constitution*, which was a key outcome of the Bougainville Peace Agreement between the state of PNG and the people of Bougainville that followed the civil conflict in the area between 1988 and 1998.

5 *Organic Law on Provincial Governments and Local-level Governments*, Pt III Divisions 3–4.

6 ibid ss 41, 42 and 44.

7 *Constitution*, ss 9–12.

There are two governmental bodies that administer public tenders for works and services on behalf of the state. These are the National Procurement Commission and the Authority to Pre-Commit Committee:

- National Procurement Commission established under the *National Procurement Act 2018* – the Commission is responsible for administering public procurement and tenders. Importantly, the Commission is responsible for public tenders for procurements of a value of 500,000 Kina (**PGK**) (US$140,000) or more.
- Authority to Pre-Commit Committee established under the *Public Finances (Management) Act 1995* – the Committee (which comprises the heads of the government departments for treasury, finance, and planning) oversees the activities of the National Procurement Commission and verifies whether any proposed expenditure of public monies is in line with the national government's budget allocations before the Commission or a public body[8] or statutory body[9] can undertake the procurement.

Contracts for the procurement of goods or services of a value in excess of PGK10 million (US$2.8 million) are subject to the approval of the national executive on recommendation of the national Procurement Commission and will require legal clearance from the State Solicitor before it is executed by the Governor General (acting on the advice of the national executive) on behalf of the state.[10]

The *National Procurement Act 2018* also introduced certain protections for national companies and citizens. These are summarised below:[11]

- Tenders for procurements relating to cottage business activities prescribed by the *Investment Promotion Act 1992* and *Investment Promotion Regulations 1992* are reserved for citizens and national companies. These are mostly small-scale activities in agriculture, forestry, fishing and wholesale and retail trade sectors.
- Procurements with an estimated value of up to PGK10 million (US$2.8 million) will have a technical evaluation requirement that the public tender be open only to national companies and citizens.
- Procurements with an estimated value of between PGK10 million (US$2.8 million) and PGK30 million (US$8.5 million) will have a technical evaluation requirement that the public tender be open only to tenderers where at least 50 per cent of the procurement is proposed to be undertaken by national companies and citizens, or where the tender is made by a partnership or joint venture, at least 50 per cent of that partnership or joint venture is held by national companies or citizens.
- Procurements with an estimated value equal to or greater than PGK30 million (US$8.5 million), and those that were unsuccessful/cancelled and retendered by the Commission, will not be subject to the national content restrictions above.

8 A 'public body' is an agency which is part of the State services established under Part VII of the *Constitution* and a provincial government and local-level government: *Public Finances (Management) Act 1995*, s 2.

9 A 'statutory body' is (a) a body, authority, or instrumentality (corporate or unincorporated) established under an Act of the Parliament for governmental or official purposes; (b) a body, authority, or *instrumentality* (corporate or unincorporated) established by a provincial government or local-level government; or (c) a subsidiary of a statutory body: *Public Finances (Management) Act 1995*, s 2.

10 *National Procurement Act 2018*, ss 12(6) and (7).

11 ibid Pt XI.

Most arms/departments of the national government and the provincial and local-level governments are subject to the *National Procurement Act* and the *Public Finances (Management) Act*. Majority state-owned enterprises (ie government-owned entities that perform public functions eg provision of utilities such as power and water) and certain statutory bodies are subject to different regulatory regimes and may tender for works and services directly (rather than through the Commission). For instance, majority state-owned enterprises are exempt from the application of the *Public Finances (Management) Act* and are instead governed by the *Kumul Consolidated Holdings Act 2002*, pursuant to which they are required to submit an annual plan each year to the national executive for approval. The annual plan must include, among other things, a business plan and expenditure budget for the next financial year. Provided the annual plan is approved by the national executive, a majority state-owned enterprise may undertake work projects contained in the annual plan.

Contractors should be aware that, where the Employer is a governmental body/agency, the laws that apply to the procurement of goods and services by the Employer and rules regarding execution of the construction contract by the governmental body/agency may vary depending on the legislation establishing or otherwise governing that governmental body/agency.

17.1.3 The court system of Papua New Guinea

17.1.3.1 Overview

The national judicial system of PNG is established by the *Constitution* and certain statutes.[12] It consists of the Supreme Court, the National Court, and other courts established by Acts of Parliament (see below).

The Supreme Court is the nation's highest judicial authority and the final court of appeal. It has the inherent jurisdiction to hear matters of constitutional interpretation and enforcement and to review all judicial decisions of the National Court.

The National Court has appellate jurisdiction to review any exercise of judicial authority in the lower courts such as the District Court and Village Courts. It has unlimited jurisdiction in criminal and civil matters and can review administrative decisions of state bodies/agencies.

17.1.3.2 Key issues/comments

Contractors should be aware that, unlike other jurisdictions, there are no construction tribunals or other quasi-judicial bodies set up specifically to determine construction disputes.

Disputes are usually dealt with in accordance with the mechanisms agreed by parties under contract or, if unresolved, the aggrieved party may file proceedings in the National Court.

17.2 The construction industry in Papua New Guinea

17.2.1 Construction industry and the economy

The construction industry is a significant contributor to the PNG economy. While there is limited data from government sources available on the subject, research by

12 Part VI Division 5 of the *Constitution*, *Supreme Court Act* (*Chapter 37*), *National Court Act* (*Chapter 38*), *District Courts Act* (*Chapter 40*), *Village Courts Act 1989*, *Land Disputes Settlement Act* (*Chapter 45*).

private sector analysts reported that in 2018 the construction sector accounted for about 6.8 per cent of PNG's gross domestic product.[13]

PNG currently has a population estimated at 9.02 million and an average population growth rate of 3 per cent.[14] Most of the country's formal working population is concentrated in and around its two largest cities, Port Moresby and Lae. The Department of Treasury projected that the construction sector would grow by 3.5 per cent in 2020 driven by private sector spending on commercial and residential buildings and the anticipated government-led projects earmarked in the 2020 National Budget.[15]

The onset of the Covid-19 pandemic and measures taken by the PNG government to combat it have slowed economic growth, with one survey revealing that 73 per cent of business leaders expecting a reduction in revenue by 20–50 per cent in the 2020 financial year.[16]

17.2.2 Local and international players working in partnership

The construction industry has a number of national contractors but few have the technical knowledge, capital equipment and financial means to execute large civil works projects. It is therefore common for national companies to team up with more experienced (and well-resourced) international contractors to deliver large construction and infrastructure projects, particularly those funded by international organisations such as the Asian Development Bank (where stringent requirements for technical expertise and capacity make it difficult for national companies bidding alone to be competitive).

As discussed in paragraph 17.1.2.2 above, there are statutory requirements that seek to foster participation by local companies in contracts tendered by government. Similarly, though more a matter of policy than a statutory requirement, the government encourages industry sectors such as mining and oil and gas to ensure that their projects have a national content element to help develop local industries and contractors.

Effective joint ventures between international and local construction companies are therefore essential to the industry and doing business in PNG.

17.2.3 No separate licensing regime or regulation

Unlike in some other jurisdictions, the construction industry is not separately regulated in PNG. There is no specific licensing regime or regulatory oversight for projects and participants in the industry. Contractors and participants must comply with the laws and requirements generally applicable to all businesses.

With respect to tenders for public work projects, the National Procurement Commission maintains a register of qualified bidders under the *National Procurement Act 2018* but it is not a regulator per se. To qualify for registration, a bidder:

- Must have the legal capacity to enter into a contract and more than 3 years' experience

13 ANZ Research, *Pacific Economic Outlook – Papua New Guinea* (December 2019).

14 https://data.adb.org/dashboard/papua-new-guinea-numbers (accessed 22 September 2020).

15 2020 National Budget Volume 1: Economic and Development Policies, prepared by the Department of Treasury, 25. The 2020 National Budget was tabled in Parliament on 28 November 2019.

16 https://www.pwc.com/pg/en/publications/COVID-19-updates/pwc-survey--73--of-png-business-leaders-expect-revenue-decline-t.html (accessed 22 September 2020).

- Show that it has registered in PNG to pay taxes and it is not otherwise insolvent/bankrupt or its business is suspended.[17]

The Commission and public and statutory bodies cannot receive bids or contracts from unregistered bidders.

17.2.4 Labour and workplace relations

In terms of labour, skilled workers in the industry will require licences from professional bodies to perform work in particular professions or trades. These bodies include:

- Institute of Engineers – licensing of engineers
- Board of Architects – registration and licensing of architects
- PNG Surveyors Board – licensing of surveyors
- PNG Power Limited – licensing of electricians
- National Apprenticeship and Trade Testing Board – testing and certification of trades personnel.

PNG labour laws are derived from statute as well as principles of common law. The key pieces of legislation are:

- *Employment Act*
- *Employment of Non-Citizens Act*
- *Migration Act*
- *Industrial Relations Act*
- *Industrial Organisations Act*

The *Employment Act* sets certain minimum terms and conditions of employment. More generous terms and conditions can apply for employees in urban centres such as Port Moresby and Lae pursuant to common rules established under the *Industrial Relations Act*. In addition, non-citizens will require appropriate visas and work permits before being employed in PNG.

See also paragraph 17.6.7 with respect to occupational, health and safety laws.

17.3 The impact of Covid-19 in Papua New Guinea

17.3.1 The impact of Covid-19 on the execution of construction projects in Papua New Guinea

Papua New Guinea recorded its first Covid-19 case on 20 March 2020. By August 2020, the total official number of positive cases grew to 459 (mostly concentrated in the capital city, Port Moresby).[18]

In response to the health risks posed by the disease, the national government enacted legislation and imposed a range of measures to control the spread of the virus. These included:

- Restrictions on international travel as early as January 2020
- The declaration of a national emergency and enactment of emergency laws under the PNG *Constitution* in March 2020

17 Section 58, *National Procurement Act 2018*.

18 See the national government's official website: https://covid19.info.gov.pg

- Upon expiry of the period of national emergency and related emergency laws in accordance with the *Constitution*, the passage and commencement of new legislation, the *National Pandemic Act 2020*, to allow the government to continue to implement health and safety measures to control the spread of Covid-19.

Figure 17.1 is a timeline of the key dates and events.

Efforts to mitigate the spread of Covid-19 in Papua New Guinea and elsewhere have had a material impact on the country's economy. Projections by the World Bank in its half year update suggest that Papua New Guinea's real GDP will drop by 4.2 percentage points (to –1.3 per cent), the current account surplus will decline by 11 percentage points (to about 15 per cent of GDP), and the country's fiscal deficit will widen by 0.6 percentage points (to –6.4 per cent of GDP).[19] The general outlook though remains positive with real GDP growth expected to rebound and expand by more than 3 per cent in 2021, driven by foreign direct investment in the resources sector.[20]

A number of the national government's measures have adversely impacted business in general in Papua New Guinea, such as the lockdowns and curfews in Port Moresby, suspension of non-essential services and a general reduction in the workforce both in private and public sectors to adhere to social distancing rules, restrictions on public gatherings, sporting events and the operation of restaurants and bars, all of which have contributed to weaker external and domestic demand.

For foreign investors including contractors, perhaps the measures that have had the greatest impact are the restrictions on international and domestic travel. International flights were banned at one point before being reopened subject to strict approval and monitoring by local authorities and quarantine requirements both offshore

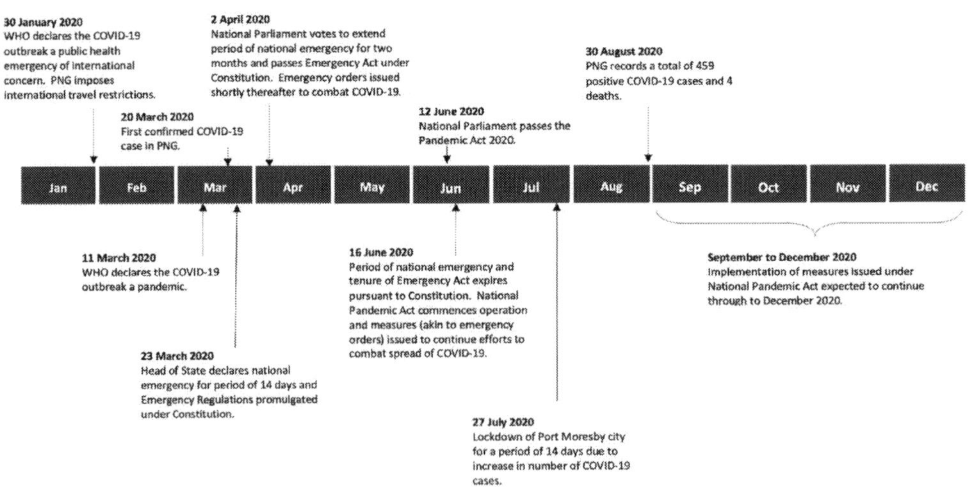

Figure 17.1 Timeline of the key dates and events in the PNG government's response to the Covid-19 pandemic

19 https://www.worldbank.org/en/country/png/publication/papua-new-guinea-in-the-time-of-covid-19---from-relief-to-recovery (accessed 22 September 2020).

20 ibid.

and in-country.[21] These restrictions have led to ongoing difficulties for companies whose businesses rely on foreign skilled labour, with contracts lost due to the general unavailability of key personnel on the ground.

The closure of borders has also affected the supply chains in the construction industry. It has become difficult to procure building materials from other countries in a timely manner due to the delay on the delivery of imported building materials or products.[22]

Accordingly, the indirect economic impact of Covid-19 in Papua New Guinea and internationally has meant Employers and Contractors alike are re-evaluating the feasibility of new construction projects and the timing and delivery of existing projects given the uncertainties of the current environment.

17.3.2 The impact of Covid-19 on the operation of construction contracts in Papua New Guinea

As noted in paragraph 17.2.1 above, the construction industry in Papua New Guinea has not been immune to the broader economic impacts of Covid-19. Disruption and delays can result in increased costs and in some instances Contractors may be prevented from performing work altogether.

From a contractual perspective, this requires parties to carefully review the terms and conditions of construction contracts and the options available to them to address challenges as they arise. Accordingly, Employers and Contractors are taking a more cautious approach to drafting of contracts with a view to ensuring rights and obligations are clear and unambiguous, and that there is an equitable sharing/allocation of risk. Provisions that typically require greater focus include *force majeure*, extensions of time, rights to vary the work scope and rights of suspension and termination.

In the absence of specific express contractual rights, renegotiation will often be required to achieve acceptable outcomes, but this obviously necessitates commercial efficacy and cooperation.

Even where there is absence of agreement, activating dispute resolution mechanisms and resorting to litigation are only considered in worst-case scenarios as parties will generally prefer to avoid the time and cost implications of disputes, especially given the subdued economic conditions.

17.4 Papua New Guinea governing law of the contract

17.4.1 Constraints on the governing law of a construction contract

Contract law in PNG is based on English common-law principles similar to those of Australia and New Zealand and recognises the Parties' freedom of contract to choose the law of their governing jurisdiction.

17.4.2 Formal requirements for a construction contract

A construction contract in PNG must have the requisite elements that form a valid contract at common law: ie that the parties are legal persons who intend to be legally

21 See Measure No 2 International Travel Measures dated 4 August 2020, issued by the Controller under s 9 of the *National Pandemic Act 2020*.

22 National Research Institute, 'Impact of the Covid: 19 Pandemic on Papua New Guinea's International Trade' (2020) Volume 13 Issue 2.

bound by an agreement, supported by valuable (but not necessarily monetary) consideration, and the terms of the agreement must be certain.

There are no specific statutory requirements in PNG governing the execution of a construction contract between private parties. Therefore, the execution of construction contracts will be governed by the general law, which in PNG requires that:

- Where the document is expressed to be a deed, it must be executed under seal or
- Where the document is expressed to be an agreement, it must be executed by a person acting under the Company's express or implied authority.[23]

Execution and enforceability of construction contracts with public/government bodies is more complex given the statutory laws governing the management of public monies (see the commentary at paragraph 17.1.2 above). Contractors should seek legal advice if they have any questions regarding execution and/or enforceability of construction contracts where the counterparty is a public/government body.

Contractors should also note that PNG's foreign investment law, the *Investment Promotion Act 1992*, requires that a foreign enterprise (ie an enterprise that is more than 50 per cent owned, directly or indirectly, by a non–PNG citizen) be certified prior to commencing to carry on business in the country. The *Act* is administered by the PNG Investment Promotion Authority.[24]

'Carrying on business' is broadly defined and includes:

- Making an application to the government for any permit, licence, authority or lease for commercial purposes
- Administering, renting, managing, or otherwise dealing with property in the country and
- Certain construction activities.

Non-compliance amounts to a breach of the law and may expose the foreign enterprise to adverse regulatory action.

Also note the commentary at paragraph 17.1.2 regarding public procurement laws.

17.5 What Special Provisions in the Particular Conditions are necessary for consistency with applicable laws in Papua New Guinea?

17.5.1 FIDIC General Conditions are incompatible or inconsistent with Papua New Guinea governing law of the contract

No Special Provisions in the Particular Conditions are essential for consistency with mandatory PNG law.

17.5.2 FIDIC General Conditions are incompatible or inconsistent with the law of the Site/Country

No Special Provisions in the Particular Conditions are essential for consistency with the law of the Site/Country.

23 *Companies Act 1997*, s 155.
24 See www.ipa.gov.pg (accessed 14 July 2019).

17.5.3 FIDIC General Conditions are incompatible or inconsistent with relevant laws on dispute determination in Papua New Guinea

No Special Provisions in the Particular Conditions are essential for consistency with the laws of the seat of the arbitration or relevant laws on dispute determination.

17.6 What Special Provisions in the Particular Conditions are desirable for consistency with applicable laws in Papua New Guinea?

It is desirable that certain specific aspects of PNG law be provided for in Special Provisions in the Particular Conditions. The following sections highlight the main issues that should be considered to ensure that the Contract clarifies the Parties' roles and responsibilities and the agreed risk allocation. Special Provisions that cover these issues will ensure that the Contract assists those personnel with the responsibility to administer the Contract in understanding their legal obligations under the applicable PNG law.

17.6.1 Clause 1.6 [Contract agreement and stamp duty]

With respect to clause 1.6 of the FIDIC General Conditions, a construction contract, in itself, is unlikely to attract stamp duty (although it is possible that a related transaction could be dutiable, eg dealings in land).

Contractors should seek professional advice from a PNG tax advisor on stamp duty and other taxes (such as foreign contractor's withholding tax, customs duties, and goods and services tax). General information regarding stamp duty and taxes can be obtained from the PNG Internal Revenue Commission's website.[25]

17.6.2 Clause 4.15 [Access route]

The majority of land in PNG is held by its traditional owners under oral/unwritten customary principles of landownership. Though they may vary from place to place, principles of customary ownership generally recognise the personal and communal use of the land by its traditional owners. The identity of one or more traditional owners of customary land in connection with a development project can be problematic due to the fluid concepts of user rights and the general lack of recorded information concerning boundaries of customary land.

The balance of land in PNG is alienated land (ie land acquired by the state of PNG from its traditional owners), most of which is held as leasehold estates from the state under a Torrens-type system of land registration similar to that in many states in Australia.[26]

Land within or immediately surrounding PNG's cities and towns is typically alienated land, and land in rural areas is likely to be customary land.

The availability and utilisation of access routes are comparatively simple if the Site and route are situated on alienated land. This is more complex if the Site and route

25 See www.irc.gov.pg (accessed 14 July 2019).

26 See *Land Registration Act* (*Chapter 191*), which sets out a Torrens-type system of land title registration.

are on customary land as rights of access are dependent on arrangements with the traditional owners of the land.

For this reason, where the Site and access route(s) are on customary land, it might be preferable to amend clause 4.15 of the FIDIC General Conditions and/or include Special Provisions in the Particular Conditions to contractually assign the risk of the access route being unavailable (in whole or in part) due to disputes with or restrictions imposed by traditional owners of the customary land to the Employer or for the Parties to proportionately share that risk.

17.6.3 Clause 4.18 [Protection of the environment]

Under the *Environment Act 2000*, carrying on an activity (which includes construction of works, land clearance, demolition, and excavation and the installation and operation of plant and equipment) without an environment permit where one is required is an offence. Offenders may be liable on conviction to significant penalties.[27]

The types of activities that require an environment permit are set out in the *Environment (Prescribed Activities) Regulation 2000* and are referred to as Level 2 and Level 3 activities.[28] Examples include construction of new national roads, aerodromes, or airfields; electricity transmission lines and pipelines greater than 10 kilometres in length; and housing estates with an area of more than five hectares.

The Employer is usually better placed to determine if an environment permit is required by law with respect to the Permanent Works and should ensure that it obtains the environment permit prior to commencement of Works. A Contractor might therefore consider amending clause 4.18 of the FIDIC General Conditions to oblige the Employer to obtain all such permits and approvals and to indemnify the Contractor against the consequences for failing to do so.

17.6.4 Insurance

PNG's insurance industry is regulated by the *Insurance Act 1995*. The *Act* requires that all risks situated in PNG for which insurance or reinsurance is required shall be insured with a local licenced insurer unless an exemption is obtained from the Insurance Commissioner to insure risks offshore.[29]

Exemptions are available only in limited circumstances where the facilities and available capacity of local licenced insurers are fully utilised.[30]

Further, it is compulsory for all workers' compensation insurance to be placed with a local licenced insurer in accordance with the *Workers Compensation Act (Chapter 179)* – failure to do so is an offence.[31]

17.6.5 Foreign exchange control

Regulatory power with respect to foreign exchange control is vested in the Bank of Papua New Guinea (**Central Bank**) under the *Central Banking Act 2000*.

27 *Environment Act 2000*, ss 41–44.
28 *Environment (Prescribed Activities) Regulation 2002*, ss 3 and 4.
29 *Insurance Act 1995*, s 36.
30 ibid s 37.
31 *Workers Compensation Act (Chapter 179)*, s 89.

The Central Bank has broad power to grant exemptions under the *Central Banking Act* and regulations, which may be conditional. In the exercise of this power, the Central Bank promulgated a broad, general, but conditional exemption in 2007 (the **General Exemption**).

A key condition to the General Exemption is a requirement to comply with the Foreign Exchange Manual (**Forex Manual**) published by the Central Bank, the most recent version of which was issued in March 2015.[32] The Forex Manual is subject to change from time to time.

The Central Bank may appoint authorised dealers in foreign exchange (**Authorised Dealers**) and may regulate their powers, rights, and duties – these include the four main commercial banks in PNG. The Central Bank may also impose restrictions and conditions on Authorised Dealers.[33]

Authorised Dealers must themselves comply with the Forex Manual, which restricts them from involvement in foreign exchange transactions by others that would be a breach by those persons of the Forex Manual. Accordingly, Authorised Dealers in a practical sense effectively administer the Forex Manual.

Note also that under the General Exemption, Central Bank approval is required where a person, being a resident (this includes companies and other bodies corporate):

- Opens and operates a foreign currency account outside PNG or
- Enters into a guarantee or grants security over assets in PNG in favour of a non-resident (or enters into a transaction having a similar effect) where such guarantee or security is part of a transaction which is not for the direct benefit of a person or business in PNG.[34]

Further, the Forex Manual:

- Imposes restrictions on the opening of onshore foreign currency accounts by Authorised Dealers and
- Stipulates that the authority of the Central Bank is required for a resident to enter into an agreement which creates an obligation in favour of another resident in a foreign currency. Obligations under such agreements must be settled in PNG Kina.[35]

17.6.6 Tax clearance for remittance of funds offshore

The *Central Banking Act 2000* and the *Income Tax Act 1959* form the legal basis for taxation surveillance in PNG. Under these laws, the government has prescribed, by notice in the *National Gazette*, certain transactions that require an original tax clearance certificate from the PNG Internal Revenue Commission before an Authorised Dealer may remit funds offshore from PNG. These include the transfer of capital funds; payment of dividends, royalties and management fees; and the repayment of loans.[36]

32 A copy of the Foreign Exchange Manual may be obtained from the Bank of PNG's website: www.bankpng.gov.pg/monetary-policy/exchange-control (accessed 14 July 2019).
33 Foreign Exchange Manual, FE Notice 1.
34 ibid FE Notice 22.
35 ibid FE Notices 11 and 23.
36 ibid FE Notice 19.

Separately, clearance is required from the PNG Internal Revenue Commission for the remittance of monies to certain jurisdictions, namely:

- Any amount, if it is to be paid to the Bahamas, Bermuda, British Channel Islands, British Virgin Islands, Gibraltar, Grenada, Hong Kong, the Isle of Man, Liberia, Liechtenstein, Luxembourg, Nauru, the Netherlands Antilles, Norfolk Island, Panama, Switzerland, Tonga or Vanuatu.
- For amounts exceeding PGK500,000 (US$140,000) annually, all jurisdictions other than those mentioned above.[37]

17.6.7 Occupational, health and safety

In 1992, the national legislature passed the *Occupational Health, Safety and Welfare Act 1992*. The *Act* is intended to govern standards for occupational health, safety, and welfare and to establish the Occupational Health and Safety Council but, since its passage, has not been promulgated to commence operation. PNG therefore does not have a specific statutory regime governing workplace health and safety.

Consequently, the English common-law rules that impose a general duty of care on an employer to provide employees with a safe system of work apply in PNG.[38] This includes taking reasonable steps to ensure or protect the safety of an employee from unnecessary risk of injury.

Note that another law that is relevant to workplace health and safety is the *Industrial Health, Safety and Welfare Act* (*Chapter 175*). The statute, however, is generally limited to factories in the scope of its application.[39]

17.6.8 Arbitration Act

In PNG, the subsisting legislation is the *Arbitration Act* (*Chapter 46*), a statute which predates PNG's independence and was adopted by virtue of Schedule 2.6 of the *Constitution*. In this regard, it is somewhat archaic in contrast to other legislative regimes elsewhere pertaining to arbitration that have adopted the UNCITRAL rules on arbitration.

At the time of writing, a review of the *Arbitration Act* by the national government is in progress with the stated intention of adopting the UNCITRAL rules (bringing PNG in line with most global arbitration regimes).

Until such time as the proposed reforms to the *Arbitration Act* have been introduced, the existing scheme under the *Act* refers to 'submissions', which are defined as written agreements to submit present or future differences to arbitration, whether or not an arbitrator is named in the submission.

37 *Income Tax* (*2018 Budget*) (*Amendment*) *Regulation 2017*.

38 *Esther Kuri v Trans Niugini Airways Ltd* (2006) N3084; cited in *Karawari Lodge Pty Ltd v Bernard Luck* (1998) SC553.

39 A 'factory' is defined to mean a building or place:

- in which employees are engaged directly or indirectly in a manufacturing process or in the generation of power (other than for private domestic purposes of the owner); or
- declared by the Minister by notice in the National Gazette to be a factory for purposes of the Act.

Generally, a submission is irrevocable, except by leave of the court, and has the same effect in all respects as if it had been made an order of the court.

There are instances where parties may opt to enter into litigation for breach of contract regardless of the contract in question requiring arbitration in the event of a dispute arising. The National Court held in *Mauga Logging Co Pty Ltd (Receiver/ Manager Appointed) v Okura Trading Co Ltd*[40] that the court has inherent discretionary power to stay a court action commenced in breach of a requirement to arbitrate (to see that parties abide by their contractual obligations).

Section 4 of the *Arbitration Act* allows a party against whom legal proceedings are commenced in relation to a contract to apply to the court for a stay of proceedings if the contract provides that present or future differences are to be submitted for arbitration.

Importantly, the court has also held that a stay of proceedings is not automatic, and the court has a discretion to exercise. There are a number of considerations the court may take into account when deciding whether to grant a stay. Some are set out in section 4 of the *Act* while others have been established by the courts.

The case of *Niugini Civil & Petroleum Ltd v West New Britain Development Corporation Ltd*[41] lists eight requirements, including (relevantly):

- Each arbitration clause must be interpreted on its merits to glean the intention of the parties to the contract.
- If an arbitration clause makes arbitration necessary, an application for a stay of proceedings can still be refused if it is not made promptly.
- It is reasonable to presume that if a party commences court proceedings notwithstanding the existence of an arbitration clause and the other parties do not object to that course of action within a reasonable time, that they acquiesce to the court proceedings.

The arbitration clause in each contract was interpreted and applied in light of those principles, the court in each case concluding that a stay of proceedings was not warranted and that the dispute would not be referred to arbitration.

Arbitration awards may be enforced in the same manner as a judgment or court order to the same effect.

In addition to arbitration, it is open to parties to agree to other alternate methods of dispute resolution under the contract – these may include mediation or determination by an expert, panel, or other independent third party. Generally, such alternate dispute resolution clauses are enforceable. Further, the principle of law (discussed above) that allows a party to compel the other party to adhere to an arbitration clause is also applicable and extends to other alternate dispute resolution mechanisms such as those mentioned.

40 [1978] PG Law Rp 538, [1978] PNGLR 259.

41 [2005] PGNC 64 N2909.

17.7 Summary of applicable legislation for Papua New Guinea governing law of the contract

17.7.1 Entry into a construction contract

Construction contracts	*Companies Act 1997* *Public Finances (Management) Act 1995*

17.7.2 Termination of a construction contract

Bankruptcy, insolvency, liquidation	*Companies Act 1997*

17.7.3 Dispute resolution

Limitation periods	*Frauds and Limitations Act 1988* *Claims By and Against the State Act 1996*
Liability	*Wrongs (Miscellaneous Provisions) Act (Chapter 179)*
Arbitration	*Arbitration Act (Chapter 46)*

17.8 Summary of applicable legislation if the Site/Country is in Papua New Guinea

17.8.1 Operation of a construction contract

Registration and administration of professionals – Engineers and Architects	*Professional Engineers (Registration) Act 1986* *Architects (Registration) Act 1989* *Survey Act 1969*
Registration/licensing of Contractors and Subcontractors	No applicable licensing regime
Labour	*Employment Act (Chapter 373)* *Employment of Non-citizens Act 2007* *Industrial Organizations Act (Chapter 173)* *Industrial Relations Act (Chapter 174)* *Migration Act (Chapter 16)*
Copyright	*Copyright and Neighbouring Rights Act 2000* *Patents and Industrial Designs Act 2000* *Trade Marks Act 1978*
Planning	*Physical Planning Act 1989*
Environment	*Environment Act 2000*
Local Procurement	*Public Finances (Management) Act 1995*
Building and construction work	*Building Act (Chapter 301)*
Standard of construction work	*National Institute of Standards and Industrial Technology Act 2009*
Health and Safety	*Industrial Safety, Health and Welfare Act (Chapter 175)* As noted in paragraph 17.5.7 above, the scope of this *Act* is generally limited to factories.
Ownership of Plant and Materials	*Personal Property Security Act 2011*

Employer's sale of Contractor's Equipment, surplus material, wreckage and Temporary Works	*Personal Property Security Act 2011*
Insurance	*Insurance Act 1995* *Worker's Compensation Act (Chapter 179)* *Motor Vehicles (Third Party) Insurance Act (Chapter 295)*
Statutory rights that coexist with contractual rights	*Fairness of Transaction Act 1993* *Goods Act (Chapter 251)*
Liability for defective work	*Wrongs (Miscellaneous Provisions) Act (Chapter 179)*

17.8.2 Termination of a construction contract

Bankruptcy, insolvency, liquidation	*Companies Act 1997*
Decennial liability and liability generally for the total or partial collapse of structures	No applicable licensing regime

17.8.3 Dispute resolution

Limitation periods	*Frauds and Limitations Act 1988* *Claims By and Against the State Act 1996*

17.9 Summary of applicable legislation if the 'seat' of the dispute determination is in Papua New Guinea

Limitation periods	*Frauds and Limitations Act 1988* *Claims By and Against the State Act 1996*
Arbitration	*Arbitration Act (Chapter 46)*

17.10 Issues that a court or arbitrator may construe differently to that expected from the words of the Contract because of local law or custom

17.10.1 Fairness of Transactions Act 1993

The *Fairness of Transactions Act 1993* is an Act:

> [r]elating to the effect of certain transactions, to ensure that they operate fairly without causing undue harm to, or imposing too great a burden on, any person, and in such a way that no person suffers unduly because he is economically weaker than, or is otherwise disadvantaged in relation to, another person.

A 'transaction' is defined under the *Act* as being:

> any contract, promise, agreement, dealing or undertaking of an economic or commercial nature whether supported by consideration or not entered into between parties.

The *Act* goes further to raise four exceptions to the definition of transaction, one of which may be relevant in the context of construction contracts. The definition excludes:

> [a] transaction between a government body and a non-citizen or a foreign State or between a government body and a foreign enterprise within the meaning of the *Investment Promotion Act 1992*, so far as it does not involve a PNG person, company or joint-venture.

Where the *Act* applies, the National Court is able to review a transaction, on application by a party, if it is satisfied that the transaction was not genuinely mutual or was manifestly unfair to a party. The *Act* imposes a burden of proof on the party alleging the unfairness of a transaction.

The *Act* is peculiar in that it imposes a mandatory duty on the court to refer parties to mediation where it is satisfied that a transaction was manifestly unfair or not genuinely mutual. If mediation fails, the court may proceed to issue such orders as it thinks conform with the purpose of the *Act*.

Whilst it is not common that an argument under the *Fairness of Transactions Act* will be raised before a court or arbitrator, it is important to be aware of the potential issue. The Supreme Court has also held that it does not accept that there is a general defence of 'unfairness' to a claim in contract in PNG.[42]

17.10.2 Proportionate liability

PNG does not have a specific statutory regime relating to proportionate liability. What presently subsists is the *Wrongs (Miscellaneous Provisions) Act* (*Chapter 179*), which provides that a party liable for damages may recover contribution from any other party who is, or if sued would have been, liable in respect to the same damage. Contribution can also be sought against a third party.

In contrast with certain other common law jurisdictions such as Australia, where State-based proportionate liability legislation allows the court to apportion liability in 'building actions', the *Wrongs (Miscellaneous Provisions) Act* places the onus on the liable party to seek apportionment. In practical terms, this may be done through the joining of additional parties in court actions or subrogated claims in the case of insurers.

In scenarios where the *Wrongs (Miscellaneous Provisions) Act* is silent, the rules of common law and equity in England, as adopted under Schedule 2 of the *Constitution*, will apply insofar as these rules are:

- Not inconsistent with Constitutional law or statute.
- Not inapplicable or inappropriate to the circumstances of the country from time to time.
- Not inconsistent with custom.

17.10.3 Claims against the state

A statute peculiar to PNG is the *Claims By and Against the State Act 1996*. Its relevance insofar as claims pertaining to contracts with the state is the time limitation imposed on parties intending to sue the state for breach of contract.

The *Act* imposes a mandatory requirement of notice of intention to sue the state within six months after the claimant became aware of the alleged breach, if the claim is one for breach of contract.

The Supreme Court has held that the proper and valid service of notice under section 5 of the *Claims By and Against the State Act 1996* is a condition precedent to competency of any civil suit against the state.

---

42 *Bank of South Pacific Limited v Robert Tingke* (2012) SC1355 and SCA 141 of 2012; *Bank of South Pacific Limited v Casper CS Apundamatiet* (2014) SC1355 (Salika DCJ), (Manuhu, Collier JJ).

17.10.4 Statutory time bar

In contracts between parties where the state is not involved, there exists a statutory time bar on claims based on contract.

The *Frauds and Limitations Act 1988* provides in section 16(1)(a) that:

> [a]n action that is founded on simple contract . . . shall not be brought after the expiration of six years commencing on the date on which the cause of action accrued.

A simple contract is distinct from a contract that is considered a 'specialty' under the *Act*, which prescribes a time limit of 12 years to bring an action for a specialty contract.

The National Court held in *Bank of South Pacific v Leahy*[43] that a guarantee was a specialty because of its nature and form, it being in the form of a deed. The Supreme Court upheld the view that any contract in the form of a deed is a specialty.

A construction contract is generally executed as a simple contract and would be subject to the 6-year time limitation under the *Act*. Parties may consider executing a construction contract as a deed, which arguably could be considered by a court to be a specialty contract and therefore attract the longer 12-year time-limitation period for claims. (However, the PNG courts have not specifically considered this point – note that the Supreme Court judgement mentioned above concerned a guarantee as opposed to a construction or other contract.) Any claim for breach of contract made outside of time would be statute-barred and unenforceable.

In instances where the time of the cause of action occurring is in issue, the Supreme Court has held that in determining whether an action involving an alleged breach of contractual obligations is time-barred under sections 16(1) or 16(3) of the *Frauds and Limitations Act*, it necessarily involves a finding on three matters:

- What is the 'cause of action'?
- What is 'the date on which the cause of action accrued'?
- Is the action 'founded on a simple contract' (in which case the 6-year limitation period in section 16(1) will apply), or is it 'an action upon a specialty' (in which case section 16(3) applies, and the limitation period is 12 years)?

17.10.5 Extension of time

Local PNG jurisprudence has yet to develop a body of authority that deals specifically with the peculiar aspect of extensions of time in construction contracts. The courts have, however, established principles relating to the variation of terms of contracts.

In *Thiess Watkins (PNG) Ltd v Papua New Guinea Electricity Commission,*[44] Hinchliffe J held that:

- In the absence of express agreement to the contrary, time limitations in contracts should be strictly complied with.
- A party to a contract will not be estopped from relying on strict compliance with time limitations in that contract unless there is evidence:

43 [2002] N2263.
44 [1989] PGNC 111; [1988-89] PNGLR 454; N768.

- of a clear and unambiguous representation, either express or implied, that the time limits will be extended or waived: failure to make any statement in relation thereto will not suffice and
- that the party seeking to rely upon the estoppel has placed himself in a position of material disadvantage as a result of reliance upon the representation.

Further, in *Nivani Ltd v China Jiangsu International (PNG) Ltd*, [45] the National Court held that:

- Parties may, by agreement, vary a contract made by them.
- Where a contract makes no provision for variation, there must be a contract of variation to bind the parties.
- A contract of variation can be formed by the conduct of the parties.
- A Contractor is entitled to perform all of the works contained in his contract but is not entitled to perform any new and additional works which the Employer may decide upon, except by agreement.
- All of the facts necessary to establish a claim for damages must be proven.
- A claim for loss of profit or overheads must include proof of the actual percentage of profit or overhead applicable to the Contractor as a percentage of gross turnover.

In this particular case:

- The facts established that the lump-sum contract was amended by the conduct of the parties to be a contract to be paid by rates against measured work.
- The contract included work which had not been completed when the works were suspended, and subsequently, the contract was terminated by the defendant. Consequently, the defendant repudiated the contract.
- The claim for work done but not paid for was not proven. The other heads of damage were only partially proven.
- The court can make an award of damages where the evidence establishes that a loss has been sustained but the evidence is inadequate to calculate a specific figure.

It is an aspect of contract law that requires judicial consideration and development in PNG, but, generally, the common-law position (as adopted by the *Constitution*) will be applied in the absence of local authorities or subsequent PNG legislation on point.

17.10.6 The prevention principle

Related to the issue of extension of time is that of the 'prevention principle'.

The prevention principle, derived from the maxim 'no person can take advantage of his or her own wrong' is not an aspect of law that has been considered by courts in PNG. Although there is authority that contracts can be varied by consent of the parties, as in the case of an extension of time, the prevention principle has been applied

45 [2007] PGNC 46, N3147.

by courts where the right to an extension of time exists. With this context in mind, it is reasonable to anticipate that the prevention principle may be considered in the context of delays in completion of work, variations of contracts, and damages. However, there is not yet any authority expressly confirming that the prevention principle would be applied.

The prevention principle is illustrated in the case of *Peak Construction (Liverpool) Ltd v McKinney Foundations Ltd*.[46] The court rejected an apportionment of damages between Employer and Contractor in that case, finding that it was not open for the Employer to seek an apportionment when it was the cause of delay.

Generally, the principles in *Peak Construction (Liverpool) Ltd v McKinney Foundations Ltd* would be applied in PNG given that they form a part of the adopted common law by virtue of the *Constitution*. This contention is also supported by the fact that courts in England and Australia have upheld the prevention principle as well.

However, there are opposing views in the courts of some common-law jurisdictions that state that damages should be apportioned, and the prevention principle is not sound law – while those judgements are not binding in PNG, they nevertheless have persuasive value. Until such time that PNG courts have decided the issue, it would be premature to state that the 'prevention principle' will definitely be applied in PNG.

17.10.7 Delay damages and liquidated damages

The issue of Delay Damages or prolongation costs and liquidated damages is another area of law that has received little or no judicial consideration in PNG. However, there is still well-established authority with respect to damages and their assessment generally.

The law as established in PNG with regard to damages is that where a plaintiff claims damages, the onus is on the plaintiff to prove the loss. This principle was discussed and applied in *Nivani Ltd v China Jiangsu International (PNG) Ltd*, [47] where the court held that, though the defendant was liable in damages to the plaintiff, the plaintiff had to prove its losses as claimed. This case involved a claim for damages for delay caused by the Employer's alterations to drawings and, ultimately, the scope of the contract.

Considering the overarching principles of the proof and assessment of damages, a claim by a Contractor for Delay Damages will be considered by the PNG courts. If a Contract allows for Delay Damages, whether for critical or non-critical delays or both, the courts will consider and assess the claim. Similarly, a claim for liquidated damages by an Employer will also be considered by the courts in the same manner.

The Supreme Court[48] has considered the distinction between a penalty and liquidated damages and cited common-law authority in *Law v Redditch Local Board*, [49] in that a penalty may be distinguished from a genuine pre-estimate of damages for breach of contract in the following manner:

> If the intention is to secure performance of the contract by the imposition of a fine or penalty, then the sum specified is a penalty; but if, on the other hand, the intention is to assess the damages for breach of the contract, it is liquidated damages.

---

46 (1970) 69 LGR 1.

47 [2007] PGNC 46, N3147.

48 *Breckwoldt & Co (NG) Pty Ltd v Gnoyke (No 2)* [1975] PNGLR 195.

49 [1892] 1 QB 127, 132 (Lopes J).

In drawing a distinction between a penalty and damages, the Supreme Court has further held that it can make inquiry into whether clauses in contracts provide for penalties or genuine pre-estimates of damage.[50]

Generally, PNG courts recognise the common-law doctrine of penalties and will not enforce a clause of a contract if it is found to be a penalty as opposed to a clause providing for a genuine assessment of damages.[51] Unlike commonwealth jurisdictions elsewhere, the body of case authority in PNG that considers the specific issue of penalty clauses and liquidated damages in construction contracts and the distinction between the two is scant. To this end, whilst case authorities on the point from jurisdictions such as Australia are not binding on PNG courts, they can nonetheless be relied on to provide persuasive value in disputes, which, in turn, over time will develop local jurisprudence on the subject.[52]

17.11 Additional references

17.11.1 Books

Port Moresby Chamber of Commerce and Industry, *The PNG Investor's Manual* (3rd edn, BusinessAdvantage 2013).

17.11.2 Case law

Bank of South Pacific v Leahy [2002] N2263.
Mauga Logging Co Pty Ltd (Receiver/Manager Appointed) v Okura Trading Co Ltd [1978] PG Law Rp 538, [1978] PNGLR 259.
Nivani Ltd v China Jiangsu International (PNG) Ltd [2007] PGNC 46, N3147.
Peak Construction (Liverpool) Ltd v McKinney Foundations Ltd [1970] 69 LGR 1.
Thiess Watkins (PNG) Ltd v Papua New Guinea Electricity Commission [1989] PGNC 111, [1988–1989] PNGLR 454, N768.

17.11.3 Internet

Internal Revenue Commission: www.irc.gov.pg (accessed 14 July 2019).
Investment Promotion Authority: www.ipa.gov.pg (accessed 14 July 2019).
PNG case law and legislation: www.paclii.org (accessed 14 July 2019).

50 *Post PNG Ltd v Yama Security Services* (2000) (unreported and unnumbered judgment of 26 July 2001; SCA 80 of 2000).
51 ibid.
52 *Law v Redditch Local Board* [1892] 1 QB 127, 132.

CHAPTER 18

Applying FIDIC contracts in the Philippines

Salvador P. Castro, Jr.[1]

1 The author acknowledges and thanks the members of his research team for their assistance: Mary Sheryl Grace A Realce, Gilleanne Chayne Q Ladan, Esmeralda C Fernandez, Roger G Antonio and Ma Nora Zenaida C Roxas.

DOI: 10.4324/9781003200901-18

18.1 Outline of the legal environment in the Philippines

18.1.1 The constitutional structure of the Philippines

The Philippines is a democratic and republican state with a presidential form of government, wherein power is equally divided among its three independent branches: executive, legislative and judicial.[2]

The fundamental law of the Philippines is in a written *Constitution*. The Philippines has had a total of six constitutions since the Proclamation of Independence on 12 June 1898, namely the *1899 Malolos Constitution* (1899–1901), the *1935 Constitution* (1935–1943, 1945–1973), the *1943 Constitution* (1943–1945), the *1973 Constitution* (1973–1986), the *1986 Provisional 'Freedom' Constitution* and the *1987 Constitution* (1987–present). The *Malolos Constitution*, the first Philippines Constitution – the first republican constitution in Asia – was drafted and adopted by the First Philippine Republic.[3]

Since the 1986 EDSA People Power Revolution, the *1987 Philippine Constitution* is the supreme law of the land. It is composed of a Preamble and 18 articles.[4] One of the important features of this *1987 Constitution* is the specific powers assigned to each

2 *Philippine Constitution 1987*.

3 https://www.officialgazette.gov.ph/constitutions/constitution-day/ (accessed 6 June 2020).

4 Article I – National Territory, Article II – Declaration of Principles and State Policies, Article III – Bill of Rights, Article IV – Citizenship, Article V – Suffrage, Article VI – Legislative Department, Article VII – Executive Department, Article VIII – Judicial Department, Article IX – Constitutional Commissions, Article X – Local Government, Article XI – Accountability of Public Officers, Article XII – National Economy and Patrimony, Article XIII – Social Justice and Human Rights, Article XIV – Education, Science and Technology, Arts, Culture and Sports, Article XV – The Family, Article XVI – General Provisions, Article XVII – Amendments or Revisions, and Article XVIII – Transitory Provisions.

branch that make up the system of checks and balances in the government and create the separation of powers between the three branches. The executive branch implements the laws. The legislature enacts the laws. The judiciary interprets the meaning of the laws.

Executive power is vested in the President. The President is the head of state and of the government within a pluriform multi-party system, and functions as the Commander-in-Chief of the Armed Forces of the Philippines (**AFP**).[5]

Legislative power is vested in Congress, except to the extent reserved to the people by the provision of initiatives and referenda. Congress is a bicameral body consisting of the Senate (upper chamber) and the House of Representatives (lower chamber).[6]

Judicial power is vested in one Supreme Court and in such lower courts as may be established by law.[7]

18.1.2 The legal system of the Philippines

The Philippine legal system is a mixture of customary usage, Roman (civil law), Anglo-American (common law) systems and Islamic law.

Civil law operates in areas such as family relations, property, succession, contract and criminal law, while statutes and principles of common law origin are evident in such areas as constitutional law, procedure, corporations law, negotiable instruments, taxation, insurance, labour relations, banking and currency.[8]

There are two main sources of these laws: statutes and jurisprudence.[9] Statutes or statutory law are defined as the written enactments by the legislative branch of the government. They consist of the *1987 Constitution* and legislative enactments such as treaties, statutes proper or legislative enactments, municipal charters and municipal legislation,. whereas jurisprudence or case law are those judicial decisions of the Supreme Court used in applying or interpreting the laws or the *Constitution*.

The laws governing the construction industry can be found in both civil law and common law.

18.1.3 The court system of the Philippines

The judicial branch is composed of one Supreme Court and other lower courts established by law, ie the Court of Appeals and the Sandiganbayan; Second Level Courts or the Regional Trial Courts (**RTC**); and the First Level Courts consisting of the Metropolitan Trial Courts (**MeTC**), Municipal Trial Court (**MTC**), Municipal Trial Courts in Cities (**MTCC**) and the Municipal Circuit Trial Courts (**MCTC**). The Supreme Court, the highest court of the land, consists of one Chief Justice and 14 Associate Justices.

Article VIII of the *1987 Constitution* provides:

> Judicial power includes the duty of the courts of justice to settle actual controversies involving rights which are legally demandable and enforceable, and to determine whether or not there has been a grave abuse of discretion amounting to lack or excess of jurisdiction on the part of any branch or instrumentality of the Government.

5 ibid.
6 ibid.
7 ibid.
8 https://unimelb.libguides.com/c.php?g=402982&p=5443355 (accessed 25 June 2020).
9 https://www.nyulawglobal.org/globalex/Philippines1.html#_Legal_System (accessed 6 June 2020).

Hence, the judge determines all questions of law and fact in a case brought before him or her. In doing so, the *Rules of Court* govern the pleadings, practice and procedure before all courts. These rules consist of four major parts dealing with civil actions, criminal actions, special civil actions and evidence.

On 1 May 2020, the Supreme Court approved the proposed amendments to the *Rules on Evidence*[10] and *Rules of Civil Procedure*[11] for the purpose of speeding up the disposition of cases and decongestion of court dockets.

Any action or suit arising from a construction contract is considered as a civil action which is governed by the *Rules of Civil Procedure* and falls under the original jurisdiction of either the RTC or the First Level Courts, depending on the value of the claim. Any decision rendered by the lower courts is appealable before the higher court, provided that the parties' litigants are required to observe the hierarchy of courts in filing appeals. However, in cases where pure questions of law are raised, the final order or resolution of a lower court may only be appealed through Petition for Review on Certiorari to the Supreme Court under Rule 45 of *Rules of Civil Procedure*.

As early as 1953, arbitration of civil actions was recognised in the Philippines through the *Arbitration Law (Republic Act No 876)*. In 2004, Congress enacted the *Alternative Dispute Resolution Act* (***ADR Law***) which institutionalised the use of an alternative dispute resolution system – arbitration, mediation and conciliation as alternative modes.

The use of mediation in trial courts, both as a mode of settling disputes and as a means to reduce court dockets, is also recognised by the Supreme Court through the *Implementing Rules and Regulations Governing Mediation in Trial Courts*, commonly known as Court-Annexed Mediation (**CAM**).[12] In CAM, the trial judge refers the parties and their counsel to the Philippine Mediation Center (**PMC**) for mediation, and if it fails, refers the case to the Branch Clerk of Court to assist the parties in reaching a settlement and to mark the documents or exhibits to be presented. The trial judge should exert all efforts to arrive at a settlement of the dispute or, if it fails, adopt measures to facilitate the disposition of the case.

18.2 The construction industry in the Philippines

18.2.1 Overview

The construction industry has the distinct advantage of being the fastest growing industry in the country for the last six years, having the second highest multiplier impact to the economy (next to manufacturing), and being a top contributor to gross value added.

The industry has the second highest output multiplier of 2.2, which means that a PHP1 investment in construction will, in return, generate a total of PHP2.2 to the national economy inclusive of all direct and indirect effects.

The Build Build Build (**BBB**) Infrastructure Program (2016–2022), the centrepiece program of President Duterte's administration, aims to usher in the 'golden age of infrastructure' in the Philippines. Lack of infrastructure has long been cited as the

10 http://sc.judiciary.gov.ph/9282/ (accessed 8 September 2020).
11 ibid.
12 Supreme Court Resolution AM No 04-3-15-SC-PHILJA (23 March 2004).

'Achilles' heel' of Philippine economic development. The BBB Program seeks to accelerate public infrastructure expenditure from an average of 2.9 per cent of gross domestic product (GDP) during the previous administration to about 7.3 per cent at the end of the Duterte administration.'[13]

In the early months of 2019, the Philippine construction industry had been projected to grow 10.9 per cent that year because of the establishment of much-needed transport infrastructure, such as the Metro Manila Subway project which was already underway. According to a Fitch Solutions report, foreign direct investments were also growing. The report highlighted how the sector would be boosted by progress made on Phase 1 of the US$75 billion Metro Manila Subway project, a 25 km-long fully underground subway system that will run from Quezon City's Mindanao Avenue to Manila International Airport. The system will link key districts within Metro Manila to alleviate traffic congestion once it is completed in 2025. This was considered as the largest project of President Rodrigo Duterte's BBB Infrastructure Program. The project was partially financed by a US$985 million loan disbursed by Japan International Cooperation Agency.[14]

The report also pointed out how the country has 64 transportation projects in the pre-construction phase, which accounts for more than 75 per cent of the total value of construction projects in the pipeline. These projects include the US$14 billion new Manila International Airport, which will add an estimated capacity of 100 million passengers annually and complement the operations of the Ninoy Aquino International Airport. A memorandum of understanding was signed between the Incheon International Airport Corporation and San Miguel Corporation for the development and operation of the new airport. Other projects include the Makati City Subway project valued at US$3.7 billion for Metro Manila's financial district, whilst the estimated US$1 billion Metro Cebu Expressway project, which started minor engineering works in 2018, aims to connect Naga City to Danao City in the Visayas region. Furthermore, Fitch Solutions also noted the administration's efforts to ease ownership restrictions for foreign contractors in selected construction projects from 25 per cent to 40 per cent as the government aims to enhance the country's competitiveness.[15]

In real terms, the Philippine construction industry expanded by 9.4 per cent in 2019. Growth during the period 2015–2019 was driven by the continuous spending on large-scale transportation and energy projects under the BBB Infrastructure Program. Although the overall spending on infrastructure remained strong in 2019, a delay in approval of the 2019 budget and the 45-day ban on public works – due to the prohibition of disbursement of public funds and materials – had an impact on the country's investment on infrastructure in the first half of the year.[16]

In March 2019, the government launched the Philippine Construction Industry Roadmap 2020–2030, with an aim to increase the construction industry's contribution to the Philippine economy from PHP2.3 trillion (US$44.1 billion) in 2018 to

13 https://cpbrd.congress.gov.ph/2012-06-30-13-06-51/2012-06-30-13-36-50/982-ff2019-07-build-build-build-bbb-program.

14 https://hongkongbusiness.hk/transport-logistics/asia/philippines-construction-sector-grow-109-in-2019 (accessed 8 July 2020).

15 ibid.

16 https://www.giiresearch.com/report/time237680-construction-philippines-key-trends-opportunities.html (accessed 9 July 2020).

PHP130 trillion (US$2.5 trillion) by 2030. Furthermore, it will also increase the job opportunities for construction from four million in 2018 to seven million by 2030.[17]

Prior to the Covid-19 pandemic, the Philippines had a very strong economy and fast- growing construction industry according to a study conducted by the Philippine Economy and Construction Industry submitted in July 2020. The World Bank likewise projected the Philippine economy to grow 6.0 per cent in 2020 and 2021.[18] Unfortunately, the impact of the Covid-19 crisis did not spare the Philippine economy. In the Asian Development Bank annual flagship economic publication, it projects the Philippines' gross domestic product (GDP) to grow at 2.0 per cent in 2020 following the 'enhanced community quarantine' imposed by the government in March to combat the spread of Covid-19. But ADB expects a strong recovery in 2021, assuming that Covid-19 infections in the country are controlled by June 2020.[19]

In order to save the economy from collapsing, the Philippine government came up with a recovery program comprising of three big areas: The *Bayanihan to Recover as One Act* (discussed below), the ambitious BBB Infrastructure Program and the 2021 budget.[20] As noted above, the economic recovery also rests on sustaining President Duterte's signature program 'Build, Build, Build' as sound infrastructure investments provide the largest multiplier effect on the economy in the form of more jobs, increased consumption, and generation of additional productive activities.[21]

The Presidential Adviser for Flagship Programs has advised that despite the pandemic, the government is pursuing flagship infrastructure projects and vows to bolster the Build, Build, Build program and generate local employment.[22]

During the virtual unveiling of a completed tunnel boring machine (TBM) in Japan, the DOTr Secretary noted that there will be delays in implementing the Metro Manila subway project because of the pandemic, but there are no plans of stopping or suspending the project. The project is expected to be completed by 2024 or 2025.[23]

There are currently 92 projects under the Build Build Build program amounting to PHP4.1 trillion (US$78.7 billion).[24]

18.2.2 Licensing of contractors

The Philippine Contractors Accreditation Board (**PCAB**)[25] is a statutory licensing and regulatory body charged with licensing and regulating contractors in the Philippines. The PCAB is an implementing agency of the Department of Trade and Industry (**DTI**).

For the purpose of engaging in construction contracts, contractors must be duly accredited and licensed by the PCAB of the Construction Industry Authority of

---

17 ibid.

18 https://www.worldbank.org/en/country/philippines/publication/philippine-economic-updates (accessed 1 September 2020).

19 https://www.adb.org/news/philippine-gdp-growth-slide-2020-due-covid-19-strong-rebound-seen-2021-adb.

20 https://www.pna.gov.ph/articles/1113381 (25 August 2020).

21 https://www.pna.gov.ph/articles/1114542 (6 September 2020).

22 https://www.pna.gov.ph/articles/1114288 (3 September 2020).

23 https://www.pna.gov.ph/articles/1114458 (4 September 2020).

24 https://www.pna.gov.ph/articles/1114288 (3 September 2020).

25 The PCAB was formed by virtue of *Republic Act No 4566* passed by Congress in 1965. It was originally called the Philippine Contractors License Board and fell under the Office of the Board of Examiners (now Professional Regulation Commission (PRC).

the Philippines (**CIAP**).[26] The PCAB issues the following two types of Contractor's licence:[27]

1. Regular Licence, which is issued to a domestic construction firm and authorises the licensee to engage in construction contracting within the field and scope of its licence classification(s) for as long as the licence validity is maintained through annual renewal; unless renewal of the licence is denied, suspended, cancelled or revoked for cause(s).
2. Special Licence, which is issued to a joint venture, consortium, foreign contractor, or project owner and authorises the licensee to engage only in the construction of a single, specific project/undertaking.

   (a) Consortium – a cooperative arrangement between licensed constructor(s) and non-constructor(s) to jointly perform a single specific undertaking/project with the licensed constructor(s) as managing and operating partner(s) and others as financier(s) or any such other construction supportive role.[28]
   (b) Joint Venture – a cooperative arrangement between licensed construction contractors (all Filipinos, all non-Filipinos, or a combination of Filipinos and non-Filipinos) to perform jointly a single specific undertaking/project with each of the partners contributing to the performance.[29]
   (c) New Special License of a Foreign Contractor Application.[30]

It is considered an offence to engage in a contracting business without first obtaining a licence.[31] The objective of this regulation is primarily to ensure public safety, that only qualified and reliable contractors are allowed to undertake construction.

The Contractors' Licence is categorised according to the financial capability of the contractor. Currently, there are seven categories of licence, namely:

Licence Category	**Minimum Net Worth/Equity**
AAAA	PHP1 billion (US$19.2 million)
AAA	PHP180,000,000 (US$3.5 million)
AA	PHP90,000,000 (US$1.7 million)
A	PHP30,000,000 (US$575,000)
B	PHP10,000,000 (US$192,000)
C	PHP6,000,000 (US$115,000)
D	PHP2,000,000 (US$38,000)

26 *Republic Act No 4566*, as amended by *Presidential Decree No 1746*.

27 http://ciap.dti.gov.ph/sites/default/files/Rules%20and%20Regulation%20Governing%20Licensing%20of%20Constructos.pdf (accessed 12 August 2020).

28 PCAB, New Special License of a Consortium Application, PCAB-F-SVD-011. Revision No 00 (19 November 2018).

29 PCAB, New Special License of a Joint Venture Application, PCAB-F-SVD-009. Revision No 00 (10 November 2018).

30 PCAB, New Special License by a Foreign Contractor Application, PCAB-F-SVD-007. Revision No 00 (19 November 2018).

31 *Republic Act No 4566*, as amended by *Presidential Decree No 1746*.

The inter-Agency Committee for Registration of Contractors initially formulated 6 categories of Contractors' licence – AAA, AA, A, B, C and D.[32] In 2013, consistent with the policy to promote the influx of foreign investments and accelerate the growth of the construction industry in the Philippines, CIAP created a new licence category, Quadruple A (AAAA) with an upgraded capitalisation net worth/equity of at least one billion Pesos. The new licence category can be participated in by foreign contractors with more than 40 per cent (40 per cent) up to 100 per cent (100 per cent) foreign equity under specific conditions. It is noteworthy that a foreign contractor may be granted a Special License to engage in the construction of a single specific undertaking/project with a project cost of at least PHP1 billion where there is limited local capability in technology as determined by the Philippine Domestic Construction Board.[33]

In 2017, CIAP issued Guidelines for the licensing of Category Quadruple A (AAAA) contractors. It categorised the new Quadruple A licence category into:

1. Quadruple A Platinum – locally owned licensed contractors with at least PHP1 billion (US$19.2 million) equity, and
2. Quadruple A Gold – foreign-owned domestic corporations with at least PHP1 billion equity.[34]

Quadruple A Platinum contractors may undertake government and private projects of any contract cost. Quadruple A Gold Contractors may undertake private projects under the following contract cost:

- For vertical projects – minimum contract cost of PHP5 billion (US$96 million)
- For horizontal projects – minimum contract cost of PHP3 billion (US$58 million).

The Quadruple A category is limited to general contractors. However, Quadruple A contractors may engage licensed subcontractor/speciality contractors to work on portions of its projects.[35]

Contractors accredited by PCAB are, by default, governed by the Code of Ethics for Philippine Contractors. The Code mandates that contractors, inter alia, adhere to the ideals of the contracting industry in terms of fairness, honesty and professional integrity in all their business dealings. Otherwise, they may be subject to Disciplinary Actions under Article VI of RA No 4566.

18.2.3 Licensing of professionals

In the Philippines, the practice of professions is governed by the Professional Regulation Commission (**PRC**).[36] PRC also recognises the practice of foreign professionals, provided they secure a special licence from the PRC and that their country honours the bilateral agreement on 'mutual recognition' policy or the principle of reciprocity.

32 PCAB Revised Guidelines for Registration and Classification of Contractors.
33 PCAB Board Resolution No 333 Series of 2013.
34 CIAP Board Resolution No 079, Series of 2017.
35 ibid.
36 *Republic Act No 8981*: *PRC Modernization Act of 2000*.

18.2.4 Labour relations

Recognising labour as a primary social economic force, the state's role is to protect workers' rights and promote their welfare. The *Labor Code of the Philippines* is the applicable law that governs the labour standards and labour relations between employer and employee.[37] It sets the minimum standard of conditions such as work hours, health and safety and wages.

The Department of Labor and Employment (**DOLE**) Department Order No 19–93 provides the Guidelines governing the employment of workers in the construction industry.

18.2.5 Modular construction using factory-fabricated components

The Philippines experiences an average of 20 typhoons every year, five of which are destructive.[38] This causes devastating floods and continuous rains which almost always affect the construction timetable due to suspension of work. To deal with these inevitable circumstances, Contractors need to provide measures to catch up lost time; thus, the introduction of different methods/strategies, one of which is the use of factory-fabricated components. These factory-fabricated components are easy to install.

Factory-fabricated components were first used in mass housing projects for safe and inexpensive living spaces. They have since been used for the construction of malls, condominiums, hospitals, and other infrastructure projects.

18.2.6 Technology/innovation/BIM

Engineering and architectural design firms use different technological innovations to improve delivery of design requirements with minimal to zero conflicts among disciplines. Collaborative software applications provide consultants ease in collaborating while monitoring and tracking the changes each member of the design team makes. Building Information Management (**BIM**), which has now become a popular byword in construction is also being utilised by Filipino designers and Contractors to create a 3D model of the design, monitor design changes (RFIs and RFAs) and construction progress, prepare estimates as well as extract quantities, facilities management, contracts management, progress payments, and other processes in construction.

With sustainability in the forefront, local developers have also adopted the concept of green building technology (ie rain harvesting and energy efficient specifications).

18.2.7 Government/private sector procurement

In the Philippines, government procurement of goods, infrastructure projects, and consulting services is governed by *Republic Act No 9184*, otherwise known as the *Government Procurement Reform Act*, and its implementing Rules and Regulations.

37 https://www.dole.gov.ph/php_assets/uploads/2017/11/LaborCodeofthePhilippines20171.pdf (accessed 26 October 2020).

38 https://www.adrc.asia/nationinformation.php (accessed 27 August 2020).

Private sector procurement is not bound by this law and parties are free to adopt their own rules in procurement subject to the provisions of the *Civil Code*.

The Public–Private Partnership Center of the Philippines was created in September 2010 through Executive Order (EO) No 8 series of 2010. The PPP Center is an agency attached to the National Economic and Development Authority (**NEDA**). It was founded to allow the allocation of public funds for other local priorities because of limited funding resources for Philippine local infrastructure or development projects in the public sector,

The Public–Private Partnership Center is a government institution that serves as the central coordinating and monitoring agency for all PPP projects in the country. It facilitates the implementation of the country's PPP Program by enabling the implementing agencies (**IA**s) in all aspects of project preparation and by providing project advisory and facilitation services.[39]

The PPP Center provides technical assistance to national government agencies (**NGA**s), government-owned and controlled corporations (**GOCC**s), government financial institutions (**GFI**s), state universities and colleges (**SUC**s), and local government units (**LGU**s) to help them develop and implement PPP projects. It also manages the Project Development and Monitoring Facility, a revolving pool of funds meant to be accessed by IAs in order to engage consultants and transaction advisors to help them undertake project preparation and transaction support for their PPP projects.

The PPP Center has no mandate to assist the private sector in undertaking PPP projects. It only provides its technical advisory services to IAs. Hence, private partners can participate in PPP projects without certification. They only need to purchase the pre-qualification documents of the project for them to understand the bidding requirements and participate in the project's tender process.

18.2.8 Insurance requirements

In the Philippines, it is generally the Contractor that has the obligation to obtain insurances such as the following:

(a) Contractor's All Risk Insurance
(b) Transportation to the project Site of Equipment, Plant, and Materials owned by the Contractor
(c) Personal injury or death of the Contractor's employees;
(d) Comprehensive insurance for third party liability for the Contractor's direct or indirect acts or omissions causing damage to third persons; and
(e) Fire insurance.

In addition to the above-mentioned insurance, professionals in construction may obtain Professional Liability Insurance because under Article 1723 of the *Civil Code of the Philippines*, engineers or architects can be held liable for damages when the building collapses:

> The engineer or architect who drew up the plans and specifications for a building is liable for damages if within fifteen years from the completion of the structure, the same should collapse by reason of a defect in those plans and specifications, or due to the defects in the

39 https://ppp.gov.ph/about-the-ppp-center/ (accessed 11 August 2020).

ground. The contractor is likewise responsible for the damages if the edifice falls, within the same period, on account of defects in the construction or the use of materials of inferior quality furnished by him, or due to any violation of the terms of the contract. If the engineer or architect supervises the construction, he shall be solidarily liable with the contractor.

Acceptance of the building, after completion, does not imply waiver of any of the cause of action by reason of any defect mentioned in the preceding paragraph.

The action must be brought within ten years following the collapse of the building.

Professional Liability Insurance covers professionals for claims made against them for economic losses resulting from the advice and services that they had provided to their clients. It also provides financial support to meet the costs of defending legal actions and any damages that are required to be paid.[40]

In any case, insurance is obtained in accordance with *The Insurance Code*.[41]

18.2.9 Common forms of contract

In the Philippine construction industry, parties to a construction contract use the following standard forms:

1. The proforma General Conditions of Contract embodied in the Philippine Bidding Documents (**PBDs**). This form of contract is used by the government in its procurement of: a) Goods, b) Infrastructure Projects, and c) Consulting services. The governing law for this contract is the *Government Procurement Reform Act*[42] and its *2016 Revised Implementing Rules and Regulations.*
2. The Uniform General Conditions of Contract for Private Construction, otherwise known as CIAP Document 102 (**CIAP 102**). This governs the construction of private construction projects, which may include residential houses, high-rise buildings, commercial complexes, institutions and the like. This document embodies fair and reasonable contract terms and conditions and was jointly formulated by the representatives of the multilateral sectors comprising a broad cross-section of the local construction industry, (i.e. project owners/developers, contractors, professional organisations of engineers, and the legal profession).
3. The FIDIC rainbow suite 1999 is widely used in international and domestic contracts, i.e. private companies whose projects involve foreign parties, mostly in energy and utilities. The Red, Yellow or Silver Books are used, depending upon the requirements of the contracting parties.
4. The Pink Book 2010 is used as part of the Standard Bidding Documents on Government projects funded by the Multilateral Development Banks (Asian Development Bank, World Bank, Black Sea Bank) and Bilateral Development Banks (JICA, China, South Korea) under ODA loans.

On 27 June 2019, FIDIC signed a memorandum of understanding with the DTI to train government engineers and other construction professionals in the use of

40 https://www.aig.com.ph/business/product-categories/financial-lines/professional-liability#:~:text=Professional%20Liability%20covers%20professionals%20for,are%20required%20to%20be%20paid. (accessed 19 August 2020).

41 *Republic Act No 10607*, amending *Presidential Decree No 612.*

42 *Republic Act No 9184.*

FIDIC contracts.[43] This two-year MoU was signed following detailed discussions between FIDIC and DTI and has been ratified by CIAP, the policy-making body for construction in the country. The agreement will assist in the implementation of the Philippine Construction Industry Roadmap 2020–2030, which aims to improve the quality of construction services and promote integrity, professionalism and innovation across the supply chain. Under the terms of the MoU, the DTI will conduct a national awareness campaign on FIDIC contracts amongst construction industry stakeholders and include contracts in its regular training programmes. It will also provide training on FIDIC contract modules for government engineers and other professionals involved in procurement, contract drafting and administration of contracts for government infrastructure contracts. Hence, the use of FIDIC was included in the Philippine Construction Industry Roadmap 2020–2030 and its Action Plans.

These pro forma General Conditions are either simply adopted by the Employer and Contractor in drafting their construction contract or modified to suit the peculiarities of a particular project through Particular Conditions.

In some cases, there are a number of bespoke contracts crafted by consultants and lawyers specifically engaged by either private Employer or Contractor for a specific project.

18.2.10 Dispute resolution

18.2.10.1 Construction mediation and arbitration

Executive Order No 1008 (1985) created the Construction Industry Arbitration Commission (**CIAC**) to provide the construction industry with another method of speedy and equitable settlement of construction disputes other than court litigation – arbitration.

Subject to the agreement of the parties to submit their dispute to voluntary arbitration, the CIAC was given the 'original and exclusive' jurisdiction over all construction disputes. The decisions of the CIAC are appealable to the Court of Appeals but are limited to questions of law.[44]

On the one hand, a decision or an award rendered by arbitrator/s in arbitration proceedings is enforceable by a writ of execution.[45] On the other hand, a decision resulting from conciliation/mediation is not binding on the parties but merely recommendatory.

In order for CIAC to acquire jurisdiction over construction disputes, the contract between the parties must contain an arbitration clause stating, inter alia, that in case a dispute arises from the contract, it will be resolved by arbitration. If the contract has no arbitration clause, both parties must sign an agreement to arbitrate. One of the parties must file a case or Request for Adjudication with the CIAC. Hence, if a contract contains an arbitration clause and one of the parties files a case with the trial court without first filing a request for adjudication with CIAC, the case will be dismissed by the trial court for lack of jurisdiction.

43 https://fidic.org/node/23956?fbclid=IwAR2a5Ns5zuArQIPNYdRHD0WfFfjIz7k6NBJjmJn_augzSuruYO0Ymr26Sbc (accessed 13 August 2020).

44 *Executive Order No 1008*, s 19.

45 *CIAC Revised Rules of Procedure Governing Construction Arbitration*, s 18.5.

It should be noted that prior referral of a dispute to a Dispute Adjudication Board is not a condition precedent to the jurisdiction of CIAC,[46] in the same way that other ADR mechanisms are not conditions precedent to acquiring CIAC jurisdiction. The mere existence of an arbitration clause in the construction contract is considered by law as an agreement by the parties to submit existing or future controversies between them to CIAC jurisdiction, without any qualification or condition precedent. To affirm a condition precedent in the construction contract, which would effectively suspend the jurisdiction of the CIAC until compliance therewith, would be in conflict with the recognised intention of the law and rules to automatically vest CIAC with jurisdiction over a dispute should the construction contract contain an arbitration clause.

However, not all construction-related disputes are admitted by the CIAC. CIAC's jurisdiction may include but is not limited to the following issues:

(1) Violation of specifications for materials and workmanship
(2) Violation of the terms of agreement
(3) Interpretation and/or application of contractual provisions
(4) Amount of damages and penalties
(5) Commencement time and delays
(6) Maintenance and defects
(7) Payment default of Employer or Contractor
(8) Changes in contract cost.

The jurisdiction of CIAC was further upheld with the passage of *Republic Act No 9285* or the *Alternative Dispute Resolution Act (ADR)* of 2004. It reinforced CIAC's jurisdiction over construction disputes and expanded CIAC's ADR services to include mediation; CIAC has conducted mediation training for its accredited arbitrators.

The Implementing Rules and Regulations of the *ADR Act* of 2004 is governed by Department of Justice (**DOJ**) Department Order No 98 dated 4 December 2009. It promotes party autonomy in the resolution of disputes or the freedom of the parties to make their own arrangements to resolve their disputes.[47]

The CIAC fulfills its mandate through its pool of accredited arbitrators and mediators, who, after having been trained and accredited by CIAC, organised themselves into what is now known as the Philippine Institute of Construction Arbitrators and Mediators, Inc. (**PICAM**).

18.2.10.2 Dispute Boards

The use of Dispute Boards to resolve construction disputes during the construction phase as they occur or are about to occur is now mandated in government projects funded by multilateral and bilateral development banks and other financial institutions.

Where 1999 FIDIC Contracts and the MDB Harmonised Edition are used in foreign-funded projects under the BBB Infrastructure Program, the application of a standing Dispute Board approach is enshrined, which then demands trained practitioners in this field.

46 *HUTAMA-RSEA Joint Operations Inc v CITRA Metro Manila Tollways Corporation*, GR No 180640 (24 April 2009).

47 DOJ Department Order No 98 (4 December 2009 Article 1.2.

With the new 2017 FIDIC Contracts focusing on dispute avoidance, it is further anticipated that there will be more training of practitioners in the field of dispute avoidance.

18.3 The impact of Covid-19 in the Philippines

18.3.1 The impact of Covid-19 on the execution of construction projects in the Philippines

During the Covid-19 outbreak the government issued a series of Guidelines to intensify safety and health standards in order to prevent the spread of the virus. Although the provisions of the *Labor Code of the Philippines*, domestic laws, and internationally recognised standards on occupational safety and health were being fully enforced, these were not enough to protect workers from the threat of the virus.

As early as January 2020, preparatory recommendations/guidelines were issued by the different implementing agencies of the government, such as the Inter-Agency Task Force (**IATF**), the Department of Health (**DOH**), the Department of Interior and Local Government (**DILG**), the DOLE, the Department of Public Works & Highways (**DPWH**), Department of Transportation (**DOTr**), among others. The **IATF** (created in 2014) was instructed by the President to facilitate intersectoral cooperation to establish preparedness and ensure efficient government response, assess, monitor, contain, control and prevent the spread of Covid-19 in the Philippines.

On 8 March 2020, Philippine President Rodrigo Roa Duterte issued *Proclamation No 922* declaring the Philippines under a state of public health emergency due to corona virus disease 2019 (Covid-19). It was only on 11 March 2020 that the WHO declared Covid-19 as a pandemic that calls for preventive measures, globally and locally.[48] In response to this, on 16 March 2020, President Duterte issued *Presidential Proclamation No 929* declaring a State of Calamity throughout the Philippines due to Covid-19 and imposed Enhanced Community Quarantine (**ECQ**) or lockdown throughout Luzon, effective on 17 March 2020.[49]

On 16 March 2020, a Memorandum from the executive Secretary was issued directing the IATF for the Management of Emerging Infectious Diseases through the DOH to disseminate information to the public on the steps and measures to be undertaken relative to the Covid-19 situation during the period of ECQ for the entire Luzon area. The ECQ was originally from 17 March to 13 April 2020, which was further extended to 31 May 2020.

During ECQ, the following restrictions were implemented, among others:

- Prohibition of mass gatherings
- Strict home quarantine
- Suspension of mass public transport facilities
- Only private establishments providing basic necessities could remain open and
- Restriction of land, air and sea travel.[50]

48 https://www.theguardian.com/world/2020/mar/11/who-declares-coronavirus-pandemic (accessed 25 June 2020).

49 *Presidential Proclamation No 929* (16 March 2020).

50 Memorandum from the executive secretary (16 March 2020).

On 25 March 2020, the *Bayanihan to Heal as One Act* was implemented. This new law was enacted primarily to give authority to President Duterte for a limited period and subject to restrictions, to exercise powers necessary and proper in carrying out the declared national policy to mitigate, if not contain, the transmission of Covid-19 and for other purposes.[51] '*Bayanihan* is a traditional system of mutual assistance in which the members of a community work together to accomplish a difficult task. A spirit of civic unity and cooperation among Filipinos.'[52]

On 30 April 2020, the DTI and the DOLE issued the Interim Guidelines on Workplace Prevention and Control of Covid-19. These Guidelines aimed to assist private institutions allowed to operate during the ECQ and General Community Quarantine (**GCQ**) in developing health protocols and standards in light of the Covid-19 pandemic.[53] The Interim Guidelines provided for the following:

- Reducing transmission of Covid-19 through wearing of facemasks, checking body temperature and sanitation prior to entrance in buildings or workplaces, and mandatory 1 metre physical distance between co-workers, disinfecting all work areas and frequently handled objects such as doorknobs at least every two hours, among other things.
- Minimise contact rate through alternative work arrangement, video-conferencing, etc.
- Reducing the risk of infection from Covid-19 through isolation of suspected Covid-19 positive workers and decontamination of workplace.

The IATF issued Omnibus Guidelines on the Implementation of Community Quarantine in the Philippines on 15 May 2020. These Guidelines were a consolidation of all Guidelines/Recommendations for community quarantine issued from March to 14 May 2020 as preparation for the lifting of ECQ in Metro Manila and other low-risk areas, further classifying the community quarantine according to the severity of Covid-19 threat or number of cases, as follows:

- *Modified Enhanced Community Quarantine* (**MECQ**) – transition phase between ECQ and GCQ, when these temporary measures are relaxed: stringent limiting movement and transportation of people, strict regulation of operating industries, provision of food and essential services, and heightened presence of uniformed personnel to enforce the community quarantine protocols.
- *General Community Quarantine* (**GCQ**) – implementation of temporary measures limiting movement and transportation, regulation of operating industries and presence of uniformed personnel to enforce community quarantine protocols.
- *Modified General Community Quarantine* (**MGCQ**) – transition phase between GCQ and New Normal, when these temporary measures are relaxed: limiting movement and transportation, the regulation of operating industries, and the

51 *Republic Act No 11469*.
52 https://www.lexico.com/definition/bayanihan (accessed 28 October 2020).
53 http://ncr.dole.gov.ph/fndr/mis/files/DTI-and-DOLE-Interim-Guidelines-on-Workplace-Prevention-and-Control-of-COVID-19.pdf (accessed 26 October 2020).

presence of uniformed personnel to enforce community quarantine protocols become less necessary.

- *New Normal* – emerging behaviours, situation, and minimum public health standards that will be institutionalised in common or routine practices and remain even after the pandemic while the disease is not totally eradicated through means such as widespread immunisation. These include actions that will become second nature to the general public as well as policies such as bans on gatherings that will continue to remain in force.

On 19 May 2020, when the entire Luzon was placed under MECQ, the DPWH issued Revised Construction Safety Guidelines for the Implementation of Infrastructure Projects During the Covid-19 Public Health Crisis, defining the type of construction that could operate under different types of community quarantine, subject to mandatory requirements of physical distancing (at least 1 metre), wearing of face mask, frequent handwashing and regular sanitation of workplaces, among others.[54] One of the obligations of the Contractors in these Guidelines was to provide their workers with welfare facilities and amenities which will be used during the duration of the project and comply with social distancing and proper hygiene. The Guidelines are as follows:

- Only construction of essential facilities (such as health care and isolation facilities), sewerage projects, water service facilities projects, digital works, and priority infrastructure projects (public and private) are allowed to operate during ECQ.
- Only small-scale construction activities which are intended for private and personal use are allowed to operate during MECQ.
- All types of government and private construction projects may be allowed to continue during GCQ.

The cost of Covid-19 prevention and control measures such as testing, disinfection facilities, hand sanitisers, personal protective equipment (PPEs, i.e. face mask), signages, proper orientation and training of workers, including IEC materials on Covid 19 prevention and control, are shouldered by the Employers or clients of the construction/service Contractor.[55]

Moreover, employers were authorised to adopt more flexible work arrangements (such as work from home, telecommuting or rotating workers) as an alternative to termination of employment or closure of business. Employers were permitted to reduce work hours and/or workdays and require employees to take leave for several days per week or weeks using their leave credits. In this way, different industries had the option to resume their respective businesses rather than closing them.[56]

On 29 May 2020, DPWH issued Approval of Work Suspension Order, Work Resumption Order, and Contract Time Extension for Civil Works Projects, to streamline the processes of DPWH and afford authority and accountability to the Implementing Offices to act on matters relating to work suspension, resumption and

54 DPWH Department Order No 39, series of 2020 (19 May 2020).
55 DOLE Labor Advisory No 18, series of 2020 (16 May 2020).
56 DOLE Labor Advisory No 17, series of 2020 (16 May 2020).

contract time extension for civil works projects, locally-funded and foreign-assisted projects.[57] DPWH further issued Guidelines on Covid-19 Management on the following:

- Workplace health
- Covid suspected case
- Covid confirmed case
- Work suspension due to confirmed Covid cases and
- Information disclosure.[58]

On 1 June 2020, Metro Manila was put under GCQ while other high-risk areas and provinces remained in other community quarantine levels. Nonetheless, the spread of Covid-19 had not flattened, and the government had not totally relaxed the restrictions in the country at the time of writing (October 2020).

On construction sites the following preventive measures against spread of Covid-19 were required to be implemented:[59]

a. Prior to entrance in buildings or workplaces, the workers are required to:
    - Wear face masks
    - Check body temperature
    - Disinfect/sanitise hands and feet
    - Answer the health symptom questionnaire
    - Be isolated and not allowed to enter the premises if temperature is >37.5C
    - Not share construction and office equipment
    - Equipment and vehicle must go through disinfection process.

b. Inside workplace:
    - All work areas and frequently handled objects such as doorknobs, shall be disinfected regularly, at least every 2 hours
    - All washrooms and toilets shall have sufficient clean water and soap
    - Sanitisers shall be made available in corridors, conference areas, elevators, stairways and areas where workers pass
    - Mandatory 1 metre physical distance
    - Clustered and staggered deployment of employees within the construction site shall be observed
    - Eating in communal areas is discouraged
    - Canteens and kitchens should be cleaned and disinfected regularly.
    - In the event that a worker is suspected of having Covid-19:[60]
        - Workplace shall be decontaminated with appropriate disinfectant;
        - After decontamination of the area, work shall resume after 24 hours;
        - Workers present in the work area with the suspect Covid-19 worker shall go on 14 days' home quarantine.

57 DPWH Department Order No 42, series of 2020 (29 May 2020).
58 DPWH Department Order No 83, series of 2020 (25 August 2020).
59 Interim Guidelines on Workplace Prevention and Control of Covid-19 issued by DTI and DOLE (30 April 2020).
60 ibid.

On 11 September 2020, the *Bayanihan to Recover as One Act* (also known as ***Bayanihan 2***) was enacted by the Congress and was signed by President Duterte.[61] This law provides for Covid-19 response and recovery interventions and mechanisms to accelerate the recovery and bolster the resiliency of the Philippine economy, and provides funds for that and other purposes.[62]

The Office of the President has advised that the government remains committed to implementing its ambitious Build, Build, Build Infrastructure Program to revive the country's economy which entered recession due to the Covid-19 pandemic.[63]

Based on the circumstances, construction works have slowed down. In effect, there are delays to the time of completion. Furthermore, in compliance with the above-mentioned Orders issued by the implementing government agencies, additional costs have been incurred by both parties, the Contractor and the Employer. Accordingly, the current challenge in the Philippine construction industry is the new normal brought by the Covid-19 pandemic.

18.3.2 The impact of Covid-19 on the operation of construction contracts in the Philippines

There was no express declaration that Covid-19 was considered as *force majeure* under Philippine Law. However, as noted earlier, different government agencies issued department orders/advisories that impose on the Employer the cost of Covid-19 prevention and control measures such as testing, disinfection facilities, hand sanitisers, personal protective equipment i.e. face masks, signages, proper orientation and training of workers including Information Education Communication materials on Covid 19 prevention and control.[64]

On 29 May 2020, the DPWH issued an Order relating to Approve Work Suspension Order, Work Resumption Order, and Contract Time Extension for Civil Works Project:

> In view of the Covid-19 pandemic, there is a need to streamline the processes of this Department and afford authority and accountability to the Implementing Offices to act on matters relating work suspension, resumption and contract time extension. This will not only reduce logistics challenges brought about by the Covid-19 pandemic when it comes to requests for suspension, resumption and contract time extension, it will also strengthen the accountability of Implementing Offices in ensuring that infrastructure projects are effectively and efficiently implemented to contribute to the country's economic growth and people's livelihood.[65]

No new provision was issued to specifically cover the effects of Covid-19, as the *Civil Code of the Philippines* arguably provides relief in this situation:

> **Article 1174 Obligations and Contracts**
>
> Except in cases expressly specified by the law, or when it is otherwise declared by stipulation, or when the nature of the obligation requires the assumption of risk, no person shall be responsible for those events which could not be foreseen or which, though foreseen, were inevitable.

61 https://www.pna.gov.ph/articles/1115210 (accessed 17 September 2020).

62 *Republic Act No 11494*.

63 https://www.pna.gov.ph/articles/1108492 (accessed 20 July 2020).

64 Guidelines on the Cost of Covid-19 Prevention and Control https://www.dole.gov.ph/news/labor-advisory-no-18-series-of-2020-guidelines-on-the-cost-of-covid-19-prevention-and-control-measures/.

65 Department Order No 42 (2 June 2020) https://www.dpwh.gov.ph/DPWH/sites/default/files/issuances/DO_42_s2020.pdf.

Parties to a contract may invoke the ground of *force majeure* or fortuitous event under the *Civil Code* as a defence, because under this doctrine, neither party is liable for breach of contract and are accordingly excused from the performance of their contractual obligations during the duration of *force majeure*/fortuitous events.

In 2016, the government promulgated the *2016 Revised Implementing Rules of Republic Act No 9184, otherwise known as the Government Procurement Reform Act* 'with the commitment of the GoP to promote good governance and its effort to adhere to the principles of transparency, accountability, equity, efficiency, and economy in its procurement process'. Those *Rules* provided that in the case of total suspension, which is not due to any fault of the Contractor, the elapsed time between the effective order of suspending operation and the order to resume work shall be allowed the Contractor by adjusting the contract time accordingly. Should the amount of additional work of any kind occur, the procuring entity shall determine the amount of such extension.[66] Accordingly, it appears that Contractors on public projects will receive extensions of time as a result of the impact of the Covid-19 pandemic under existing laws.

18.4 Philippines governing law of the contract

18.4.1 Constraints on the governing law of a construction contract

The Philippine Laws, particularly the *Civil Code of the Philippines* (***CCP***), give parties the freedom to choose the terms and conditions of their construction contract as follows:

> **Art. 1305.** A contract is a meeting of minds between two persons whereby one binds himself, with respect to the other, to give something or to render some service.
> **Art. 1306.** The contracting parties may establish such stipulations, clauses, terms and conditions as they may deem convenient, provided they are not contrary to law, morals, good customs, public order, or public policy.

The stipulations, clauses, terms and conditions in construction contract entered into and between parties shall be the law between them:

> **Art. 1159.** Obligations arising from contracts have the force of law between the contracting parties and should be complied with in good faith.

Courts recognise this and determine the rights and obligations of Employer and Contractor in accordance with the contractual provisions. However, in accordance with Article 1306 these must not be illegal nor immoral and not against good customs, public order or public policy; otherwise, it will not be enforceable.

Under the *CCP*, a construction contract is considered as a Contract for a Piece of Work, that is:

> **Art. 1713.** By the contract for a piece of work the contractor binds himself to execute a piece of work for the employer, in consideration of a certain price or compensation. The contractor may either employ only his labor or skill, or also furnish the material.

Hence, primarily Articles of 1713–1731 of the *CCP* shall govern the rights and obligations of the parties in a construction contract and shall be supplemented by the laws on Obligations (Articles 1156–1304) and Contracts (Articles 1305–1422).

66 https://www.gppb.gov.ph/laws/laws/RevisedIRR.RA9184.pdf (accessed 27 October 2020).

In accordance with the freedom of contract enshrined in the *CCP*, parties to a construction contract may choose the governing law of their contract; they may even choose governing law of a jurisdiction other than the Philippines. However, this freedom is not without restriction. Article 1306 of the *CCP* is explicit in stating that stipulations of a contract shall not be contrary to law, morals, good customs, public order or public policy. Hence, the parties, in drafting their contract, should observe the Philippine law, morals, good customs, public order or public policy.

In a private construction contract, parties may stipulate terms and conditions as they may deem convenient and that includes the governing law of their contract since there is no law is prohibiting it. However, in public construction contracts, parties are required to observe the 2016 Revised IRR of *RA No 9184* in drafting their contract since such contract is imbued with public interest.

Furthermore, regardless of the governing law of the contract, the parties may choose the seat of arbitration other than the Philippines. This is based on the doctrine of separability, or severability as other writers call it, which enunciates that an arbitration agreement is independent of the main contract. However, it is worth noting that the Philippines follows the first-to-file rule.[67] Where the arbitration clause of the parties in a construction contract stipulates that any dispute arising therefrom shall be referred to another arbitral institution, other than CIAC, the contracting party which is first to file a request for arbitration gets the opportunity to determine which arbitral institution – as between the CIAC and stipulated arbitral institution. This means that the arbitral institution who first acquires jurisdiction shall take cognisance of the arbitration proceedings.

18.4.2 Formal requirements for a construction contract

Pursuant to Article 1318 of the *CCP*, there is no contract unless the following preconditions are satisfied:

(1) Consent of the contracting parties
(2) Object certain which is the subject matter of the contract
(3) Cause of the obligation which is established.

There is consent when the following concur: first, the consent must be manifested by the concurrence of the offer and the acceptance; second, the contracting parties must possess the necessary legal capacity; and third, the consent must be intelligent, free, spontaneous, and real.[68]

Whilst the *CCP* states that a contract is perfected by mere consent, a construction contract must be put into writing.

As a general rule, contracts shall be obligatory, in whatever form (oral or written), provided all the essential requisites for their validity are present, namely: consent, proper subject matter, and consideration or cause for the obligation assumed.[69] However, this general rule is not without exception. 'When the law requires that a contract be in some form in order that it may be valid or enforceable, or that a contract

67 *China Chang Jiang Energy Corporation (Philippines) v Rosal Infrastructure Builders*, GR No 125706 (30 September 1996).

68 Desiderio P Jurado, *Comments and Jurisprudence on Obligations and Contracts* (12th edn, REX Printing Company Inc 2010) 397.

69 See *Civil Code of the Philippines*, art 1356.

be proved in a certain way, that requirement is absolute and indispensable.'[70] Thus, the parties must observe Article 1403 paragraph 2(a) of the *CCP* which provides that, in order to be enforceable by action, an agreement that by its terms is not to be performed within a year from the making thereof, shall be in writing. This is in compliance with the *Statute of Frauds*.

The purpose of the *Statute* is to prevent fraud and perjury in the enforcement of obligations depending for their evidence on the unassisted memory of witnesses by requiring certain enumerated contracts and transactions to be evidenced by a writing signed by the party to be charged.

Furthermore, Article 1358 of the *CCP* provides that: 'All other contracts where the amount involved exceeds five hundred pesos must appear in writing, even a private one.'

Therefore, a construction contract that by its terms cannot be performed within one year from the day of its execution or with a contract amount exceeding PHP500, must be in writing.

18.5 What Special Provisions in the Particular Conditions are necessary for consistency with applicable laws in the Philippines?

18.5.1 FIDIC General Conditions are incompatible or inconsistent with Philippines governing law of the contract

No Special Provisions in the Particular Conditions of FIDIC rainbow suite contracts are necessary for consistency with applicable laws if Philippines law is the governing law of the Contract.

18.5.2 FIDIC General Conditions are incompatible or inconsistent with the law of the Site/Country

No Special Provisions in the Particular Conditions of FIDIC rainbow suite contracts are necessary for consistency with applicable laws if the Site is in the Philippines.

18.5.3 FIDIC General Conditions are incompatible or inconsistent with the relevant laws on dispute determination in the Philippines

18.5.3.1 The seat of arbitration

Where construction work is carried out in the Philippines, the FIDIC General Conditions on dispute resolution may be incompatible or inconsistent with the laws of the Philippines.

In the Philippines, *Executive Order 1008* provides that the CIAC has 'original and exclusive' jurisdiction over disputes arising out or in connection with a construction contract:

> **Section 4. Jurisdiction** – The CIAC shall have original and exclusive jurisdiction over disputes arising from, or connected with, contracts entered into by parties involved in construction in the Philippines, whether the disputes arises before or after the completion of the contract, or after the abandonment or breach thereof. These disputes may involve government or private contracts. For the Board to acquire jurisdiction, the parties to a dispute must agree to submit the same to voluntary arbitration.

70 ibid.

> The jurisdiction of the CIAC may include but is not limited to violation of specifications for materials and workmanship; violation of the terms of agreement; interpretation and/or application of contractual provisions; amount of damages and penalties; commencement time and delays; maintenance and defects; payment default of employer or contractor and changes in contract cost.
>
> Excluded from the coverage of this law are disputes arising from employer-employee relationships which shall continue to be covered by the Labor Code of the Philippines.[71]

The 'original and exclusive' jurisdiction of CIAC over construction disputes was affirmed by the Philippine Supreme Court in the case of *China Chang Jiang Energy Corporation (Philippines) v Rosal Infrastructure Builders*.[72] Subsequently, CIAC's jurisdiction was further affirmed by the passage of *Republic Act No 9285*, otherwise known as the *'Alternative Dispute Resolution Act of 2004'*:

> **SEC. 35. Coverage of the Law.** – Construction disputes which fall within the original and exclusive jurisdiction of the Construction Industry Arbitration Commission (the 'Commission') shall include those between or among parties to, or who are otherwise bound by, an arbitration agreement, directly or by reference whether such parties are project owner, contractor, subcontractor, quantity surveyor, bondsman or issuer of an insurance policy in a construction project.
>
> The Commission shall continue to exercise original and exclusive jurisdiction over construction disputes although the arbitration is 'commercial' pursuant to Section 21 of this Act.

In the case of *China Chang Jiang Energy Corporation (Philippines) v Rosal Infrastructure Builders*, the Supreme Court held that:

> What the law merely requires that for a particular construction contract will to fall within the jurisdiction of CIAC if is for the parties agree to submit their dispute the same to voluntary arbitration.
>
> The law does not mention that the parties should agree to submit disputes arising from their agreement specifically to the CIAC for the latter to acquire jurisdiction over such disputes. Rather, it is plain and clear that as long as the parties agree to submit to voluntary arbitration, regardless of what forum they may choose, their agreement will fall within the jurisdiction of the CIAC, such that, even if they specially choose another forum, the parties will not be precluded from electing to submit their dispute before the CIAC because this right has been vested upon each party by law, ie E.O. No 1008.[73]

Thus, even if the Parties to a contract for construction works in the Philippines choose the seat of arbitration to be that of another jurisdiction, the seat will be in the Philippines, provided that the request for arbitration was first filed before the CIAC. *Republic Act No 9285* does, however, allow for a foreign arbitrator in an international contract:

> **SEC. 37. Appointment of Foreign Arbitrator**. – The Construction Industry Arbitration Commission (CIAC) shall promulgate rules to allow for the appointment of a foreign arbitrator or coarbitrator or chairman of a tribunal a person who has not been previously accredited by CIAC: Provided, That:
>
> (a) the dispute is a construction dispute in which one party is an international party

71 *Executive Order No 1008 Construction Industry Arbitration Law* s 4 Jurisdiction. https://ciap.dti.gov.ph/sites/default/files/E.O.%201008_0.pdf (accessed 27 October 2020).

72 GR No 125706 (30 September 1996).

73 ibid.

(b) the person to be appointed agreed to abide by the arbitration rules and policies of CIAC;
(c) he/she is either coarbitrator upon the nomination of the international party; or he/she is the common choice of the two CIAC-accredited arbitrators first appointed one of whom was nominated by the international party; and
(d) the foreign arbitrator shall be of different nationality from the international party.

Accordingly, it is advisable to insert a Special Provision in the Particular Conditions to make it clear that the arbitration of a dispute in respect of construction works in the Philippines will be subject to the jurisdiction of the CIAC and the applicable Philippine laws.

18.6 What Special Provisions in the Particular Conditions are desirable for consistency with applicable laws in the Philippines?

18.6.1 Force majeure – fortuitous events (Civil Code)

The term *force majeure* is not expressly defined in the *CCP* however, it has been used synonymously with the term fortuitous events in construction contracts and jurisprudence. Fortuitous events are defined as events which could not be foreseen or which, though foreseen, were inevitable.[74]

Based on the foregoing, FIDIC Conditions of Contract must include the term fortuitous event in drafting the *force majeure* clause.

18.6.2 FIDIC SC 8.7 Delay Damages vs Liquidated Damages

In the Philippines, Delay Damages are governed by Article 2226–2228 of the *CCP*:

> Art. 2226. Liquidated damages are those agreed upon by the parties to a contract, to be paid in case of breach thereof.
> Art. 2227. Liquidated damages, whether intended as an indemnity or a penalty, shall be equitably reduced if they are iniquitous or unconscionable.
> Art. 2228. When the breach of the contract committed by the defendant is not the one contemplated by the parties in agreeing upon the liquidated damages, the law shall determine the measure of damages, and not the stipulation.

Based on the above provision of the law, the parties to a construction contract are allowed to stipulate on liquidated damages to be paid in case of breach. It is attached to an obligation in order to ensure performance. The most common stipulation in relation to this is the amount agreed upon to answer for damages suffered by the Employer due to delays in the completion of the project. This is known as Delay Damages in FIDIC General Conditions. Hence, the FIDIC General Conditions must be consistent with the above-mentioned provisions, especially Article 2227, where it is required that the amount should not be unconscionable.

74 See *Civil Code of the Philippines*, art 1174.

18.7 Summary of applicable legislation for Philippines governing law of the contract

18.7.1 Entry into a construction contract

Contracts generally	*Republic Act No 386* *Civil Code of the Philippines*, art1305–1422
Construction contracts	*Republic Act No 386* *Civil Code of the Philippines*, art 1305–1422 and art 1713–1731

18.7.2 Termination of a construction contract

Frustration	*Republic Act No 386* *Civil Code of the Philippines*, art 1156–1422 and art 1713–1731
Bankruptcy, Insolvency, Liquidation	*Republic Act No 386* *Civil Code of the Philippines*, art 1156–1422
Guarantees under forms of Security (Tender Security, Demand Guarantee, Surety, Bond, Advance Payment Guarantee, Retention Money Guarantee, Payment Guarantee by Employer)	*Republic Act No 386* *Civil Code of the Philippines*, art 1156–1422, art 1713–1731 and art 2047–2081 *The 2016 Revised Implementing Rules and Regulations of RA No 9184*

18.7.3 Dispute resolution

Limitation Periods	*Republic Act No 386* *Civil Code of the Philippines*, art 1444 *Implementing Rules and Regulations of Alternative Dispute Resolution Act of 2004* AM No 07–11–08-SC *Special Rules of Court on Alternative Dispute Resolution* (01 September 2009) AM No 04-3-15-SC-PHILJA *Implementing Rules & Regulations on Mediation in the Trial Courts* (23 March 2004) *CIAC Revised Rules of Procedure Governing Construction Arbitration* (28 February 2019) AM No 19-10-20-SC *2019 Amendments to the 1997 Rules of Civil Procedure*
Liability	*Republic Act No 386* *Civil Code of the Philippines*, art 1156–1422 and art 1713–1731
Alternative dispute resolution	*Implementing Rules and Regulations of Alternative Dispute Resolution Act of 2004* AM No 07–11–08-SC *Special Rules of Court on Alternative Dispute Resolution* (01 September 2009) AM No 04-3-15-SC-PHILJA *Implementing Rules & Regulations on Mediation in the Trial Courts* (23 March 2004)

Arbitration	*Executive Order No 1008* *Construction Industry Arbitration Law* *CIAC Revised Rules of Procedure Governing Construction Arbitration* (28 February 2019)

18.8 Applicable legislation if the Site/Country is in the Philippines

18.8.1 Operation of a construction contract

Registration and administration of professionals – engineers, architects, quantity surveyors, certifiers, building surveyors, surveyors[75]	*Republic Act No 8981* *PRC Modernization Act of 2000* *PRC Resolution No 1 series of 2001* (IRR of RA No 8981)
Registration/licensing of contractors and subcontractors[76]	*Republic Act No 4566* *Contractors' License Law*
Use of liens/Assignment of Debts	*Republic Act No 386* *Civil Code of the Philippines*, art 1255
Labour	*Presidential Decree No 442*, as amended *Labor Code of the Philippines* *Republic Act No 386* *Civil Code of the Philippines*, art 1727–1728
Design/Moral Rights	*Republic Act No 10372*, amending *Republic Act No 8293* *Intellectual Property Code of the Philippines*
Copyright	*Republic Act No 10372*, amending *Republic Act No 8293* *Intellectual Property Code of the Philippines*
The product being produced from the Works	*Republic Act No 10372*, amending *Republic Act No 8293* *Intellectual Property Code of the Philippines*
First nation people's land rights	*Republic Act No 8371* *The Indigenous Peoples' Rights Act of 1997*
Planning	*Presidential Decree No 1096* *National Building Code of the Philippines* (amending *Republic Act No 6541*) *Implementing Rules and Regulations of Presidential Decree No 1096* (2005 Revised Edition)
Works affecting adjacent property to the Site	*Republic Act No 386* *Civil Code of the Philippines*, art 414–693
Heritage	*Presidential Decree No 1505* amending *Presidential Decree No 260* *Republic Act No 10066* *National Cultural Heritage Act of 2009*

75 See para 18.2.1.2 above.
76 See para 18.2.1.1 above.

Environment	*Republic Act No 9003* *Ecological Solid Waste Management Act of 2000* *Republic Act No 9275* *Philippine Clean Water Act of 2004* *Republic Act No 8749* *Philippine Clean Air Act of 1999* *Republic Act No6969* *Toxic Substances, Hazardous and Nuclear Waste Control Act of 1990* *Presidential Decree No 1586 Environmental Impact Statement (EIS) System of 1978* *Republic Act No 9512* *Environmental Education Act of 2008*
Building and construction permits, Execution of construction work, Standard of construction work	*Presidential Decree No 1096* *National Building Code of the Philippines* (amending *Republic Act No 6541*) *Implementing Rules and Regulations of Presidential Decree No 1096* (2005 Revised Edition)
Healthy and safety	*Republic Act No 11058* *An Act Strengthening Compliance with Occupational Safety and Health Standards*
Employer's sale of Contractor's Equipment, surplus material, wreckage and Temporary Works	*Republic Act No 386* *Civil Code of the Philippines*, art 1306
Insurance[77]	*Republic Act No 10607* *The Insurance Code*
Statutory rights that coexist with contractual rights	*Republic Act No 386* *Civil Code of the Philippines*, art 1156–1422
Liability for defective work	*Republic Act No 386* *Civil Code of the Philippines*, art 1715 and 1719
Liability for nuisance	*Republic Act No 386* *Civil Code of the Philippines*, art 694–707
Construction for Government Employer	*Republic Act No 9184* *Government Procurement Reform Act* The *2016 Revised Implementing Rules and Regulations of RA No 9184* *Republic Act No 8371* *The Indigenous Peoples' Rights Act of 1997* *Presidential Decree No 1096* *National Building Code of the Philippines* *(amending Republic Act No 6541)* [This includes the referral Codes such as Fire, Structural Engineering, Electrical, Plumbing, etc.] *Implementing Rules and Regulations of Presidential Decree No 1096* (2005 Revised Edition) *BATAS PAMBANSA Bilang 344* *The Accessibility Law* and its Implementing Rules and Regulations

77 See para 18.2.7 above.

18.8.2 Termination of a construction contract

Bankruptcy, insolvency, liquidation	*Republic Act No 386* *Civil Code of the Philippines*, art 1156–1422
Stay on enforcing rights against an entity that has publicly announced it will be making an application to avoid being wound up in insolvency	*Implementing Rules and Regulations of Alternative Dispute Resolution Act of 2004* AM No 07–11–08-SC *Special Rules of Court on Alternative Dispute Resolution* (1 September 2009) AM No 04-3-15-SC-PHILJA *Implementing Rules & Regulations on Mediation in the Trial Courts* (23 March 2004) *CIAC Revised Rules of Procedure Governing Construction Arbitration* (28 February 2019) AM No 19-10-20-SC *2019 Amendments to the 1997 Rules of Civil Procedure*
Decennial liability and liability generally for the total or partial collapse of structures	*Republic Act No 386* *Civil Code of the Philippines*, art 1723

18.8.3 Dispute resolution

Alternative dispute resolution	*Implementing Rules and Regulations of Alternative Dispute Resolution Act of 2004* AM No 07–11–08-SC *Special Rules of Court on Alternative Dispute Resolution* (1 September 2009) AM No 04-3-15-SC-PHILJA *Implementing Rules & Regulations on Mediation in the Trial Courts* (23 March 2004)
Limitation periods	*Republic Act No 386* *Civil Code of the Philippines*, art 1444 *Implementing Rules and Regulations of Alternative Dispute Resolution Act of 2004* AM No 07–11–08-SC *Special Rules of Court on Alternative Dispute Resolution* (1 September 2009) AM No 04-3-15-SC-PHILJA *Implementing Rules & Regulations on Mediation in the Trial Courts* (23 March 2004) *CIAC Revised Rules of Procedure Governing Construction Arbitration* (28 February 2019) AM No 19-10-20-SC *2019 Amendments to the 1997 Rules of Civil Procedure*

18.9 Summary of applicable legislation if the 'seat' of the dispute determination is in the Philippines

Limitation periods	*Republic Act No 386* *Civil Code of the Philippines* art 1444 *Implementing Rules and Regulations of Alternative Dispute Resolution Act of 2004* AM No 07–11–08-SC *Special Rules of Court on Alternative Dispute Resolution* (1 September 2009) AM No 04-3-15-SC-PHILJA *Implementing Rules & Regulations on Mediation in the Trial Courts* (23 March 2004) *CIAC Revised Rules of Procedure Governing Construction Arbitration* (28 February 2019) AM No 19-10-20-SC *2019 Amendments to the 1997 Rules of Civil Procedure*
Alternative Dispute Resolution	*Implementing Rules and Regulations of Alternative Dispute Resolution Act of 2004* AM No 07–11–08-SC *Special Rules of Court on Alternative Dispute Resolution* (1 September 2009) AM No 04-3-15-SC-PHILJA *Implementing Rules & Regulations on Mediation in the Trial Courts* (23 March 2004) AM No 19-10-20-SC *2019 Amendments to the 1997 Rules of Civil Procedure*
Arbitration	*Executive Order No 1008* *Construction Industry Arbitration Law* *CIAC Revised Rules of Procedure Governing Construction Arbitration* (28 February 2019)

18.10 Issues that a court or arbitrator may construe differently to that expected from the words of the Contract, because of local law or custom

18.10.1 Disputes relating to non-contractual claims may not be arbitrable

In the Philippines, not all construction-related disputes are arbitrable by the CIAC. CIAC's jurisdiction may include but is not limited to the following issues:

1. Violation of specifications for materials and workmanship
2. Violation of the terms of the agreement
3. Interpretation and/or application of contractual provisions
4. Amount of damages and penalties
5. Commencement time and delays
6. Maintenance and defects

7. Payment default of employer or contractor and
8. Changes in contract cost.[78]

18.11 References

18.11.1 Internet

Constitution, Acts, Executive Orders, Presidential Decrees, Proclamations: http://www.asianlii.org/resources/247.html

Court of Appeals decisions 2004 – http://www.asianlii.org/ph/cases/PHCA/

Supreme Court decisions 1901 – http://www.asianlii.org/ph/cases/PHSC/

78 *Executive Order No 1008*, s 4. https://ciap.dti.gov.ph/sites/default/files/E.O.%201008_0.pdf (accessed 27 October 2020).

CHAPTER 19

Applying FIDIC contracts in Singapore[1]

Yvonne Foo

1 The author acknowledges and thanks Justin Tan and Lloyd Tan for their assistance.

DOI: 10.4324/9781003200901-19

19.1 Outline of the legal environment in Singapore

19.1.1 The constitutional structure of Singapore

Singapore's *Constitution* sets out the fundamental principles and framework for the three branches of government, ie the legislature, the executive and the judiciary.

The legislature is made up of a single House of Parliament and the President. Laws are enacted through Parliament and assented to by the President.

The executive is headed by the President, who is Singapore's head of state. In practice, the President's authority is exercised through the Cabinet of Singapore, which is in turn led by the Prime Minister, who is the head of government. Cabinet ministers are drawn from Members of Parliament.

The judiciary is the final branch of government and is headed by the Chief Justice. The judiciary's role is to administer justice via the court system so as to ensure that justice is accessible to all.

19.1.2 The legal system of Singapore

Singapore uses the common law legal system. Much of Singapore's common law principles are like those of the English common law (particularly in areas of contract, tort and restitution). However, Parliament has also supplemented or replaced the common law in many areas via statute.

The Singapore courts have also developed Singapore's own case law, especially in statute-based areas such as company law, criminal law and evidence. At times and as appropriate, the Singapore courts still refer to case law across the Commonwealth (particularly from England, Australia, New Zealand, Canada, Hong Kong, India and Malaysia) where they may be persuasive or otherwise helpful in any particular case.

19.1.3 The court system of Singapore

Broadly, the Singapore judiciary has two tiers – the State Courts and the Supreme Court. This chapter focuses on the judiciary's civil jurisdiction and will not delve into the other aspects of the judiciary (such as family or criminal law, and the Syariah courts).

The State Courts form the lower tier in the judicial hierarchy and handle the bulk of all court matters. Over 95 per cent of all judicial cases in Singapore are heard in the State Courts.[2] It comprises the small claims tribunals, Magistrates' Courts and District Courts, which hear civil disputes which do not exceed the amounts of SG$20,000, SG$60,000 and SG$250,000 (US$15,000, US$45,000 and US$187,000) respectively.

The Supreme Court is made up of the High Court and Court of Appeal. The High Court can hear all civil claims, but usually hears those exceeding SG$250,000 (US$187,000). The High Court also has general supervisory and revisionary jurisdiction over all State Courts in any civil matter and can therefore reverse decisions from the State Courts or ask for a new trial to be conducted.

The Singapore International Commercial Court (**SICC**) has recently been set up as a division of the High Court. The SICC is designed to deal with transnational commercial disputes as an alternative to international arbitration, particularly in resolving the typical issues encountered such as the rising costs of arbitration and increasing lack of speediness in resolution of disputes.

The Court of Appeal is the highest court in the land and Singapore's final court of appeal. The Court of Appeal is usually made up of three judges, although there may be five or any greater uneven number of judges if required to pass judgment on issues of significance.

19.2 The construction industry in Singapore

The construction industry plays an important role in the continued development of Singapore. There was encouraging growth in the industry as the number of contracts awarded came in at a total of about SG$33.5 billion (US$25 billion) in 2019, with an expectation of a steady increase in the demands for construction in Singapore in the following years, especially for public infrastructure projects. Some of the major infrastructure projects which were awarded in 2019 included the Integrated Waste Management Facility at Tuas, infrastructure works for Changi Airport Terminal 5, the Jurong Region MRT Line and Cross Island MRT Line. In the private sector, projects including the redevelopment of en-bloc sites, developments at Mandai Park, Jurong Port and Tanjong Pagar Terminal were announced within the same year. Expansion of two integrated resorts were also in planning.

The Covid-19 pandemic which started in early 2020 inevitably impacted the construction industry's recent growth trajectory. The projected construction demand was initially forecast by the Building and Construction Authority (**BCA**) to be between SG$28 billion and SG$33 billion (US$20.9 billion and US$24.7 billion) for 2020. However, this forecast was revised to between SG$18 billion and SG$23 billion (US$13.5 billion and US$17.2 billion) after a mid-year review by BCA – due largely to a drop in private sector contracts which were for example, postponed in the midst of market uncertainty during the pandemic.

2 https://www.supremecourt.gov.sg/who-we-are/the-supreme-court/supreme-court-jurisdiction (accessed 7 December 2020).

Notwithstanding that, there is a pipeline of public infrastructure projects such as public residential developments, new healthcare facilities and transport infrastructure projects including the Cross Island MRT line which are still slated to proceed and thus, anticipated to aid in the recovery of the construction industry. The silver lining in the sudden onset of the pandemic can be found in the acceleration of the industry's focus on strengthening resilience and competitiveness such as exploring the innovative use of technology and digitalisation to improve construction productivity and quality, increasing the awareness and implementation of business continuity plans, and enhancing environmental sustainability. The construction industry has in fact already started on its transformation efforts since the launch of the Construction Industry Transformation Map in 2017. For example, with the Design for Manufacturing and Assembly initiative, a substantial portion of work can be done in a controlled manufacturing environment using methods such as Prefabricated Pre-finished Volumetric Construction (**PPVC**) and Advanced Precast Concrete System (**APCS**), before transportation to the construction site to be assembled. The industry has also been encouraged to continue building up a skilled and competent local workforce which would take the lead in a modernised construction industry in the near future. Stepping up on the industry's efforts in this direction would drive a positive transformation and produce results sooner rather than later.

Generally, there is a good mix of domestic and international developers and main contractors, as well as specialist sub-contractors in fields such as geotechnical, foundation and underground works, in the local construction industry, whereas the sub-contracting level consists mainly of domestic contractors.

Procurement of construction contracts is typically on a design and build or build only basis for local projects involving local stakeholders. However, where international parties are involved, other contracting methods such as on an EPC basis are also commonly used. The most common standard forms of contracts used in Singapore include the Public Sector Standard Conditions of Contract (**PSSCOC**) for Construction Works,[3] PSSCOC for Design and Build, the Singapore Institute of Architects (**SIA**) Building Contracts,[4] the Real Estate Developers' Association of Singapore (**REDAS**) Design & Build Conditions of Contract (and with an Option Module with Employer's Architectural Design),[5] and REDAS Design & Build Conditions of Sub-Contract.[6] There is, however, also an observable increase in the use of the FIDIC Contracts for construction projects in Singapore, and in particular, the 2017 Second Edition has already been used locally.

Multi-tiered dispute resolution clauses are common in construction contracts in Singapore. Mediation or settlement by amicable negotiations between the contracting parties is often stipulated as the first step in the dispute resolution process. It is common for disputes to be referred to and finally resolved by arbitration or litigation. Since the introduction of the *Building and Construction Industry Security of Payment Act* (***SOP Act***) on 1 April 2005, however, statutory adjudication is the most frequently used

3 Latest revised edition of the PSSCOC for Construction Works is the 8th Edition, July 2020.

4 Latest revised edition of the suite of SIA Building Contracts was launched in 2016 and 2017 and comprises the SIA Building Contract 2016 Without Quantities (Domestic & International), SIA Building Contract 2016 With Quantities 2016 (Domestic & International), SIA Building Contract 2016 Design & Build (Domestic & International) and SIA Sub-Contract 2016.

5 Latest revised edition of the REDAS Design & Build Conditions of Contract is the 3rd edition (October 2010).

6 Introduced in July 2013.

method of dispute resolution for construction contracts in Singapore. Adjudication determinations are binding on the contracting parties until and unless enforcement of the determination is refused by a court, the dispute is finally determined by a court or tribunal or at any other dispute resolution proceeding, or the parties settle the dispute by agreement.

19.3 The impact of Covid-19 in Singapore

19.3.1 The impact of Covid-19 on the execution of construction projects in Singapore

Covid-19 impacted (and is continuing to impact at the time of writing) the execution of construction projects in Singapore in many different ways, including issues relating to the restrictions on manpower resources, new requirements for safe management measures at project sites and in offices, and challenges with timely procurement of materials, plant and equipment. The key problems which have arisen are mainly cashflow issues, added complexity for project management, and the uncertainty due to the continuous introduction of new legislation (although necessary for responding adequately to the constantly developing Covid-19 circumstances).

In Singapore, construction projects faced a slew of difficulties relating to manpower resources and in particular, foreign manpower due to drastic measures introduced by the government to curb the rampant spread of the Covid-19 virus among foreign workers (and in particular within the worker dormitories housing the majority of these foreign workers). The Singapore Ministry of Manpower reported that as at June 2020, there were 351,800 foreign work permit holders in the construction, marine shipyard and process sectors.[7]

Initially, there was a lack of manpower resources from countries such as China and Malaysia due to the movement restrictions imposed by these countries. Manpower who would otherwise have arrived or returned from these countries to work on construction projects in Singapore were unable to travel out of these countries. For example, the Movement Control Order was implemented in Malaysia on 18 March 2020 such that travel out of Malaysia (and even out of the particular State that a person was in) was strictly disallowed. Subsequently, large numbers of foreign workers in Singapore were diagnosed as Covid-19 positive. These numbers quickly escalated and remained high for a prolonged period of many months. A key contributing factor was the close proximity that the foreign workers were living with each other in their living quarters, which promoted the rapid spread of the Covid-19 virus. Most of the foreign workforce in the construction industry was therefore quarantined (and also given suitable alternative accommodation with reduced density) during the Circuit Breaker period from 7 April 2020 to 1 June 2020 (essentially a government mandated 'stay-at-home' order with non-essential businesses closed and non-essential movement discouraged). Medical support has also been made available at all worker dormitories so that workers are able to receive the medical attention they need.

Regular Covid-19 testing has since been implemented for all construction workers. In relation to protection of the workers' salaries, the government required employers

7 https://www.mom.gov.sg/documents-and-publications/foreign-workforce-numbers (accessed 10 December 2020).

to continue providing the upkeep and maintenance of Work Permit holders while they are in Singapore and to continue paying the prevailing salaries of foreign employees (wherever possible). To assist employers, the government introduced waivers and rebates of Foreign Worker Levy currently lasting until December 2021. Additionally, the Jobs Support Scheme was also announced by the government to support employers in retaining and continuing to pay their local employees. Although the government took on the initial financial brunt of complying with these new requirements, the buck is still eventually passed to the individual employers of these workers.

New protocols for safe management measures at project sites and in offices are still in place at the time of writing (December 2020). For employer-provided transportation for example, the Ministry of Manpower and the Land Transport Authority issued an advisory requiring the clear floor space of the deck available for each seated passenger to be at least 0.496 square metre, which equates to a 25 per cent reduction of the Maximum Passenger Capacity allowed for each lorry or van. Further, employers are required to procure private transportation for workers staying in the same dormitory to commute to and from their workplaces with no other passengers. Project costs are thus conceivably increased, and productivity is inevitably affected.

Procurement of materials, plant and equipment was also affected since Covid-19 first surfaced in Singapore as the supply chain lies predominantly outside Singapore. For instance, factories in China were shut down by the Chinese government for a period of time, thus affecting the availability of the requisite materials, plant and equipment to be produced in China. Securing alternative sources of supply was tough as Covid-19 hit globally. Moreover, most if not all the projects in Singapore were impacted at the same time and procuring from alternative suppliers was highly competitive and/ or extremely costly.

In order to keep up with the developments on the ground, the BCA in Singapore regularly introduced new directives to manage and control the Covid-19 situation on construction projects. The uncertainty that this brings to the execution of construction projects is inevitable and creates mounting challenges for construction stakeholders who have to ensure they are keeping up to date with the latest developments, regulations and guidelines, or otherwise face heavy fines, suspensions or even revocation of licenses.

19.3.2 The impact of Covid-19 on the operation of construction contracts in Singapore

19.3.2.1 Covid-19 (Temporary Measures) Act 2020

A key measure taken in Singapore to combat the impact of Covid-19 was the passing of the *Covid-19 (Temporary Measures) Act 2020* (***Covid-19 Act***). The *Covid-19 Act* provides temporary relief for a contracting party's inability to perform its contractual obligations if such inability was to a material extent caused by a Covid-19 event, and where a notification for relief is served in accordance with the *Covid-19 Act*. A Covid-19 event is defined under section 2 of the *Covid-19 Act* as follows:

(a) the Covid-19 epidemic or pandemic; or
(b) the operation of or compliance with any law of Singapore or another country or territory, or an order or direction of the Government or any statutory body, or of the government or other public authority of another country or territory, being any law, order or direction that is made by reason of or in connection with Covid-19.

Construction contracts (entered into before 25 March 2020) are included as specified contracts (referred to as **scheduled contracts**) that are afforded temporary relief under the *Covid-19 Act* for the prescribed period, which at the time of writing expires on 31 March 2021.

Generally, the temporary relief that is available to a party unable to perform its contractual obligations under the *Covid-19 Act* (**affected party**) includes relief from the other party commencing or continuing court or arbitration proceedings against the affected party, enforcing a court judgment, arbitral award under the *Arbitration Act* or an adjudication determination under the *SOP Act* against the affected party or its guarantor or surety, enforcing any security over immoveable or moveable property used for the purpose of a trade, business or profession, applying for schemes of arrangement, judicial management, winding up or bankruptcy in relation to the affected party or its guarantor or surety, appointing a receiver or manager over any property or undertaking of the affected party or its guarantor or surety, commencing or levying of execution, distress or other legal proceedings against the property of the affected party of its guarantor or surety, except with leave of court.

Relief specific to construction contracts is set out at section 6 of the *Covid-19 Act*. Firstly, bond calls on performance bonds or 'equivalent' are disallowed until seven days before the expiry date of the said bond as stated on the bond or as extended pursuant to section 6(3) of the *Covid-19 Act*. A bond may be extended by way of an application for extension made to the issuer of the bond not less than seven days before the expiry date stated on the bond. The extension application has to be served on the other contracting party at the same time in order for the bond to be extended to seven days after the end of the prescribed period or such other date agreed between the contracting parties and the issuer of the bond. Secondly, notwithstanding what is stated in the contract, any period between 1 February 2020 and the end of the prescribed period for which the inability to perform the contract is due, to a material extent, to a Covid-19 event is to be disregarded for the purposes of calculating the liquidated damages or other damages payable under the contract. Thirdly, an inability to supply goods or services under a construction or supply contract caused to a material extent by a Covid-19 event is a defence to a claim for the breach of contract in relation to that inability. There is, however, no temporary relief from adjudication proceedings under the *SOP Act*.

Some other key provisions of the *Covid-19 Act* which relate to construction contracts include the implementation of Part 8 of the *Act* on 30 September 2020, pursuant to which relief is afforded to the renter of goods used for construction work where the affected goods rental contract was entered into before 25 March 2020 and was in force at any time from 1 February 2020 to 31 March 2021, and the delay or breach in the contract occurred within the aforesaid period. The *Covid-19 (Temporary Measures) (Amendment No 3) Bill* which was passed on 3 November 2020, also introduced further relevant relief including in Parts 8A and 8B of the *Covid-19 Act* relating to the automatic extension of the project completion date by 122 days (subject to stipulated conditions), and the co-sharing of specified additional costs due to project delays respectively.

To qualify for temporary relief under the *Covid-19 Act*, the affected party must ensure that its inability to perform a contractual obligation started from 1 February 2020 and is materially due to a Covid-19 event, and that a notification for temporary relief is served on all other parties to the contract, any guarantor or surety for the affected party's obligation under the contract, and such other person as prescribed under the *Act*, for example the issuer of a related performance bond. A contracting party who receives a notification for relied is entitled to apply for an assessor's binding determination as to whether the affected party is entitled to temporary relief under the *Covid-19 Act*.

19.4 Singapore governing law of the contract

19.4.1 Constraints on the governing law of a construction contract

Under Singapore law, there is generally no constraint on the contracting parties' choice of the governing law of a construction contract. Party autonomy is typically recognised such that the contracting parties' choice of the governing law is upheld, unless the choice is not *bona fide* or legal, or if there are public policy grounds requiring otherwise.[8]

When contracting parties have not expressly chosen a governing law, the construction contract will be governed by the law with the closest and most real connection to the transaction and the parties.[9]

19.4.2 Formal requirements for a construction contract

For a construction contract, the usual requirements for a valid contract governed by the laws of Singapore will apply – offer and acceptance, consideration, certainty of the essential terms, completeness of the agreement and the intention to create legal relations between parties who have the capacity to contract. There is no formal requirement for a construction contract to be in writing, although most are.

19.5 What Special Provisions in the Particular Conditions are necessary for consistency with applicable laws in Singapore?

19.5.1 FIDIC General Conditions that are incompatible or inconsistent with Singapore governing law of the contract

No FIDIC General Conditions are incompatible or inconsistent with Singapore laws as the governing law of the contract.

19.5.2 FIDIC General Conditions that are incompatible or inconsistent with the law of the Site/Country

No FIDIC General Conditions are incompatible or inconsistent with Singapore laws as the law of the Site/Country.

19.5.3 FIDIC General Conditions that are incompatible or inconsistent with relevant laws on dispute determination in Singapore

No FIDIC General Conditions are incompatible or inconsistent with Singapore laws as the law of the seat of the arbitration or relevant laws on dispute determination.

8 The leading Singapore case in this regard is *Peh Teck Quee v Bayerische Landesbank Girozentrale* [2000] 1 SLR 148 (CA). Subsequent cases have similarly affirmed party autonomy in the choice of governing law for contracts.

9 Tiong Min YEO, 'The Effective Reach of Choice of Law Agreements' (2008) 20(2) *Singapore Academy of Law Journal* 723.

19.6 What Special Provisions in the Particular Conditions are desirable for consistency with applicable laws in Singapore?

19.6.1 Building and Construction Industry Security of Payment Act, Chapter 30B

Since its introduction in Singapore on 1 April 2005, the *SOP Act* has played a significant part in many construction projects in Singapore – to say the least, in ensuring that 'everyone in the industry gets paid honest wages for an honest day's work', as Dr Amy Khor Lean Suan aptly expressed at the Second Reading of the *Building and Construction Industry Security of Payment Bill* on 16 November 2004. The primary purpose of the *SOP Act* is to protect the rights to payment for work done and goods supplied in the construction industry. It governs the adjudication process regarding interim payments for work done and goods supplied so as to facilitate cashflow within the construction industry in Singapore.

Pursuant to section 4 of the *SOP Act*, the provisions of the *SOP Act* apply to any contract for the carrying out construction work and/ or supply of goods and services for construction work requiring building plan approval in Singapore.

The *SOP Act* was most recently amended on 15 December 2019 such that its application is now extended to also cover contracts relating to the prefabrication of components (whether in or outside Singapore) for construction work to be carried out on a construction site in Singapore. It is noteworthy that the *SOP Act* applies to any written contract which falls within the aforesaid ambit, even if the governing law is not Singapore law.

The *SOP Act* sets out strict procedural requirements for the adjudication process in order to ensure that the process remains a speedy one. For example, section 11 of the *SOP Act* provides that a payment response to a payment claim served in relation to a construction contract shall be served according to the terms of the construction contract, but no later than 21 days after the payment claim is served under section 10. For the sake of completeness, where the construction contract does not contain such terms, the payment response is required to be served within 14 days after the payment claim is served. As stated in section 36 of the *SOP Act*, contracting parties are not allowed to contract out of the provisions of the *SOP Act*.

The Contractor's application for interim and final payment under clauses 14.3 and 14.11 respectively of the General Conditions and the Engineer's issuance of a corresponding Interim Payment Certificate and Final Payment Certificate under clauses 14.6 and 14.3 respectively of the General Conditions may constitute the Payment Claim and Payment Response respectively for the purposes of an adjudication under the *SOP Act*. The timeline stipulated for the Engineer's issuance of Interim Payment Certificates and a Final Payment Certificate (ie within 28 days after receiving the relevant Statement) should therefore be reviewed to determine whether it is appropriate in light of this legislation. Otherwise, section 11 of the *SOP Act* will operate to reduce the time for issuance of the relevant Payment Certificate from 28 days to 21 days.

19.6.2 Cross-construction contract claims not allowed in SOP adjudication

The same contracting parties could enter into various construction contracts in relation to different projects, or for different phases or parts of the same project. For the purposes of a SOP adjudication, the respondent is not entitled to withhold or set-off claims under a separate contract from the monies due to a claimant under the contract that an SOP adjudication has been brought. In the case of *Civil Tech Pte Ltd v Hua Rong Engineering Pte Ltd Civil* [2018] SGCA 12, the Court of Appeal referred to such a claim as a Cross-Construction Contract Claim and held on the narrow issue of law that a Cross-Construction Contract Claim is not a valid withholding reason pursuant to sections 17(3) and 11 of the *SOP Act*. Otherwise, it would lead to an inconsistency with the primary purpose of the *SOP Act* to facilitate cash flow as adjudicators could potentially be required to consider extensive documentation relating to claims arising under contracts other than the one to which the adjudication relates. Respondents may also attempt to evade the deadlines under the *SOP Act* in relation to such Cross-Construction Contract Claims if they are allowed to be considered for adjudications that did not arise out of the Cross-Construction Contract itself. Note, however, that the Court of Appeal specifically left open the issue of whether 'the only valid reasons under the *Act* were those arising from the Payment Claim Contract ("the Single Contract Interpretation") was correct'.

In light of the current position under Singapore law as to Cross-Construction Contract Claims, clauses 14.3(vi) and 14.6(b) of the General Conditions should be reviewed to determine if it is appropriate to set out Special Provisions to clarify the Parties' intention in this regard, and in particular if it is intended that the Employer would have a right to make deductions which have become due 'otherwise' than under the FIDIC Contract, ie deductions due under a separate contract.

19.6.3 Right to serve a payment claim after contract termination for SOP adjudication

In the case of *Shimizu Corporation v Stargood Construction Pte Ltd* [2020] SGCA 37, the Court of Appeal considered the issue of whether the terms of the subcontract entitled the Subcontractor, ie Stargood Construction Pte Ltd, to serve payment claims following termination of the contract by the Contractor, ie Shimizu Corporation, under clause 33.2 of the contract in question. The relevant provision highlighted by the court concerning the effect of a termination of the contract under clause 33.2 was set out in clause 33.4 as follows:

> Upon termination of the [Subcontract] under clauses 33.2 or 33.3 hereof:
>
> (a) [Shimizu] shall be entitled to damages on the same basis as if [Stargood] had wrongfully repudiated the Sub-Contract …

Importantly, there was no entitlement for the Subcontractor to make a payment claim in the event of a termination of the contract under clause 33.2. This was contrasted with the provision under clause 33.5 in relation to a termination of the Subcontract due to the termination of the main contract, where '[Stargood] shall in that event be entitled to payment for work done and materials supplied by him on the [Subcontract] Prices and Rates' if the termination of the main contract was for some reason unconnected to the Subcontractor's default.

Accordingly, the Court of Appeal held that the Subcontractor had no right to serve a payment claim for work done prior to termination if the subcontract is terminated for its default, ie pursuant to clause 33.2.

In light of the above, contracting parties to a FIDIC contract ought to be cognisant of the differing rights arising from the various methods of termination. In particular, when the Contract is terminated for the Contractor's default, clause 15.3 requires the Engineer 'to agree or determine the value of the Permanent Works, Goods and Contractor's Documents, and any other sums due to the Contractor for work executed in accordance with the Contract'. Although the aforesaid provision arguably gives the Contractor an entitlement to be paid the value for the work executed according to the Contract, contracting parties may wish to consider making such entitlement explicit if the intention is to allow the Contractor to serve a payment claim after termination of the Contract and to avail of the adjudication regime. Note, however, that pursuant to section 4(2)(c) of the *SOP Act*, clause 15.4 would likely be construed to postpone the Contractor's right to serve a payment claim and to commence an adjudication until after 'all the costs, losses and damages (if any) described in' clause 15.4 are established.

For completeness, it appears that the Contractor has an express entitlement to submit 'detailed supporting particulars' (ie which could be construed as a payment claim under the *SOP Act*) for payment subsequent to a termination if the Employer terminates the Contract for convenience pursuant to clause 15.6, if the Contractor terminates the Contract pursuant to clause 16.4, or if the either Party invokes optional termination pursuant to clause 18.5.

The relevant termination and payment clauses in the FIDIC Contract should be reviewed to determine whether they are appropriate in light of the above.

19.6.4 Priority of specially drafted terms over general conditions

Where there is conflict between the standard terms incorporated into a contract and the specific terms drafted for the contract, the Court of Appeal in Singapore have held that the latter will take precedence.

In the case of *Ser Kim Koi v GTMS Construction Pte Ltd* [2016] 3 SLR 51, it was held by the Court of Appeal that a specially drafted term should take precedence over the printed conditions. This was further reinforced in the case of *Grouteam Pte Ltd v UES Holdings Pte Ltd* [2016] 5 SLR 1011, where there was a dispute between the main Contractor and the subcontractor. The timeline for the service of payment claims stated in the Summary of Contract Negotiations annexed to the Subcontract Agreement, which was signed by the parties just two days before the subcontract was executed, was held to take precedence over that stated in the Preliminaries, which was taken from the main contract which the subcontractor was not a party to.

The priority of documents forming the Contract stated at clause 1.5 of the FIDIC General Conditions allows Parties to include 'other documents forming part of the Contract'. Where such other documents are not specifically listed in order of priority, it is likely that specially drafted terms will take precedence over General Conditions. Accordingly, it will be prudent for contracting parties to review terms which are specifically drafted for the Contract to ensure that these terms conform with the Parties' agreement.

19.6.5 Frustrated Contracts Act, Chapter 115

Under section 2 of the *Frustrated Contracts Act*, contracting parties to contracts which have 'become impossible of performance or been otherwise frustrated' would for that reason be discharged from the further performance of the contract, subject to section 3 of the *Frustrated Contracts Act*. Consequences of such discharge are also stipulated within the *Frustrated Contracts Act*.

Section 3(3) states that where a contract contains provisions which operate in the event that circumstances arise (or not) in relation to frustration of the contract, section 2 would only be given effect 'to such extent, if any, as appears to the court to be consistent with that provision'.

Clause 18 of the General Conditions should therefore be reviewed to determine if it is appropriate in light of this legislation.

19.6.6 Gross negligence

There is no settled meaning for 'gross negligence' under Singapore law. On the contrary, the High Court held in the case of *Sie Choon Poh (trading as Image Galaxy) v Amara Hotel Properties Pte Ltd* [2005] 3 SLR(R) 576 that to determine 'whether there had been gross negligence, the particular circumstances in each case had to be examined' and that it is not 'possible to lay down a standard, derived logically from past cases, by which a court can confidently rule when negligence should be deemed to be gross negligence'.[10]

Parties may wish to prescribe, in the FIDIC Contract, more clarity to the ambit of term 'gross negligence' used in clause 1.15 of the General Conditions.

19.6.7 Contracts (Rights of Third Parties) Act, Chapter 53B

Section 2(1) of the *Contracts (Rights of Third Parties) Act* allows 'a person who is not a party to a contract' to 'enforce a term of the contract' in his own right if:

(a) the contract expressly provides that he may; or
(b) subject to subsection (2), the term purports to confer a benefit on him.

Section 2(2) of the *Act* states that section 2(1)(b) 'shall not apply if, on a proper construction of the contract, it appears that the parties did not intend the term to be enforceable by the third party'.

The contracting parties may consider inserting Special Provisions excluding the application of the *Contracts (Rights of Third Parties) Act*. Clause 4.5.3 of the General Conditions should be reviewed to determine if it is appropriate in light of this legislation.

19.7 Summary of applicable legislation for Singapore governing law of the contract

19.7.1 Entry into a construction contract

Contracts generally	Common law principles
Construction contracts	Common law principles

19.7.2 Termination of a construction contract

Frustration	*Frustrated Contracts Act* (Cap 115, 2014 Rev. Ed.)
Bankruptcy, insolvency, liquidation	*Insolvency, Restructuring and Dissolution Act 2018* (No. 40 of 2018) *Companies Act* (Cap 50, 2006 Rev. Ed.)

10 At paragraph 6.

19.7.3 Dispute resolution

Limitation periods	*Limitation Act* (Cap 163, 1996 Rev. Ed.)
Liability	*Civil Law Act* (Cap 43, 1999 Rev. Ed.) *Contributory Negligence and Personal Injuries Act* (Cap 54, 2002 Rev. Ed.) *Unfair Contract Terms Act* (Cap 396, 1994 Rev. Ed.)
Adjudication	*Building and Construction Industry Security of Payment Act* (Cap 30B, 2006 Rev. Ed.)
Arbitration	*Arbitration Act* (Cap 10, 2002 Rev. Ed.) *International Arbitration Act* (Cap 143A, 2002 Rev. Ed.)

19.8 Summary of applicable legislation if the Site/Country is in Singapore

19.8.1 Operation of a construction contract

Registration and administration of professionals – Engineers, Architects, Building Surveyors, Surveyors	*Building Control Act* (Cap 29, 1999 Rev. Ed.) *Professional Engineers Act* (Cap 253, 1992 Rev. Ed.) *Architects Act* (Cap 12, 2000 Rev. Ed.) *Land Surveyors Act* (Cap 156, 2012 Rev. Ed.)
Registration/ licencing of Contractors and subcontractors	*Building Control Act* (Cap 29, 1999 Rev. Ed.) *Building Control (Licensing of Builders) Regulations* 2008 *Building Control (Value of Significant General Building Work Projects) Order 2008* *Building and Construction Authority (Registration of Construction Personnel) Regulations 2008*
Use of liens/ Assignment of debts	*Building and Construction Industry Security of Payment Act* (Cap 30B, 2006 Rev. Ed.)
Labour	*Employment Act* (Cap 91, 2009 Rev. Ed.) *Employment of Foreign Manpower Act* (Cap 91A, 2009 Rev. Ed.) *Workplace Safety and Health Act* (Cap 354A, 2009 Rev. Ed.) *Work Injury Compensation Act 2019* (No 27 of 2019)
Design/Moral rights	*Registered Designs Act* (Cap 266, 2005 Rev. Ed.) *Building Control Act* (Cap 29, 1999 Rev. Ed.)
Copyright	*Copyright Act* (Cap 63, 2006 Rev. Ed.)
The product being produced from the Works	*Environmental Protection and Management Act* (Cap 94A, 2002 Rev. Ed.) *Environment Protection and Management (Hazardous Substances) Regulations* (2008 Rev. Ed.) *Fire Safety Act* (Cap 109A, 2000 Rev. Ed.) *Workplace Safety and Health Act* (Cap 354A, 2009 Rev. Ed.)
Planning	*Planning Act* (Cap 232, 1998 Rev. Ed.) *Land Acquisition Act* (Cap 152, 1985 Rev. Ed.) *Land Titles (Strata) Act* (Cap 158, 2009 Rev. Ed.) *Residential Property Act* (Cap 274, 2009 Rev. Ed.) *Building Maintenance and Strata Management Act* (Cap 30C, 2008 Rev. Ed.)
Work affecting adjacent property to the Site	*Conveyancing and Law of Property Act* (Cap 61, 1994 Rev. Ed.) Common law principles

Heritage	*Preservation of Monuments Act* (Cap 239, 2011 Rev. Ed.) *National Heritage Board Act* (Cap 196A, 2014 Rev. Ed.) *Planning Act* (Cap 232, 1998 Rev. Ed.)
Environment	*Environmental Protection and Management Act* (Cap 94A, 2002 Rev. Ed.) *Environmental Public Health Act* (Cap 95, 2002 Rev. Ed.) *Transboundary Haze Pollution Act 2014* (No. 24 of 2014)
Local procurement	*Government Procurement Act* (Cap 120, 1998 Rev. Ed.) *Prevention of Corruption Act* (Cap 241, 1993 Rev. Ed.)
Building and construction permits, Execution of construction work, Standard of construction work	*Building Control Act* (Cap 29, 1999 Rev. Ed.)
Health and safety	*Workplace Safety and Health Act* (Cap 354A, 2009 Rev. Ed.) *Work Injury Compensation Act 2019* (No 27 of 2019) *Electricity Act* (Cap 89A, 2002 Rev. Ed.) *Gas Act* (Cap 116A, 2002 Rev. Ed.) *Fire Safety Act* (Cap 109A, 2000 Rev. Ed.)
Calibration of testing apparatus, equipment and instruments	*Sale of Goods Act* (Cap 393, 1999 Rev. Ed.) *Workplace Safety and Health Act* (Cap 354A, 2009 Rev. Ed.)
Insurance	*Insurance Act* (Cap 142, 2002 Rev. Ed.) *Work Injury Compensation Act 2019* (No 27 of 2019)
Statutory rights that coexist with contractual rights	*Building and Construction Industry Security of Payment Act* (Cap 30B, 2006 Rev. Ed.)
Liability for defective work	*Building Maintenance and Strata Management Act* (Cap 30C, 2008 Rev. Ed.)
Liability for nuisance	*Miscellaneous Offences (Public Order and Nuisance) Act* (Cap 184, 1997 Rev. Ed.) Common law principles

19.8.2 Termination of a construction contract

Bankruptcy, insolvency, liquidation	*Insolvency, Restructuring and Dissolution Act 2018* (No. 40 of 2018) *Companies Act* (Cap 50, 2006 Rev. Ed.)

19.8.3 Dispute resolution

Dispute before a local board/ Adjudication	*Building and Construction Industry Security of Payment Act* (Cap 30B, 2006 Rev. Ed.)
Limitation periods	*Limitation Act* (Cap 163, 1996 Rev. Ed.)

19.9 Summary of applicable legislation if the 'seat' of the dispute determination is in Singapore

Dispute resolution	*Building and Construction Industry Security of Payment Act* (Cap 30B, 2006 Rev. Ed.)
Limitation periods	*Limitation Act* (Cap 163, 1996 Rev. Ed.)
Adjudication	*Building and Construction Industry Security of Payment Act* (Cap 30B, 2006 Rev. Ed.)
Arbitration	*Arbitration Act* (Cap 10, 2002 Rev. Ed.) *International Arbitration Act* (Cap 143A, 2002 Rev. Ed.)

19.10 Issues that a court or arbitrator may construe differently to that expected from the words of the Contract, because of local law or custom

19.10.1 Exercise of Engineer's duties

In relation to the Engineer's exercise of its duties, Clause 3.2 of the General Conditions provides that:

> Except as otherwise stated in these Conditions, whenever carrying out duties or exercising authority, specified in or implied by the Contract, the Engineer shall act as a skilled professional and shall be deemed to act for the Employer. …

Further, as provided under Clause 3.7 of the General Conditions:

> **When carrying out his/ her duties under this Sub-Clause, the Engineer shall act neutrally between the Parties and shall not be deemed to act for the Employer. …**

These clauses are consistent with how a court or arbitrator may construe that stipulated in the words of the Contract. However, it would be worthwhile to note that it is possible for the Engineer to also be expected to exercise his/her function in good faith.

As the High Court stated in the case of *Aoki Corp v Lippoland (Singapore) Pte Ltd* [1995] 1 SLR(R) 314 at paragraph 36, '[n]eedless to say, the architect must exercise his function as the certifier in good faith and to the best of his uninfluenced professional judgment, even though he is usually appointed by the employer. Otherwise, the object of the provisions for temporary finality could be defeated'. The SIA contract form was used in this case, under which the architect was obliged to issue a delay certificate if the Contractor failed to complete the building work by the original date for completion in the contract or by any extended date for completion. The Court of Appeal's holding in the case of *Hiap Hong & Co Pte Ltd v Hong Huat Development Co (Pte) Ltd* [2001] SGCA 17 was also instructive in this regard. The Court recognised that the architect (also under an SIA contract form in this case) has a dual function. At paragraph 16, the Court of Appeal stated that:

> [i]t is equally settled law that an owner and a contractor would have made their contract on the understanding that in all matters where the architect has to apply his professional skill and judgment, the architect will act in a fair and unbiased manner in applying the terms of the contract. Such matters will include the issue of certificates for payments and the grant of extension of time. While an architect under such a contract is the employer's agent, in the exercise of his function requiring skill and judgment, he must act fairly and

professionally and neither party should seek to unfairly or unduly influence him in the discharge of those functions.

Note that in the same case, the Court rejected the submission that there was an implied duty on the Employer to oversee the certification function of the architect such that the Employer is liable for the architect's failure to issue an interim certificate at the prescribed time regardless of the reasons for the failure and whether the Employer knew of the cause of the delay.

19.11 References

19.11.1 Journals

Tan Chau Yee, Justin Tan, Andrea Koh, 'Summarising the Covid-19 (Temporary Measures) Act 2020 for the Construction Industry [2020] Singapore Academy of Law, *SAL Prac* 10
Singapore Academy of Law Annual Review of Singapore Cases

19.11.2 Internet

Case law: www.lawnet.sg (accessed 6 December 2020)
Legislation: www.sso.agc.gov.sg (accessed 6 December 2020)
www.singaporelawwatch.sg (accessed 6 December 2020)
www.bca.gov.sg (accessed 6 December 2020)
www.mom.gov.sg (accessed 6 December 2020)

CHAPTER 20

Applying FIDIC contracts in Sri Lanka

Dr Harsha Cabral PC, Malith Mendis and Chamaka Ambagahawita

DOI: 10.4324/9781003200901-20

20.1 Outline of the legal environment in Sri Lanka

20.1.1 The constitutional structure of Sri Lanka

In the political history of Sri Lanka, under the 'dominium' of the British Empire for centuries, various forms of 'Constitutional Documents' were formulated from time to time in an attempt to structure a 'workable' system of governance for Sri Lanka. Although Sri Lanka achieved independence on 4 February 1948, it was not until 1972 that Sri Lanka had a 'Constitutional Document of its own'- the first autochthonous Constitution. Thereafter, in 1978 the second autochthonous Constitution (*Second Republican Constitution of Sri Lanka 1978,* the present ***Constitution***) was enacted which is currently in force together with 19 amendments to date.[1]

In terms of the *Constitution*, Sri Lanka is a free, sovereign, independent and democratic Socialist Republican State which is a unitary State comprised of 24 Administrative Districts and 9 Provinces.[2] Further, in terms of the *Constitution* the inalienable sovereignty of the State vests with the People which comprises the powers of Government, fundamental rights and the franchise exercised and enjoyed by the People in the form of Legislative Power, Executive Power, Judicial Power and Fundamental Rights.[3]

20.1.2 The legal system of Sri Lanka

The legal system of Sri Lanka is a composite of Roman-Dutch law, English law, Sinhalese/Kandyan law, Theswalamai law and Muslim law. The common law of Sri Lanka has been the Roman-Dutch law, and constitutes the residuary law of the land applicable in the absence of specific or general statutory provisions. However, with the 'dominium' of the British Empire, principles of English law were infiltrated to the legal system through a series of codification of statutes such as the *Penal Code*, the *Evidence Ordinance* and the *Sale of Goods Ordinance.* Through the provisions of the *Introduction of English Law Ordinance*[4] the English law for the time being applicable in the United Kingdom was incorporated to determine disputes in specific areas of

1 Sinhalese and Tamil are official languages, with English as the link language; see art 18 of the *Second Republican Constitution of Sri Lanka 1978* (the *Constitution*).

2 *Constitution*, arts 1, 2 and 5. See also the Sch 5 and the 13th Amendment to the *Constitution.*

3 See ibid arts 3 and 4.

4 *Civil Law Ordinance* (also known as the *Introduction of English Law Ordinance) No 5 of 1852*, as subsequently amended.

the law such as banks and banking, corporations and partnerships, agency, life and fire insurance and maritime matters (including marine insurance). Furthermore, English law was infiltrated into the country through judicial incorporation by case law. Therefore, although the subject of contract law is governed by the Roman-Dutch law, being the common law and/or residual law of the country, almost all of the principles of contract law well established in Sri Lanka are principles incorporated through judicial incorporation of English law on the subject. Therefore, it is safe to draw the conclusion that, principles of English law apply to contracts subject to few exceptions.[5]

Principles of customary law such as Sinhalese or Kandyan law, Theswalamai law and Muslim law apply only to the extent permitted by statutory provisions and these laws are not of general application but apply to sections of the community.[6]

20.1.3 The court system of Sri Lanka

The *Constitution* declares that the judicial power of the People shall be exercised by Parliament through courts, tribunals and institutions, created or recognised by the *Constitution* or by law, except in regard to parliamentary privileges.[7] The *Constitution*, moreover, contains detailed legal provisions ensuring the independence of the Judiciary,[8] which comprises Courts exercising both original jurisdiction and appellate jurisdiction. While the original civil jurisdiction is exercised by Primary Courts, Family Courts, District Courts, and Commercial High Courts, the original criminal jurisdiction is exercised by Magistrates' Courts and High Courts in Sri Lanka. In addition to these courts, there are also Labour Tribunals which deal with private sector employment related issues.

Before the enactment of the Thirteenth Amendment to the *Constitution*, persons aggrieved by decisions of original courts, had the right to appeal to the Court of Appeal, and therefrom to the Supreme Court.[9] The Thirteenth Amendment to the *Constitution* established the Provincial High Courts to hear appeals from decisions of Primary Courts, Magistrates' Courts, and Labour Tribunals.[10] Following the Thirteenth Amendment, a litigant can also appeal from the Provincial High Court directly to the Supreme Court. Further, a litigant aggrieved by a decision of the District Court can also lodge an appeal to the Provincial Civil Appellate High Court and obtain relief from it.

The Supreme Court being the apex court in Sri Lanka exercising final appellate jurisdiction, is also constitutionally vested with the exclusive original jurisdiction on constitutional matters and applications relating to violations of the Fundamental Rights. On the other hand, the Court of Appeal in Sri Lanka is vested with the writ jurisdiction except where it is provided in any law that such jurisdiction shall be exercised exclusively by the Supreme Court.[11]

---

5 See eg the notion of ***justa causa*** [just cause] under Roman-Dutch Law is applicable under the law of contract in Sri Lanka. Hence, the notion of consideration of English law is not applicable in Sri Lanka.

6 See LJM Cooray, *An Introduction to the Legal System of Sri Lanka* (Stamford Lake 1992)

7 *Constitution*, art 2.

8 ibid arts 105–17.

9 ibid art 127 read with art 138.

10 ibid art 154P(3)(b) read with s 4 of the High Court of the *Provinces (Special Provisions) Act No 19 of 1990*.

11 ibid arts 140–41.

20.2 The construction industry in Sri Lanka

20.2.1 Overview

Sri Lanka has a long history of construction of cities, religious monuments and reservoirs, steeped in its ancient hydraulic civilisations.

The current construction industry has weathered many storms and was subjected to the economic cycles mostly affected by the civil war that lasted for 25 years. With the periodic absence of a peaceful environment combined with a shortage of material and labour, Sri Lanka's domestic construction industry has seen its ups and downs. For many years, while foreign consultants and contractors succeeded in securing the larger aid-funded and investment projects, the local subcontractors and the lsocal sub-consultants, for the most part, played a limited role in such projects.

The construction industry in Sri Lanka contributes approximately 9% of Sri Lanka's GDP, employing around 600,000 personnel. In the past few years, the total annual construction turnover has been approximately LKR 800b (equivalent to US$ 4.3b). A comparison of the construction costs of middle-class housing, reveals that the unit cost of construction in Sri Lanka is the highest in the region, ranked second only to Singapore, a well-developed country with a very high GDP per capita.[12] The comparatively higher costs of construction in Sri Lanka, is manifested by the costs incurred in setting up industrial ventures. This could discourage direct foreign investment, which would be detrimental to the economic growth of Sri Lanka.

20.2.2 Construction Industry Development Authority

The *Construction Industry Development Act No 33 of 2014* (the *Construction Industry Development Act*) gave birth to the Construction Industry Development Authority (**CIDA**), formerly known as the Institute for Construction Training and Development (ICTAD). With the enactment of the *Construction Industry Development Act*, the Sri Lankan construction industry has been blessed with orderly and tightened regulation. Regulations introduced by the *Construction Industry Development Act* include, inter alia, provisions for registration, formalisation and standardisation of the activities within the construction industry. Further, it introduced provisions for the improvement and wellbeing of industry related professionals, manufacturers, suppliers, contractors and craftsmen. Notable among the features introduced by the *Construction Industry Development Act* was the formation of a mechanism to settle disputes related to construction activities. These regulations have however, faced criticism from time to time, such as CIDA's attempts to register adjudicators and consulting engineers, and legislation that only CIDA Works Contract Forms are to be used for non-MDB or direct foreign investment projects. These are seen as over-regulation by the industry. The contractual documents promulgated by the CIDA, namely the CIDA Works Contracts, require further development in order to facilitate EPC/turnkey or design, build and operate projects. This is regardless of the amendments brought in, from time to time, to such CIDA Works Contracts.[13]

---

12 Chamber of Construction Industry Sri Lanka, Proposals for Budget 2019 (27 September 2018).

13 Some 'players' in the construction industry are of the view that certain amendments introduced as such have been detrimental to certain stakeholders in the construction industry. By and large CIDA Works Contracts have been inspired by the FIDIC Contracts forms which are widely used, especially in foreign funded projects. CIDA Standard Bidding Documents are available at: http://www.cida.gov.lk/sub_pgs/publications.html (accessed 15 September 2020).

CIDA performs the task of evaluating and grading local construction contractors based on pre-qualification for size and specialisation. There are over 2,500 construction contractors registered with CIDA. Among them are approximately 60 contractors registered under Grade C1, out of which 29 contractors are considered major contractors and are represented by their association – the Major Constructors of Sri Lanka (MCSL). The specialised contractors for Electrical & Mechanical Services (EM), for piling works and other specialised construction contractors (such as for aluminium work, floor and ceiling finishes etc.) are graded separately.[14] CIDA has also started registering qualified persons, such as engineers, architects and quantity surveyors from 2019.

CIDA facilitates and regulates the construction industry by setting standards, providing advisory services, facilitating alternative dispute resolution procedures, conducting technical auditing and research on construction economics, registration and monitoring of qualified persons and designating Identified Construction Works. Activities of this entity extend to the stakeholders of the construction industry, such as clients, consultants, contractors, policymakers, investors, planners etc. contributing to the development of the construction industry. These activities are aimed at regularising, harmonising and systematising construction activities to make the construction industry more effective and efficient. Whilst promoting and facilitating local consultancy services and work of locally registered contractors, this entity also assists by promoting and facilitating them to undertake construction work overseas.[15]

20.2.3 Industry associations

The Chamber of Construction Industry (**CCI**) is the Sri Lankan construction industry's apex association body, with the National Construction Association of Sri Lanka (**NCASL**) being the representative association of the construction contracting industry. The Association of Consulting Engineers Sri Lanka (**ACESL**) is a member association of FIDIC and represents the consulting engineering industry of Sri Lanka in many fora. The prominent professional bodies are the Engineering Council of Sri Lanka (**ECSL**), the Institution of Engineers Sri Lanka (**IESL**), the Sri Lanka Institute of Architects (**SLIA**) and the Institution of Quantity Surveyors of Sri Lanka (**IQSSL**).

20.2.4 Current status and growth of the Sri Lankan construction industry

The construction industry of Sri Lanka operates in both the private and the public sectors, across three broad areas of activity, namely, in the engineering construction (usually major infrastructure), in the non-residential building (including offices, shops, hotels, industrial premises, hospitals, entertainment facilities, etc.) and in the residential building (houses, apartments, housing schemes etc.) spheres.

The industry is currently regulated by the CIDA and most developmental activities require approvals from, inter alia, the Urban Development Authority of Sri Lanka (UDA), the Municipal Councils and various other local government bodies established

14 http://www.cida.gov.lk/sub_pgs/con_registration.html (accessed 15 September 2020).
15 http://www.cida.gov.lk/sub_pgs/advisory.html (accessed 15 September 2020).

for specific purposes. Most of the major developments require an environmental impact assessment (EIA) and such other permissions issued by the Central Environmental Authority of Sri Lanka (CEA).

Multilateral Development Banks (**MDBs**), such as the Asian Development Bank and the World Bank are active in many infrastructure development projects, as well as various aid-agencies such as JICA, OPEC, Kuwait Fund etc. In addition, many infrastructure projects are being funded by loans from various Chinese banks, which have become prominent since the end of the civil war in 2009. The MDBs and other aid-agencies have been instrumental in promoting the appointment of Dispute Adjudication Boards in their project contracts for dispute avoidance and resolution. Currently, Sri Lanka lacks legislative measures for the provision of statutory adjudication.

The consulting industry in construction largely remains small, usually playing the role of sub-consultants to foreign consultants. Other than a few large firms, most are small firms. The SLIA regulation that architectural firms remain owned by Chartered Architects to maintain registration with SLIA may be a disincentive to their growth. Similar moves are expected for engineering consultancies, which may also hinder their growth. A large government owned entity which secures negotiated consultancy contracts with the government, also seem to hinder the growth of private sector and independent consultants. The MDBs also have influence in this area, where they grant consultancy contracts only to independent private firms if the implementing agency is the Government of Sri Lanka (**GOSL**), together with encouragement to international consultants to engage local consultants as sub-consultants. Some local consulting firms are known to engage in work overseas, although the GOSL has been slow to see this as an area of export.

The imposition of high taxes, resulting in increased cost of imported material, shortages and high costs associated with construction sand, high competition between local construction firms and foreign construction firms which enjoy various incentives from their governments, competition to and access to low cost capital are some of the factors which undermine the growth of the construction industry, especially the local industry.

There are a variety of incentives offered for foreign funded projects, including those approved by the Board of Investment of Sri Lanka (BOI) and the Special Development Projects. These incentives include VAT and tax exemptions, duty free import of material and equipment and other incentives. The majority of such projects are handled by foreign consultants and contractors, with the local industry playing a subcontract role. As a result, one can observe an unequal bargaining power between the local and the foreign participants. In the last few years, the GOSL has initiated locally funded infrastructure projects with projects divided into smaller sections contracted to local consultants and contractors, with the intention of promoting growth of the local industry and to garner experience.

Salaries of workers are regulated by the *Wages Boards Ordinance No 27 of 1941* (as amended) and health and safety is regulated by the *National Institute of Occupational Safety and Health Act No 38 of 2009*.

Insurance for workers is covered by the *Workmen's Compensation Ordinance No 19 of 1934* (as amended) and is offered by most insurance firms operating in Sri Lanka, as well as Personal Accident Insurance cover and Contractor's All Risk Insurance cover. Professional Indemnity Insurance is offered by a few insurance firms, with little or no coverage for practice outside Sri Lanka. Insurance Guarantees as Performance and Tender Securities are also offered by insurance firms in Sri Lanka, although they are not accepted by most Employers.

There is an increased use of DABs in most MDB supported projects as the first tier of dispute resolution and also the adoption of standing boards. The *Arbitration Act No 11 of 1995* governs arbitral proceedings in Sri Lanka. Where parties agree in the Contract, arbitral proceedings can be utilised for the purposes of enforcing DAB decisions.

The FIDIC 1999 Contract forms and the MDB Harmonised editions are widely used. The CIDA Contract forms of SBD 2 (similar to the Red Book), SBD 3 (similar to the Green Book) and SBD 4 (similar to the Yellow book) are also widely used. For house constructions architects tend to use a SLIA approved/formulated contract form. The subcontracts for Red and Yellow Books, Dredging Contract and 2017 edition contracts are not used at the time of writing (2020).

There is little adoption of innovation in construction in Sri Lanka, with construction being site based and using labour extensively. Modular construction is rarely used. BIM is rarely adopted, although the CCI has proposed a BIM Centre to propagate its use.

20.3 The impact of Covid-19 in Sri Lanka

20.3.1 The impact of Covid-19 on the execution of construction projects in Sri Lanka

Lockdown and island-wide curfew was imposed on Sri Lanka in March 2020 and was not lifted for several months. Construction projects were stalled with workers and supplies not available at Sites. The curfew was lifted in outlying provinces earlier than the other provinces, and projects in these areas were re-started earlier. Sri Lanka closed its airports for inward travel (except approved repatriation flights) and this was still in force at the time of writing in September 2020.

These measures meant that the Engineer/Project Manager could not issue any specific instructions to secure and protect works. The Contractor's fixed costs remained the same although no work was done at Sites, with some workers isolated at Site. Many Contractors reduced workers' pay for the duration of these locked down months.

Even before the pandemic effects were felt, there were large amount of outstanding payments to Contractors, the GOSL being the biggest defaulter, with many Contractors suffering cash flow deficits and inability to continue work.

After construction resumed after the lockdown was lifted, construction projects were subject to mandatory health and cleaning protocols, including social distancing, face masks, checking of employees' health, increased record keeping and stringent cleaning protocols to guard against transmission of Covid-19 from contact surfaces. These new measures adversely affected productivity and added significantly to the costs of construction

At the time of writing (September 2020), apart from general legislation for health protection applying to the whole community, the GOSL had not passed any specific legislation in respect of the impact of Covid-19 on construction projects, and has not provided any financial assistance to Contractors.

20.3.2 The impact of Covid-19 on the operation of construction contracts in Sri Lanka

Most Contractors declared *force majeure* provisions of their Contracts during the curfew. Whilst they are certainly entitled to an extension of time for completion, it is not clear who will meet the costs during this period.

Several Contractors have claimed costs under change in legislation provisions in the contracts, with the expectation that imposition of the lock-down and curfew will be considered a change in law. The GOSL may give directives on this matter. This may include financial assistance as provided to hotels, airlines etc. Insurance may also be directed to cover costs under the risk of perils.

Sri Lanka will need to ensure a continuing volume of work for Sri Lankan contractors and also financial and other assistance to Contractors to enable them to resume operations. In these writers' view, Sri Lanka/CIDA will need to develop sub-contract forms similar to FIDIC to ensure that where Sri Lankan contractors are subcontractors to foreign Contractors, their rights are safeguarded. It is important for Sri Lanka that the construction industry returns to the same position in terms of employment and contribution to GDP as it was in March 2020.

At the time of writing (September 2020), the GOSL had not passed any specific legislation in respect of the impact of Covid-19 on construction contracts.

20.4 Sri Lankan governing law of the contract

20.4.1 Constraints on the governing law of a construction contract

Since matters relating to all commercial and business activities in Sri Lanka are governed by English law,[16] the principle of freedom of contract, it is submitted, is embedded in the legal system of Sri Lanka subject to limited vitiating elements recognised under English law principles relating to the subject of contract law.

However, the principle of freedom of contract may not itself entail the logical conclusion that parties to a contract, in particular a construction contract, would necessarily be free to choose the law that governs the contract itself - the substantive law of the contract.[17] Sri Lanka, however, following the *United Nations Commission on International Trade Law (UNCITRAL) Model Law*, has enacted in 1995, the *Arbitration Act No 11 of 1995* which expressly allows for the freedom of parties to select a discretionary substantive law to govern their contract. Section 24(1) of the *Arbitration Act No 11 of 1995* reads as follows:

> An arbitral tribunal shall decide the dispute in accordance with such rules of law as are chosen by the parties as applicable to the substance of the dispute. Any designation of the law or legal system of a given State shall be construed, unless otherwise expressed as referring to the substantive law of that State and not to its conflict of laws rules (emphasis added).

Therefore, in Sri Lanka, unlike in certain other jurisdictions, party autonomy is expressly recognised in relation to the choice of law where the parties have agreed

16 W Weerasooria, *A Textbook of Commercial Law (Business Law)* (The Post Graduate Institute of Management 2010) 66–68.

17 See eg certain arguments advanced by courts of law in other jurisdictions: *Vita Foods Products Inc v Unus Shipping Co Ltd* [1939] ACC 277, 290 (Wright LJ).

to settle their disputes by arbitration. This position remains applicable regardless of the form of arbitration conducted in Sri Lanka, be it a domestic arbitration or international arbitration. If there is no agreement to arbitrate, the dispute would be referable to court and therefore, the dispute would be governed by the law of Sri Lanka.

20.4.2 Formal requirements for a construction contract

Contracts by their nature can be broadly categorised as either simple contracts and/or contracts entered into through notarially executed deeds.[18] Simple contracts are either verbal or written. Construction contracts, being contracts entered for and in relation to construction work, can be categorised as simple contracts.[19] The term 'construction work' has a very wide ambit and it generally includes not only construction activities, but services provided as well:

> [a]n agreement with a person or entity for . . . (a) the carrying out of construction work; (b) arranging for the carrying out of construction work by others, whether under sub-contract or otherwise to such person or entity, as the case may be; (c) providing his own labour or labour owned by the entity or the labour of others, for carrying out of construction work.[20]

Since construction contracts are matters relating to commercial and business activities, English law governs their formation, performance, termination and consequences thereof in Sri Lanka.[21] However, inter alia where a party to a construction contract comprises a juristic body, ie a company, provisions of the *Companies Act No 7 of 2007* and Articles of Association of such juristic body stipulate as to who is authorised to sign on behalf of such juristic body.

Where deeds affect immovable properly, ie a transfer of a land, then such deeds are required to be executed before a Notary and to be witnesses.[22]

> No sale, purchase, transfer, assignment, or mortgage of land or other immovable property, and no promise, bargain, contract, or agreement for effecting any such object . . . nor any contract or agreement for the future sale or purchase of any land or other immovable property, . . . shall be of force or avail in law unless the same shall be in writing and signed by the party making the same, or by some person lawfully authorized by him or her in the presence of a licensed notary public and two or more witnesses present at the same time, and unless the execution of such writing, deed, or instrument be duly attested by such notary and witnesses.[23]

---

18 Notarially executed deeds are not relevant to the formation of a construction contract for present purposes since 'construction work' for which construction contracts are entered may not involve the transferal of lands.

19 Therefore, statutory requirement in Sri Lanka for notarial execution does not apply, see, *Prevention of Frauds Ordinance No 7 of 1840* (as amended).

20 *Construction Industry Development Act No 33 of 2014* (CIDA), s 67. In this regard, see further, MDTE Abeynayake and C Weddikkara, 'An Analysis of Construction Law and Disaster Management Law Relating to Sustainable Development of Sri Lanka' (World Construction Symposium, Cinamon Grand, Colombo, Sri Lanka 2012).

21 Elaboration on the intricacies of the law of contract is beyond the scope of this book. An English law textbook on the subject of contract law is an appropriate reference for Sri Lankan contract law.

22 For formalities of notarial execution see *Notaries Ordinance No 1 of 1907* (as amended), s 31(8).

23 *Prevention of Frauds Ordinance No 7 of 1840* (as amended), s 2.

20.5 What Special Provisions in the Particular Conditions are necessary for consistency with applicable laws in Sri Lanka?

20.5.1 FIDIC General Conditions are incompatible or inconsistent with Sri Lankan governing law of the contract

No Special Provisions in the Particular Conditions are necessary for consistency with applicable laws in Sri Lanka if the governing law of the contract is Sri Lanka.

20.5.2 FIDIC General Conditions are incompatible or inconsistent with the law of the Site/Country

No Special Provisions in the Particular Conditions are necessary for consistency with applicable laws in Sri Lanka if the Site is in Sri Lanka.

20.5.3 FIDIC General Conditions are incompatible or inconsistent with the relevant laws on dispute determination in Sri Lanka

No Special Provisions in the Particular Conditions are necessary for consistency with applicable laws in Sri Lanka if the seat is in Sri Lanka.

20.6 What Special Provisions in the Particular Conditions are desirable for consistency with applicable laws in Sri Lanka?

In Sri Lanka, disputes that crop up in the construction industry are resolved by various methods, including formal and informal means. While negotiation and resolution of disputes by chartered surveyors, independent personnel, and adjudication advisers are common informal means used, conciliation, mediation and arbitration are recognised as formal means of resolving disputes in the field of construction in Sri Lanka.

It must be noted that even though adjudication as a means of resolving and/or avoiding disputes is on the rise at present, in contrast with other jurisdictions Sri Lanka is yet to enact legislation on adjudication and the procedures relating thereto.[24]

The *Construction Industry Development Act No 33 of 2014* in Part IX under the heading Settlement of Disputes provides as follows:

> 50. *If the parties so desire* any dispute relating to a contract for construction works, if it is not provided for in the contract, *may be settled* through conciliation or mediation by the Authority.
>
> 51(1). A party to any contract relating to an identified construction work, if unable to settle any dispute by conciliation or mediation by the Authority, *may* refer such dispute for *adjudication*.
>
> (2). The procedure for adjudication of any dispute under this section shall be as prescribed (emphasis added).

Therefore, in the absence of specific detailed statutory provisions for the regulation of adjudication proceedings in Sri Lanka at present, it is submitted that no Particular

24 In other jurisdictions, the applicability of adjudication (scope), the way in which the contracts ought to be drafted to suit the availability of adjudication, who can invoke adjudication, and the time frames within which adjudication must be conducted etc. are detailed in statute. See further PC Vajira Dayaratne, 'Statutory Adjudication as a means of resolving disputes in the Construction Industry' (2013) *Attorney General's Law Review* 53.

Conditions are necessary to be adopted for ensuring consistency with the law relating to adjudication in Sri Lanka.

By contrast, in Sri Lanka arbitral proceedings are governed by the *Arbitration Act No 11 of 1995* (***Arbitration Act***), which clearly sets out the substantive and the procedural aspects thereof, from the commencement to the delivery of the arbitral award and thereafter the enforcement thereof. Therefore, Special Provisions are desirable to bring Clause 21 (Disputes and Arbitration) in line with the law relating to arbitration in Sri Lanka.

Primarily, the appropriate Special Provisions relate to the arbitral award and the nature and enforceability thereof. In terms of section 26 of the *Arbitration Act*, an award delivered by an arbitrator or an arbitral tribunal is final and binding on the disputing parties. That is, an arbitral award is not subjected to challenge before a Court on its merits.[25]

Nevertheless, it must be noted that, in terms of the Sri Lankan *Arbitration Act*, an arbitral award is a 'mere piece of paper' until it is enforced in a court of law. Therefore, for an arbitral award to have the force of law, it is required to be filed in court for enforcement.[26] Thus, a successful party to an arbitration cannot compel the defeated party to execute payment contained in an arbitral award until the award is recognised by a court as a decree of court executable through judicial process.[27]

20.7 Summary of applicable legislation for Sri Lankan governing law of the contract

20.7.1 Entry into a construction contract

Contracts generally	*Sale of Goods Ordinance No 11 of 1896* *Consumer Affairs Authority Act No 9 of 2003* *Consumer Credit Act No 29 of 1982* *Public Contracts Act No 3 of 1987* *Service Contracts Ordinance No 11 of 1865* (as amended).
Construction contracts	No particular legislation in Sri Lanka governing the entry into construction contracts.

20.7.2 Termination of a construction contract

Frustration	No particular legislation in Sri Lanka
Bankruptcy, insolvency, liquidation	*Companies Act No 7 of 2007.*
Guarantees under forms of Security (Tender Security, Demand Guarantee, Surety Bond, Advance Payment Guarantee, Retention Money Guarantee, Payment Guarantee by Employer)	*Prevention of Frauds Ordinance No 7 of 1840.*

25 'Subject to the provisions of Part VII of this Act, the award made by the arbitral tribunal shall be final and binding on the parties to the arbitration agreement', s 26 of the *Arbitration Act*. However, an arbitral award can be set aside on 'procedural defects' contained therein by a Court; see ss 32 and 34 of the *Arbitration Act*.

26 See *Arbitration Act*, s 31.

27 For further discussion, see H Cabral, *Law and Practice of Commercial Arbitration in Sri Lanka* (2018); K Kanag-Isvaran, SS Wijeratne (eds), *Arbitration Law in Sri Lanka* (4th edn, ICLP 2016).

20.7.3 Dispute resolution

Limitation periods	*Prescriptions Ordinance No 22 of 1871* (as amended).
Liability	*Unfair Contract Terms Act No 26 of 1997* *State (Liability in Delict) Act No 22 of 1969.*
Adjudication	*Construction Industry Development Act No 33 of 2014* (does not have substantive provisions governing the area).
Arbitration	*Arbitration Act No 11 of 1995.*

20.8 Summary of applicable legislation if the Site/Country is in Sri Lanka

20.8.1 Operation of a construction contract

Registration and administration of professionals - Engineers, Architects, Quantity Surveyors	*Construction Industry Development Act No 33 of 2014.*
Registration/licencing of Contractors	*Construction Industry Development Act No 33 of 2014.*
Subcontractors	No applicable legislation in Sri Lanka.
Use of liens/ Assignment of debts	No applicable legislation in Sri Lanka.
Labour	*The Constitution of the Democratic Socialist Republic of Sri Lanka (1978)* *Human Rights Commission of Sri Lanka Act No 21 of 1996* *Industrial Disputes Act No 43 of 1950* (as amended) *Industrial Disputes (Hearing and Determination of Proceeding) (Special Provisions) Act No 45 of 1971* *Termination of Employment of Workmen (Special Provisions) Act No 45 of 1971* (as amended) *Workmen's Compensation Ordinance No 19 of 1934* (as amended) *Protection of Rights of Persons with Disabilities Act No 28 of 1996* (as amended) *Employees' Trust Fund Act No 3 of 1982* (as amended) *Employees Provident Fund Act No 15 of 1958* (as amended) *Employees' Provident Fund (Special Provisions) Law No 6 of 197* *Mines and Minerals Act No 33 of 1992* *Payment of Gratuity Act No 12 of 1983* (as amended) *Wages Boards Ordinance No 27 of 1941* (as amended) *Factories Ordinance No 45 of 1942* (as amended) *Employment of Women, Young Persons and Children Act No 47 of 1956* *Shop and Office Employees (Regulation of Employment and Remuneration) Act No 19 of 1954* (as amended) *Trade Unions Ordinance No 14 of 1935* *Employment of Trainees (Private Sector) Act No 8 of 1978.*
Design/Moral rights	*Intellectual Property Act No 36 of 2003.*
Copyright	*Intellectual Property Act No 36 of 2003.*
The product being produced from the Works	*Electricity Act No 20 of 2009* *Sri Lanka Standards Institution Act No 6 of 1984* *National Medicines Regulatory Authority Act No 5 of 2015.*

First nation people's land rights	No applicable legislation in Sri Lanka.
Planning	*Urban Development Authority Law No 41 of 1978* (as amended) *Town and Country Planning Ordinance No 13 of 1946* (as amended) *Municipal Council Ordinance No 29 of 1947* (as amended) *Urban Council Ordinance No 61 of 1939* (as amended) *Pradeshiya Sabhas Act No 15 of 1987* (as amended) *Tsunami (Special Provisions) Act No 16 of 2005* *Sri Lanka Disaster Management Act No 13 of 2005* *Sri Lanka Land Reclamation and Development Corporation Act, 15 of 1968* (as amended).
Work affecting adjacent property to the Site	No applicable legislation in Sri Lanka.
Heritage	*Antiquities Ordinance No 9 of 1940* (as amended) *Archaeological Sites of National Importance Act No 16 of 1990.*
Environment	*The Constitution of the Democratic Socialist Republic of Sri Lanka (1978)* (Chapter VI and the Thirteenth Amendment to the Constitution) *Penal Code No 2 of 1883* (as amended) (Chapter XIV) *Code of Criminal Procedure Act No 15 of 1979* (as amended) (Chapter IX) *Nuisance Ordinance No 15 of 1862* (as amended) *Police Ordinance No 16 of 1885* (as amended) *National Environmental Act No 47 of 1980* (as amended) *Forest Ordinance No 16 of 1907* (as amended) *Plant Protection Act No 35 of 1999* *Fauna and Flora Protection Ordinance No 2 of 1937* (as amended) *Fisheries and Aquatic Resources Act No 2 of 1996* (as amended) *Coast Conservation Act No 57 of 198*1(as amended) *Soil Conservation Act No 25 of 1951* (as amended) *Felling of Trees (Control) Act No 9 of 1951* (as amended) *Marine Pollution Prevention Act No 35 of 2008* *Mines and Minerals Act No 33 of 1992* (as amended) *Sri Lanka Land Reclamation and Development Corporation Act No 15 of 1968* (as amended) *Agrarian Development Act No 46 of 2000* *Irrigation Ordinance No 32 of 1946* (as amended) *Water Resource Board Act No 29 of 1964* (as amended) *Environment Conservation Levy Act No 26 of 2008* *National Heritage and Wilderness Areas Act No 3 of 1988* *Department of Coast Guard Act No 41 of 2009* *Factories Ordinance No 45 of 1942* (as amended) *Urban Development Authority Law No 41 of 1978* (as amended) *Sri Lanka Atomic Energy Act No 40 of 2014.*
Local procurement	No applicable legislation in Sri Lanka.
Building and Construction Permits, Execution of construction work, Standard of construction work	*Construction Industry Development Act No 33 of 2014.*

Health and Safety	*National Institute of Occupational Safety and Health Act No 38 of 2009* *National Authority on Tobacco and Alcohol Act No 27 of 2006* *Prevention of Mosquito Breeding Act No 11 of 2007.*
Calibration of testing apparatus, equipment and instruments	*Sri Lanka Standards Institution Act No 6 of 1984.*
Ownership of Plant and Material	No applicable legislation in Sri Lanka.
Employer's Sale of Contractor's Equipment, Surplus Material, Wreckage and Temporary Works	No applicable legislation in Sri Lanka.
Insurance	*Regulation of Insurance Industry Act No 43 of 2000* *Workmen's Compensation Acts of No. 19 of 1946* (as amended).
Statutory rights that coexist with contractual rights	*Construction Industry Development Act No 33 of 2014* *Commercial Mediation Centre of Sri Lanka Act No 44 of 2000* *Mediation Boards Act No 72 of 1988* (as amended) *Mediation (Special Categories of Disputes) Act No 21 of 2003.*
Liability for defective work	No applicable legislation in Sri Lanka.
Liability for nuisance	*Penal Code No 2 of 1883* (as amended) (Chapter XIV) *Code of Criminal Procedure Act No 15 of 1979* (as amended) (Chapter IX) *Nuisance Ordinance No 15 of 1862* (as amended).
Other issues	*Civil Procedure Ordinance No 2 of 1889* (as amended) *Mortgage Ordinance No 6 of 1949* (as amended) *Debt Recovery (Special Provisions) Act No 2 of 1990* (as amended) *Recovery of Loans by Banks (Special Provisions) Act No 4 of 1990* (as amended) *Trust Ordinance No 9 of 1917* *Customs Ordinance No 17 of 1869* *Inland Revenue Act No 24 of 2017* *Registration of Documents Ordinance No 23 of 1927.*

20.8.2 Termination of a construction contract

Bankruptcy, insolvency, liquidation	*Companies Act No 7 of 2007.*
Decennial liability and liability generally for the total or partial collapse of structures	No applicable legislation in Sri Lanka.

20.8.3 Dispute resolution

Dispute before a local board/Adjudication	*Construction Industry Development Act No 33 of 2014* *Commercial Mediation Centre of Sri Lanka Act No 44 of 2000* *Mediation Boards Act No 72 of 1988* (as amended) *Mediation (Special Categories of Disputes) Act No 21 of 2003.*
Limitation periods	*Prescriptions Ordinance No 22 of 1871*(as amended).

20.9 Summary of applicable legislation if the 'seat' of the dispute determination is Sri Lanka

Dispute resolution	*Arbitration Act No 11 of 1995* *Construction Industry Development Act No 33 of 2014* *Commercial Mediation Centre of Sri Lanka Act No 44 of 2000* *Mediation Boards Act No 72 of 1988 (as amended)*
Limitation periods	*Prescriptions Ordinance No 22 of 1871*(as amended).
Adjudication	*Construction Industry Development Act No 33 of 2014* (does not have substantive provisions governing the area).
Arbitration	*Arbitration Act No 11 of 1995.*

20.10 Issues that a court or arbitrator may construe differently to that expected from the words of the Contract, because of local law or custom

There are no particular customs and/or local laws which would influence the way in which an arbitrator and/or court would determine an issue. The customary laws referred to above are applicable on a communal basis and are personal in nature. Commercial transactions are predominantly governed by English law as stated above.

20.11 References

20.11.1 Books

H Cabral, *Law and Practice of Commercial Arbitration in Sri Lanka* (2018)

K KanagIsvaran, SS Wijeratne (eds), *Arbitration Law in Sri Lanka* (4th edn, ICLP 2016)

LJM Cooray, *An Introduction to the Legal System of Sri Lanka* (Stamford Lake 1992)

W Weerasooria, *A Textbook of Commercial Law (Business Law)* (The Post Graduate Institute of Management 2010)

20.11.2 Internet

Sri Lankan legislation and cases:
http://www.lawlanka.com/
https://www.lawnet.gov.lk

CHAPTER 21

Applying FIDIC contracts in Vietnam

Nguyen Nam Trung, Le The Hung and Dr Nguyen Thi Hoa

DOI: 10.4324/9781003200901-21

21.1 Outline of the legal environment in Vietnam

21.1.1 The constitutional structure of Vietnam

Vietnam is a socialist republic state. Its birth was declared on 2 September 1945 as the Democratic Republic of Vietnam, which is now officially known as the Socialist Republic of Vietnam. The *Constitution of Vietnam* was first enacted on 9 November 1946 with amendments made respectively in 1959, 1980, 1992 and 2013. The latest 2013 version of the *Constitution* was passed on 28 November 2013 by the XIIIth National Assembly of Socialist Republic of Vietnam at the 6th Session. The contemporary *Constitution* includes 11 chapters with 120 articles. Notably, under Article 3 of the *Constitution*, the state shall guarantee and promote the people's right to mastery; recognise, respect, protect and guarantee human rights and citizens' rights; and pursue the goal of a prosperous society, strong democratic, equitable and civilised country, where all citizens enjoy an abundant, free and happy life for their comprehensive development.

21.1.2 The legal system of Vietnam

Vietnam has a codified legal system in which, apart from customary and case law,[1] codified legal instruments remain the primary source of law prevailing over other

1 The Supreme People's Court is a competent authority to collect and anounce judgments considered as case law when they satisfy the three criteria specified in art 2 of the Resolution No 04/2019/NQ-HDTP on 18 June 2019 of the Council of Judges of the Supreme People's Court on the process of collection, announcement and implementation of case law.

secondary sources. In that sense, under Articles 5 and 6 of *Civil Code 2015*,[2] a judge may only resort to customary, case law and basic principles of civil law where the legal text itself is silent on a respective matter and there is also an absence of the parties' agreement. According to Article 119 of the *Constitution*, the *Constitution* affirms itself as the fundamental and supreme law of the Socialist Republic of Vietnam to which all other legal documents must conform. Thus, Vietnam adopted the *Law on International Treaties* in 2016 providing the principle under which the conclusion and implementation of international treaties cannot be contrary to the *Constitution*. Except for the *Constitution*, any normative text must be enacted by the competent authorities in strict conformity with the processes provided in the *Law on Enactment of Legislation* in 2015.

21.1.3 The court system of Vietnam

According to Article 102 of the *Constitution*, the People's Courts are the judicial bodies of the Socialist Republic of Vietnam and exercise judicial power. The People's Courts[3] includes the Supreme People's Court, the High People's Court and the People's Courts which are organised at two administrative levels (provincial and district levels), amongst which the Supreme People's Court is the highest judicial body.[4] Military courts are a special branch divided into three levels, not according to administrative levels.

21.2 Outline of the construction industry in Vietnam

21.2.1 Overview

There were approximately 112,000 businesses in the Vietnam construction industry by 2019. The construction sector is the fourth largest employer in Vietnam, employing 4,615,200 people,[5] equal to 8.4 per cent of the work force[6]. However, only 14 per cent[7] of the employees are trained (second lowest sector), and the average annual labour productivity is only 77.7 million Vietnam Dong (**VND**)[8] (US$3,260), the third lowest sector.[9] In 2019, the gross domestic product of the construction sector was 358,684 billion Vietnam Dong (US$15 billion), and maintained a positive growth rate of 9.1 per cent, contributing 0.66 percentage points to the overall GDP growth rate of 7.06 per cent.[10]

The area of floors of residential buildings constructed in 2018 gained 103.8 million square metres, an increase of 1.3 per cent compared to 2017. The area of apartment buildings reached 3.3 million m^2, declining by 28.6 per cent compared to 2017 and accounting for 3.1 per cent of the total areas of floors of residential buildings, of which high apartment building (from nine floors and above) occupied a large share. The area of single detached houses reached 100.6 million m^2, increasing by 2.7 per

2 In the civil field, the *Civil Code 2015* is considered as a common law which provides the basic principles governing all civil relationships to which the other texts of law can not be contrary.

3 *Law on the Organisation of the People's Courts 2014*, art 3.

4 *The Constitution of the Socialist Republic of Vietnam*, art 104.

5 General Statistics Office, *Statistical Yearbook of Vietnam 2019* (Statistical Publishing House 2020) 157.

6 ibid 159.

7 ibid 94.

8 Vietnam Dong.

9 General Statistics Office, *Statistical Yearbook of Vietnam 2019* (Statistical Publishing House 2020) 97.

10 ibid 27.

cent compared to the previous year and accounting for 96.9 per cent of the total areas of floors of residential buildings. Less than four floor single detached houses reached 98.1 million m², accounting for 97.5 per cent of the total areas of single detached houses. In 2019, more than 14,000 social apartments/houses were completed with a total floor area of 701,500 m².

As of 2016, the total length of the road network (excluding village roads) totalled over 300,000 km, notably the development of about 1,000 km of expressways. Vietnam's railway network has a route length of 2,609 km, with total trackage of 3,300 km. Vietnam's extensive seaport system includes 45 ports and nearly 200 terminals; the first deep-sea port, the Vung Tau seaport complex, has been developed to handle up to 180,000 DWT vessels. Vietnam's aviation sector has seen rapid growth in recent years, both in passenger and freight segments with 22 airports.[11] Social housing is publicly procured, while single detached houses are mostly private.

21.2.2 Contracts

Parties can enter into a contract established on the basis of the common forms of construction contract as follows:

Publisher	*Available language*	*Consulting Services*	*Procurement of Goods*	*Construction of Works*	*Non-Consulting Services*
Ministry of Planning and Investment (**MPI**)	Vietnamese	01/2015/TT-BKHDT	05/2015/TT-BKHDT	03/2015/TT-BKHDT	14/2016/TT-BKHDT
Ministry of Construction (**MoC**)	Vietnamese	08/2016/TT-BXD	-	09/2016/TT-BXD	-
	Vietnamese	30/2016/TT-BXD for EPC Contract			
World Bank and Asian Development Bank in Vietnam	English Vietnamese	-	Standard Conditions of Contracts for Procurement of Good and Construction in the Harmonized Bidding Documents, 2 July 2015		
FIDIC	English Vietnamese	White Book 2017 (2006)	-	Red Book 2017 (1999)	
	English Vietnamese			Green Book 1999 Yellow Book 1999 (2017) Silver Book 1999 (2017)[12]	

With promotion and a roadmap for e-bidding,[13] MPI forms are the most common forms for local contracts procured under *Bidding Law 2013*, while FIDIC forms are

11 World Bank Group, *Vietnam Development Report 2019: Connecting Vietnam for Growth and Shared Prosperity* (Hong Duc Publishing House) 17–21.

12 Silver Book 1999 (Vietnamese edition, translated by VECAS) is recommended by the Ministry of Planning & Investment for EPC Contracts in Circular 11/2016/TT-BKHDT.

13 Circular 11/2019/TT-BKHDT elaborating online supply and posting of procurement information, roadmap for application of e-selection of preferred bidders and management and use of non-returnable bid security and performance security, art 29.

the preferred contracts for projects funded by Official Development Assistance (**ODA**) from donors such as the World Bank, Asia Development Bank, JICA, Credit Institute of Reconstruction (**KfW**).

21.2.3 Roles and obligations of construction participants

Regarding contractual relationships, in Vietnam the roles and functions of Employer under the Contract are usually performed by project management units (**PMU**), involved in procuring the engineering design consultants, supervision consultants and various contractors for the projects. It is usually not possible for the PMU and the Engineer to make decisions or give approvals without reference to higher authority, and this leads to slow decision-making processes, especially in claim agreement.[14]

The roles and obligations of relevant parties as per *Construction Law 2014* can be seen in the following table, with stage descriptions: (1) Feasibility Study (including Basic Design), (2) Survey and Investigation, (3) Design and Engineering, (4) Construction permit, (5) Construction, (6) Acceptance, (7) Handing-over, (8) Warranty, (9) Maintenance.

Investment- Construction Stage	**(1)**	**(2)**	**(3)**	**(4)**	**(5)**	**(6)**	**(7)**	**(8)**	**(9)**
Government agencies	X		X	X		X			
Investment Decider	X								
Owner	X	X	X	X	X	X	X	X	X
Project Management Unit (PMU)	X	X	X	X	X	X	X	X	
Project Management Consultant	X	X	X		X	X			
Consultant for Feasibility Study (FS)	X								
Consultant for FS Appraisal	X								
Survey and Investigation Consultant		X							
Design and Engineering Consultant			X		X	X			
Design Reviewing Consultant			X						
EPC Contractor			X		X	X	X	X	
Construction Contractor					X	X	X	X	
Supervision Consultant					X	X			

Construction Law 2014 also provides requirements for licensing, both for individuals and organisations. Construction Practicing Certificates are required for professionals in respect of the following works:

- Project Managers of Project Management Units, Project Management Consultants; Survey and Geotechnical Investigation Consultant
- Project Managers and Team Leaders of Planning Consultant, Design and Engineering Consultant, Design Reviewing Consultant

14 David Lockwood, 'The use of FIDIC forms in Vietnam' in Lukas Klee (ed), *International Construction Contract Law* (2nd edn, Wiley Blackwell 2018).

- Supervisors of Supervision Consultant
- Team Leaders of Quantity Surveying Consultant.

Construction Activities Eligibility Certificates are required for the following organisations:

- Contractor
- Project Management Consultant
- Survey and Geotechnical Investigation Consultant
- Design and Engineering Consultant
- Design Reviewing Consultant
- Supervision Consultant.

Asian international contractors (Japanese, Korean, Chinese) are quite active in Vietnam, and they participate in many Overseas Development Assistance projects (funded by the World Bank, JICA, ADB, etc.). There are also many international consultants in Vietnam, especially in consulting and engineering services. Foreign contractors, consultants and professionals working in the Vietnam construction industry are also required to possess operation licenses granted by authorities in charge of construction, either Ministry of Construction or provincial Department of Construction.

21.2.4 Innovation and BIM

The Vietnamese construction industry is quick to apply innovation and BIM. In 2016, the Vietnam government declared decision 2500/QD-TTg which established steps for the application of BIM in the Vietnam construction industry. The expected timeline for the plan is to prepare necessary conditions and skill training sessions for application of BIM from 2017 to 2019, initiate pilot BIM projects during 2018 to 2020; and introduce regulations and guidelines on universal utilisation of BIM in construction and operating management activities from 2021.[15] This ambitious plan was adjusted in 2020 by Decision 1004/QD-BXD on Digitalisation Plan for the Construction Industry between 2020–2025, with vision to 2030.

One key milestone for the legal framework for BIM projects was in December 2017, when the MoC issued Interim Guidelines for pilot BIM projects by Decision 1057/QD-BXD. The BIM Protocol was provided in Part II of Interim Guidelines, with six articles to be included as an Appendix to Contract between parties in pilot BIM Projects:

1. Definitions
2. General Principles
3. BIM Management
4. BIM Execution Plan
5. Risk Allocation
6. Intellectual Property Rights.[16]

15 Decision 2500/QD-TTg approving the Plan to utilize Building Information Modelling (BIM) for construction activities, management and operation of buildings/facilities, 2016

16 Decision 1057/QD-BXD Interim Guidelines for Projects involved Building Information Modelling (BIM) during pilot stage, 2017.

21.3 The impact of Covid-19 in Vietnam

21.3.1 The impact of Covid-19 on the execution of construction projects in Vietnam

Regarding the impact of Covid-19, Vietnam has well controlled the spread of the Covid-19. The virus cases came mostly from abroad and were isolated immediately. To achieve this success, the government operated timely and effective policies as follows.

21.3.1.1 Constraints on travel

At the beginning of the spread of Covid-19 on 31 January 2020,[17] when there were only two virus cases in Vietnam, the government suspended licensed flights to and from pandemic areas of China. This policy was also applied from 25 February 2020 to flights from other countries such as Korea, Japan, Italy, Iran and others with spread of Covid 19.[18] Moreover, the government advised nationals not to travel to pandemic areas and people returning from these countries to Vietnam had to be quarantined for 14 days in a common area. After that, when the situation deteriorated in the world as well as in Vietnam, the government[19] announced on 21 March 2020 that:

> Temporary suspension of entry for all foreigners shall be applied since 12:00AM on March 22, 2020 to prevent and control Covid-19. This shall not be applied for those entering Vietnam for diplomatic, official purposes and other special circumstances (such as for participation in major diplomatic events; being experts, business managers, highly-skilled workers…). However, these entrants shall be subject to mandatory medical declaration, other effective regulations at designated areas at ports of entry and shall have to isolate themselves at places of residence as currently regulated… Temporary suspension of entry due to Covid-19 shall also be applied to all overseas Vietnamese and their relatives who have been granted with certificate of visa – exemption since 12:00AM on March 22, 2020.

Even under this announcement the experts, business managers and highly skilled workers were able to enter Vietnam after being isolated at an accommodation establishment in accordance with regulations. In practice, there were cases where construction projects' implementation were affected as a result of lack of experts who could not travel due to frontier closure of other countries. For instance, more than 100 Chinese experts for the Cat Linh – Ha Dong railway project[20] could not return to work from China as a result of its exit restriction policy due to Covid-19. On 22 April 2020, the Ha Noi Metropolitan Railway Management Board (Ha Noi MRB) reported that nearly 20 consultants and safety management experts in France, Italy and Korea for Nhon-Ha Noi railway Station project were unable to come to Vietnam because of border closures of these countries.[21]

---

17 *Prime Minister, Order 06/CT-TTg dated 31 January 2020 on strengthening prevention and control measures against the nCoV epidemic, Point 3.*

18 *Prime Minister, Order 10/CT-TTg dated 25 February 2020 on enhancement of Covid-19 prevention and control.*

19 The Government Office, Notice 118/TB-VPCP (21 March 2020).

20 See information on the website of the Ha Noi Metropolitan Railway Management Board: https://mrb.hanoi.gov.vn/thong-tin-hoat-dong/-/view_content/3635356-chuyen-gia-tuyen-metro-chua-the-den-viet-nam.html (accessed 17 December 2020).

21 Moreover, for Ha Noi MRB, there was a lack of domestic as well as imported materials and equipement as a result of pandemic: See information on the website of the Ha Noi Metropolitan Railway Management Board https://mrb.hanoi.gov.vn/thong-tin-chuyen-nganh/-/view_content/3764050-ban-tin-du-an-thang-5-2020.html (accessed 15 November 2020).

21.3.1.2 Prohibition on construction

Inside the country, there were two notable periods. First, a social distancing for 15 days from 1 April 2020 imposed by the government.[22] To implement this Order of the government, certain provinces announced temporary lockdown of construction sites such as the case of the Ha Noi People's Committee.[23] In this context, three days later, the government[24] specified that 'the construction works continue to be carried out' subject to health measures and safe constraints on employees such as wearing a face mask. Consequently, on 6 April 2020, the Ha Noi People's Committee instructed that the construction works continue to be in operation but must strictly comply with the requirements for ensuring safety against the spread of Covid-19, otherwise, it will be stopped. Therefore, in practice, the fact that construction works were affected during this quarantine[25] was inevitable.

Apart from the social distancing at the national level, there was a social distancing at provincial level in Da Nang City from 28 July 2020[26] to 5 September 2020. However, there was no lockdown of construction sites but health and safety constraints on the normal operation of a construction site imposed such as: physical distancing; cleaning and disinfection; wearing a face mask; measuring body temperature.[27]

21.3.1.3 Health and safety constraints on the normal operation of a construction site

With regard to health and safety constraints on the normal operation of a construction site, under the Directive of the Ministry of Health, [28] working on construction sites was not included in the list of occupations and jobs with a high risk of exposure and infection. Therefore, there were no special constraints for construction sites and the relevant subjects were only required to implement measures to prevent and control the epidemic in a general manner as discussed above such as: physical distancing; cleaning and disinfection; wearing a face mask; measuring body temperature.

21.3.1.4 Financial support

Dealing with this Covid outbreak, the government adopted the following policies to support employees and businesses.

First, for employees required to stop work, the Ministry of Labour-Invalids and Social Affairs gave an instruction[29] on the payment of wages and benefits for employees during work stoppage time. If a work stoppage results from an employee's fault, she/he cannot be paid under Article 98 of *Labour Code*. In the absence of her/his own fault, there are two situations as follows: if employees cannot come to work because of

22 Order No 16/CT-TTg (31 March 2020).

23 Ha Noi People's Committee, Order 05/CT-UBND (31 March 2020).

24 The Government Office, Letter 2601/VPCP-KGVX (3 April 2020).

25 Ministry of Construction http://moc.gov.vn/vn/tin-tuc/1184/62281/tang-cuong-phong--chong-dich-COVID-19-tai-cac-cong-trinh-xay-dung.aspx (accessed 17 November 2020).

26 Da Nang People's Committee, Order 4930/UBND-SYT (27 July 2020).

27 Da Nang Construction Department, Letter 5396/SXD-CCGD (27 July 2020).

28 Ministry of Health, Directive No 1133/BYT-MT on 9 March 2020 on desease prevention at workplaces and worker's dormitories, Appendix, p 3.

29 Ministry of Labour-Invalides and Social Affairs, Letter 1064/BLĐTBXH-QHLĐTL (25 March 2020).

complying with a decision of the authorities, they can be paid under their agreement with the employer but the wages must not be lower than the regional minimum wage set by the government; if due to difficulties of material supply or market pressure arising during Covid outbreak the employer cannot create a job for an employee, the employer can transfer the employee to a job differing from the job in the employment contract or terminate the employment contract under Articles 38 and 49 of the *Labour Code*. Moreover, these employees could receive financial support from the government[30] from 500,000 VND to 1,800,000 VND (US$21 to US$77) per month for up to three months beginning from 1 April 2020, depending on the case listed in section II of the Resolution of the Government No 42/NQ-CP on 9 April 2020 on assistance for people affected by the Covid-19 pandemic.

Secondly, employers could apply for an unsecured loan that is worth up to 50 per cent of the total region-based minimum wages of suspended employees over the suspension period (but not exceeding three months) at an interest rate of 0 per cent with a loan terms of up to 12 months from the Bank for Social Policies. For a household business who earned an annual revenue of under 100 million VND/year (US$4,300) and had to suspend business operation from 1 April 2020, they will receive 1,000,000 VND (US$43) per month. The period of this financial assistance depends on the pandemic situation.[31] Furthermore, they can receive other financial support such as reducing 15 per cent land rents in 2020, and a reduction of 2 per cent of the interest rate of direct and indirect lending for small and medium enterprises taken from the medium and small enterprise development fund.[32]

21.3.2 The impact of Covid-19 on the operation of construction contracts in Vietnam

As analysed above, the Vietnamese government did not declare a *force majeure* due to the Covid-19 pandemic. Moreover, in the Order on 3 April 2020, the government[33] specified that 'the construction works continue to be carried out' with respect to health and safe constraints on employees. So, the question arising is whether the parties to a construction contract can be freed from damages for non-performance of their contractual obligations due to difficulties arising from the Covid-19 outbreak. To respond to this question, it is necessary to explore conditions for the exemption of liability for non-performance of the contractual obligation under Vietnamese law. In principle, the parties can sign a waiver listing the circumstances that allow one party to be exempted from contractual liabilities. Such a clause is very popular in construction contracts such as in clause 19.1 of the 1999 FIDIC Red Book and in other standard contracts published by the Vietnamese authorities. For example, a *force majeure* clause of a sample contract defines: '*force majeure* is unforeseen events beyond control of the parties such as war, riot, strike, fire, natural disaster, flood, epidemic, isolation due to

30 Section II, points 4, 5, 6, 7 of the Resolution of the Government No 42/NQ-CP on 9 April 2020 on assistance for people affected by the Covid-19 pandemic.

31 Section II, points 2, 3 of the Resolution the Government No 42/NQ-CP on 9 April 2020 of on assistance for people affected by Covid-19 pandemic.

32 Section II, point 1 of Resolution of the Government No 84/NQ-CP on 29 May 2020 on task and solutions for dealing with difficulties in business operations, promoting disbursement of public investment and ensuring social order and safety during the Covid-19 epidemic.

33 The Text No 2601/VPCP-KGVX (3 April 2020).

quarantine.'[34] Under this clause in this type of contract, Covid-19 or quarantine as a result of Covid-19 spread is able to be considered as a *force majeure* event.

In the absence of agreement of the Parties, *force majeure* under Article 156 of the *Civil Code 2015* can be applied if there is 'an event which occurs in an objective manner which is not able to be foreseen by the parties to contract and which is not able to be remedied by all possible necessary and admissible measures being taken'. So, a *force majeure* is composed of three elements – objectivity, unpredictability and irresistibility – of an event. Therefore, whether an event is characterised as a *force majeure* depends on the particular context because the obligor must prove that it could not reasonably overcome the consequences as a result of this event despite taking all possible necessary and admissible measures. If this is the case, under Article 351 of the *Civil Code*, the obligor is exempted from damages as a consequence of non-performance of contract obligations due to *force majeure*. During the Covid-19 outbreak, this provision has attracted the attention of parties to construction contracts such as the case of the Arena Project[35] in Khanh Hoa province. This project involves construction of a hotel which could not be completed on time because employees and materials which must be imported from other countries having spread of Covid-19 could not come to work due to complying with quarantine imposed by the government in Order No16/CT-TTg on 31 March 2020. Therefore, for the Contractor, extension of time is necessary and legitimate and 'this subject are also working hard to overcome all difficulties caused by the epidemic and focus on implementing the works, maximizing the construction time to ensure the general progress of the project, preserving interests of client of the project'. Lack of labour and materials was inevitable[36] during the Covid-19 outbreak and where the Contractor on this project had good faith in its efforts to remedy the damage, the request for extension of time is acceptable on the basis of *force majeure* existing.

Apart from *force majeure*, a party disadvantaged by the Covid-19 outbreak can resort to 'the fundamental change of circumstances' under Article 420 of the Vietnamese *Civil Code 2015* in order to preserve its interests. Under this Article 420, 'the fundamental change of circumstances' occurs if all the following requirements met:

(a) The circumstances change due to objective reasons occurred after the conclusion of the contract
(b) At the time of concluding the contract, the parties could not foresee this change
(c) This change is such great that if the parties knew in advance, the contract would not be concluded or would be concluded but with completely different content
(d) The continuation of the contract without the modification would cause serious damage to one party
(e) The disadvantaged party which has adopted all the necessary measures, in accordance with the nature of the contract, cannot prevent or minimize damage.

34 See art 1.3 of Chapter VI if general conditions of type of contract published by the the Ministry of Planning and Investment on 6 May 2015 in the Circular No 03/2015/TT-BKHĐT detailing the preparation of construction and installation bidding documents.

35 Nhat My, 'Legal and schedule updates of Arena project' *Economy-Environment Magazine* (3 October 2020) https://kinhtemoitruong.vn/thong-tin-phap-ly-va-tien-do-du-an-the-arena-50123.html (accessed 19 November 2020).

36 It is also the case of Vietnam Electricity, see on its website https://www.evn.com.vn/d6/news/Dich-COVID-19-anh-huong-den-tien-do-trien-khai-nhieu-du-an-luoi-dien-6-13-25592.aspx (accessed 19 November 2020).

With these requirements, 'the fundamental change of circumstances' under the Vietnamese *Civil Code* can be seen as a hardship which alters the equilibrium of the contract. Paragraph 2 of Article 420 permits the parties to re-negotiate or terminate a contract due to the fundamental change of circumstance. This is a recent provision of the Vietnamese *Civil Code 2015* and has not yet been applied in practice.

In summary, the Vietnam State did not create a new law to intervene in civil relationships in general and in construction contracts in particular as a consequence of the Covid-19 pandemic. Therefore, performance of contracts depends on good faith of the parties during the Covid-19 outbreak, otherwise, the disadvantaged party is able to apply existing legal rules in order to preserve its interests.

21.4 Vietnamese governing law of the contract

21.4.1 Constraints on the governing law of a construction contract

The first paragraph of Article 138 of the *Construction Law 2014* provides that a construction contract is a civil contract and due to this civil character, the construction contract must be subject to the *Civil Code 2015* and not to the *Commercial Law 2005* of Vietnam. However, in practice, this provision was not applied in a uniform way between provincial courts. For instance, the People's Court of Ha Noi[37] quashed a prior judgment because of the application of the *Commercial Law* to a construction contract. In contrast, the People's Court of Da Nang approved a prior judgment that applied the *Commercial Law* in order to determine deferred interest.[38] It is regrettable that there is no guidance from the People's Supreme Court on this matter yet. Apart from the *Construction Law*, a construction contract is also subject to the *Law on Public-Private Partnership Investment* (*PPP Law*)[39] if there is a state party to the contract; under the fifth paragraph of Article 97 of this Law, a dispute relating to a PPP contract is a commercial dispute.

The second paragraph of Article 138 referred to above expressly allows and recognises the parties' autonomy to contract, subject to the limits of law under the fifth paragraph of the same Article. Regarding the governing law of a construction contract, it is necessary to differentiate between two types of the contract. For a construction contract in which there is a state party, or the contract is for execution of a project using state capital, corporate capital from 30 percent or under 30 percent but over VND 500 billion (US$21.5 million) of the total project investment capital, it must conform to the legal system of the Socialist Republic of Vietnam and the provisions thereof.[40] For the second type of construction contract, its governing law can be chosen by the Parties if there is one of the three elements stated in Article 663 of *Civil Code 2015*, namely: 'At least, one party is a foreign individual or a legal entity; or all parties to the contract are Vietnamese but establishment, amendments, implementation or termination of the contractual relationship occurs in a foreign country; or the subjects of such relationship are overseas'. In that case, the application

37 Judgment 64/2017/KDTM-ST regarding construction contract disputes by the People's Court of Ha Noi City.

38 Judgment 09/2020/KDTM-PT regarding construction contract disputes by the People's Court of Da Nang City.

39 This *PPP Law* was recently enacted and will take effect from 1 January 2021.

40 *Decree No 37/2015/ND-CP*, art 11.

of a foreign law is permissible on condition that it does not violate the fundamental principles[41] of Vietnamese laws.

21.4.2 Formal requirements for a construction contract

As noted in paragraph 21.4.1 above, although there are two types of construction contract, the written formal requirement is only imposed on a construction contract for which there is a state party or the contract is for the execution of a project using state capital, corporate capital from 30 percent or under 30 percent but over VND 500 billion (US$21.5 million) of total project investment capital, pursuant to point c of the first paragraph of Article 6 Decree No 37/2015/NĐ-CP on 22 April 2015 detailing regulations on construction contracts. For the other type of construction contract, there is no formal requirements so that it implies the recognition of parties' autonomy in this case.

21.4.3 Contract agreement

In sub-clause 1.6 of the FIDIC 2017 rainbow suite, the Parties shall sign a Contract Agreement within 35 days after the Contractor receives the Letter of Acceptance, unless they agree otherwise, and the Contract Agreement shall be based on the form annexed to the Particular Conditions (Red Book and Yellow Book).

The *Construction Law* provide prerequisites for the Contract before it comes into full force and effect:

- The signees of the Contract must have authorised power in accordance with the law
- The Contractor has Construction Activities Eligibility Certificates in accordance with the *Construction Law*
- Assurance of adequate funds for payment according to the contractual agreement
- The selection of bidders is completed and the contract negotiations concluded
- If the Contractor is a JV, there must be a JV agreement attached to the Contract Agreement.

For public projects governed by *Bidding Law 2013*, there is no such Letter of Acceptance, while the Contract Agreement is required to be in compliance with standard forms issued by the Ministry of Planning and Investment.[42] Within the process under *Bidding Law 2013*, after the evaluation of bidders, the first-ranked bidder will be invited for negotiations. After the Employer and bidder agree the contents of the Minutes of Contract Negotiation, the Employer will submit its Bidding Evaluation, Minutes of Contract Negotiation and draft Contracts for approval.[43]

Bidding Law requires some prerequisites for Parties at the time of signing the Contract Agreement:

- The bidding documents of the Contractor are still valid.
- The Contractor has ensured it meets the requirements on technical and financial capability for implementation of the procurement. If necessary, the Employer shall conduct a verification of information provided by the Contractor.

---

41 In practice, the content of 'fundamental principles' are difficult to identify.

42 *Decree 63/2014/ND-CP*, art 89.

43 *Bidding Law 2013*, art 38.

- The Employer has ensured the conditions on funding for advance payment, interim payments, construction site and access routes, as well as other necessary conditions for carrying out the project in accordance with the schedule.[44]

21.5 What Special Provisions in the Particular Conditions are necessary for consistency with applicable laws in Vietnam?

21.5.1 FIDIC General Conditions are incompatible or inconsistent with Vietnamese governing law of the contract

The following are examples of FIDIC General Conditions that may be incompatible or inconsistent with the governing law of the contract in Vietnam and may therefore need to be modified by Particular Conditions.

21.5.1.1 Performance security

FIDIC General Conditions provide that the Performance Security remains valid and enforceable until the issue of the Performance Certificate and the Contractor has complied with sub-clause 11.11 [*Clearance of Site*].[45] The Contractor has an obligation to extend the validity of the Performance Security until the issue of the Performance Certificate and the Contractor has complied with sub-clause 11.11 [*Clearance of Site*]. This concept is illustrated diagrammatically in the 'Typical Sequence of Principal Events during Contracts for Construction' in the Foreword to the 1999 Red Book and the 2017 Red Book.[46]

FIDIC General Conditions are based on the concept that 'the Contractor's proper performance of the Contract' includes the obligation to remedy any defects during the Defects Notification Period and until the Performance Certificate is issued (or deemed to have been issued). This concept is, however, not consistent with applicable law in a number of aspects, such as:

- The existence of the so-called Performance Certificate: the law of Vietnam does not recognise this Performance Certificate concept, which consequently leads to a confusion to apply the Final Payment Statement concept under sub-clause 14.11, sub-clause 14.12 and sub-clause 14.13 of the FIDIC General Conditions.
- The shorter validity of the Performance Security: the law of Vietnam specifies that the Performance Security shall be valid and enforceable until the issue of the Taking-Over Certificate and the Contractor undertakes the remedying obligations and the Defects Notification Period commences.[47][48] In respect of this approach, it has its pros and cons, eg the Contractor can reduce its financial cost in obtaining, securing and maintaining the Performance Security, but the Employer sees the risk of disputing with the Contractor if and to the extent

44 ibid art 64.

45 See sub-clause 4.2.1 [*Contractor's obligations*] in the Red Book 2017, Yellow Book 2017 and Silver Book 2017.

46 Similar diagrams are in the Foreword to the 1999 Yellow and Silver Books, and the 2017 Yellow and Silver Books.

47 *Bidding Law 2013*, art 72.

48 *Decree 37/2015/ND-CP*, art 16(2).

(i) the Contractor refuses to remedy defects, and (ii) the Retention Money is not sufficient for the Employer (or any contractor engaged by the Employer) to remedy the defects during the Defects Notification Period which is now extended to a minimum five years for high-rise residential projects, and two years for other residential projects such as detached houses.[49]

- The role of the Performance Security: construction contracts for state-funded projects require the submission/delivery of the Performance Security to make the construction contracts valid, eg a contractual obligation under a construction contract to secure a proper Performance Security must be performed prior the effective date of that construction contract.[50, 51]

21.5.1.2 Condition precedent for issuance of Taking-over Certificate for the Works or Sections

The FIDIC General Conditions set out a number of clear conditions precedent under sub-clause 10.1 [*Taking Over the Works and Sections*] to determine whether the Taking-over Certificate is issued or deemed to have been issued to enable the Parties to consider whether the Contractor has any liability to the Employer in respect of Delay Damages (eg obligation to complete the Works in a specific time),[52] the commencement of the Defects Notification Period (eg the remedying obligations of the Contractor under the contract),[53] and the release of the first Retention Money to the Contractor.[54] There are a number of ways of applying the conditions precedent under Vietnam law, and the application of sub-clause 10.1 therefore requires due care.

In particular, the application of this sub-clause will not be fully consistent with applicable law in respect of the following issues:

- The role of the Engineer to issue the Taking-over Certificate: applicable law specifies that[55] the Taking-over Certificate should be signed by the authorised persons of the Employer, the supervision consultant, the main Contractor, the design consultant, the chief designer, and the investor (under the public-private partnership agreement). The involvement of those persons are notably different to the processes in FIDIC General Conditions in which the Taking-over Certificate is to be issued by the Engineer.[56]
- The form and process: Likewise, a condition precedent for any final inspection before taking over the Works under the law of Vietnam is that the competent authority in the Construction Department or Ministry of Construction (depending on the grade of the project) should have inspected and verified the Works by issuing an approval on the inspection reports.[57]

49 *Law on Housing 2014*, art 85(2).
50 *Bidding Law 2013*, art 72.
51 *Decree 37/2015/ND-CP*, art 16(2).
52 Sub-clause 8.7 [*Delay Damages*].
53 Sub-clause 1.1.27 [*Defects Notification Period*] FIDIC Red Book 2017, FIDIC Yellow Book 2017 and sub-clause 1.1.24 [*Defects Notification Period*], FIDIC Silver Book 2017.
54 Sub-clause 14.9 [*Release of Retention Money*].
55 Circular 26/2016/TT-BXD, art 9.
56 Sub-clause 10.1 [*Taking Over the Works and Sections*], FIDIC Red Book 2017, FIDIC Yellow Book 2017.
57 *Circular 26/2016/TT-BXD*, art 13.

- The prolongation associated with the inspection and acceptance to the Works: it is hard for either the Employer or the Contractor to specify an appropriately sufficient float time for the parties to get all the documents signed by the relevant persons. This makes the 28 days for the Engineer to respond in sub-clause 10.1 practically if not actually impossible. Therefore, local practitioners creatively define a variant to the completion status, eg 'physical completion' to enable the Contractor to discharge its liability to Delay Damages (and to a certain extent, to release the first half of the Retention Money to the Contractor), but to prevent the Employer from commencing its entitlement to remedy defects; this is the best practically possible solution.

21.5.1.3 Delay Damages

Under Vietnam's legal framework, two typical monetary legal remedy methods are recognised, ie a penalty imposed for breach of contract obligations regardless of whether consequential damages or losses are incurred or not[58] and the other is the mandatory compensation[59] required for any and all actual damages and/or loss the aggrieved party suffers.

Common applicable practice for these two monetary legal remedies are as follows:

- For the penalty: The Parties agree on a percentage or an amount which is subject to a cap of 8 per cent of breached parts under the *Commercial Law*[60] or 12 per cent of breached parts under the *Construction Law* for a project funded by the state.[61] Whenever a breach of the contract occurs, the agreed percentage or amount will automatically apply.
- For the compensation: The Parties could agree on a pre-estimated amount to be considered as compensation that the defaulting party pay the non-defaulting party, or in case there is no such agreement, the actual compensation for the damages or losses will apply.

Accordingly, whilst drafting the Particular Conditions of a construction contract, the drafter, depending on who s/he is working for, will need to make sure the intention of the Delay Damages concept is accurately reflected. This may be achieved by replacing Delay Damages with 'fine' or 'penalty' if the Delay Damages represents a penalty rather than damages or a loss. Conversely, if Delay Damages represents damages or losses, then there should be a clear reference to the *Civil Code 2015* to state that under no circumstance shall the Delay Damages be construed as a penalty or fine, and for that reason the Contractor is liable for any actual damages the Employer might have suffered from the delay.

21.5.1.4 Roles of the Engineer

In the modern world of construction contract administration, especially for those administering FIDIC contracts, the roles of the Engineer have become vital. FIDIC

58 *Civil Code 2015*, art 418.
59 ibid arts 13 and 360.
60 *Commercial Law 2005*, art 301.
61 *Construction Law 2014*, art 146(2).

General Conditions provide that the Engineer 'shall be deemed to act for the Employer',[62] but when carrying out his/her duties in reaching agreement or making a determination 'shall act neutrally' and 'shall make a fair determination'.[63]

Therefore, FIDIC General Conditions allow or vest in the Engineer the power, duties and authority necessary to perform its roles under the Contract, eg the authority to issue the necessary clarification or instruction to resolve any ambiguity or discrepancy found in the contract documents;[64] the independence of the Engineer to make a determination;[65] issuing an instruction to approve a Variation or to request a proposal for a Variation.[66] The Engineer has the authority to issue important certificates or instructions during the whole process of the Works such as a Notice of Commencement Date,[67] an instruction to suspend the Works or any part thereof,[68] the Taking-over Certificate certifying the date on which the Works or Section are handed-over,[69] and the Performance Certificate confirming the completion of the Works.[70]

However, due care must be taken in the application of those FIDIC General Conditions as there are constraints imposed by applicable law or the uncertainty of those provisions under Vietnam's legal framework and/or practice itself. Particularly:

- No Notice of Dissatisfaction: The FIDIC concept where neither Party, within 28 days, gives any Notice of Dissatisfaction to the Engineer's determination, this determination shall be deemed to have been accepted by both Parties and shall be final and binding on them[71] might be challenged by applicable law due to two factors: (i) one is that the Engineer is not a contracting party, and has 'no authority to amend the Contract',[72] and (ii) the other ground is that scope of project management defined in Article 66 [*Scope of the Project Management*], *Construction Law 2014* does not provide clear provisions to determine whether the Engineer has the authority to do so.
- Determination: Likewise, the Engineer is not defined under the law of Vietnam as an official dispute resolver nor an alternative dispute resolver whose decisions or awards are enforceable before the civil enforcement body.[73] In order to request enforcement of a decision by the Civil Enforcement Body/Unit, such request must be made and based on a successful mediation agreement, and/or an arbitral award. An Engineer's decision is not recognised as final and binding upon parties as it is neither commercial arbitration[74] nor commercial mediation.[75]

62 Sub-clause 3.2 [*Engineer's Duties and Authority*].
63 Sub-clause 3.7 [*Agreement or Determination*], FIDIC Red Book 2017, FIDIC Yellow Book 2017.
64 Sub-clause 1.5 [*Priority of Documents*], FIDIC Red Book 2017, FIDIC Yellow Book 2017.
65 Sub-clause 3.7 [*Agreement or Determination*], FIDIC Red Book 2017, FIDIC Yellow Book 2017.
66 Sub-clause 13.1 [*Right to Vary*], sub-clause 13.3.1 [*Variation by Instruction*], and sub-clause 13.3.2 [*Variation by Request for Proposal*], FIDIC Red Book 2017, FIDIC Yellow Book 2017.
67 Sub-clause 8.1 [*Commencement Date*], FIDIC Red Book 2017, FIDIC Yellow Book 2017.
68 Sub-clause 8.9 [*Employer's Suspension*], FIDIC Red Book 2017, FIDIC Yellow Book 2017.
69 Sub-clause 10.1 [*Taking Over the Works and Sections*], FIDIC Red Book 2017, FIDIC Yellow Book 2017.
70 Sub-clause 11.9 [*Performance Certificate*], FIDIC Red Book 2017, FIDIC Yellow Book 2017.
71 Sub-clause 3.7.5 [*Dissatisfaction with Engineer's determination*], FIDIC Red Book 2017, FIDIC Yellow Book 2017.
72 Sub-clause 3.2 [*Engineer's Duties and Authority*], FIDIC Red Book 2017, FIDIC Yellow Book 2017.
73 *Civil Enforcement Law 2018*, art 1.
74 *Commercial Arbitration Law 2010*, art 1-2, art 4.5, art 6, art 8.
75 *Decree 22/2017/ND-CP*, arts 1–2.

- Assessment of a provisional measurement[76] or an appropriate rate or price[77] for the purpose of an Interim Payment Certificate: Although *Construction Law 2014*[78] states that 'The payment for the Variation Orders having no relevant unit prices shall be made in accordance with the construction contract terms', the practice suggests that under projects funded by the state that (i) the Engineer normally shall not issue the Interim Payment Certificate for those Variation works, or (ii) even if an Interim Payment Certificate could be issued by the Engineer, it shall not be easily accepted by the investigator, the treasurer and other competent authorities as it might involve civil or criminal liability at the closing-out stage of the project where investigators, auditors etc, will finally review the final payments and liquidation of the construction contracts.[79]
- The use of a provisional index for the issue of Interim Payment Certificates when current cost index is not available: This is the same issue as the assessment of a provisional measurement or an appropriate rate or price.

21.5.1.5 Contract liquidation

As the Performance Certificate does not exist under Vietnam's legal framework, the issuance of a Performance Certificate which consequently enables the Engineer to issue the Final Payment Certificate[80] (after the Defects Notification Period) seems contradictory to the timeframe for the parties to discharge each other's liability under *Construction Law 2014*.

In particular, *Construction Law 2014* specifies that:

> The time limit for the parties to liquidate the contracts and discharge liability of each other is those set out in the contracts. For the project funded by the State, the time limit will not exceed 60 days since the Taking-Over Certificate for the Works, including the varied works, if any. For large construction contracts, the time limit could be extended but under no circumstance will last more than 120 days.

This means (i) the contract liquidation shall use the issuance of the Taking-Over Certificate for the Works as the starting point to calculate the number of days for which the parties have the obligation to discharge the other of the liability and (ii) the timeframe for the parties to liquidate the contract and discharge the liability of the other, as specified, is much shorter and comes much earlier than the time for the Engineer to issue the Performance Certificate (after the expiry date of the Defects Notification Period).

Therefore, an Employer being a state-owned organisation will likely encounter a very difficult situation where it has an obligation to liquidate the contract as the law requires (eg within 120 days after the issuing date of the Taking-Over Certificate), but if it liquidates the contract so, it is against the FIDIC General Conditions, specifically those stated in sub-clause 11.9 [*Performance Certificate*], sub-clause 11.11 [*Final*

76 Sub-clause 12.1 [*Works to be Measured*], FIDIC Red Book 2017.

77 Sub-clause 12.3 [*Valuation of the Works*], FIDIC Red Book 2017.

78 *Construction Law 2014*, art 144(8).

79 *Circular 10/2020/TT-BTC*, art 7.

80 Sub-clause 14.13 [*Issue of FPC*], FIDIC Red Book 2017, FIDIC Yellow Book 2017, FIDIC Silver Book 2017.

Statement], sub-clause 14.12 [*Discharge*], sub-clause 14.13 [*Issue of FPC*], and sub-clause 14.14 [*Cessation of Employer's Liability*].

21.5.1.6 Notice of claim

Despite the various enhanced provisions in the 2017 rainbow suite pertaining to the serving a Notice of Claim being the condition precedent for either the Employer or the Contractor to entitle itself to a cost and time claim,[81] failure by either Party to provide a timely notice to the Engineer might result in a loss of rights and entitlement.

The above concept might not be compatible with applicable law and could be challenged not only by the parties but also the competent settlement bodies such as the courts and arbitral tribunals.

One of the grounds helping those entities to rely on and challenge this concept is that the time limitation to bring a lawsuit against the other is explicitly defined by law, but not by a contract term.[82, 83] Sometimes limitations are even unlimited:[84] three years if it is a compensation claim;[85] two years if it is a claim for invalidity of a contract;[86] and three years if it is a contractual dispute claim.[87]

This means that agreeing to a time limit for a party to raise a claim (i) is either an invalid term as it is contradictory to the applicable law, or (ii) even if it is valid under the construction contract, it might still be accepted by the competent settlement bodies provided that such claim is brought to their attention prior to the expiry of those specified time limitations under the law.

21.5.2 FIDIC General Conditions are incompatible or inconsistent with the law of the Site/Country

21.5.2.1 Employer's sale of Contractor's equipment, surplus material, wreckage and Temporary Works (11.11)

The *Civil Code 2015* determines the transfer of ownership rights by an owner as follows:

> Where an owner transfers its ownership rights to another person through a contract for sale and purchase, by exchange, gift or loan, or through inheritance, the ownership rights of the owner with respect to the property shall terminate from the time when the ownership rights of the transferee arise.[88]

In case the transfer of ownership right of property in order to fulfill obligations:

> 1. Ownership rights with respect to property shall terminate when such property is realized in order to fulfill the obligations of the owner pursuant to a decision of a court or another competent authority, unless otherwise provided by law.

81 Sub-clause 20.2.1 [*Notice of Claims*], sub-clause 20.2.2 [*Engineer's initial response*], sub-clause 20.2.4 [*Fully detailed Claim*], sub-clause 20.2.5 [*Agreement or Determination of the Claim*], sub-clause 3.7 [*Agreement or Determination*], sub-clause 21.4 [*Obtaining DAAB's Decision*], sub-clause 3.7.5 [*Dissatisfaction with Engineer's determination*], sub-clause 21.6 [*Arbitration*].

82 *Civil Code 2015*, art 149.

83 *Civil Procedure Code 2015*, art 184.

84 *Civil Code 2015*, art 155.

85 ibid art 588.

86 ibid art 132(1).

87 ibid art 429.

88 ibid art 238.

2. Property which the law provides is not able to be seized may not be realized in order to fulfill the obligations of the owner.
3. The ownership rights with respect to property realized in order to fulfill the obligations of the owner shall terminate at the time when the ownership rights of the recipient of such property arise.[89]

From the above, it is clear that the Employer's sale would only have been realized if the requirements for transfer of ownership have been met under the *Civil Code 2015*, either by purchasing contract(s) between Employer and Contractor, or by order of the court or a competent authority.

21.5.2.2 Ownership of Plant and Materials

Sub-clause 7.7 of the FIDIC 2017 rainbow suite provides criteria for changing the ownership of Plant and Materials as follows:

> Item of Plant and Materials shall, to the extent consistent with the mandatory requirements of the Laws of the Country, become the property of the Employer at whichever is the earlier of the following times, free from liens and other encumbrances:
>
> (a) when it is delivered to the Site;
> (b) when the Contractor is paid the value of the Plant and Materials under sub-clause 8.11 [Payment for Plant and Materials after Employer's Suspension]; or
> (c) when the Contractor is paid the amount determined for the Plant and Materials under sub-clause 14.5 [Plant and Materials intended for the Works].

Depending on which law will be applied to the Contract, *Civil Code 2015, Commercial Law 2005* or *Construction Law 2014*, this sub-clause should be reviewed and revised to comply with relevant laws.

In *Commercial Law 2005*, the point of time for transferring ownership of goods passing from the Contractor to the Employer shall be the time of handover of the goods, unless otherwise agreed.[90] As the Contractor manages the entire construction Site in accordance with *Construction Law* until acceptance and handing-over, limb (a) of 'when it is delivered to the Site' can be revised accordingly.[91]

21.5.3 FIDIC General Conditions are incompatible or inconsistent with the relevant laws on dispute determination in Vietnam

There are some cases where the FIDIC General Conditions can be incompatible or inconsistent with the laws of the seat of the arbitration or relevant laws on dispute determination in Vietnam jurisdiction as follows:

21.5.3.1 DAB/DAAB

Under Vietnamese law, adjudication by a DAB is not a mandatory procedure. Moreover, the term 'DAB' needs to be understood in a sense different from DAB under English law. Specifically, under Vietnam legislation, a DAB is considered to be a mediation procedure.[92] This means that a DAB cannot issue a final and binding

---

89 ibid art 241.
90 *Commercial Law 2005*, art 62.
91 *Construction Law 2014,* art 109.
92 Decree 37/2015/ND-CP, art 45(2).

decision for the parties and therefore implementation of its decision is at the will of the parties only. The government agency also considers a DAB as a mediation process, and therefore prefers the ad-hoc DAB over a standing DAB.[93]

In practice, there was a case that one party to a construction contract bypassed the DAB procedure and referred the dispute directly to The Vietnam International Arbitration Centre (**VIAC**). The opposing party then appealed to the People's Court of Ha Noi to set aside the arbitral award due to the incompetence of the arbitral tribunal. However, this appeal was not admitted, and the court held that referring the dispute to the DAB was infeasible because prior to arbitration, both parties did not obtain a consensus in spite of the exchanges between them. The word 'consensus' in this judgment emphasises that a DAB is only a mediation procedure under Vietnamese law. [94]

21.5.3.2 Arbitration

In Vietnam, there is only one law on arbitration, a law called *Commercial Arbitration Law 2010*. As analysed above, under Vietnamese *Construction Law*, a construction contract is a civil contract, therefore a question might be raised whether disputes relating to a construction contract can be arbitrable under the *Commercial Arbitration Law 2010*. The answer to this question must be positive because even though this law of 2010 is named the *'Commercial' Arbitration Law*, under the second and third paragraphs of Article 2, this law applies to disputes amongst parties at least one of whom conducts commercial activities and disputes are legislatively arbitrable. Under the eighth paragraph of Article 146 of Vietnamese *Construction Law*, disputes relating to a construction contract are arbitrable and so an arbitration clause in the construction field must be subject to the *Commercial Arbitration Law 2010*.

One point to be noted is that as a construction contract has a civil character, any foreign arbitral awards on this matter cannot be recognised or enforced under the *New York Convention* in Vietnam; Vietnam reserves the *New York Convention* for diputes arising from commercial legal relationships.[95] So, *exequatur*[96] of foreign arbitral awards in the construction domain is subject to Chapter XXXVII of the *Code of Civil Procedure*. However, it is important to observe that this *Code* does not impose more severe requirements than the *New York Convention* in order to enforce a foreign arbitral award.

21.6 What Special Provisions in the Particular Conditions are desirable for consistency with applicable laws in Vietnam?

The following sections highlight certain issues where it is desirable for consistency with applicable Vietnamese law to provide Special Provisions in the Particular Conditions.

21.6.1 Compensation for damages

The *Construction Law 2014* requires compensation for damages, where the breaching party shall compensate for damages caused to the other party and a third party (if any).[97]

---

93 Decision 4835/BTC-QLN of the Ministry of Finance.

94 Judgment No 2/2020/QD-PQTT dated 23 April 2020 of the People's Court of Ha Noi.

95 Article 2 of the Decision of the President of Vietnam No 453/QĐ-CTN on 28 July 1995.

96 ***Exequatur***: A Latin expression meaning an official recognition by a government of a consul or other representative of a foreign state, authorizing them to exercise office.

97 *Construction Law 2014*, art 146(3).

Damage compensation by the Contractor to the Employer is required in the following cases:

(a) The work quality fails to ensure the agreements reached in the contract or the completion time is prolonged due to the fault of the Contractor;
(b) Human and property losses are caused due to the fault of the Contractor during the warranty period.

Damage compensation by the Employer to the Contractor is required in the following cases:

(a) Due to the fault of the Employer, the contractual work is discontinued or performed behind schedule, encounters risks or machines, equipment, supplies and structures of the Contractor are left unused;
(b) The Employer provides documents and conditions necessary for the jobs not in accordance with the contractual agreements, making the Contractor re-implement construction, suspend or adjust its job;
(c) The Employer supplies raw materials, materials and equipment and meets other requirements not according to the time and requirements stated in the construction contract;
(d) The Employer fails to make payment as agreed upon in the contract.

The *Civil Code 2015* requires compensation for total damage, unless otherwise agreed by the Parties or unless otherwise prescribed by law.

21.6.2 Effectiveness and effective date of the Contract

The preconditions for the Contract to come into full force and effect are discussed in paragraph 21.4.3 above. It may be desirable to include these preconditions in a Special Provision for consistency with the formal requirements of Vietnamese Laws.

21.6.3 Insurance to be provided by the Contractor

This section discusses Insurances for Works to be provided by the Contractor under the FIDIC 2017 rainbow suite General Conditions and relevant laws and regulations. Sub-clause 19.2 of FIDIC 2017 provides that the Contractor shall insure and keep insured in the joint names of the Contractor and the Employer from the Commencement Date against various risks.

Decree 119/2015/ND-CP requires that the Employer shall be the Party who will provide insurance for the Works. The Contractor shall provide insurance for the Works if insurance for Works had been mentioned and included in the Contract Price.[98] Insurance for the Works shall be kept from the start until completion of construction works. Circular 329/2016/TT-BTC clarified 'completion of construction works' shall be the Handing-over Certificate for each section/structure or when that section/structure was taking-over.

Moreover, the insurer shall be freed from the liability to indemnify for the following losses:

(a) Loss caused by intentional acts. To be specific:

- Loss incurred due to riots, strikes and hostilities

98 *Decree 119/2015/ND-CP*, art 4.

- Loss caused by intentionally illegal acts committed by the policyholder or the insured
- Loss caused by the consultants' errors in design.

(b) Loss caused by nature: loss due to corrosion, abrasion, redox, and material defects.

(c) Loss dues to catastrophic events: Loss caused by wars, terrorism, nuclear reaction, nuclear radiation and radioactive contamination.[99, 100]

21.7 Summary of applicable legislation for Vietnamese governing law of the contract

21.7.1 Entry into a construction contract

Contracts generally	*Civil Code 2015*, art 385 to art 408 *Commercial Law 2005*, art 24, art 74 *Bidding Law 2013*, art 62 to art 65 *Law on Public-Private and Partnership 2020*.
Construction contracts	*Civil Code 2015*, art 385 to art 408 *Construction Law 2014*, art 138 to art 142 *Commercial Law 2005*, art 74 *Bidding Law 2013*, art 62 to art 65

21.7.2 Termination of a construction contract

Frustration	*Civil Code 2015*, art 420 *Commercial Law 2005,* art 296
Bankruptcy, insolvency, liquidation	*Law on Bankruptcy 2014* *Construction Law 2014*, art 145
Guarantees under forms of Security (Tender Security, Demand Guarantee, Surety Bond, Advance Payment Guarantee, Retention Money Guarantee, Payment Guarantee by Employer)	*Bidding Law 2013*, art 66 *Decree 37/2015/ND-CP* detailed guidance on construction contracts, art 16 to art 18 *Ordinance on Foreign Exchange Control 2005* and Amendment 2013 *Circular 07/2015/TT-NHNN* stipulating the Bank Guarantee

21.7.3 Dispute resolution

Limitation periods	*Civil Code 2015*, art 429, art 588 and art 688 *Commercial Law 2005,* art 318 to art 319 *Commercial Arbitration Law 2010*, art 33
Liability	*Construction Law 2014*, art 146 *Commercial Law 2005*, art 302 to art 316 *Civil Code 2015*: Contractual liability: art 13, art 360, and art 419 Non-contractual liability: art 584 to art 608

99 *Decree 119/2015/ND-CP*, art 6(2).
100 *Circular 329/2016/TT-BTC*, art 5.

Adjudication	*Construction Law 2014,* art 146 *Decree 37/2015/ND-CP* detailed guidance on construction contracts, art 45
Arbitration	*Construction Law 2014*, art 146 *Civil Procedure Code 2015*, arts 414 to 415: domestic arbitration, arts 423 to 431 and arts 451 to 463: foreign arbitration *Commercial Arbitration Law 2010*

21.8 Summary of applicable legislation if the Site/Country is in Vietnam

21.8.1 Operation of a construction contract

Registration and administration of professionals – Project Manager, Design Engineers, Supervisors, Architects, Quantity Surveyors, Certifiers, Topographical Surveyors, Geotechnical Investigator	*Construction Law 2014* and Amendment 2020, art 148 to art 159 *Law on Architecture 2019*, art 19 to art 35
Registration/licensing of Contractors and subcontractors	*Law on Enterprises 2020*, art 17 to art 45 *Construction Law 2014* and Amendment 2020, art 157 *Bidding Law 2013*, art 5
Subcontractors	*Bidding Law 2013* *Decree 63/2014/ND-CP* detailing the implementation of several provisions of the *Bidding Law* regarding the selection of Contractors, art 128 *Decree 37/2015/ND-CP* detailed guidance on construction contracts, art 47
Labour	*Labour Code 2019*
Design/Moral rights	*Intellectual Property Law 2005* and Amendment 2009 *Construction Law 2014* and Amendment 2020 art 86
Copyright	*Intellectual Property Law 2005* and Amendment 2009 *Construction Law 2014* and Amendment 2020 art 86
Planning	*Law on Planning 2017* *Law on Urban Planning 2009* *Construction Law 2014* and Amendment 2020, art 13 to art 44
Work affecting adjacent property to the Site	*Civil Code 2015*, art 245 to art 256 *Construction Law 2014* and Amendment 2020
Heritage	*Law on Cultural Heritage 2001* and Amendment 2009 *Construction Law 2014* and Amendment 2020
Environment	*Law on Environmental Protection 2014* and Amendment 2018 *Construction Law 2014*, art 116
Local procurement	*Bidding Law 2013* *Decree 63/2014/ND-CP* detailing the implementation of several provisions of the *Bidding Law* regarding the selection of Contractors.
Building and construction permits, Execution of construction work, Standard of construction work	*Construction Law 2014* and Amendment 2020, art 89 to art 106 *Construction Law 2014* and Amendment 2020, art 107 to art 124 *Law on Standards and Technical Regulations 2006*

Health and safety	*Labour Code 2019:* Working hours: art 105 to art 116 Health and Safety: art 132 to art 134 Female labours: art 135 to art 142 *Law on Occupational Safety and Hygiene 2015* *Construction Law 2014* and Amendment 2020, art 115 *Decree 37/2015/ND-CP* detailed guidance on construction contracts art 48 *Decree 44/2016/ND-CP* details some articles of the *Law on Occupational Safety and Hygiene*, technical inspection of occupational safety, training of occupational safety and hygiene and monitoring of occupational environment.
Calibration of testing apparatus, equipment and instruments	*Law on Measurement 2011*
Ownership of Plant and Materials	*Civil Code 2015*, art 158 to art 244 *Commercial Code 2005*, art 62
Insurance	*Law on Insurance Business 2000* with Amendments 2010, 2019 *Decree 119/2015/ND-CP* regulating compulsory insurance for construction investment activities *Law on Occupational Safety and Hygiene 2015*, art 41 to art 62 *Decree 37/2015/ND-CP* detailed guidance on construction contracts art 46
Statutory rights that coexist with contractual rights	*Construction Law 2014* and Amendment 2020 Design: art 83a and art 87 Construction: art 123 *Law on State Audit 2015* and Amendment 2019 *Law on Inspection 2010*
Liability for defective work	*Construction Law 2014* and Amendment 2020, art 119 to art 125 *Commercial Law 2005*
Liability for nuisance	Public nuisance: *Law on Handling Administrative Violations 2012* Private nuisance: *Civil Code 2015*, art 589 and art 605
Other issues	*Decree 139/2017/ND-CP* regarding penalties for administrative violations against regulations on investment and construction; extraction, processing and trading of minerals used in construction, production and trading of building materials; management of infrastructural constructions; real estate business, housing development, management and operation of apartment buildings and office buildings.

21.8.2 Termination of a construction contract

Bankruptcy, insolvency, liquidation	*Law on Bankruptcy 2014*
Decennial liability and liability generally for the total or partial collapse of structures	*Law on Housing 2014*, art 85 *Construction Law 2014*, art 119 and art 127

21.8.3 Dispute resolution

Dispute before a local board/ Adjudication	*Construction Law 2014*, art 146 *Commercial Law 2005*, art 317 *Decree 37/2015/ND-CP* detailed guidance on construction contracts, art 45
Limitation periods	*Civil Code 2015*, art 429, art 588 and art 688 *Commercial Law 2005*, art 318 to art 319

21.9 Summary of applicable legislation if the 'seat' of the dispute determination is in Vietnam

Dispute resolution	*Civil Procedure Code 2015* *Commercial Arbitration Law 2010*
Limitation periods	*Civil Code 2015*, art 429, art 588 and art 688 *Commercial Law 2005*, art 319 *Commercial Arbitration Law 2010*, art 33
Mediation	*Law on Mediation or Dialogue at Court 2020* Decree 22/2017/ND-CP on Commercial Mediation
Arbitration	*Civil Procedure Code 2015* Domestic arbitration: arts 414 to 415 International arbitration: arts 423 to 431 and arts 451 to 463 *Commercial Arbitration Law 2010* *Civil Enforcement Law 2008* and Amendment 2014
Litigation	*Civil Procedure Code 2015* *Law on Mediation or Dialogue at Court 2020* *Law on Judicial Expertise 2012* and Amendment 2020

21.10 Issues that a court or arbitrator may construe differently to that expected from the words of the Contract, because of local law or custom

21.10.1 Delay damages

As discussed in paragraph 21.5.1.3 above, the *Construction Law 2014* provides that, for public funded projects, the penalty shall not exceed 12 per cent of the value of the breached contractual obligation portion,[101] while the *Commercial Law 2005* states that the penalty or sum of penalties shall not exceed 8 per cent of the value of the breached contractual obligation portion.[102]

Previously there seemed to be no confusion in the application of those two monetary legal concepts under the law of Vietnam until the so-called 'liquidated damages', 'Delay Damages' (under FIDIC Contracts), and/or other like pre-agreed amounts were introduced to Vietnam. This is now a controversial topic for scholars, practitioners, judges, arbitrators and all other players to discuss and the outcome remains unclear.

101 *Construction Law 2014*, art 146, s 2.
102 *Commercial Law 2005*, art 301.

For example, the Supreme People's Court's decision dated 9 June 2020[103] on appeal from the decision of a lower court regarding the dispute between Yen Sao Sai Gon Co Ltd and Yen Viet Joint Stock Company has concerned the public the most. In this appeal decision, the Supreme Court held that the pre-agreed/estimated amount of the damages were uncertain and that it contradicted the application of the principle of law and required the lower court to open the case again.

A possible reason explaining why the courts, judges and arbitrators apply the concept of 'liquidated damages', 'Delay Damages' (under FIDIC Contracts), and/or other like pre-agreed amounts differently is because the freedom to contract concept is not yet commonly accepted and strictly adhered to, so that each judge or arbitrator will adapt those concepts in a way which is closest to their position on the case.

Existing disputes require an immediate settlement/conclusion to determine whether or not the freedom to contract concept to agree on the pre-estimated amount of damages is applicable. In addition, it is important, urgent and necessary to make sure that application of the Delay Damages are consistent and updated to legal developments in the world in upcoming disputes, especially international disputes requiring the recognition and enforcement of a foreign arbitral award or court decision.

Furthermore, the court may adjust the capped percentage of delay damage based on the value of a delayed part (or breached part) instead of a percentage of the whole Contract Price. In a case with a FIDIC contract with Delay Damages capped at 5 per cent of the Contract Price, the Council of Justices of the Supreme Court commented that:

> The First-Instance Court and the Appeal Court failed to review and clarify percentages of completed works and remained works of the Contractor, to determine value of violated part of contract, and the courts requested the Contractor to pay 5% of the whole contract price is not correct.[104]

21.10.2 Financing charges in delayed payment

Sub-clause 14.8 entitles the Contractor to financing charges compounded monthly on the unpaid amount during the delayed period of the payment. The FIDIC 2017 rainbow suite and the FIDIC 2010 Pink Book provide two different references.

Sub-clause 14.8 of 2010 2017 FIDIC Red, Yellow, and Silver Book provides that:

> These financing charges shall be calculated at the annual rate of three percent (3%) above: (a) the average bank short-term lending rate to prime borrowers prevailing for the currency of payment at the place for payment, or (b) where no such rate exists at that place, the same rate in the country of the currency of payment, or (c) in the absence of such a rate at either place, the appropriate rate fixed by the law of the country of the currency of payment.

Sub-clause 14.8 of 2010 FIDIC Pink Book provides that:

> These financing charges shall be calculated at the annual rate of three percentage points above the discount rate of the central bank in the country of the currency of payment, or if not available, the interbank offered rate, and shall be paid in such currency.

103 Decision No11/2020/KN-KDTM dated 9 June 2020 of the Supreme People's Court.

104 Decision 15/2016/KDTM-GDT 'regarding construction contract dispute' of Council of Justices of the Supreme People's Court.

In Vietnam law, different rates on financing charges apply depending on which laws will be applied for that particular contract. If the contract is within the scope of the *Commercial Law*, when the Employer delays making payment, the Contractor may claim interest on such delayed payment at the average interest rate applicable to overdue debts in the market at the time of payment for the delayed period.[105] If the contract is funded by public-investment projects or state-owned enterprises, then *Decree 37/2015/ND-CP* requires that interest at the commercial bank where the Contractor opens its payment accounts will be applied for delayed payment.[106]

In many cases, the courts prefer to apply an average interest rate according to the *Commercial Law 2005*,[107] or even adjust excessive interest rates to this average interest rate.[108]

For contracts for the supply of goods and services, the courts prefer to apply an average interest rate as per *Commercial Law 2005*, and even adjust excessive interest rates to this average interest rate[109]. This is confirmed by Precedent 09/2016/AL where the Supreme Court referred to Article 306 of the *Law on Commerce 2005* in returning the judgment of the Court of First Instance (when applying basic interest rate quoted by the State Bank) and requested that the court should have applied average overdue interest of at least three local banks (Agribank, Vietcombank, Vietinbank, etc.) to calculate the interest on late payment.[110]

However, for construction contracts, the conclusions are varied. There are cases where the court preferred to apply average interest rates according to the *Commercial Law 2005*.[111] However, there are other cases where the court preferred the interest from *Decree 37/2015/ND-CP* over interest from *Commercial Law* for a dispute between private enterprises, on the argument that a construction contract should be interpreted under *Construction Law* and its detailed guidance of construction contract instead of *Commercial Law*.[112]

The *Civil Code 2015* requires that the delayed payment interest shall not exceed the maximum loan interest of 20 per cent.[113, 114] During determination of the interest for financing charges, some courts agreed with maximum interest of 20 per cent set by the *Civil Code 2015*, while other courts agreed with average interest of three local banks (Agribank, Vietcombank, Vietinbank, etc.).

---

105 *Commercial Law*, art 306.

106 *Decree 37/2015/ND-CP*, art 43(2).

107 Judgment 37/2018/KDTM-PT regarding disputes in construction contract by People's Court of Hai Phong City.

108 Judgment 09/2018/KDTM-PT regarding disputes in property purchasing contract by People's Court of Hanoi City.

109 ibid.

110 Precedent 09/2016/AL on Commercial case concerning dispute over purchase agreement.

111 Judgment 37/2018/KDTM-PT regarding disputes in construction contract by People's Court of Haiphong City.

112 Judgment 130/2019/KDTM-PT regarding construction contract dispute by People's Court of Hanoi City.

113 *Civil Code 2015*, art 357.

114 ibid art 468.

21.10.3 Exceptional events

Exceptional Events in FIDIC 2017 used to be *Force Majeure* in FIDIC 1999. Under Vietnam law, there are two types of exceptional events: *force majeure* and fundamental change of circumstances.

> *Force majeure* is an event which occurs beyond the control of Parties, which is not able to be foreseen and which is not able to be remedied by all possible necessary and admissible measures being taken.[115]

When an event is considered as *force majeure*, the *Construction Law* provides a mechanism for both Parties to adjust the construction contract[116] and the Employer can adjust the construction project. *Commercial Law 2005* goes further by providing an exemption of liability for a party who breached a contract due to *force majeure*, [117] while the *Bidding Law* provides an option for extension of time agreed by both Parties.[118]

Another term worth noting is 'fundamental change of circumstances', or hardship, which is defined in paragraph 21.2.5 above. Article 420 of the *Civil Code* provides the following tools for Parties under such hardship:

> 2. In the case of basic circumstances change, the affected party may request the other party to re-negotiate the contract in a reasonable period of time.
> 3. If the parties cannot reach an agreement on amending the contract within a reasonable period of time, any of the parties may request a court to:
> (a) Terminate the contract at a specific time;
> (b) Amend the contract to balance the lawful rights and interests of the parties due to basic change of circumstances.

The court may only decide to amend the contract in the event that the termination of the contract would cause greater damage than the cost to perform the contract if it is modified.

> 4. In the process of negotiating amendments and termination of the contract and the court handling the case, the parties must continue to perform its obligations under the contract, unless otherwise agreed.

Table 21.1 compares the criteria for the application of hardship provisions in the *Civil Codes* of various countries.

From the table, one point to be highlighted is that criteria (a1) and criteria (đ) are not common in the *Civil Codes* of civil law countries. Criteria (a1) on 'objective reasons' has been used by a court to reject a request for fundamental change of

115 ibid art 156.
116 *Construction Law 2014*, art 143(2)(d).
117 *Commercial Law 2005*, art 294.
118 *Bidding Law 2013*, art 67(6)(a).

Table 21.1 Comparison of criteria for hardship in various *Civil Codes*

No	Criteria for hardship	Vietnam	UNIDROIT [119]	France [120]	Russia [121]	Germany [122]	China [123]
(a1)	The circumstances change due to objective reasons	X	X				X
(a2)	occurred after the conclusion of the contract	X	X		X	X	X
(b)	At the time of concluding the contract, the parties could not foresee a change in circumstances	X	X	X			X
(c)	The circumstances change such greatly that if the parties knew in advance, the contract could not be concluded or could be concluded, but with completely different content	X			X	X	
(d)	The continuation of the contract without modification would cause serious damage to one party	X		X		X	X
(d)	The disadvantaged party has adopted all the necessary measures in its ability, in accordance with the nature of the contract but cannot prevent or minimize damage.	X					

circumstances[124]. Criteria (d) have put a burden on a disadvantaged party to prove that all measures within its ability have been adopted. Scholars have argued that this article should be revised.[125]

21.10.4 Indemnities by the Contractor

Sub-clause 17.4 of FIDIC 2017 requires that the Contractor shall indemnify and hold harmless the Employer and the Employer's Personnel against and from all third party claims, damages, losses and expenses in respect of damage to or loss of any property, to the extent that such damage or loss arises out of or in the course of or by reason of the Contractor's execution of the Works.

Indemnity is a common law term which does not have an equivalent term in Vietnam civil law and may be not recognized by the court. In one case where the Contractor's execution of the Works caused damage to a neighbour's building, and the neighbour

119 UNIDROIT Principles of International Commercial Contracts 2016, cl 6.2.2.

120 *French Civil Code* 2016, art 1195.

121 *Russian Civil Code* 1994, art 451.

122 *German Civil Code* (BGB) 2002, art 313.

123 Interpretation of the Supreme People's Court on Several Issues Concerning Application of the 'Contract Law of the People's Republic of China', art 26.

124 Judgment 01/2018/KDTM-PT regarding disputes in loan contract by People's Court of Danang City

125 Dam Thi Diem Hanh and Le Thi Kim Oanh, 'Identification of Fundamental Change Circumstance under German Civil Code and Lessons for Vietnam' [2019] *State and Law* 9.

brought a claim in court against the Contractor under the *Civil Code* on liability for compensation for non-contractual damages, the judge determined that:

> As per article 605 of the *Civil Code*, the Owner of a house or Employer of construction work must compensate for damage if such building or construction works causes damage to other person. If the Contractor is partly at fault that such house or construction works causes damage, he must jointly compensate for such damage. This article in the *Civil Code* does not allow exceptional case where there is other agreement between the Owner and the Contractor. As per article 370 of the *Civil Code*, the Employer, or the Contractor, can only transfer the obligation for compensation liability with the consent of the obligee.[126]

21.11 References

21.11.1 Books

Truong Nhat Quang, *Contract Law- Fundamental Legal Principles* (1st edn, Dan Tri Publishing House 2020).

21.11.2 Journals

The People's Court Journal
Legal Studies
State and Law

21.11.3 Internet

Vietnamese Codes, Laws and Regulations: http://congbao.chinhphu.vn/ (accessed 23 November 2020)

Precedents adopted by the Supreme People's Court of Vietnam: https://anle.toaan.gov.vn/ (accessed 23 November 2020)

E-portals on publication of judgments and decisions of the court: https://congbobanan.toaan.gov.vn/ (accessed 23 November 2020)

126 Judgment 23/2019/KDTM-PT regarding compensation for non-contractual damages caused by construction works by People's Court of Danang City.

GLOSSARY

Term	Meaning	Defined in Section
1977 Red Book	**FIDIC**[1] Conditions of Contract for Works of Civil Engineering Construction – Third Edition 1977.	**1.3.1**
1987 Red Book	**FIDIC** Conditions of Contract for Works of Civil Engineering Construction – Fourth Edition 1987.	**1.3.1**
1987 Yellow Book	**FIDIC** Conditions of Contract for Electrical and Mechanical Works – Third Edition 1987	**1.3.1**
1995 Orange Book	**FIDIC** Conditions of Contract for Design-Build and Turnkey – First Edition 1995.	**1.3.1**
1999 Arrangement	The Arrangement Concerning Mutual Enforcement of Arbitral Award Between the Mainland and Hong Kong (1999).	**9.2.5**
1999 Red Book	**FIDIC** Conditions of Contract for Construction – First Edition 1999.	**1.3.1**
1999 Silver Book	**FIDIC** Conditions of Contract for EPC/Turnkey Projects – First Edition 1999.	**1.3.1**
1999 Yellow Book	**FIDIC** Conditions of Contract for Plant and Design-Build – First Edition 1999.	**1.3.1**
2017 Red Book	**FIDIC** Conditions of Contract for Construction – Second Edition 2017.	**1.3.1**
2017 Silver Book	**FIDIC** Conditions of Contract for EPC/Turnkey Projects – Second Edition 2017.	**1.3.1**
2017 Yellow Book	**FIDIC** Conditions of Contract for Plant and Design-Build – Second Edition 2017.	**1.3.1**
AABE	The *Act on Architects and Building Engineers* (Act No 202 of 1950) (Japan).	**12.6.9**
ABCC	Australian Building and Construction Commission.	**6.2.3**
ABLIS	Australian Business Licence and Information Service.	**6.2.2**
Abrahamson Principles	Principles of fair and balanced risk allocation, articulated in Max W Abrahamson, 'Risk Management' (1983) *International Construction Law Review* 241, 244.	**2.4**
Accepted Contract Amount	FIDIC definition (Red,[2] Pink, Yellow,[3] Gold and Emerald Books).	**FIDIC GCs**
ACESL	Association of Consulting Engineers Sri Lanka.	**20.2.3**
ACI	Arbitration Council of India.	**10.2.8**
ACL	*Australian Consumer Law.*	**6.10.1**
adhesion contract	A contract in which its essential clauses are imposed or are drafted by one party, by a third person especially for a party, or as a result of its instructions, the other party having only the possibility to accept the contract as such.	
ADR	Alternative dispute resolution – alternative to resolution by litigation in court.	
ADR Law	*Alternative Dispute Resolution Act* (Philippines).	**18.1.3**
Advance Payment Certificate	FIDIC definition (2017 Red, 2017 Yellow and Emerald Books).	**FIDIC GCs**

(Continued)

1 Terms in bold are defined elsewhere in the Glossary.
2 Red Book refers to 1999 Red Book and 2017 Red Book.
3 Yellow Book refers to 1999 Yellow Book and 2017 Yellow Book.
4 Silver Book refers to 1999 Silver Book and 2017 Silver Book.

Term	Meaning	Defined in Section
Advance Payment Guarantee	FIDIC definition (2017 Red, 2017 Yellow, 2017 Silver[4] and Emerald Books).	**FIDIC GCs**
AFP	Armed Forces of the Philippines.	**18.1.1**
AIAC	Asian International Arbitration Centre (Malaysia).	**14.2.9**
amiable compositeur	The power given by parties to an arbitrator to decide a dispute equitably or ***ex aequo et bono*** without strict regard to the rules of law that would otherwise apply.	
Antitrust Act	*Act on Prohibition of Private Monopolisation and Maintenance of Fair Trade* (Act No 45 of 1947) (Japan).	**12.2.7.1**
APCS	Advanced Precast Concrete System (Singapore).	**19.2**
APEC	Asia-Pacific Economic Cooperation Forum.	**14.2.3**
Appendix to Tender	FIDIC definition (1987 Red, 1999 Red and 1999 Yellow Books).	**FIDIC GCs**
ARTC	*Act on the Regulation of Terms and Conditions* (Korea).	**13.6.5**
ASEAN	Association of Southeast Asian Nations.	**14.2.1**
Authorised Dealer	Authorised dealer in foreign exchange appointed by the **Central Bank**. (Papua New Guinea).	**17.6.5**
Authorised Person	An Architect, Engineer or Surveyor registered under the Hong Kong *Buildings Ordinance*.	**9.6.4**
Bank	FIDIC definition (Pink Book).	**FIDIC GCs**
Base Date	FIDIC definition (Red, Pink, Yellow, Silver, Gold and Emerald Books).	**FIDIC GCs**
Basic Law	*Basic Law of the Hong Kong Special Administrative Region of the People's Republic of China.*	**9.1.1**
BBB	The Build Build Build Infrastructure Program (2016–2022) (Philippines).	**18.2.1**
BCA	Building and Construction Authority (Singapore).	**19.2**
BCISPA	*Building and Construction Industry Security of Payment Act 1999* (NSW) (Australia).	**6.6.1**
BDD	Building Dispute Department (*kenchiku-bu*) of the Tokyo and Osaka District Courts (Japan).	**12.2.10.2**
Bill of Quantities	FIDIC definition (1987 Red, Red, Pink and Emerald Books).	**FIDIC GCs**
BIM	Building information modelling or building information management.	**4.8**
Blue-Green Book	FIDIC Form of Contract for Dredging and Reclamation Works – First Edition 2006, Second Edition 2016.	**1.3.1**
BNM	Bank Negara Malaysia.	**14.3.1**
BOO	Build-Own-Operate.	**10.2.1**
BOOT	Build-Own-Operate-Transfer.	**10.2.1**
BoQ	**Bill of Quantities**.	
Borrower	FIDIC definition (Pink Book).	**FIDIC GCs**
BOT	Build-Operate-Transfer.	**10.2.1**
BPKP	Financial and Development Supervisory Agency (Indonesia).	**11.5.3.2**
BS	*Bikram Sambat* calendar used officially by the Government of Nepal. It is a solar calendar based on Hindu traditions.	**15.1.1**
BSA	The *Building Standards Act* (Act No 201 of 1950) (Japan).	**12.6.9**
BUJKA	Foreign construction services business entity (Indonesia).	**11.2.1**
Bumiputra	Native Malays (Malaysia).	**14.6.6**
causa	A lawful cause required for the existence of a contract in a civil law system.	
CAM	Court-Annexed Mediation (Philippines).	**18.1.3**
CAN	Contractor's Association of Nepal.	**15.2.1**
CAR	Contractors' All Risk insurance policy.	**10.2.2.4**
CBA	*Construction Business Act* (Act No 100 of 1949) (Japan).	**12.2.2.1**
CBDC	Construction Business Development Council (Nepal).	**15.2.1**

CCI	Chamber of Construction Industry. (Sri Lanka)	**20.2.3**
CCP	*Civil Code of the Philippines.*	**18.4.1**
CCP	*Code of Civil Procedures* (Act No 109 of 1996) (Japan).	**12.1.3**
Central Bank	The Bank of Papua New Guinea, exercising regulatory power in respect of foreign exchange control under the *Central Banking Act 2000* (PNG) (Papua New Guinea).	**17.6.5**
CIAC	Construction Industry Arbitration Commission (Philippines).	**18.2.10.1**
CIAP	Construction Industry Authority of the Philippines.	**18.2.2**
CIAP 102	Uniform General Conditions of Contract for Private Construction (Philippines).	**18.2.9**
CIArb	Chartered Institute of Arbitrators.	**14.2.9**
CIC	Fiji Construction Industry Council.	**8.2**
CIDA	Construction Industry Development Authority (Sri Lanka).	**20.2.2**
CIDB	Construction Industry Development Board (Malaysia).	**14.2.2**
CIETAC	China International Economic and Trade Arbitration Commission.	**7.2.9**
CIM	**BIM** like technologies (Japan).	**12.2.6**
CIICA	Centre for International Investment and Commercial Arbitration (Pakistan).	**16.2.2**
CIMP	Construction Industry Master Plan (Malaysia).	**14.2.2**
CIRP	Corporate Insolvency Resolution Process (India).	**10.2.6**
CITF	Construction Innovation and Technology Fund (Hong Kong).	**9.2.2**
CITP	Construction Industry Transformative Plan (Malaysia).	**14.2.2**
civil law	A system of law in which the laws are codified in a large number of general rules and principles.	**1.1.2**
CLAB	Construction Labour Exchange Centre (Malaysia).	**14.2.2**
Claim	FIDIC definition (2017 Red, 2017 Yellow, 2017 Silver and Emerald Books).	**FIDIC GCs**
CLQ	Centralised Labour Quarter (Malaysia).	**14.3.1**
CMCO	Conditional Movement Control Order (Malaysia).	**14.3.1**
CNI	Confederation of Nepalese Industries.	**15.2.8**
Commencement Date	FIDIC definition (1987 Red, Red, Pink, Yellow, Silver, Gold and Emerald Books).	**FIDIC GCs**
common law	The body of law developed by judges from around the 11th century in England, and later exported to its various colonies such as Canada, the USA, Australia, Fiji, Hong Kong, India, Malaysia and Singapore.	**1.1.2**
Completion Schedule	FIDIC definition (Emerald Book).	**FIDIC GCs**
Compliance Verification System	FIDIC definition (2017 Red, 2017 Yellow, 2017 Silver and Emerald Books).	**FIDIC GCs**
Conditions of Contract	FIDIC definition (2017 Red, 2017 Yellow, 2017 Silver and Emerald Books).	**FIDIC GCs**
Construction Work Contract	A contract for construction works regulated by *Law No 2 of 2017 Construction Services* (Indonesia).	**11.4.1**
Contract	The construction contract being referred to.	**1.1.1**
Contract	FIDIC definition (1987 Red, Red, Pink, Yellow, Silver, Gold and Emerald Books).	**FIDIC GCs**
Contract Agreement	FIDIC definition (1987 Red, Red, Pink, Yellow, Silver, Gold and Emerald Books).	**FIDIC GCs**
Contract Data	FIDIC definition (2017 Red, Pink, 2017 Yellow, 2017 Silver, Gold and Emerald Books).	**FIDIC GCs**
contract of adhesion	See **adhesion contract**.	
Contract Participants	All the persons referred to in a **FIDIC Contract**.	**2.4**

(Continued)

Term	Meaning	Defined in Section
Contract Price	FIDIC definition (1987 Red, Red, Pink, Yellow, Silver, Gold and Emerald Books).	**FIDIC GCs**
Contract Risk Management Plan	FIDIC definition (Emerald Book).	**FIDIC GCs**
Contract Risk Register	FIDIC definition (Emerald Book).	**FIDIC GCs**
Contractor	The party to a construction contract (the **Contract**) who carries out the work.	**1.1.1**
Contractor	FIDIC definition (1987 Red, Red, Pink, Yellow, Silver, Gold and Emerald Books).	**FIDIC GCs**
Contractor's Documents	FIDIC definition (Red, Pink, Yellow, Silver, Gold and Emerald Books).	**FIDIC GCs**
Contractor's Equipment	FIDIC definition (1987 Red, Red, Pink, Yellow, Silver, Gold and Emerald Books).	**FIDIC GCs**
Contractor's Key Equipment	FIDIC definition (Emerald Book).	**FIDIC GCs**
Contractor's Key Personnel	FIDIC definition (Emerald Book).	**FIDIC GCs**
Contractor's Personnel	FIDIC definition (Red, Pink, Yellow, Silver, Gold and Emerald Books).	**FIDIC GCs**
Contractor's Proposal	FIDIC definition (Yellow, Gold and Emerald Books).	**FIDIC GCs**
Contractor's Representative	FIDIC definition (Red, Pink, Yellow, Silver, Gold and Emerald Books).	**FIDIC GCs**
Cost	FIDIC definition (1987 Red, Red, Pink, Yellow, Silver, Gold and Emerald Books).	**FIDIC GCs**
Cost Plus Profit	FIDIC definition (2017 Red, 2017 Yellow, 2017 Silver, Gold and Emerald Books).	**FIDIC GCs**
Country	FIDIC definition (Red, Pink, Yellow, Silver, Gold and Emerald Books).	**FIDIC GCs**
Covid-19 Act	*Covid-19 (Temporary Measures) Act 2020* (Singapore).	**19.3.2.1**
CPEC	China Pakistan Economic Corridor.	**16.2.1**
crore	Ten million (India, Sri Lanka).	**10.2.7**
CTEVT	Council of Technical Education and Vocational Training (Nepal).	**15.2.4**
curial law	The law governing the existence and operation of the arbitral tribunal, generally the law of the 'seat' of arbitration. Also known as the *lex arbitrii*.	**1.5.5**
DAAB	**Dispute Avoidance/Adjudication Board**.	**FIDIC GCs**
DAAB Agreement	FIDIC definition (2017 Red, 2017 Yellow, 2017 Silver and Emerald Books).	**FIDIC GCs**
DAB	FIDIC definition (1999 Red, 1999 Yellow, 1999 Silver and Gold Books).	**FIDIC GCs**
Date of Completion	FIDIC definition (Red, Yellow, Silver and Emerald Books).	**FIDIC GCs**
day	FIDIC definition (1987 Red, Red, Pink, Yellow, Silver, Gold and Emerald Books).	**FIDIC GCs**
Daywork Schedule	FIDIC definition (Red, Pink, 2017 Yellow, 2017 Silver and Emerald Books).	**FIDIC GCs**
DB	FIDIC definition (Pink Book).	**FIDIC GCs**
Defects Notification Period	FIDIC definition (Red, Pink, Yellow, Silver and Emerald Books).	**FIDIC GCs**
Delay Damages	FIDIC definition (2017 Red, 2017 Yellow, 2017 Silver and Emerald Books).	**FIDIC GCs**
dekigata	The product being produced from the Works (Japan).	**12.9.1**

Delayed Payment Act	The *Act against Delay in Payment of Subcontract Proceeds, Etc. to Subcontractors* (Act No 120 of 1956) (Japan).	**12.4.1**
design	All plans, drawings, sketches, instructions, and descriptions that determine the way the **Works** (or parts of it) are to be constructed. Design includes the writing or selection of specifications as well as the production of plans and drawings and any element of choice on the part of the designer, such as requirements as to materials or working methods.	
design contract	A contract for the preparation of a **design** to be constructed under a construction contract.	
Dewan Sengketa	**Dispute Board** (Indonesia).	**11.10.1**
DILG	Department of Interior and Local Government (Philippines).	**18.3.1**
Dispute	FIDIC definition (2017 Red, 2017 Yellow, 2017 Silver, Gold and Emerald Books).	**FIDIC GCs**
Dispute Avoidance /Adjudication Board	FIDIC definition (2017 Red, 2017 Yellow, 2017 Silver and Emerald Books).	**FIDIC GCs**
Dispute Adjudication Board	A **Dispute Board** that provides a provisionally binding decision on a dispute referred to it; if neither party issues a notice of dissatisfaction within a defined time, the decision becomes final and binding.	
Dispute Board	A panel of one or three suitably qualified and experienced independent persons appointed under the **Contract** to provide a determination of a dispute referred to it. A Dispute Board may be a **Dispute Avoidance/Adjudication Board (DAAB)**, a **Dispute Adjudication Board (DAB)**, a **Dispute Review Board (DRB)** or a **Dispute Resolution Board (DRB)**.	
DNP	**Defects Notification Period.** FIDIC definition (2017 Red, 2017 Yellow, 2017 Silver and Emerald Books).	**FIDIC GCs**
doctrine of separability	The generally recognised principle of the law of international arbitration that an arbitration agreement incorporated in a contract is treated for legal purposes as a separate and independent agreement for the purpose of determining its validity or enforceability.	**1.5.6**
DOH	Department of Health (Philippines).	**18.3.1**
DOJ	Department of Justice (Philippines).	**18.2.10.1**
DOLE	Department of Labor and Employment (Philippines).	**18.2.4**
DOSH	Department of Occupational Safety and Health (Malaysia).	**14.2.6**
DOTr	Department of Transportation (Philippines).	**18.3.1**
DPWH	Department of Public Works and Highways (Philippines).	**18.3.1**
Drawings	FIDIC definition (1987 Red, Red and Pink Books).	**FIDIC GCs**
DRB	Dispute Review Board or Dispute Resolution Board.	**15.2.11**
DRC	Dispute Resolution Committee.	**15.2.11**
DTI	Department of Trade and Industry (Philippines).	**18.2.2**
DWSS	Digital Works Supervision Systems (Hong Kong).	**9.2.2**
EA	Project Executing Agency (Japan).	**5.3.1**
East Coast model	The scheme of statutory adjudication legislated in the New South Wales, Queensland, South Australia, Victoria, Tasmania and the Australian Capital Territory (Australia).	**6.6.1**
ECQ	Enhanced Community Quarantine (Philippines).	**18.3.1**
ECSL	Engineering Council of Sri Lanka.	**20.2.3**
EIA	*Environmental Impact Assessment Notification* 2006 issued by Ministry of Environment and Forest under the *Environment (Protection) Act* 1986 (India).	**10.2.2.5**
EMCO	Enhanced Movement Control Order (Malaysia).	**14.3.1**

(Continued)

Term	Meaning	Defined in Section
Emerald Book	FIDIC Conditions of Contract for Underground Works, First Edition 2019.	**1.3.1**
Employer	The party to a construction contract for whom the work is done. Also referred to as the Principal or sometimes the Owner or Client.	**1.1.1**
Employer	FIDIC definition (1987 Red, Red, Pink, Yellow, Silver, Gold and Emerald Books).	**FIDIC GCs**
Employer's Equipment	FIDIC definition (Red, Pink, Yellow, Silver, Gold and Emerald Books).	**FIDIC GCs**
Employer's Personnel	FIDIC definition (Red, Pink, Yellow, Silver, Gold and Emerald Books).	**FIDIC GCs**
Employer's Representative	FIDIC definition (2017 Silver and Gold Books).	**FIDIC GCs**
Employer's Requirements	FIDIC definition (Yellow, Silver, Gold and Emerald Books).	**FIDIC GCs**
Employer-Supplied Materials	FIDIC definition (2017 Red, 2017 Yellow, 2017 Silver and Emerald Books).	**FIDIC GCs**
ENAA	Engineering Advancement Association (Japan).	**12.2.9.2**
ENAA-Domestic	**ENAA** General Conditions for Domestic Plant Construction Work (last amended in 2020) (Japan).	**12.2.9.2**
ENAA-Internationals	International construction contract forms published by **ENAA** (Japan).	**12.2.9.2**
Engineer	FIDIC definition (1987 Red, Red, Pink, Yellow and Emerald Books).	**FIDIC GCs**
Engineer's Representative	FIDIC definition (1987 Red, 2017 Red, 2017 Yellow and Emerald Books).	**FIDIC GCs**
EOT	Extension of time.	
EPB	Earth pressure balance tunnelling machines.	**4.1**
EPC contract	Engineer, procure and construct contract. A construction contract (also referred to as a turnkey contract) in which the **Contractor** takes total responsibility for the engineering (**design**), procurement and construction, and provides a fully equipped facility ready for operation (at the 'turn of the key').	**1.1.1**
EPCM contract	Engineer, Procure and Construction Management contract. A construction contract in which the **Contractor**, as Construction Manager, designs, procures and manages the construction as agent of the **Employer**.	**1.1.1**
ePenjana	National Short-Term Economic Recovery Plan (Malaysia).	**14.3.1**
ESS	Employment Support Scheme (Hong Kong).	**9.3.1**
ex aequo et bono	A Latin phrase meaning according to the right and good.	**11.12**
exequatur	An official recognition by a government of a consul or other representative of a foreign state, authorising them to exercise office (Latin).	**21.5.3.2**
Excavation	FIDIC definition (Emerald Book).	**FIDIC GCs**
Exceptional Event	FIDIC definition (2017 Red, 2017 Yellow, 2017 Silver, Gold and Emerald Books).	**FIDIC GCs**
Extension of Time or **EOT**	FIDIC definition (2017 Red, 2017 Yellow, 2017 Silver and Emerald Books).	**FIDIC GCs**
FATA	Federally Administered Tribal areas (Pakistan).	**16.1.1**
FCAN	Federation of Contractor's Association of Nepal.	**15.2.1**
FDI	Foreign Direct Investment.	**10.2.3**
FIDIC	International Federation of Consulting Engineers (Fédération Internationale des Ingénieurs-Conseils).	**1.3.1**

FIDIC	FIDIC definition (Red, Pink, Yellow, Silver, Gold and Emerald Books).	**FIDIC GCs**
FIDIC Golden Principles	The essential features of a FIDIC Contract that make the risk/reward allocation fair and balanced.	**2.1**
Final Payment Certificate or **FPC**	FIDIC definition (1987 Red, Red, Pink, Yellow and Emerald Books).	**FIDIC GCs**
Final Statement	FIDIC definition (Red, Pink, Yellow, Silver and Emerald Books).	**FIDIC GCs**
force majeure	In civil law, *force majeure* applies to situations where the performance of a contract is substantially impossible, not merely something different from what was originally contemplated by the parties. In civil law systems, *force majeure* operates independently of party agreement, which means that it will protect an obligee even if the contract does not contain a *force majeure* clause.	
Force Majeure	FIDIC definition (1999 Red, Pink, 1999 Yellow and 1999 Silver Books).	**FIDIC GCs**
Foreign Currency	FIDIC definition (1987 Red, Red, Pink, Yellow, Silver, Gold and Emerald Books).	**FIDIC GCs**
Forex Manual	Foreign Exchange Manual published by the **Central Bank**. Papua New Guinea).	**17.6.5**
fukakoryoku	***Force majeure*** (Japan).	**12.6.11**
Fundamental Change in Circumstances	A **civil law** principle similar to the principle of frustration of contract in **common law** countries. If the circumstances change fundamentally after the execution of a contract so that the performance of the contract would be onerous for one Party, that Party has the right to terminate the contract or to modify some articles of the contract.	**7.10.2**
Gam-Li	A third-party supervisor of a construction contract. *Gam-Li* under the *Construction Technology Promotion Act* applies to construction projects in which the Employer is a State, a Local Government, or a public institution, and *Gam-Li* of the *Building Act* applies to private construction projects (Korea).	**13.10.1**
GBR	**Geotechnical Baseline Report**. FIDIC definition (Emerald Book).	**FIDIC GCs**
GCCC	General Conditions for Construction Contract (last amended in April 2020) published by the Committee of Seven Associations of Architects and Contractors (Japan).	**12.2.9.2**
GCDB	General Conditions for Design/Build Contract published by the Japan Federation of Construction Contractors.	**12.2.9.2**
GCQ	General Community Quarantine (Philippines).	**18.3.1**
GCs	**General Conditions**. FIDIC definition (Emerald Book).	**FIDIC GCs**
GDP	Gross Domestic Product.	
GDFCF	Gross domestic fixed capital formation.	**9.3.1**
GDR	**Geotechnical Data Report.** FIDIC definition (Emerald Book).	**FIDIC GCs**
General Conditions	FIDIC definition (2017 Red, 2017 Yellow, 2017 Silver and Emerald Books).	**FIDIC GCs**
General Exemption	The broad, general but conditional exemption to foreign exchange regulations under the *Central Banking Act* promulgated by the **Central Bank** in 2007. A key condition to the General Exemption is a requirement to comply with the **Forex Manual**. (Papua New Guinea).	**17.6.5**

(Continued)

Term	Meaning	Defined in Section
Geotechnical Baseline Report or **GBR**	FIDIC definition (Emerald Book).	**FIDIC GCs**
Geotechnical Data Report or **GDR**	FIDIC definition (Emerald Book).	**FIDIC GCs**
GFI	Government Financial Institution (Philippines).	**18.2.7**
giso-ukeoi	Camouflaged Contractor (Japan).	**12.2.3**
GNP	Gross National Product.	
GOCC	Government-Owned and Controlled Corporation (Philippines).	**18.2.7**
Gold Book	**FIDIC** Conditions of Contract for Design, Build and Operate Projects – First Edition, 2008.	**1.3.1**
Goods	FIDIC definition (Red, Pink, Yellow, Silver, Gold and Emerald Books).	**FIDIC GCs**
GoN	Government of Nepal.	**15.2.1**
governing law of the contract	The law that governs the Parties' contractual relations. Also known as the **proper law of the contract.**	**1.1.6**
GPs	**FIDIC Golden Principles**.	**2.1**
Green Book	**FIDIC** Short Form of Contract – First Edition, 1999.	**1.3.1**
Green Card	Construction Personnel Registration Card issued by CIDB (Malaysia).	**14.2.6**
Hague Principles	*Principles on Choice of Law in International Commercial Contracts* (2015) published by the Hague Conference on Private International Law.	**3.2.1**
haken-rodo	Labour hire (Japan).	**12.2.3**
HKIAC	Hong Kong International Arbitration Centre.	**9.2.5**
Head Contract	A contract for construction of a facility between the owner or user of the facility (**Employer**) and a contractor (**Contractor**) who takes responsibility for construction of the complete **Works** in accordance with the requirements of the **Contract**. The **Contractor** generally employs one or more **Subcontractors** to execute some (but not all) of the **Works**.	**1.1.1**
HPS	Self-estimated Price (Indonesia).	**11.6.4**
i-construction	**BIM** like technologies (Japan).	**12.2.6**
IA	Implementing Agency (Philippines).	**18.2.7**
IAA	*International Arbitration Act 1974* (Cth) (Australia).	**6.4.1**
IATF	Inter-Agency Task Force (Philippines).	**18.3.1**
IBS	Industrialised Building System (Malaysia).	**14.2.2**
ICAC	Independent Commission Against Corruption (Hong Kong).	**9.2.4**
ICB	International Competitive Bidding (JICA, Nepal).	**5.3.1**
ICC	International Chamber of Commerce.	**9.2.5**
ICE	Institution of Civil Engineers.	**4.2.5**
IESL	Institution of Engineers Sri Lanka.	**20.2.3**
IIDS	Institute for Integrated Development Studies (Nepal).	**15.2.8**
***in rem* claim**	A claim *in rem* literally means 'against the thing'. It is taken directly against property and it can be brought even though the owner has no personal liability.	**1.5.5**
inin	Mandate contract (Japan).	**12.6.10**
Interim Payment Certificate or **IPC**	FIDIC definition (1987 Red, Red, Pink, Yellow, Gold and Emerald Books).	**FIDIC GCs**

international construction contract	An international construction contract is a contract for the provision of goods and services in which: (a) the parties to the Contract have, at the time of the conclusion of their agreement, their places of business in different legal jurisdictions; or (b) one of the following places is situated outside the legal jurisdiction in which the parties have their places of business: (i) the Site; or (ii) any place where a substantial part of the obligations for the Works is to be performed.	**1.1.7**
IP	Intellectual property.	
ipso facto	By the fact itself (Latin).	
ipso jure	By the operation of the law itself (Latin).	
IQSSL	Institution of Quantity Surveyors of Sri Lanka.	**20.2.3**
ITA-AITES	International Tunnelling and Underground Space Association – Association Internationale des Tunnels et de L'Espace Souterrain.	**4.2.1**
ITA Contractual Framework Checklist	The ITA Contractual Framework Checklist for Subsurface Construction Contracts published by ITA-AITES in 2011.	**4.2.2**
***iTaukei* land**	Native land in Fiji.	**8.5.1**
IUJK	Construction Service Business License (Indonesia).	**11.2.1**
JCSS	The Japan Calibration Service System (Japan).	**12.8.1**
JCT Contracts	Joint Contracts Tribunal suite of standard form contracts (UK).	**14.2.5**
JFY	Japanese Fiscal Year.	**5.1**
Jian Li	Supervising engineer with contractual authority as Employer's agent, and statutory duties and obligations in respect of safety, quality, project management, cost control and coordination between Employer and Contractor (China).	**7.10.1**
JICA	Japan International Cooperation Agency.	**1.3.2**
Joint Venture or **JV**	FIDIC definition (2017 Red, 2017 Yellow, 2017 Silver and Emerald Books).	**FIDIC GCs**
jorei	Local laws (Japan).	**12.1.2**
jumbi-shomen	Memorials in court proceedings (Japan).	**12.2.10.1**
justa causa	A just cause or legal ground (Roman–Dutch law). *Justa causa* is applicable under the law of contract in Sri Lanka; hence, the English contract law notion of consideration is not applicable in Sri Lanka.	**20.1.2**
JV Undertaking	FIDIC definition (2017 Red, 2017 Yellow, 2017 Silver and Emerald Books)	**FIDIC GCs**
kankyo-eikyo-hyoka	Environment impact assessment (Japan).	**12.9.1**
kanri-gijiutsu-sha	Supervising engineer (Japan).	**12.9.1**
kashitsu-sosai	Comparative negligence (Japan).	**12.5.6**
keiyaku-futekigo	Non-conformance (Japan).	**12.5.1.2.1**
kenchiku-kakunin	Building confirmation (Japan).	**12.6.14**
kenchiku-shi	Architect (Japan).	**12.9.1**
KFSK	*Kensetsu-Funso-Shinsa-Kai* – Construction Dispute Adjudication Board (Japan).	**12.2.10.3**
KfW	Credit Institute of Reconstruction (Vietnam).	**21.2.2**
KLRCA	Kuala Lumpur Regional Centre for Arbitration (Malaysia).	**14.2.9**
koyo	Employment contract (Japan).	**12.6.10**
lakh	100,000 (India, Sri Lanka).	**10.2.6**
law of the forum	The law of the place in which court or arbitral proceedings are conducted.	**1.5.5**

(Continued)

Term	Meaning	Defined in Section
Laws	FIDIC definition (2017 Red, Pink, 2017 Yellow, 2017 Silver, Gold and Emerald Books).	**FIDIC GCs**
LDs	Liquidated damages.	
Letter of Acceptance	FIDIC definition (1987 Red, Red, Pink, Yellow, Gold and Emerald Books).	**FIDIC GCs**
Letter of Tender	FIDIC definition (Red, Pink, Yellow, Gold and Emerald Books).	**FIDIC GCs**
lex arbitrii	The law governing the existence and operation of the arbitral tribunal, generally the law of the 'seat' of arbitration. Also known as the **curial law**.	**1.5.6**
lex fori	See **law of the forum**.	
lex loci rei sitae	A Latin phrase meaning law of the place where the property is situated.	**1.5.5**
lex loci solutionis	A Latin phrase meaning law of the place where relevant performance occurs.	**7.4.1**
LGU	Local Government Unit (Philippines).	**18.2.7**
Lining	FIDIC definition (Emerald Book).	**FIDIC GCs**
LKPP	Government Procurement Policy Agency (Indonesia).	**11.3.2**
Local Currency	FIDIC definition (Red, Pink, Yellow, Silver, Gold and Emerald Books).	**FIDIC GCs**
Lok Sabha	House of the People (India).	**10.1.1**
LPJK	Construction Development Board (Indonesia).	**11.2.1**
LSA	The *Labour Standard Act* (Act No 49 of 1947) (Japan).	**12.5.2.1**
MACC	Malaysian Anti-Corruption Commission.	**14.2.8**
MAMPAN	Sustainable Construction Excellence Centre (Malaysia).	**14.2.2**
Management Guidelines	Covid-19 Management Guidelines in Malaysia No 5/2020 published by the Ministry of Health (Malaysia).	**14.3.1**
mandatory law or **mandatory rules of law**	Provisions of a statute which the parties to a contract may not derogate from.	**1.5**
Materials	FIDIC definition (Red, Pink, Yellow, Silver, Gold and Emerald Books).	**FIDIC GCs**
MCO	Movement Control Order (Malaysia).	**14.3.1**
MCTC	Municipal Circuit Trial Court (Philippines).	**18.1.3**
MDB	Multilateral Development Bank.	**1.3.2**
MECQ	Modified Enhanced Community Quarantine (Philippines).	**18.3.1**
MeTC	Metropolitan Trial Courts (Philippines).	**18.1.3**
MHA	Ministry of Home Affairs, Government of India.	**10.3.1**
MHR	Ministry of Human Resources (Malaysia).	**14.3.1**
MIArb	Malaysian Institute of Arbitrators.	**14.2.9**
MiC	Modular Integrated Construction (Hong Kong).	**9.2.2**
Milestone	FIDIC definition (Emerald Book).	**FIDIC GCs**
Milestone Certificate	FIDIC definition (Emerald Book).	**FIDIC GCs**
MKN	National Security Council (Malaysia).	**14.3.1**
MLIT	Ministry of Land, Infrastructure, Transport and Tourism (Japan).	**12.1.1**
MLIT Covid-19 Guideline	**MLIT** Guideline regarding the preventive measures against Covid-19 dated 14 May 2020 (Japan).	**12.3.1.2**
MLIT Minister	The head of the Ministry of Land, Infrastructure, Transport and Tourism (Japan).	**12.1.1**
MMC	Malaysian Mediation Centre.	**14.2.9**
Model Law	1985 UNCITRAL Model Law on International Commercial Arbitration.	**Annexure to Chapter 1**

MoC	Ministry of Construction (Vietnam).	**21.2.2**
MoEF	Ministry of Environment and Forest (India).	**10.2.2.5**
mokuji-no-goi	Implied agreement (Japan).	**12.11.3**
month	FIDIC definition (2017 Red, 2017 Yellow, 2017 Silver and Emerald Books).	**FIDIC GCs**
MoPIT	Ministry of Physical Infrastructure and Transport (Nepal).	**15.2.1**
MPI	Ministry of Planning and Investment (Vietnam).	**21.2.2**
MQCQ	Modified General Community Quarantine (Philippines).	**18.3.1**
MTC	Municipal Trial Court (Philippines).	**18.1.3**
MTCC	Municipal Trial Courts in Cities (Philippines).	**18.1.3**
MTR	Mass Transit Railway (Hong Kong).	**9.2.1**
mutatis mutandis	Notwithstanding differences between two things being compared because of their different situations, the basic point remains the same.	
NCASL	National Construction Association of Sri Lanka.	**20.2.3**
NCB	National Competitive Bidding (Nepal).	**15.2.10**
NEDA	National Economic and Development Authority (Philippines).	**18.2.7**
NEPCA	Nepal Council for Arbitrators.	**15.2.11**
New York Convention	United Nations *1958 New York Convention on the Recognition and Enforcement of Foreign Arbitral Awards.*	**1.8.1**
NGA	National Government Agency (Philippines).	**18.2.7**
NGT	National Green Tribunal, a specialised body under the *National Green Tribunal Act* 2010 (India).	**10.2.2.5**
No-objection	FIDIC definition (2017 Red, 2017 Yellow, 2017 Silver and Emerald Books).	**FIDIC GCs**
NOC	No Objection Certificate (India, Pakistan).	**10.2.2.7**
NOD	**Notice of Dissatisfaction.**	**FIDIC GCs**
non-mandatory law or **non-mandatory rules of law**	Provisions of a statute which the parties can opt out of by appropriate agreement otherwise in their contract.	**1.5**
Notice	FIDIC definition (2017 Red, 2017 Yellow, 2017 Silver, Gold and Emerald Books).	**FIDIC GCs**
Notice of Dissatisfaction or **NOD**	FIDIC definition (2017 Red, Pink, 2017 Yellow, 2017 Silver and Emerald Books).	**FIDIC GCs**
NPCSC	Standing Committee of the National People's Congress. (China).	**9.1.3**
NSTB	National Skill Testing Board (Nepal).	**15.2.4**
OBOR	China's One Belt One Road initiative.	**14.2.10**
ODA	Official Development Assistance.	**5.1**
Orang Asli	Indigenous people of Malaysia.	**14.8.1**
ordre public	Public policy (French).	**3.2.1**
pacta sunt servanda	A Latin phrase that means that agreements are to be kept.	**1.1.5**
P3DN	Increased Use of Domestic Products (Indonesia).	**11.6.3**
PAM	Pertubuhan Arkitek Malaysia (Malaysian Institute of Architects).	**14.2.5**
Part	FIDIC definition (2017 Red, 2017 Yellow and Emerald Books).	**FIDIC GCs**
Particular Conditions	FIDIC definition (2017 Red, 2017 Yellow, 2017 Silver and Emerald Books).	**FIDIC GCs**
Party	FIDIC definition (Red, Pink, Yellow, Silver, Gold and Emerald Books).	**FIDIC GCs**
Payment Certificate	FIDIC definition (Red, Pink, Yellow and Emerald Books).	**FIDIC GCs**
PBD	Philippine Bidding Document.	**18.2.9**
PCAB	Philippine Contractors Accreditation Board.	**18.2.2**
PCs	**Particular Conditions**.	**2.3**

(Continued)

Term	Meaning	Defined in Section
PEC	Pakistan Engineering Council.	**16.2.2**
Performance Certificate	FIDIC definition (Red, Pink, Yellow, Silver and Emerald Books).	**FIDIC GCs**
Performance Damages	FIDIC definition (2017 Yellow, 2017 Silver and Emerald Books).	**FIDIC GCs**
Performance Guarantees	FIDIC definition (1999 Silver Book).	**FIDIC GCs**
Performance Security	FIDIC definition (Red, Pink, Yellow, Silver, Gold and Emerald Books).	**FIDIC GCs**
Permanent Works	FIDIC definition (1987 Red, Red, Pink, Yellow, Silver, Gold and Emerald Books).	**FIDIC GCs**
PFI	Private Finance Initiative.	
PGK	Papua New Guinea Kina.	**17.1.2.2**
PICAM	Philippine Institute of Construction Arbitrators and Mediators.	**18.2.10.1**
Pink Book	**FIDIC** Conditions of Contract for Construction MDB Harmonised Edition for Building and Engineering Works Designed by the Employer (MDB Harmonised Edition 2010).	**1.3.1**
PKK	Contractors Services Centre (Malaysia).	**14.2.3**
Plant	FIDIC definition (1987 Red, Red, Pink, Yellow, Silver, Gold and Emerald Books).	**FIDIC GCs**
PMC	Philippine Mediation Center.	**18.1.3**
PMU	Project Management Unit (Vietnam).	**21.2.3**
PNG	The Independent State of Papua New Guinea.	**17.1.1.1**
PPA	*Public Procurement Act 2063 (2006)* (Nepal).	**15.1.2**
PPVC	Prefabricated Pre-finished Volumetric Construction (Singapore).	**19.2**
PPE	Personal protective equipment.	**1.6.6**
PPMO	Public Procurement Monitoring Office (Nepal).	**15.2.8**
PPP	Public Private Partnership.	**10.2.1**
PPR	*Public Procurement Rules 2064 (2007)* (Nepal).	**15.1.2**
PPRA	Public Procurement Regulatory Authority (Pakistan).	**16.2.1**
PRC	Professional Regulation Commission (Philippines).	**18.2.3**
Programme	FIDIC definition (2017 Red, 2017 Yellow, 2017 Silver and Emerald Books).	**FIDIC GCs**
proper law of the contract	The law that governs the parties' contractual relations. Also known as the **governing law of the contract.**	**1.1.6**
Provisional Sum	FIDIC definition (Red, Pink, Yellow, Silver, Gold and Emerald Books).	**FIDIC GCs**
PSSCOC	Public Sector Standard Conditions of Contract (Singapore).	**19.2**
PT PMA	A joint venture between a foreign entity and a local contractor (Indonesia).	**11.2.1**
public policy	Public policy is largely concerned with the potential for manifest unfairness or injustice within a given situation. Courts may disregard or refuse to give effect to contractual obligations which, whilst not directly contrary to any express or implied statutory prohibition, nevertheless contravene 'the policy of the law' as discerned from a consideration of the scope and purpose of the particular statute.	**1.1.4**
PWSC	Public Work Standard Contract published by the Central Government (Japan).	**12.2.9.1**

Quality Management or **QM System**	FIDIC definition (Emerald Book).	**FIDIC GCs**
QM System	FIDIC definition (2017 Red, 2017 Yellow and 2017 Silver Books).	**FIDIC GCs**
rainbow suite	The construction contracts published by **FIDIC**: • **Red Book** • **Yellow Book** • **Silver Book**	**1.3.1**
Rajya Sabha	Council of States (India).	**10.1.1**
rebus sic stantibus	The civil law doctrine or rules relating to changed circumstances.	**1.2.3**
Red Book	**FIDIC** Conditions of Contract for Construction for Building and Engineering Works Designed by the Employer – First Edition 1999 and Second Edition 2017.	**1.3.1**
REDAS	Real Estate Developers' Association of Singapore.	**19.2**
Retention Money	FIDIC definition (1987 Red, Red, Pink, Yellow, Silver, Gold and Emerald Books).	**FIDIC GCs**
Review	FIDIC definition (2017 Red, 2017 Yellow, 2017 Silver and Emerald Books).	**FIDIC GCs**
RFA	Request for approval.	
RFI	Request for information.	
RMCO	Recovery Movement Control Order (Malaysia).	**14.3.1**
Rome I	*Convention on the Law Applicable to Contractual Obligations. Regulation (EC) No 593/2008* of the European Parliament and of the Council of 17 June 2008 on the law applicable to contractual obligations.	**1.1.4**
roshi-kyotei	Labour management agreement (Japan).	**12.5.2.1**
RPTKA	Employment Plan of Foreign Workers (Indonesia).	**11.6.2**
RTC	Regional Trial Courts (Philippines).	**18.1.3**
saimu-furiko	Non-performance of obligations (Japan).	**12.8.4**
san-mitsu	'Three Cs' – closed spaces, crowded places, close-contact settings (Japan).	**12.3.1.2**
SBD	Standard Bidding Document.	**1.3.2**
SBD Design Build	**SBD** for Design Build, Plant and Works (Japan).	**5.3.2**
SBD Works	**SBD** for Procurement of Works (Japan).	**5.3.2**
SBU	Business Entity Certificate (Indonesia).	**11.2.1**
Schedules	FIDIC definition (Red, Pink, Yellow, 2017 Silver, Gold and Emerald Books).	**FIDIC GCs**
Schedule of Baselines	FIDIC definition (Emerald Book).	**FIDIC GCs**
Schedule of Contractor's Key Equipment	FIDIC definition (Emerald Book).	**FIDIC GCs**
Schedule of Guarantees	FIDIC definition (1999 Yellow Book).	**FIDIC GCs**
Schedule of Payments	FIDIC definition (Red, Yellow, Silver, Gold and Emerald Books).	**FIDIC GCs**
Schedule of Performance Guarantees	FIDIC definition (2017 Yellow, 2017 Silver and Emerald Books).	**FIDIC GCs**
Schedule of Rates and Prices	FIDIC definition (2017 Yellow, 2017 Silver and Emerald Books).	**FIDIC GCs**

(Continued)

Term	Meaning	Defined in Section
Schedule, Payment Currencies	FIDIC definition (Pink Book).	**FIDIC GCs**
SDR	Special Drawing Rights.[5]	**9.2.3**
Section	FIDIC definition (1987 Red, Red, Pink, Yellow, Silver, Gold and Emerald Books).	**FIDIC GCs**
SEDA	Sustainable Development Authority (Malaysia).	**14.2.2**
sekou-kanri-gishi	Managing engineer (Japan).	**12.9.1**
SEZ	Special Economic Zone (India).	**10.2.4**
Shinkansen	Bullet train (Japan).	**12.3.2**
shometsu-jiko	Statute of limitation (Japan).	**12.5.1.2.1**
SIA	Singapore Institute of Architects.	**19.2**
SIAC	Singapore International Arbitration Centre.	**15.2.1.1**
SICC	Singapore International Commercial Court.	**19.1.3**
Site	FIDIC definition (1987 Red, Red, Pink, Yellow, Silver, Gold and Emerald Books).	**FIDIC GCs**
Silver Book	**FIDIC** Conditions of Contract for EPC/Turnkey Projects – First Edition 1999, Second Edition 2017.	**1.3.1**
SLIA	Sri Lanka Institute of Architects.	**20.2.3**
SME	Small and medium enterprise.	
SOCSO	Social Security Organisation (Malaysia).	**14.6.7**
SOE	State of Emergency.	**12.3.1.1**
sojo	Complaint in court proceedings (Japan).	**12.2.10.1**
SOP	Standard Operating Procedure.	**14.3.1**
SOP Act	*Building and Construction Industry Security of Payment Act (2005)* (Singapore).	**19.2**
sosai-tekijo	Set-off (Japan).	**12.8.3**
Special Provisions	FIDIC definition (2017 Red, 2017 Yellow, 2017 Silver and Emerald Books).	**FIDIC GCs**
specialty	A contract executed under seal.	**6.4.2**
Specification	FIDIC definition (1987 Red, Red, Pink and Yellow Books).	**FIDIC GCs**
SPR	*Stores and Procurement Regulations* issued by the Financial Secretary under the *Public Finance Ordinance* (Cap 2) (Hong Kong).	**9.2.3**
stare decisis	'The decision stands' (Latin). The doctrine under which a **common law** court is required to follow previous decisions, unless they are inconsistent with a higher court's decision or determined to be wrong in law.	**1.1.2**
Statement	FIDIC definition (Red, Pink, Yellow, Silver, Gold and Emerald Books).	**FIDIC GCs**
Subcontractor	FIDIC definition (1987 Red, Red, Pink, Yellow, Silver, Gold and Emerald Books).	**FIDIC GCs**
SUCs	State Universities and Colleges (Philippines).	**18.2.7**
SWP	'Safe Work Procedure for Prevention of Covid-19 at Workplace' published by **DOSH** (Malaysia).	**14.3.1**
Taking-Over Certificate	FIDIC definition (1987 Red, Red, Pink, Yellow, Silver and Emerald Books).	**FIDIC GCs**
TBM	Tunnel boring machine.	**4.1**
TDS	Tax Deducted at Source (India, Nepal).	**10.2.2.3** **15.6.1**
Temporary Works	FIDIC definition (Red, Pink, Yellow, Silver and Emerald Books).	**FIDIC GCs**

5 https://www.imf.org/en/About/Factsheets/Sheets/2016/08/01/14/51/Special-Drawing-Right-SDR (accessed 30 November 2020).

Tender	FIDIC definition (1987 Red, Red, Pink, Yellow, Silver, Gold and Emerald Books).	**FIDIC GCs**
Tests after Completion	FIDIC definition (Red, Pink, Yellow, Silver and Emerald Books).	**FIDIC GCs**
Tests on Completion	FIDIC definition (1987 Red, Red, Pink, Yellow, Silver and Emerald Books).	**FIDIC GCs**
TG15	**FIDIC** Task Group 15, responsible for articulating the **FIDIC Golden Principles**.	**2.3**
Time for Completion	FIDIC definition (1987 Red, Red, Pink, Yellow, Silver and Emerald Books).	**FIDIC GCs**
TKDN	Domestic Component Level (Indonesia).	**11.6.3**
tobensho	Answer in court proceedings (Japan).	**12.2.10.1**
tojisha-no-goriteki-ishi	A party's reasonable intention (Japan).	**12.11.3**
ukeoi	Contract for Work (Japan).	**12.6.10**
UNCITRAL	United Nations Commission on International Trade Law.	**1.5.6**
UNCITRAL Model Law	*UNCITRAL Model Law on International Commercial Arbitration 1985* with Amendments as adopted in 2006.	**Annexure to Chapter 1.**
Underground Works	FIDIC definition (Emerald Book).	**FIDIC GCs**
Unforeseeable	FIDIC definition (Red, Pink, Yellow, Silver, Gold and Emerald Books).	**FIDIC GCs**
UNIDROIT	International Institute for the Unification of Private Law.	
Variation	FIDIC definition (Red, Pink, Yellow, Silver, Gold and Emerald Books).	**FIDIC GCs**
VIAC	Vietnam International Arbitration Centre.	**21.5.3.1**
VND	Vietnam Dong.	**21.2.1**
WACIA	*Worker's Accident Compensation Insurance Act* (Act No 50 of 1947) (Japan).	**12.2.8.1**
West Coast model	The scheme of statutory adjudication legislated in the Northern Territory (Australia).	**6.5.1**
WHO	United Nations World Health Organization.	**10.3.1**
WHS	Workplace health and safety.	**6.2.2**
WMA	The *Waste Management and Public Cleaning Act* (Act No 137 of 1970) (Japan).	**12.6.13**
Works	FIDIC definition (1987 Red, Red, Pink, Yellow, Silver, Gold and Emerald Books).	**FIDIC GCs**
writing	FIDIC definition (1987 Red Book).	**FIDIC GCs**
WSHA	*Workers Safety and Health Act* (Act No 57 of 1972) (Japan).	**12.2.4**
WTO	World Trade Organization – the only global international organisation dealing with the rules of trade between nations.[6]	**1.8.2**
WTO GPA	**WTO** Agreement on Government Procurement.	**1.8.2**
year	FIDIC definition (Red, Yellow, Silver, Gold and Emerald Books).	**FIDIC GCs**
Yellow Book	**FIDIC** Conditions of Contract for Plant and Design-Build for Electrical and Mechanical Plant and for Building and Engineering Works, designed by the Contractor – First Edition 1999, Second Edition 2017.	**1.3.1**

6 https://www.wto.org/english/thewto_e/thewto_e.htm (accessed 9 November 2020).

INDEX

Kolibri 360 GmbH
Ferdinand-Jühlke-Straße 7
99095 Erfurt, Deutschland
produktsicherheit@kolibri360.de